Black Labor and the American Legal System

Books by Herbert Hill

Black Labor and the American Legal System:
Race, Work, and the Law

Employment, Race, and Poverty
(with Arthur M. Ross)

Anger, and Beyond: The Negro Writer in the
United States (editor)

Soon, One Morning: New Writing by Black Americans
(editor)

The Citizen's Guide to Desegregation: A Study of
Social and Legal Change in American Life
(with Jack Greenberg)

No Harvest for the Reaper: The Story of the Migratory
Agricultural Worker

Black Labor

and the

American Legal System

Race, Work, and the Law

HERBERT HILL

The University of Wisconsin Press

Published 1985
The University of Wisconsin Press
114 North Murray Street
Madison, Wisconsin 53715

The University of Wisconsin Press, Ltd.
1 Gower Street
London, WC1E 6HA, England

Originally published in 1977 by The Bureau of National Affairs, Inc.

The epigraph by Orde Coombs is from "Three Faces of Harlem," *The New York Times*, November 3, 1974. © 1974 by The New York Times Company. Reprinted by permission.

Printed in the United States of America

ISBN 0-299-10590-3 cloth, 0-299-10594-6 paper
LC 85-40762

This book is dedicated to those workers—black, Chicano, women, Asian, and Puerto Rican—who through the long years when it seemed no one listened, persisted in attempts to use the law in seeking redress for their grievances and made the history that is the material of this book.

The voice of the majority may be that of force triumphant, content with the plaudits of the hour, and recking little of the morrow. The dissenter speaks to the future, and his voice is pitched to a key that will carry through the years. Read some of the great dissents, the opinion, for example of Judge Curtis in Dred Scott v. Sandford, *and feel after the cooling time of a better part of a century the glow and fire of a faith that was content to bide its hour. The prophet and the martyr do not see the hooting throng. Their eyes are fixed on the eternities.*

—Benjamin N. Cardozo
Associate Justice
United States Supreme Court
1932–1938

Those who love their work may sometimes forget that a successful human community requires the performance of many vapid and colorless tasks. Even the most tedious physical labor is endurable and in a sense enjoyable, however, when the laborer knows that his work will be appreciated and his progress rewarded. "Work without hope," said Coleridge, "draws nectar in a sieve, and hope without an object cannot live." The ethic which permeates the American dream is that a person may advance as far as his talents and his merit will carry him. And it is unthinkable that a citizen of this great country should be relegated to unremitting toil with never a glimmer of light in the midnight of it all.

—Judge Walter Pettus Gewin
United States Court of Appeals
for the Fifth Circuit

Of all the evils heaped upon black people in this country in the 20th century, it seems to me that job discrimination, more than anything else, broke the resilience of many black men. Men need to work. They need to know that the sounds of their own exhaustion help to create the kind of world in which they live. The refusal to honor a black man's work—to let him know that the smell of his sweat led to just recompense, that his hands were his survival, and his sinews his passport to success—has led to the degradation, the hostility and lethargy now threatening to engulf us.

—Orde Coombs

Acknowledgments

This volume and its companion volume, the result of many years of research and writing, could not have gone forward without the assistance and encouragement of many persons to whom I am deeply grateful. I wish to acknowledge a major debt to James E. Jones, Jr., Professor of Law at the University of Wisconsin, Madison, and to Russell Specter, former Deputy General Counsel of the Equal Employment Opportunity Commission, for reading extensive portions of the manuscript, giving me valuable criticism and suggestions, and sharing many insights with me.

For their generous assistance and many kindnesses, my sincere appreciation to: Derrick A. Bell, Jr., Professor of Law, Harvard University; Alfred W. Blumrosen, Acting Dean of the Law School, Rutgers University, formerly Chief of Conciliations, EEOC; David R. Cashdan, formerly Acting Chief, District Court Litigation, Office of the General Counsel, EEOC; Eugene Cotton, attorney for the United Packinghouse Workers of America; Harold Goodman, attorney, Community Legal Services, Inc., Philadelphia; Barbara A. Morris, Adjunct Professor of Law, Rutgers University, formerly Associate General Counsel, NAACP; Marshall Patner, Professor, Department of Criminal Justice, University of Illinois, Chicago Circle; Sanford Jay Rosen, Legal Director, Mexican-American Legal Defense and Education Fund, formerly Professor of Law, University of Maryland; William A. Wells, Assistant Counsel, NAACP; Ruth Weyand, Associate General Counsel, International Union of Electrical Radio and Machine Workers; and Dennis R. Yeager, Director, National Employment Law Project.

I have also greatly benefited from the advice of Albert Fried, Professor of Political Science, Sarah Lawrence College; Barry L. Goldstein, Associate Counsel, NAACP Legal Defense and Educational Fund, Inc.; Alvin Golub, Deputy Executive Director, EEOC; Charles V. Hamilton, Professor of Government, Columbia University; Milton R. Konvitz, Professor of Law, Cornell University; Stanford M. Lyman, Professor of Sociology, Graduate Faculty, New School for Social Research; Joseph L. Rauh, Jr., of Rauh and Silard, Washington, D.C.; David Copus, Deputy Chief, National Programs Division, EEOC; Charles L. Reischel, Assistant General Counsel, EEOC; and William Robinson, Associate Counsel, NAACP Legal Defense and Educational Fund, Inc.

Among those who encouraged this work and shared their knowledge with me were: Jerold S. Auerbach, Professor of History, Wellesley College; Don Elisburg, counsel, Committee on Labor and Public Welfare, U.S. Senate; Ralph Helstein, former President, United Packinghouse Workers of America; Ronald W. Haughton, Vice President, Wayne State University; Whitney Adams and Jeffrey M. Miller of the staff of the U.S. Commission on Civil Rights; Whitney Walker, formerly Chief, Field Operations, EEOC; and David B. Parker, editor, BNA's *Daily Labor Report*.

In the course of field research, many persons across the country were interviewed. These interviews provide an important dimension to the book and in some instances were crucial to my study. Although space does not permit a complete listing, I should like to express my thanks to the following: Mrs. Frances Albrier, Oakland, Calif.; Clifford L. Alexander, Washington, D.C.; William H. Brown, III, Washington, D.C.; Horace Cayton, Berkeley, Calif.; Joseph Carnegie, New York; Edward E. Doty, Chicago; Orrin Evans, Philadelphia; Martin Gopen, Boston; John Heneghan, Washington, D.C.; Vivian W. Henderson, Atlanta; Samuel C. Jackson, Washington, D.C.; Herbert March, Los Angeles; Will Maslow, New York; James F. McNamara, New York; Ted Poston, New York; Frank Quinn, San Francisco; Eli Rock, Philadelphia; Tyree C. Scott, Seattle; Grover Smith, Jr., Birmingham; George Staab, Philadelphia; Bennett O. Stalvey, Philadelphia; Edward Sylvester, Washington, D.C.; Shelton Tappes, Detroit; James F. Warren, Seattle; and to William H. Friedland, Professor of Sociology, University of California, Santa Cruz, for kind permission to quote from his master's thesis on the United Auto Workers.

Research for this book was done in many libraries and archives and I wish especially to acknowledge the kind and generous help of Mrs. Roberta McBride, Archives of Labor History and Urban Affairs, Wayne State University; Mrs. Jean Blackwell Hutson, the Schomberg

Collection, New York; Joseph B. Howerton, The National Archives, Washington, D.C.; Mrs. Dorothy Porter, Moorland-Spingarn Collection, Howard University, Washington, D.C.; and James D. Abajian, the California Historical Society, San Francisco. I also thank the staffs of the Library of Congress, the New York Public Library, and The State Historical Society of Wisconsin.

To Mrs. Hazel N. Lewis and Mrs. Judith Douw, who typed various drafts of the manuscript, my sincere appreciation.

In this long and difficult manuscript, the editorial contribution of Mary T. Heathcote and Berenice Hoffman has been incalculable. I am much indebted to Louise Rosenblatt, my editor at BNA Books, for her diligence and superb editorial judgment. I also wish to note my appreciation to Donald F. Farwell, Manager, BNA Books, for his patience and understanding.

It is my hope that all those who helped will feel that this book justifies their encouragement, and that together we have made a scholarly contribution worthy of one another.

It should be understood that the views expressed in this book are entirely my own and do not in any way express the program or policies of any organization of which I am an officer or member. Furthermore, while I acknowledge the kind assistance of many, the opinions expressed are mine and I accept full responsibility for any errors of fact or judgment.

A Note on Terminology

Regarding the use of the terms "Negro," "colored," "black," and "Afro-American," I have, with the exception of the Introduction, generally used the form most common to each historical period.

Contents

Race, Work, and the Law

Introduction

Historical Sources of Resistance to Change

A great irony lies at the heart of slavery in the United States. Although slaves were not legally recognized as persons, central to the institution of slavery was the requirement that these less-than-human chattels, or "articles of commerce" (by legal definition), perform one of the most creative of human tasks: work. It was largely in the condition of involuntary servitude that black people in America acquired a great variety of skills by which they labored for their masters and were instrumental in creating their masters' wealth.

In 1965, a hundred years after the end of the Civil War and the abolition of slavery, federal legislation went into effect to eliminate the continuing barriers that deny black citizens equal opportunity to work and to share in the rewards of work. By then, many forces had combined to push the descendants of black men and women, both slave and free, into a subordinate position in the American labor force. A dual racial labor system had been established. Whites derived substantial economic and social gains from the subordination of blacks, and both employers and organized white workers repeatedly resisted compliance with new civil rights statutes.

By 1975, a decade had passed since the first comprehensive civil rights law in almost a century was enacted. The Civil Rights Act of 1964 and its Title VII, which prohibits employment discrimination, have had a direct impact on the operations of employers and labor unions in virtually every sector of the economy.

The interpretation and application of the law has caused conflict and public contention that go far beyond the world of industrial relations. This book explores the roots of that ferment, the perceptions of black workers, and the remedies they sought over the years to eliminate job discrimination. It is an interpretive history of the evolution of American law concerning employment discrimination, and of the response of employers and organized labor to the legal prohibitions against discrimination, past and present.

This volume deals mainly with developments from the abolition of slavery to the present, and with the events that preceded and affected the enactment of Title VII, including the consequences for nonwhite workers of the operation of the National Labor Relations Act. In addition, it evaluates government efforts to eliminate job discrimination through administrative agencies, with special attention to the work of the original Fair Employment Practice Committee during the 1940s.

The companion volume is a study of the contending forces in the legislative history of Title VII, an examination of the statue as amended, and an analysis of the extensive body of case law that has developed in litigation under the Act. It indicates the potential as well as the limitation of law as an instrument for social change. The book concludes with a perspective for the future and suggests new approaches for action against job discrimination.

After the Thirteenth Amendment prohibited involuntary servitude, the ensuing patterns of occupational segregation and discrimination succeeded in circumscribing black workers within a system of deprivation that remained, with rare exceptions, untouched by the law for almost a century. In fact, the early judicial interpretations of the Fourteenth Amendment and the Reconstruction civil rights acts—which did not directly relate to employment discrimination—served substantially to nullify the intention of the amendment and the acts to benefit blacks as a class. In combination with prevailing custom and entrenched racial attitudes, North and South, the absence of judicial affirmation of the purposes of the Fourteenth Amendment functioned to further institutionalize the subordination of blacks in the era when the initial freedom from bondage held out hope for ameliorative conditions. Realization of the potential of the Constitution and the Reconstruction civil rights acts in litigation against employment discrimination had to await the changed judicial climate after the passage of the Civil Rights Act of 1964, when they gained some acceptance as alternatives or supplements to modern equal employment legislation. The end of the first decade since Title VII went into effect brings us to the threshold of new litigation on behalf of blacks and other minorities on such issues as eliminating the present effects of past discrimination, especially on the question of seniority as it relates to the "last-hired, first-fired" principle during periods of mass unemployment. Judicial retreat on the protection of racial minorities has occurred with dismaying frequency in the history of the American legal system. Nevertheless, the extensive body of case law that has evolved over a ten-year period establishes judicial precepts that cannot be easily dismantled or ignored.

Title VII, with its 1972 amendments,[1] has led to a new stage in the struggle against job discrimination. Prior to the emergence of this law federal executive orders requiring nondiscrimination in employment by government contractors were honored more in the breach than in the observance, and although many states had fair employment laws, they were seldom enforced. In practice, employers and organized labor had little to fear from federal contract compliance orders and even less from state antidiscrimination laws. Only after Title VII of the Civil Rights Act of 1964 was adopted, defining and prohibiting unlawful racial employment practices, was a national legal instrument forged to abolish such practices and redress the grievances of the victims. The response of employers and labor unions to this new law must be measured by their resistance to compliance, as expressed in the extensive record of litigation in the past decade.

Abstract principles of racial equality change nothing. Judicial orders that enforce such principles are quite another matter. Title VII, interpreted and enforced by the courts, has become qualitatively different from previous fair employment practice laws, with substantial consequences that cannot be lightly dismissed by the affected institutions.

Employer resistance to the requirements of Title VII of the Civil Rights Act often came from a desire to maintain labor tranquility by not disturbing established systems of hiring, promotion, and job assignment. Stiff resistance also resulted from attempts to perpetuate the racial exclusiveness of certain all-white occupations, especially among professional, technical, and supervisory personnel. National corporations—in heavy industry, public utilities, banking and insurance, retailing, consumer goods manufacturing, transportation, and elsewhere—not only failed to use their power and influence to obtain compliance with the new law but instead persisted in retaining and defending illegal discriminatory employment practices. This resistance was intensified by assumptions of the inferiority of nonwhite workers and in some instances by management's commitment to racial segregation.

Widespread resistance occurred in industries where overall labor costs were rationalized by a low wage base for an entire subclass of workers, traditionally composed of blacks and other minority groups, whose lower wage scales subsidized the higher pay of white workers. To preserve these advantages, and to prevent complex and costly changes in traditional production and personnel practices, both employers and labor unions vigorously defended their racial practices in Title VII lawsuits. After several years of such litigation, when it became clear that the federal courts would continue to order far-reaching changes in racial employment patterns and would impose substantial compensatory awards— often involving millions of dollars for an entire class of workers— some deterrent effect was discernible. By the mid-1970s the impact of the law was evident as court orders began to make the elimination of racial discrimination an economic necessity.

Many employers and labor unions responded, however, by attempting to ward off judicial interference through negotiated settlements with federal agencies. These settlements usually provided inadequate remedies and inadequate compensation for past discrimination (substantially less than the courts frequently require) and also offered immunity from further litigation. As a result, in the steel industry, for example, the affected workers— excluded from negotiations among the major steel corporations, the Steelworkers union, and government agencies—challenged in the courts the validity of the 1974 industrywide agreement.

Whatever the consequences of Title VII for employers, for those in supervisory, technical, and professional classifications, as well as for unorganized white workers, organized labor is more vulnerable and is affected more directly and on a larger scale. The response of unions as defendants in Title VII cases repeatedly revealed that labor organizations have become the institutional defenders of white male workers' job expectations, expectations which have become the norm and are based in large part upon the systematic deprivation of black workers; any alteration of this norm is considered to be "reverse discrimination." An account of organized labor's resistance to Title VII must take into consideration the advantages that discriminatory employment patterns give to white male workers in training, promotion, higher job status, and better wages. In fact, organized labor's efforts to evade the new legal requirements are incomprehensible without an understanding of its history in both generating and codifying the job expectations of white workers at the expense of blacks.

White workers' claims to more desirable job classifications and to "inherent" white employment privileges—which had a long history in the contentions for access to work between whites and blacks—were reinforced by labor unions in a variety of crafts and industries. In most craft occupations, if blacks were excluded from union membership they were thereby almost entirely excluded from the craft labor force; and when they were included in industrial unions on a segregated or inferior basis, they did not share equally in the benefits of unionization. Through the collective bargaining process, organized labor has played a crucial role in institutionalizing a variety of discriminatory practices in diverse sectors of the economy. Labor-management agreements covering both craft and industrial jobs frequently codified and structured discriminatory racial patterns. Many labor unions have been involved as defendants in Title VII litigation, much of the case law as it developed directly affected unions, and some of the most important decisions—especially those dealing with seniority and job-assignment practices and preferential hiring remedies—involved labor organizations. Furthermore, major elements of organized labor have determinedly resisted compliance with a law that opens collective bargaining agreements to judicial scrutiny and threatens the power of unions to perpetuate hitherto unregulated discriminatory racial practices. It is precisely for these reasons that much of the litigation described in this study has involved labor unions as defendants or codefendants with employers in Title VII cases.

The collective bargaining process as presently constituted, that is, without provision for the adequate representation of the interests of blacks and other minorities, serves not only to regulate the relation between workers and employers but also, all too often, to reinforce traditional discriminatory patterns. When these discriminatory job practices are eliminated, white workers believe that preferential treatment is being given to blacks, when it is, in fact, removal of the preferential treatment traditionally enjoyed by whites at the expense of black wage earners that is at issue. Enforcement of the law by the judiciary not only affects the traditional racial practices of employers and organized labor but, more important, threatens the structure that gave white workers valuable advantages as a result of these practices. These self-generated factors—the result of the historical dual labor system based on race—account for the resistance by labor unions to judicial orders that require changes in the status of the black labor force.

Ten years after passage of the Civil Rights Act of 1964, it is evident that employers and labor unions in many industries are so interlocked in the collective bargaining nexus that they frequently make a joint defense in Title VII litigation and use a joint legal strategy to resist compliance.

When Title VII became effective—on July 2, 1965—two centuries of American history had created formidable obstacles to its acceptance. Not only were many powerful institutions involved in perpetuating the racial status quo in employment, but popular belief had come to question the capacity of blacks to do acceptable work. Consistent with the self-fulfilling prophecy, the high rates of black unemployment and the concentration of black workers in low-wage occupations were considered proof of their inherent limitations. The condition of black workers was increasingly held to be a deserved consequence of the overall inadequacy of the black population.

To appreciate fully the influences that fostered the notion that low job status is a result of black cultural attitudes toward work, and to trace to some degree the history of black labor, it is necessary to go back to the period of slavery. It was the "peculiar institution," slavery itself, that created not only the familiar images of field hands and domestic servants but, far less widely depicted in popularizations of the American past, the skilled workers and artisans of the southern labor force. The more skilled the slave, the more profit for the master.

Although there is tangible evidence of the presence of skilled slave craftsmen in the American colonies during the seventeenth century, Negro mechanics and craftsmen did not become important factors in the colonial economy before the eighteenth century. In the earliest period slaveowners feared, as historian Leonard Stavisky argues, that educating slaves and giving them access to tools might provide them with weapons to be used against their masters. The hostility of white artisans and general assumptions about the Negro's inferior capacity contributed to the reluctance to employ slaves in any pursuit other than heavy agricultural labor.[2] Declining tobacco prices and a concurrent shortage of skilled labor during the early eighteenth century, however, forced reconsideration of the issue, and plantation owners in Virginia and elsewhere began to train their slaves in the home manufacture of shoes and cloth goods, as well as building construction. Another scholar, Marcus W. Jernegan, argues that the diversification of Virginia's agriculture and the expansion of tanneries, ship's stores, leather production, and other craft enterprises were directly responsible for the employment of slave labor in nonagrarian occupations.[3]

Stavisky also reminds us that a minimum of specialization existed in the eighteenth century crafts, so that every trade embraced a wide variety of operations.[4] A Negro blacksmith, for example, could work in iron and fashion his own tools. A carpenter would also be a wood turner, pattern maker, and so on.

The use of slaves in the wide range of skilled work required on the colonial plantation is illustrated by advertisements for the sale of slaves. An advertisement in the *South Carolina Gazette* in 1751 offered "About Fifty Valuable Slaves, among which are sundry tradesmen, such as Bricklayers, Carpenters, Coopers, Sawyers, Shoemakers, Tanners, Curriers, and Boatmen." A 1768 advertisement in the same paper announced the sale of "A Parcel of Slaves belonging to the estate of Mrs. Mary Frost, deceased, consisting of sawyers, mowers, a very good caulker, a tanner, a compleat tight cooper, a sawyer, squarer and rough carpenter."[5] Slaves also worked at manufacturing trades in the colonial towns. A *Gazette* advertisement in that same year offered the shoemaking business of John Matthews for sale, the purchase to include slaves "who have done all my business, for nine years past, and are at least equal to any negroes of the trade in this province. . . ."[6]

A significant characteristic of the southern economy in the eighteenth and early nineteenth centuries was that large plantations functioned virtually as self-contained economic units.* Writing of the colonial period, Eugene D. Genovese observes that "the wealthier plantations resembled industrial villages and substantial numbers of slaves acquired a high level of skill in a wide variety of trades."[7] By 1850 more than 20 percent of the 3.2 million slaves in the South were engaged in activities other than large-scale

---

*An eighteenth century Irish traveler in the United States, Isaac Weld, observed that "[t]he principal planters in Virginia have nearly everything they can want on their own estates. Amongst their slaves are found taylors, shoemakers, carpenters, smiths, turners, wheelwrights, weavers, tanners, and etc. I have seen patterns of excellent coarse woolen cloth made in the country by slaves, and a variety of cotton manufactures. . . . The work is done wholly by slaves, whose numbers are in this part of the country more than double that of white persons. . . ."—Isaac Weld, *Travels through the States of North America and the Provinces of Upper and Lower Canada*, Vol. 1 (London: 1799), pp. 145–152, Letter XI.

agriculture. It has been estimated that 400,000 of these were urban slaves and the balance were in rural areas.[8] Altogether, blacks performed a large share of the nonagricultural labor tasks in the antebellum South. Domestic and personal service accounted for the largest number of nonagricultural jobs for Negroes,[9] but slaves, both rural and urban, as well as free blacks in the towns, also engaged in a variety of other occupations too. Slaves built the plantations and at a later period kept the large ones supplied through small-scale local manufacturing.[10] Slave artisans were worth considerably more money than ordinary field hands; well-trained mechanics sometimes sold for as much as $2,000, compared to a price of $800 to $1,000 for a strong plantation hand.[11]

In the cities, black mechanics were usually "even better trained and more competent workmen than the slave artisans on the plantations."[12] There they usually worked directly for the masters who owned them, but some were hired out as apprentices to white master craftsmen.[13] Although the practice of binding a slave over to another white person, not his owner, was more widespread in the cities, it also occurred in rural areas.

Another kind of hiring-out system, confined almost exclusively to the cities, permitted the slaves to hire out their own time and work for different masters.[14] The slave found his own jobs, paid his owner a fixed weekly or monthly sum or a certain percentage of his earnings, and kept the remainder for himself.

Frederick Douglass in his autobiography describes the system of hiring out that made it possible for him to obtain employment as a caulker in a Baltimore shipyard:

> I was to be allowed all my time, make all contracts with those for whom I worked, and find my own employment; and, in return for this liberty, I was to pay him [Master Hugh] three dollars at the end of each week; find myself in calking tools, and in board and clothing. My board was two dollars and a half per week. This, with the wear and tear of clothing and calking tools, made my regular expenses about six dollars per week. This amount I was compelled to make up, or relinquish the privilege of hiring my time. Rain or shine, work or no work, at the end of each week the money must be forthcoming, or I must give up my privilege. This arrangement, it will be perceived, was decidedly in my master's favor. It relieved him of all need of looking after me. His money was sure. He received all the benefits of slaveholding without its evils; while I endured all the evils of a slave and suffered all the care and anxiety of a freeman. I found it a hard bargain. But, hard as it was, I thought it better than the old mode of

getting along. It was a step towards freedom to be allowed to bear the responsibilities of a freeman, and I was determined to hold upon it.[15]

Whether owned directly by their employers or hired out, urban blacks followed a wide variety of occupations. The relative status of some of these trades is indicated by the different fees the city of Savannah charged for badges (passes) carried by slaves whose masters hired them out by the day instead of by yearly contract. In the highest category a badge cost

> ten dollars for any slave to exercise the trade of cabinetmaker, house or ship carpenter, caulker, bricklayer, blacksmith, tailor, barber, baker or butcher; eight dollars for pilots, fishermen, boatmen, grass cutters and hucksters, four for a porter or other daily laborer but only two and a half for females in the same job.[16]

There was a heavy concentration of blacks in the building trades, including the most highly skilled classifications. The Charleston, South Carolina, municipal census for 1848, for example, showed that black workers outnumbered whites as bricklayers, house and ship carpenters, plasterers, wharf builders, and coopers, and that as many blacks as whites were painters and millwrights.[17] The same general pattern was true for Savannah, New Orleans, and other urban communities. Quite frequently private companies bought black workers to build canals,[18] and most of the railroads in South Carolina were to a large extent constructed with slave labor.[19] In many instances cities, towns, and villages purchased slaves for the purpose of building municipal projects.[20] One visitor to New Orleans was "surprised to discover colored labor running the town's gas works and even more surprised to find a black superintendent who could explain the whole process 'with striking precision and clearness.' "[21]

Slaves also followed maritime pursuits. One estimate puts the number working in internal navigation in the mid-1850s at 5,000.[22] Many thousands of blacks worked in a variety of mining occupations, as in the iron, salt, and lead mines in Missouri, and were hired out to work coal mines in other states.[23]

As the Civil War approached, prominent southern editors, politicians, and industrialists advocated the wider use of slaves in industry. J. D. B. De Bow argued in his influential *Review* that the South could thereby reduce its dependence on northern manufactured goods.[24] In Richmond "the two key industries, tobacco and iron, depended on the Negro."[25] At the Tredegar Iron Works, "blacks did skilled work such as puddling, heating, and rolling as well as the usual common tasks."[26]* In Charleston a newspaper reported in 1853 that slaves in the mills and furnaces had become "expert workers in iron" and urged employers to use slaves more widely.[27] Blacks were also frequently employed in foundries and as blacksmiths.

Slaves worked at iron furnaces in Missouri,[28] where "[s]everal thousand men were employed in the mining of iron and in conducting the iron furnaces . . . and without a single exception the employees were slaves. One company, which was capitalized at $700,000, owned seven hundred slaves."[29] In Alabama, too, the iron industry employed black workers extensively. The Ware family of Birmingham arranged for their slaves to be trained as foundrymen, colliers, furnace engineers, chief coal teamsters, and top fillers and keepers. John Ware wrote that "[t]hey proved faithful and efficient in these places of responsibility and when they became free after the war, their knowledge of such work stood them well in hand and they easily secured remunerative employment with furnace operators."[30]

Slaves were even more common in the tobacco industry. "Nearly all the labor in the tobacco factories of pre-Civil War Virginia and North Carolina . . . was performed by Negro slaves hired out to the manufacturers by their owners. By 1860, these factories employed 12,843 hands."[31] Blacks were employed as twisters, stemmers, screwmen, and jobbers; in fact they performed nearly all the skilled and unskilled tasks in the tobacco industry.[32]

Though historians have held conflicting views regarding the degree and the significance of southern industrialization in the antebellum period, a growing body of evidence establishes that, to the extent that southern industry existed, slaves constituted the basic work force at virtually all levels. The employment of slaves in industry was not merely an extension of the "southern way of life" and less costly than the use of wage workers. It was, from the viewpoint of the slaveowners, an essential instrument for maintain-

---

*The Tredegar Iron Works, in Richmond, was the most important industrial establishment of the antebellum South. Over a period of years the company expanded its slave labor force, and in 1847 a conflict with white workers on this issue arose. When whites were directed to train slaves in skilled occupations such as "puddler" they organized a strike. The strikers were dismissed, and the company continued to employ an increasing number of slaves. See Kathleen Bruce, *Virginia Iron Manufacture in the Slave Era* (New York: The Century Company, 1930), pp. 224–237; Charles B. Dew, *Ironmaker to the Confederacy* (New Haven: Yale University Press, 1966), pp. 22–32. See also S. Sydney Bradford, "The Negro Ironworkers in Ante-Bellum Virginia," *Journal of Southern History*, May 1959, pp. 194–206.

ing their hegemony over the flow of capital in the South and securing their class position against the emergence of independent entrepreneurial groups.

Robert S. Starobin, in his extensively documented study, *Industrial Slavery in the Old South,* concludes:

> By the time of the Civil War, the struggle for southern self-sufficiency had reached a climax. Slaveowning agriculturalists were now vigorously campaigning for slave-based industrialization and they were investing some of their surplus capital in southern industries. Such men, who included many influential Southerners, had overcome their traditional agrarianism and whatever backward-looking tendencies they may have had. They were seeking to create a balanced economy in which the South's great natural potential for agriculture would be complemented by its opportunities for extracting, processing, manufacturing, and transporting its resources and staples. Indeed, one reason why they wanted to expand slavery into the territories, and if possible to reopen the African slave trade, was to accelerate the development of southern industries.
>
> Slaveowners were determined to industrialize the South under their own auspices exclusively, however, so that existing class and caste relationships would remain unchanged. They, therefore, opposed the creation not only of a slaveless industrial bourgeoisie independent of planter control, but also of a free industrial labor force. Had either of these two groups come into being, it might have challenged the slaveowners' domination of southern society. Unless slaveowners directed industries themselves, their ultimate security as a class was in jeopardy.[33]

The widespread domination by slaves of the skilled trades in the South impeded the growth of a free white working class, so that by the beginning of Reconstruction the great majority of skilled workers in the South were black. A federal census of occupations taken in 1865 revealed 100,000 blacks among the 120,000 artisans in the South.[34] It is as though history were making sport of present-day shibboleths when we read the accounts and warnings in antebellum records of the undesirability of employing white immigrants—among them the Dutch and the Irish—as industrial workers and craftsmen in the South because of their drunkenness, shiftlessness, instability, and lack of commitment to what now would be described as the "work ethic," along with the fear that free whites would demand "rights" as workers, including the right to organize, strike, and command higher wages. White immigrants with skills were in the minority. The few who were master craftsmen were valued for training other workers, but proper training was long and costly. The belief in the unreliability of white workers (a consequence of slavery was that it demeaned work and workers), the higher wage base required, and white workers' insistence on better living conditions than slaves combined to discourage the training and hiring of whites for skilled employment.[35]

In the North, where free persons of color were denied equal citizenship rights and where free blacks were not the essential human tool in industrialization, black workers were concentrated in a variety of service and unskilled jobs but were also part of the skilled labor force, especially in the early part of the nineteenth century. In Philadelphia, which had the largest free black population of any northern city, the Society of Friends compiled in 1838 a hierarchy of black occupations that included such skilled jobs as cabinetmaker, plumber, printer, sailmaker, ship's carpenter, and stone cutter, among other crafts.[36]

At the same time, especially in the South, there was a growing movement toward displacing the black worker and restricting permissible occupations. The conversion of "Negro jobs" to "white jobs" actually began before Emancipation. In 1845, for example, Georgia enacted a law prohibiting white persons from entering into a labor contract "with any slave, mechanic or mason, or free person of color, being a mechanic or mason."[37] During this period Virginia and other states enacted similar legislation to prevent the employment of black artisans.

A major example of how considerations of race subsumed conflicts of class occurred in South Carolina in the early 1850s, when widespread action was taken to eliminate black workers from the textile industry. The decision of employers to manufacture textiles with white workers exclusively was based upon the warnings of James H. Hammond and other political leaders, who perceived a potential danger to the stability of the social order if poor whites continued to be excluded from the textile industry.[38] Thus was begun the practice of black exclusion from the major manufacturing industry of South Carolina, a practice which was to be adopted later in other southern states, and which would accelerate in the post-Reconstruction era.

The effects of these legal and social prohibitions were prophetically described by Frederick Douglass in 1853:

> The old avocations, by which colored men obtained a livelihood, are rapidly, unceasingly and inevitably passing into other hands; every

hour sees the black man elbowed out of employment by some newly arrived emigrant, whose hunger and whose color are thought to give him a better title to the place; and so we believe it will continue to be until the last prop is levelled beneath us. . . . It is evident, painfully evident to every reflecting mind, that the means of living, for colored men, are becoming more and more precarious and limited. Employments and callings, formerly monopolized by us, are so no longer.[39]

A typical example of black occupational eviction occurred just after Emancipation, when newly freed blacks in Richmond, Virginia, on August 5, 1865, presented a petition asking for jobs in the tobacco industry which they had formerly held as slaves. They "had been engaged in the tobacco business exclusively before the war," but white workers had been substituted in their places.[40] In the same year, blacks in Baltimore organized a shipyard, the Chesapeake Marine Railroad and Dry Dock Company, because black carpenters and caulkers had been driven from other yards by the refusal of whites to work with them as free men.[41] Nevertheless, as southern industry expanded, black workers were to play an important, but changing, role in the economy, a factor that was to have continuing consequences in the postbellum period.

The Thirteenth Amendment legally ended the institution of slavery, but left unresolved the fundamental issues of land reform and the protection of black labor. The former slaveowners made a successful and determined effort to salvage what they could of their "security as a class" by forcing inferior caste status on the newly emancipated slaves and thwarting the legal rights guaranteed by the Thirteenth, Fourteenth, and Fifteenth Amendments.

The failure to "reconstruct" the South left the black freedman without an independent economic or political base. Once the emancipated black was defined as inferior in a series of court decisions and by social practice, and the Federal Government did little or nothing to insure equal treatment, his economic position continued to deteriorate, thus reinforcing the notion of racial inferiority. In the North (as southern leaders never tired of repeating as evidence of Republican Party hypocrisy) the rights of blacks had seldom been protected—either before Emancipation or after Reconstruction.

After 1877 the willingness of national Republican administrations to make local and state governments responsible for law enforcement on racial matters contributed to the steady and disastrous degeneration of the freedman's political and economic condition; one of the results was the extension of segregated racial employment patterns in the North and South alike. In the latter, it was further institutionalized by law; in the former, it was served by custom. In both, it was enforced by violence. In the post-Reconstruction era, national economic and social forces, together with the proliferation of the infamous Black Codes and Jim Crow laws, conspired to deliver newly freed blacks to the statutory status of nonslaves but not to the equal rights of American citizenship; they were still the bondsmen of subjugation and exploitation.

By the 1880s, with the failed effort of Reconstruction ended and with urbanization and industrialization well under way, black wage earners, in the face of overwhelming difficulties, struggled to participate in the industrial transformation of the nation.

At the beginning of the twentieth century, although already displaced from many skilled occupations and diminished in numbers in others,

> 1,200,000 Afro-Americans worked in the manufacturing, mining, and transportation industries of the United States, most of them in Southern states. With the exception of the cotton textile industry, unskilled black workers played an important part in the development of all major Southern industries. By 1910 almost one-third of the railroad firemen and brakemen and well over half the trackmen in the South were black. In Alabama 55 percent of the coal miners and 80 percent of the iron ore miners were Afro-Americans. They also held a majority of the unskilled jobs in the Gulf Coast lumber industry and in the iron and steel industry of Alabama. Two-thirds of the Virginia shipbuilders, the New Orleans dock workers, and the North Carolina tobacco workers were Afro-Americans. Even the ranching and cattle industry of the Southwest, especially along the Texas Gulf Coast, depended upon black labor; more than one-fourth of the 35,000 cowboys who drove cattle north from Texas between 1866 and 1895 were black. Black drivers predominated as teamsters and draymen in Southern cities. In Atlanta, Memphis, and Birmingham, for example, they held over 80 percent of those jobs. And black craftsmen played a significant role in the construction of Southern cities. By 1910, 15 percent of the carpenters, 35 percent of the brickmasons and 38 percent of the plasterers were blacks.[42]

The status of black workers was becoming increasingly tenuous, however, as the process of racial occupational eviction was accelerated. After Reconstruction, as industrialization increased in the South, new jobs were created that required new skills. White artisans learned their trades under the apprenticeship system of the advancing craft unions, which usually excluded blacks. Black workers "had to depend upon good will and philanthropy," mainly from a diminishing number of neo-abolitionists.[43]

During this period of industrial expansion, white labor unions organized strikes and took other action to force the displacement of black workers from jobs they had long held. In 1890 the Brotherhood of Locomotive Trainmen petitioned the Houston and Texas Central Railroad demanding that all black workers be replaced by whites,[44] and in 1909 white workers struck against the Georgia Railroad to protest the company's practice of hiring black firemen.[45]

Violence frequently accompanied organized labor's efforts to replace black men with white union members, as in a strike called in 1911 to protest the employment of blacks by the Cincinnati, New Orleans and Texas Pacific Railroad, which resulted in the killing of ten black firemen.[46] Similar events were to occur in the railroad industry over a period of many years.

By the turn of the century the process of racial job displacement that had begun in the South was also well under way in the North. Here too economic expansion and the quickened pace of industrialization gave rise to new and more attractive jobs, to which blacks were denied entry. As Gunnar Myrdal wrote in *An American Dilemma,* "[p]rogress itself seems to work against the Negro."[47] At the same time, the emergence of labor unions that excluded blacks on the basis of race also hastened the occupational eviction of northern blacks from skilled jobs.

These trends were accelerated by fluctuations in business cycles. In times of industrial expansion, when labor was scarce, the black "labor reserve" was utilized. But the concomitant losses in periods of recession more than canceled the short-term gains.

When employers wished to hire blacks, white workers frequently protested. Between 1882 and 1900 there were at least fifty strikes by white workers against the hiring of blacks.[48] Some of these strikes failed, but the success of a number of them meant that blacks were effectively barred from almost all the higher paid skilled work in iron and steel manufacturing, in tobacco factories, and in other industries. They also lost their near-monopoly of personal service jobs such as barber, waiter, and porter.[49]

Commenting on developments in the southern states during the early 1900s, C. Vann Woodward writes:

> A large body of law grew up concerned with the segregation of employees and their working conditions. . . . In most instances seg-

regation in employment was established without the aid of statute. And in many crafts and trades the written or unwritten policies of Jim Crow unionism made segregation superfluous by excluding Negroes from employment.[50]

Blacks in tobacco manufacturing lost "what had once been almost a Negro monopoly" as mechanization increased,[51] but, unlike black textile employees, they were assigned to some machine operations. Work in tobacco factories in any department was generally "monotonous, [with] little or no opportunity for advancement, often carried on in badly lighted factories under the worst conditions."[52] Predictably, blacks were concentrated mainly in the stemming divisions, where dust hazards were highest and rates of pay lowest. In iron and steel, most jobs were hot and heavy, and many blacks found employment there, "but most of the higher paid skilled jobs (even if they were both hot and heavy) were exclusively for the white worker."[53]

A similar process was taking place in the North. According to the Philadelphia *Press* in 1894:

> Negroes are tacitly but nonetheless completely excluded from railroad positions on most Northern lines. No Negro is ever seen in a position on a railroad. This industrial exclusion is a most serious injustice and with other like exclusions, lies at the bottom of much of the industrial deficiencies of the Negro.[54]

The emergence of the organized labor movement in the post-Reconstruction period was an important factor in the process of racial occupational eviction. A few unions succeeded in organizing both black and white workers and for a relatively brief period tried to build labor organizations based upon interracial working class unity. Among these were the Knights of Labor, the Brotherhood of Timber Workers, the Industrial Workers of the World, and in its early years the United Mine Workers of America, founded in 1890. But the dominant labor influence at the beginning of the twentieth century, the American Federation of Labor, was to have an adverse effect on the status of black workers, both in the North and South.

In the 1880s and 1890s the success of the American Federation of Labor* as a national organization also led to its power and to its ability to determine the policies and practices around which labor unions were to coalesce. With the rise of the

---

*The American Federation of Labor was founded in 1881 and was originally known as the Federation of Organized Trades and Labor Unions of the United States of America and Canada. In 1886 the name was changed.

AFL, organized labor could have chosen to include black workers in a single, racially unified labor movement. Instead, most unions chose to drive black workers out of competition with white organized workers. This end was achieved with the assent and cooperation of employers, who saw benefits to themselves in policies that guaranteed a supply of cheap black labor, unorganized and unprotected.

The unions affiliated with the AFL and the independent railroad brotherhoods attained their restrictive goals by a variety of methods. These included exclusion of blacks from membership through racial provisions in union constitutions or in the ritual bylaws of local unions; exclusion by tacit agreement in the absence of written provisions; racially segregated units; separate racial lines of seniority and job assignment in union contracts; union control of licensing boards; refusal to admit nonwhites into union-controlled apprenticeship training programs; negotiating discriminatory labor agreements that directly affected black workers while excluding them from union membership and preventing their participation in collective bargaining; and denial of access to hiring halls and other union-controlled job referral systems.

Early in its history, the American Federation of Labor affirmed the principle that "working people must unite and organize, irrespective of creed, color, sex, nationality or politics."[55] The 1890 AFL convention passed a resolution declaring that the federation "looks with disfavor upon trade unions having provisions which exclude from membership persons on account of race or color."[56] At the same convention the AFL refused to admit the National Association of Machinists (later the International Association of Machinists) because the national constitution of the Machinists union limited membership to white persons exclusively. During the 1890s some unions affiliated with the AFL helped black workers in their struggle for labor organization and union recognition. Most important was the historic New Orleans General Strike of 1892, in which thousands of black and white workers joined together in an expression of interracial unionism.[57] But for the most part these were brief and episodic events that soon gave way to the conservative and racially exclusive craft union policies of the AFL.

At the beginning of his long career, Samuel Gompers, the first president of the American Federation of Labor (whose tenure lasted almost uninterruptedly from 1886 to 1924), stated that exclusion of blacks was inimical to the best interests of labor, as a matter of principle and of common sense, because employers would continue to exploit both black and white labor so long as they remained divided. "Wage-workers," Gompers wrote in 1890, "like many others may not care to socially meet colored people, but as working men we are not justified in refusing them the right of the opportunity to organize for their common protection. Then again, if organizations do, we will only make enemies of them, and of necessity they will be antagonistic to our interests."[58] In 1896 he reiterated the necessity of including blacks, again on the grounds of organized labor's perceived self-interest. Otherwise, he said, employers would hire black workers at lower wage rates, thereby defeating union efforts at labor organization.[59]

Nevertheless, Gompers had already begun to compromise his expressed desire to organize black labor by at first covertly—and later openly—acquiescing in the discriminatory practices of many labor unions. Not irrelevantly, as early as the 1870s Gompers had become a leader in organized labor's anti-Oriental campaigns, and soon afterward he advanced vitriolic racist arguments against Asian workers.* By 1905 Gompers was firmly asserting the superiority of Caucasians over black workers. That year, in the September issue of the *American Federationist,* the official journal of the AFL, Gompers declared that the federation did not desire controversy with blacks, "but if the colored man continues to lend himself to the work of tearing down what the white man has built up, a race hatred far worse than any ever known will result. Caucasian civilization will serve notice that its uplifting process is not to be interfered with in any way."[60]

This unabashed avowal of white racial superiority and its "uplifting" ethos came ten years after Gompers had cautiously begun the process of admitting into AFL affiliation those unions that had previously been rejected because of "white-only" membership clauses in their constitutions. By the turn of the century, Gompers and his colleagues had embraced a concept of narrow business unionism on behalf of skilled workers. They used prevalent ideas of white supremacy as an important element in creating a trade union consciousness, rather than a working-class consciousness, among organized wage earners. In the process,

---

*For a study of organized labor's role in the anti-Oriental agitation from the 1850s on, see Alexander Saxton, *The Indispensable Enemy: Labor and the Anti-Chinese Movement in California* (Berkeley: University of California Press, 1971); see also Herbert Hill, "Anti-Oriental Agitation and the Rise of Working Class Racism," *Transaction/Society,* January 1973, pp. 43–54.

Gompers and other leaders of the AFL rejected the goal of building an interracial labor movement.

The incorporation of restrictive racial membership clauses in trade union constitutions antedated the formation of the American Federation of Labor and continued long after its establishment. A typical example of early restrictive membership practices is to be found in the 1864 constitution of the Cigar Makers Union, of which Gompers was a high-ranking official. Article IX stated that "unless said person is a white practical cigar maker," he could not belong to the union.[61] In 1871 the Cigar Makers Union convention transferred the racial exclusion provision from the national union's constitution to the admission ritual of the local union, where it performed the same function,[62] and the International Typographical Union resorted to the same device, as did other unions later on, including the Iron Molders Union, the National Carpenters Union, the Bricklayers and Masons Union, and, in 1895, the National Association of Machinists. Professor Frank E. Wolfe's study of union membership exclusion sums up the racial practices of this period: "Indeed, all available evidence supports the conclusion that Negroes were seldom admitted into a union in any part of the country."[63]

That these exclusionary racial practices continued into the twentieth century is evident from an examination of the constitutions of several important national unions, both AFL and independent. Among the independent unions was the Brotherhood of Locomotive Firemen and Enginemen. Their constitutional provision in 1906 regarding membership qualifications was typical: "He shall be white born, of good moral character, sober and industrious, sound in body and limb, his eyesight shall be normal, not less than eighteen years of age, and able to read and write the English language."[64]

The AFL's Brotherhood of Railway Carmen listed in its constitution the following qualifications for membership:

> Any white person between the ages of 16 and 65 years, who believes in the existence of a Supreme Being, who is free from hereditary or contracted diseases, of good moral character and habits. . . .[65]

The Clerks and Freight Handlers stipulated:

> All white persons, male or female, of good moral character. . . .[66]

The Order of Sleeping Car Conductors:

The applicant for membership shall be a white male, sober and industrious, and must join of his own free will. He must be sound in mind and body.[67]

The Masters, Mates and Pilots:

White person of good moral character, in sound health, and a firm believer in God, the Creator of the Universe.[68]

The Wire Weavers:

Christian, white, male of the full age of 21. . . . Foreigners applying for admission must declare citizenship intentions and pay an initiation fee of $1,000.[69]

During this period the AFL had to decide its policy with respect to segregated Negro locals, since in the past it had revoked charters of some central labor bodies that would not accept delegates from all-Negro units. Segregated locals were originally intended to be temporary, but soon after the AFL constitution authorized them, their establishment became the preferred practice.*

In reality, these segregated locals functioned under restrictions and standards imposed by the same international unions that refused to admit black workers. Thus in 1903 the International Brotherhood of Electrical Workers stated that "we do not want the Negro in the International Brotherhood of Electrical Workers, but we think they should be organized into locals of their own. . . ."[70] One of the major purposes of creating segregated locals and auxiliary units was to prevent blacks from exercising any control over their condition and from participating equally in the labor-management relationship. The existence of segregated locals and racial auxiliaries usually prohibited blacks from gaining knowledge of, and intervening in, the collective bargaining process.

Where black labor unions had already existed and were crucial to AFL organizing efforts, as among longshoremen in New Orleans, Charleston, and other southern cities, they entered AFL-affiliated national unions as segregated locals. Where blacks were admitted into union membership, AFL leaders quickly enforced the segregation of locals as a matter of common practice, and this became the prevailing pattern within the federation.

*Article 12, Section 6, of the AFL constitution, as revised in 1900, reads: "Separate charters may be issued to central labor unions, local unions or federated labor unions, composed exclusively of colored workers, where in the judgment of the executive council it appears advisable."

The aim of white labor organizations to restrict black workers to the lowest rungs of the job ladder was successful. C. Vann Woodward trenchantly sums up the interplay of organized labor's racial caste policies, black occupational eviction, and the emergence of fixed patterns of job deprivation:

> The caste system, the color line, and the new spirit of racial aggression were strongly felt in labor relations and in trade unions. Caste sanctioned a division of labor into white men's jobs and black men's jobs. Sometimes aided by an employer's policy of hiring, sometimes encouraged by politicians, white labor kept up an unremitting pressure to drive Negroes out of the better paid, more attractive work, and further down in the job hierarchy.[71]

Early in the twentieth century the configuration of the racial employment pattern was fixed. The changes in the economic, political, and social order begun after Reconstruction had become clearly defined. Immigrant workers satisfied the increased demand for labor and further served to displace black workers. Despite early hostility toward the impoverished new arrivals who were willing to work for a pittance, the trade union movement was ultimately willing to absorb them while still denying membership, and thus access to skilled craft jobs and labor union protection, to blacks. Farm labor, domestic service, and menial jobs in industry were all that remained open to the black wage earner.

John Stephens Durham described in the *Atlantic Monthly* the persistence with which the Negro's industrial advancement was "now checked by the interference of the labor organizations."[72] Durham proceeded to give example after example of how AFL unions prevented blacks in the North and South from working in a variety of occupations, among them those of baker, confectioner, printer, cooper, painter, and carpenter. Durham concluded that in the past, blacks had worked harmoniously alongside whites in many skilled craft occupations and industries when they had been given an equal chance; now the black artisan class was

> forced to work along menial lines . . . the colored man has come to be associated with this kind of work, and his effort to secure the opportunity to do better is regarded with indifference or with a sense of helplessness. Thus, the Negro as a group is denied the work which it is capable of doing and detesting the work it is forced to do.[73]

Almost as quickly as blacks were displaced from skilled jobs, the myth that they were incapable of doing skilled work was born and took root in the American consciousness, among whites and even among some blacks. During the early 1900s, as blacks were being more and more restricted to menial and unskilled jobs at the lowest pay and losing the share of skilled jobs they had once possessed even as slaves, Booker T. Washington was calling upon blacks to demonstrate their virtues by discipline and hard work in occupations that would keep them out of competition for jobs with whites. According to his precepts, the black who was willing to work diligently within limited job contexts—performing either humble jobs or work that serviced only the black community—was precisely the black who did not threaten the white worker and who could elicit benevolent tolerance from the white establishment.

The great majority of blacks still lived in the South, where they worked mainly in agriculture or domestic service. But throughout the country they were without the protection of organized labor and were prevented from holding any but the meanest jobs. They were compelled to accept whatever wages they were offered or not work at all. When blacks were able to enter new industries, they were limited almost exclusively to inferior positions with little chance of advancement. At the same time, displacement from their traditional work in the railroad industry, in the longshore industry, in skilled construction work, and in the higher status service occupations continued—reaching its peak in the 1930s.

In a study of the racial practices of labor unions published in 1930, Dr. Ira De A. Reid noted that even though some unions had removed racial exclusion provisions from their constitutions, they continued to exclude nonwhites by tacit consent:

> The absence of constitutional clauses discriminating against Negro workers implied their admission into these unions. Tacit agreement, examinations and local determination of eligibility for membership serve as deterrents to Negro exclusion in many unions. The Plumbers have never made an issue of the question of admitting Negroes, though it is generally understood that they are not admitted. Despite persistent efforts of Negro plumbers in Philadelphia, New York, and Chicago to secure membership, they have not succeeded. . . . In Philadelphia, the licensing board will not grant licenses to Negro plumbers.[74]

Under the Wagner-Connery Act of 1935, which became the National Labor Relations Act, the right of workers to organize into unions of their own choosing was given legal sanction and the employer's obligation to engage in "good faith" collective bargaining was established within a comprehensive legal structure. As a result of the failure of Congress to address issues of racial discrimination in the Act—despite pressure from civil rights organizations that it do so—the power of labor unions to engage in a variety of discriminatory racial practices was reinforced by law.

This was also the period when the industrial unions, with a different approach from that of the AFL craft unions, made their great drives to organize industrial workers. Arriving late on the labor scene, the Congress of Industrial Organizations* had fresh possibilities of pursuing nondiscriminatory policies. When the industrial union movement arose the CIO adopted a formal policy of racial equality. Although unevenly implemented and often ignored by its affiliates, the CIO's egalitarian program was an important break with the AFL tradition. The protectionist, guildlike spirit of the AFL craft unions was contrary to the aims and growth potential of industrial unionism, which required the inclusion of all employees in large collective bargaining units as a source of plantwide unity (and then industrywide unity) to exert pressure on employers. Within the industrial unions, organized on vertical lines rather than in the horizontal craft structure of the AFL unions, the forms of racial discrimination changed. Informal discriminatory job practices often became more rigid when separate seniority and promotional lines based on race were structured through provisions in collective bargaining agreements of many CIO industrial unions.

Despite some skepticism based upon their earlier experiences with labor unions, thousands of black workers soon came to accept the CIO. But within a few years they found that they had again become the victims of a different kind of discriminatory pattern. For example, in the southern steel industry, where racial job assignment had been somewhat casual, more classifications had been available to black workers before unionization. In many industries collective bargaining agreements systematized seniority practices in which job assignment, promotion, furlough, and dismissal were based on race. Furthermore, such discriminatory systems were routinely enforceable through union contracts. In the South this was done explicitly by designating racial lines of job progression; in the North, through a variety of euphemisms and through the operation of departmental seniority.

---

*Formed in 1935, as the Committee for Industrial Organization, the CIO was expelled from the AFL and reorganized in November 1938 as the Congress of Industrial Organizations. In 1955 it merged with the AFL to form the AFL-CIO.

Protests by black industrial workers against such discriminatory practices in the North as well as in the South began in the 1940s. The *First Report* of the Fair Employment Practice Committee, established by a federal executive order in 1941, provides the details of a work stoppage by black steelworkers that began on February 25, 1944, at the coke plant of the Carnegie-Illinois Steel Corporation in Clairton, Pennsylvania:

> The stoppage in the coke plant which occurred at midnight, February 25, 1944, was the result of a long series of incidents dating back as far as 1933. Prior to 1933 the entire coke works was manned by Negroes, but thereafter management began to introduce white workers who were taught the various processes in the plant by Negroes. As soon as the white workers became proficient in the operations of the various machines, the Negro workers were transferred to other departments and jobs of a lower classification. Various incidents of this type continued to occur up to December 1943.
>
> The Negro workmen, realizing that they were being steadily barred from all the higher jobs formerly held by them, decided that the only way to regain what they had lost was to tie up the plant by striking. However, by this time, the United Steel Workers of America, Local #1557, had completed an agreement with the management which provided for a definite line of progression from laborers to the top machine jobs in the plant. But because of the fact that all the top jobs were already in the hands of white operators who had displaced Negroes, it appeared that there was little opportunity for Negro workmen to regain these jobs in spite of the new agreement. Moreover, very few of the workmen knew anything at all about this agreement and there had been insufficient time to show any definite improvements attributable to the agreement. Negro workmen on the midnight shift at the byproducts plant refused to work, claiming that they were denied promotions and were actually being passed over by white men with far less seniority.[75]

Typical of action by black steelworkers during the 1950s and early 1960s was the petition to the national offices of the Steelworkers union dated February 5, 1958, from black members of Local 2401 of the United Steelworkers of America, which stated in part that "all the undersigned are employed at the Atlantic Steel Company plant in Atlanta, Georgia, and are members of the Steelworkers Union. For many years we have been denied the right to be upgraded and promoted . . . all the colored workers are kept in laborer jobs while the whites with less seniority are promoted over us."[76] Interestingly enough, many of the aggrieved black workers had played a decisive role in organizing the union at this plant. When the international union failed to respond, the black workers filed complaints with the President's Committee on Government Contracts[77] and the National Labor Relations Board against both the company and the union.[78] But despite the protests of black workers against the discriminatory pattern, local and national union leaders in Atlanta and elsewhere continued to trade off the rights of black workers to obtain greater benefits for whites.

Thus it becomes evident that the exclusionary racial practices of craft unions are but one aspect of the discriminatory activities of organized labor. In contrast to the craft unions, which generally refuse membership to blacks, the industrial unions do organize black workers but often discriminate against them in several ways after they have been admitted into the collective bargaining unit. The discriminatory practices of industrial unions have significant consequences for black and other minority workers as a class.

Frequently these unions actively prevent the participation of nonwhites in union leadership positions and fail to process the grievances of black workers. New testing devices and other non-work-related qualifications, although nondiscriminatory on their face, have kept black workers out of desirable jobs just as effectively as the "white-only" clauses did in the past. Segregated seniority lines openly labeled "white" and "colored" have been eliminated, but separate lines of promotion are maintained in more subtle ways. The wording has changed, but the results for black workers are usually the same.

As black workers in the steel industry, in pulp and paper manufacturing, in oil and chemical refineries, in tobacco factories, and in other industries have learned, what exclusion is to the craft unions, separate lines of promotion and seniority are to the industrial unions.

Organized labor has been able to directly affect the condition of the black worker in regard to seniority and other terms of employment because it has long been a significant factor in the contending aggregations of power within the American polity. This view has been cogently expressed by Carl Brent Swisher:

> Indeed, if we view government in the United States in terms of aggregations of power rather than in terms of concepts of sovereignty, we may say that recent years have brought the development of a new type of federalism. Below the government, however, we find not only the states but also, and often on lines roughly parallel with the states, the more powerful corporations of the country, with labor unions in some instances not much lower than the same parallel lines. A prop-

erly descriptive chart might show a pipeline carrying supplemental power from the federal government to labor unions, to inflate them up to positions of equality with employing corporations so that the process of collective bargaining can be carried on between parties at the same bargaining level.[79]

Elaborating on the contemporary legal implications of this development, Professor Alfred W. Blumrosen has written:

> One objective of the labor policy adopted in 1935 was to create a power unit in the union strong enough to counterbalance the power of the corporation over the employment relation. But once this relationship had developed, the underlying conditions tended to force these conflicting power units, union and employer, into ever broader areas of agreement. They found that, by acting together, they could accomplish mutually shared objectives at the expense of third parties. Law regulating such concerted action between union and employer is only beginning to unfold in this decade.[80]

Aside from such exceptional issues as public health, child labor, and minimum wage and hour requirements, national labor law was, until 1964, concerned almost exclusively with the regulation of relations between management and organized labor, leaving such "third parties" as blacks and women unprotected from discriminatory employment practices.

A consequence of federal labor laws that gave unions legal privileges and immunities was that the government itself became a party to the discriminatory practices of organized labor. In recent years government involvement in the collective bargaining process has greatly increased and takes many forms. In addition to conferring legal authorization upon a union to act as exclusive bargaining agent and providing protection from competing unions, it also requires employers to engage in collective bargaining and makes possible the filing of unfair labor practice charges with the National Labor Relations Board. Agencies of government intervene in wage disputes, mediate labor conflicts, require reporting of union election procedures and disclosure of expenditures, and perform many other regulatory functions. Government also influences labor-management relations through the awarding of contracts and through far-reaching economic policies.

Nearly thirty years ago, C. Wright Mills anticipated that the collective bargaining process would eventually become part of the regulatory function of the state:

One of the trends characterizing U.S. society and accelerated by the New Deal is the increasing integration of real and, more particularly, potential democratic forces into the apparatus of the political state. . . .

The New Deal was an attempt to subsidize the defaults of the capitalist system. Part of this attempt consisted in the effort to rationalize business and labor as systems of power in order to permit a continued flow of profits, investments, and employment. . . .

The power of the union is thus in part dependent upon the continuation of the governmental framework and in part upon the majority will of the employees. Union power is no longer directly dependent upon the strength it has accumulated and put into a direct arrangement with the employer.[81]

With the passage of Title VII, the government's role as protector and regulator of the collective bargaining process came into conflict with its legally mandated responsibility to enforce equal employment opportunity. It may be anticipated that the government will move to accommodate these conflicting functions and, as it has done so often in the past, compromise on the civil rights issue. If this occurs, once again the vital interests of the black population will be sacrificed as a result of the greater political power of employers and organized labor.

The National Labor Relations Board, the major governmental agency directly involved in labor-management affairs, has existed for forty years and has accumulated extensive power and influence. Its policies and practices directly affect employers and organized labor and, indeed, the entire functioning of the collective bargaining system. By contrast, the Equal Employment Opportunity Commission, the major government agency responsible for the elimination of discriminatory employment practices, is a new federal agency that came into being in mid-1965. It is, by any standard of comparison, a weak and administratively awkward agency. By 1974 it was suffering from a crisis of leadership, serious internal conflicts, a huge backlog of unresolved cases, and diminishing authority and influence within the government and the industrial relations community.

Black workers and others have repeatedly found it necessary to initiate litigation in the federal courts to obtain enforcement of their legal rights, and it is the courts, not the administrative agencies of government, that have played the decisive role in interpreting and enforcing Title VII. In this context, the 1974 ruling of the Supreme Court in *Alexander* v. *Gardner-Denver Co.*[82]

is extremely important. By implication, the decision in this case went far beyond the narrow issue presented to the Court—the relationship of arbitration to Title VII procedures—as the opinion suggests that prior agreements of parties and agencies cannot bar access to the courts, and that in Title VII litigation the courts will retain final jurisdiction and the substantive issues will be decided through the judicial process. Although this and related decisions augur well for Title VII plaintiffs, it is doubtful that the protracted, expensive, and difficult process of individual case law can compel a reluctant government to pursue a broad and effective civil rights policy.

Civil rights statutes, federal executive orders, and other restraints on discriminatory practices in the vital area of employment depend in large part on administrative agencies of government for enforcement. Before the emergence of judicial decisions based on Title VII of the Civil Rights Act of 1964, legal prohibitions against job discrimination were for the most part declarations of public policy that rarely became operative. Moreover, federal, state, and municipal governments themselves continued to violate the law by subsidizing in many ways widespread discriminatory employment practices in both public and private sectors of the economy.

Pronouncement of the law may have some symbolic significance, but it is only a beginning. Immediately following the enactment of a civil rights law, a great victory over racism seems to have been won and compliance with the law is anticipated. But the apparent victory is later revealed to be illusory or extremely limited; the forces of tradition and resistance soon act to maintain the status quo. The ability of the government to enforce its laws in the face of pervasive racial patterns is particularly relevant to the subject of employment discrimination.

Compliance with the requirements of the law as it developed in Title VII litigation has been resisted by the two organized groups that have repeatedly been ordered to initiate changes by the courts: employers and labor unions. There are, however, certain notable differences in the forms and the degree to which each has resisted compliance.

As the following chapters demonstrate, employer resistance to change is in large part based on the desire to keep an enterprise operating with a minimum of disruption to established methods. The legally required elimination of discriminatory practices may involve extensive financial costs and the dismantling of long-established employment procedures. In these terms, employer resistance to change is not only a mirror of the racial prejudice of the society at large, it is also rooted in traditional management objections to government interference, although corporate enterprise is the direct beneficiary of many forms of vital government assistance.

The resistance of organized labor is far more complex. For example, because of his race the white worker historically has enjoyed certain specific benefits in employment which, in turn, have created a highly exploited class of black labor that is rigidly blocked from advancing into the all-white occupations. The white plumber, printer, or electrician, by virtue of the exclusion of blacks from the trade, does not have to compete with an entire subclass within the working population. Similarly, in desirable classifications in industrial plants white workers are also exempted from competition with blacks; they are assigned job classifications with a high wage base and have access to better paying, more skilled jobs. Thus white workers have expectations of both the opportunity for employment and the opportunity for earnings and promotion which are based in varying degrees (depending on the industry) on the denial of equal opportunity to blacks. The elimination of racial disadvantages in employment necessarily affects the expectations of white workers, since it compels competition with black workers and other minority group members where none previously existed. White workers, therefore, feel directly "victimized" by legislation, administrative action, and court orders that provide not only for equal job opportunity but for measures that attempt to compensate for the present effects of past discrimination. What the white male worker believes to be at stake is his likelihood of getting a job, his status in the job, his promotion, seniority, and susceptibility to layoff—the entire constellation of expectations which he tacitly assumes are his rights.

Thus the nature and the forms of discriminatory employment practices created in the past by both management and organized labor motivate their resistance to change. These practices have also contributed significantly to the reasons why, more than a century after Emancipation, "the badges and incidents" of slavery remain attached to the black worker.[83] And the meaning of this continuing deprivation in the day-to-day lives of blacks is singularly evident in the destructive relationship between the systematic denial of economic justice to black workers and the denial of equality to black people as a class.

At the beginning of 1975 the black community was again experiencing a crisis of unemployment and underemployment. The national rate of black unemployment was more than double the white rate, and in areas of black urban population concentration, far greater. Official figures do not include large numbers of blacks, especially young workers who have never entered the labor force, "discouraged workers"* who are no longer in the labor force, part-time workers, and the many black underemployed—that is, those who work at less than their highest skills—who have full-time jobs but remain in a permanent condition of poverty. As a result of traditional patterns of job discrimination, blacks are more vulnerable to economic dislocation than any other group of workers, and many of the gains made during the past two decades are rapidly being erased.†

Although the serious economic recession did not begin to affect white workers until mid-1974, a pronounced deterioration of the economic status of blacks was well under way much earlier. Between 1969 and 1972, the number of blacks living in poverty (as conservatively defined by the Federal Government) increased by 600,000 to a total of 7.7 million, while the number of poor whites declined by 500,000.[84] In 1973, blacks made up 30 percent of those living in poverty, about three times their proportion of the total population.[85] Also in that year, "about 8 percent of white persons and 31 percent of black persons were below the poverty level."[86]

The highest unemployment rate during 1973, 34.5 percent, was for minority teenage females. Unemployment for white teenage females was 13.0 percent. The unemployment rate for minority teenage males was 26.9 percent; for white teenage males, 12.3 percent. The unemployment rate in 1973 for black teenagers of

---

*For information on the concept of the "discouraged worker" and its significance, see the following articles which appeared in *Monthly Labor Review* (Washington, D.C.: Bureau of Labor Statistics, March 1973): Paul O. Flaim, "Discouraged Workers and Changes in Unemployment," pp. 8–16; Joseph L. Gastwirth, "Estimating the Number of 'Hidden Unemployed,' " pp. 17–26; and Jacob Mincer, "Determining the Number of 'Hidden Unemployed,' " pp. 27–30.

†The distribution of unemployment and the persistence of the black-white differential is significant. "The U.S. data for 1974 show a wide disparity in unemployment among demographic groups. The unemployment rate is higher for teenagers than for adults, for women than for men, for blacks than for whites, and for unskilled workers than for skilled. These differentials have endured in U.S. labor markets for a long time. Even in 1969, a year of extremely tight labor markets, when the unemployment rate for adult men was 2.1 percent, the unemployment rate was 3.7 for adult women, 6.4 percent for blacks, and 12.2 percent for teenagers."—*Economic Report of the President* (Washington, D.C.: U.S. Government Printing Office, 1975), p. 102.

both sexes was 31.4 percent in contrast to the white teenage unemployment rate for both sexes of 12.6 percent.[87] In early 1975 the rate of unemployment among black teenagers reached 41.1 percent.[88]

At the beginning of the 1970s, black family income for the nation was 61 percent of white family income—an all-time high.[89] In 1971 black family income fell to 60 percent,[90] in 1972 to 59 percent,[91] in 1973 and 1974 to 58 percent.[92] In the past twenty-five years black family income relative to white family income has fluctuated between a low of 51 percent and a high of 61 percent.[93] Furthermore, the disparity in dollar income between blacks and whites has increased. In 1947 the difference between black and white family income was $2,700;* by 1970 the disparity had risen to $3,700.[94] And it is the relative position of blacks to whites that is the crucial factor in measuring progress.†

The "circle of poverty" theory has been in vogue since the late 1950s. Blacks, it is held, are "disadvantaged" because of poor education, poor housing, and poor family life as well as because of overt racial discrimination. Until all these ills are remedied, so the argument goes, no progress is possible. This theory minimizes the fact that racial discrimination is the greatest single cause of black "disadvantage" and is therefore the major factor upon which government policy, if enforced, could have the greatest impact. A nationwide survey conducted by the Equal Employment Opportunity Commission refutes the notion that the lower employment attainment of blacks is due primarily to their inferior education:

> The lower education level of some minority groups is a factor in their lower occupational status, but statistical analyses using two different approaches show that it accounts for only about one-third of the difference in occupational ranking between Negro men and majority group men; the inevitable conclusion is that the other two-thirds must be attributed to discrimination, deliberate or inadvertent.[95]

Since the commission issued this report in 1966, blacks have made dramatic strides in education which have not been equally reflected in employment patterns. If the study were repeated ten years later, one might hypothesize that the difference in occupa-

---

*In 1970 dollars.

†The Federal Government's study based on the 1970 census revealed that in 1969 "[t]he income of the average Negro family with three earners is not significantly different from the family income of the average white family with one earner."—*Current Population Reports,* Series P-23, No. 38, "The Social and Economic Status of Negroes in the United States, 1970" (Washington, D.C.: U.S. Bureau of the Census, 1971), p. 32.

tional attainment between blacks and whites found in the EEOC study would be even less attributable to the lower educational levels of blacks. In other words, the differences in 1975 might be a result of intensified racial discrimination.

In the mid-1970s most jobs were still largely regarded as "black" or "white," and those designated black were inferior in wages and status relative to white labor classifications. In relation to the occupational and income status of whites, black workers are on a treadmill, with no possibility—within the prevailing pattern—of achieving parity with whites.

As certain industries decline, or as the traditional white labor force is no longer available in sufficient numbers, black workers are permitted to move into vacated jobs; for example, in the southern textile industry in the late 1960s black workers became the last available source of cheap labor. The movement of whites out of low-paying textile jobs into new, cleaner, and higher paying industries created a labor shortage, and black workers replaced departing whites.

In the North as well some industries have changed from a white to a predominantly black labor force in a similar pattern. As their status and wages relative to other industries decline, black labor is utilized to replace upwardly mobile whites.* A classic

---

*A striking example of this development may be found in the telephone industry. According to a study made by the Equal Employment Opportunity Commission, "[i]n the last 10 years turnover among Operators has continued to escalate, reaching astounding levels in major urban areas. It is these areas that are becoming increasingly black and in which the Operator's wage is no longer attractive to whites. The combination of these factors is rapidly converting the Traffic Department from simply a 'nunnery' into a 'ghetto nunnery.' This conclusion has been reached repeatedly by persons at the highest levels within the Bell System itself. In October 1969, an extremely important 'Report on Force Loss and the Urban Labor Market' was presented by AT&T Vice President Walter Straley to the assembled Presidents of all Bell companies. According to the report, 'What a telephone company needs to know about its labor market [is] who is available for work paying as little as $4,000 to $5,000 a year.' According to Straley's remarks, two out of three persons available at that wage were black: 'It is therefore just a plain fact that in today's world, telephone company wages are more in line with black expectations—and the tighter the labor market the more this is true.' The AT&T report continues, 'It is therefore perfectly plain that we need nonwhite employees. Not because we are good citizens. Or because it is the law as well as the national goal to give them employment. We need them because we have so many jobs to fill and they will take them.' " The EEOC study concludes that "the increased black employment during the 1960s was dictated by labor market conditions which forced the Bell System to hire black females as Operators. Similar economic factors did not apply to Plant craft jobs and consequently few black males were hired. It is reasonable, therefore, to conclude that the Bell System hired blacks only when there were no economically viable alternatives."— *A Unique Competence: A Study of Equal Employment Opportunity in the Bell System* (an investigative report undertaken by the EEOC pursuant to a petition filed with the Federal Communications Commission, Docket No. 19143, n.d.), pp. 203–206.

example has occurred in the ladies garment manufacturing industry in New York City, whose labor force has become increasingly black, Puerto Rican, and low paid. In 1947, dressmakers earned an average of 42 cents an hour more than steelworkers but in 1967 earned 95 cents *less.* The garment industry paid 33 cents an hour more than the auto industry in 1947; twenty years later, it paid $1.17 less. A study done for this industry by the economist Leon Keyserling was so damaging that it has not been released to the public. It showed that wages have declined in real terms though productivity has been rising, and that the working conditions in garment manufacturing may be among the worst of any unionized industry.[96] By mid-1975, the average earnings in the apparel trades, with its concentration of black and Spanish-speaking workers, had declined to less than half the earnings of workers in the auto and steel industries. The configuration of the black labor force has been changing in some respects, but the pattern of relative deprivation has not.

The *Report of the National Advisory Commission on Civil Disorders* in 1968 summed up the data on the occupational characteristics of the black labor force as follows:

> Even more important perhaps than unemployment is the related problem of the undesirable nature of many jobs open to Negroes. Negro workers are concentrated in the lowest skilled and lowest paying occupations. These jobs often involve substandard wages, great instability and uncertainty of tenure, extremely low status in the eyes of both employer and employee, little or no chance for meaningful advancement, and unpleasant or exhausting duties. Negro men in particular are more than three times as likely as whites to be in unskilled or service jobs which pay far less than most. . . .[97]

For the majority of blacks, little has changed in the years since the commission warned the nation of the potential consequences of continued black deprivation. As a result of litigation and affirmative action programs some modest, if tenuous, progress in job advancement was made by black workers and members of other minority groups. Although not yet fully realized, the potential of Title VII of the Civil Rights Act of 1964 to eliminate widespread discriminatory patterns and to obtain broad relief for the victims of employment discrimination was established. But the decline of the economy and the nation's general retreat from the goal of a humane and just society has resulted in the erosion of past gains. The patterns of employment discrimination continue as employers, labor unions, and government agencies circumvent or resist compliance with the law, and oppose the efforts of black workers and other minority groups to eliminate the dual racial labor system of the American economy.

.The enactment of civil rights laws, especially those prohibiting racial discrimination in employment, in conjunction with a variety of social programs begun during the past two decades, promised a new and better future for black Americans. Because the hope is so great, the promise becomes all the more vivid. But as the promise and the hope fail to materialize, the despair and alienation become more profound. This alienation is rooted in the most significant source of identity for western men and women—work.

Part 1

National Policy and Employment
Discrimination

1

The Judicial Process

The judicial system of the United States has been the major institution of government through which necessary but long-postponed social change has been made, especially in the area of race relations, since the end of World War II. The judiciary not only responded to emerging social forces but also helped create them. Federal court decisions on complex and controversial racial issues in the past thirty years have ushered in a new period in the history of the judicial system and begun a new era in American life. This profound change in judicial perception is all the more significant when we consider the record of racial conflict in American society and the traditional conservatism of the courts.

Historically, the federal courts were primarily concerned with safeguarding property rights and protecting a laissez-faire economy. More recently, the judiciary, especially the Supreme Court, was for two decades concerned with inequality and injustice. In large part, the changed perception of the courts on racial issues was the result of decades of sustained programs of litigation in conjunction with a rising movement of racial protest.

The American judicial system, rooted in the English common law tradition, was rarely a vehicle for major social change. Adherence to precedent, expressed in the principle *stare decisis*—let the decision stand—was a powerful factor in the courts' reluctance to depart sharply from established concepts. Another tradition was that in resolving conflicts between private parties the courts should be socially neutral. There were certain exceptions, but generally, when courts were presented with questions of public policy involving complex social issues, they either decided in favor of the

37

status quo or declined to act on the grounds that such matters were nonjusticiable, that they should be resolved by legislation. Changes in this legal tradition since the early 1950s are notably expressed in the Supreme Court's decisions, under the leadership of Chief Justice Earl Warren, on questions of criminal law, the right to privacy, the "one man, one vote" issue in legislative reapportionment cases, and, most important of all, in race relations.

In the matter of civil rights, the decisions of the Supreme Court and of the federal courts in interpreting the "equal protection of the laws" specified in the Fourteenth Amendment to the Constitution have played a major role in articulating and encouraging social change. Because, as Professor Vern Countryman has noted, "our constitutional system was not founded upon the proposition that racial discrimination should be forbidden,"[1] Supreme Court decisions on segregation in schools and public accommodations and on the issue of voting rights have been rendered not only in the absence of federal legislation but also against many state and local statutes. They have been based on creative constitutional interpretations of the law and on the knowledge that there was an acute social need for these decisions.

The penetrating nature of such judicial orders, and the extent to which they can successfully rend the fabric of tacit legal sanction for widespread patterns of racial discrimination, can be seen in *Hawkins* v. *Town of Shaw*,[2] in which the patterns were attacked on a communitywide basis. In early 1971 the U.S. Court of Appeals for the Fifth Circuit applied the equal protection clause of the Fourteenth Amendment to enjoin the manner in which Shaw, Mississippi, had provided a range of public services.* The court received detailed statistical evidence that the small Delta town of 2,500 persons discriminated against its 1,500 black residents in providing various municipal services, including street paving, lighting, sanitary sewers, surface water drainage, water mains, and fire hydrants, and that there existed a general pattern of unequal treatment based on race. The appellate court stated that the characterization of a segment of society as being "on the other side of the tracks . . . has for too long been a familiar expression to most Americans." It concluded: "Surely, this was enough evidence to establish a prima facie case of racial discrimination." The court held that the correction of such inequalities is, under the

---

*The 1971 decision was made by a three-judge panel of the court. On March 27, 1972, the full circuit court reaffirmed its original order by a 13-to-3 ruling.

Constitution, a proper judicial function. Here the court clearly conceived of its constitutional role as protecting minorities from broad and pervasive patterns of discrimination:

> The separation of powers principle assumes that we have a system of checks and balances. In Madisonian terms, each department or power center is to act as a curb on other departments or centers. Indeed, "unless these departments be so far connected and blended, as to give to each a constitutional control over the others, the degree of separation which the maxim requires as essential to a free government, can never in practice, be duly maintained." Madison, *The Federalist,* No. 48. Utilizing the power vested in this court to check an abuse of state or municipal power is, in effect, consistent with the separation of powers principle.[3]

State and federal statutes prohibiting discrimination in public accommodations, voting, and education were enacted only after a series of Supreme Court decisions during the 1940s and 1950s. The constitutional basis for the Court's decisions in these areas did not seem to be applicable to the question of employment discrimination. A legal distinction had traditionally been drawn between public and private acts of discrimination; hence the discriminatory practices of such "private" parties as employers and labor unions were long held to be free of any constitutional compulsion. The terms of this distinction have changed significantly in the past thirty years. Labor unions, for example, derive their power to act as exclusive representatives of employees from federal law[4]—that power is a consequence of government action. The employer's duty to bargain collectively with unions is enforced by the National Labor Relations Board and the federal courts, fitting the problem squarely within the rule of *Shelley* v. *Kraemer,*[5] a 1948 Supreme Court decision which held that the power of the state cannot be invoked to enforce a "restrictive covenant," a voluntary discriminatory agreement by private parties.

As to employers, many of them—certainly all the major corporate enterprises—have a variety of subsidies, licenses, certificates, government contracts, special tax considerations, and the like, any or all of which may be essential to their business operations, all of which involve government action. In fact, the operation of a business as a corporation is the result of a privilege granted by the state.

Nevertheless, until the enactment of Title VII of the Civil Rights Act of 1964, there was no recognized basis for legal action against employment discrimination by private parties in the federal courts. Litigation against employment discrimination was limited to lawsuits involving various forms of governmental action. A few of these cases were based on the doctrine of the "duty of fair representation," which began to evolve in the federal courts during the 1940s, and others were based on state and local fair employment practice laws.

The Supreme Court decision that established "fair representation" as a possible means of redress was *Steele* v. *Louisville & Nashville R.R. Co.*[6] In that case, black railway workers raised the issue of discriminatory labor unions operating under the mantle of governmental authority. Charles H. Houston, vice dean of the Howard University Law School, originated the concept of applying the "duty of fair representation" required by the Railway Act of 1926 and the National Labor Relations Act of 1935 to discriminatory employment practices based on race. The Supreme Court said in its decision:

> We think that the Railway Labor Act imposes upon the statutory representative of a craft at least as exacting a duty to protect equally the interests of the members of the craft as the Constitution imposes upon a legislature to give equal protection to the interests of those for whom it legislates. Congress has seen fit to clothe the bargaining representative with powers comparable to those possessed by a legislative body both to create and restrict the rights of those whom it represents. . . . [B]ut it has also imposed on the representative a corresponding duty. We hold that the language of the Act to which we have referred, read in the light of the purposes of the Act, expresses the aim of Congress to impose on the bargaining representative of a craft or class of employees the duty to exercise fairly the power conferred upon it in behalf of all those for whom it acts, without hostile discrimination against them.[7]

Application of the fair representation doctrine resulted in several important court decisions, but the doctrine itself was sharply limited because it did not deal with such essential questions as union membership for black workers and segregated locals. In addition, for many years the National Labor Relations Board did not apply the duty of fair representation in the area of racial discrimination.

In a study of decisional law under the doctrine of fair representation, Neil Herring wrote:

> Certainly judicial remedies for racial discrimination have been of some value. . . . The threats of money damages and embarrassing litigation have been useful even against unions that acknowledged

their *Steele* obligations. In *all* cases, Negro plaintiffs have improved their situation over what it would have been without solicitation of judicial rescue. But viewed from the evidence here presented or from Negro workers' ambitions, judicial relief has been fragmentary in scope and accomplishment.[8]

The very nature of the judicial process has retarded enforcement of the duty of fair representation. Lawsuits are expensive and time consuming. Reliance on the case-by-case method to enforce any law guarantees that enforcement will neither be uniform nor have a consistent direction. Furthermore, in fair representation cases involving racial issues the courts were not concerned with the underlying social patterns that fostered discrimination.

In every successful case brought under the fair representation doctrine, the defendant union was ordered to protect the plaintiff in the collective bargaining process; but there was never an affirmation of the right of black workers to participate directly in the bargaining process through access to union membership, much less to leadership positions within the union.

The concept of the duty of fair representation has been significantly changed by Title VII litigation. Whereas under the doctrine of the *Steele* case the duty was interpreted negatively, under Title VII the doctrine was interpreted affirmatively. Thus a union is at least technically liable for discriminatory terms and conditions of employment when it has given its active or tacit consent to such discrimination. For example, a union's execution of a collective bargaining agreement which contains discriminatory provisions violates the duty of fair representation laid down by Title VII even when the union's role is passive. Because Title VII creates an affirmative duty not to discriminate, if standard labor law is applied the union is liable under Title VII when it enters into a contract containing discriminatory provisions.*

State fair employment practice laws, the second means of redress for discrimination in employment before the passage of Title VII, were as inadequate as the fair representation doctrine.

*For example, in *Myers* v. *Gilman Paper Co.*, 392 F. Supp. 413, 10 FEP Cases 220, 9 EPD para. 9920 (S.D. Ga. 1975), a federal court held that the passive role of unions in failing to renegotiate contracts which discriminated against black workers made the unions, along with the employer, liable for monetary damages under Title VII. The court further held that local unions have an affirmative duty to eliminate discriminatory practices based upon provisions in collective bargaining agreements and that an international union violates Title VII when it fails to act to obtain compliance with the law by its locals, notwithstanding the contention of the international union that no agency relationship exists between it and local affiliates.

Here too a major problem was the limitation of the law in recognizing the social nature of employment discrimination, and the resulting limitation of judicial remedy. State agencies and courts in states with fair employment practice laws viewed—and still tend to view—racial discrimination in employment as a consequence of individual acts of bigotry, with the result that only extremely limited relief was provided for the victims. On the federal level, after the doctrine of fair representation was interpreted to prohibit discriminatory racial practices, successful plaintiffs were awarded individual relief, while the broad patterns of discrimination remained untouched by the courts.

But job discrimination does not—as spokesmen for employers and labor unions would have it—occur "in isolated pockets."*. Rather, these "pockets" reveal the operation of racial employment patterns which can be broken only by sweeping measures. Specific instances of discrimination are the product of long-established employer and labor union practices involving the basic institutions of the work place and the very structure of labor-management relations, including the collective bargaining process itself.

The extent to which state antidiscrimination agencies have failed to perceive that individual acts of employment discrimination usually indicate systematic patterns is underscored by their emphasis on voluntarism rather than on law enforcement—on voluntary settlements that invariably provide less than the law requires and that often perpetuate the discriminatory pattern. Even the few states with strong civil rights statutes have persisted in avoiding enforcement.

Among the reasons why municipal and state civil rights commissions failed to enforce the law is that such administrative agencies usually became vehicles of social control, primarily concerned with reducing community tensions instead of achieving the goals for which the agencies were supposedly created. Clearly, strong laws are not enough. Most state fair employment practice agencies have never lacked the *power* to function as instruments of social change. Professor Countryman writes that "[t]he chief shortcoming of the states as a source of protection against discrimination in employment, then, does not lie in their want of power to act. It lies, rather, in the unwillingness of some of them to

*For example, see Brief of State of New York in *Carr* v. *Rockefeller*, Civil Action No. 1970–521 (W.D. N.Y.). The Civil Rights Resolution adopted by the eighth AFL-CIO convention, October 1969, refers to "pockets of discrimination."—Publication No. 8F, AFL-CIO, Washington, D.C., unpaged.

do so."[9] Timothy Jenkins, a consultant to the Equal Employment Opportunity Commission, has detailed the charge:

> Thirty-three states now have fair employment practice commissions. Without exception each of these has proved a dismal failure in altering patterns of employment for minority group workers within their jurisdiction. . . .
>
> Symptoms of their malfunctioning are the few cases they handle, the large percentage of those cases dismissed for lack of jurisdiction, the large percentage of those in which they find no cause, the few successful cases they conclude annually, and the low level of relief they grant to charging parties and their class as well as the impractical delays intervening between the filing and the final decree.[10]

Considering these basic defects in the administrative processing of complaints of employment discrimination during the twenty years preceding Title VII, it is hardly surprising that the record of both federal contract compliance agencies and state civil rights commissions demonstrates that the public policy against employment discrimination has been unenforceable by administrative means.* These agencies have been unwilling to understand the social and institutional character of employment discrimination.

---

*Alfred W. Blumrosen, former chief of conciliations of the Equal Employment Opportunity Commission, concludes that the "dismal history" of administrative civil rights agencies "is one of timidity in investigation, vacillation in decision-making, and soft settlements which failed to aid the victims of discrimination and did not remedy the broader social problems. . . . A quarter century of administrative effort has failed to produce a body of law which defines discrimination. . . . The pure administrative process has proved incapable of coping with employment discrimination."—Alfred W. Blumrosen, *Black Employment and the Law* (New Brunswick, N.J.: Rutgers University Press, 1971), pp. 6–7. See also Herbert Hill, "Twenty Years of State Fair Employment Practice Commissions: A Critical Analysis with Recommendations," *Buffalo Law Review,* Fall 1964, pp. 22–69; Joseph Minsky, "FEPC v. Illinois: Four Stormy Years," *Notre Dame Lawyer,* December 1965, pp. 152–181; Alfred W. Blumrosen, "Antidiscrimination Laws in Action in New Jersey: A Law-Sociology Study," *Rutgers Law Review,* Winter 1965, p. 187; Richard B. Couser, "The California FEPC: Stepchild of the State," *Stanford Law Review,* November 1956, pp. 187–212; Arthur Frakt, "Administrative Enforcement of Equal Opportunity Legislation in New Jersey," *Rutgers Law Review,* Winter 1967, p. 442; Jay Anders Higbee, *Development and Administration of the New York State Law Against Discrimination* (University, Ala.: University of Alabama Press, 1966). For the history of fair employment practice laws, see Arthur E. Bonfield, "The Origin and Development of American Fair Employment Practice Legislation," *Iowa Law Review,* June 1967, pp. 1043–1092; Michael I. Sovern, *Legal Restraints on Racial Discrimination in Employment* (New York: The Twentieth Century Fund, 1966); Sanford Jay Rosen, "The Law and Racial Discrimination in Employment," in Arthur M. Ross and Herbert Hill, eds., *Employment, Race, and Poverty* (New York: Harcourt, Brace & World, 1967), pp. 479–540. See also Vern Countryman, "Discrimination in Employment," in Vern Countryman, ed., *Discrimination and the Law* (Chicago: University of Chicago Press, 1965), pp. 20–35.

Their reliance on voluntarism rather than on law enforcement has itself been an effect of the failure to perceive that discrimination is not a consequence of random acts of malevolence. As a result of protest and exposure, an employer or union may, on occasion, be expected to remedy single acts of discrimination, but to uproot a basic pattern of industrial activity obviously requires the will to apply the full power of the law, a will that has been singularly absent.

Samuel C. Jackson, a former EEOC commissioner, had evaluated pre-Title VII handling of employment discrimination:

> Looking back at efforts aimed at employment discrimination antedating Title VII, one perceives that they were, by and large, ineffective, not because the law lacked strength, but because of the failure of the administrator and the courts to see the shape of the target. Enforcement focused on individual acts of discrimination and failed to perceive that a specific act of discrimination was often embedded into the institutions of an employment relationship, such as the collective bargaining agreement . . . one might say that prior to the enactment of Title VII, compliance activity was concerned with the wrong done the complainant—an issue of no slight importance—to the virtual exclusion of the subject matter of the dispute, the *practice* of employment discrimination.[11]

A striking example of this may be found in the state of New York. The New York antidiscrimination law adopted in 1945 was the first such state statute, and it remains potentially the strongest fair employment practice legislation enacted by any state. But its powers have rarely been invoked, and the state human rights commission has long been a passive, complaint-taking agency.[12]

Two classic instances of the failure of a state civil rights agency, even one with extensive statutory powers, to enforce the law appear in the response of the New York State Commission for Human Rights to long-standing complaints of black workers against labor unions with collective bargaining agreements in two major sectors of the economy of New York City—construction and garment manufacturing.

As early as 1948 the state commission ordered Local 28 of the Sheet Metal Workers International Association, AFL, to desist from "executing and/or maintaining constitution or by-law provisions which exclude Negroes," and the "Caucasian-only" clause was removed from the local union's constitution. Fifteen years later, however, not a single Negro had been admitted to union membership and union-controlled employment. In 1963

James Ballard, a twenty-two-year-old black Air Force veteran, initiated a complaint against Local 28 before the state commission with the assistance of the Civil Rights Bureau of the state attorney general's office. In 1964, after an extensive investigation and public hearings, the commission ruled that Local 28 had "automatically excluded" blacks over the entire seventy-eight years of its existence and ordered the union to cease and desist from such practices.[13] But after more than two decades of conferences, negotiations, administrative procedures, litigation in the state courts, and repeated antibias pledges by the union, the racial pattern in this construction union remained basically unchanged. In 1974 the Federal Government brought suit against Local 28 under Title VII,[14] charging the union with, among others, the following unlawful practices: failing and refusing to admit, refer, and recruit blacks on the same basis as whites; failing and refusing to permit contractors with whom the union had collective bargaining agreements to fulfill affirmative action obligations imposed upon those contractors by Executive Order 11246 by refusing to refer to jobs blacks whom such contractors wished to employ; and failing and refusing to make known to nonwhite workmen employment opportunities or otherwise to take affirmative action to overcome the effects of past racially discriminatory policies and practices. The suit against Local 28, with the city of New York an intervening plaintiff, was scheduled for trial early in 1975.

A discriminatory pattern in a different context occurs in New York's garment industry, which, unlike the construction industry, employs many nonwhite workers. This history too can be documented from the inception of the state antidiscrimination law.

In 1946 a formal complaint was filed by a black worker against the International Ladies' Garment Workers' Union, AFL, because Local 89, the Italian Dressmakers Union, had barred her from membership.[15] After the New York State commission had notified the ILGWU that nationality locals violated the state law, the commission sought to conciliate the case. It failed to perceive that the worker's complaint—as subsequent investigation revealed—was a response to systematic policies and practices which had serious discriminatory consequences for black and Puerto Rican garment workers. Rather than use the specific complaint to eliminate the discriminatory pattern, the commission entered into a conciliation agreement. But twenty-five years later not a single black or Spanish-speaking person held membership in the Italian locals, and the ILGWU had taken no action to comply with the state law.*

In 1961 a young black worker, Ernest Holmes, filed a complaint against the Cutters Union, Local 10 of the ILGWU, with the New York state commission charging that he had been denied membership in this craft local because of his race.[16] After trying for more than a year to conciliate the case, the commission made a formal finding of "probable cause" and ordered the union to accept Holmes into membership. A year after that, the ILGWU finally entered into a stipulation agreement regarding Holmes and the complaint was withdrawn.

Like the Local 28 case, *Holmes* is typical of cases handled by state fair employment practice agencies. Long-drawn-out attempts at conciliation took precedence over enforcement of the law, and although there was overwhelming evidence of discrimination, the commission centered its efforts on resolving the single pending case, ignoring the context of years of discriminatory practices that excluded blacks and Puerto Ricans from skilled, higher paying jobs in the major manufacturing industry of New York City.

As in the construction industry, garment workers belonging to minority groups are still seeking relief. Between 1968 and 1975 many charges were filed with the Equal Employment Opportunity Commission against the ILGWU and its locals in the New York area.[17] These included *Tucker* v. *Pickwick Knitting Mills and Local 155, ILGWU, and International Ladies Garment Workers Union, AFL-CIO,*[18] in which black and Puerto Rican workers in Brooklyn, New York, charged the union and the company with racial discrimination in job classification and wages. There were, in addition, more than thirty-five charges pending against the ILGWU and employers in other cities.[19]

In the twenty years preceding the enactment of the Civil Rights Act of 1964, there was little advance beyond the limited holdings in the "duty of fair representation" cases and the state fair

*Nationality locals have been illegal since 1945 in New York under the state antidiscrimination law. Title VII further requires the elimination of such locals, and some unions have moved to disband them. In 1966 the New York Furriers Union Joint Council, affiliated with the Amalgamated Meat Cutters and Butcher Workmen of North America, AFL-CIO, dissolved its forty-year-old Greek Fur Workers local. The 1,500-member local went out of existence, and its members transferred to other locals as a result of action taken by the international union to comply with Title VII. Although the Furriers union and other labor organizations have moved to disband nationality locals because of legal requirements, the ILGWU maintains two Italian-language locals in New York City—Local 89, called the Italian Dressmakers Union, and Local 48, the Italian Cloakmakers Union.

employment practice laws. In the early 1960s, however, a nationwide protest movement began to draw serious attention to the legitimate grievances of black Americans. In addition to other civil rights demands, the black community, again faced with unemployment and underemployment in the midst of a high-water mark of prosperity and affluence for the rest of the country, demanded an end to racial discrimination in employment.

In belated response to this intensive national protest, the Congress adopted the Civil Rights Act of 1964. The Act is the most important and comprehensive civil rights legislation since the ratification of the Thirteenth, Fourteenth, and Fifteenth Amendments to the Constitution. Among its eleven major sections is Title VII, the Equal Employment Opportunity Act.[20] With its amendments, known as the Equal Employment Opportunity Act of 1972,[21] Title VII prohibits unlawful forms of discrimination in private and public employment and makes such discrimination, whether as a result of actions by employers or by labor unions, a federally judiciable matter.

Title VII was a compromise measure and was among the most fiercely challenged portions of the entire Civil Rights Act; indeed, its enforcement powers were limited and its effective date was postponed for a year after passage. The 1972 amendments extending its coverage were also hard-fought. Although some parts of Title VII provide for delays and awkward enforcement procedures, it must be recognized that whatever its shortcomings, Title VII has directly involved the Federal Government in eliminating job discrimination more forcefully than ever before. It has provided for the first time a usable statutory basis for attacking discriminatory practices throughout the American economy.

Title VII prohibits discrimination in employment because of race, color, religion, sex, or national origin. It covers the employment practices of employers with more than fifteen employees, employment agencies servicing employers covered by the Act, and labor organizations with fifteen or more members. As amended in 1972, the law gives the Civil Service Commission authority to enforce equal employment requirements within the Federal Government and it also covers agencies of state and local governments and most educational institutions.*

*Title VII became effective on July 2, 1965. During its first year the law was limited to employers with 100 or more employees and labor organizations with 100 or more members. In July 1968 the law became applicable to employers of twenty-five or more and labor organizations with twenty-five or more members, and in March 1973 the number was reduced

The basic obligations imposed upon employers under the law are set forth in Section 703(a), which declares that it is an unlawful practice for an employer

1. To fail or refuse to hire or to discharge any individual, or otherwise to discriminate against any individual with respect to his compensation, terms, conditions, or privileges of employment, because of such individual's race, color, religion, sex, or national origin; or
2. To limit, segregate, or classify his employees or applicants for employment in any way which would deprive or tend to deprive any individual of employment opportunities or otherwise adversely affect his status as an employee, because of such individual's race, color, religion, sex, or national origin.

The same restrictions apply to discrimination in apprenticeship and other training programs undertaken by employers, labor unions, or joint labor-management committees. In addition, retaliation against those who seek to invoke the law is expressly forbidden.

Administrative responsibility for the operation of Title VII rests with the five-person Equal Employment Opportunity Commission appointed by the President. The commission itself has no direct enforcement powers; its functions consist of investigation, persuasion, conciliation, and initiation of lawsuits in the federal courts.*

By the time Title VII became law, judicial experience in other areas of racial discrimination had had an important effect on the determination of employment discrimination issues. For example, court decisions interpreting Title II of the Civil Rights Act of 1964, which prohibits segregation in public facilities, forestalled potential defense arguments in employment cases based on the commerce clause.[22] More importantly, the line of segregation cases beginning with *Brown* v. *Board of Education*[23] created a judicial climate in which the class character of racial discrimination was recognized in

---

to fifteen. Labor organizations are included within the law if they operate hiring halls or represent or seek to represent employees of a covered employer, even if the membership of a local labor organization is less than the established minimum.

*Under the 1972 amendments, the EEOC was given authority to litigate against private parties under Section 706 of the Act, involving failure of respondents to comply with the law. Only the Attorney General is permitted to sue agencies of government. Effective March 24, 1974, the authority to file a lawsuit in the private sector under Section 707, concerned with "pattern or practice" violations, was transferred from the Department of Justice to the commission. (For a detailed discussion, see Volume II, Chapter 1.)

the early decisions under Title VII. In *Hall* v. *Werthan Bag Corp.*,[24] a district court said that "[r]acial discrimination in employment is by definition a class discrimination. If it exists, it applies throughout the class."

During the first decade of the law's existence, the primary method of enforcement of Title VII was through private litigation brought by victims of discrimination. There is some reason to believe that Congress meant Title VII to be enforced through the case-by-case method, but because the debates on Title VII do not adequately reveal congressional intent, or show much understanding of the nature of the problem of employment discrimination, it is impossible to determine Congress's precise view of the law.

Frequent references to the various state agencies in the debates preceding its passage indicate, however, that Congress assumed that the effect of Title VII would not be substantially different from that of state and municipal antidiscrimination laws. Accordingly, the question of whether the Equal Employment Opportunity Commission would have direct enforcement powers was not seriously debated. Congress was aware that such powers are rarely, if ever, exercised by state agencies, and it had no reason to believe that a federal agency would act differently. However, the denial of cease-and-desist powers to the EEOC, demanded as the price for ending a filibuster against the original bill, was legislative excess, designed to protect employers and unions from "harassment" (the concern with "harassment" was frequently stressed by Senate Minority Leader Everett M. Dirksen of Illinois during hearings on EEOC appropriations). Congressional compromises on the enforcement provisions of Title VII were intended to foreclose any possibility of a meaningful attack on institutional discrimination.

Until the 1972 amendments authorized the Equal Employment Opportunity Commission to initiate lawsuits, Title VII was among the weakest of the fair employment practice laws. The EEOC was charged primarily with conciliation and negotiation and, unlike some state agencies, lacked enforcement powers. The Attorney General of the United States was authorized to bring "pattern or practice" suits, but the Department of Justice filed few cases in the first years after the enactment of Title VII. In 1972, when Congress amended Title VII, direct enforcement in the form of cease-and-desist powers was again denied.

Like many private groups, Congress apparently viewed employment discrimination as random rather than systematically structured. The initial separation of EEOC processes and those of the Department of Justice was evidence of this. The commission was restricted to the voluntary resolution of claims through conciliation, and the Department of Justice alone could seek judicial relief. The EEOC was funded to process 2,000 claims in its first year of operation, with a budget of two and a quarter million dollars,[25] but the Department of Justice was given only trivial extra moneys for its responsibilities under the newly enacted law.

All this, plus the background of the general failure of state agencies, argues strongly for the conclusion that although Congress had some awareness of the existence of institutional discrimination, it did not consider such discrimination the major problem. It is probably safe to say that Congress never imagined Title VII would be any more effective in dealing with discriminatory patterns than the state antidiscrimination laws from which it was drawn.*

The Act specified that if the EEOC did not find a "pattern or practice" violation, it could not refer the complaint to the Department of Justice for action. Nothing in our legal tradition suggests that an individual case is assumed to be of little consequence and that a pattern must be established before judicial enforcement can be sought. But ironically, the restriction placed on the EEOC to refer only those cases involving a "pattern or practice" of discrimination was used by the courts to initiate broad social change. The very weakness of the Title VII statute precluded the commission's following the usual course of state agencies in using its administrative powers to "patch over" employment discrimination problems. Respondents before the EEOC had so little to fear in the form of enforcement, and so little awareness of the threat inherent in private litigation, that many of them were

---

*During the congressional debates on Title VII there were many references to state fair employment practice agencies. For example, Senator Leverett Saltonstall of Massachusetts, in discussing the relationship of conciliation to court enforcement of antidiscrimination laws, stated that "[i]n Massachusetts, we have had experience with an arrangement of this sort for 17 years; and, as I recall, approximately 4,700 unfair practices complaints have been brought before our Massachusetts Commission Against Discrimination. Only two of them have been taken to court for adjudication. One has been decided, and a second is now in court, but has not yet been decided. That procedure is the basis and theory of this part of the bill, and that is why I support it."—*Legislative History of Titles VII and XI of Civil Rights Act of 1964* (Washington, D.C.: Equal Employment Opportunity Commission, n.d.), p. 3311. Congressman Ogden R. Reid of New York, arguing for the passage of Title VII, placed in the record documentation showing the disposition of complaints filed with the New York State Commission on Human Rights from its inception and stated that "[f]rom 1945 to 1963— 10,869 total complaints were filed—over 8,000 of these on employment—and the vast majority were settled voluntarily by conference, conciliation, and persuasion. Of the some 1 percent that finally went to public hearings only 12 today are still pending."—*Id.*, p. 3346.

unwilling to submit to the commission's persuasion or recommendations for conciliation. Because the EEOC had no power to enforce its recommendations, a meaningful threat of court action was imperative to make Title VII administratively workable. And because it could not initiate litigation, this was accomplished by a joining of privately initiated litigation with legal support from the EEOC; that is, by the commission providing investigative reports and filing briefs *amicus curiae.*

Invoking the decision in *Udall* v. *Tallman*[26]—in which the Supreme Court in 1965 ruled that "great weight" must be given to an agency's view of the statute under which it operates (thereby establishing an important general principle for administrative agencies)—the commission urged the courts toward strong enforcement. This approach, in conjunction with aggressive private party litigation, produced a new body of law which transcends anything known before under fair employment practice laws.

First the courts were urged by the EEOC and by private litigants to give little or no weight to the administrative process itself. Procedural or other deficiencies in the administrative process were of no consequence to the plaintiffs because it was they and not the commission who bore the real burden of enforcing the law through the courts. The standard of relief to be applied to Title VII cases, it was successfully argued, was not to be determined by administrative "expertise" or the lack of it, but essentially by a constitutional test. The range of the judicial proceeding was not to be restrained by the administrative process but could only be expanded by it. Early in its organizational stage, the EEOC decided to take measures that would facilitate rather than frustrate the broad application of the law. The statute's requirement of deferral of complaints to state fair employment practice agencies was interpreted by the commission in such a manner as to minimize administrative delay; the commission deferred charges for the statutory period only and then routinely began its own processing of the case.

In *Crosslin* v. *Mountain States Telephone & Telegraph Company*[27] the Supreme Court in 1971 modified the requirement that charging parties defer their complaints to a state agency when that agency has no authority to provide adequate relief. This was the first time the Supreme Court decided a procedural question involving Title VII. In the early period of the evolution of the law under Title VII, court decisions on procedural matters were extremely important in forming the substance of the law.*

The requirement of filing a sworn charge was also liberally interpreted, with support from the courts,† and the commission initiated the concept of "continuing violations," so that the Act's statute of limitations cannot frustrate implementation of the law.‡ In addition, the investigation and reasonable cause phases of the EEOC process were separated from the conciliation process. Most state fair employment practice agencies, by contrast, combine the investigation and conciliation processes, with the result that inadequate investigations, protracted delays, and irresolute conciliations occur. In the seven-year absence of direct enforcement powers, the EEOC adopted measures that—while leaving much to be desired—simplified the administrative procedures of Title VII and facilitated court enforcement of the law.

Litigation arising under Title VII began appearing in the federal courts as early as the fall of 1966, and despite some early adverse decisions by district judges, it was clear almost from the beginning that plaintiffs in Title VII cases would be beneficiaries of the favorable judicial climate generated by the body of law which developed out of the school segregation cases.** The mood of the courts was expressed in 1970 by the Court of Appeals for the Fifth

---

*The EEOC, through briefs *amicus curiae,* argued that charging parties should have direct and rapid access to courts. The most important cases in this regard were those in which the commission took the position that an EEOC finding of no cause should not preclude access to the courts. See *Fekete* v. *United States Steel Corp.,* 424 F.2d 331, 2 FEP Cases 540 (3rd Cir. 1970); *Flowers* v. *Laborers International Union of North America, Local 6,* 431 F.2d 205, 2 FEP Cases 881 (7th Cir. 1970), *reversing and remanding,* 2 FEP Cases 235 (N.D. Ill. 1969); *Robinson* v. *P. Lorillard Corp.,* 444 F.2d 791, 3 FEP Cases 653 (4th Cir. 1971), *affirming in part and reversing in part, and remanding,* 2 FEP Cases 465 (M.D. N.C. 1970); and *Beverly* v. *Lone Star Lead Construction Corp.,* 437 F.2d 1136, 3 FEP Cases 74 (5th Cir. 1971).

†See, for example, *Blue Bell Boots, Inc.* v. *EEOC,* 418 F.2d 355, 2 FEP Cases 228 (6th Cir. 1969), *affirming* 295 F. Supp. 1060, 1 FEP Cases 346, 69 LRRM 2009 (M.D. Tenn. 1968); and *Georgia Power Co.* v. *EEOC,* 412 F.2d 462, 1 FEP Cases 787, 71 LRRM 2614 (5th Cir. 1969), *affirming* 295 F. Supp. 950, 1 FEP Cases 351, 69 LRRM 2017 (N.D. Ga. 1968).

‡See *Cox* v. *U.S. Gypsum Co.,* 409 F.2d 289, 1 FEP Cases 714, 70 LRRM 3278 (7th Cir. 1969), *affirming as modified,* 284 F. Supp. 74, 1 FEP Cases 602, 70 LRRM 2423 (N.D. Ind. 1968); and *Macklin* v. *Spector Freight Systems, Inc.,* 478 F.2d 979, 5 FEP Cases 994 (D.C. Cir. 1973), *reversing and remanding,* 4 FEP Cases 662 and 663 (Dist. Col. 1971).

**For historical data on the development of programs of litigation by civil rights organizations that culminated in the Supreme Court decision in *Brown* v. *Board of Education,* see Herbert Hill and Jack Greenberg, *Citizen's Guide to Desegregation: A Study of Social and Legal Change in American Life* (Boston: Beacon Press, 1955); Clement E. Vose, "Litigation as a Form of Pressure Group Activity," *Annals of the American Academy of Political and Social Science,* September 1958, pp. 20–31. For a history of the continuity of efforts to utilize the law against racial discrimination, see Loren Miller, *The Petitioners: The Story of the Supreme Court of the United States and the Negro* (New York: Pantheon Books, 1956).

Circuit in *Culpepper* v. *Reynolds Metals Company:* "Title VII of the Civil Rights Act provides us with a clear mandate from Congress that no longer will the United States tolerate this form of discrimination. It is, therefore, the duty of the courts to make sure that the Act works."[28] Given the weakness of the statute, the significant decisions that developed out of Title VII litigation— which the *Culpepper* case typifies—are at first surprising, but only if changes in the judicial perception of racial issues since *Brown* v. *Board of Education*[29] are ignored.

The courts are increasingly aware of the fact that acts of racial discrimination in employment take place in a broad context of social behavior which promotes discrimination. The entire structure of employment practices is seen as more the "enemy" than the individual discriminator (for example, *Parham* v. *Southwestern Bell Telephone Company*[30]). In Title VII cases the federal courts are now recognizing the significance of institutional patterns and are fashioning remedies which go far beyond redress to individual plaintiffs.* A major example of this was the decision of the Supreme Court in *McDonnell Douglas Corp.* v. *Green*[31] where the Court recognized the relevance and importance of "pattern" evidence in an individual case.

The first major case in which the courts began to recognize that justice required a remedy beyond redressing individual complaints was *Jenkins* v. *United Gas Corporation.*[32] Here an appellate court perceived that if Title VII suits were to effect social change, they should be classwide.

Thomas L. Jenkins, a black employee of the United Gas Corporation, had been refused a promotion to the job category of serviceman with the company. After the EEOC found "reasonable cause" to sustain the allegations of his charge, and after he had filed suit in a federal district court in Texas, the company offered Jenkins the position he had sought, and he accepted. The company then successfully argued in the district court that his promotion

---

*A review of Title VII litigation will demonstrate that the Department of Justice has not often been responsible for innovative law in this field; most major developments have grown out of private litigation by civil rights organizations. Until 1972 the Department of Justice was hesitant in seeking back pay in Title VII cases, although the right to back pay was well established as part of the total equitable relief to which the victims of employment discrimination are entitled. See *Bowe* v. *Colgate-Palmolive Company,* 416 F.2d 711, 2 FEP Cases 121, 223 (7th Cir. 1969). See also *Albemarle Paper Co.* v. *Moody,* 422 U.S. 405, 10 FEP Cases 1181, 9 EPD para. 10,230 (1975), *vacating and remanding,* 474 F.2d 134, 5 FEP Cases 613 (4th Cir. 1973).

rendered the matter moot, and the court dismissed the case. This action resembled those in state fair employment practice cases; presented with an opportunity to inquire into and eliminate an entire range of discriminatory practices affecting a large number of black employees, the court held to a narrow concern with the standing of the individual before it.

In 1969, setting an important precedent for future Title VII cases, the Court of Appeals for the Fifth Circuit reversed the district court's holding, stating that "[t]he suit is therefore more than a private claim by the employee seeking the particular job which is at the bottom of the charge of unlawful discrimination filed with the EEOC. . . . And the charge itself is something more than the single claim that a particular job has been denied him."[33] The EEOC, which had entered the case on appeal as *amicus curiae,* argued:

> We are concerned, too, with the possibility that the effect of the decision of the district court will be to burden the federal courts with a multiplicity of cases seeking individual relief. If, for example, a company resists the promotion of its Negro employees until, one by one, they go through the Commission and into the courts, the very purpose of Title VII could be defeated. It is true that the Attorney General is authorized to bring "pattern or practice" suits under section 707, but he is not, and should not have to be, in a position to bring all such suits.[34]

The court of appeals agreed with this EEOC position that a single Title VII suit should be applied as broadly as possible: "In dollars Employee's claim for past due wages may be tiny. But before a Court as to which there is no jurisdictional minimum, it is enough on which to launch a full scale inquiry into the charged unlawful motivation in employment practices."[35]

The court of appeals ruled that it would consider both the individual and the class aspects of the suit in further proceedings, even though Jenkins had obtained the job he originally sought:

> Although the moving papers warranted the Judge to conclude that there was no dispute about the offer and acceptance of this individual promotion, the court without more—and without ever making any factual inquiry into the broad charges affecting others system-wide— entered an outright judgment of dismissal.[36]

By its very nature, a suit alleging employment discrimination was a class action demanding redress for a pattern of acts in addition to individual relief:

The Federal Judge—awesome as are his responsibilities and powers when invoked by a timely, proper suit—does not sit as a sort of high level industrial arbiter to determine whether employee X rather than Y should have a promotion. Relative competency and qualification, are involved, to be sure. But they are relevant in determining whether denial of the coveted promotion was motivated by unlawful discrimination of race, color, sex or national origin. This is the familiar problem in §8(a)(3) discharges in NLRB cases and, closer home, voter registration cases in which, of course, the class-action-sought-for voting right is the most highly personalized, individualized thing imaginable.[37]

Citing *Potts* v. *Flax*,[38] an earlier case that established the class nature of racial discrimination, the court noted that redressing individual claims and leaving the broader patterns of discrimination untouched would result in the courts themselves being passive participants in perpetuating those patterns:

Indeed, if class-wide relief were not afforded expressly in any injunction or declaratory order issued in Employee's behalf, the result would be the incongruous one of the Court—a Federal Court, no less—itself being the instrument of racial discrimination, which brings to mind our rejection of like arguments and result in *Potts* v. *Flax*.[39]

Thus the court indicated the direction the law was to take. In *Jenkins* the court of appeals stated that Title VII was to be used as a means of securing redress and eliminating discrimination that is rooted in social patterns. And the major shortcoming of state fair employment practice agencies—their failure to apply and enforce the law—was about to be overcome by an extended judicial awareness of the nature of the problem.*

*On September 4, 1973, the fifth circuit court stated that "[t]he standard for determining whether a plaintiff may maintain a class action is not whether he will ultimately prevail on his claim. . . . The court should not exclude plaintiff as a representative because he cannot succeed on the merits of his individual claim." Where the state had failed to move against racial discrimination, it added that "[w]e have applied a broad approach to standing, stressing the individual's role as private attorney general taking on the mantle of the sovereign."—*Huff* v. *N.D. Cass Company of Alabama*, 4 FEP Cases 740, 4 EPD para. 7833 (N.D. Ala. 1971); *affirmed*, 468 F.2d 172, 4 FEP Cases 741 (5th Cir. 1972); *rehearing granted*, 468 F.2d at 180, 4 FEP Cases at 1269, 4 EPD at para. 7775 (5th Cir. 1972); *affirmed in part, vacated in part on rehearing*, 485 F.2d 710, 6 FEP Cases 400 (5th Cir. 1973). In a later decision, the fifth circuit held that voluntary dismissal of an individual charge filed with the EEOC does not in itself preclude subsequent action by the commission if action is not limited to matters contained in the original charge. The court stated that "[i]f upon investigating a particular charge of racial discrimination (which itself might be relatively minor) the EEOC discovers other discriminatory practices, surely the EEOC should not be prevented from taking appropriate action on those newly discovered practices simply because the charging party settles his suit

In *Sanchez* v. *Standard Brands*[40] the Court of Appeals for the Fifth Circuit further developed its judicial philosophy in interpreting Title VII. In *Sanchez* the plaintiff had filled in the wrong boxes on the standard EEOC charge form, and she had failed to particularize the nature of the discriminatory act she suffered. When she later corrected her mistakes on a new form, the statutory time period for filing a charge with the commission had passed. Although the EEOC processed her case, the district court dismissed it on grounds of failure to comply with the time limitations and the plaintiff's failure to include the specific acts of discrimination in her original charge.

In this 1970 decision the court of appeals again reversed the district court, stating that "[i]t is obvious that the private litigant's right of access to the courts must be vigilantly protected, for if the courthouse door closes in his face, enforcement of the Act ceases to exist."[41] The court continued:

> Mindful of the remedial and humanitarian underpinnings of Title VII and of the crucial role played by the private litigant in the statutory scheme, courts construing Title VII have been extremely reluctant to allow procedural technicalities to bar claims brought under the Act. Consequently, courts confronted with procedural ambiguities in the statutory framework have, with virtual unanimity, resolved them in favor of the complaining party.[42]

The court of appeals concluded that the purpose of Title VII was to prevent the worker who is a member of a minority from becoming an "industrial pariah" and that complaints of discrimination should therefore not fail on the basis of mere technicalities. Liberality was required:

> In the context of a statute like Title VII it is inconceivable that a charging party's rights should be cut off merely because he fails to articulate correctly the legal conclusion emanating from his factual allegations. . . . We must ever be mindful that the provisions of Title VII were not designed for the sophisticated or the cognoscenti, but to protect equality of opportunity among all employees and prospective employees. This protection must be extended to even the most unlettered and unsophisticated. . . . In the context of Title VII, no one—not even the unschooled—should be boxed out.[43]

This judicial philosophy, and the changing perception of the courts, was also expressed by the Court of Appeals for the Fifth

---

with the employer."—*EEOC* v. *Huttig Sash and Door Co.*, 511 F.2d 453, 10 FEP Cases 529, 9 EPD para. 10,065 (5th Cir. 1975).

Circuit in *Culpepper v. Reynolds Metals Company.*[44] "Title VII should receive a liberal construction while at all times bearing in mind that the central theme of Title VII is 'private settlement' as an effective end to employment discrimination."[45]

The question involved in *Culpepper* was the denial of a preliminary injunction by the district court on the grounds that, while such a measure was proper in a class suit, it was not permissible in an individual claim. The court of appeals reversed the district court's ruling, stating that its interpretation of the Act had not been the "generous interpretation which a humane and remedial statute should receive."[46] The court held:

> If the need exists, we find little distinction in the issuance of a preliminary injunction in a class action under Title VII and in an action by an individual. Such a distinction based on numbers alone is artificial and does not lend itself to the ultimate aim of the statute— full enjoyment of employment rights to all (and each) employees.[47]

The artificial distinction which state fair employment practice agencies had traditionally drawn between the individual complaint and its social context was finally obliterated.

Interestingly enough, it was the U.S. Court of Appeals for the Fifth Circuit, whose jurisdiction is in the Deep South, that led the way in establishing a broad interpretation of Title VII. Other courts deciding Title VII cases were also becoming aware that they must consider the larger patterns of racial discrimination in employment which go beyond the specifics of the individual complaint. In *Gunn v. Layne & Bowler, Inc.,*[48] a 1967 case in Tennessee, the substance of the complaint, that of discriminatory discharge, was denied by the district court, but an injunction was issued against the company's entire discriminatory seniority system and apprenticeship program. Although the facts presented had failed to substantiate the plaintiff's individual allegation, the evidence elicited at trial demonstrated an extensive pattern of discrimination which this court could not ignore.

Gregory v. Litton Systems, Inc.,[49] a later case decided by a district court in California, also illustrates that courts are considering individual acts in the context of patterns of discrimination in order to find and provide remedies for the root causes. In *Gregory* the black plaintiff seeking a job at the defendant company had a record of fourteen arrests—thirteen of which had occurred several years before he applied for the job—and no convictions. The company refused to hire the plaintiff, stating that its policy was not to hire persons who had been arrested "on a number of occasions." The court held that in the context of this case, which did not involve national security, "information concerning a prospective employee's record of arrest without conviction is irrelevant to his suitability or qualifications for employment."[50] Although the individual act of denial of employment was nondiscriminatory on its face, the court considered the social context of the refusal and concluded that it did in fact violate Title VII:

> Negroes are arrested substantially more frequently than whites in proportion to their numbers. The evidence on this question was overwhelming and utterly convincing. . . . Thus, any policy that disqualifies prospective employees because of having been arrested once, or more than once, discriminates in fact against Negro applicants. This discrimination exists even though such a policy is objectively and fairly applied as between applicants of various races.[51]*

The *Gregory* case is important too because it demonstrates that the reasoning in the earlier decision in *Quarles* v. *Philip Morris Company*[52]—the court's recognition that the imposition of selection standards with discriminatory consequences is in itself discriminatory—has been established in the law. For example, refusing to hire any person with an arrest record would appear to have no racial significance, but considered in its social context, the company's policy clearly discriminated against blacks as a class. Apparent neutrality or lack of specific intent to discriminate can no longer be asserted as a defense for any "neutral" act which has discriminatory consequences. Furthermore, federal appellate courts have repeatedly held that "neutral" employment practices are unlawful when they perpetuate the effects of past discrimination. This has been expressed in an extensive line of cases involving seniority systems in industrial plants,[53] and a similar approach was also applied in litigation against craft unions in the building trades.[54] Because the basic concern is with the consequences of any act or practice, it becomes necessary for the courts to consider the patterns of discrimination that exist in American society.

---

*The decision of the district court in *Gregory* v. *Litton Systems, Inc.*, 316 F. Supp. 401, 2 FEP Cases 842 (D.C. Cen. Calif. 1970), was sustained by the Court of Appeals for the Ninth Circuit, 472 F.2d 631, 5 FEP Cases 267 (1972). In this context, see also *Green* v. *Missouri Pacific Railroad Co.*, 523 F.2d 1290, 10 FEP Cases 1409, 11 FEP Cases 658 (8th Cir. 1975); and *Wallace* v. *Debron Corp.*, 494 F.2d 674, 7 FEP Cases 595 (8th Cir. 1974).

The process of judicially inquiring into underlying racial patterns in an individual case began early in the history of Title VII. The question of seniority came first. Decisions rendered in *Quarles* and in *United States* v. *Local 189, United Papermakers and Paperworkers*[55] examined seniority systems which appeared to be fair on their face and were uniformly applied. In both cases, however, considered against a historical background of racial exclusion, the seniority systems perpetuated past overt discriminatory practices.

Later seniority cases filed in private Title VII lawsuits have caused federal courts to consider *primarily* the social context of such systems and to regard as secondary the claims of the individual plaintiff. In the 1970 case *Jones* v. *Lee Way Motor Freight, Inc.,*[56] a private party suit, the Court of Appeals for the Tenth Circuit concluded that a seniority system violated Title VII although *no specific acts* of past discrimination were shown. The individual plaintiff, a black employee of the company, did not charge the company with failure to promote or transfer him individually. He simply alleged that the company maintained a discriminatory seniority system that violated the rights of all black employees as a class. Virtually the only proof offered to substantiate his claim was statistics showing the employment pattern of blacks and whites. In ordering an injunction against use of the company's seniority system, the court stated:

> The company's conclusory claims that it has never discriminated against Negroes in hiring line drivers does not overcome this prima facie case. . . . True, no specific instances of discrimination have been shown. However, because of the historically all-white make-up of the company's line driver category, it may well be that Negroes simply did not bother to apply. . . . In any event, lack of specific instances does not rebut the fact that at no time before the institution of this action had the company employed a Negro line driver. The company's claimed recent efforts to recruit Negro line drivers and its hiring of two in August, 1968, do not change the situation, because our concern is with the employment practices at the time when the plaintiffs were hired.[57]

Because such crucial issues had not previously been attacked by state fair employment practice agencies or even by the federal courts before Title VII, the *Jones* decision is a significant advance in the evolution of Title VII law. It demonstrates that there is no distinction between private litigation and "pattern or practice" suits brought by the Department of Justice. The burden of proof upon the plaintiff in such cases will tend to be statistical in nature, and the relief obtained will focus on class concerns as much as or more than on the specific interests of the named plaintiff.[58] In the progression of litigation, Title VII will have an increasing impact as federal courts inquire more deeply into national racial employment patterns.

Interpretation of Title VII in this direction was not entirely uniform, however. Some courts continued to construe the Act narrowly and thus restrict its scope. In *Dewey* v. *Reynolds Metals Company*,[59] a case in Michigan involving religious discrimination, the plaintiff filed a grievance against his employer claiming that overtime rules violated his religious principles. He carried his grievance through an unsuccessful arbitration and then filed suit in court under Title VII. The district court allowed relief, but the Court of Appeals for the Sixth Circuit denied his claim *inter alia* on the ground that the arbitration decision was final and binding. The applicability of *Culpepper* v. *Reynolds Metals Company*[60] and *Hutchings* v. *U.S. Industries*,[61] in which the courts held that a party may pursue both arbitration and a Title VII suit, was denied on the grounds that they were cases of racial discrimination and the *Dewey* suit was not. The second question in *Dewey*—whether it is the employer's duty to make reasonable changes in normal working hours to accommodate the religious beliefs of his employees—was finally resolved in the affirmative by Section 701(j) of the Equal Employment Opportunity Act of 1972, which had the effect of reversing *Dewey*.

In January 1971 the Supreme Court granted a petition for certiorari (request for review) in *Dewey*. This was compelled by the conflict between *Dewey*, on the one hand, and *Hutchings* v. *U.S. Industries* and *Bowe* v. *Colgate-Palmolive Company*,[62] on the other. The sixth circuit's view in *Dewey* was that when grievances are based on an alleged civil rights violation, and parties consent to arbitration by a mutually agreed upon arbitrator, the arbitrator has a right to finally determine the grievance. Accordingly, a suit alleging discriminatory discharge could not be sustained after an arbitrator had already concluded that the employee's discharge was lawful.[63]*

*The EEOC has noted that "the fundamental relationship between the union contract-grievance procedure and Title VII rights and remedies was tested in the case of *Hutchings* v. *U.S. Industries*. . . . [T]he Court also held that an adverse arbitration award obtained through the grievance procedure is not a bar to the maintenance of a suit under Title VII, reasoning

The Supreme Court affirmed *Dewey* by a 4-to-4 ruling but the divided vote eliminated the legal significance of the decision.[64] Although the issue remained in controversy for some time, by 1973 most other courts did not hold that arbitration forecloses a Title VII proceeding. In 1974, in *Alexander* v. *Gardner-Denver Co.,*[65] the Supreme Court reversed the Court of Appeals for the Tenth Circuit, which had sustained a district court's ruling based upon the approach in *Dewey*—that an employee who voluntarily submits his charge of discrimination to arbitration is bound by the arbitrator's decision. The Supreme Court held that neither the doctrine of election of remedies, the doctrine of waiver, nor federal labor policy regarding arbitration prevents an employee whose charge of racial discrimination is rejected by an arbitrator from filing a lawsuit under Title VII. In its unanimous decision the Court also ruled that while federal courts may give some deference to an arbitrator's findings of fact they are not required to defer to the arbitrator's decision but instead should consider the employee's claim *de novo.* Furthermore, there can be no implied waiver of an employee's rights under Title VII, and submission to arbitration does not eliminate that right. (The Supreme Court stated, however, that there can be an express waiver if it is voluntary and informed.) This decision indicates that the private right of action is the primary form of enforcement of Title VII and that all other forms are supplementary. It also implies that neither labor-management agreements nor any other agreements can set aside the right to sue under Title VII. This case also resolved certain procedural issues of Title VII litigation.

The broadening impact of Title VII cases is best exemplified by the Supreme Court's 1971 decision in *Griggs* v. *Duke Power Company,*[66] a case in North Carolina whose resolution is described by EEOC attorney Philip B. Sklover as "a momentous decision, one of the ten most important civil rights opinions ever made by the Supreme Court."[67] The *Griggs* decision held that the use of tests by employers to make hiring and promotion decisions violates Title VII when such tests have no relationship to successful job performance and operate to disqualify blacks at a substantially higher rate than white applicants. In calling into question the

---

that 'determinations under a contract grievance-arbitration process will involve rights and remedies separate and distinct from those involved in judicial proceedings under Title VI. . . .' The Court concluded that these separate rights could be independently pursued, each in its appropriate forum."—*Fifth Annual Report* (Washington, D.C.: Equal Employment Opportunity Commission, April 1, 1971), p. 18.

validity of such standards as intelligence tests or high school diplomas and college degrees as predictors of job performances, the Supreme Court stated:

> The facts of this case demonstrate the inadequacy of broad and general testing devices as well as the infirmity of using diplomas or degrees as fixed measures of capability. History is filled with examples of men and women who rendered highly effective performance without the conventional badges of accomplishment in terms of certificates, diplomas, or degrees. Diplomas and tests are useful servants, but Congress . . . mandated the common-sense proposition that they are not to become the masters of reality.[68]

When such tests or other standards are applied in the absence of evidence that they are job related, and even when neutral in their intent, they are illegal under Title VII if they result in the exclusion of a disproportionate number of minority group applicants. Given the widespread use of such tests and standards, the *Griggs* decision requires a fundamental change in testing and related procedures by virtually every private employer, government agency, and labor union in the United States.

The significance of the vast majority of the cases decided in the first decade of litigation under Title VII is that the trend of decisions is toward attacking the inherently discriminatory aspects of employment systems. In *Griggs* and in other decisions, the courts have focused on consequences that are rooted in historical social patterns of racial discrimination. For the first time, the federal courts are doing what state fair employment practice commissions and previous rulings failed to do—confronting the systematic structure of discriminatory practices instead of merely providing limited relief for individual plaintiffs.

In litigation under Title VII the courts are providing new legal definitions of job discrimination and they are fashioning remedies based on the concept that acts of employment discrimination are *not* isolated, individual occurrences but are manifestations of institutionalized, pervasive patterns. Furthermore, the courts have repeatedly held that intent is irrelevant, that it is the consequences of employment practices that matter, and that these considerations are the proper concern of the judicial system.

2

The Contemporary Application of the
Civil Rights Act of 1866

Until the beginning of the Civil War, all three branches of the U.S. Government had encouraged and vigorously protected the institution of slavery. The fugitive slave acts of 1793 and 1850, providing for the forcible return of escaped slaves as the property of their masters, were passed by Congress, enforced by the executive branch, and upheld by the courts.[1] In the *Dred|Scott*[2] decision of 1857 the Supreme Court ruled that Negroes and their children living in free territory were not "citizens" and could claim no constitutional rights or privileges. In that case, Chief Justice Roger Taney told Negroes, free or slave, that they had no rights that white men were bound to respect.[3]

Even after the Thirteenth, Fourteenth, and Fifteenth Amendments were incorporated into the Constitution (in 1865, 1868, and 1870, respectively) and the enforcing civil rights acts of 1866, 1870, and 1875 were passed, the Supreme Court continued to interpret narrowly all legislation intended to abolish the vestiges of slavery. The decisions of the Supreme Court in the *Civil Rights|Cases*[4] and subsequent related cases nullified for almost a century one of the most important legislative acts of the Reconstruction period, the Civil Rights Act of 1866. The Thirteenth Amendment had formally abolished the institution of slavery, and the Civil Rights Act of 1866 was passed to destroy the remnants—the "badges and incidents" of slavery perpetuated by the discriminatory practices of private individuals. But only with the Supreme Court's decision of 1968 in *Jones* v. *Mayer*[5] was the long-dormant 1866 law revived.

In that case, applying the antislavery statute to a suburban St. Louis community of the 1960s, the Court broadly interpreted the concept of "badges and incidents" of slavery to include the depressed social condition of black Americans in the twentieth century. Justice William O. Douglas, in a concurring opinion, stated that the racially motivated denial of housing opportunities was, in fact, a vestige of slavery.[6] Barred from opportunities to live and work where they pleased, Negroes, he wrote, had retained the inferior economic and social status which the institution of slavery imposed on them. The *Jones v. Mayer* decision, and its interpretation of the 1866 statute, is a major development in contemporary civil rights law.*

Before the *Jones* decision, acts of private discrimination had been considered beyond the reach of federal law until the passage of the Civil Rights Act of 1964. It is ironic that four years after the passage of Title VII of the Act, which was itself born only after an intense eighty-three-day congressional debate, the Supreme Court indicated that much of what was declared unlawful by Title VII had been unlawful for a century.

*Relevant parts of the legislative history of the 1866 Act are given in the Supreme Court's decision in *Jones* v. *Mayer*. The briefs *amicus curiae* filed by the U.S. Department of Justice, the National Committee Against Discrimination in Housing, and the National Association for the Advancement of Colored People also contain interpretations of the legislative history of the 1866 Act. Many legal historians share the view of Professor Arthur Larsen that the *Jones* v. *Mayer* case "by infusing new vitality both into the early Reconstruction statutes and into the Thirteenth Amendment will prove to be the most far-reaching race relations case since the Civil War."—Arthur Larsen, "The New Law of Race Relations," *Wisconsin Law Review*, No. 2 (1969), pp. 470–524. However, Professor Charles Fairman is more critical: "In *Jones* v. *Mayer* the Court appears to have had no feeling for the truth of history, but only to have read it through the glass of the Court's own purpose. It allowed itself to believe impossible things—as though the dawning enlightenment of 1968 could be ascribed to the Congress of a century ago."—Charles Fairman, *Reconstruction and Reunion 1864–1888*, Vol. VI, *History of the Supreme Court of the United States* (New York: Macmillan, 1971), p. 1258. Two later Supreme Court decisions also discuss the legislative history of Section 1981. *Tillman* v. *Wheaton-Haven Recreation Assn., Inc.*, 410 U.S. 431, 41 LW 4311 (1973), deals primarily with Section 1982, but states (41 LW p. 4314) that "[i]n light of the historical interrelationships between Section 1981 and Section 1982, we see no reason to construe these sections differently. . . ." Footnote 11 of that decision traces the legislative history of Section 1981 and concludes that it enforces the Thirteenth, rather than the Fourteenth, Amendment. This first Supreme Court case dealing specifically with Section 1981 confirms the legislative analyses made by various appeals courts in their interpretations of the statute. *District of Columbia* v. *Carter*, 409 U.S. 418, 41 LW 4127 (1973), deals primarily with Section 1983, holding that the District is not a "State or Territory" under that statute. The decision also distinguishes between the effects of the 1866 and 1871 civil rights acts and retraces their legislative histories. This important decision, by stating (41 LW p. 4128) that Section 1982— and by analogy Section 1981—applies to federal as well as state and private acts of discrimination, suggests that an employment discrimination suit may be filed against the Federal Government under Section 1981.

The passage of the Civil Rights Act of 1866 reflected the concern of Congress, just after the Civil War, that the southern states would resist altering the slave-labor system which had been the basis of their economy for many generations. On December 18, 1865, the Thirteenth Amendment, prohibiting slavery and involuntary servitude, was ratified by twenty-seven states. The amendment itself expressly granted Congress the authority to give it force "by appropriate legislation."[7] Accordingly, five days after official certification of the Thirteenth Amendment, a bill was introduced in the Senate. Section I stated:

> [A]ll persons born in the United States and not subject to any foreign power, excluding Indians not taxed, are hereby declared to be citizens of the United States; and such citizens, of every race and color, without regard to any previous condition of slavery or involuntary servitude, except as a punishment for crime whereof the party shall have been duly convicted, shall have the same right, in every State and Territory in the United States, to make and enforce contracts, to sue, be parties, and give evidence, to inherit, purchase, lease, sell, hold, and convey real and personal property, and to full and equal benefit of all laws and proceedings for the security of person and property, as is enjoyed by white citizens, and shall be subject to like punishment, pains, and penalties, and to none other, any law, statute, ordinance, regulation, or custom, to the contrary notwithstanding.[8]

With this law Congress intended to provide specific implementation to the mandate of the Thirteenth Amendment. Since the essence of the institution of slavery is forced, involuntary labor, Congress had to guarantee that Negroes would be free to bargain for their labor and to seek maximum employment opportunities on an equal basis with whites. Because the sale of one's labor was generally regarded as a matter of bargaining and contracting, Congress included the prohibition of discrimination in employment by stating that Negroes "shall have the same rights . . . to make and enforce contracts."[9] The evidence that Congress considered this point during the extensive debates on statutory language emphasizes that the law's prohibitions were meant to include discrimination in employment.

When the war ended, President Andrew Johnson had sent Major General Carl Schurz on a mission through the southern states to report on conditions there and suggest measures to overcome the effects of the war. Schurz's report to the President was prophetic:

It would be presumptuous of me to speak of the future with absolute certainty; but it may safely be assumed that the same causes will always tend to produce the same results. As long as a majority of the southern people believe that "the negro will not work without physical compulsion," and that "the blacks at large belong to the whites at large," that belief will tend to produce a system of coercion, the enforcement of which will be aided by the hostile feeling against the negro now prevailing among the whites, and by the general spirit of violence which in the south was fostered by the influence of slavery exercised upon the popular character. It is, indeed, not probable that a general attempt will be made to restore slavery in its old form, on account of the barriers which such an attempt will find in its way; *but there are systems intermediate between slavery as it formerly existed in the south, and free labor as it exists in the north, but more nearly related to the former than to the latter, the introduction of which will be attempted.* [Emphasis added.][10]

Schurz described one such semislave relationship, in which South Carolina planters intended to keep "free" Negro labor under permanent control "by introducing into the contracts provisions leaving only a small share of the crops to freemen, subject to all sorts of constructive charges, and then binding them to work off the indebtedness they might incur."[11] He also reported:

There appears to be another popular notion prevalent in the south, which stands as no less serious an obstacle in the way of a successful solution of the problem. It is that the negro exists for the special object of raising cotton, rice, and sugar for the whites, and that it is illegitimate for him to indulge, like other people, in the pursuit of his own happiness in his own way. Although it is admitted that he has ceased to be the property of a master, it is not admitted that he has a right to become his own master.[12]

Schurz's report made clear to the President and to Congress that the South would not voluntarily permit economic freedom and equality for its black freedmen. Through private acts of discrimination and racially discriminatory legislation, improvement of the Negroes economic status was, in effect, already prohibited. Negroes were not allowed to own land or operate businesses. The Negro freedmen were working for their former masters and were bound by discriminatory labor contracts. The unfair contracts insured that such Negroes would never have the freedom or the financial means necessary to leave the plantation.

The Bureau of Freedmen, Refugees and Abandoned Lands, established by the government before the end of the war, was intended to protect Negroes from such exploitation. Originally planned as a relief operation, the bureau functioned as an agency of the Union army in the defeated South, with broad powers over race relations. The bureau tried to protect the rights of Negroes in negotiating contracts and in obtaining a fair price for their labor, but southern resistance was firm and bitter throughout the three years of its existence.*

The bureau's provision that freedmen could lease with an option to buy "not more than forty acres" was intended to be the foundation of a new economic order, but President Johnson's amnesty proclamation restoring property rights to former slave-owners sharply limited the availability of good land. In all, fewer than 40,000 Negro families were resettled on their own land, mostly on the basis of the early land seizures authorized by a field order of General W. T. Sherman. But the former landowners soon regained control and the dream of "forty acres and a mule" never materialized. The historian James M. McPherson has written of the failure to redistribute land:

> As a result, the Negroes remained economically a subordinate class, dependent on the white landowners or employers for their livelihood. The South was not reconstructed economically, and consequently the other measures of reconstruction rested upon an unstable foundation.[13]

As a whole, the mission of the bureau was to make order out of a shattered southern social system. Upholding the rights of blacks was secondary. Even while the bureau was supposedly protecting Negro employment rights, its commissioner, General Oliver O. Howard, discouraged the appointment of Negroes to positions within the bureau, claiming that this would increase white hostility toward it.

In 1868 the bureau employed nearly 1,000 agents. Although some of its representatives made genuine efforts to protect Negroes from exploitation, the Steedman-Fullerton report of 1866 noted wide disparities in its operations. In some areas bureau officials were reported to have arbitrarily "interfered" with planters in favor

---

*For studies of the Bureau of Freedmen, Refugees and Abandoned Lands, see W. E. B. Du Bois, "The Freedmen's Bureau," *Atlantic Monthly*, March 1901, pp. 354–365; Luther P. Jackson, "The Educational Efforts of the Freedman's Bureau and Aid Societies in South Carolina, 1862-1872," *Journal of Negro History*, January 1923, pp. 1–40; Martin Abbott, "Free Land, Free Labor, and the Freedmen's Bureau," *Agricultural History*, October 1956, pp. 150–156. Perhaps the most complete study is George R. Bentley's *A History of the Freedmen's Bureau* (Philadelphia: University of Pennsylvania Press, 1955).

of freedmen, while in others the bureau seemed little more than a reenslavement agency operating in the interests of the planters.[14]

According to a history of the bureau, "[b]y 1868, both planters and Negroes had become quite disinterested in the Bureau's [labor] contracts. . . . Apparently the planters felt they no longer needed the Bureau's help in working the Negro, and probably most Freedmen had become disillusioned about its effectiveness in securing for them more than subsistence wages."[15]

Most activity had halted by 1869; by 1872 the bureau had ceased to function. The enactment of the Black Codes rapidly subverted the bureau's limited accomplishments.*

The notorious Black Codes, which most southern states began enacting as soon as the Union armies withdrew, severely restricted the newly freed Negro workers' employment rights. According to John Hope Franklin:

> More important to the former slaveholders . . . were the laws covering contracts between Negro laborers and white employers. Mississippi authorized "any person" to arrest and return to his employer any Negro who quit before the expiration of his contracted term of labor. For this the person was to receive $5.00. Most states had stern provisions against enticing or persuading a Negro to desert his legal employment before the expiration of his contract. There were also apprentice laws that gave preference to former owners in hiring minors whose parents were not providing for their support. A final feature of the labor provisions of the black codes was the vagrancy laws. In Mississippi all persons not lawfully employed by January, 1866, were to be arrested as vagrants and, if convicted and unable to pay the fine of $50.00, were to be hired out to the person who would pay the fine and require the shortest period of labor in return. Similar laws were enacted in other states.
>
> Other state laws and town ordinances were designed to maintain what the legislators considered due subordination of the Freedmen. . . . Most of the laws employed such terms as "master" and "servant" and clearly implied a distinction that consigned the Negro to a hopelessly inferior status. . . .
>
> The enactment of these black codes confirmed the North's worst fears. Reformers believed that the former Confederates were attempting to re-establish slavery.[16]

---

*See W. E. B. Du Bois, *Black Reconstruction,* Harbor Scholar's Classics ed. (New York: S. A. Russell Company, 1956), pp. 128–181; Theodore B. Wilson, *The Black Codes of the South,* Southern Historical Publications No. 6 (University, Ala.: University of Alabama Press, 1965); William B. Hesseltine, "Economic Factors in the Abandonment of Reconstruction," *Mississippi Historical Review,* September 1935, pp. 191–210; Roger W. Shugg, "Survival of the Plantation System in Louisiana," *Journal of Southern History,* August 1937, pp. 311–325.

It was evident early in the Reconstruction period that unless forthright measures were taken, the precarious gains Negroes had obtained would soon be lost. The Civil Rights Act of 1866 was intended to safeguard the future, when there would be no federal military agents to protect the rights of Negroes. The Act sought to protect their property rights, their legal competence in court, and their future employment status.

Although Congress did not explicitly define the scope of the term "contracts" in the 1866 Act, the only contract referred to and discussed during the congressional debates was the employment contract. Speaking for the necessity to include in the Act a prohibition against discrimination in employment, Representative William Windom of Minnesota stated:

> Planters combine together to compel them [Negroes] to work for such wages as their former masters may dictate, and deny them the privilege of hiring to anyone without the consent of the master; and in order to make it impossible for them to seek employment elsewhere, the pass system is still enforced. . . . Do you call that man free who cannot choose his own employer, or name the wages for which he will work?[17]

The object of the bill, he said, was "to secure to a poor, weak class of laborers the right to make contracts for their labor, the power to enforce the payment of their wages, and the means of holding and enjoying the proceeds of their toil."[18] Representative William Lawrence of Ohio supported the inclusion of employment rights:

> It is idle to say that a citizen shall have the right to life, yet deny him the right to labor, whereby alone he can live. It is a mockery to say that a citizen may have a right to live, and yet deny him the right to make a contract to secure the privilege and rewards of labor.[19]

Supporters of the Act felt that the freedom guaranteed by the recently adopted Thirteenth Amendment would be meaningless without the protection of the fundamental right of Negroes to bargain for their labor on an equal basis with whites. The essence of the 1866 statute, therefore, was the fundamental right to obtain employment without discriminatory conditions based on race. The freedom to acquire and dispose of property and to appear in court was necessary to guarantee the enjoyment of the fruits of labor, but the primary purpose of the statute was to allow Negroes to contract for their labor without being impeded because of their race or former status.

Two years after the passage of the Civil Rights Act of 1866, the Fourteenth Amendment was enacted and ratified. It conferred citizenship status upon the former slaves and prohibited the states from denying them the "privileges or immunities" belonging to other citizens. The Fourteenth Amendment repeated many of the prohibitions contained in the Civil Rights Act of 1866, which had also conferred citizenship status. Milton R. Konvitz, an authority on constitutional law, discussing the similarities and overlapping coverage, explains:

> In view of the existence of the Civil Rights Act, what was the need of the amendment? The answer is that, although the act was upheld by the federal circuit court in two cases in 1866 and 1867, its constitutionality was doubtful; at any rate, it was thought safer to place the substance of the act beyond the reach of the Supreme Court and the Congress of a later time.[20]

In introducing the Fourteenth Amendment, Congress reinforced its intention to grant Negroes equal rights in specific areas and placed those rights above the power of the states to alter.

In 1870 the Fifteenth Amendment was ratified and Negroes received the right to vote. Two months later Congress passed the Civil Rights Act of 1870.[21] The new Act reinforced the Civil Rights Act of 1866 by providing that all citizens were qualified to vote without regard to race.

In 1875 Congress passed "An Act to Protect All Citizens in Their Civil and Legal Rights,"[22] which extended the civil rights acts of 1866 and 1870 to give all citizens equal rights to public accommodations.*

*Section 1981, applicable to private acts of employment discrimination, was originally part of the Civil Rights Act of 1866, as was Section 1982, which provides that "[a]ll citizens of the United States shall have the same right, in every state and territory, as is enjoyed by white citizens thereof to inherit, purchase, lease, sell, hold, and convey real and personal property." Section 1983, however, derives from the Ku Klux Klan Act of 1871 (42 U.S. Section 1983). Since the 1866 Act was intended to enforce the Thirteenth Amendment, and the 1871 Act to enforce the Fourteenth Amendment, the courts have interpreted these sections to have separate statutory meaning and application. See *District of Columbia* v. *Carter,* 409 U.S. 418, 41 LW 4127 (1973), *reversing* 447 F.2d 358 (D.C. Cir. 1971); *Tillman* v. *Wheaton-Haven Recreation Association, Inc.,* 410 U.S. 431, 41 LW 4311. See also *Waters* v. *Wisconsin Steel Works, et al.,* 427 F.2d 476, 2 FEP Cases 574 (7th Cir. 1970), *cert. denied,* 400 U.S. 911, 2 FEP Cases 1059 (1970). For the historical development of Reconstruction civil rights laws, see Jacobus tenBroek, *The Anti-Slavery Origins of the Fourteenth Amendment* (Berkeley: University of California Press, 1951; rev. ed., *Equal Under Law,* New York: Collier Books, 1965). For the congressional debates on the civil rights legislation of this period, see Bernard Schwartz, ed., *Statutory History of the United States, Civil Rights, Part I* (New York: Chelsea House, 1970). See also Note, "*Jones* v. *Mayer:* The Thirteenth Amendment and the Federal Anti-Discrimination Laws," *Columbia Law Review,* June 1969, pp. 1019–1056; Richard E. Larson, "The Development of Section 1981 as a Remedy for Racial

Congress intended the three civil rights acts to be cumulative in effect, not to supersede one another. During debate over the Civil Rights Act of 1875, Congressman John Storm of Pennsylvania, after citing the Thirteenth, Fourteenth, and Fifteenth Amendments, observed:

> These amendments were and are now enforced by the rigid acts of Congress, which are still in force. We have also in force the civil rights bill of April 9, 1866, passed over the veto of President Johnson, which places upon the broad basis of equal rights every citizen of the United States and furnishes a complete remedy for their vindication.[23]

Discussing the reasons for the three civil rights acts which were substantially restatements of the Thirteenth, Fourteenth, and Fifteenth Amendments, Konvitz comments:

> After the South lost the Civil War it continued its efforts to keep the Negro "in his place." Four states flatly refused to accept the Thirteenth Amendment. . . . All of the Southern and Border states refused to ratify the Fourteenth Amendment. The South opposed freedom, but freedom was achieved notwithstanding; then the South determined that freedom meant only the absence of slavery as it had been known before Emancipation: no political or civil rights. The North felt, on the other hand, that freedom without these rights was only an illusion and a snare; that a civil rights law was required to override the effect of the Black Codes which the Southern States adopted as soon as the North relaxed its vigilance: codes which fixed on the Negro all the badges of servitude. It was to meet this situation that Congress passed the various civil rights laws, culminating in the Act of 1875.[24]

Through the three civil rights acts Congress implemented a positive approach to the protection of the rights of citizens. The Thirteenth, Fourteenth, and Fifteenth Amendments conferred political and social rights in a broad but essentially negative manner. Under the enabling clauses of the amendments, Congress sought to convert those general rights into an enforceable body of law. The radical Republicans in Congress, who had spearheaded the passage of strong civil rights laws, were anticipating a post-Reconstruction turn of attitude away from civil rights and toward the problems of nation building, the healing of old wounds, and an accommodation with the South.

Discrimination in Private Employment," *Harvard Civil Rights-Civil Liberties Law Review,* January 1972, pp. 56–102.

Indeed, cases subsequently decided by the Supreme Court greatly narrowed the applicability of the Reconstruction civil rights laws. Eight years after the Civil Rights Act of 1875 the Supreme Court had its first opportunity to consider the constitutionality of that statute. In the *Civil Rights Cases*[25] the Court had before it seven consolidated cases involving discrimination in public accommodations, which was expressly forbidden under the 1875 law. It was argued on behalf of Negroes that under the Thirteenth Amendment Congress had the power and the duty to enact all legislation necessary and proper for abolishing all "badges and incidents" of slavery, and that the definition of slavery and "badges and incidents" of slavery should be broadened to include the postwar factors that forced Negroes to remain in essentially the same depressed economic and social condition to which they had been consigned under the slave system.

Justice Joseph P. Bradley, writing for the majority, rejected a broadened definition of slavery and the concept of "badges and incidents." He felt that although it was entirely proper to prohibit the institution of slavery itself,

> [i]t would be running the slavery argument into the ground to make it apply to every act of discrimination which a person may see fit to make as to the guests he will entertain, or as to the people he will take into his coach or cab or car, or admit to his concert or theatre, or deal with in other matters of intercourse or business.[26]

Bradley's explicit reasoning was that broadening the rights of newly freed slaves to include equal access to public accommodations was unwarranted because even free blacks had been barred from many public places during the period of slavery. Since the 1875 law attempted to extend the rights conferred by the Thirteenth Amendment to an area that free Negroes had not enjoyed, it could not be upheld. And since it attempted to reach private acts of discrimination, which the Court considered denial of access to public accommodations to be, it could not be upheld under the Fourteenth Amendment, which prohibits state action only.

In his historic dissent Justice John Marshall Harlan argued for a much broader interpretation of the constitutional amendments and of the intent of Congress when it passed the civil rights laws, stating that the government's function should be to eradicate all the consequences of slavery as vigorously as it had earlier defended the institution.[27] He attacked the majority's opinion as proceeding upon grounds

> [e]ntirely too narrow and artificial. I cannot resist the conclusion that the substance and spirit of the recent amendments of the Constitution have been sacrificed by a subtle and ingenious verbal criticism. Constitutional provisions, adopted in the interest of liberty, and for the purpose of securing through national legislation, if need be, rights inhering in a state of freedom, and belonging to American citizenship, have been so construed as to defeat the ends the people desired to accomplish, and which they supposed they had accomplished by changes in their fundamental law.[28]

Harlan analyzed the Court's history of upholding the fugitive slave acts of 1793 and 1850 and its *Dred Scott* decision, which had stripped blacks living in free territory of the status of citizenship. If Congress had the power to legislate in the interest of the private ownership of slaves, he wrote in his forty-page document, there was no reason why Congress could not legislate toward a contrary result by directing the activities of private individuals. If Congress had the power to support slavery, surely it had the power to prohibit it and all of its attendant characteristics.

Harlan noted that the Constitution had recognized the existence of slavery and that the Supreme Court had held, therefore, that Congress had the implied authority to protect the institution. But when the Thirteenth Amendment abolished slavery, he pointed out, it also expressly gave Congress the authority to implement its abolition:

> I do not contend that the Thirteenth Amendment invests Congress with authority, by legislation, to define and regulate the entire body of civil rights which citizens enjoy, or may enjoy, in the several states. But I hold that since slavery, as the court has repeatedly declared, was the moving or principal cause of the adoption of that amendment, and since that institution rested wholly upon the inferiority, as a race, of those held in bondage, their freedom necessarily involved immunity from, and protection against, all discrimination against them, because of their race, in respect of such civil rights as belong to freemen of other races.[29]

Harlan recognized that the primary purpose of the legislation was to enable Negroes to take the rank of citizen on an equal basis with whites with respect to their fundamental rights and privileges:

> At every step, in this direction, the nation has been confronted with class tyranny. . . . If the constitutional amendments be enforced,

according to the intent with which, as I conceive, they were adopted, there cannot be, in this republic, any class of human beings in practical subjection to another class, with power in the latter to dole out to the former just such privileges as they may choose to grant.[30]

If the amendments were not so enforced, he concluded, they would become no more than "splendid baubles, thrown out to delude those who deserved fair and generous treatment at the hands of the nation."[31]

The decision in the *Civil Rights Cases* considered only the constitutionality of the Civil Rights Act of 1875, which dealt with discrimination in public accommodations. The civil rights acts of 1866 and 1870 were not struck down or narrowed in their applicability. On the contrary, Justice Bradley specifically stated in the decision that they were properly enacted pursuant to the Thirteenth Amendment and were properly concerned with the true "badges and incidents" of slavery: the denial of the right to make contracts, to take and hold property, and to sue in court.

The *Civil Rights Cases* did not narrow the interpretation of "badges and incidents" of slavery in the area of employment discrimination. Another case achieved that distinction in 1906— *Hodges* v. *United States.*[32] When a group of Arkansas white men terrorized several Negroes to prevent them from working at a sawmill, the white men were charged under a section of the United States Code that prohibited anyone from abridging the rights of individuals secured by the Civil Rights Act of 1886—in this case, that portion dealing with the right to make contracts.* The majority opinion went far beyond the *Civil Rights Cases* in interpreting the Thirteenth Amendment as proscribing only such conduct as *actually enslaved* someone. This decision in effect eliminated from the concept of "badges and incidents" of slavery all inferior social and economic conditions of Negroes and so prohibited only the direct imposition of slavery itself. No Negro who was not actually the slave property of a master could be considered as suffering in any way from the "badges and incidents" of slavery.

The decisions in the *Civil Rights Cases* and *Hodges* were to dominate judicial thinking until 1968, when the *Jones* v. *Mayer*

---

*For a description of *Hodges* and other cases of violence against black workers in labor contract controversies, see Loren Miller, *The Petitioners* (New York: Pantheon Books, 1966), pp. 186–198. See also Mary Frances Berry, *Black Resistance and White Law* (New York: Appleton-Century-Crofts, 1971), especially Chap. 10, "Riots, Lynchings, and Federal Quiescence."

case reintroduced arguments based on the Civil Rights Act of 1866. The provisions of the 1866 law had been incorporated in Title 42 of the United States Code in two sections:

1981.   All persons within the jurisdiction of the United States shall have the same right . . . to make and enforce contracts. . . .

1982.   All citizens of the United States shall have the same right, in every State and Territory, as is enjoyed by white citizens thereof to inherit, purchase, lease, sell, hold and convey real and personal property.

In *Jones* v. *Mayer* the Court considered only Section 1982, which applies to the taking and holding of real and personal property.

Mr. and Mrs. Jones had been denied the purchase of a home from a private developer in suburban St. Louis because of their race. Their complaint, based on Section 1982, was dismissed by the trial court, and the decision was affirmed by the Court of Appeals for the Eighth Circuit.[33] But the Supreme Court, instead of extending the "state action" concept of the Fourteenth Amendment, chose to determine the constitutionality and effect of Section 1982. The Court stated: "We hold that Sect. 1982 bars *all* racial discrimination, private as well as public, in the sale or rental of property, and that the statute, thus construed, is a valid exercise of the power of Congress to enforce the Thirteenth Amendment."[34] Affirming that the participation of a public official or agency was not a necessary condition of violation of the statute, the Court reiterated that the law prohibits "*all* discrimination against Negroes in the sale or rental of property—discrimination by private owners as well as discrimination by public authorities."[35] Responding to objections by the defendants, the Court held:

Stressing what they consider to be the revolutionary implications of so literal a reading of Sect. 1982, the respondents argue that Congress cannot possibly have intended any such result. Our examination of the relevant history, however, persuades us that Congress meant exactly what it said.[36]

The defendants argued that the intent of Congress in enacting the Civil Rights Act of 1866 was merely to counteract the proliferation of the Black Codes. On this contention, the Court stated:

But the Civil Rights Act was drafted to apply throughout the country, and its language was far broader than would have been necessary to strike down discriminatory statutes. . . . For the same Congress that wanted to do away with the Black Codes *also* had before it an imposing body of evidence pointing to the mistreatment of Negroes by private individuals and unofficial groups, mistreatment unrelated to any hostile state legislation.[37]

In the area of employment, the Court found the congressional debates to be "replete with references to private injustices against Negroes—references to white employers who refused to pay their Negro workers, white planters who agreed among themselves not to hire freed slaves without the permission of their former masters."[38] From the congressional debates the Court concluded that Congress clearly intended the Act to apply to private, individual acts of discrimination. Justice Potter Stewart added:

> In light of the concerns that led Congress to adopt it and the contents of the debates that preceded its passage, it is clear that the Act was designed to do just what its terms suggest: to prohibit all racial discrimination, whether or not under color of law, with respect to the rights enumerated therein—including the right to purchase or lease property.[39]

The Court concluded that Congress did in fact have the power to enact legislation pursuant to the Thirteenth Amendment to abolish all of the remnants and consequences of the institution of slavery. Referring to the *Civil Rights Cases,* the Court noted that such "badges and incidents" of slavery included denial of the right to purchase property. The Court's majority opinion concluded with a quotation from Representative James Wilson of Iowa, House floor manager of the 1866 bill: " 'A man who enjoys the civil rights mentioned in this bill cannot be reduced to slavery. . . . This settles the appropriateness of this measure, and settles its constitutionality.' We agree."[40] Accordingly, the Supreme Court reversed the lower courts' rulings in *Jones* v. *Mayer.* *

*In *Jones* v. *Mayer* the Supreme Court included a discussion of *Hodges* v. *United States* and expressly overruled the 1906 decision: "This Court reversed [that] conviction," said the majority decision. "The majority recognized that 'one of the disabilities of slavery, one of the indicia of its existence, was a lack of power to make contracts.'. . . And there was no doubt that the defendants had deprived their Negro victims, on racial grounds, of the opportunity to dispose of their labor by contract. Yet the majority said that 'no mere personal assault or trespass or appropriation operates to reduce the individual to a condition of slavery'. . . and asserted that only conduct which actually enslaves someone can be subjected to punishment under legislation enacted to enforce the Thirteenth Amendment. . . . Mr. Justice Harlan, joined by Mr. Justice Day, dissented. In their view, the interpretation the majority placed upon the Thirteenth Amendment was 'entirely too narrow and . . . hostile to the freedom established by the supreme law of the land.'. . .

"The conclusion of the majority in *Hodges* rested upon a concept of congressional power under the Thirteenth Amendment irreconcilable with the position taken by every member of this Court in the *Civil Rights Cases* and incompatible with the history and purpose of the

In dealing with the relationship of the Civil Rights Act of 1866 to Title VII, it is important to note that when the Court decided the *Jones* case it took into account the possible preemptive effects of the Civil Rights Act of 1968, dealing with housing discrimination, over Section 1982 of the 1866 Act. The Civil Rights Act of 1968, like Title VII, provides for the prohibition of private acts of discrimination and sets forth a complex system of administrative procedures to be exhausted before the statute is enforceable in court. The Court noted that the 1866 statute was not specific about types of discrimination in housing, and that the 1968 Act was, but the Court said that "[i]t would be a serious mistake to suppose that Sect. 1982 in any way diminishes the significance of the law recently enacted by Congress,"[41] and added:

> Its [the 1968 Act's] enactment had no effect upon this litigation, but it underscored the vast differences between, on the one hand, a general statute applicable only to racial discrimination in the rental and sale of property and enforceable only by private parties acting on their own initiative, and, on the other hand, a detailed housing law, applicable to a broad range of discriminatory practices and enforceable by a complete arsenal of federal authority.[42]

The decision in *Jones* revived the use of the Civil Rights Act of 1866 and Section 1982 as vehicles for antidiscrimination litigation. By extension—although not a direct issue in the *Jones* case—Section 1981, which includes the right to make and enforce contracts, was also revived and has evolved in a progression of cases, culminating in the Supreme Court's 1975 decision in *Johnson* v. *Railway Express Agency Inc.*[43] as a valuable independent cause of action in the federal courts. In some instances litigation under Section 1981 will have advantages over suits based on Title VII.[44] This may be of significance in relation to procedural prerequisites, where, for example, plaintiffs who do not qualify for a proper suit under Title VII for reasons of late filing or failure to exhaust administrative remedies can go into court under the 1866 Act.* Section 1981 also provides an excellent vehicle for bringing before the court respondents not known or not named in the administrative charge.†

Amendment itself. Insofar as *Hodges* is inconsistent with our holding today, it is hereby overruled."—392 U.S. 409, 441 n.78 (1968).

*For a discussion of the complex filing procedures of Title VII, see Volume II, Chapter 3. See also Volume II, Appendix A, the text of Title VII, especially Section 706.

†See, for example, *Sabala* v. *Western Gillette, Inc.,* 516 F.2d 1251, 11 FEP Cases 98 (5th Cir. 1975), *affirming in part, reversing in part, and remanding,* 371 F. Supp. 385, 7 FEP Cases 443 (S.D. Tex. 1974).

Until 1975, however, most lawsuits concerning discrimination in employment filed under the 1866 statute were also filed under Title VII, and the courts, with some exceptions, rendered their decisions under Title VII.

The first case to present the question of whether the Civil Rights Act of 1866 applies concurrently with Title VII was *Dobbins* v. *Local 212, IBEW.*[45] Shortly after the Supreme Court's decision in *Jones* v. *Mayer,* Anderson L. Dobbins, a black electrician in Cincinnati, Ohio, filed suit under both Title VII and Section 1981. Although Congress had assumed in 1866 that employment was a matter of contract, it had not directly anticipated the question of racial restrictions by labor unions. It is generally accepted, however (as implied in both the National Labor Relations Act and the Labor-Management Reporting and Disclosure Act of 1959), that since union membership and apprenticeship practices which determine access to employment are of a contractual nature, the 1866 law should apply to union membership and apprenticeship training. It was therefore argued in *Dobbins* that the Act prohibited racial discrimination by private parties, including denial of the right to enter into union membership or an apprenticeship agreement. The district court held that the case was properly brought under Section 1981 and that

> [a]t least since *Jones* v. *Mayer,* a strictly private right, be it in the property field as such, or the contract field as such, is within the protection of the Civil Rights Act of 1866 against interference by a private citizen or a group of citizens. Governmental sanction or participation is no longer a necessary factor in the assertion of a Sect. 1981 action.[46]

The rediscovery of Section 1981, more than three years after the effective date of Title VII, caused the courts to focus initially on the interplay of Section 1981 with Title VII and later on its potential as a separate statute. Title VII does not have the effect of repealing Section 1981. Pointing out that in *Jones* v. *Mayer* the Supreme Court explicitly rejected the contention that the Civil Rights Act of 1964 had preempted the 1866 law, the Court of Appeals for the Fifth Circuit said in *Boudreaux* v. *Baton Rouge Marine Contracting Co.*[47] that "[t]he specific remedies fashioned by Congress in Title VII were not intended to preempt the general remedial language of Section 1981."[48] This view was expressed earlier in *Dobbins,* in which Section 1981 was asserted as a separate and concurrent ground for federal jurisdiction. In a later case, however, *Young* v. *International Telephone & Telegraph*,[49] the plaintiff did not invoke Title VII but filed a complaint in federal court under Section 1981 exclusively. The district court dismissed the complaint, with the opinion that

> the failure of the plaintiff to have invoked the administrative process covered by Title VII is fatal to his cause. It is our further opinion that the Civil Rights Act of 1866 is not applicable to discrimination in private employment. An action for alleged employment discrimination because of race must be pursued under the authority granted by Congress when it passed the Civil Rights Act of 1964 and in so doing the administrative procedures are mandatory and cannot be ignored.[50]

On appeal, the Court of Appeals for the Third Circuit applied the *Jones* rationale and reversed and remanded the case to the district court: "We conclude, therefore, that this case falls within the holding of *Jones* v. *Mayer* [392 U.S. 409 (1968)] and *Sullivan* v. *Little Hunting Park* [396 U.S. 229 (1969)], and Section 1981 is applicable to private acts of discrimination."[51]

In *Sanders* v. *Dobbs Houses*[52] the plaintiff filed\ suit under Title VII sixteen days after the statutory period of limitations had expired. Faced with a motion to dismiss for untimeliness, she requested leave to amend the complaint to establish jurisdiction under Section 1981. The trial judge allowed the amendment but dismissed the case on the grounds that the plaintiff had failed to file a timely complaint under the statutory provisions specified by Title VII, and that the 1981 claim could not be maintained against a private employer in the absence of some element of state action. The Court of Appeals for the Fifth Circuit reversed and remanded the action, holding *inter alia* that the provisions of the 1866 law, guaranteeing all persons equal rights to make and enforce contracts, were available to support an employee's action against a private employer, and that the specific remedies provided in Title VII of the Civil Rights Act of 1964 were not intended to preempt the general remedies available under the 1866 law for the violation of rights by either private or state action. However, in *Waters* v. *Wisconsin Steel Works*,[53] in which suit was brought under both Section 1981 and Title VII, the Court of Appeals for the Seventh Circuit ruled that a basis for federal jurisdiction was established only where the plaintiff "pleads a reasonable excuse for his failure

to exhaust EEOC remedies."⁵⁴* But this part of the holding was
not sustained by a subsequent decision of the appellate court which
stated that "exhaustion of Title VII remedies, or reasonable excuse
for failing to do so, is not a jurisdictional prerequisite to an action
under section 1981."⁵⁵ The Supreme Court in *Johnson* v. *Railway
Express Agency Inc.*⁵⁶ resolved this and related questions by ruling
that Section 1981 was separate and independent.

   In *Clark* v. *American Marine Corporation*⁵⁷ a district court in
Louisiana reviewed Section 1981 and found it applicable in a case
of discriminatory discharge; but, as in *Dobbins*, it awarded relief
based on a Title VII claim. Three black employees of the company
had been discriminatorily discharged from their jobs before the
effective date of Title VII, and white workers were hired to fill
their jobs after the effective date of the Act. The discharged black
employees filed suit under both Title VII and Section 1981. The
court found that "[t]he discharge of Turner and Magee did not
itself violate Title VII since it occurred after the enactment of that
Title but five months before it became effective. However," it
continued, "plaintiffs assert that it violated a portion of the 1870
Civil Rights Act, Section 1981. . . ."⁵⁸ The court stated that after
Jones v. *Mayer,* the Reconstruction statute has been held to
prohibit all racially motivated deprivations of the rights enumerated in the statute. It concluded that "[i]t follows inescapably
therefore that, if . . . Sect. 1982 covers private discrimination in
housing, . . . Sect. 1981 covers private discrimination in making
and enforcing contracts."⁵⁹ The court found that the contractual
prohibitions of the statute were intended to include employment
matters:

> "The right to make and enforce contracts," afforded all persons by
> Section 1981, applies to contracts of employment as well as to other
> kinds of contracts. When Congress enacted the 1866 Act, it was con-
> cerned with the employment difficulties of the freedmen. . . . Fur-

---

*In suits filed under Section 1981 before the Supreme Court decided *Johnson* v. *Railway
Express Agency Inc.,* 421 U.S. 454, 10 FEP Cases 817 (May 19, 1975), the courts relied on the
four primary cases of *Waters* v. *Wisconsin Steel, supra; Young* v. *International Telephone &
Telegraph, supra;* *Sanders* v. *Dobbs Houses, supra;* and *Boudreaux* v. *Baton Rouge Marine,
supra.* But see also *Caldwell* v. *National Brewing Co.,* 443 F.2d 1044, 3 FEP Cases 600 (5th
Cir. 1971), *cert. denied,* 405 U.S. 916, 4 FEP Cases 324 (1972); *Carter* v. *Gallagher,* 452 F.2d
315, 3 FEP Cases 900, 4 FEP Cases 121 (8th Cir. 1971), *cert. denied,* 406 U.S. 950, 4 FEP
Cases 771, 4 EPD para. 7818 (1972); *Beverly* v. *Lone Star Lead Construction Corp.,* 437 F.2d
1136, 3 FEP Cases 74 (5th Cir. 1971); *Brown* v. *Gaston County Dyeing Machine Co.,* 457 F.2d
1377, 4 FEP Cases 514, 4 EPD para. 7737 (4th Cir. 1972), *cert. denied,* 409 U.S. 982, 93 S. Ct.
319, 5 FEP Cases 149 (1972); *Brady* v. *Bristol-Myers, Inc.,* 459 F.2d 621, 4 FEP Cases 749 (8th
Cir. 1972).

thermore, in *Jones* the Court expressly overruled *Hodges* v. *United States* . . . which had indicated that Section 1981 did not apply to a conspiracy by private individuals to interfere with a contract of employment. Subsequently, in *Dobbins* v. *Local 212*, . . . the only case to rule on Section 1981 since *Jones* v. *Mayer, supra,* private employment contracts were held to be covered by the Act. Thus the termination of Turner's and Magee's contractual relationship for racially discriminatory reasons would violate Section 1981, as interpreted in the light of *Jones* v. *Mayer.*[60]

Although the district court held that the 1866 statute would support the claims of the plaintiffs in *Clark,* it applied rather tortuous logic to avoid granting relief under the statute. The court ruled that failure to reemploy the plaintiffs was due to their race and therefore constituted a violation of Title VII. "Hence," the court concluded, "relief should be granted under that Title whether or not it is also mandated by Section 1981."[61] But the court avoided the question of the nature of the relief available under Section 1981. The decision of the district court in *Clark,* although of little significance in the evolution of the case law, was an example of lower court opinions on the relationship of Section 1981 to Title VII before the appellate courts decided these questions.

In *Waters* v. *Wisconsin Steel Works*[62] the district court dismissed the plaintiffs' complaint of discriminatory hiring and furlough. It held that *Jones* v. *Mayer*[63] could not be extended to create a cause of action for "private" racial discrimination in employment; that if such an action existed prior to 1964, Title VII preempted it; and that the plaintiffs' action in this case would be barred by the 120-day filing period of the Illinois Fair Employment Practices Act. The Court of Appeals for the Seventh Circuit rejected the lower court's conclusions and reversed and remanded the case for further proceedings under Section 1981 and Title VII.

The court of appeals agreed with the plaintiffs' analogy to the *Jones* case: Section 1981 was a "valid exercise of congressional power under the Thirteenth Amendment: and that it is intended to prohibit private racial discrimination in employment by companies and unions."[64] Here for the first time a federal court included discriminatory activities of unions in the prohibitions of Section 1981:

> Racial discrimination in employment by unions as well as by employers is barred by Section 1981. The relationship between an employee and a union is essentially one of contract. Accordingly, in the per-

formance of its functions as agent for the employees a union cannot discriminate against some of its members on the basis of race.[65]

Since the lower court had dismissed the Section 1981 claim partly on the ground that the statute had been preempted by Title VII, the court of appeals considered that issue also. The court noted that although Congress had been unaware of the existence of Section 1981 during the Title VII debates, it had been aware of an alternate remedy for employment discrimination found in the National Labor Relations Act. Congress had rejected a proposal to exclude agencies other than the Equal Employment Opportunity Commission from dealing with employment discrimination, and the court stated that Congress's refusal "demonstrates an intent to preserve previously existing causes of action," including Section 1981. In addition, although the numerous detailed prohibitions in Title VII, as well as its administrative requirements, did contain a potential for conflict with Section 1981, nevertheless, "[w]e cannot conclude that the possibility of conflict demonstrates that section 1981 was wholly repealed by implication. . . . Therefore, we hold that conflicts must be resolved on a case-by-case basis."[66] Although Congress had clearly indicated that conciliation and opportunities for voluntary compliance with Title VII were highly desirable, the court stated that where a plaintiff could show a good reason for bypassing the EEOC's administrative procedures, he should be allowed to prosecute his claim under Section 1981.

Since the 1866 law contains no time limitation, courts must apply the most relevant statute of limitations of the state in which the claim arises. The appeals court dealt with the contention of the defendants that the Illinois Fair Employment Practices Act's period of limitation of 120 days barred suit under Section 1981. The district court had chosen the state's fair employment practice law as the basis for determining the limitation period. The court of appeals disagreed, however: "We are not convinced that the Illinois F.E.P.A. is the most analogous state action under these provisions."[67] The court noted the dissimilarity between the state's fair employment practices law and Section 1981—the former providing much weaker solutions to employment discrimination—and held that the state's general statute of limitations which governs all civil suits should apply to Section 1981 suits also. Thus the statute of limitations pertaining to Section 1981 suits in the state of Illinois was held to be five years as compared with the ninety-day limitation under Title VII.

The decision in *Waters* v. *Wisconsin Steel Works* is one of the most important applications of Section 1981 to questions of employment discrimination. The court clearly stated that the administrative mandates of Title VII were not absolute jurisdictional prerequisites as long as the plaintiff "provides a reasonable excuse for his failure" to comply with them. The *Waters* decision itself held that the failure to name a union as a corespondent before the EEOC did not preclude suing the union in an action under Section 1981.

The scope of relief available under the statute has not been fully developed by the courts. It seems that at the very least injunctive relief will be available, and it is probable that other remedial relief can be obtained as well.* Unlike Title VII, the statute does not contain an "affirmative action" provision directed to the courts, but the clear intent of Congress in enacting the statute of 1866 was to take active measures to place blacks suffering from the "badges and incidents" of slavery in competition with whites for equal employment. This congressional intent would seem to require courts to grant broad relief such as has been awarded in many Title VII cases.

Finally, there has been virtually no indication from the courts of the limits to which Section 1981 may be used to attack discriminatory employment practices. The statute has been held applicable in cases alleging discriminatory hiring, discharge, and union membership and apprenticeship practices, and increasingly in cases involving complex and subtle forms of discrimination.†

The Court of Appeals for the Fifth Circuit has extended the reasoning of the seventh circuit's opinion in *Waters*. In *Sanders* v. *Dobbs Houses*,[68] when the plaintiff's amended complaint was dismissed on the basis that Section 1981 could not be maintained against a private employer in the absence of some element of state action, the court of appeals reversed the trial court, stating that "[t]he quickening of this statutory Lazarus necessarily revived the congressional prohibition against purely private racial discrimina-

---

*See, for example, *Sanders* v. *Dobbs Houses,* 431 F.2d 1097, 2 FEP Cases 942 (5th Cir. 1970), *cert. denied,* 401 U.S. 948, 3 FEP Cases 193, 3 EPD para. 8127 (1971). See also *Carter* v. *Gallagher,* 452 F.2d 315, 3 FEP Cases 900, 4 FEP Cases 121 (8th Cir. 1972), *cert. denied,* 406 U.S. 950, 4 FEP Cases 771, 4 EPD para. 7818 (1972), *judgment entered,* ——F. Supp. ——, 9 FEP Cases 1191, 4 EPD para. 7853 (D. Minn. 1972); and *James* v. *Ogilvie,* 310 F. Supp. 661, 664, 2 FEP Cases 697 (D.C. N. Ill. 1970). Both these cases were brought under Section 1981 and Section 1983 of the Civil Rights Act of 1866.

†See, for example, *Sabala* v. *Western Gillette, supra;* and *Waters* (II), 502 F.2d 1309, 8 FEP Cases 577 (7th Cir. 1974).

tion in contracts of employment." Citing the court's reasoning in
Waters v. *Wisconsin Steel Works,* the fifth circuit court held that
Section 1981 prohibited private acts of discrimination in employment. By 1972, then, both district and circuit courts, buttressed by
the Supreme Court's opinion in *Jones* v. *Mayer,* were applying the
hundred-year-old law against private acts of racial discrimination
in employment.* This provides an additional means of attack upon
the discriminatory practices of both employers and labor unions,
which until recently have been free of judicial restraint.

Section 1981 also gives legal justification for considering past
acts of discrimination in finding and providing remedies for present
violations of law. In some of the earliest Title VII cases, such as
Quarles[69] and *Crown Zellerbach,*[70] which in part dealt with the
issue of whether courts could examine alleged discriminatory
actions occurring before July 2, 1965, the defense argued
successfully that the Act could not reach back past its effective
date. Although courts are now in agreement that the present effects
of past discrimination should be dealt with under Title VII, the
revival of Section 1981 as an independent basis for litigation
provides an effective means to reach past actions even if they have
no present effects.†

Soon after the enactment of Title VII it was argued that the
statute could not be used to remedy the present effects of past
discriminatory practices. The debates and memoranda in the
legislative history of Title VII were sufficiently ambiguous to lend

---

*Among these cases are: *Brown* v. *Gaston County Dyeing Machine Co.,* 457 F.2d 1377, 4
FEP Cases 514 (4th Cir. 1972), *cert. denied,* 409 U.S. 982, 5 FEP Cases 149, 5 EPD para. 7990
(1972); *Brady* v. *Bristol-Myers, Inc.,* 459 F.2d 621, 4 FEP Cases 749 (8th Cir. 1972); *Young* v.
International Telephone & Telegraph Co., 438 F.2d 757, 3 FEP Cases 146 (3rd Cir. 1971);
Boudreaux v. *Baton Rouge Marine Contracting Co.,* 437 F.2d 1011, 3 FEP Cases 99 (5th Cir.
1971); *Caldwell* v. *National Brewing Co.,* 443 F.2d 1044, 3 FEP Cases 600 (5th Cir. 1971), *cert.
denied,* 405 U.S. 916, 92 S. Ct. 560, 4 FEP Cases 324 (1972); *Carter* v. *Gallagher,* 452 F.2d
315, 3 FEP Cases 900, 4 FEP Cases 121 (8th Cir. 1971), *cert. denied,* 406 U.S. 950, 4 FEP
Cases 771, 4 EPD para. 7818 (1972); *Beverly* v. *Lone Star Lead Construction Corp.,* 437 F.2d
1136, 3 FEP Cases 74 (5th Cir. 1971); *Waters* v. *Wisconsin Steel Works,* 427 F.2d 476, 2 FEP
Cases 574 (7th Cir. 1970), *cert. denied,* 400 U.S. 911, 2 FEP Cases 1059 (1970); *Sanders* v.
Dobbs Houses, 431 F.2d 1097, 2 FEP Cases 942 (5th Cir. 1970), *cert. denied,* 401 U.S. 948, 3
FEP Cases 193, 3 EPD para. 8127 (1971); *Copeland* v. *Mead Corp.,* 51 F.R.D. 266, 3 FEP
Cases 333 (N.D. Ga. 1970); *Washington* v. *Baugh Construction Co.,* 313 F. Supp. 598, 2 FEP
Cases 271, 278 (W.D. Wash. 1969); *Central Contractors Ass'n* v. *Local 46, IBEW,* 312 F. Supp.
1388, 2 FEP Cases 189 (W.D. Wash. 1969); *Clark* v. *American Marine Corp.,* 304 F. Supp.
603, 2 FEP Cases 198 (E.D. La. 1969); *Dobbins* v. *Local 212, IBEW,* 292 F. Supp. 413, 1 FEP
Cases 387, 69 LRRM 2313 (S.D. Ohio 1968).

†See, for example, *Brown* v. *Gaston County Dyeing Machine Co.,* 457 F.2d 1377, 4 FEP
Cases 514 (4th Cir. 1972), *cert. denied,* 409 U.S. 982, 5 FEP Cases 149, 5 EPD para. 7990
(1972).

some support to contradictory interpretations of this problem. A memorandum filed by the Department of Justice during congressional consideration of the bill stated:

> First, it has been asserted that Title VII would undermine rights of seniority. This is not correct. Title VII would have no effect on seniority rights existing at the time it takes effect. If, for example, a collective bargaining contract provides that in the event of layoffs, those who were hired last must be laid off first, such a provision would not be affected in the least by Title VII. This would be true even in the case where owing to discrimination prior to the effective date of the title, white workers had more seniority than Negroes.[71]

Another memorandum, submitted by Senators Clark of Pennsylvania and Case of New Jersey, in an attempt to end a filibuster against Title VII stated:

> Title VII would have no effect on established seniority rights. Its effect is prospective and not retrospective. Thus, for example, if a business has been discriminating in the past and as a result has an all-white working force, when the title comes into effect the employer's obligation would be simply to fill future vacancies on a nondiscriminatory basis. He would not be obliged—or indeed, permitted—to fire whites in order to hire Negroes, or to prefer Negroes for future vacancies, or, once Negroes were hired, to give them special seniority rights at the expense of the white workers hired earlier.[72]

In *Quarles* the district court found it necessary to interpret the law differently, stating that "the legislative history indicates that a discriminatory seniority system established before the act cannot be held lawful under the act."[73] The court also said:

> Obviously one characteristic of a bona fide seniority system must be lack of discrimination. Nothing in [Section] 703(h), or in its legislative history, suggests that a racially discriminatory seniority system established before the act is a bona fide seniority system under the act. . . . The Court holds that a departmental seniority system that has its genesis in racial discrimination is not a bona fide seniority system.[74]

"Congress," it said flatly, "did not intend to freeze an entire generation of Negro employees into discriminatory patterns that existed before the act."[75]

Going beyond the *Quarles* decision, the courts in *United States v. Local 189, United Papermakers,*[76] *Taylor v. Armco Steel,*[77] and in other cases have defined as illegal present discriminatory practices rooted in segregated seniority systems negotiated prior to Title VII.*

Many courts confronted with the problem of the present effects of past discrimination in a seniority context have decided that the present system must be altered to provide full relief to black workers long confined to segregated lines of job progression. Commenting on the fundamental importance of such interpretations, Gould writes:

> Title VII of the Civil Rights Act of 1964 has provided the judiciary with a fairly broad mandate to remedy employment discrimination. But the greatest uncertainty in the interpretation of the statute surrounds the extent to which the courts may correct the evils of past discrimination which are embodied in present practices. It is becoming clear that unless the courts have the authority to reach back and deal with the past, institutional discrimination reflected in seniority and referral systems, as well as apprenticeship and journeyman examinations, cannot be remedied effectively.[78]

Section 1981 has become important in attacking those effects in the broadest terms. It can also invalidate arguments condoning discrimination that took place before Title VII.

The courts have allowed evidence of past discriminatory practices to be brought into Title VII trials for purposes of examining the effects of present practices; but relief that would fully compensate victims of discrimination for many years of economic deprivation has been avoided. By filing suit under both Title VII and Section 1981, black plaintiffs could expect the possible benefits of both statutes in terms of available relief.

As an independent basis for federal jurisdiction, Section 1981 may reach areas not covered by Title VII and be capable of providing relief not available under other statutes.

For example, the Equal Employment Opportunity Commission in its *Sixth Annual Report,* covering the fiscal year ending June 30, 1971, stated:

> It is possible to challenge deprivation of federally protected rights, such as those under Title VII, in the U.S. courts independently of the complex requirements of Title VII (thus, without filing with the Commission). The Civil Rights Acts of 1866 and 1871 create causes of action to redress deprivation of civil rights which have been held

---

*But compare *Jones* v. *Lee Way Motor Freight, Inc.,* 431 F.2d 245, 2 FEP Cases 895 (10th Cir. 1970), *cert. denied,* 401 U.S. 954, 3 FEP Cases 193 (1971); and *U.S.* v. *St. Louis-San Francisco Ry. Co.,* 464 F.2d 301, 4 FEP Cases 853 (8th Cir. 1972), *cert. denied,* 409 U.S. 1116, 5 FEP Cases 299, 5 EPD para. 8099 (1973).

in cases decided during 1970–71 to be available as the basis for a suit in employment-discrimination cases.[79]

On November 6, 1972, the Supreme Court in *Brown* v. *Gaston County Dyeing Machine Co.*[80] let stand a decision of the Court of Appeals for the Fourth Circuit which ruled that the Civil Rights Act of 1866 allows black workers to collect damages from employers who engage in job discrimination. The circuit court held that the company had violated the 1866 law and that the black plaintiff was entitled to back pay exclusively under Section 1981 because of discriminatory practices which took place before Title VII went into effect. In 1974 the Court of Appeals for the Fifth Circuit in *Johnson* v. *Goodyear Tire & Rubber Co.*[81] held that classwide back pay is valid to remedy employment discrimination found to be in violation of Section 1981.

Some district courts have ordered punitive damages in suits arising under both Title VII and Section 1981. Punitive damages in Title VII cases were awarded under Section 706(g), which authorizes the court to enjoin an unlawful employment practice and to "order such affirmative action as may be appropriate, which may include, but is not limited to, reinstatement or hiring of employees, with or without back pay . . . or any other equitable relief as the court deems appropriate."* The relief provisions of Title VII are drawn from the National Labor Relations Act, and the Supreme Court has held that under the NLRA only compensatory damages are available and punitive damages are prohibited.[82] However, the antipunitive damage provisions of the labor law, as amended by the Taft-Hartley Act, have been interpreted to apply solely to the jurisdiction of the National Labor Relations Board. But by mid-1975 it was clearly established that punitive damages are to be awarded exclusively under Section 1981 and not under Title VII.

In 1975 in *Johnson* v. *Railway Express Agency*[83] the Supreme Court explicitly held that punitive damages were available under Section 1981. The Court held that "[a]n individual who establishes a cause of action under Section 1981 is entitled to both equitable and legal relief, including compensatory and, under certain circumstances, punitive damages. . . . And a backpay award

---

*See, for example, *Waters, Plaintiff; EEOC, Applicant for Intervention* v. *Heublein Inc., et al.*, ——F. Supp. ——, 8 FEP Cases 908, 8 EPD para. 9522 (N.D. Calif. 1974). For discussion of these matters, see Comment, "Implying Punitive Damages in Employment Discrimination Cases," *Harvard Civil Rights-Civil Liberties Law Review*, March 1974, pp. 325–371.

under Section 1981 is not restricted to the two years specified for backpay recovery under Title VII." In this case the Court also decided that the filing of a charge with the Equal Employment Opportunity Commission under Title VII does not delay the running of the applicable state statute of limitations for the 1866 Act. Title VII, as amended, limits back-pay liability to not more than two years prior to the filing of a charge with the commission.

In the only explicit ruling by an appellate court on the subject, *EEOC* v. *Detroit Edison Co.,*[84] the sixth circuit court rejected the remedy of punitive damages in Title VII cases on the ground that Congress had not provided for it in the legislation. While denying punitive damages under Title VII alone or in conjunction with the Civil Rights Act of 1866, it is possible that such relief could be obtained in a lawsuit brought exclusively under the 1866 statute, but only if the defendant is afforded an opportunity for a jury trial.*

Under Section 1981, employers who maintain segregated facilities may be subject to money damages, and labor unions are also likely to feel the impact of the law. In *Dobbins*[85] the court ruled that exclusion from union membership is subject to the provisions of Section 1981. This is clearly within the concept that the relationship between a union and its membership is contractual in nature. Under Section 1981 it is likely that money damages will be available to blacks and others who are excluded from union membership, denied training because of their race, or placed in segregated locals, although such damages could not be viewed as back pay.

Section 1981 would also appear to be a vehicle for obtaining damages when a union directly denies a black worker the opportunity to contract with an employer on a nondiscriminatory basis. Such situations would arise, for example, where a union operates a hiring hall that is the exclusive source of labor. Discrimination by labor unions in referral opportunities is unlawful

---

*On the issue of attorneys' fees there is a significant distinction between Title VII and Section 1981. The awarding of such fees is clearly established in Title VII litigation. Among such cases, see *Robinson* v. *P. Lorillard Co.,* 444 F.2d 791, 3 FEP Cases 653 (4th Cir. 1971); *Lea* v. *Cone Mills,* 467 F.2d 277, 4 FEP Cases 1259 (4th Cir. 1972); *Johnson* v. *Georgia Highway Express,* 417 F.2d 1122, 2 FEP Cases 231 (5th Cir. 1969), attorneys' fees awarded, —— F. Supp. ——, 5 FEP Cases 776, 5 EPD para. 8444 (N.D. Ga. 1972), *vacated and remanded,* 488 F.2d 714, 7 FEP Cases 1 (5th Cir. 1974). In contrast, the decision of the Supreme Court in *Alyeska* v. *Wilderness Society,* 421 U.S. 240, 7 ERC 1849, 43 LW 4561, 10 FEP Cases 826 (1975), implies no attorneys' fees under Section 1981.

under Title VII, and back pay is available, but under Section 1981 the union's conduct could be viewed as a tortuous interference with the right of contract, for which punitive damages would be an acceptable form of relief. Prolonged, discriminatory apprenticeship or other training requirements would also be subject to attack in this fashion.

Section 1981 also provides an opportunity for immediate judicial relief which may not be available under Title VII. The language and legislative history of Title VII indicate that judicial proceedings may not be commenced under the Act until a period for administrative resolution of the case has passed. This problem is especially troublesome when the EEOC is required to defer to state agencies which often results in protracted delays. The 1972 amendments to Title VII modified this difficulty to some degree, but it is still a handicap. Such delays may be extremely damaging when mass furlough or dismissal is threatened or when the work opportunity is of relatively short duration—as on a construction job—or when members' rights are violated in the internal affairs of a union. Although no court has said that the administrative time delays built into Title VII may not be waived in appropriate circumstances, the statute would require special construction to permit judicial intervention in a Title VII proceeding before the period allowed for administrative handling of the case expires. Section 1981, on the other hand, as interpreted by a majority of the circuit courts and the Supreme Court, can be an entirely separate cause of action, without the administrative inhibitions of Title VII.* Its use in obtaining immediate judicial relief appears to fit precisely into the kind of jurisdictional problem the court described in *Waters* v. *Wisconsin Steel Works.*[86] Accordingly, Section 1981

---

*In *Alpha Portland Cement* v. *Reese,* 507 F.2d 607, 10 FEP Cases 126 (5th Cir. 1975), the fifth circuit court held that the 1866 law is separate from Title VII and that issues raised in class action litigation under the earlier Act are not limited to discrimination charges filed by an individual claimant with the EEOC. The commission's *Seventh Annual Report* observes that "[s]ix circuits now recognize the right to bring an action against discrimination in private employment under the Civil Rights Act of 1866. In addition to the Third, Fourth, Sixth and Seventh Circuits, the Fifth Circuit in *Caldwell* v. *National Brewing Co.* (443 F.2d 1044, 3 FEP Cases 600 (5th Cir. 1971); *cert. denied,* 405 U.S. 916, 4 FEP Cases 324 (1972)) and the Eighth Circuit in *Brady* v. *Bristol-Myers Inc.* (459 F.2d 621, 4 FEP Cases 749, 4 EPD para. 7808 (8th Cir. 1972)) have also recognized this right independent of Title VII rights."—*Seventh Annual Report* (covering the fiscal year ended June 30, 1972) (Washington, D.C.: Equal Employment Opportunity Commission, n.d.), p. 17. In 1975 the Supreme Court stated that "[a]lthough this Court has not specifically so held, it is well settled among the federal courts of appeals—and we now join them—that Section 1981 affords a federal remedy against discrimination in private employment on the basis of race."—*Johnson* v. *Railway Express Agency Inc.,* 421 U.S. 454, 10 FEP Cases 817 (May 19, 1975).

represents a sure avenue to immediate judicial consideration in cases where delay is intolerable.

A subsequent decision in *Waters,*[87] rendered in 1974 by the Court of Appeals for the Seventh Circuit, expands the applicability of Title VII case law and advances the utility of Section 1981. In the second *Waters* case the court removed the prior qualification of "reasonable excuse" to invoke Section 1981, and made that section totally independent of Title VII. Thus plaintiffs can use either approach, or both simultaneously. The decision of the appellate court in this case also held that the body of the law established under Title VII and EEOC regulations applied with equal force to cases arising under Section 1981.

Before the 1972 amendments to Title VII authorized litigation against governmental bodies, Sections 1981 and 1983 of the Civil Rights Act of 1866 were especially useful in such suits. In *Carter* v. *Gallagher,*[88] a case involving discriminatory employment practices by the Minneapolis Fire Department, action was brought under both sections of the 1866 statute, and the trial court decreed "[t]hat the defendants . . . give absolute preference in certification of fire fighters with the Minneapolis Fire Department to twenty (20) Black, American Indian or Spanish-surnamed American applicants who qualify for such a position."[89]

On appeal, the defendants alleged that the lower court lacked jurisdiction, abused its discretion, and erred in ordering absolute preference to minorities. The defendants' most vigorous attack was directed toward the preferential hiring issue. The appeals court held:

> The trial court's determination that past racial discrimination against minority persons applying for fire fighters' positions has been established is *affirmed.* The court's decree to the extent that it gives absolute preference to twenty applicants is *reversed* and *vacated.*[90]

The court did, however, grant a petition for rehearing *en banc* on the sole issue of the rejection of the trial court's quota standard for remedial relief, and in its full-court decision said:

> Admittedly, the District Court has wide power sitting as a court of equity to fashion relief enforcing the congressional mandate of the Civil Rights Act . . . and clearly, courts of equity have the power to eradicate the effects of past discrimination. . . .
>
> . . . [I]n making meaningful in the immediate future the constitutional guarantees against racial discrimination, more than a token representation should be afforded. For these reasons we believe the

trial court is possessed of the authority to order the hiring of 20 qualified minority persons. . . .

In reaching our conclusions . . . we have been guided to some extent by the following considerations:

(1) It has now been established by the Supreme Court that the use of mathematical ratios as "a starting point in the process of shaping a remedy" is not unconstitutional and is within the equitable remedial discretion of the District Court. . . .

(4) . . . Thus we conclude that a one-to-two ratio would be appropriate here, until 20 qualified minority persons have been hired.[91]*

In 1971 in *Chance* v. *Board of Examiners*,[92] a case brought under both Sections 1981 and 1983, a district court applied the Supreme Court's decision in *Griggs* to invalidate testing procedures which had discriminatory consequences for nonwhite teachers in New York City who were seeking promotion. The court ruled that the city's educational system must stop using its traditional examinations in selecting school principals because the tests had an "[e]ffect of discriminating significantly and substantially against qualified black and Puerto Rican applicants." The court concluded that the procedures of the Board of Examiners, allegedly based upon the merit system, could not be justified as being reasonably related to job performance and the decision was sustained by the Court of Appeals for the Second Circuit.

Although the importance of Section 1983 as applicable to discrimination by public agencies will perhaps be lessened as a result of the expanded jurisdiction of Title VII, Section 1981 involving private acts continues to develop apart from Title VII. Section 1981 is especially important because it establishes that the employment relationship is a contractual relationship and that black workers "have the same right in every State and Territory to make and enforce contracts. . . ." Thus, if a labor union, or any other agency, interposes itself between contracting parties and uses its power to inhibit that right, it may be assumed that there is a violation of the law.

As the law has evolved, Section 1981, although it may be used as a supplement to Title VII, also stands separate and apart from any other statute. The dual character of Section 1981 is indicated by the decision in *Waters* (I),[93] which recognized it in its supplementary relationship, and the opinion in *Young*,[94] which perceived it to be completely independent. This latter line of

*For a discussion of preferential hiring remedies, see Volume II, Chapter 5.

development culminated in the Supreme Court's decision in *Johnson* v. *Railway Express Agency Inc.*[95] It may be some time before the possibilities implicit in Section 1981 are fully realized. But, quite clearly, it provides a most important legal instrument for successful attacks on discriminatory employment practices and opens up new approaches under the revitalized Civil Rights Act of 1866.

3

The National Labor Relations Act and the Emergence of Civil Rights Law

Until Title VII of the Civil Rights Act of 1964 was adopted, the National Labor Relations Act (Wagner Act)[1] of 1935 and the Railway Labor Act,[2] dating from 1926, were the only potential means of redress based on federal legislation available to victims of racial discrimination in employment. The NLRA established the National Labor Relations Board, with three members (increased to five in 1947) plus a general counsel with broad authority, all appointed by the President. The Railway Labor Act set up two boards, the National Railroad Adjustment Board for minor disputes in the railroad industry, and the National Mediation Board for major disputes and for appeals from the adjustment board.

The history of the National Labor Relations Board in regard to racial discrimination may be characterized as the slow transformation of a vague public policy into a judicially developed body of law reluctantly enforced by an administrative agency. For many years the board remained unresponsive to complaints of racial discrimination. Evolution from a generalized policy, abstractly requiring nondiscrimination, to law, and then to practice has occurred in several distinct phases, each one marked by the board's general unwillingness to use its powers against discriminatory employment practices.

From its inception the NLRB could have applied its extensive administrative resources against the more overt discriminatory practices of employers and labor unions. As history shows,

93

however, the interests of employers and labor unions were directly represented within the board, but the community of black workers had neither such representation nor the institutions and the power that both management and labor possessed and used. Black wage earners were repeatedly forced to go to the federal courts in an often vain attempt to get protection of their rights from an agency dominated by organized employers and organized labor.

The National Labor Relations Act was, of course, primarily concerned with regulating relationships between employers and labor unions.* This, however, does not excuse the board's failure to use the potential of the Act in connection with racial discrimination, especially after 1944, when the federal courts began to develop the judicial remedy of the "duty of fair representation" for certain forms of racial discrimination in employment. Although the courts found an applicable prohibition among the interstices of both the National Labor Relations Act and the Railway Labor Act, the only remedies available remained judicial. Negro workers experiencing discrimination were forced to bear the expense and the protracted delay of court suits in seeking enforcement of their legal rights. The NLRB refused to use its powers for swift and pervasive action against the discriminatory racial practices of management and organized labor. For years it rejected the numerous petitions it received charging racially motivated employment abuses. The board has not merely been neutral in its response to the issue of discriminatory practices based on race; it has provided vital protection and a full range of government services to both labor unions and employers engaged in discrimination.

Because the Act itself deals inadequately with the entire problem of racial discrimination in employment, and because the NLRB has been loath to bring its administrative power to bear on the problem, "creative interpretation" by the courts has been necessary, but it has emerged very slowly.

---

*Section 7 of the NLRA declares a right to self-organization and to engage in "concerted activities for the purpose of collective bargaining or other mutual aid or protection." Section 8(a) makes it an unfair labor practice for the employer to coerce employees in the exercise of these rights, or to discriminate in employment "to encourage or discourage membership in any labor organization," or to refuse to bargain collectively with the representatives designated by the employees. Section 8(b) makes it an unfair labor practice for unions to coerce employees in the exercise of the rights guaranteed in Section 7 or to coerce employers to discriminate in violation of the provision of Section 8(a). Section 9 confers exclusive representation rights on the bargaining agent designated by the majority of the employees in an appropriate unit. The phrase "other mutual aid or protection" in Section 7 can be used to protect those seeking aid against racial discrimination.

The railway labor boards, to an even greater degree than the NLRB, have been and remain unresponsive to the discriminatory practices of both employers and labor unions. Within the railroad industry there was a high concentration of Negro workers with unique traditions and status in their communities. This, combined with the harsh injustices they suffered, impelled them to initiate the early court cases that brought racial discrimination within the duty of fair representation. The issue of fair representation was forced into the courts because the administrative processes of all the federal regulatory boards were closed to Negro workers.[3]

As initially expressed by the courts, the only labor law prohibiting racial discrimination in employment was an ambiguous doctrine requiring labor unions to treat whites and Negroes alike in the collective bargaining process. Although black employees were denied membership in the white-only operating railroad brotherhoods, the unions negotiated terms and conditions of employment for black workers which directly—and adversely—affected many aspects of their job status. (See Chapter 13.) The doctrine of fair representation was not applied to exclusionary union membership practices for many years; unions that were free to exclude Negroes from membership were somehow expected to treat them fairly in other vital phases of the employment relationship.

This contradiction in the law remained in force until 1964, when the NLRB indicated that it would begin inquiring into the racial practices of labor unions if complaints of discrimination were properly filed.[4] The federal courts were quick to confirm the board's authority to deal with problems of job discrimination based on race, but up to 1975 the board's power in such areas had been infrequently used. Since the NLRB has the administrative power to conduct investigations at its own expense,[5] to issue cease-and-desist orders,[6] and to proceed directly to federal court for enforcement of its orders,[7] it has the potential to serve as an important vehicle for the redress of racial discrimination in employment, but its history in the area of civil rights has been one of great possibility and little practical effect.

The Negro and the New Deal

When Franklin D. Roosevelt became President in 1932, the white population was suffering serious privation, but for Negroes the Depression was catastrophic. Much of Roosevelt's New Deal was a variety of efforts to generate new employment. The New Deal sought to provide economic stabilization and security as well as emergency relief and new jobs through a series of laws and programs.[8] In general, these efforts improved conditions for whites but had little impact on the status of Negro workers. Because the Federal Government failed to require or enforce equal racial access to government-created jobs, the ultimate effect of the New Deal employment programs was to widen the gap between the economic condition of black and white workers.* And because of the massive federal impact on the national economy that began in the 1930s, the initial failure of executive power to enforce equal treatment in federal programs established a new degree of government complicity in economic racial discrimination.

Such an indictment may seem paradoxical, especially when one considers the Roosevelt Administration's much-publicized compassion for the conditions of blacks. Relief agencies such as the Works Progress Administration (WPA) did provide desperately needed help in many cities. And the so-called "Black Cabinet," consisting of about two-dozen Negro advisers, did succeed in obtaining some assistance for at least a portion of the black community not, in fact, by abolishing discrimination but by managing on occasion to make it less flagrant. Several members of the Black Cabinet agreed later[9] that at best the emergency assistance they obtained was on a segregated basis. In the context of the period, however, this was no mean achievement. To bring about genuinely equal treatment in New Deal programs would have required a political price the Roosevelt Administration was not willing to pay, notwithstanding the presence of a few whites

---

*Arthur M. Ross, a former commissioner of the Bureau of Labor Statistics, noted that the significant disparity between black and white unemployment rates did not begin until the Depression of the 1930s. See "The Negro in the American Economy," in Arthur M. Ross and Herbert Hill, eds., *Employment, Race, and Poverty* (New York: Harcourt, Brace & World, 1967), pp. 14–15. The Federal Government's failure to enforce public policy declarations of nondiscrimination in employment at the beginning of the period of vast government involvement in the national economy has been a major factor in the perpetuation of racial job patterns. For studies of the effect of New Deal policies on the black community, see Raymond Wolters, *Negroes and the Great Depression: The Problem of Economic Recovery* (Westport, Conn.: Greenwood Publishing Corp., 1970); Allen Francis Kifer, "The Negro Under the New Deal, 1933–1941," unpublished Ph.D. dissertation, University of Wisconsin, 1961; Leslie H. Fishel, Jr., "The Negro in the New Deal Era," *Wisconsin Magazine of History,* Winter 1964–1965, pp. 111–121; and Frank Freidel, *F.D.R. and the South* (Baton Rouge, La.: University of Louisiana Press, 1965), pp. 71–102.

like Harold Ickes who were sympathetic and concerned with the plight of Negroes, and Mrs. Roosevelt's acts of friendship.*

The practices of the many New Deal agencies in relation to Negroes varied, but in no case was there equality of treatment. The programs seeking to establish economic stabilization and security either excluded Negroes from their benefits or accepted (and thereby gave federal sanction to) inferior standards for them. The industry codes of the National Recovery Administration of 1933 did not regulate wages and hours for agricultural or domestic labor, where over 70 percent of black workers were concentrated. These two labor groups were similarly excluded from the Fair Labor Standards Act of 1938. The National Labor Relations Act itself gave immense power to organized labor without any concomitant requirement that the unions cease their long-standing discriminatory practices. The general result of this group of New Deal laws was to provide a series of legal protections and benefits to white workers and to make black workers more vulnerable to job discrimination. The only areas in which Negroes even approached equal treatment with whites were the emergency relief and welfare programs.†

The National Recovery Administration was the first and most extensive of the New Deal agencies. It established a system of

---

*Mrs. Roosevelt addressed conventions of the National Association for the Advancement of Colored People; invited Mrs. Oscar De Priest, wife of the only Negro congressman (R-Illinois), to tea with other congressional wives; and canceled her membership in the Daughters of the American Revolution when it excluded Marian Anderson from Constitution Hall. These actions were of great symbolic importance in the civil rights struggles of the period and were reflected in the Negro press's affection for Mrs. Roosevelt.

†In the New Deal period there was a short-lived attempt to use the NLRB's powers on behalf of nonwhite workers. In the words of former NLRB attorney Ruth Weyand, "[t]he Board reinstated thousands of blacks who were discriminatorily discharged or refused reinstatement after strikes in the late thirties and early forties. However, the fact that NLRB records of that period so often gave a vivid picture of the mistreatment of blacks makes even more legitimate criticism of the Board's failure to protect the rights of minorities and their fair representation by unions that it certified."—Letter to author from Ruth Weyand, April 29, 1973. Ruth Weyand's observation is underscored by several strong early holdings of the NLRB, which suggest that the board later retreated on these issues. In 1938, in *American Tobacco Company* (9 NLRB 579, 3 LRRM 308), the board refused to conduct a certification election because of racial segregation, and in 1943, in *Bethlehem Alameda Shipyard, Inc.* (53 NLRB 999, 13 LRRM 139), the board deferred an election because the petitioning union had refused to admit black and Chinese employees into union membership. In *Bethlehem Alameda Shipyard* the board expressed "grave doubt whether a union which discriminatorily denies membership to employees on the basis of race may nevertheless bargain as the exclusive representative in an appropriate unit composed in part of members of the excluded race." Furthermore, it noted that if a union-shop contract were executed by a union denying membership to nonwhites, the legal validity of such a contract, under Section 8(a)(3), was questionable.

industry-by-industry regulation of prices, wages, and working conditions. It was inevitable that in a society where Negroes were traditionally either limited to inferior jobs or paid inferior wages for the same work as whites, such standardized regulations would collide with social norms.

Although racial discrimination was prohibited in the general language of the NRA, in practice the Act discriminated against Negro workers in several ways. Companies not engaged in interstate commerce were frequently able to circumvent the law. Regional wage differentials were permitted, and minimum wages were lowest in the South, which had the greatest concentration of the black population. Furthermore, jobs held by Negroes were often reclassified so that they received the lowest minimums. In 1934, *Opportunity,* the organ of the National Urban League, published an article called "Black Wages for Black Men," by Dr. Ira De A. Reid, in which he said:

> Negro workers are automatically classed as sub-standard or sub-normal workers, and are given an initial wage lower than that prescribed by industrial codes or professional standards. The indirect methods include such devices as changing the title of an occupation while authorizing the same performance as existed in a higher occupation for which there was a higher wage.[10]

Reid also cited the practice of distributing lower paying piece work to Negroes and favoring whites with overtime.

Frequently Negroes were forced, as they had been ever since Emancipation, to either accept lower wages or be displaced by whites.[11] In the absence of federal enforcement of the Act's antidiscrimination provisions, the ban on differentials only accelerated Negro displacement.

The NRA was viewed with great skepticism by Negro groups during that period. The executive director of the Labor Advisory Board of the NRA, Gustave Peck, writing in *Crisis,* the publication of the National Association for the Advancement of Colored People, acknowledged that the choice was between racial wage differentials and displacement. However, he rationalized it on the ground that "in the South, public opinion makes it necessary for employers to take on unemployed white workers at jobs formerly performed by colored workers at lower wages."[12] The public opinion referred to, needless to say, was white public opinion.* A

---

*The Federal Re-employment Service director for Savannah, Georgia, put it more bluntly: "Any nigger who gets over $8 a week is a spoiled nigger."—Arthur M. Schlesinger, Jr., *The Politics of Upheaval,* Sentry ed. (Boston: Houghton Mifflin, 1960), p. 433.

later article in *Crisis,* "NRA Codifies Wage Slavery,"[13] was typical of the critical attitude of Negro organizations. It asserted not only that black workers' hold on inferior jobs was threatened but that discriminatory labor unions were given new power through the industry committees, and that organized labor was generally hostile to the interests of Negro workingmen and workingwomen.

Peck's article also disclosed that "[w]e have had to make a number of exceptions or allowances for firms employing Negro workers exclusively, if these firms were to continue to exist in codified industries."[14] This was tacit acceptance of the customary practice of paying Negro workers less than white workers, even when prohibited by law.

Such were the arguments presented to leaders of the Negro community in justification of federal acquiescence to wage differentials: the tradition that Negroes are usually paid less; the contention that Negroes are, after all, less efficient than whites; the argument that Negroes do not require as high a standard of living as whites; and the risk of displacement by unemployed whites, with the implication that whites deserve preferential treatment in the allocation of jobs.[15]

The danger inherent in the Federal Government's compromise and abuse of its own laws was summed up by the National Urban League's representative, T. Arnold Hill:

> The large number of [Negro] employees who are worked longer hours and paid smaller wages than the regulations dictate constitute a much more serious violation of public trust and legal statute than do the dismissals of Negro workers by employers who are against paying them wages equal to those paid whites. And more serious is the failure of NRA to enforce compliance, thus tacitly condoning the violation.[16]

The worst abuses were in the South, where flagrant violations established the precedent that such abuses were to be tolerated. Although Negro advisers to some agencies were able to exercise a slight salutary influence on officials, pressing them to show some concern for Negro workingmen, that was not the case in the NRA. There the sole Negro employee, Miss Mabel Byrd, who worked in the Division of Research, was dismissed after she asked to investigate, personally, code violations in the South.[17]

During NRA's short life hundreds of complaints charging racial discrimination were filed with the agency. Retaliation against those who complained was widespread. A typical case was that of

200 women factory workers in Arkansas who were summarily dismissed for "inefficiency" after one of them complained to Washington that their wage was $6.16 per week compared to the $12.00 minimum set by the code.[18]

Civil Rights Opposition to the Wagner Act

When the NRA was struck down by the Supreme Court in 1935,[19] there was cause for celebration in the Negro community. The legislation intended to be the keystone of President Roosevelt's program to protect and uplift the working class had already become a millstone around the black worker's neck. The Wagner Act, which replaced Section 7a of the NRA, gave organized labor legitimacy within the legal structure and increased its power enormously. It was intended to fill the gaps left by the demise of the NRA but was also viewed by blacks with considerable hostility. Now discriminatory labor agreements negotiated under the National Labor Relations Act were sanctioned by government agencies.* The NLRB was not set up to supervise negotiations or approve collective bargaining agreements, but it was authorized to deal with specific issues arising collaterally when charges were filed claiming violations of the agreement. Although the original Wagner Act made no provision for enforcing collective bargaining agreements, Section 301 of the Taft-Hartley Act of 1947 made collective bargaining agreements enforceable by the federal courts. Under the Railway Labor Act, the National Railway Adjustment Board adjudicates breaches of agreements, but all union security agreements were illegal until 1951.†

*As demonstrated in this instance, legal institutions as they develop may also legitimize injustice. The National Labor Relations Act not only imposed limits on conflict in industrial relations and provided a mechanism for resolving labor-management disputes, it also had the effect of legitimizing racial discrimination. After passage of the Act, informal discriminatory practices became structured and legally sanctioned by government action. Max Weber writes of "domination by virtue of 'legality,' by virtue of the belief in the validity of legal statute and functional 'competence' based on rationally created *rules*. . . . This is domination as exercised by the modern 'servant of the state' and by all those bearers of power who in this respect resemble him."—*Max Weber: Essays in Sociology,* trans. and eds. H. H. Gerth and C. Wright Mills (New York: Oxford University Press, 1946), p. 79.

†The NLRA and the RLA may be regarded as companion acts in the sense that the courts did not uphold the collective bargaining provisions of the RLA until March 1937 (in *Virginia Ry. Co.* v. *System Federation,* 300 U.S. 515, 1 LRRM 743), after the Supreme Court had heard oral argument on the constitutionality of the Wagner Act; decision on the latter was issued in April 1937 (in *Jones & Laughlin Steel Corp.* v. *NLRB,* 301 U.S. 1, 1 LRRM 703).

Thus the two federal acts increased and institutionalized the collective bargaining strength of organized labor. Both provided for elections among employees to determine their bargaining representative and for an agency to determine such a representative should a dispute arise. Since most unions at that time excluded Negro workers, limited them to segregated locals, or confined them to auxiliary units,* the white majority in any one craft was able to elect and control the bargaining agent. Negroes were thus unable to alter racial practices within unions, and they were denied representation in the collective bargaining process. In fact, certification by the National Labor Relations Board provided unions with a broad range of powers that enabled them to enforce and extend discriminatory labor practices. Neither the National Labor Relations Act nor the Railway Labor Act contained provisions for the protection of minority interests from the rule of the majority; neither specifically prohibited racial discrimination in employment; and neither contained express provisions requiring unions to represent their constituents fairly in negotiating and executing bargaining agreements.

A significant aspect of the public controversy surrounding the passage of the National Labor Relations Act was the intense opposition of the NAACP, the National Urban League, and other Negro interest groups. The most important feature of the Act was taken from Section 7a of the National Industrial Recovery Act (which became Section 9 of the NLRA). This section established labor unions as exclusive collective bargaining agents through a process of governmental certification by the National Labor Relations Board. Because most of the unions affiliated with the American Federation of Labor either excluded Negro workers from membership (the United Mine Workers of America was the major exception), thus preventing their employment in union-controlled jobs, or engaged in other discriminatory practices, spokesmen for the black community vigorously opposed Section 7a. W. E. B. Du Bois wrote in *Crisis:*

Politically the Railway Labor Act was the product of an earlier period, but the judicial imprimatur on its collective bargaining provisions was part of the "post-NRA New Deal." Anticoercion parts of the RLA had been held constitutional earlier, in 1929 (in *Texas & N. O. Ry.* v. *Railway Clerks,* 281 U.S. 548).

*See Sterling D. Spero and Abram L. Harris, *The Black Worker* (New York: Columbia University Press, 1931); Herbert R. Northrup, *Organized Labor and the Negro* (New York: Harper & Brothers, 1944); and Herbert Hill, "The Racial Practices of Organized Labor—In the Age of Gompers and After," in Arthur M. Ross and Herbert Hill, eds., *Employment, Race, and Poverty* (New York: Harcourt, Brace & World, 1967), pp. 365–397.

The American Federation of Labor is not a labor movement. It is a
monopoly of skilled laborers, who joined the capitalists in exploiting
the masses of labor, whenever and wherever they can. . . . The AF
of L has from the beginning of its organization stood up and lied bra-
zenly about its attitude toward Negro labor. . . . They have affirmed
and still affirm that they wish to organize Negro labor when this is a
flat and proven falsehood.[20]

Du Bois also said "the most sinister power that the N.L.R.A. has
reinforced is the American Federation of Labor."[21]

The National Urban League protested in a memorandum to
President Roosevelt that Section 7a failed to protect "minority
groups of workers whom the union wishes, for racial or religious
reasons, to exclude from employment."[22] Roy Wilkins, at that time
assistant secretary of the NAACP, stated its position in a letter to
the journalist Horace Cayton:

When the New Deal Program was launched, we realized as did all
other persons interested in the labor movement that Section 7a of the
National Industrial Recovery Act was a powerful weapon for the
workers if they would use it and fight for the correct interpretation of
it. We came shortly to realize, however, that while the American
Federation of Labor was seizing upon Section 7a to carry on the most
stupendous drive for membership in its history it was doing little or
nothing to include Negroes in the organizing. As a matter of fact, we
strongly suspect, although we cannot prove, that AF of L unions
have attempted to use Section 7a to drive Negroes out of certain
occupations.

The strategy was to organize a union for collective bargaining, to
claim the right to speak for all the workers, and then to either agree
with the employers to push Negroes out of the industry or, having
effected an agreement with the employer, to proceed to make the
union lily-white.[23]

The southern field secretary of the National Urban League,
Jesse O. Thomas, observed in a report that "while Section 7a has
greatly increased the security of labor in general, insofar as the
different labor organizations thus benefitted deny and exclude
Negroes from their membership by constitutions or rituals, the
position of Negro labor has been made less favorable." Thomas
added that as a result of the "anti-social attitude of the majority of
the membership and heads of the many unions and crafts, the
position of Negroes has been made even more disadvantageous."[24]
An influential Negro newspaper, the Baltimore *Afro-American*,
editorialized that "[u]nless the AF of L is able to make its locals

throughout the country open their doors to colored members in all crafts, it may be necessary for colored labor to organize and join in a country-wide fight on the union."[25]

The apprehension of Negroes throughout the country about Section 7a was fully justified. The historian Raymond Wolters wrote:

> During the 1930's several examples of trade unions using their power to force the dismissal of black workers came to the attention of Negro leaders, an experience which understandably served to confirm their original pessimistic suspicions. In Long Island City, New York, the Brotherhood of Electrical Workers, Local No. 3, organized several electrical supply shops, refused membership to the Negro workers already employed there, and used its newly won power to force the managements to discharge several dozen Negro employees. In Manhattan, some locals of the Building Service Employees' Union demanded that employers discharge Negro workers and fill the vacancies with white unionists. As a result, several hotels, restaurants and office buildings were forced to discharge Negro elevator operators and restaurant workers and hire whites. . . . In St. Louis the depth of this anti-Negro sentiment was strikingly illustrated when all the AFL men working on the Homer Phillips Hospital (a $2 million hospital for blacks built in the middle of a Negro neighborhood) walked off the job and halted construction for two months in protest against the General Tile Company's decision to employ a Negro as a tile setter. Examples such as this naturally made other contractors reluctant to hire black labor.[26]

The NAACP had organized mass demonstrations at the AFL's 1934 convention in protest against the federation's racial practices. Negro workers picketed the San Francisco convention hall with banners proclaiming "White Unions Make Black Scabs." Subsequently the convention passed a resolution authorizing a "Committee of Five to Investigate Conditions of Negro Workers," but not before rejecting the proposal of A. Philip Randolph, president of the Brotherhood of Sleeping Car Porters, that the AFL expel "any union maintaining the color bar."[27]

William Green, president of the AFL, called a meeting of the Committee of Five in Washington at which Charles H. Houston, then an NAACP attorney, the Urban League's Reginald Johnson, and A. Philip Randolph, together with groups of black workers, presented their grievances against AFL affiliates. Houston reported that signed statements testifying to specific acts of racial discrimination by AFL affiliates were being collected by NAACP branches all over America for presentation at subsequent hearings. But Green announced soon afterward that no further hearings would be held. On September 26, 1935, Walter White, executive secretary of the NAACP, telegraphed Green that his refusal to proceed with the investigation and to take action on "this vitally important question" would be "construed as justification of the skepticism widely expressed of the sincerity of the American Federation of Labor's action."[28]

John Brophy, of the United Mine Workers of America, who had been appointed secretary of the Committee of Five, resigned in protest. "The maneuvering on the part of the Executive Council," said Brophy, "plainly indicated that [Green] wanted the 'Committee of Five to Investigate Conditions of Negro Workers' to be merely a face-saving device for the AFL rather than an honest attempt to find a solution to the Negro problem in the American labor movement."[29] Later, in his autobiography, *A Miner's Life,* Brophy explained: "None of the unions that practiced discrimination appeared . . . the others were afraid that we would be exceeding our commission unless Green approved. Green did not approve, so that ended that."[30]

White wrote to John L. Lewis, president of the United Mine Workers, that he approved of Brophy's resignation, adding that "the recent hypocritical attitude of the American Federation of Labor in suppressing the report of the Committee . . . has destroyed the last vestige of confidence which Negro workers ever had in the AFL."[31]

In 1934, after much public debate, Senator Robert F. Wagner proposed a new bill intended to reformulate Section 7a, authorizing creation of an independent agency, the National Labor Relations Board. This board would have the power to certify unions as exclusive collective bargaining agents; to order elections among competing unions so that workers could choose a collective bargaining agent or "no union"; and to insure that after a union was certified as the exclusive representative, employers legally obliged to recognize the union would engage in collective bargaining. The proposed law gave labor unions great power to directly determine the job status of workers in many industries.

Negro leaders responded by insisting upon the inclusion of an antidiscrimination clause in Senator Wagner's revised proposal. The NAACP, the Urban League, and other civil rights organizations began a nationwide campaign to obtain the "inclusion of an amendment that would have denied the benefits of the legislation to any union which discriminated on the basis of race."[32]*

On behalf of the NAACP, Roy Wilkins objected that the proposed Wagner bill in reality "rigidly enforces and legalizes the closed shop," and that "the Act plainly empowers organized labor to exclude from employment in any industry those who do not belong to a union." Wilkins noted "the fact that thousands of Negro workers are barred from membership in American labor unions and, therefore, if the closed shop is legalized by this act, Negro workers will be absolutely shut out of employment."[33] Harry E. Davis, a member of the NAACP's board of directors, in a letter to Walter White urging a vigorous battle against the Wagner Act, argued that "it is not a 'closed' shop which is in the offing, but a 'white' shop."[34] T. Arnold Hill of the Urban League warned that "if the Wagner bill passes in its present form, the power and influence of the labor movement will be greatly enhanced with the consequent danger of greater restrictions being practiced against Negro workers by organized labor."[35] He wrote:

> Under NRA, Labor has been a silent partner along the entire recovery front. The Wagner bill elevates labor to the dominant position of an active, operating co-partner with the employer and the public, each having equal rights and authority. If, as it has been pointed out above, the NRA under the guidance of General Hugh S. Johnson has permitted labor unions to continue their restrictions against Negroes, what might not be expected when organized labor is given greater prestige and control?[36]

Dean Kelly Miller of Howard University wrote in the Norfolk *Journal and Guide* that "every effort should be made to amend the Wagner bill so as to safeguard the rights of the Negro. . . . Unless this is done it is easy to foretell the doom of the Negro in American industry."[37]

In the midst of the campaign for the inclusion of an antidiscrimination amendment, Leon Keyserling, then Senator

---

*Walter White, acting on the instructions of the board of directors of the NAACP, proposed to Senator Wagner that no union be defined as a "labor organization" if it, "by its organic law, or by any rule or regulation, or any practice precludes any employee or employees from membership in the organization or from equal participation with other employees by reason of race, creed, or color."—Letter from Walter White to Senator Robert F. Wagner, April 17, 1934 (NAACP files). The Urban League proposed an amendment stating "[i]t shall be an unfair labor practice for a labor organization to bar from membership any worker or group of workers for reason of race or creed."—*Legislative History of the National Labor Relations Act, 1935* (Washington, D.C.: National Labor Relations Board, 1949), pp. 1058–1060.

Wagner's secretary, informed Walter White that "the Act as originally drafted by Senator Wagner provided that the closed shop should be legal only when there were no restrictions upon members in the labor union to which the majority of workers belonged." But, according to Keyserling, "the American Federation of Labor fought bitterly to eliminate this clause and much against his will Senator Wagner had to consent to the elimination in order to prevent scuttling of the entire bill."[38]

In a telegram to President Roosevelt dated March 21, 1934, Walter White asked the support of the President, saying "we rely on you to prevent [the] sacrifice of [the] Negro to Jim Crow unionism."[39]

Negro workers suffered a major legislative defeat, a defeat with grave long-term consequences, when in 1935 Congress adopted and President Roosevelt signed into law the National Labor Relations Act without the NAACP-Urban League antidiscrimination amendment. Wolters explains:

> The reason for this [defeat] seems clear; the American Federation of Labor had more political power and influence than the two Negro protest organizations. . . . Negro leaders had appealed for an amendment on grounds of equity and justice, but their request was not granted because it conflicted with the claims of better organized, more powerful white interests.[40]

As passed, the National Labor Relations Act, like the earlier Railway Labor Act, gave unions virtually unrestricted power to negotiate on behalf of all employees under their jurisdiction.

Federal legislation had now legitimized the powers that discriminatory unions exercised over Negro workers. It was not until the next decade, when the Supreme Court began to interpret liberally the doctrine of the duty of fair representation, that Negroes were able to obtain some minimal redress for their inequitable employment status.

From *Steele* to *Hughes Tool*

Between 1941 and 1946 the World War II Fair Employment Practice Committee—able to investigate, hold hearings, and issue directives but lacking any enforcement powers—demonstrated that major sections of organized labor systematically deprived Negroes of employment rights with impunity. In its railroad industry hearings[41] the FEPC documented the relationship between the collective bargaining status conferred on railroad unions by the Railway Labor Act and the power of those unions to negotiate with railroad companies agreements that systematically segregated blacks in some crafts and excluded them from others in an industry in which there had formerly been a substantial proportion of jobs available to them. Here the Railway Labor Act not only helped maintain employment discrimination but, through its very existence, increased employment discrimination by legally sanctioning the unions' power to displace employed Negroes and transfer their jobs to whites. The Supreme Court, aware of "the Committee's outstanding failures"[42] in trying to enforce federal executive orders prohibiting discrimination as they related to the railroad industry, in 1944 provided a limited remedy through the doctrine of the duty of fair representation.

In 1941 the Brotherhood of Locomotive Firemen and Enginemen and twenty-one railroad companies negotiated an agreement, sanctioned by the National Mediation Board, that would have systematically eliminated Negroes from the position of fireman. At the time the agreement was negotiated the union as a matter of policy excluded Negro workers from membership, and it did not give notice of the impending agreement to the thousands of nonunion Negro firemen working under its jurisdiction. Two Negro firemen who were displaced from their jobs as a result of the agreement filed suit, and ultimately, after many years of litigation, the issue was resolved by the Supreme Court. Although the Railway Labor Act contained no express provisions requiring nondiscrimination in the industry's employment practices, the United States entered the case as *amicus curiae,* urging the Court to infer from the Act a duty of fair representation.* The government's brief stated:

*Both the Justice Department and the NAACP filed briefs *amicus curiae* in *Steele* v. *Louisville & Nashville R.R. Co.* The NAACP brief sought a ruling that a racially exclusionary union could not constitutionally bargain for excluded employees. The NAACP had earlier filed a brief *amicus curiae* with the NLRB making the same argument in *Bethlehem Alameda Shipyard Inc.,* 53 NLRB 999, 13 LRRM 139 (1943). The brief of the United States in *Steele* took the opposite view, asserting that fair representation "does not mean that a labor union as a private organization has no power to fix its own eligibility requirements, even if the result is to discriminate against persons because of their race" (p. 38). The opinion of the Court, written by Chief Justice Stone, generally followed with only slight rephrasing the brief of the United States (including the language quoted in the text). The Court's rephrasing in this particular reads: "The statute does not deny to such a bargaining labor organization the right to determine eligibility to its membership." —323 U.S. 204, 15 LRRM 713. Ruth Weyand, at that time an attorney for the NLRB, writes: "Those of us from the NLRB who

The right of the organization chosen by the majority to be the exclusive representative of a bargaining unit exists only by reason of the Railway Labor Act. Implicit in the grant of such right is a correlative duty of the representative to act in behalf of all the employees in the unit without discrimination. Congress would not have incapacitated a minority or an individual from representing itself or his own interests without imposing upon the craft representative a duty to serve on behalf of the craft as a whole, and not merely for the benefit of certain portions of it favored as a result of discrimination against others.[43]

In its first major decision involving employment discrimination in the modern period, the Supreme Court announced in 1944, in *Steele* v. *Louisville & Nashville R.R. Co.*[44] and its companion case, *Tunstall* v. *Brotherhood of Locomotive Firemen and Enginemen*,[45] that the duty of the certified collective bargaining agent to represent members and nonmembers alike fairly and without discrimination when negotiating a bargaining agreement was implicit in the Railway Labor Act. Thus began the interpretation of the statutory duty of fair representation as providing a means of judicial redress to victims of racial discrimination in employment.[46] Professor Harry H. Wellington writes:

It is extraordinary, if one thinks about it for a moment, that neither the Labor-Management Relations Act nor its counterpart, the Railway Labor Act, has an express provision requiring that the union of the majority exercise its power to represent all employees in a unit with absolute fairness and impartiality. That this is the case speaks rather badly for the Congress of the United States which did write into law the majority rule concept. This congressional lapse, however, was to afford the Supreme Court in *Steele* v. *Louisville & N.R.R.* . . . a brilliant opportunity to display the creative art of statutory interpretation.[47]

Since the Railway Labor Act did not contain an express limitation on the power of the majority of workers in a craft to represent all the workers, the Supreme Court was forced to find the source of authority for the doctrine of fair representation in the Act as a whole, "read in the light of the purpose of the Act."[48] The Court likened the unions' duty to that of a legislature, which is

had participated in drafting the brief for the United States as *amicus curiae* all agreed at the time the opinion was handed down that if we had been successful in our attempt to persuade the Department of Justice to argue for the right to membership as a prerequisite to representation by the union, the Supreme Court's opinion would have gone along."—Letter from Ruth Weyand to author, November 22, 1973.

under a constitutional mandate to provide equality of protection. The reference to equal protection was an analogy only, however, and the Court did not decide the case on constitutional grounds. It recognized that Congress had conferred on unions "powers comparable to those possessed by a legislative body," but it did not extend the requirement of equal protection to unions on the basis of "state action."[49] Professor Wellington, in his discussion of the *Steele* opinion, suggests that the Court was wise not to extend the equal protection clause to apply to the Brotherhood of Locomotive Firemen and Enginemen:

> Observe, however, what the Court is not deciding. *Steele* does not hold that the equal protection clause of the Constitution applies to the Brotherhood of Locomotive Firemen and Enginemen. The equal protection clause regulates state action—including, through the due process clause, the actions of the United States itself. It would require some rather sophisticated doctrinal analysis of the most far-reaching constitutional, and, therefore, fundamentally political, sort to equate Brotherhood action to state action. Perhaps the equation is possible, but the Court was careful not to attempt it. The equal protection clause was employed as an analogy, not as a constitutional requirement. By analogy it served as a standard with which the Court was able to inform itself as to the meaning of fairness in the industrial setting with which it was concerned. And a perfectly splendid analogy it was! A legislature may not draw distinctions on the basis of color; such distinctions are barred absolutely. Labor unions when negotiating collective agreements are engaged in essentially legislative activity, prospectively establishing the terms and conditions of employment. Nothing in the union's structure or function suggests that it should be held to a less exacting standard of conduct in its legislative activities than state or federal legislatures.[50]

Justice Frank Murphy, in a separate concurring opinion, differed with the Supreme Court majority in believing the case should have been decided on constitutional grounds. In his view, economic discrimination against Negroes practiced under the guise of congressional authority was constitutionally prohibited, so that interpretation of the statute in a way that authorized discrimination would, in effect, make the statute unconstitutional. Although the Act "contains no language which directs the manner in which the bargaining representative shall perform its duties . . . I am willing to read the statute as not permitting or allowing any action by the bargaining representative in the exercise of its delegated powers which would in effect violate the constitutional rights of individuals."⁵¹ Justice Murphy saw the "utter disregard for the dignity and well-being of colored citizens" as a condition demanding "the invocation of constitutional condemnation";⁵² and that economic discrimination should be met with constitutional disapproval whenever applied "under authority of law."⁵³

This was the first time a Supreme Court justice declared that a union, which owes its status as exclusive bargaining agent to a federal statute, violates the Constitution when it discriminates against a minority group it is supposed to represent. While the Court majority found the duty of fair representation in the commands of the statute, Justice Murphy believed that, because the union operated under authority delegated by Congress, it had a duty to comply with the same constitutional standards imposed on Congress; since Congress was precluded from authorizing discriminatory action on the basis of race, so too were labor unions. From the conviction with which Justice Murphy set forth his separate opinion in *Steele,* it is apparent that the constitutional issues were considered and rejected by the other members of the Court, and they have never been successfully raised in a federal court since that time. Resolution of racial discrimination cases arising under national labor legislation by the NLRB and the federal courts is usually based on statutory interpretations and not directly on constitutional grounds. Labor unions that receive public funds and government approval for union-controlled training programs, federal protection in organizing and bargaining, and jurisdiction over a substantial number of jobs deriving from publicly financed programs often continue to operate without regard for the legal prohibitions against racial discrimination.

A second notable omission in the *Steele* opinion was the lack of any condemnation of the union's discriminatory membership practices. The exclusion of Negroes from membership effectively denied them notice of pending agreements or participation in the internal political affairs of the union and denied them a voice in the negotiating process. The doctrine of fair representation as thus interpreted was therefore tantamount to an application of the "separate but equal" doctrine. The union was allowed to treat Negroes as a separate class, excluded from membership, but was expected to negotiate equally on their behalf. The Court was aware that the union's constitution contained a "white-only" membership clause and that the union adhered to it. By condoning such practices, the Court permitted them to continue:

While the statute does not deny to such a bargaining labor organization the right to determine eligibility to its membership, it does require the union, in collective bargaining and in making contracts with the carrier, to represent non-union or minority union members of the craft without hostile discrimination, fairly, impartially, and in good faith. Wherever necessary to that end, the union is required to consider requests of non-union members of the craft and expressions of their views with respect to collective bargaining with the employer and to give them notice of an opportunity for hearing upon its proposed action.[54]

Even under the doctrine of the duty of fair representation, unions were free to exclude Negroes from membership solely on the basis of race. The duty of fair representation as it emerged from *Steele* was extremely limited in scope. It was not based on constitutional grounds, and it did not apply to the membership practices of labor unions. In the context of the *Steele* case, the duty of fair representation was imposed only in the negotiation of collective bargaining agreements. In addition, the doctrine bore the disadvantages inherent in judicial initiation and enforcement. Professor Sanford Jay Rosen has written:

The basic weaknesses of the judicially nurtured and enforced duty are interrelated. First, courts are essentially neutral agencies that do not customarily engage in prosecutional activities; they merely adjudicate claims that are brought before them on a case-by-case basis. Such adjudications are exceedingly time consuming, for extensive inquiry into the facts is necessary and there are endless procedural ways in which proceedings can be lengthened. Moreover, attempted suits may fail without decision on the merits, for it is within the power of unfriendly judges to impose procedural and technical impediments. Second, there is no government apparatus to prosecute fair representation claims in the courts; consequently, there is no centralized enforcement of the duty.[55]

Rosen emphasizes that where the government fails to prosecute,

the individual Negro worker and such civil rights or other organizations as are willing to support him bear the burden of initiating and prosecuting claims and stand the risk of paying for enforcement. Because these adjudications are expensive, time consuming and precarious, suit is undertaken only by the most outraged of individuals and only in critical circumstances.[56]

Later decisions extended the doctrine of fair representation beyond the prohibition of a discriminatory contract as stated in the *Steele* decision, but until 1955 all decisions interpreting the doctrine were limited to consideration of the union's duty during the collective bargaining process. Unions were required in the abstract to bargain fairly on behalf of their Negro members or nonmembers, but the duty did not extend to other forms of racial discrimination in employment.

In 1949, in *Graham* v. *Brotherhood of Locomotive Firemen and Enginemen*,[57] the Supreme Court held that the Norris-La Guardia Act* did not prevent federal courts from enjoining labor unions because of discriminatory racial practices. As in *Steele*, a railway union that excluded Negroes from membership was nevertheless the certified bargaining representative for white and Negro workers. The union had negotiated with the carrier an agreement establishing two classifications for workers: promotable and nonpromotable. Since "nonpromotable" applied exclusively to Negro employees, the eventual effect of the agreement, if implemented as intended, would have been to eliminate all blacks from employment with the railroad. The Court reaffirmed its position in *Steele* that because the union derived its authority as bargaining agent from a federal statute, and was therefore the beneficiary of a federal grant of power, it could not abuse its position by depriving Negro workers of their rights. Racial minorities subjected to discriminatory practices were allowed to sue labor unions, and the courts retained their injunctive power to protect the Negro worker.

Although the Supreme Court did not identify a specific section of the Railway Labor Act as a basis of the duty of fair representation, the implication of the *Graham* case, as with *Steele*, was that the requirement of fair representation must be operative even if a prohibition against discrimination does not expressly exist in the Act. If the requirement were not implicit, it could be inferred that Congress had given unions unlimited power—including authorization to deny equal representation to a class of employees, a power which would deny workers the right to seek legal remedies to limit the abuse of that power or to seek redress for their grievances.

---

*The Anti-Injunction Act (Norris-La Guardia Act) of 1932 limits the use of the injunction against labor organizations. Section 1 of the Act provides that "[n]o court of the United States, as herein defined, shall have jurisdiction to issue any restraining order or temporary or permanent injunction in a case involving or growing out of a labor dispute, except in strict conformity with the provisions of this Act; nor shall any such restraining order or temporary or permanent injunction be issued contrary to the public policy declared in this Act."

The Supreme Court extended the doctrine of fair representation in 1952 in *Brotherhood of Railroad Trainmen* v. *Howard.*[58] The *Steele* doctrine was interpreted to include the union's obligation to workers who were not members of the union, who did not work under the union's jurisdiction, and who were not even represented by the union in the bargaining process.

The railroad had employed white union members as trainmen and nonunion Negro workers as train porters, although each group performed virtually identical tasks. (See Chapter 13 and Volume II, Chapter 4.) After resisting the union's demands for more than twenty years, the company acquiesced to a labor agreement which eliminated the job classification of train porter and notified its Negro employees that, under its agreement with the Brotherhood of Railroad Trainmen, their services were no longer required. The white trainmen, of course, would now perform the porters' duties.

Under the doctrine as set forth in *Steele,* it would seem that a union owed a duty of fair representation only to those members and nonmembers who worked in the craft in which the union had jurisdiction. In the *Howard* case, the union argued that it owed no duty to the Negro train porters—they were not members of the union, and furthermore they belonged to a different craft, and the union was in fact accomplishing a legitimate bargaining function by expanding the employment opportunities of the white workers under its jurisdiction. Since both groups had performed the same tasks, it was evident that race was the only reason Negro train porters were excluded from the craft of trainman and so were not within the brotherhood's jurisdiction. Justice Hugo L. Black, speaking for the majority, penetrated the artificiality of the craft distinction, finding that it was an "unsound" basis on which to differentiate the case from *Steele.* Instead, he broadened the union's responsibility; "bargaining agents who enjoy the advantages of the Railway Labor Act's provision must execute their trust without lawless invasions of the rights of other workers."[59] In spite of the arguments for craft distinction presented before the Court, the majority found that considerations of race were the sole reason for the arbitrary separation of the crafts:

> [T]hese train porters are threatened with loss of their jobs because they are not white and for no other reason. The job they did hold under its old name would be abolished by the agreement; their color alone would disqualify them for the old job under its new name. The end result of these transactions is not in doubt; for precisely the same reason as in the *Steele* case "discriminations based on race alone are

obviously irrelevant and invidious. Congress plainly did not undertake to authorize the bargaining representative to make such discrim-
inations." . . . The Federal Act thus prohibits bargaining agents it
authorizes from using their position and power to destroy colored
workers' jobs in order to bestow them on white workers. And courts
can protect those threatened by such an unlawful use of power granted by a federal act.[60]

Three justices dissented from the majority's decision. Justices
Sherman Minton, Fred M. Vinson, and Stanley Reed wrote that
since the Negroes were classified as train porters, not trainmen,
they were not entitled to representation by the brotherhood; they
held that the case should have been dismissed as nonjusticiable.
These justices believed that the Court majority had invalidated the
contract not because the porters were equal to trainmen and
entitled to fair representation but because they were Negroes
discriminated against at the behest of a labor union. This minority
opinion held that private parties could discriminate on grounds of
race and that the majority's decision was consequently in error.

The *Howard* decision did not settle the matter. Despite that
ruling, lower federal courts refused to expand the fair representation doctrine as a means of protecting the interests of Negroes and
other minorities in the collective bargaining process. In *Williams* v.
Yellow Cab Company of Pittsburgh, Pa.,[61] the Court of Appeals for
the Third Circuit indicated that it did not subscribe to the
implications of Justice Black's theory in *Howard.* Negro taxi
drivers were seeking an injunction to prevent the International
Brotherhood of Teamsters from implementing a contract designed
to limit their employment to Negro residential districts in the city
of Pittsburgh and, in general, to give them undesirable assignments.
The Negro drivers were full dues-paying members of an integrated
local of the Teamsters union, and the union operated under
National Labor Relations Board certification. The third circuit
court's opinion cited the *Steele* case and acknowledged that a union
operating under a federal statute was indeed bound by the duty of
fair representation. But it held that, since the Negro cab drivers
had voluntarily joined the union, the union's authority over them
derived from voluntary membership rather than compulsion under
federal labor laws. Therefore, no federal statute was involved and
no controversy cognizable in a federal court existed. The case was
dismissed, and the Supreme Court refused to review the decision.[62]

Both a district court and the Court of Appeals for the Fifth
Circuit relied on the *Williams* decision as authority for their

decisions in *Syres* v. *Oil Workers, Local 53.*[63] In that case an all-white and an all-Negro local of the Oil Workers International Union, CIO, had agreed to "amalgamate" in order to negotiate a single labor agreement with their employer, the Gulf Oil Company. Despite limited participation by black workers, the combined bargaining committee negotiated a contract that established segregated lines of promotion, confining Negroes to the "dead-end" jobs they had traditionally held. In response to a suit brought by black workers to protest these actions, the Court of Appeals for the Fifth Circuit affirmed the district court's dismissal of the case, finding that no federal statute or constitutional provision applied to the union's actions. The courts believed that the only issue was a breach of agreement between the two segregated locals and that federal courts did not have jurisdiction to hear such a claim.

Judge Richard T. Rives, in his dissenting opinion in *Syres,* conceded that as private parties employers and unions could discriminate against Negro workers free of constitutional restraints. However, he argued, once the Federal Government is called upon to sanction their racially discriminatory practices or to assist them in their ability to so discriminate, then constitutional limitations arise; and once a labor union has sought the services and protection of the National Labor Relations Board and of national labor legislation, it becomes subject to such restrictions as the duty of fair representation in acting as a representative in the bargaining process. When a union is given exclusive collective bargaining rights by the NLRB, which has conducted an election and has certified the winning organization as exclusive agent under the National Labor Relations Act, the federal authority is directly involved. Both employer and union then engage in collective bargaining, and the NLRB is empowered to compel such bargaining. In effect, Judge Rives wrote, the government has taken part; because the government gives the majority union the right to act for all workers in the unit, it imposes on the agent the duty not to abuse its status by engaging in racial discrimination.

By 1955 it seemed well established that both the Railway Labor Act and the National Labor Relations Act contained prohibitions against certain forms of racial discrimination.[64] But because of *Williams* in the third circuit and *Syres* in the fifth circuit, the duty of fair representation did not apply to situations where Negro workers had voluntarily placed themselves under the bargaining authority of a white-controlled union that was responsible for discriminatory racial practices. This limitation was surmounted when the Supreme Court reversed *Syres* in a one-sentence, *per curiam* opinion (a decision "by the court," whose author is not identified), rendered without argument.[65] Judge Rives was at least partly vindicated and the concept that discriminatory representation by labor unions was a matter under the jurisdiction of the National Labor Relations Act as well as the Railway Labor Act was advanced.*

In 1957, two years after the *Syres* decision, the Supreme Court further expanded the concept of the union's duty of fair representation. In *Conley* v. *Gibson,*[66] another railroad case, the union had failed to process the grievance filed by Negro workers discharged and replaced by whites. The Supreme Court held that the union's failure to process grievances was a proper cause for litigation under the duty of fair representation, thus extending the doctrine beyond the bargaining process.

However, the Court continued to refuse to apply the doctrine of fair representation to require unions to admit Negroes into equal membership with whites. In *Oliphant* v. *Brotherhood of Locomotive Firemen and Enginemen* (1958),[67] several Negro firemen employed by southern railroads brought suit to compel the brotherhood to admit them to membership. The union was their exclusive bargaining agent under the Railway Labor Act, but they alleged that lack of membership denied them participation in collective bargaining negotiations which resulted in a contract that caused them loss of income. The district court did in fact find discrimination both in the union's representation of the Negro workers and in the conditions of employment at the railroad; but it dismissed the case, holding that certification as exclusive bargaining agent by the National Labor Relations Board did not make the union an agent of the government and therefore no governmental action was involved. Sustaining the district court, the court of appeals stated that "the Brotherhood is a private association, whose membership policies are its own affair, and this is not an appropriate case for interposition of judicial control."[68] Certiorari was denied by the Supreme Court, which noted the "abstract

---

*The judicial interpretation of the duty of fair representation under the Railway Labor Act and the National Labor Relations Act occurred in a progression of cases, some of which did not involve racial issues. Among these are *Ford Motor Co.* v. *Huffman,* 345 U.S. 330, 31 LRRM 2548 (1953); *Humphrey* v. *Moore,* 375 U.S. 335, 55 LRRM 2031 (1963); *NLRB* v. *Miranda Fuel Co., Inc.,* 326 F.2d 172, 54 LRRM 2715 (2nd Cir. 1963); *Vaca* v. *Sipes,* 386 U.S. 171, 64 LRRM 2369 (1967).

context in which the questions sought to be raised are presented by this record."[69] *Oliphant* was the first case that directly presented the question of discriminatory denial of union membership to the Supreme Court.

Despite certain setbacks, it is significant in considering the slow evolution of legal doctrine on employment discrimination to note that, although Congress did not specifically provide an administrative remedy for the protection of minorities against discrimination by labor unions or employers until the Civil Rights Act of 1964, the courts in the interim interpreted the duty of fair representation so as to grant minorities a measure of judicial protection. A labor union cannot expect to gain the status of exclusive bargaining agent granted by the authority of federal law and then engage in a racially discriminatory pattern of conduct.

The social consequences of labor union actions, through the collective bargaining process, are such that unions have become, in effect, public bodies, that is, extensions of governmental power, and thus they are not private "voluntary associations," free to segregate and discriminate at will. It should follow, therefore, that black workers or members of other minority groups can resort to the federal courts for relief under existing national labor legislation.

Throughout the period when the concept of the duty of fair representation was evolving in the federal courts, there was a concurrent abdication by the National Labor Relations Board of its obligation to assist workers subjected to racial abuses. The board early adopted a neutral position when presented with issues of discriminatory racial employment practices, and it remained closed for many years as a forum for the redress of grievances based upon race. The Court has implied the possibility of a violation of the "due process" protection of the Fifth Amendment on the basis that the NLRB is an instrument which provides significant governmental involvement in the discriminatory racial practices of labor unions, and it may be that the application of the Fifth Amendment to this issue will be tested in future NLRB litigation.

Empowered under the National Labor Relations Act to certify unions as exclusive collective bargaining agents,[70] the NLRB is equally empowered to enforce[71] the unfair labor practice sections of the Act.[72] The board conducts investigations and holds elections, at government expense, to determine collective bargaining agents. It then certifies the union elected by the majority of employees as the exclusive representative for all workers in the bargaining unit. Upon certification, the board protects the newly elected union from "raids" or appeals to workers by competing unions. When a certified union enters into an agreement with an employer, the contract must contain a specified period of duration.* The "contract-bar" rule protects the certified union from rival unions for the term of the contract, up to three years.[73] Once a union has been certified, this contract-bar rule insures that a union remains the exclusive bargaining agent for the specified period. Indeed, the law has been interpreted as forbidding any negotiations between the employer and individual employees or groups of employees that may have the effect of circumventing a collective bargaining agreement.† The certified union is also in a position to compel an unwilling employer to bargain collectively in good faith, and it may ask the NLRB to issue an unfair labor practice charge against a noncomplying employer.[74]

Thus in a very real sense the board is the instrument that sanctions and regulates virtually all important labor-management relations. When a union seeks certification from the board or files an unfair labor practice complaint with it against another party, the board provides a variety of services as well as legal protection to enable the union to retain its status as a certified collective bargaining representative. But for years the board refused to use the panoply of remedies at its disposal when Negro workers asked for assistance. Even after it had become quite clear as a result of court decisions that the board had not only the power and authority but, indeed, the obligation to impose sanctions against labor unions found guilty of racial discrimination, the board refused to do so.

In its earliest decisions in cases involving racial discrimination, the board acknowledged the judicial interpretation of the doctrine of fair representation but failed to implement it. In 1945 in *Larus & Brother Co.*[75] the board cited previous cases and stated that "these holdings give support to many decisions in which we have said that there is a duty on the statutory bargaining agent to represent all members of the unit equally and without discrimination on the basis of race, color, or creed."[76] But in *Larus* it also held that neither the segregation of Negro workers nor their exclusion from

---

*This was administratively established in *Pacific Coast Assn. of Pulp and Paper Mfrs.*, 121 NLRB 990, 42 LRRM 1477 (1958); and *Kroger Co.*, 173 NLRB 397, 69 LRRM 1333 (1968).

†The Supreme Court has held that employer negotiations with individual employees are "subversive of the mode of collective bargaining which the statute has ordained."—*Medo Photo Supply Corp. v. NLRB*, 321 U.S. 678, 684, 14 LRRM 581, 584 (1944). See also *J. I. Case Co. v. NLRB*, 321 U.S. 332, 14 LRRM 501 (1944).

union membership constituted a violation of the duty of fair representation.[77] The board continued to certify as exclusive collective bargaining agents unions with segregated locals and unions that excluded Negroes from membership. It consistently held that "neither exclusion from membership nor segregated membership *per se* represents evasion on the part of a labor organization of its statutory duty to afford 'equal representation.' "[78] Rather, "in each case where the issue [of discrimination] is presented the Board will scrutinize the contract and the conduct of a representative organization and withhold or withdraw its certification if it finds that the organization has discriminated against employees in the bargaining units through its membership requirements or otherwise."[79] The board did not even threaten to decertify a union because of racial practices until 1962.

With the Supreme Court's important 1948 decision in *Shelley* v. *Kraemer*,[80] the board's policy on racial discrimination became even less defensible. In *Shelley*, an effort was made to uphold a state court's enforcement of a racial covenant in a deed of real property. It was argued that the discriminatory practice originated with private parties who were constitutionally free to discriminate and that no state action was involved. State court enforcement of the restriction did not create unlawful discrimination but merely enforced an agreement in which the parties had lawfully entered. The Supreme Court disagreed with this reasoning and ruled that the act of a court was as much state action as the act of a legislature. The judicial branch was not permitted to impose a racially discriminatory system upon real property, even when it took the form of enforcing contracts between private parties. The Court held that court enforcement of restrictions based on race was a violation of the equal protection clause of the Fourteenth Amendment. The covenant itself was not invalid; rather, enforcement of the covenant by the state through the courts was declared to be unconstitutional.

In a companion case, *Hurd* v. *Hodge*,[81] the Supreme Court made a similar finding based on facts comparable to those in *Shelley* and decided that federal courts could not, under the Fifth Amendment, be used to enforce discriminatory racial covenants in the District of Columbia.

The implications of *Shelley* and *Hurd* for the NLRB were self-evident. Although government agencies themselves did not originate discriminatory practices, they were prohibited by the Fifth Amendment from giving powers derived from governmental authority to private parties who practiced racial discrimination. Through the National Labor Relations Act, Congress has given the established union great powers over the welfare of large groups of workers. By its decisions in *Steele, Howard,* and *Syres* the Supreme Court indicated that unions may not accept the preferred status of exclusive bargaining agents and exercise direct authority over employees without accepting the concurrent obligation to carry out their duty of fair representation without discrimination on the basis of race. However, when the NLRB issues a certification establishing exclusive status for unions that engage in racially discriminatory practices, the board functions as an instrument of government to assist unions in violating their duty of fair representation. If a legal collective bargaining agreement exists, the board effectively protects the union against defections by dissatisfied Negro workers, and the union may call upon the NLRB to sustain its power. The state through the NLRB and other government agencies participates in several decisive ways in the enforcement of discriminatory schemes. The implications of *Shelley* and *Hurd* were that the board could no longer render assistance to "private parties" such as labor unions and thereby place them in a position of power that they could abuse to the detriment of Negro workers and members of other minority groups. Thus the board's policy of routinely providing services to unions engaged in discriminatory practices should have been held to violate the Fifth Amendment.

This interpretation of NLRB policies in relation to questions of racial discrimination is given credence by a 1955 decision of the Court of Appeals for the Ninth Circuit in *NLRB* v. *Pacific American Shipowners Association.*[82] An independent Negro union of cooks and stewards challenged the NLRB's certification of the Seafarers' International Union, AFL-CIO, as the exclusive bargaining representative for all workers aboard ship, which included the Negro stewards. On the basis of past experience, the black workers feared that they would suffer from the discriminatory practices of the Seafarers' union if they were placed under its jurisdiction. The Negro plaintiffs' motion for a show cause order was denied by the court, however, and Judge Walter L. Pope, in a concurring opinion, wrote that the NLRB had exclusive jurisdiction to determine such questions. Referring to the board's duty when faced with questions involving racial discrimination, Judge Pope stated:

> I think the last chapter on this question has not been written. When *Shelley* v. *Kraemer* . . . held that the Fourteenth Amendment pro-

hibited state courts from enforcing restrictive covenants based on race or color, the Court in *Hurd* v. *Hodge* . . . declared such covenants equally unenforceable in the federal courts. . . . A union which practices racial discrimination as a practical matter carries its policy into its collective bargaining agreements. It is a nice question whether the Labor Board may recognize or enforce such an agreement any more than a federal court may lend its aid to a racial restrictive covenant.[83]

By deferring the decision to the NLRB in this case, the court clearly placed on it the responsibility for resolving the racial dispute. In view of the Seafarers' International Union's assurances to the board that it would not discriminate,[84] the court was satisfied that the board had at least considered its constitutional duty when faced with the question of participation in discriminatory actions.[85]

In the late 1950s the NLRB attempted to institute a practice which would have benefited many thousands of black workers who were denied equal employment rights because they were discriminatorily denied union membership. As demonstrated by the extensive hearings of the Fair Employment Practice Committee during World War II (see Part 2), closed-shop agreements were effectively used in many instances to prevent Negro workers from obtaining employment. Under the closed-shop arrangement, the employer agreed not to hire anyone who was not a member of the union. Therefore, through exclusionary membership policies, many labor unions prevented the employment of Negro workers.

Although the closed shop was prohibited by the Taft-Hartley Act in 1947,[86] the practice continued and violations of the law were frequent. The Act's application to racial questions was considered by Congress before it was passed. Senator Robert A. Taft, the bill's coauthor, stated before its passage:

Let us take the case of unions which prohibit the admission of Negroes to membership. If they prohibit the admission of Negroes to membership, they may continue to do so; but representatives of the union cannot go to the employer and say "You have got to fire this man because he is not a member of our union."[87]

The Taft-Hartley Act made the operation of closed-shop agreements that excluded nonunion members from employment an unfair labor practice to be eliminated by the board. One of the features of the closed shop which continued was the exclusive hiring-hall arrangement, in which employers agreed to hire workers exclusively through the union's referral facilities. It is illegal under the Act for a union to give preference to its members in job referral and to refuse to refer nonmembers.[88] In practice, however, black workers, long barred from membership in the construction unions, for instance, where hiring halls predominate, are frequently denied referral for employment.*

---

*For data on the racial practices of referral unions in the building trades, see *Local Union Equal Opportunity Report,* EEO-3 (1968), EEO-3 (1969), EEO-3 (1970), EEO-3 (1971), EEO-3 (1972) (Washington, D.C.: Equal Employment Opportunity Commission); *Minorities and Women in Referral Units in Building Trade Unions 1972,* Research Report No. 44 (Washington, D.C.: Equal Employment Opportunity Commission, 1974); Massachusetts State Advisory Committee to the U.S. Commission on Civil Rights, *Hearings,* Boston, June 25–26, 1969; Herbert Hill, "Labor Union Control of Job Training: A Critical Analysis of Apprenticeship Outreach Programs and the Hometown Plans," Occasional Paper, Vol. 2, No. 1 (Washington, D.C.: Howard University, Institute for Urban Affairs and Research, 1974); New York City Commission on Human Rights, *Bias in the Building Trade— An Updated Report,* 1963–1967 (1967); U.S. Commission on Civil Rights, *Hearings,* San Francisco, May 1–3, 1967, pp. 286–371; U.S. Commission on Civil Rights, *Hearings,* Cleveland, April 1–7, 1966, pp. 443–491. See also the following cases: *Lefkowitz, etc. v. Farrell, et al.* (New York State Commission for Human Rights, Case No. C 9287–63), *affirmed sub nom. New York State Commission for Human Rights v. Farrell,* 43 Misc.2d 958, 252 N.Y.S.2d 649, 1 FEP Cases 100, 59 LRRM 3050 (N.Y. Sup. Ct. 1964), *affirmed,* 24 A.D.2d 128, 264 N.Y.S.2d 489, 1 FEP Cases 112, 60 LRRM 2509 (N.Y. App. Div. First Dept. 1965) (*Farrell* was brought against Sheet Metal Workers, Local 28, a defendant in the original actions brought in the *Local 638* cases *infra*); *U.S. v. Building & Construction Trades Council of St. Louis,* 271 F. Supp. 454, 1 FEP Cases 902, 71 LRRM 3168 (E.D. Mo. 1966); *Ethridge v. Rhodes,* 268 F. Supp. 83, 1 FEP Cases 185, 65 LRRM 2331 (S.D. Ohio 1967); *Dobbins v. Electrical Workers (IBEW), Local 212,* 292 F. Supp. 413, 1 FEP Cases 387, 69 LRRM 2313 (S.D. Ohio 1968); *Asbestos Workers, Local 53 v. Vogler,* 407 F.2d 1047, 1 FEP Cases 577, 70 LRRM 2257 (5th Cir. 1969), *affirming* 294 F. Supp. 368, 1 FEP Cases 197, 65 LRRM 2554 (E.D. La. 1967); *U.S. v. Plumbers (PPF), Local 73,* 314 F. Supp. 160, 2 FEP Cases 81 (S.D. Ind. 1969); *Central Contractors Assn., et al. v. Local 46, Electrical Workers (IBEW),* 312 F. Supp. 1388, 2 FEP Cases 189 (W.D. Wash. 1969); *U.S. v. Sheet Metal Workers Int'l Assn. (SMW), Local 36,* 416 F.2d 123, 2 FEP Cases 127 (8th Cir. 1969); *U.S. v. Ironworkers (BSOIW), Local 392,* 3 EPD para. 8063 (E.D. Ill. 1970) (Consent Decree); *Ironworkers, Local 67 v. Hart and Iowa Civil Rights Commission,* 3 FEP Cases 204, 3 EPD para. 8148 (Iowa Dist. Ct., Polk County 1970); *EEOC v. Plumbers, Local 189, et al.* (*Locke* case), 438 F.2d 408, 3 FEP Cases 193 (6th Cir. 1971), *cert. denied,* 404 U.S. 832, 3 FEP Cases 1030 (1971); *U.S. v. Ironworkers (BSOIW), Local 86,* 443 F.2d 544, 3 FEP Cases 496 (9th Cir. 1971), *affirming* 315 F. Supp. 1202, 2 FEP Cases 741 (W.D. Wash. 1970); *Southern Illinois Builders Assn. v. Ogilvie,* 471 F.2d 680, 5 FEP Cases 229 (7th Cir. 1972), *affirming* 327 F. Supp. 1154, 3 FEP Cases 571 (S.D. Ill. 1971); *U.S. v. Lathers (WWML), Local 46,* 471 F.2d 408, 5 FEP Cases 318 (2nd Cir. 1973); *U.S. v. Sheet Metal Workers, Local 10,* 6 FEP Cases 1037, 1043, 6 EPD para. 8715, 8718 (D. N.J. 1973); *Byrd v. Local 24, Electrical Workers (IBEW),* 375 F. Supp. 545, 8 FEP Cases 399 (D. Md. 1974); *Rios, et al. v. Enterprise Assn. Steamfitters, Local 638,* 326 F. Supp. 198, 3 FEP Cases 349 (S.D. N.Y. 1971); *U.S. v. Local 638, Plumbers, et al.,* 337 F. Supp. 217, 4 FEP Cases 213 (S.D. N.Y. 1972), 347 F. Supp. 164, 4 FEP Cases 1025 (S.D. N.Y. 1972) (permission granted to New York City Human Rights Commission to intervene), 347 F. Supp. 169, 4 FEP Cases 1009 (S.D. N.Y. 1972), 360 F. Supp. 979, 6 FEP Cases 319 (S.D. N.Y. 1973) (*U.S.* and *Rios* cases consolidated prior to this trial), *remanded for mod. and affirmed sub nom., Rios v. Enterprise Assn. Steamfitters, Local 638, et al.,* 501 F.2d 622, 8 FEP Cases 293 (2nd Cir. 1974), *on remand,* 400 F. Supp. 983, 10 FEP Cases 796 (S.D. N.Y. 1975), *affirmed,* 520 F.2d 352, 10 FEP Cases 1223 (2nd Cir. 1975), 400 F. Supp. 988, 10 FEP Cases 1278 (S.D.

In 1957 in *Mountain Pacific*,[89] the board decided that an agreement requiring an employer to hire only through a union hiring hall constituted an unfair labor practice unless the agreement specifically provided that selection of applicants for referral would not favor union members and that a notice to that effect would be prominently posted. The Supreme Court soon rejected this approach,[90] holding that the board could strike down a hiring-hall arrangement only after specific evidence of preferential referral of union members had been presented. Had the NLRB's interpretation in *Mountain Pacific* been allowed to stand, it would not have insured equality for Negroes at union hiring halls, but it would, as Professor Michael I. Sovern noted, have provided some benefit:

> At the very least, the requirement that "the parties to the agreement post . . . all provisions relating to the functioning of the hiring agreement" would have made it easier for Negroes to detect refusals to refer because of their race, which would in turn have facilitated remedial action by other agencies. Moreover, by diminishing the chances of discrimination against nonunion workers, the *Mountain Pacific* safeguards would have increased the chances that Negroes excluded from union membership would nevertheless have been referred to jobs.[91]

Although the board failed in its attempt to open up exclusive hiring halls to nonunion workers—which in the construction trades especially meant a large percentage of blacks—*Mountain Pacific* and some later decisions indicated that it was at least considering its constitutional duty when dealing with unions that maintained discriminatory practices. In the *Pioneer Bus Company* case,[92] the NLRB ruled that if a labor union's contract with a company sanctions discrimination, another union is free at any time to seek the right to represent the company's workers. The Pioneer Bus Company of Houston had a two-unit bargaining relationship with racially segregated locals of an independent union. The company bargained separately with each local and made separate contracts providing for segregated promotion and seniority lines for white and Negro employees. The Transport Workers Union, AFL-CIO,

---

N.Y. 1975) (award of back pay), 400 F. Supp. 993, 10 FEP Cases 1282 (S.D. N.Y. 1975) (award of attorneys' fees), 401 F. Supp. 467, 12 FEP Cases 712 (S.D. N.Y. 1975) (trial for Sheet Metal Workers, Local 28, previously severed from *Local 638* cases), *affirmed as modified*, 532 F.2d 821, 12 FEP Cases 755 (2nd Cir. 1976).

filed a complaint before the board, seeking to withdraw the protection of the contract-bar rule from the independent union and to allow the TWU to hold an election in competition with the segregated locals.

The board agreed with the argument that it could no longer permit the contract-bar rule to protect discriminatory practices from challenge:

> Consistent with clear court decisions in other contexts which condemn governmental sanctioning of racially separate groupings as inherently discriminatory, the Board will not permit its contract-bar rules to be utilized to shield contracts such as those here involved from the challenge of otherwise appropriate election petitions. We therefore hold that, where the bargaining representative of employees in an appropriate unit executes separate contracts, or even a single contract, discriminating between Negro and white employees on racial lines, the Board will not deem such contracts as a bar to an election.[93]

The board also noted that execution of contracts of this nature was in "patent derogation of the certification"[94] given unions as exclusive agents, and decertification was threatened. The board apparently believed, however, that the impending election was a sufficient remedy in this case.[95] Its reference to "clear court decisions" was to the developing *Shelley* doctrine. Presumably the implication of the reference was a realization by the board that protecting the legitimacy of a discriminatory union through application of the contract-bar rule would constitute "state action" to enable unions to deprive Negro workers of their equal employment rights. Under the doctrine of *Shelley*, the board, as an agency of the state, could not render vital assistance to unions practicing racial discrimination. Still, the compulsion of the doctrine did not apply to the union itself but only to the actions of the board that conferred the power of the state upon the union, thus making it possible for the union to discriminate.

After it has certified a union, the National Labor Relations Board has at its disposal various remedies for correcting racial abuses. It can rescind the union's certification as exclusive collective bargaining agent, as was threatened in *Pioneer Bus,* and/or it can refuse to render valuable services such as applying the contract-bar rule, accepting unfair labor practice complaints, and providing assistance to enforce union security agreements.

Alternately, and more effectively, the board can interpret the racially discriminatory actions of labor unions as unfair labor practices and can issue complaints, hold administrative hearings, issue cease-and-desist orders, and seek injunctions in courts of appeals to enforce its orders. Finally, it has the power to disestablish a labor union, that is, to divest the union of its status as a labor organization and to order the employer to sever all relations with it.*

The first type of remedy, withholding services and protections, would allow the board to maintain its position of neutrality while fulfilling minimum compliance with its constitutional obligations under the Fifth Amendment. The second method, a more punitive one, would require the board to define a union's violation of the duty of fair representation as an unfair labor practice under Section 8 of the NLRA.† Barbara A. Morris, former associate general counsel of the NAACP, points out, however, that to make this latter method useful, the board would have to improve its administrative practices. As it is, "any effective remedy is obviated by the length of time it takes the Board to act."[96]

Until 1962 none of these remedies had been directly applied by the board in cases involving racial discrimination. In one case, *Pioneer Bus,* the contract-bar rule had been lifted and decertification threatened, but the method of allowing victims of racial discrimination to present unfair labor practice charges to the board—and of acting on such charges by full prosecution of the defendants—had never been tried. Although minority groups did

---

*Although the board has disestablished unions that failed to represent their members fairly because of participation in union affairs by company representatives, it has never suggested that it might disestablish a union that failed to represent a racial minority fairly. Decertification may make the union vulnerable to challenge in a representation election, but disestablishment is a much more severe form of relief than decertification. Because the right of a union which represents a majority of the employees to be the exclusive representative is based entirely on the provisions of the National Labor Relations Act—see *Arkansas Oak Flooring* v. *UMW,* 351 U.S. 62, 37 LRRM 2828 (1956)—and enforced by actions of the NLRB, it appears that the principle laid down in *Shelley* v. *Kraemer,* 344 U.S. 1 (1948), requires disestablishment of the bargaining representative which fails to represent fairly rather than the ambiguous remedy of decertification. For a detailed analysis, see James E. Jones, Jr., "Disestablishment of Labor Unions for Engaging in Racial Discrimination—A New Use for an Old Remedy," *Wisconsin Law Review,* 1972, pp. 351–381.

†See Section 8(d) and Section 9(a) of the National Labor Relations Act. See also *Arkansas Oak Flooring* v. *United Mine Workers,* 351 U.S. 62, 37 LRRM 2828 (1956); *NLRB* v. *Miranda Fuel Co.,* 366 U.S. 763, 48 LRRM 2277 (1961); *Independent Metal Workers Union, Locals 1 and 2 (Hughes Tool),* 147 NLRB 1573, 56 LRRM 1289; and *Vaca* v. *Sipes,* 386 U.S. 171, 64 LRRM 2369 (1967). For comments, see Benjamin Aaron, "The Union's Duty of Fair Representation Under the Labor Relations Act," *Journal of Air Law & Commerce,* Vol. 34 (1968), p. 167; Benjamin Aaron, "Some Aspects of the Union's Duty of Fair Representation," *Ohio State Law Journal,* Vol. 22 (1961), p. 39; and Archibald Cox, "The Duty of Fair Representation," *Villanova Law Review,* Vol. 2 (1957), p. 151.

have a route available for obtaining relief from the discriminatory practices of unions and employers, it was very costly and time-consuming, and the results were unpredictable. They could sue directly in the federal courts, basing their cause of action on the duty of fair representation. The board had many times acknowledged the right of Negroes and other minorities to present it with complaints of discrimination, but it had remained virtually closed to charges based upon the duty of fair representation.

In 1962, however, the NLRB defined violation of the duty of fair representation as an unfair labor practice. In *Miranda Fuel Company*[97]—a nonracial case involving an internal dispute between a white worker and a union—the board interpreted the duty of fair representation as being implicit in the unfair labor practice sections of the National Labor Relations Act. Following the principle laid down by the Supreme Court in *Steele* v. *Louisville & Nashville R.R. Co.*, the board held that Section 9(a) of the National Labor Relations Act, which grants unions the right to be exclusive bargaining representatives, creates the concomitant duty to represent all employees fairly. In essence, that duty, as defined in *Miranda Fuel Co.*, is to *not* make invidious and irrelevant distinctions among employees concerning their interests, which the union, by asserting its status as exclusive representative, has undertaken to protect. When the union fails to protect those interests on impermissible grounds it violates the law; and by authorizing, encouraging, or conspiring in the action, the employer shares the liability. Further, it was held in *Miranda Fuel Co.* that by subjecting the employer to economic pressure to discriminate against employees, the union engages in an illegal act, and that the employer by acquiescing is also guilty of committing an unfair labor practice.

Unfortunately, the Court of Appeals for the Second Circuit, in an evenly divided court, failed to uphold the specific ruling in *Miranda Fuel Co.* However, the language of the decision and the division of the vote reduce the significance of the circuit court's ruling. The additional fact that only the Supreme Court can issue a rule of law which is binding on the board encouraged the board to continue to apply the *Miranda Fuel Co.* principle to other cases; and it appears, the second circuit's decision notwithstanding, that the board has for the most part retained the legal definition of the duty of fair representation established in *Miranda Fuel Co.**

*For additional information on *Miranda Fuel Co.*, see Michael I. Sovern, "Race Discrimination and the National Labor Relations Act: The Brave New World of Miranda," in

Nevertheless, when the board was later presented with a case involving a question of a violation of the duty of fair representation as an unfair labor practice in a racial context, it avoided consideration of the basic issue. At the Atlantic Steel Company, in Atlanta, Georgia, black workers, who were members of the United Steelworkers of America, were confined to all-black labor classifications, with limited opportunities for promotion and with no provisions for transfer into the higher paying, all-white seniority lines. In 1962 the union and the company signed a new labor agreement that provided for transfers out of the all-Negro line but required those who transferred to forfeit their accrued seniority. This elimination of the valuable seniority of black workers (many of them older men with long years of employment), and their consequent lower initial pay in the former all-white line, effectively dissuaded them from transferring out of the laborers' department. Thirteen Negro employees of the company filed unfair labor practice charges with the board, claiming that the union had breached its duty of fair representation.[98] Seeking the unprecedented remedy of union decertification for discriminatory racial practices, they alleged that by negotiating the 1962 agreement the union had not bargained fairly on their behalf; that since the union had violated its duty, it had committed an unfair labor practice and the board, under the compulsion of the Fifth Amendment, could no longer continue certification of the union as exclusive bargaining agent.

Narrowly interpreting relevant sections of the National Labor Relations Act, the NLRB's regional director in Atlanta refused to issue complaints against the union. The complainants had alleged that the discrimination practiced against them was continuing in nature, as indeed it was, but the board official dismissed their charge on the ground that the complaints had not been filed within the statutory period. He also expressed the opinion that the union had eliminated some of the manifest discriminatory features of its promotion system. A subsequent NLRB press release quoted the official as saying:

> Aside from the fact that the negotiation of such an agreement might well subject the union to a charge of unfair representation of the white employees, it is not the function of the Board to sit in judgment

Sixteenth Annual New York University Conference on Labor, 1963, pp. 10–13. For the contrary view, see Note, "Administrative Enforcement of the Right to Fair Representation: The *Miranda* Case," *University of Pennsylvania Law Review,* March 1964, p. 711.

over the substantive terms of a collective agreement, absent evidence that such agreement is either discriminatory on its face or in its practical application.[99]

Here, sharply presented with the question of whether a union's racially discriminatory practices violated the union's duty of fair representation and constituted an unfair labor practice, the board resorted to a procedural technicality to avoid deciding the issue.

The NLRB finally dealt with the basic problem in a racial context on July 1, 1964, in the *Hughes Tool Company* case.[100] The Hughes Tool Company of Houston, Texas, a manufacturer of drilling equipment, had since 1928 segregated and racially classified all jobs in its plant. Negroes filled only the lowest paying jobs; they were barred from all other positions. In 1941 the company's two original labor unions, the Employees Welfare Organization and the Hughes Tool Colored Club, had been disestablished by the NLRB on the grounds that they were company-dominated. Locals 1 and 2 of the Independent Metal Workers Union were organized in their places. From their inception until after the issuance of a complaint, membership in Local 1 was open only to white employees and Local 2 was exclusively for black workers.

Both locals of the Independent Metal Workers Union had been repeatedly certified as exclusive bargaining agents by the NLRB. In 1961 the board once again certified the segregated locals. In the course of negotiations with the company, black employees sought to have Local 1 initiate steps to eliminate the discriminatory racial pattern in the plant, but Local 1 took the position that it was too late in the bargaining process to raise the issue with the company. The all-white local signed a labor agreement with the company restricting Negro employees to the lowest five labor grades, whereas opportunities for promotion for whites extended through Labor Grade 12. Local 2, the all-Negro local, had customarily been a joint party and signatory of all previous agreements with the company; now it refused to sign the new agreement on the ground that it perpetuated racial discrimination.

In addition, Local 1 and the company negotiated a separate agreement providing for apprenticeship training, but the agreement did not call for signature by Local 2. The effect of this agreement was to provide a training program for white apprentices only.

In 1962 the company posted a notice inviting bids for six apprenticeship vacancies. Ivory Davis, a Negro employee who had worked for the company since 1942 and who was treasurer of Local 2, filed an application for the training program. He met all the qualifications stated in the notice except that the job fell within the category reserved exclusively for white employees by the contract with Local 1. The company-issued list of employees who had applied did not include Davis's name. The grievance committee of Local 2 discussed the matter with the company, which took the position that the apprenticeship program was covered by its contract with Local 1 and not by any contract with Local 2. Davis took appropriate procedural steps to have his grievance processed by Local 1, but it refused to consider his complaint. Local 2 subsequently filed unfair labor practice charges with the NLRB, basing its complaint on the refusal of Local 1 to process the grievances of the members of Local 2. Local 2 also filed a motion to rescind both unions' certification, alleging that the practices of Local 1 in discriminating against Negroes and the existence of the segregated locals rendered the certification invalid.

As was required at this stage in the development of labor law, the question of the NLRB's duty to take affirmative action on complaints of Negro workers charging racial discrimination was sharply presented. The complainants were calling for both types of redress—rescinding the union's certification and issuing cease-and-desist orders—available under the NLRA; more significantly, they were asking the board, not the federal courts, to order the relief. Furthermore, the plaintiffs were seeking a definition of the violation of a union's duty of fair representation as an unfair labor practice under Section 8 of the National Labor Relations Act; and they were requesting decertification as the remedy under Section 9. The NAACP, representing the complainants in the *Hughes Tool* case, argued that in a practical sense the duty of fair representation was of no avail in securing redress for black workers unless the discriminatory membership practices of labor unions were included. Robert L. Carter, general counsel of the NAACP, stated:

> Racial exclusion is both the symptom and the cause of unfair treatment of Negro workers. On the one hand, it is racial discrimination which leads to the establishment of racial criteria for full membership. On the other hand, the fact that Negroes have no role in the formulation of bargaining policies in an all-white union leads to discrimination in the contract and in its administration.[101]

The NLRB's trial examiner accepted the argument of the complainants that the existence of segregated locals violated the duty of fair representation and therefore constituted an unfair labor practice. In his report to the board recommending decertification of the segregated locals he wrote:

> Such "separate but equal" treatment resulted in this case in Negroes being precluded from eligibility for the higher paid jobs and even training as apprentices. Similar results of "separate but equal" locals were condemned by the courts in *Betts* v. *Easley.* . . . Assuming *arguendo* that the doctrine of "separate but equal" retains any vitality in this area, the record here shows that separateness was accompanied by inequality. In any event, the same logic which led to the overruling of [the doctrine in education cases]—namely that "separate but equal" in the area of race relations is self-contradictory and that separateness of itself both connotes and creates inequality—leads here to the conclusion that racial discrimination in membership in itself creates an inequality inconsistent with the bargaining agent's duty of fair representation.[102]

The American Civil Liberties Union, entering the case as *amicus curiae,* supported the NAACP's arguments that racial discrimination by labor unions should constitute an unfair labor practice under the National Labor Relations Act and should precipitate the application of the routine remedies for unfair labor practices, including decertification. The ACLU's brief to the board stressed throughout that the NLRB was under constitutional compulsion to so decide the case:

> Under the principles enunciated by recent Supreme Court decisions the National Labor Relations Board itself violates the Fifth Amendment if it certifies or continues in effect a certification of a union which refuses to admit Negroes to full membership in the union or practices racial discrimination in its collective bargaining, unless the Board also issues an order enforceable in the courts which requires the union as a condition of continuing as the certified representative to admit Negroes to full membership and to cease discriminating in its representation of the Negro employees within the unit.[103]

Arguing that the board could no longer follow the practice of deferring to the courts for enforcement of the duty of fair representation, the ACLU placed the responsibility squarely on the board:

> To meet its constitutional obligations, the Board cannot place such power as a certification affords in the hands of a union without policing the union to prevent racial discrimination. Leaving the policing to the courts is an obvious evasion of constitutional responsibility. The "time-consuming expensive litigation" involved in resorting to

the courts is not any remedy to the "low income worker" who is usually the victim of racial discrimination by unions against employees they are bound by law to represent.[104]

Further arguing that the lack of precedent in this case was solely the fault of the NLRB, the ACLU contended that "[t]he failure of this issue to have been presented to the Board at an earlier date is due to the fact that prior to 1947, unions were not subject to the unfair labor practice sections of the statute and since 1947, the General Counsel never saw fit to issue a complaint charging a union with failure to represent fairly."[105] The ACLU also argued that the board's responsibility for enforcing the judicially developed racial prohibitions of the NLRA was much broader than the facts presented in this particular case, and that in many cases decertification as a method for remedying unfair labor practices based on racial discrimination was not a wholly satisfactory remedy. The board had at its disposal a variety of remedies which it had not hesitated to employ in unfair labor practice cases not involving racial discrimination. The ACLU argued that the board's entire arsenal of weapons should be used in racial cases as well:

> While we are in full accord that no union which denies Negroes membership or discriminates against them should serve as a collective bargaining agent, in many instances orders requiring unions as a condition of bargaining to admit Negroes and to cease discriminating, and orders requiring unions to give back pay to workers suffering job discrimination, may be much more effective remedies.[106]

In the *Hughes Tool* decision, which represented a major turning point in the board's evolution toward an affirmative policy in protecting the rights of black workers, the NLRB held that the refusal of a union to process a worker's grievance because of race was an unfair labor practice subject to established legal remedy. The board affirmed the trial examiner's findings "that the certification should be rescinded because [the segregated locals] discriminated on the basis of race in determining eligibility for full and equal membership, and segregated their members on the basis of race."[107] Not only did the board overrule its earlier decisions condoning the segregation of Negro workers,[108] but, significantly, a majority of the board went beyond the *Pioneer Bus* doctrine to invoke *Shelley* v. *Kraemer* and other cases having constitutional implications:

> Specifically, we hold that the Board cannot validly render aid under Section 9 of the Act to a labor organization which discriminates

racially when acting as a statutory bargaining representative. Cf. *Shelley* v. *Kraemer,* 334 U.S. 1; *Hurd* v. *Hodge,* 334 U.S. 24; *Bolling* v. *Sharpe,* 347 U.S. 497 . . . .

We hold too, in agreement with the Trial Examiner, that the certification should be rescinded because . . . [the segregated locals] discriminated on the basis of race in determining eligibility for full and equal membership, and segregated their members on the basis of race. In the light of the Supreme Court decisions cited herein and others to which the Board adverted in *Pioneer Bus,* we hereby expressly overrule such cases as *Atlanta Oak Flooring Company,* 62 NLRB 973, 16 LRRM 235; *Larus & Brother Co.,* 62 NLRB 1075, 16 LRRM 242; and other cases epitomized by the language of the Board's Tenth Annual Report . . . insofar as such cases hold that unions which exclude employees from membership on racial grounds, or which classify or segregate members on racial grounds, may obtain or retain certified status under the Act.[109]

The National Labor Relations Board thus reversed a long-standing policy. For the first time in its history it ruled that discrimination by labor unions is an unfair labor practice; that racial discrimination by a union in membership practices—such as exclusion or segregation of Negroes—is a violation of the duty of fair representation under Section 9(a) of the NLRA. A new principle in administrative labor law was established.

Perhaps the NLRB's original perseverance in aiding unions which practiced racial discrimination resulted from the Supreme Court's initial reluctance to interfere with union membership policies. And possibly the board's change in policy with respect to the rights of black workers was at least in part a response to social forces, such as the civil rights protest movement of the early 1960s and the virtual certainty of some form of congressional legislation dealing with discrimination in employment. Wellington, discussing the evolution of the doctrine of the duty of fair representation, comments:

One wonders why the Board took twenty years, the time between *Steele* and *Hughes Tool,* to reach this conclusion. It was not for lack of professional urging. During the years many disinterested commentators had argued the position to the Board. The unhappy fact is that the National Labor Relations Board failed during those twenty years to perform its task properly, to display the courage required of it, to provide leadership in the fight against discrimination; and leadership, nothing less, was what was required. Indeed, it was not until the civil rights movement caught up with the fair representation doctrine that the Board accepted its responsibility. At this point in time it would have taken misguided courage not to have decided the fair representation question as the Board did in *Hughes Tool.*[110]

In deciding *Hughes Tool,* the board was acting under its recently discovered constitutional obligations. Going beyond the requirements of the facts in the case, and citing *Shelley* v. *Kraemer* and other cases interpreting the concept of "state action," the board stated: "Specifically, we hold that the Board cannot validly render aid under Section 9 of the Act to a labor organization which discriminates racially when acting as a statutory bargaining representative."[111] Given the facts presented and the relief requested by the plaintiffs, the board could have limited itself to decertification of the segregated locals. However, the board's decision made it clear that practices of racial discrimination maintained by labor unions in whatever form were unfair labor practices, and made it equally clear that the board would not hesitate to apply remedies, including decertification, injunction, back-pay orders, and other affirmative relief, to correct such practices. For the first time, then, the NLRB complied with the constitutional obligation to withdraw legal protections and services from unions which engage in discriminatory racial practices. It went beyond the negative duty of ceasing assistance to discriminatory labor organizations and adopted the affirmative position that it was obliged to take measures to halt racial discrimination by labor unions.

The board's decision in *Hughes Tool* was of great significance for black workers (for example, the thirteen complainants employed by the Atlantic Steel Company had previously been denied this means of redress for their grievances). As a result of this decision, black complainants for the first time had available to them an administrative forum which, at government expense, provided investigations, hearings, and powerful remedies enforceable in the federal courts.

Job Discrimination as an Unfair Labor Practice

In cases that followed *Hughes Tool,* the board expanded the applicability of unfair labor practice sections of the NLRA to reach other forms of racial discrimination in employment. In its 1964 decision in *Local 1367, International Longshoremen's Association*[112] the board found that a labor agreement restricting the employment opportunities of black workers constituted an unfair labor practice.

Segregated locals of the Longshoremen's union had divided employment opportunities on a racial basis. The white local enforced a 75- to 25-percent distribution of work between the two locals, thus allotting three fourths of the work to its own members. The agreement also contained a "no-doubling" clause which prohibited white and Negro units from working together. The board found that Section 8(d)'s commandment to unions and employers "to confer in good faith" and to sign "any agreement reached" did not contemplate the signing of racially discriminatory agreements. The board's decision that the signing of such an agreement was an unfair labor practice stated:

> Because collective bargaining agreements which discriminate invidi-ously are not lawful under the Act, the good-faith requirements of Section 8(d) necessarily protect employees from infringement of their rights; and both unions and employers are enjoined by the Act from entering into contractual terms which offend such rights.[113]

Concluding that "it is not in the public interest for patently invalid provisions to be included in collective labor agreements," the board implied that unions were under an affirmative obligation to oppose discrimination by employers in terms and conditions of employment and that they could no longer remain passive toward employer-initiated discriminatory practices against black workers under their jurisdiction. The elimination of racial abuses in employment was therefore implied to be as valid a subject for collective bargaining as increased wages and greater employment security.

In a subsequent case, before the Court of Appeals for the Fifth Circuit, it was decided that a union did in fact have an affirmative obligation to eliminate racial discrimination. Local 12 of the United Rubber, Cork, Linoleum and Plastic Workers of America, AFL-CIO, had been the exclusive bargaining agent for employees of the Goodyear Tire and Rubber Company at its Gadsden, Alabama, plant since 1943. Until March 1962 there were three seniority rolls that segregated workers on the basis of race. Black employees with greater seniority had no rights in relation to white employees with less seniority involving promotions, transfers, layoffs, and recall to employment. Eight black workers were furloughed in 1960 while white workers with less seniority retained their jobs. The blacks presented their grievances to Local 12, which refused to process them, even when ordered to do so by the president of the international union. Upon petition by the complainants, the NLRB found that the union had committed an unfair labor practice by failing to process the grievances and present them to the company for arbitration. The board ordered the union to process the grievances through to arbitration and to propose to the employer specific contractual provisions prohibiting racial discrimination.

The local appealed the board's order, and in *Local 12, United Rubber Workers* v. *NLRB*[114] the Court of Appeals for the Fifth Circuit framed the question presented as being the degree to which the duty of fair representation compelled a union to protect the employment status of its black workers:

> The vital issue in this area resolves itself into that of determining at what point the exclusive bargaining agent's duty to represent fairly the interests of each individual employee must bow to the equally comprehensive obligation of negotiating and administering the bargaining contract in accordance with the act's primary policy of fostering union-employer relations.[115]

The court agreed with the board's interpretation of the union's duty of fair representation and found that the union's failure to process the grievance constituted an unfair labor practice. The *Local 12, United Rubber Workers* decision stands for the proposition that unions are under an affirmative obligation to oppose the discriminatory practices of employers and that failure to do so violates the unfair labor practice sections of the NLRA.[116] The decision is thus a further extension—by both the NLRB and the courts—of the duty of unions with respect to discriminatory employment practices.

Local 12, United Rubber Workers was the first case in which the federal courts sustained the National Labor Relations Board's power to act against racial discrimination in employment as an unfair labor practice. The court of appeals stated:

> More specifically, we must determine whether a breach of the duty of fair representation in itself constitutes an unfair labor practice within contemplation of the National Labor Relations Act, as amended. We are convinced that the duty of fair representation implicit in the exclusive-representation requirement in section 9(a) of the act comprises an indispensable element of the right of employees "to bargain collectively through representatives of their own choosing" as guaranteed in section 7. We therefore conclude that by summarily refusing to process the complainants' grievances concerning back wages and segregated plant facilities, petitioner thereby violated section

8(b)(1)(A) of the act by restraining those employees in the exercise of their section 7 rights.[117]

For years the federal courts had been the primary forum for redressing breaches of the duty of fair representation. The board's recognition in *Hughes Tool, ILA Local 1367,* and *Local 12, United Rubber Workers* that violations of the duty constituted unfair labor practices necessitated a new approach, with the board now having primary jurisdiction in such cases.[118] Recognizing the consequences of its holding that a breach of the duty of fair representation was in fact an unfair labor practice, the court of appeals stated that its interpretation "will have the necessary effect of bringing such controversies within the primary jurisdiction of the Board, thus requiring some degree of reorientation of current jurisdictional practices."[119]

The court recalled that in the past the board had avoided its duty to decide such questions effectively and that the plaintiffs had then been forced to seek redress in the courts. A Negro worker could present his case to the board "with the bleak prospect of beginning anew in the courts if the Board concludes that the only violation involved in his claim is a breach of the union's duty of fair representation."[120] Now, however, the court noted that the board was willing to serve as a forum for the redress of racial issues, stating that "[r]ecognizing a violation of the duty of fair representation as an unfair labor practice will avoid this jurisdictional predicament of 'sending the impecunious plaintiff back to the courts when the Board finds the union's action to have been wholly arbitrary.' "[121] The court concluded that the board was a superior forum for deciding such questions since it had great expertise in adjusting employment rights in other contexts:

> In light of these considerations, we are convinced that the rights of individual employees to be fairly represented can be more fully achieved within the spirit of the act by recognizing the Board as the appropriate body to meet the challenge of uniformly administering standards of fair representation. Its peculiar expertise with respect to the complexities of the bargaining process, its broad powers of investigation, and most importantly, its power to encourage informal settlements at the regional director level render it better qualified than the necessarily diverse system of state and federal tribunals to meet the task of formulating and applying uniform standards of fair representation in such manner as to afford adequate protection to employee rights without unduly impeding the collective bargaining process.[122]

The task of persuading the board that it was empowered and obligated to decide questions of racial discrimination in employment was long and difficult, but at least the initial barriers seem to have been overcome. That the board has the authority to deal with such issues has now been stated by the courts; whether it will do so often and effectively remains an open question.

Farmers' Cooperative Compress (United Packinghouse Workers)[123] presented a new situation, one of an employer alone engaging in discriminatory racial practices, while the labor union opposed these practices. In 1968 the United Packinghouse Workers of America, AFL-CIO, filed unfair labor practice charges with the board alleging that the company had, among other things, refused to eliminate a variety of discriminatory practices against black and Mexican-American workers. The board determined that the company had violated Sections 8(a)(1) and 8(a)(5) of the National Labor Relations Act and ordered the company to cease and desist from certain of its anti-union practices, but, as to racial discrimination, it ordered the company only to bargain in good faith with the union. Before the U.S. Court of Appeals for the District of Columbia, the union appealed the board's failure to find that the company's discriminatory racial practices were in and of themselves an unfair labor practice, and its failure to order the company directly and specifically to cease and desist from racially discriminatory conduct. The company, on the other hand, filed its own appeal, raising more routine lines of objection to the board's finding that it was guilty of anti-union coercion and refusal to bargain.

The court of appeals very quickly disposed of the routine issues, sustaining the board's findings of anti-union conduct by the company. The largest portion of the decision was addressed to the union's appeal, which presented the question of whether racial discrimination in and of itself is an unfair labor practice. The employer was accused of having parceled out preferred job assignments and promotions in ways that discriminated against both black and Spanish-speaking workers, and even of having engaged in discriminatory practices in arranging plant outings.

All the previous cases and board decisions interpreting racial abuses as unfair labor practices and as breaches of the duty of fair representation had involved union activity, and a union had been the defendant in each case. The court's decision, remanding the case to the board to take evidence on racial discrimination as a violation of the unfair labor practice sections of the Act, is significant because it marked the first time any court had stated that the board may issue cease-and-desist orders based on an employer's record of discriminatory racial practices.[124] The board had earlier considered only the company's refusal to bargain fairly, but the court decision forced the board to confront the issue of discriminatory practices by an employer alone.*

Since the company's efforts to perpetuate discriminatory racial practices were overt and diverse, Judge J. Skelly Wright framed the issue broadly: "Can an employer's policy and practice of invidious discrimination against its employees on account of race or national origin violate Section 8(a)(1)† of the National Labor Relations Act? . . . [W]e answer this question in the affirmative."[125] Ordering the board to reopen the case, the court stated:

> It is apparent that the Board has not felt itself unable to examine charges of union racial discrimination to determine whether they are true, and, if true, what the effect is on the discriminated employees. No reason appears why employer discrimination is exempt from Board scrutiny.[126]

As a guideline to the board in inquiring into Section 8(a)(1) violations, the court pointed out that the employer's discrimination must have had the effect of inhibiting employees from asserting their Section 7 rights, the rights to organize and bargain collectively:

> This effect is twofold: (1) racial discrimination sets up an unjustified clash of interest between groups of workers which tends to reduce the likelihood and the effectiveness of their working in concert to achieve their legitimate goals under the Act; and (2) racial discrimination creates in its victims an apathy or docility which inhibits them from asserting their rights against the perpetrator of the discrimination. *We find that the confluence of these two factors sufficiently deters the exercise of Section 7 rights as to violate Section 8(a)(1).* . . .

---

*Subsequently, following a further hearing after the case was remanded, the board's trial examiner found that the company had engaged in racial discrimination and again issued a cease-and-desist order; but the board reversed his findings, decided the facts did not show a pattern of race discrimination, and dismissed the charge on this item, thereby avoiding the legal question. *Farmers Cooperative Compress,* 194 NLRB 85 (1971).

†29 U.S.C. Section 158(a)(1) (1964): "It shall be an unfair labor practice for an employer—(1) to interfere with, restrain or coerce employees in the exercise of the rights guaranteed in section 157 of this title." 29 U.S.C. Section 157 (1964) (Section 7 of the Act): "Employees shall have the right of self-organization, to form, join, or assist labor organization, to bargain collectively through representatives of their own choosing, and to engage in other concerted activities for the purpose of collective bargaining or other mutual aid or protection. . . ."

> . . . [W]e are not holding that all discrimination, even where justified, is by itself sufficient to make out a violation. Rather . . . it is the conjunction of the unreasonable and illegal discrimination with the induced docility in the discriminated group which is the basis of our unfair labor practices holding. [Emphasis added.][127]

A Section 8(a)(1) violation is thereby established because of the suppressant effect of the discrimination on the employees' Section 7 rights. Although this effect is usually seen as an inevitable consequence of the act itself, William B. Gould makes the following observation about this novel application of the National Labor Relations Act:

> Does discrimination always result in apathy and docility on the part of black workers and other minority groups? The militance of a good number of black workers leads one to believe that there are some contexts in which Judge Wright's conclusions may not hold water. Since we now know that the extent and severity of racial discrimination varies in different circumstances, might not also the response of black workers vary as well? One wonders whether a black militant in an auto plant in Detroit will respond in the same manner as the newly hired Negro textile hand in South Carolina. The result in *United Packinghouse Workers* is a laudable one, but the rationale is somewhat questionable.[128]

As a result of the decision in *United Packinghouse Workers,* victims of racial discrimination in employment should be able to obtain redress in the form of cease-and-desist orders from the board as well as other forms of affirmative relief against union and employer practices. Although the board has not probed into the forms of and proper remedies for employment discrimination as carefully as the courts have in their decisions on Title VII cases, processing a discrimination case through the board does offer certain advantages over methods possible through the Equal Employment Opportunity Commission. The board can issue cease-and-desist orders,[129] an enforcement power that the EEOC lacks. It can petition federal courts to compel affirmative relief, such as ordering back pay to an employee. In addition, the board's general counsel bears the responsibility and the board bears the cost of prosecuting the case through the courts. But the board's movement in the field of unfair representation in racial issues has been demonstrably slow and cautious in the past, so that interminable procedural requirements often negate the virtues of the NLRA as written. And the fact that the board vigorously argued against the conclusion reached by the court in *United Packinghouse Workers* should not be ignored.[130] Moreover, the NLRB has refrained from applying the principle established in that case to use its powers against employers who alone engage in discrimination based on race.

Title VII and the NLRA

Prosecuting charges of racial discrimination in employment before the board offers black workers an *additional* remedy, not an *alternative* remedy. Cases brought under the National Labor Relations Act and Title VII confirm the fact that the NLRB and the EEOC often have concurrent jurisdiction and that black workers may simultaneously approach both forums to obtain redress. In *Local 12, United Rubber Workers,*[131] in which the board's authority to deal with discriminatory practices as unfair labor practices was first affirmed by the courts, the Court of Appeals for the Fifth Circuit noted: "In thus concluding that a breach of the duty of fair representation constitutes an unfair labor practice, we are not unmindful that Title VII . . . makes it an 'unlawful employment practice' for a union to discriminate. . . ."[132] Despite the existence of legislation aimed specifically at racial discrimination in employment, "[n]evertheless, it is equally clear that had these claims arisen after [the effective date of Title VII], the complainants . . . would be at liberty to seek redress under the enforcement provisions of Title VII or to assert unfair labor practice charges before the Board."[133] The court concluded that the board was in some respects a superior forum to the EEOC for the resolution of racial questions:

> We recognize that while Title VII represents an appreciable addition to the protection afforded employee rights in the specific areas of discrimination covered by the Civil Rights Act, there continues to exist a broad potential range of arbitrary union conduct not specifically covered by Title VII which may also violate the union's duty of fair representation. . . . The mere fact, therefore, that Congress has seen fit to provide specific protection to employees from union and employer discrimination in the area of civil rights in no way detracts from the legal and practical bases of our determination that a breach of the union's duty of fair representation constitutes a violation of section 8(b)(1)(A).[134]

Here, with respect to questions of racial discrimination in employment, the court clearly stated that the board possessed concurrent jurisdiction with the EEOC and with the courts.

But only one week after the *Local 12, United Rubber Workers* decision the board indicated its intention to retreat from the court's broad interpretation of its authority. Arnold Ordman, the NLRB's general counsel at that time, in reply to an inquiry from Senator Jacob Javits of New York stated that the board would continue to follow the practice of "deferring" to the EEOC in cases of racial discrimination:

> *The National Labor Relations Act is primarily designed as a law concerned with problems of labor-management relations and organizational rights rather than racial discrimination.* On the other hand, Title VII . . . is aimed directly at racial discrimination. . . . Administrative agencies have been adjured to accommodate the policies developed in the administration of the law to be administered by the agency with the policies of other federal agencies administering other federal statutes in appropriate cases. . . . In any particular case, therefore, my policy is to examine the particular factual situation and to make a determination to defer or not to defer, as the case may be, on the basis of my judgment as to whether deferral will best effectuate the intent of Congress. I have deferred action in some cases on charges involving racial discrimination where charges have also been filed with the Equal Employment Commission where it appears that the Commission is actively investigating and if permitted to act might well be able to dispose of the case more expeditiously or more effectively than the Board could. [Emphasis added.][135]

The NLRB's general counsel is responsible for issuing a complaint against a union or an employer when a charge alleging an unfair labor practice is filed with the board; without his complaint, the case cannot proceed. Therefore, the general counsel's view that the resolution of racial issues is not an important purpose of the board means that few such cases will be brought.

Despite both the clear implications of an emerging body of law over a twenty-five-year period and the explicit statements of the court in *Local 12, United Rubber Workers,* the board has refrained from adopting a policy requiring the exercise of its powers in complaints alleging racial discrimination. The long line of cases beginning with *Steele* at the judicial level, and with *Pioneer Bus* and *Hughes Tool* at the administrative level, makes it evident that the board's constitutional duty to take affirmative action when presented with evidence of racial discrimination by unions and employers is mandatory, *not* discretionary. Yet the board has continued, since 1965, when Title VII became effective, to refuse to issue complaints and to defer to the EEOC. With the exception of a small number of cases, the board has rejected jurisdiction in questions of racial discrimination.

In a 1970 case, *Asbestos Workers Local 53 and Paul Vogler, Jr.,*[136] the board indicated that it intended to continue deferring consideration of racial discrimination whenever possible. The related Title VII suit arose in Louisiana, in 1967, when a complaint was filed by black and Spanish-surnamed construction workers who were barred from membership in Local 53 of the International Association of Heat and Frost Insulators and Asbestos Workers, AFL-CIO. The union also refused to issue temporary work permits to Mexican Americans and blacks so that they could obtain employment without joining the union. The district court in New Orleans enjoined further exclusion of minority workers from membership and ordered four blacks into membership and nine others to immediate referral. In addition, the court granted sweeping relief that virtually stripped the union of its discretionary powers in admitting new members, determining the size of its membership, and controlling employment in the trade in the New Orleans-Baton Rouge area. This was also the first case in which a court issued a temporary restraining order barring a union from holding an internal election scheduled for the purpose of closing its membership rolls. The court of appeals affirmed the order of the district court.

In response to unfair labor practice charges filed with the NLRB, the trial examiner concluded that, because the district court had enjoined the operation of the discriminatory hiring hall by the union, there was no need for any additional remedy.* He failed to recommend cease-and-desist orders against racial discrimi-

---

*Philip Ross, professor of industrial relations at the State University of New York at Buffalo, concluded in an interesting analysis of the NLRB's regulation of union hiring-hall procedures: "There is at least one feature about hiring-hall cases which deserves special attention. This is the perpetuation of past discrimination through the use of currently applied objective standards. The law is clear that if the true purpose and intent of such standards is to disguise otherwise unlawful tests of discrimination such as race a violation has taken place. It is at least arguable that the NLRB and the courts have unrealistically and passively accommodated themselves in their interpretation and application of section 8(b)(2) to systems of job discrimination which are inconsistent with the act and the public policy on equal employment opportunity."—Philip Ross, "NLRB's Regulation of Union Job Control," *Monthly Labor Review* (Washington, D.C.: U.S. Department of Labor, Bureau of Labor Statistics, March 1971), pp. 59–62.

nation because "as a matter of comity between branches of the federal government, it was not proper to rule on these matters which were similar to the racial issues before the United States District Court."[137] A majority of the board disagreed with the trial examiner, ruling that cease-and-desist orders were necessary. The orders were limited, however, to the union's practice of giving preference to union members in referrals for employment—they did not deal with racial issues. Board member Howard Jenkins dissented from "the Board's unwillingness to find the conduct violative of these same sections of the Act for the additional reason that the discrimination was based on race and national origin."[138]

Citing *Local 12, United Rubber Workers,* Jenkins said: "The Board has already held, with Court approval, that Title VII of the Civil Rights Act of 1964 in no way limits the Board's powers and duties under the National Labor Relations Act." He thus addressed himself to the board's duty to consider and resolve racial disputes even when they were being considered in other forums. On the basis of the facts presented by the charging parties, Jenkins believed the board should issue cease-and-desist orders against the union's "maintaining a hiring arrangement which gave preference on the basis of race or national origin as well as preference on the basis of union membership. . . ."[139] But the board limited the grounds of its orders to the practice of union preference in referral. The board's failure to base its orders, at least in part, on racial practices—on grounds that racial questions had been resolved by the court—is therefore a further indication that the board intends to continue its resistance to involvement in racial issues.

Two cases decided under Title VII in 1969 have further clarified the role of the EEOC and the NLRB as administrative agencies with dual and concurrent responsibilities to redress acts of discrimination. In *Bowe* v. *Colgate-Palmolive Company,*[140] a case in Indiana involving sex discrimination, the federal district court required the plaintiff to elect, prior to trial, whether to proceed with the case in court or to seek a remedy under the collective bargaining agreement through arbitration.[141] The court of appeals reversed the district court's requirement of election of forums: "[I]t was error not to permit the plaintiffs to utilize dual or parallel prosecution both in court and through arbitration so long as election of remedy was made *after* adjudication so as to preclude duplicate relief. [Emphasis added.]"[142] The court therefore held that a plaintiff alleging discrimination in employment may prosecute his case in more than one forum at once and may choose the more desirable relief offered. Although this holding would subject defendants to multiple prosecution, other considerations were more important: "While we recognize that there is a burden placed on the defendant who must defend in two different fora, we also note that there may be crucial differences between the two processes and the remedy afforded by each."[143]

The court's decision would seem to support the proposition that minority workers may pursue their cases both before the commission (and, subsequently, through the courts under Title VII) and before the board.* They may be awarded relief under both the NLRA and Title VII and then choose the more complete form of redress. The *Bowe* case suggests that the NLRB should no longer abdicate its responsibility by deferring cases to the EEOC. Regardless of the commission's investigations and other administrative procedures, the board should proceed separately to hear and determine charges of racial discrimination in employment.†

Another Title VII decision rendered in 1969 confirms by implication the court's ruling in *Bowe* that Title VII and other labor legislation may be used simultaneously to resolve questions of racial discrimination in employment. In *Norman* v. *Missouri Pacific Railroad*[144] the question before the Court of Appeals for the Eighth Circuit was whether black employees of the railroad were limited to seeking relief for racial discrimination under the Railway Labor Act or whether they could also seek redress under Title VII. The court's holding in *Norman* dealing with the relationship between the Railway Labor Act and Title VII are of great significance to NLRB cases involving racial discrimination, since the Railway Labor Act (drawn under the influence of the major rail unions and companies) is considerably more restrictive and affords more limited remedies than the National Labor Relations Act.

The *Norman* case was decided in a context of almost thirty years of litigation on the issue. As the eighth circuit court stated,

---

*This principle was later explicitly established in *Alexander* v. *Gardner-Denver Co.*, 415 U.S. 36, 7 FEP Cases 81 (1974).

†The Equal Employment Opportunity Commission's *Sixth Annual Report,* released in 1972, states: "The National Labor Relations Board has jurisdiction over cases which involve failure of a union to represent all employees fairly and over cases where the unfair labor practice involves the assertion of Title VII rights in a contract grievance proceeding. In *Tipler* v. *duPont Co.* [443 F.2d 125, 3 FEP Cases 540 (6th Cir. 1971)] the court found that the jurisdictions of the NLRB and the EEOC were concurrent, though not identical. Thus, certain acts of racial discrimination not within the ambit of the NLRB still are proscribed by Title VII."—*Sixth Annual Report* (Washington, D.C.: Equal Employment Opportunity Commission, March 30, 1972), p. 20.

the case represents "another chapter in the long, arduous litigation of the train porters against the railroads, and at times against railroad unions, in an attempt to preserve the train porters' position against adverse changes in the operation of passenger trains and predatory raids by their alleged white counterparts, the railway brakemen."[145] The craft of train porter has been recognized since 1918, and Negroes alone have traditionally been employed as train porters. Train porters perform braking work on the front end of passenger trains; brakemen, who are traditionally white, perform the same task on the back end of passenger trains and on freight trains. White brakemen have been represented by the Brotherhood of Railroad Trainmen, but black train porters have been denied membership in the union. The separate labor classifications of train porters and brakemen and the division of representation have always been drawn along racial lines. Even though the two classifications represent performance of virtually identical tasks, train porters receive lower wages; and because they are restricted to passenger trains, they are facing a rapid attrition of job opportunities. The thirty-year history of case law dealing with the conflict between black train porters and white brakemen shows the need for Title VII legal remedies to redress racial employment grievances.[146]

The Brotherhood of Railroad Trainmen has repeatedly attempted to use its collective bargaining power with the railroads to discontinue the train porters' jobs entirely and replace them with jobs for white brakemen. In 1942, in *Howard*,[147] the Supreme Court saved the train porters from displacement by holding that the duty of fair representation under the Railway Labor Act prohibited the brakemen's union from transferring black workers' jobs to whites. The same problem recurred in 1946.[148] In 1966, in *Howard* v. *St. Louis-San Francisco Ry. Co.*,[149] the Court of Appeals for the Eighth Circuit denied relief to train porters seeking as a class to be placed in the job category of brakeman with preservation of seniority rights and security in job assignments. The court ruled that only the National Mediation Board had the power to make craft or class determinations and that without a change in classification, the issues between the parties represented a minor dispute under the Railway Labor Act, with final jurisdiction resting in the Railroad Adjustment Board. Also in 1966, in *Nunn* v. *Missouri Pacific Railroad Co.*,[150] black train porters unsuccessfully fought the elimination of their jobs on ten passenger trains of the defendant railroad. The district court held that the case constituted a minor dispute subject to the jurisdiction of the Railroad Adjustment Board. A year earlier, in *Neal v. System Board of Adjustment (Missouri Pacific Railroad)*,[151] black employees of the Missouri Pacific Railroad had also filed suit to prevent the abolition of their job classification and establishment of new classifications to be filled by white workers. The eighth circuit dismissed their suit, holding that they had failed to exhaust the administrative remedies available in their union grievance procedures before proceeding to court.

None of the administrative complaints and lawsuits involving railroads and railroad unions since the 1940s have brought protection for the black train porters. Courts interpreting the duty of fair representation have refused to confront the fact that the two craft classifications, brakeman and train porter, are based solely on racial distinction and have deferred resolution of the segregated classification system to the National Mediation Board and the Railroad Adjustment Board, both of which have refused to consider consolidation of the classifications and protection of the seniority rights of black workers.

In 1969, when the question was again presented to the Court of Appeals for the Eighth Circuit in *Norman,* this time under Title VII rather than under the Railway Labor Act, the court said: "It appears clear, however, that even though train porters are foreclosed from judicial relief by way of merger or reclassification of craft, the plaintiffs have certain protections under the Railway Labor Act and under Title VII of the Civil Rights Act of 1964."[152] The plaintiffs argued that although prior cases had held that the courts could not tamper with established crafts or classifications and had relegated black workers to the unsympathetic mediation and adjustment boards for relief, they were now entitled to seek new relief under Title VII. The defendant railroad tried to persuade the court to require the plaintiffs to turn once again to the two boards. The court of appeals replied to the defendant's arguments:

> No exclusivity can be placed in the Railway Labor Act over racial discrimination complaints. . . . We think the earlier cases clearly demonstrate and hold that the Railway Labor Act had not preempted jurisdiction over all racially based grievances arising out of the operation of the railroads nor is it set up to determine all types of racial complaints.[153]

Appellants' brief to the Court of Appeals for the Eighth Circuit in *Howard* noted, the curtailing of mileage and the substitution of white brakemen for train porters on the continuation of runs, reduces the remuneration paid to those Negroes who are retained and terminates the services of others. On each occasion when mileage was shortened no notice was given to appellant and his class regarding abolition of positions or termination of services. Appellant and his class have no administrative relief and must rely on the courts to remedy the racially discriminatory practices which are responsible for both their classification and their inferior contractual rights and remedies.[154]

The brief states that an earlier decision by the Interstate Commerce Commission had authorized termination of many passenger trains, and that "[i]n August, 1966, the Railway is authorized to [give] notice of discontinuance of the remaining trains. Unless this matter is disposed of promptly and relief afforded, appellant and the class he represents will have their employment terminated."[155]

When the *Norman* case was decided in December 1974,[156] numerous passenger trains had ceased to operate, several of the plaintiffs had retired, and three others had been transferred to brakemen's jobs without seniority, but they too were soon forced to retire because of age. The argument against racial discrimination in the railroad industry—the issue that led initially to the application of the fair representation doctrine to employment discrimination—will be substantially moot by the time a measure of relief is finally available to black workers.

As a result of *Steele, Hughes Tool,* and subsequent judicial and administrative cases, the National Labor Relations Board could become a channel through which workers experiencing racial discrimination might seek effective relief. Its availability as a powerful administrative agency to decide such questions is firmly established. Its possibilities for effective action in this area have not yet been fully explored because the quest for administrative relief has shifted to Title VII and the Equal Employment Opportunity Commission, designed specifically to deal with discrimination in employment.[157] This shift has taken place despite the fact that the EEOC has no means of enforcing its decisions short of litigation,[158] and plaintiffs are required to exhaust administrative procedures before litigating to obtain relief.[159] Although the EEOC has been strengthened by the Equal Employment Opportunity Act of 1972[160] which gives it authority to initiate lawsuits, the NLRB's capacity for effectively and creatively obtaining the lawful rights of minorities remains of continuing importance. The board has the power, already exercised in nonracial contexts, to enjoin discriminatory bargaining agreements,[161] to decertify unions engaged in discriminatory practices,[162] and to compel unions and employers—through the issuance of cease-and-desist orders enforceable by the board in the federal courts—to alter their illegal racial practices.[163]

The National Labor Relations Board can offer cost-free procedures to victims of racial discrimination, but there is an administrative barrier; the right to go to court under the National Labor Relations Act is conditioned on the issuance of a complaint by the general counsel of the board.[164] The general counsel may at his discretion refuse to issue a complaint on any ground. Furthermore, with the exception of cases involving picketing,[165] preliminary relief under the Railway Labor Act is rarely available.[166]

Broad powers to deal with racial questions have been demonstrated to be available under *Steele* and the National Labor Relations Act, but the board's full potential under the principle of *Shelley* v. *Kraemer* has yet to be explored, and the board has resisted such exploration. In other areas, the board's enforcement mechanisms have been effective. For example, the Taft-Hartley Act of 1947 required unions to file reports of activities[167] and union officers to sign non-Communist affidavits.[168] Failure to comply with these requirements deprived unions of the services of the NLRB.[169] A noncomplying union could not, for example, receive the board's help in holding an election and thus could not be certified.[170] Moreover, the NLRB would not issue an unfair labor practice complaint at the request of a noncomplying union but would prosecute it for violation of the Act.[171] Although the Landrum-Griffin Act of 1959[172] repealed the non-Communist provision, it extended the reporting requirements;[173] while the unions are no longer penalized, stiff penalties are imposed upon individuals found to be violating the Act.[174] These sanctions have induced most unions to comply with the filing requirements, and logic suggests that such measures would be just as effective against unions that practice racial discrimination.

The NLRB, as we have seen, has decertified a union and taken other steps to eliminate racial abuses only when presented with overwhelming evidence of discrimination. However, the board could require written assurances, stating that they are not engaged in racially discriminatory practices, from all unions it certifies as exclusive bargaining agents and from all employers and unions filing unfair labor practice complaints. The board would then have the responsibility of policing the written assurances, and upon a finding of violation could invoke stringent sanctions to bring the party into compliance. Leo Weiss, an NLRB attorney who has suggested such procedures, adds:

> There is no question that such an approach would impose upon the NLRB a substantial quantity of additional work. Nor is there any question that the penalties suggested are severe and would impose substantial hardships on unions which are guilty of racial discrimination. But there is also no question that such a program would provide unions with considerable encouragement to abandon the racially discriminatory practices in which some of them are now engaged.[175]

The doctrine of *Shelley* v. *Kraemer* has sometimes been interpreted as requiring the NLRB to cease participation in discriminatory racial practices and to cease rendering assistance to private parties that engage in such practices.[176] But other court decisions have held that labor unions and employers are private parties capable of action free of constitutional compulsion. The better view is that unions are directly subject to the restrictions of the Fifth and Fourteenth Amendments. To allow unions—whose conduct embodies characteristics of governmental action by virtue of certification and statutory protection—to engage in racially discriminatory policies and practices is to ignore the broad implications of the *Shelley* decision. Racial discrimination by labor unions cannot be distinguished from other forms of discriminatory racial practices where the power of the state is operative. The state is prohibited from acting to assist private parties engaged in racial discrimination because such action by the state is a violation of the Constitution. Unions have been empowered by the state to exercise great control over individuals and over entire classes of workers. Although they are not specifically given the right to discriminate racially, they have been given powers by the state which make it possible for them to do so. Therefore racial discrimination by labor unions may well be regarded as a form of prohibited "state action" under the *Shelley* doctrine.

The only case which squarely holds that a certified union is required by the Fifth Amendment to admit Negroes is *Betts* v. *Easley*,[177] a 1946 decision of the Supreme Court of Kansas. The state court said:

> The acts complained of are those of an organization acting as an agency created and functioning under provisions of Federal law. . . . While claiming and exercising rights incident to its designation as

bargaining agent, the defendant union cannot at the same time avoid the responsibilities that attach to such statutory status.[178]

The *Betts* case, though not a precedent in the federal courts, is consistent with federal cases which have held state requirement, involvement, sanction, ratification, support, or enforcement sufficient to convert otherwise private discrimination into that of the state.* Certainly labor unions—sanctioned, supported, and protected by the government in their collective bargaining capacities— might be held subject to constitutional standards. Professor Rosen has suggested that

> [s]uch a position, or even a more extended one, might be justified by the fact that, in our contemporary mass society, the power exercised by labor unions and corporate and other employers, and indeed by many other such "voluntary private associations," is very like the political power of government, insofar as the exercise of such associational power greatly affects important interests of the subject individuals. Starting from such a view of organizations and society, it has been recommended that significant private centers of power, as petite governments, should be subjected to constitutional requirements that protect individual rights.[179]

However, in no case have the federal courts held that constitutional compulsions directly apply to labor unions and private employers. Before such a qualitative leap in the evolution of constitutional law can be accomplished, it is necessary for the National Labor Relations Act to be interpreted as broadly as Title VII in reaching virtually all forms of discrimination in employment and in prohibiting them by the administrative process. Several cases decided under the National Labor Relations Act and under Title VII have indicated the similarity in the potential of both acts to prohibit employment discrimination. The National Labor Relations Board has never decided racial questions of such complexity and sophistication as some of those decided under Title VII, but with its expertise in labor relations and its broad administrative enforcement powers, the board could become a most important forum for the resolution of claims involving work and race. Frequent use of its powerful remedies against subtle as well as overt forms of racial discrimination could produce large-scale

---

*See, for example, *Burton* v. *Wilmington Parking Authority*, 365 U.S. 715, 81 S. Ct. 856, 6 L.Ed.2d 45 (1961); and *Evans* v. *Newton*, 382 U.S. 296, 86 S. Ct. 486, 15 L.Ed.2d 373 (1966). Both of these cases expanded the concept of state action. But see *Moose Lodge* v. *Irvis*, 407 U.S. 163 (1973).

results in eliminating patterns of employment discrimination by both unions and employers.*

Black Protest and Collective Bargaining

Although evolving case law has established that racially discriminatory employment practices by labor unions and employers are an "unfair labor practice" which the NLRB is obligated to halt, other litigation has raised the issue of whether union members who belong to minority groups may independently protest an employer's racial practices without the formal sanction of the collective bargaining agent.

Section 7 of the National Labor Relations Act guarantees workers the right to engage in concerted activity in dealing with their employer with respect to terms and conditions of employment.[180] Section 9(a) of the Act provides that when employees are represented by a certified collective bargaining representative, that union shall have the exclusive authority to bargain on behalf of those working under its jurisdiction.[181] The potential conflict between these two provisions was presented in two cases initiated by black workers, *NLRB* v. *Tanner Motor Livery,*[182] and *Western Addition Community Organization* v. *NLRB (The Emporium).*[183] The issue is the extent to which protection from dismissal will be accorded dissident minority group union members when they picket and otherwise protest the racial practices of their employer without the consent of the union to which they belong.† The legal

---

*In an isolated instance the NLRB took the unprecedented action of finding that Local 1066 of the International Brotherhood of Painters and Allied Trades, AFL-CIO, in New Castle, Pennsylvania, had violated the National Labor Relations Act both by attempting to cause a painting contractor to deny employment to a black apprentice and by reprisals against white workers who refused to support the union's position. With all five members participating, the board held that the union's conduct violated Sections 8(b)(1)(A) and (2) of the Taft-Hartley Act. In ordering a remedy, the board required the union to reimburse the contractor, with interest, for the fine levied because of alleged "contract violations" and to rescind all disciplinary proceedings against the workers. In its decision and order the board noted that the union's business agent had threatened the employer with "trouble" if black workers were hired and had said that the employer would "have a lot of union problems."— See *International Brotherhood of Painters and Allied Trades, Local Union 1066, AFL-CIO, and W. J. Stiebenoller, Jr., et al., and Benjamin D. Dematteo,* 205 NLRB No. 110, 84 LRRM 1013 (1973).

†For information on the emergence of black labor caucuses, see James B. Gannon, "Black Unionists: Militant Negroes Press for a Stronger Voice in the Labor Movement," *Wall Street Journal,* November 29, 1968, p.1, col. 1; Peter Henle, "Organized Labor and the New Militants," *Monthly Labor Review,* July 1969, pp. 20–25; A. H. Raskin, "Labor and Blacks: The Unions Wear Two Faces Where Race Is Involved," *The New York Times,* September 7,

152   *Black Labor and the American Legal System*

question is therefore whether Section 9(a), the "exclusivity" section
of the Act, restricts their right to engage in activity otherwise
protected under Section 7. The practical question is what recourse
is available to minority union members when the majority of the
union membership fails to support their demands for nondiscriminatory working conditions.

The first case to approach the problem was *NLRB* v. *Tanner
Motor Livery, Ltd.*[184] Two black union members had picketed the
company in protest against its discriminatory practices, and had
done so without trying to obtain the union's sanction or use its
grievance machinery. The company promptly dismissed them
because of their activity and they filed unfair labor practice charges
with the NLRB. The board found the activity protected, issued a
complaint against the company, and subsequently ordered it to
reinstate the protesting workers.[185]

On review, the Court of Appeals for the Ninth Circuit held
that although the picketing activity was concerted conduct under
Section 7 of the Act, it could not be protected by the NLRB
because only the union itself, the exclusive bargaining agent, was
empowered under Section 9(a) to engage in picketing. In reversing
the board's determination the court analyzed and followed judicial
precedents in cases involving similar protests by dissident union
members over nonracial issues. It gave little weight to the fact that
racial discrimination was at the heart of the protest here and that
an extensive body of federal antidiscrimination legislation—apart
from labor legislation—protected the employees from retaliatory
dismissal.

In *Western Addition Community Organization* v. *NLRB* (*The
Emporium*)[186] the Court of Appeals for the District of Columbia
relied upon the intent of Congress expressed in Title VII to reach a
decision opposite to *Tanner*. In *Emporium* several black members
of Local 1100 of the Retail, Wholesale, and Department Store
Union, AFL-CIO, which represented employees of the Emporium,
a large department store in San Francisco, filed grievances with the
union in protest against discriminatory practices by the employer.
The union initiated grievance proceedings but it presented the

1969, Section 4, p.4, col. 2; William B. Gould, "Black Power in the Unions: The Impact Upon
Collective Bargaining Relationships," *Yale Law Journal*, November 1969, pp. 46–84; Burton
H. Hall, ed., *Autocracy and Insurgency in Organized Labor*, Section II, "White Leaders and
Black Workers" (New Brunswick, N.J.: Transaction Books, 1972), pp. 137–236; Herbert Hill,
"Black Labor, the NLRB, and the Developing Law of Equal Employment Opportunity,"
Labor Law Journal, April 1975, pp. 207–223.

grievances as individual cases rather than on the storewide or pattern basis requested by the black employees. Believing that the union was not vigorously pressing their complaints, these employees then abandoned the grievance procedure and, without union sanction, picketed the store and distributed leaflets on their off-duty time. After union officials had unsuccessfully urged them to stop picketing, the Emporium management dismissed two protest leaders from their jobs. A community group, Western Addition Community Organization, then presented an unfair labor practice petition to the NLRB seeking the workers' reinstatement, but the board dismissed the complaint, holding that since they had not proceeded with their protest through the union, the protest was not protected under the National Labor Relations Act and the employer was free to dismiss them.

When the board's decision was appealed to the Court of Appeals for the District of Columbia, the EEOC filed a brief *amicus curiae* arguing that

> the Board applied the "exclusivity principle" in most inappropriate circumstances. In a case of alleged discrimination by a private employer, the Board must consider the policies underlying another federal statute, Title VII of the Civil Rights Act of 1964. Had the Board properly done so, it would have concluded that Title VII protects the individual's efforts to rectify unlawful employment practices to the extent of necessarily circumscribing the right of a labor union to serve as the only employee voice in such cases.[187]

In urging that "the Board should afford great weight to the policies underlying Title VII," the commission stated:

> It is well-established that in applying the National Labor Relations Act, the Board must give consideration to other Congressional expressions of national policy. A federal administrative agency charged with implementing the "public interest" can hardly do otherwise. . . . Thus, since the passage of Title VII, this court has ruled that racial discrimination in employment is an unfair labor practice, and the Board has taken an active role in the elimination of employment discrimination. . . . [T]he law of the land now prohibits retaliation against individuals who assert their rights to equal employment opportunity.[188]

Addressing itself to the issue of labor union responsibility for discriminatory employment practices, the commission reminded the court:

Twenty years before the passage of Title VII, the Supreme Court imposed upon labor unions the "duty to fully represent" their minority members. Despite the Court's continued insistence on the performance of this duty, the nation's labor unions have too often proven unable or unwilling to combat racial discrimination on the part of employers. Indeed Congress recognized that in many instances labor unions have been the perpetrators of discrimination. . . . In the past few years, many Black union members have formed independent labor organizations to assert their rights to equal employment opportunity. Such groups have grown dramatically in size largely because of the frustration of Black workers with the failure of their collective bargaining representatives to take the lead in assuring equal rights. This failure in turn is attributable to the fact that under the principle of majority rule, labor unions have minimal obligations to serve the interests of their minority members.[189]

The court of appeals reversed the NLRB decision, sustaining the right of "a minority group who has reasonable grounds for believing that the union is not proceeding against all discrimination . . . to assert its claim of racial discrimination in a manner which it considers would be more successful."[190] The court held that dissident minority protest over racially discriminatory employment practices stands upon a different plane in federal labor law from other types of dissident protests and that it is entitled to special protection from coercion:

The right of an employee to racially non-discriminatory treatment is unquestionably a "condition of employment," and as such the negotiation of an anti-discrimination clause in a collective bargaining agreement is within the purview of the exclusive bargaining enunciated in section 9(a). Yet, this right to non-discriminatory treatment differs significantly from other "conditions of employment" which are also the subject of exclusive bargaining, such as pension benefits or seniority rights. The right to be free of racially discriminatory employment practices does not depend upon the presence of an anti-discrimination clause in a collective bargaining agreement, but is firmly rooted in the law. . . .

Not only does concerted activity involving racial discrimination have a unique status in that the subject matter has independent statutory bases, but section 704(a) of Title VII precludes an employer from discharging employees in retaliation for peaceful picketing of the employer's business in protest of allegedly discriminatory racial practices. . . . Where, as here, both the subject matter of the concerted activity and the right to engage in such activity are safeguarded by legislation, we feel such concerted activity cannot be treated identically with other concerted activity which is not so safeguarded for the purpose of determining whether it so violated section 9(a) as to lose section 7 protection.[191]

In *Tanner* both the NLRB and the court had ignored the prohibition against racial discrimination and the protection against retaliatory firing contained in Title VII of the Civil Rights Act of 1964. The court of appeals in *Emporium,* however, ruled that Title VII was to be considered in a sense companion legislation to the NLRA when the issue of racial discrimination was raised:

> Neither the Trial Examiner nor the Board took cognizance of the statutory bases of the rights involved in their evaluation of the undermining effect of these concerted activities to section 9(a). While these activities are the subject of review by the Board only because they are deemed to be "concerted activities" within section 7 and also involving "conditions of employment" within section 9(a), the Board has an obligation in construing the acts which it administers to recognize, and sometimes reconcile, coexisting and perhaps inconsistent policies embodied in other legislation. . . . Thus, the Board should have recognized that in light of Title VII, concerted activity involving racial discrimination is quite distinct from other concerted activity.[192]

The court further stated that whenever the board was presented with facts showing that minority union members were protesting discrimination on their own, an inquiry should be conducted into the question of why the union did not sanction or support the protests: "On the issue of whether to tolerate racial discrimination in employment the individuals in a union cannot legally disagree. The law does not give the union an option to tolerate *some* racial discrimination, but declares that *all* racial discrimination in employment is illegal."[193] In such circumstances, said the court, the board should conduct its own inquiry into "whether the union was actually remedying the discrimination to the fullest extent possible, by the most expedient and efficacious means. Where the union's efforts fall short of this high standard, the minority group's concerted activities cannot lose its section 7 protection."[194] Thus the court held not only that union members who belong to a racial minority have the right to protest against racial discrimination in employment with or without the sanction of their union but further that the board itself is under an obligation to insure that the union does everything within its power to eradicate the discriminatory pattern.

On February 18, 1975, the Supreme Court, in response to an appeal from the NLRB, reversed the circuit court's decision.[195] The

Court held that while national labor policy gives the highest priority to equal employment opportunity, workers cannot bypass the exclusive bargaining agent because of dissatisfaction with efforts to eliminate discriminatory job practices through available grievance procedures. The Court noted that the labor agreement "had a no-strike or lockout clause, and it established grievance and arbitration machinery for processing any claimed violation of the contract, including a violation of the antidiscrimination clause."[196]

In response to the argument that Title VII remedies are inadequate, the Court stated:

> There are indeed significant differences between proceedings initiated under Title VII and an unfair labor practice proceeding. Congress chose to encourage voluntary compliance with Title VII by emphasizing conciliatory procedures before federal coercive powers could be invoked. Even then it did not provide the EEOC with the power of direct enforcement, but made the federal courts available to the agency or individual to secure compliance with Title VII. . . . By contrast, once the General Counsel of the NLRB decides to issue a complaint, vindication of the charging party's statutory rights becomes a public function discharged at public expense, and a favorable decision by the Board brings forth an administrative order. As a result of these and other differences, we are told that relief is typically available to the party filing a charge with the NLRB in a significantly shorter time, and with less risk, than obtains for one filing a charge with the EEOC.
>
> Whatever its factual merit, this argument is properly addressed to the Congress and not to this Court or the NLRB. . . .[197]

Justice Douglas dissented:

> The Court's opinion makes these union members—and others similarly situated—prisoners of the union. The law, I think was designed to prevent that tragic consequence. . . . In distinguishing "opposition" from participation in legal proceedings brought pursuant to the statute, it would seem that Congress brought employee self-help within the protection of Section 704. . . . The employees were engaged in a traditional form of labor protest, directed at matters which are unquestionably a proper subject of employee concern.[198]

In ruling that the black workers could not bypass the exclusive bargaining representative, the Supreme Court in *Emporium* reinforced the doctrine of union exclusivity expressed in Section 9(a) of the National Labor Relations Act. It left little doubt that the traditional interpretation of "exclusive representation" will continue to be a significant obstruction in realizing the rights of black workers.* Given the absence of internal democracy in many labor unions, where the rights of minorities are frequently violated, a more flexible interpretation of the exclusivity doctrine is essential.† This rigid concept of exclusivity is not justified. The doctrine as currently enforced does not encourage the democratic process within unions and makes effective representation of the interests of blacks and other minorities extremely difficult.‡ Adequate safeguards to protect the fundamental rights of racial minorities and others in the collective bargaining process are necessary. In practice, this means recognizing the right of minorities to engage in protected, concerted activity against discriminatory job practices with or without union approval and denying the remedial powers of the NLRA to labor organizations engaged in unlawful discrimination.

In his dissent in *Emporium* Justice Douglas argued[199] that the actions of the dismissed black employees were concerted activities protected under Section 7 of the NLRA and invoked *New Negro Alliance* v. *Sanitary Grocery Co.,*[200] a 1938 Supreme Court decision granting protection to workers engaged in concerted activity against racial discrimination in employment. In this case the Supreme Court held that picketing to protest job discrimination constituted a "labor dispute" and was therefore immune from injunctions under the Norris-La Guardia Act:

> [T]he desire for fair and equitable conditions of employment on the part of persons of any race, color, or persuasion, and the removal of discriminations against them by reason of their race and religious

---

*Judge Wyzanski's dissent in the decision of the Court of Appeals for the District of Columbia in *Emporium,* 485 F.2d at 936–938, 83 LRRM at 2749–2754, argued that in cases involving racial discrimination the exclusivity principle should be ignored.

†For information on problems of internal union democracy, see Burton H. Hall, ed., *Autocracy and Insurgency in Organized Labor* (New Brunswick, N.J.: Transaction Books, 1972); Paul E. Sultan, *The Disenchanted Unionist* (New York: Harper & Row, 1963), Chap. 7 and 9. See also Joseph Hickey, Jr., "The Bill of Rights of Union Members," *Georgetown Law Journal,* XLVIII, No. 2 (Winter 1959), pp. 231–249.

‡When the National Labor Relations Act was debated in the Congress during the early 1930s, the issue was viewed simply as a struggle between labor and management and the problems of minorities were ignored. The diversity of interests among employees and the conflicting goals within the working class were not considered. In 1944, Justice Jackson, dissenting in *Wallace Corp.* v. *NLRB,* anticipated the contemporary problem. He wrote: "The labor movement in the United States is passing into a new phase. The struggle of the unions for recognition and rights to bargain and of workmen for the right to join without interference seems to be culminating in a victory for labor forces. We appear to be entering the phase of struggle to reconcile the rights of individuals and minorities with the power of those who control the bargaining groups."—323 U.S. 248, 251, 271, 15 LRRM 697, 707 (1944).

beliefs is quite as important to those concerned as fairness and equity in terms and conditions of employment can be to trade or craft unions or any form of labor organization or association. Race discrimination by any employer may reasonably be deemed more unfair and less excusable than discrimination against workers on the ground of union affiliation.[201]

Twenty-seven years after *New Negro Alliance,* Title VII went into effect, and, under Title VII, acquiescence by a labor union in an employer's discriminatory practices, or failure by the collective bargaining representative to make an effective protest against such practices, constitutes participation in the unlawful acts.* However, it will be necessary to await the continued evolution of the law before the NLRB makes compliance with Title VII a requirement of national labor policy.

A far-reaching decision involving another aspect of the issue of the NLRB and racial discrimination was made by the Court of Appeals for the Eighth Circuit in *NLRB* v. *Mansion House Center Management Corp.*[202] In this 1973 decision the court, applying *Shelley,* held that the NLRB has an obligation to inquire into the racial practices of labor unions, and that it is constitutionally prohibited from certifying as exclusive bargaining representative a union that engages in discriminatory racial practices. In this case an employer had refused to bargain with a union that until 1968 maintained segregated locals and whose later membership practices allegedly discriminated against blacks. The union then complained to the NLRB, which ordered the company to bargain. The appellate court reversed the board's decision and denied enforcement of its order:

> In substance we hold that the remedial machinery of the National Labor Relations Act cannot be available to a union which is unwilling to correct past practices of racial discrimination. Federal complicity through recognition of a discriminating union serves not only to condone the discrimination, but in effect legitimizes and perpetuates such invidious practices. Certainly, such a degree of federal participation in the maintenance of racially discriminatory practices violates basic constitutional tenets.[203]

All decisions prior to the *Mansion House* case upheld the limited inquiry theory expressed in the findings of NLRB hearing

---

*See, for example, *U.S.* v. *Georgia Power Co.,* 474 F.2d 906, 5 FEP Cases 587 (5th Cir. 1973); *Carey* v. *Greyhound Lines, Inc.,* 500 F.2d 1372, 8 FEP Cases 1184 (5th Cir. 1974); *EEOC* v. *Detroit Edison Co.,* 515 F.2d 301, 10 FEP Cases 239, 1063 (6th Cir. 1975); and *Myers* v. *Gilman Paper Co.,* 392 F. Supp. 413, 10 FEP Cases 220 (S.D. Ga. 1975).

officers. The issue of discrimination by a union, if raised at all, went to the question of revocation of certification, not to initial certification. For various reasons—including employer reluctance to admit to interim liability, worker reluctance to defy the bargaining agent, and the paucity of minority workers' resources— suits to revoke certification on the grounds of racial discrimination have rarely been brought and the existence of the remedy has had minimal impact on the discriminatory practices of labor unions. By contrast, stringent enforcement of an antidiscrimination policy at the stage of initial NLRB certification would have a maximum effect on union racial practices, since initial certification is vital for most labor unions. *Mansion House* held for the first time that unions engaging in racial discrimination should be denied initial certification and that employers could invoke the discriminatory racial practices of a labor union as a reason for refusing to bargain.

In its opinion the court of appeals took judicial notice of the importance of discrimination by labor organizations:

> Today membership in a union is often the *sine qua non* for obtaining employment in most skilled crafts in this country . . . a union which discriminates in membership against blacks effectively deprives blacks of employment opportunities.[204]

In making a vital connection between equal employment opportunity and the role of the NLRB in the discriminatory acts of labor organizations, the court held that certification of a discriminatory union violated the right to equal protection:

> It is well settled that the Equal Protection Clause of the Fourteenth Amendment prohibits any state, or individual acting under the color of state authority, to discriminate on the basis of race, color, or religion. The Fifth Amendment's Due Process Clause has been held to legally encompass the Equal Protection Clause of the Fourteenth Amendment, thereby placing the same constitutional limitations on federal action as restricts state action.[205]

The involvement of the NLRB as a government instrumentality was noted by the court in applying the state action concept in *Mansion House:*

> When a governmental agency recognizes such a union to be the bargaining representative, it significantly becomes a willing participant in the union's discriminatory practices. Although the union itself is not a governmental instrumentality, the National Labor Relations Board is. . . . The Board seeks enforcement of its order requiring

collective bargaining in a federal court. Obviously, judicial enforcement of private discrimination cannot be sanctioned.[206]

The decision of the circuit court in *Mansion House* represents a significant departure from the traditional approach of the NLRB. As a result of *Mansion House,* the board is required to investigate the racial practices of unions before it grants certification as exclusive bargaining agent; it is prohibited from issuing such certification to discriminatory labor organizations; and, furthermore, the court suggested that the board apply Title VII standards, especially in the use of statistical evidence to establish a *prima facie* case of discrimination.

As a result of litigation, and the fact that the NLRB has found itself increasingly confronted with racial issues, the board on June 11, 1974, announced a new policy in cases involving discriminatory practices of labor unions.[207] The board stated that henceforth it would consider in its certification procedures contentions that a union should be denied certification as collective bargaining agent because of alleged discriminatory practices. However, "[w]hen an objection is filed with the NLRB in a representation election case, claiming that a union practices discrimination, the NLRB will judge the merits of the objection before issuing a certification—but only after an election the union has won."[208] Furthermore, the board refused to specify "what degree or form of invidious minority group discrimination would be sufficient to warrant withholding certification."[209]

The new policy was adopted in connection with the board's decision in a case involving a union election at Bekins Moving & Storage Co., in Miami, Florida, and Local 390 of the International Brotherhood of Teamsters.[210] The issue arose when the employer claimed that the union was disqualified from seeking a certification election under Section 9(c) of the NLRA on the ground that it engaged in discrimination on the basis of sex as well as against Spanish-speaking and Spanish-surnamed workers. In its 3-to-2 opinion, the board stated:

> The question of denying representative status through NLRB certification to unions because of discriminatory practices came before the Board after the 8th U.S. Circuit Court of Appeals issued a 1973 ruling in the *Mansion House Center Management Corporation* case. The Court declined to enforce an NLRB order that the Company bargain with Painters Union Local 115. The Company had refused to bargain on grounds of racial discrimination by the Union. The Court said a claim of racial discrimination allegedly practiced by a union is a rele-

vant area of inquiry for the NLRB when the defense is appropriately raised before the Board on an employer's refusal to bargain, and held that the remedial machinery of the Act cannot be available to a union which is unwilling to correct past practices of racial discrimination.[211]

The board acknowledged its constitutional obligations under *Mansion House* but decided to move very cautiously. It would proceed

> on a case-by-case basis, to determine whether the nature and quantum of the proof offered sufficiently shows a propensity for unfair representation as to require us, in order that our own action may conform to our constitutional duties, to take the drastic step of declining to certify a labor organization which has demonstrated in an election that it is the choice of the majority of employees. It is not our intention to take such a step lightly or incautiously, nor to regard every possible alleged violation of Title VII, for example, as grounds for refusing to issue a certificate. There will doubtless be cases in which we will conclude that correction of such statutory violations is best left to the expertise of other agencies or remedial orders less draconian than the total withholding of representative status.[212]

In the period between the announcement of the new policy and early 1976, the board did not deny certification to any labor organizations that won representation elections. In its decision in *Grant's Furniture Plaza*[213] the board held that statistical data demonstrating a discriminatory pattern, together with the Justice Department complaint documenting the international union's discriminatory practices against black and Spanish-surnamed workers, were insufficient evidence to refuse certification. A similar approach was taken in the board's action in *Bell and Howell Co.,* a sex discrimination case.[214] And in a construction union case, the full five-member board affirmed the decision of an administrative law judge that Sheet Metal Workers Local 102, in Washington, D.C., was not practicing racial discrimination even though it had repeatedly failed to refer nonwhite workers for employment. The board accepted the opinion that there was no "substantial evidentiary basis" to sustain the charge of racial discrimination.[215]

The board's refusal to act in these cases suggests that it has established excessive standards of proof. Its rejection of statistical evidence would indicate that the board is not complying with the intent of the *Mansion House* decision, which held that statistical evidence is valid in establishing that a union has been guilty of discriminatory racial practices.

Conclusion

In dealing with the issue of fair representation, the two railroad boards have demonstrated complete disregard for the needs of black workers in the railroad industry, and the National Labor Relations Board has failed to use its powers to attack discriminatory racial practices in other sectors of the economy. By neglecting the problems of black workers for so long, while encouraging and strengthening labor organizations regardless of their racial practices, all three boards have directly contributed to the severity of racial problems facing other government agencies.

One of the major reasons why labor unions have repeatedly defended discriminatory practices during the first ten years of the existence of Title VII is that the depressed condition of minority workers, in large part the result of inadequate and unfair representation in the past, has produced job expectations among white males based upon the systematic deprivation of nonwhites and women which the unions, for internal political reasons, have failed to substantially modify. This fact alone, given the influence of organized labor over the actions of the National Mediation Board and the National Labor Relations Board, warns against placing too much hope in a quick turn to effective action by these agencies.*

---

*The NLRB's limited conception of its role in eliminating racial discrimination is equally manifest in its response to charges of job bias based upon sex. The board has interpreted the NLRA in such/a narrow manner as to deprive itself of authority to remedy discriminatory practices in this area also. It has held, for example, that wage discrimination by an employer based on sex was not "inherently destructive" of employees' rights under the Act and thus could not be treated as an unfair labor practice. See *Jubilee Manufacturing Co.*, 202 NLRB No. 2, 89 LRRM 1482 (1973). Other board decisions have held that the existence of union locals segregated by sex is not per se a violation of the NLRA and does not justify decertification. See *American Mailing Corp.*, 197 NLRB No. 33, 80 LRRM 1294 (1972), and *Glass Blowers Association*, 2 CCH EPG p. 3244 (1973). The board ruled similarly in *Sheraton Park Hotel*—199 NLRB No. 104, 81 LRRM 1305 (1972)—but on the same issue a district court held that sex-segregated local unions violated Title VII. See *Evans* v. *Sheraton Park Hotel*, 5 FEP Cases 393, 5 CCH EPD para. 6290 (D. D.C. 1972), *affirmed in part, and vacated and remanded in part*, 503 F.2d 177, 8 FEP Cases 705 (D.C. Cir. 1974). In virtually every case involving racially segregated local unions, the courts have ordered integration. The ruling of the fourth circuit court in *U.S.* v. *International Longshoremen's Association* is typical: "We agree with the district judge that the maintenance of racially segregated locals inevitably breeds discrimination that violates the Act. Racial segregation limits both black and white employees to advancement only within the confines of their races. The position that would rightfully be an employee's, but for his race, may be filled by a person of lower seniority or inferior capability because the job traditionally has been reserved for either a white person from one local or a black person from the other." See 319 F. Supp. 737, 2 FEP Cases 1106 (D. Md. 1970); *aff'd*, 460 F.2d 497, 4 FEP Cases 719 (4th Cir. 1972); *cert. denied*, 409 U.S. 1007, 5

Moreover, the responsibility confronting unions and federal labor agencies has been greatly enlarged by Title VII. Under the *Steele* doctrine, the duty of fair representation was passive in nature. Title VII not only prohibits discrimination by both union and employer but changes the duty of fair representation to a requirement that the bargaining representative act affirmatively to prohibit employer discrimination.[216] Under Title VII, a union violates the law by agreeing to a collective bargaining contract that embodies racially discriminatory provisions, even if the union was not originally responsible for the discriminatory practices. Thus labor unions, which by their passivity or tacit consent allow discrimination against black workers and other minorities, are recognized as bearing equal responsibility under law with discriminatory employers.*

It is doubtful that the NLRB has grasped the full significance of the concept of the duty of fair representation as generated by cases brought under Title VII of the Civil Rights Act of 1964, and certainly it has not begun to understand the remedies required in cases of that character. The right to be the exclusive collective bargaining agent flows from a statute. The exclusive character of the bargaining relationship in turn generates the duty to represent all workers fairly. It seems quite sound to argue that where there is a failure of fair representation, the right to be the exclusive representative must be revoked.

In *Jenkins* v. *United Gas,*[217] the Court of Appeals for the Fifth Circuit laid down a constitutional standard regarding action of the courts and those administrative agencies charged with preventing and remedying employment discrimination.† In this and in other

---

FEP Cases 149 (1972). Federal courts have invariably applied precedents established in cases of racial discrimination to sex-bias rulings.

*In 1972 the EEOC extended the concept of union responsibility when it ruled that an international union had violated Title VII by failing to intervene to prevent its local from engaging in discriminatory treatment of black and Spanish-surnamed workers. The international union maintained that under the Taft-Hartley Act it was not accountable for unlawful acts of its locals unless it had ratified or authorized the conduct; but the EEOC concluded that an international union has an affirmative obligation to insure against its locals' engaging in discriminatory activity. When an international union grants a charter to a local, Title VII requires that it prohibit or eliminate practices that violate the Act, according to the ruling (EEOC Decision No. 71–1670, 4 FEP Cases 476). See also *Myers* v. *Gilman Paper Co.,* 10 FEP Cases 211 (S.D. Ga. 1974), 392 F. Supp. 413, 10 FEP Cases 220 (S.D. Ga. 1975).

†In deciding *Jenkins* the fifth circuit court drew upon its decision in *Potts* v. *Flax,* 313 F.2d 284 (5th Cir. 1963). *Jenkins* has now been explicitly or implicitly adopted by courts in four other circuits and one district of a fifth: *United States* v. *Bethlehem Steel Corp.,* 446 F.2d

decisions the courts have held that the executive and judicial arms of the government are under a constitutional duty to act affirmatively in cases involving employment discrimination and to order an end to such discrimination. The failure to act affirmatively, the court pointed out, is the equivalent of sanctioning the forbidden act. Such official sanction is, of course, constitutionally prohibited.

As has been voluminously demonstrated in a decade of litigation under Title VII, as well as in lawsuits prior to 1965, considerations of race frequently and directly affect conditions of employment. There is also a body of judicial opinion, beginning with *Steele*[218] in 1944, that requires the board to concern itself with certain aspects of the racial component in the collective bargaining process. Furthermore, the NLRB has for many years been involved in such matters and has acknowledged some responsibility in this regard. Additionally, a wide variety of racial issues are becoming increasingly pervasive in the conduct of labor-management affairs.

It is frequently argued that contentious problems of racial discrimination must not be permitted to interfere with the stability of the collective bargaining process. While many commentators generally admit the desirability of eliminating job discrimination, they warn against approaches that might have a disruptive effect upon industrial peace.* Although there now exists both constitu-

---

652, 3 FEP Cases 589 (2nd Cir. 1971); *Parham* v. *Southwestern Bell Tel. Co.,* 433 F.2d 421, 2 FEP Cases 1017 (8th Cir. 1970); *Blue Bell Boots* v. *EEOC,* 418 F.2d 355, 2 FEP Cases 228 (6th Cir. 1969); *Bowe* v. *Colgate-Palmolive Co.,* 416 F.2d 711, 2 FEP Cases 121 (7th Cir. 1969); *Rosen* v. *Public Serv. Elec. & Gas Co.,* 328 F. Supp. 454, 2 FEP Cases 1090 (D. N.J. 1970). The *Jenkins* principle was significantly reinforced and expanded in a non-Title VII case, *Adams* v. *Richardson* (HEW), 356 F. Supp. 92 (D. D.C. 1973), *modified and affirmed in part,* 480 F.2d 1159 (D.C. Cir. 1973) *(en banc), supplemented and modified on remand,* 391 F. Supp. 269 (D. D.C. 1975), relief granted.

*There is a growing body of literature on this issue. For examples of some recent interpretation and argument, see Fred J. Naffziger, "The NLRB Attitude on Discrimination and the Judicial Response," *Labor Law Journal,* January 1975, pp. 21–32; Charles B. Craven, "Minority Action Versus Union Exclusivity: The Need to Harmonize NLRA and Title VII Policies," *Hastings Law Journal,* September 1974, pp. 1–56; Bernard D. Meltzer, "The National Labor Relations Act and Racial Discrimination: The More Remedies, the Better?" *University of Chicago Law Review,* Vol. 42, No. 1 (Fall 1974), pp. 1–46; Recent Cases, "Labor Law—Protected Activity," *Harvard Law Review,* Vol. 87 (1974), pp. 656–665; Comment, "The Inevitable Interplay of Title VII and the National Labor Relations Act: A New Role for the NLRB," *University of Pennsylvania Law Review,* Vol. 123 (1974), pp. 158–186; Note, "Title VII and NLRA: Protection of Extra-Union Opposition to Employment Discrimination," *Michigan Law Review,* December 1973, pp. 313–331; Note, "Allocating Jurisdiction Over Racial Issues Between the EEOC and NLRB: A Proposal," *Cornell Law Review,* Vol. 54 (1969), pp. 943–957.

tional and statutory authority for the right of black workers and those of other minority groups to be free from job discrimination, agencies of government as well as employers and organized labor resist the changes that are required if this right is to be achieved.

Alteration of many aspects of the collective bargaining system is necessary in the light of judicial interpretation of Title VII. That the goal of equal employment opportunity must be given at least equal priority with the purposes of collective bargaining was indicated by Justice Powell on behalf of a unanimous Supreme Court in *Alexander* v. *Gardner-Denver Co.:*

> These [collective bargaining] rights are conferred on employees collectively to foster the processes of bargaining and properly may be exercised or relinquished by the union as collective bargaining agent to obtain economic benefits for unit members. Title VII, on the other hand, stands on plainly different ground; it concerns not majoritarian processes, but an individual's right to equal employment opportunities. Title VII strictures are absolute and represent a congressional command that each employee be free from discriminatory practices.[219]

Since the adoption of the National Labor Relations Act in 1935, a comprehensive system of labor-management relations has developed. Whatever the strengths and weaknesses of this structure in other areas, it is an operational system that has either ignored or resisted the requirements of contemporary civil rights law. It is within this context that the response to racial issues by the most important government agency directly involved in the conduct of collective bargaining must be viewed.

Some commentators have argued that the National Labor Relations Act should not be a vehicle for eliminating discriminatory employment practices and that Title VII should be the exclusive remedy.* This argument not only ignores the implication of *Jenkins*[220] and *Alexander* v. *Gardner-Denver Co.*[221] but also ignores the legislative history of Title VII and the board's response to the relevant aspects of that history.

In *Business League of Gadsden*[222] a majority of the board reiterated its position in *Hughes Tool*[223] that certain forms of racial discrimination by a bargaining agent, such as the refusal of a union to process the grievance of a black employee, are unfair labor

---

*See, for example, Bernard E. Meltzer, "The National Labor Relations Act and Racial Discrimination: The More Remedies, the Better?" *University of Chicago Law Review*, Vol. 42, No. 1 (Fall 1974), pp. 1–46.

practices.[224] The majority also noted the line of cases represented by *Ford Motor Co.* v. *Huffman*,[225] in which the Supreme Court defined the statutory obligations of the collective bargaining agent to represent all members equally.

In responding to the minority dissent in *Business League* the majority of the board referred to the legislative history of Title VII:

> We are not unmindful that in Title VII of the Civil Rights Act of 1964 the Congress has legislated concerning racial discrimination by labor organizations. But the reach of Title VII goes far beyond such discrimination, proscribing as it does discrimination on the basis of race, color, religion, sex, or national origin by employers, employment agencies, and joint labor-management committees, as well as labor organizations. Moreover, the Board's powers and duties are in no way limited by Title VII. On June 12, 1964, before the passage of the Civil Rights Act of 1964, the Senate rejected by a vote of 59 to 29 an amendment to Title VII which had been proposed by Senator Tower (R-Texas) and which perhaps would have had the effect of limiting the Board's powers. (See the Congressional Record (daily copy), 88th Congress, 2nd Session, pp. 13171–73.)[226]

It bears repeating that in enacting Title VII, Congress expressly refused to give exclusive jurisdiction over employment discrimination to the EEOC. The Tower amendment proposing just that was rejected by the Senate. Title VII has no preemptive effect over the National Labor Relations Act. Significantly, the board itself recognized this in *Business League of Gadsden.*[227] The Court of Appeals for the District of Columbia later emphasized this point in *United Packinghouse Workers Union* v. *NLRB (Farmers' Cooperative Compress)*,[228] in which the court held, as a matter of law, that discrimination based on race by an employer constitutes an unfair labor practice, and declared that the Civil Rights Act of 1964

> itself says nothing to indicate that the National Labor Relations Board is ousted from jurisdiction in these matters, and an examination of legislative history demonstrates that the Board was not meant to be. 110 Congressional Record (Part 6) 7207 (1964).[229]

Again in 1972 the Senate rejected an amendment that, like the Tower amendment in 1964, would have made Title VII the exclusive remedy.[230]* Furthermore, the Supreme Court in *Alexan-*

---

*The legislative history of the Equal Employment Opportunity Act of 1972, which amended Title VII (Public Law 92–261, approved March 24, 1972), is replete with references

der v. *Gardner-Denver Co.*[231] took note of these developments in the legislative history of Title VII.

Given this history, it is evident that nothing contained in Title VII detracts from the statutory authority of the NLRB to invoke its considerable powers in appropriate cases of job discrimination based on race.

Even if the EEOC were a far more effective agency, it could not by itself achieve the purposes of Title VII.* Other government agencies must accept responsibility for enforcing civil rights laws within their jurisdictions. If black workers and members of other minority groups are not to be denied the most effective remedy, the EEOC and the NLRB must function with concurrent jurisdiction.

---

to the exclusive remedy issue. Senator Hruska, speaking on behalf of his proposal to give the EEOC exclusive jurisdiction, stated: "The amendment which I have introduced on this subject would provide that, with certain named exceptions, a charge filed with the commission shall be the exclusive remedy of any person claiming to be aggrieved by an unlawful employment practice" (p. 1379). Senator Williams in his response stated that "to make Title VII the exclusive remedy for employment discrimination would be inconsistent with our entire legislative history of the Civil Rights Act. It would jeopardize the degree and scope of remedies available to workers of our country. To lock the aggrieved person into the administrative remedy would narrow rather than strengthen our civil rights enforcement effort. . . . This is especially true where the legal issues under other laws may not fall within the scope of Title VII, or where the employee, employer, or labor organization does not fall within the jurisdictional confines of Title VII. . . . The peculiarly damaging nature of employment discrimination is such that the individual who is frequently forced to face a large and powerful employer, should be accorded every protection that the law has in its purview and that the person should not be forced to seek his remedy in only one place" (p. 1404). Senator Williams called attention to the testimony previously presented before the Committee on Labor and Public Welfare by Assistant Attorney General David L. Norman, who had stated on behalf of the Department of Justice: "In the field of civil rights, the Congress has regularly insured that there be a variety of enforcement devices to insure that all available resources are brought to bear on the sources of discrimination" (p. 1401). Senator Javits, arguing against the Hruska amendment, noted that "Title VII does not have the facility to reach the bargaining process as the NLRA can where the issue heavily involves trade unions and a whole union could be decertified" (p. 1512). The view of the EEOC on the matter of exclusive jurisdiction was stated by the commission in an *ex parte* statement submitted to the Interstate Commerce Commission concerning Equal Opportunities in Surface Transportation: "Title VII of the Civil Rights Act of 1964 did not grant exclusive jurisdiction to the Equal Employment Opportunity Commission (EEOC) in all matters of employment discrimination over which it has jurisdiction. On the contrary, its very design provides for the uses of all available means to achieve the end of employment discrimination" (*ex parte* No. 278, p. 56, quoted p. 1507). The above quotations are from Committee on Labor and Public Welfare, U.S. Senate, *Legislative History of the Equal Employment Opportunity Act of 1972* (H.R. 1746, P.L. 92–261) (Washington, D.C.: U.S. Government Printing Office, November 1972).

*According to Lowell W. Perry, chairman of the EEOC, "even if we were able to successfully resolve all of the more than 280,000 individual charges filed with us over the past ten years, systematic employment practices having a disparate impact on one or more groups protected by Title VII would remain."—Statement Before the House Subcommittee on Equal Opportunities, September 22, 1975, EEOC document.

In a variety of cases that come before the NLRB, issues of race and labor are inextricably related and racial practices are indeed a "condition of employment." To regard questions of race and labor in the industrial context as separate or even separable is to ignore fundamental realities of the workplace. In many situations, resort to the board would be more effective than resort to the cumbersome and financially expensive procedures under Title VII. Of great importance to minority workers, who frequently do not have adequate resources to pursue a Title VII claim to final exhaustion, is the fact that the NLRB provides a cost-free procedure from initial investigation to litigation in an appellate court. In addition, the time lag for cases pending before the NLRB is much shorter than in district courts where an aggrieved worker is required to file suit if the EEOC is unable to obtain compliance with the law. And the NLRB, unlike the EEOC, is not required to defer to state and local fair employment practice agencies.

There are those who argue that concurrent jurisdiction would interfere with the NLRB's other traditional functions and that its efficiency would be impaired.* Such arguments are predicated on the false assumption that Title VII creates an exclusive remedy, and they also reflect a refusal to give a high priority to the goal of eliminating employment discrimination. The efficiency argument is a specious one, as involvement by the board in racial issues will make it neither more nor less efficient. The problem of the board's inefficiency and the well-known need to reform its procedures are not valid reasons for its refusal to respond affirmatively to major changes in the law and public policy. If the reordering of priorities took place and concurrent jurisdiction between the two agencies became the reality, then the necessary organizational and procedural adjustments would follow. Furthermore, the operations of the board must be generally improved if it is to effectively fulfill all of its responsibilities including the processing of complaints of race and sex discrimination that fall within its authority.

*This argument is pressed by Meltzer in his *University of Chicago Law Review* article, *supra.* Early in 1976 attorneys for the AFL-CIO and the U.S. Chamber of Commerce in oral argument before the NLRB urged the board to overturn the *Mansion House* (473 F.2d 471, 82 LRRM 2608) and *Bekins* (211 NLRB No. 7, 86 LRRM 1323) rulings. The union and employer representatives jointly argued that the involvement of the board in problems of race and sex discrimination would be "enormously time-consuming" and would adversely affect the functioning of the board. They also argued that the board is not empowered or required to condition a union's certification on the absence of discrimination—*Labor Relations Reporter,* News and Background Section, February 9, 1976, 91 LRR 102–103 (Washington, D.C.: The Bureau of National Affairs, Inc.).

At certain stages of development, policy choices become available to institutions, public and private. Either new approaches are taken as a result of developments in the law and altered social conditions, or old policies become frozen in administrative procedures and progress is obstructed. Title VII has confronted many institutions with this choice, and how they respond to the challenge reveals much about their utility and future social roles.

The history of the National Labor Relations Board in relation to problems of racial discrimination suggests that it will not rush to seize the great opportunity generated by Title VII. If the NLRB were to enforce the legal prohibitions against job discrimination that are within its authority, it would have a major impact in eliminating patterns of employment discrimination. Unfortunately, there is every reason to believe that this development will be postponed until the courts compel the NLRB to fulfill the constitutional imperative as a matter of national policy.

Part 2

Federal Administrative Action:
Executive Orders Prohibiting
Employment Discrimination
During World War II

4

The Fair Employment Practice Committee
(1941–1946)

When Title VII, the employment section of the Civil Rights Act of 1964, was adopted a quarter century of federal executive orders prohibiting discrimination in employment by government contractors had preceded it. The Fair Employment Practice Committee, which spanned the years 1941 to 1946, is of particular significance because its records document the patterns of job discrimination at that time and provide the basis for an analysis of the continuity of racial practices in many industries. In addition, the records make possible a comparison with the experience of the Equal Employment Opportunity Commission created by the Civil Rights Act of 1964.

The executive orders of the Roosevelt Administration establishing the Fair Employment Practice Committee represent the beginning of governmental intervention against racial discrimination in employment through the administrative powers of the executive branch of the Federal Government. The FEPC, with no direct enforcement power, was not able to eliminate discriminatory job patterns and, in retrospect, had little effect in changing the status of nonwhite workers. Nevertheless, for the first time the authority of federal administrative agencies was utilized to investigate, record, and, in a few instances, to act against employment discrimination.

The committee's extensive documentation and public exposure of job discrimination was an important factor in generating litigation by black workers that began the evolution of contempo-

173

rary legal prohibitions against discrimination in employment. Most important of all, the FEPC initiated the process that led to a new judicial perception of racial discrimination in employment. It was a vital link in the continuing development of the law from the early 1940s to the 1970s.

Through the records and investigative hearings of the FEPC we are able to examine nationwide patterns of discrimination against Negro workers during a period of full employment for white workers—the period of World War II. The committee's hearings in the aircraft, shipbuilding, railroad, merchant marine, and other major industries demonstrated that Negroes were excluded from jobs or limited to segregated work even in those sectors of the economy that experienced acute manpower short-ages. According to the FEPC, the "most important hearings" were those involving twenty-three railroads and the fourteen labor unions of their employees; the International Brotherhood of Boilermakers and certain west coast shipyards, including the Kaiser Company, the Oregon Shipbuilding Company, the Western Pipe and Steel Company, the shipbuilding division of the Consolidated Steel Corporation, and the California Shipbuilding Company; also the Philadelphia Transportation Company and its employees' union; the Los Angeles Railway Corporation; and the St. Louis hearings involving a variety of defense contractors.[1] Comparison of the committee's findings during the World War II period with those of the Equal Employment Opportunity Commission indicates the persistence of discriminatory patterns over a twenty-five-year period—indeed, in many industries only the names of the plaintiffs have changed.*

*In some instances, including cases that involved the International Association of Machinists, the Brotherhood of Railway Clerks, and the operating railroad brotherhoods, the racial practices were found to be virtually identical to those of twenty-five years ago. The following example illustrates a historical pattern. In the early 1940s the FEPC received complaints against the International Longshoremen's Association, AFL, charging a pattern of segregated locals and discriminatory job assignments in Atlantic coast cities and in the ILA's gulf district. Twenty-five years later the EEOC received complaints against the ILA involving several of the same locals and the same issues. In Philadelphia the commission found "reasonable cause" in charges brought by members of segregated black ILA locals that the all-white unit, Local 142, which operates the hiring hall for checkers and clerks, refused to refer black workers to these jobs. EEOC Case No. 5–11–2804 *et seq.*, filed November 28, 1966. The EEOC also found reasonable cause in charges brought by segregated black locals against white locals of the gulf district in Galveston and Port Arthur, Texas, and against local unions on the Atlantic coast. EEOC Case No. AU68–7–47, filed July 28, 1967; EEOC Case No. 7–2–110 *et seq.*, filed January 26, 1967; and EEOC Case No. 6–9–7721 *et seq.*, filed January 26, 1966. The racial practices of the ILA have changed little over the past quarter century; segregated locals with whites obtaining preferential treatment are still characteristic. In 1972 the Court of Appeals for the Fourth Circuit affirmed a decision of the district court in Baltimore that

During the era that preceded World War II—the Great Depression of the 1930s—Negro workers had suffered extreme hardship for a longer time and more extensively than any other group in the American labor force. As Irving Bernstein wrote in *The Lean Years:*

> The unemployed were distributed unevenly. The numbers increased as one descended the scales of skill, income, and ethnic origin. Managerial employees suffered least, followed in order by the clerical and manual groups, with the unskilled at the bottom. Those with higher incomes were more likely to hold on to their jobs than those with low incomes. Whites made out much better than Negroes. Since manual workers with low incomes, many of them Negroes, concentrated in the metropolitan areas, large cities were worse off than small.[2]

And Raymond Wolters has further documented the Negro workers' situation in the 1930s:

> Available statistics indicate that the position of urban Negroes during the Great Depression was particularly desperate. Reports from Urban League investigators in 106 American cities revealed that "with a few notable exceptions . . . the proportion of Negroes unemployed was from 30 to 60 percent greater than for whites.". . . The Federal Emergency Relief Administration reported that in the nation's cities the proportion of all persons on relief was almost three times as high for Negroes (26.7 percent) as for whites (9.6 percent).[3]*

---

ordered the ILA to merge segregated locals, operate a single, integrated hiring hall, institute a nondiscriminatory seniority system, and fill permanent vacancies in work crews on the basis of seniority rather than race. The appeals court said, "[s]ince there is no substantial difference in the locals except race, the evidence fully supports the trial court's finding that ILA chartered and maintained segregated locals in the port of Baltimore."—*United States* v. *I.L.A. Locals 829 and 853,* 319 F. Supp. 737, 2 FEP Cases 1106 (D.C. Md. 1970); *aff'd,* 460 F.2d 497, 4 FEP Cases 719 (4th Cir. 1972); *cert. denied,* 409 U.S. 1007, 5 FEP Cases 149, 5 EPD para. 8031 (1972). In 1971, thirty-seven locals in the gulf district were found to be engaging in unlawful discriminatory practices. In this case the court found that there was a rigid pattern of racial segregation—sixteen white locals, nineteen black locals, two Mexican-American locals—and that work was assigned on a racial basis. The court rejected the defendant unions' argument that the government was imposing an illegal quota plan in ordering the elimination of job assignments on the basis of race and held that "it is not the racial composition of the community that controls, but the number of blacks and whites that make themselves available for longshore work that counts."—*United States* v. *I.L.A., et al.,* 334 F. Supp. 976, 4 FEP Cases 6 (S.D. Tex. 1971). On April 11, 1975, the Court of Appeals for the Fifth Circuit ordered the integration of the thirty-seven local unions and stated that "the segregated unions . . . by their very nature deny equal employment opportunities. . . ." The court rejected the argument of the ILA that the unions were "separate but equal" and held that the requirements of Title VII could not be satisfied "short of the merger in each particular port of the racially segregated locals within that port."—*EEOC* v. *Longshoremen* (ILA), 511 F.2d 273, 10 FEP Cases 545, 9 EPD para. 10, 061 (5th Cir. 1975).

*For more data on this period, and for the effects of the Depression on Negro

By 1940 the situation of white workers had improved to some extent, but the black community was still experiencing the full impact of the Depression. In April 1940, 22 percent of nonwhites in the labor market were unemployed compared to 17.7 percent of white workers;[4] in August 1940, with employment increased overall by two million, the unemployment rate for whites was 13 percent, but the rate for Negroes had declined by only one tenth of 1 percent[5]—leaving 21.9 percent still unemployed.* Gunnar Myrdal wrote, in *An American Dilemma,* that "in October, 1940, only 5.4 percent of all [U.S.] Employment Service placements in 20 selected defense industries (airplanes, automobiles, shipbuilding, machinery, iron, steel, chemicals, and so on) were nonwhite, and this proportion had, by April, 1941, *declined* to 2.5 percent."[6]

Even before the United States entered World War II in December 1941, it was clear that the nation would need the maximum utilization of all available manpower, including the millions of workers who were members of minority groups, to meet anticipated war-production demands. In mid-1940 the National Defense Advisory Commission established an office in its Labor Division to advise on training and placement of Negro workers; the U.S. Office of Education announced a policy of nondiscrimination

---

communities, see Bernard Sternsher, ed., *The Negro in Depression and War* (Chicago: Quadrangle Books, 1969); Raymond Wolters, *Negroes and The Great Depression* (Westport, Conn.: Greenwood Publishing Corp., 1970). A study originally prepared by the Federal Writers Project under the working title "Harlem—The Negroes of New York (An Informal Social History)" contains a description of the largest Negro community during the years 1929 through 1935. See Chapter XVII, "The Depression," in Roi Ottley and William J. Weatherby, eds., *The Negro in New York* (New York: Praeger Publishers, 1969). According to this study, "[d]iscrimination against employment of Negroes had practically closed the doors to any and all types of occupations. Generally, the poorer half of the colored population lived on an income which was only forty-six percent of that of the poorer half of the white population.

"The people of Harlem regarded the public utilities and trade unions as the chief agencies of discrimination."—p. 268.

*For additional information on the status of Negro workers in defense industries during this period, see U.S. Bureau of the Census, *Sixteenth Census of the United States, 1940, Population,* Vol. III, *The Labor Force,* Pt. I, United States Summary, tables 60, 61, 62 (pp. 84 *et seq.*); "The Negro's War," *Fortune,* Vol. 15 (1942), pp. 79 *et seq.;* Lester B. Granger, "Negroes and War Production," *Survey Graphic,* Vol. 31 (1942), pp. 469 *et seq.; Negro Workers and the National Defense Program* (Washington, D.C.: Social Security Board, Bureau of Employment Security, September 16, 1942); Robert C. Weaver, "Racial Employment Trends in National Defense," *Phylon* (Atlanta, Georgia), Vol. 2 (1941), pp. 337–358, and Vol. 3 (1942), pp. 22–30; "The Employment of the Negro in War Industries," *Journal of Negro Education,* Vol. 12 (1943), pp. 386–390; "Employment of Negroes in United States War Industries," *International Labour Review,* Vol. 1 (1944), pp. 141–159; *Labor Supply and Demand in Selected Defense Occupations Through the Period May-November 1941* (Washington, D.C.: Federal Employment Security Agency, September 1941); Robert C. Weaver, *Negro Labor—A National Problem* (New York: Harcourt, Brace & Co., 1946).

in federally funded vocational training programs; and the U.S. Employment Service was directed to refer workers to war-production industries on a nondiscriminatory basis. But these limited governmental policies were inadequate and rarely enforced, and failed to eliminate widespread practices of job discrimination against Negroes and members of other minority groups.

Negro leaders realized that to reverse the traditional exclusion of Negroes from many job categories and labor unions would require more extensive and direct government efforts. If Negro workers were to be admitted into the expanding defense industries, the racial hiring policies of employers and the exclusionary membership practices of labor unions would have to be fundamentally changed. Typical of the racial employment practices of expanding wartime industry were these unabashed acknowledgments from major aircraft companies: "I regret to say," Vultee Aircraft's industrial relations manager wrote to an officer of the National Negro Congress, "that it is not the policy of this Company to employ people other than of the Caucasian race, consequently, we are not in a position to offer your people employment at this time."[7] The following year, 1941, the president of North American Aviation stated that "[w]hile we are in complete sympathy with the Negroes, it is against company policy to employ them as aircraft workers or mechanics . . . regardless of their training. . . . There will be some jobs as janitors for Negroes."[8]

Many labor unions, especially the craft unions of the American Federation of Labor, were committed to discriminatory policies which had a direct and adverse effect on black workers. For years A. Philip Randolph, president of the Brotherhood of Sleeping Car Porters, had tried to persuade the AFL to act against its affiliated unions that excluded Negroes or were otherwise discriminatory. In a speech at the AFL's 1940 convention Randolph continued his efforts: "We think that something should be done besides a mere perfunctory statement of this matter . . . we have from year to year made perfunctory statements about this question, we have made generalizations about it, but we have done nothing constructive."[9] In 1941 the AFL convention again rejected a resolution introduced by Randolph and Milton P. Webster, also of the Sleeping Car Porters, calling for creation of a committee to investigate the discriminatory practices of AFL unions. In debate on the resolution Randolph told the convention delegates:

I want to cite a few cases [of discrimination] . . . . The AFL unions
in the shipbuilding yards in New Orleans refuse membership to
Negro workers, although the company has expressed a willingness to
employ them.

Recently, Metal Trades Department unions have secured at some
yards, through training formulas, a monopoly on trainees who will be
upgraded in these yards.

Stabilization pacts between the O.P.M. [Office of Production
Management] and certain of the building trades have resulted in
disqualifying qualified colored artisans from defense employment and
thereby retarding defense efforts. . . . The most conspicuous and
consistent denial of employment of Negroes which can be attributed
almost directly to union influence is found at the Boeing Aircraft
Corporation in Seattle, Washington. From the very beginning of the
National defense program, the Boeing Company has given as its
excuse for not employing Negroes the fact that it had a contract with
the Aeronautical Mechanics Union, Local 751, International Association of Machinists, AFL, and that the union accepts white members
only.[10]

Randolph went on to recount the specific ways and places in which
the International Brotherhood of Boilermakers and the International Association of Machinists at the Tampa Shipbuilding
Corporation and other defense installations around the country had
forced Negroes out of their jobs during this period.

In 1942 the AFL convention rejected a resolution similar to
those Randolph and Webster had offered in previous years. It also
rejected one proposing "[t]hat workers who are now in Uncle
Sam's uniform . . . be given the freedom and eligibility to join any
union affiliated with the AFL at the end of the war without regard
to race, color, religion or national origin,"[11] together with other
resolutions condemning discrimination by affiliated unions.

The proceedings of AFL conventions during the 1940s and
after confirm Gunnar Myrdal's statement: "The fact that the
American Federation of Labor as such is officially against racial
discrimination does not mean much. The Federation has never
done anything to check racial discrimination exercised by its
member organizations."[12]

In 1941, confronted with the intransigence of powerful
industrial corporations and organized labor, as well as the
ineffectiveness of governmental policies, Randolph planned a mass
march on Washington to protest the exclusion of Negro workers
from defense and other industries. The march was scheduled for

July 1, and more than 10,000 participants were expected. Just before the march, however, after a conference with Negro leaders President Roosevelt pledged swift executive action, and the demonstration was canceled.*

On June 25, 1941, the President issued Executive Order 8802,[13] which stated that it was the "duty of employers and of labor organizations to provide for the full and equitable participation of all workers in defense industries, without discrimination because of race, creed, color or national origin," and established a five-man Fair Employment Practice Committee to "receive and investigate complaints of discrimination" and to "take appropriate steps" to obtain compliance. This was to be accomplished through investigation, public exposure, and persuasion. (See Volume II, Appendix B, for complete text of Executive Order 8802.)

In July the President increased the committee membership to six and appointed Mark Ethridge, publisher of the *Louisville Courier-Journal,* as the committee's first chairman. The other members were representatives from the American Federation of Labor, the Congress of Industrial Organizations (at that time separate organizations), and the Brotherhood of Sleeping Car Porters, as well as one from corporate management and a Negro attorney who was a member of the Chicago City Council. In May 1942 the number of committee members was increased to seven and Dr. Malcolm S. MacLean, president of Hampton Institute, became chairman.

On May 27, 1943, President Roosevelt issued Executive Order 9346,[14] which reorganized the FEPC and expanded its jurisdiction beyond defense industries to include virtually all enterprises whose functioning affected the national interest. Coverage was extended to "all employers, and the unions of their employees, engaged in the production of war materials or in activities necessary for the maintenance of such production or for the utilization of war materials, whether or not these employers have contractual relations with the Government."[15] It was "the duty of all employers, including the several Federal departments and agencies, and all labor organizations . . . to eliminate discrimination in regard to hire, tenure, terms or conditions of employment, or union membership"[16] because of race, creed, color, or national origin.

*For a history of the March on Washington Movement, see Herbert Garfinkel, *When Negroes March: The March on Washington Movement in the Organizational Politics for FEPC* (Glencoe, Ill.: The Free Press, 1959).

The first chairman of the new committee was Msgr. Francis J. Haas, dean of the School of Social Sciences at Catholic University. When he resigned, Malcolm Ross, author, journalist, and former information director of the National Labor Relations Board, was appointed chairman in October of 1943, and was to remain chairman until the FEPC was dissolved in June 1946. Ostensibly an independent agency directly responsible to the President, the FEPC was administratively in the Office of Production Management and later functioned as part of the War Production Board.

Although the committee still had no enforcement powers, other than reporting a citation of noncompliance to the President, it had investigatory jurisdiction over complaints against employers and unions. Of the 14,000 complaints handled by the committee from 1943 to 1946, 80 percent were based on race discrimination.[17]

Altogether, the nation's first Fair Employment Practice Committee received 250 complaints against labor unions,[18] well over a third of them from the South,[19] and held hearings in Los Angeles, Chicago, New York, and Birmingham to investigate the status of Negroes in defense training and employment. Complaints and investigations involving employers and labor unions jointly were among the FEPC's major cases; these demonstrated industry-wide patterns and revealed the extent and consequences of discriminatory labor-management agreements.

The most significant cases were based upon complaints filed by Negro workers in mass-production industries and related employment—such as railroad, longshore, maritime, and urban transit services—and in the building trades. Since these have long been highly unionized areas of the economy, where organized labor through its collective bargaining agreements has substantial control over initial hiring and seniority and promotion systems, the racial practices of unions in these industries were a decisive factor in the perpetuation of discriminatory racial patterns. The FEPC found that, especially in the South and West, "the craft unions which predominate in war industry either refuse to admit Negroes to membership or grant them limited status"[20] and that "in every regional office complaints of discrimination because of race were more frequent than for any other category."[21]

Not surprisingly, since initial application for employment most often had to be made directly to employers (including many who were restricted in their hiring practices by collective bargaining agreements with unions), by far the greatest number of complaints were lodged against employers. FEPC's *First Report* gave this breakdown for a one-year period:

> [M]ost of the complaints reported to the Committee alleged discrimination in private industry, described for coding purposes as "business." These charges accounted for 2,833 or 69.4 percent of all cases docketed between July 1, 1943, and June 30, 1944. Complaints filed against Federal agencies numbered 998, forming 24.5 percent of the total, and those against labor unions, 250 or 6.1 percent.[22]

These figures in themselves would constitute an impressive argument for the primary role of industry in perpetuating discriminatory employment practices were it not for the committee's findings on the disposition of charges of racial discrimination against the three categories cited above—"business," government agencies, and labor unions:

> With regard to disposition, it will be noted that the majority of cases satisfactorily adjusted involved business. Of the total 3,030 cases closed, 890 or 29.4 percent were in this category while only 192 forming 6.3 percent involved Government agencies and 17 or 0.6 percent unions. A comparison of cases docketed with cases closed showed that complaints against business were received, closed, and satisfactorily adjusted at a much faster rate than those against Government agencies and unions.[23]

The excessively low overall figure of less than 1 percent of satisfactorily adjusted cases involving charges of employment discrimination against labor unions is further scrutinized in the committee's breakdown of such figures by month: "The comparative figures for satisfactory adjustments are as follows: Business 74.2 cases per month, Government 16, and unions 1.4. It is clear that industry, when challenged, eliminated discrimination much more readily than labor unions."[24]

The same year the FEPC was established—1941—the Office of Production Management and its Labor Division, with Sidney Hillman of the Congress of Industrial Organizations as OPM codirector, were given direct administrative responsibility for obtaining maximum utilization of the labor force. In an effort to prevent labor strife, the Labor Division of the OPM negotiated a series of "stabilization agreements," which permitted unions to maintain closed-shop contracts* in shipbuilding, aircraft, construc-

---

*Closed shops were created by collective bargaining agreements specifying that only union members in good standing could be employed and that such membership was a

tion, and other industries in exchange for union "no-strike" assurances. Such agreements were signed with the AFL's Metal Trades Council as well as with the Building and Construction Trades Department of the federation. As Robert C. Weaver wrote:

> Many of the unions which were parties to these stabilization pacts either barred capable Negroes from membership, or created separate and auxiliary unions for Negroes and systematically discriminated against these Negro locals in referring men to jobs. In many instances the net result of stabilization pacts was to disqualify colored artisans and potential semi-skilled men from defense employment. . . . Where, in such instances, there was a conflict between the operation of these agreements and the announced policy of non-discrimination in defense employment, OPM supported the stabilization pacts.[25]

The closed-shop agreements encouraged by high government officials and enforced by labor unions that excluded Negroes from membership were an important factor in maintaining mass Negro unemployment as well as underemployment among skilled Negro workers qualified for placement in essential defense industries. Closed-shop agreements were one of the major devices used by unions to exclude Negro workers from jobs during World War II. By allowing and even encouraging such agreements, the government contributed greatly to the unions' power to exclude Negroes from employment.

Commenting on the condition of Negro workers at the beginning of World War II, the FEPC reported:

> The percentage of Negroes in manufacturing was lower than it had been 30 years before. Although every tenth American is a Negro, only 1 Negro in 20 was in defense industry. Every seventh white American was a skilled craftsman; only 1 Negro in 22 had skilled rating. Many trade unions had constitutional barriers to Negro membership.[26]

In its *First Report* the FEPC described in detail the status of Negro workers in the economy:

> Comparisons between the occupations of whites and Negroes in 1940 reveal that Negro labor was disproportionately concentrated in

---

condition of continued employment. The closed-shop agreement was outlawed by the Taft-Hartley Act of 1947. In *James* v. *Marinship Corporation,* 25 Cal.2d 721, 155 P.2d 329, 15 LRRM 798 (1945), the Supreme Court of California held that a union with monopoly control of jobs in its jurisdiction could not enforce a closed-shop agreement against Negro workers who were denied union membership because of their race. De facto closed shops continued to exist, especially in the construction industry.

unskilled, service, and agricultural jobs. Agricultural workers and other laborers constituted 62.2 percent of all employed Negro men but only 28.5 percent of all employed white men. Only about 5 percent of Negro men as compared with approximately 30 percent of white men were engaged in professional, semiprofessional, proprietary, managerial, and clerical and sales occupations. Skilled craftsmen represented 15.6 percent of employed white men but only 4.4 percent of employed colored men. Moreover, more than half of the Negro craftsmen were mechanics or artisans in the construction trades, further indicating the scarcity of Negro skilled workers in manufacturing industries. Striking differences also were shown between the occupations of white and colored women.

When the period of defense preparation began in 1940, local white labor was absorbed and outside white workers were imported into centers of expanding activity, but the local Negro labor supply was not utilized to any appreciable degree. Both management and the unions practiced a policy of excluding Negroes from the new job openings. The Tolan Committee found in 1941 that 9 A. F. of L. unions and the Railway Brotherhoods still had constitutional provisions barring Negroes from membership. Numerous other unions discriminated by tacit consent or by forcing Negroes into auxiliaries. A survey in the fall of 1941 by the Bureau of Employment Security of the Social Security Board revealed that Negroes would not be considered by industry for 51 percent of 282,215 job openings expected to occur by February 1942. The War Manpower Commission estimated early in 1942 that nonwhites constituted 2.5 to 3 percent of employees in war industries.[27]

As wartime employment continued to expand at a rapid rate, labor organizations that excluded or segregated Negroes began to fear that traditional discriminatory patterns and, indeed, the entire dual racial labor structure would be weakened by the urgent need to utilize all available manpower. Anticipating that union exclusionary practices and control of jobs would be abolished if the racial caste system were breached, organized labor was adamant in demanding that the color line in employment be rigidly enforced.

In the past, organized action including intimidation and violence had been used to force black workers out of many jobs they had long held, or to prevent them from entering new occupations; but, for the most part, such activity had no legal sanction. During World War II discriminatory labor-management agreements, sanctioned and protected by law, were to an unprecedented extent the principal method of exclusion. In many industries this was done overtly. In others, racial exclusion or segregation was enforced through the application of closed-shop requirements and various restrictive provisions in union contracts.

In the following chapters, which analyze the major cases of the Fair Employment Practice Committee, it becomes clear that the collective bargaining process was used jointly by management and unions in many defense and defense-related industries to the detriment of Negro workers. The extensive investigations by the FEPC document how employers and labor organizations enforced discriminatory collective bargaining agreements which codified industrywide racial practices in many sectors of the economy. This historical record also reveals much about the sources and forms of resistance to change at a later period, and the consequences of the Federal Government's failure to obtain compliance through the administrative process of the prohibitions against job discrimination during World War II.

5

The Shipbuilding Industry and the
International Brotherhood of Boilermakers

The shipbuilding industry expanded rapidly during World War II. Increased production had also taken place during World War I, when the industry hired many thousands of workers, including skilled Negro craftsmen, but after 1918 output was severely curtailed. In the late 1930s the industry once again received substantial government contracts for building military and merchant marine vessels, and an acute manpower shortage developed.

Although Negro workers had been employed in a variety of occupations in the shipbuilding industry since the nineteenth century, by the early 1940s a pattern of racial exclusion had been firmly imposed, largely as a result of discriminatory practices by the International Brotherhood of Boilermakers, Iron Ship Builders, and Helpers of America, AFL.[1] A report from the Bureau of Employment Security noted that in this industry, where twenty years earlier Negroes had composed a large portion of the skilled craftsmen, in 1941 only 1.7 percent of the workers referred by government agencies and hired by shipbuilding companies were Negroes.[2] The government report concluded that "not only are nonwhite workers not receiving many skilled or semiskilled jobs in a great many defense establishments, but they are receiving very few jobs of any type, even unskilled."[3]

From its inception in 1880 the Boilermakers union had enforced a policy of racial exclusion. When it was admitted to the American Federation of Labor in 1896 the union transferred the "white-only" membership clause from its constitution to the admission ritual of the local unions, where, according to Malcolm Ross, "as a secret rite, it could bar Negroes from the craft without making public confession of the act."[4] At the 1908 convention of the Boilermakers union, the delegates debated returning the color bar to the constitution of the international union, but decided that it should remain part of the local union ritual.[5] The racial exclusion clause remained an actively enforced part of the ritual until the 1960s.

In 1937, when production in the shipbuilding industry was increasing, the question of Negro membership became an issue at the Boilermakers convention because of growing concern that shipyards might begin hiring large numbers of Negro workers in a variety of job classifications. The fear that the color line would be breached forced some officers of the union to consider organizing Negro workers—provided that limitations were established to prevent them from achieving equal status within the industry and within the union. Some delegates from southern locals favored granting a segregated form of membership to Negroes because their lower wages impeded organizing and limited the union's effectiveness in bargaining. One delegate said: "I have been taught all my life to keep the Negro down. To keep the Negro out of our organization is arming him with a weapon that he can use for the purpose of bringing down the wages, conditions, and hours of the people that have this deplorable condition to contend with in the Southern shipyards."[6] But, as Malcolm Ross wrote:

> The last word on the subject of that convention was spoken by the chairman of the resolutions committee. "Any man who knows the Southern situation," he said, "knows that the Negro is either beneath or above the white man. He never will be his social equal."
> This delphic statement leaves a sense of bewilderment as to who might be the Negro placed above the white man in the Southern situation, but it apparently turned the trick. The convention voted to continue exclusion of Negroes from full membership. The executive committee was authorized to set up subordinate lodges for Negroes, should the occasion arise.[7]

The convention adopted a policy of limiting Negro workers to segregated auxiliary units, each under the "supervision" of a white local. The bylaws governing such auxiliaries provided that "[a]n applicant for membership must be a colored male citizen of some civilized country, between the ages of sixteen (16) and sixty (60) years."[8] The bylaws for white locals allowed membership until the age of seventy. The auxiliaries were not allowed to have their own business agents but were to use the services of their "supervising" local's agent. Grievances of the auxiliary members would be processed through the grievance committees of the white locals. Negro members were denied the right of "universal transfer" among the Boilermakers locals, retaining only the right to transfer among auxiliary units, with restrictions upon job promotion. Negro auxiliaries had no representation on any of the white locals' governing committees or at the union's international conventions. Auxiliary membership provided only half the life insurance coverage received by white members, and the auxiliary bylaws imposed a $25 fine for intoxication and disturbance of union meetings, a clause which did not appear in the white locals' bylaws.

The policy requiring separate auxiliary units within the Boilermakers union established a rigid pattern of segregation within the industry, and white control of the all-Negro auxiliaries was guaranteed. Negro workers seeking employment at major defense shipyards across the nation were therefore forced to submit to the control of the white locals or be totally deprived of jobs under the closed-shop agreements negotiated between unions and the shipbuilding companies. Auxiliary membership denied Negro workers the power to control their own working conditions and wages while forcing them to pay full dues to the union that discriminated against them.

Negro workers could not seek promotion or upgrading at a shipyard without the approval of the white supervising local, since the bylaws provided that "[a]ny member desiring a change of classification must first receive the approval of his auxiliary lodge, after which it will be necessary for him to receive the approval of the supervising lodge. The application will then be submitted to the International President for final approval."[9] White locals of the Boilermakers had secured for themselves full control of the occupational classifications of Negro workers at most major shipyards. The device of segregated auxiliaries provided a means of utilizing and controlling Negro labor in the shipbuilding industry while reserving better paying classifications for members of the white locals.

Some locals of the union resisted even the establishment of Negro auxiliaries until growing labor shortages forced them to accept this as a matter of expediency. At the Gulf Shipbuilding Corporation in Chickasaw, Alabama, there was a shortage of 10,000 skilled workers. The company maintained a preferential hiring agreement with the Mobile Metal Trades Council of the AFL, and the council refused to refer skilled Negro workers to the company despite the fact that at other yards in the area 20 percent of the skilled and semiskilled labor force were Negroes.[10]

The Delta Shipbuilding Corporation in New Orleans had a similar agreement with the New Orleans Metal Trades Council. The company was thus obligated to give hiring preference to members of the unions affiliated with the council, including the Boilermakers. Of Delta's 7,000 employees only a few hundred were Negroes, all of them in menial positions.[11] Paul Dixon, a Negro boilermaker in New Orleans, testified at a Fair Employment Practice Committee hearing that he had tried to organize an all-Negro local of the Boilermakers union at Delta and was dismissed from his job when he persisted in his efforts.[12] Labor shortages then became more acute, and the union installed an all-Negro auxiliary to accommodate the company's demand that it be allowed to hire Negroes to meet the manpower needs created by its extensive government contracts. A union representative later told the FEPC: "Our policy is very easily explained. We put in an auxiliary a few months ago, right after the negotiations of the agreement with the Delta Shipbuilding Company. If it had been our policy to discriminate, we would have never put in that lodge at all."[13]

An FEPC field representative reported wryly:

> The AFL Metal Trades Council of the union were much concerned about discrimination in the rival shipyards which had contracts with the CIO. They were much concerned about the discrimination being practiced against Negroes in that yard. I was told, however, there was no discrimination in the Gulf Shipbuilding plant because there were no Negroes there; therefore, they couldn't be discriminated against.[14]

The pattern of resistance to Negro workers' gaining equal membership rights within the union and on the job was repeated at virtually every major shipyard where the Boilermakers union obtained jurisdiction as the collective bargaining agent. Throughout the war period Negro workers were at first excluded and then limited to segregated auxiliaries and inferior job classifications.

The treatment the Boilermakers accorded Negro workers under its jurisdiction became an issue of sharp debate at conventions of the American Federation of Labor. A. Philip Randolph, Milton Webster, and other Negro delegates repeatedly condemned the establishment of Negro auxiliaries. They were particularly critical of the intolerable situation of Negro workers at shipyards in Tampa, Florida. When the Boilermakers obtained a closed-shop agreement with these yards, hundreds of Negro workers were forced out of their jobs because they were denied union membership. Negro workers who attempted to organize an all-Negro union had crosses burned on their lawns and were subjected to other threats from the Tampa Ku Klux Klan. Randolph stated at the AFL's 1940 convention:

> Negro workers were in the shipyards working at the various trades, but when the union got a closed shop in Tampa shipbuilding ‚ards Negro workers were eliminated, put out of their jobs, and the thing went so far that some of the Negro workers who were rather militant fought this condition vigorously, and the Ku Klux Klan burned the fiery cross in front of their homes. In other words, there seemed to have been a tie-up between the Ku Klux Klan in Tampa, Florida, and certain leaders of the American Federation of Labor there. That is a matter that can be verified. As a matter of fact, it is a notorious, flagrant and indefensible condition that has victimized the Negro workers of Tampa, Florida.[15]

By 1941 the union had forced the dismissal of over 600 Negro workers from the Tampa shipyards. Threats of violence against local Negro leaders were increasing, and the Boilermakers remained firmly opposed to the employment of Negro workers. At the 1941 convention Randolph again rose to attack the union's practices:

> May I say in connection with the Tampa situation I took this matter up with Mr. John Frey, President of the Metal Trades Department, and Mr. Frey took the position that unions were not responsible for the plight of the Negro workers in relation to the Tampa Shipbuilding Corporation. He assigned as the cause of the condition the general social condition of the city of Tampa, indicating Tampa was under the influence and control of the Ku Klux Klan. Now upon analysis, Mr. Frey's argument is unsound. Why? Because the Ku Klux Klan, we admit, is in control of Tampa. Incidentally, it is also in control of the Central Labor Union of the A.F. of L. in Tampa. Now, the Negro workers, 600 Negro workers were in the shipbuilding yards before the unions had negotiated a closed shop contract with the shipbuilding company. At the same time the Ku Klux Klan was in control of Tampa when these 600 Negroes were in the shipbuilding yards. Now if the Ku Klux Klan is responsible for elimination of the Negroes from the shipbuilding yards why is it they were not eliminated before the closed shop contract was negotiated and the unions won recognition with the shipbuilding company? So the position that

has been taken by Mr. Frey in this matter is entirely indefensible and as a matter of fact it will not bear examination.

And so my friends, the disposition assigned to the Ku Klux Klan as the cause for the condition of the Negro workers, which is fundamentally assignable to the Metal Trades Department that controls practically most of the shipbuilding yards, is entirely one which will not pass muster, and I think that Mr. John P. Frey is obligated to make a statement to the public, to the American people, on this question of exclusion of Negro workers from various of these shipbuilding yards.[16]

At the same convention Randolph said: "The primary purpose of auxiliary unions is to give the impression that these national unions are taking Negro workers in when they are actually keeping them out."[17]

Year after year Randolph raised the question of the Boilermakers Jim Crow auxiliaries at AFL conventions. He directly attacked the Boilermakers union and the AFL's Metal Trades Council—of which the Boilermakers was an influential affiliate—for consistently supporting the union's racial practices.

At the AFL's 1943 convention, Charles MacGowan, president of the Boilermakers international union, called Randolph a "professional Negro" and denounced his repeated criticisms of the auxiliary system:

> No act of this convention can compel our convention to do other than that which it elects to do of its own free will, and I say in all earnestness to Delegate Randolph and those of you who think as he does that the allegations made here yesterday are not helping the cause of the Negro in our International Union or in others. The statements made by him constitute one of the greatest disservices that he has ever rendered his people. . . .
>
> Mr. Chairman and delegates, no man has more sympathy and more understanding of an oppressed people's problems than I think I have. All my life I have been a champion of the underprivileged, and I say with the utmost kindness to Delegate Randolph, this Auxiliary proposition may not be the entire answer, but you have got to meet conditions as you find them, not as you would wish them to be. . . .
>
> One of the greatest causes contributing to the failure of the Negro to advance further is the professional Negro. We have no difficulty with the workers in the shipyards and plants and railroad shops. We meet with them, we confer with them and sympathetic understanding prevails, but then those people come around who seek other things than the pure and simple advancement of the economic welfare of all people—regardless of color—then the trouble begins.[18]

In 1944 MacGowan attacked Randolph again:

> Some of us are getting a bit tired of being kicked around by professional agitators when we are striving to do a job, and by some of the utterances made by Delegate Randolph, I wonder if he is in the right organization? I wonder if he is in sympathy with the American Federation of Labor or its aims and objectives?[19]

The continuing debate over the issue of Negroes relegated to inferior auxiliary status was not limited to AFL conventions. During World War II the shipbuilding industry became one of the largest in the country, and the Boilermakers union was among the most powerful unions in the AFL; the union's racial practices became a symbol to Negroes of the continuing racial barriers they faced during a period of full employment for white workers. The Michigan *Chronicle,* an influential Negro newspaper, reported the debate over the Boilermakers union within the AFL:

> Down in New Orleans last week A. Philip Randolph made a statement before the convention of the American Federation of Labor which is echoing all over America today. Mr. Randolph charged that those AFL unions which maintain jim crow auxiliaries for Negro members were practicing "trade union imperialism." Incensed by these remarks, Charles J. MacGowan of the Boilermakers Union stated that the speech of Mr. Randolph was full of "arrogant and insolent statements."
>
> The tall, dark, somber labor leader thereupon gave the AFL boss a prophetic answer, "Get as mad as you like, but the Negroes are going to fight for their rights no matter how mad you get."
>
> Each year Mr. Randolph addresses the annual AFL convention in behalf of Negro workers who are being discriminated against by several of the most powerful AFL unions. Just as regularly the same AFL bosses take offense and accuse the Negro labor leader of insolence and arrogance. How these labor leaders can twist logic and attribute to Mr. Randolph the very traits which they themselves symbolize is one of the marvels of our time.[20]

With the full support of the American Federation of Labor and through the closed-shop agreements negotiated by the AFL's Metal Trades Council with shipyards in the North as well as in the South, the International Brotherhood of Boilermakers denied Negro workers equal membership status in the union and directly curtailed their employment opportunities throughout the war period.* The FEPC held four separate hearings on the west coast,

*The FEPC noted in its *Final Report:* "About the time the hiring program started, most of the yards entered into what was known as a 'Master agreement' with the metal trades

where the most rapid increase in shipbuilding had taken place. After several years of FEPC inquiries, hearings, and directives, and after the Supreme Court of California had twice addressed itself to the racial practices of the union,* the Boilermakers made some minor accommodations but still did not give Negro workers full membership status.

The experience of Mrs. Frances Albrier, the first Negro woman to be employed as a welder in the Kaiser Shipyards in Richmond, California, illustrates in large measure the problems of Negro workers in the shipbuilding industries during World War II:

> The call came for everybody from the government, from President Roosevelt—that we should work in the shipyards to make "victory ships" which were much needed. . . . And the call came through the women's organizations that women could participate. After going through a Depression for so many years, at the time everybody was very eager to get employment. . . . In 1942 I entered the Central Trades School to study welding for the shipyards. . . . I graduated; I got a certificate after finishing a hundred and twenty hours, on September 22, 1942. [Mrs. Albrier had completed more than double the required number of hours and was certified as a trained welder under government standards.] Then I went to the Kaiser Shipyards at Richmond and passed the test there, with the instructor okaying me as excellent because I'd made such a perfect "B." Then he sent me to the employment office at Kaiser Shipyard No. 1, and there the employment officer said, "Well, we're not employing today because it's the weekend, but Monday we start employing again and you come out Monday. But first call me before you come out."
>
> The following Monday I called him, and he said that I'd better not come out today because he didn't think that he could get me on. And

---

department of the American Federation of Labor on behalf of certain AFL unions. Under this agreement the International Brotherhood of Boilermakers, Iron Shipbuilders and Helpers of America was given exclusive bargaining rights for and representation of about 65 percent of the workers in most of the shipyards. The agreement instituted a closed shop in that it provided that the 'employer agrees to hire all workmen it may require hereunder . . . through and from the unions and to continue in its employ . . . only workmen who are members in good standing of the respective unions signatory hereto.'

"When Negroes were first hired, the boilermakers opposed their employment in any other capacity than that of laborer, threatening otherwise to invoke the closed shop provisions (which was possible because Negroes at the time could not become members of the boilermakers union under its ritual)."—*Final Report,* June 28, 1946 (Washington, D.C.: Fair Employment Practice Committee, 1947), p. 20.

*See *James* v. *Marinship Corp.,* 25 Cal.2d 721, 155 P.2d 329, 15 LRRM 798 (1945); *Williams* v. *International Brotherhood of Boilermakers,* 27 Cal.2d 586, 165 P.2d 903, 17 LRRM 771 (1946); see also *Thompson* v. *Moore Drydock Company,* 27 Cal.2d 595, 165 P.2d 901, 17 LRRM 776 (1946).

I asked him why. And he was very reluctant, and I said, well now, is it the unions? And he said, "Yes. . . . You have to go through the unions, and the unions are not employing Negro women as burners or welders." So I said, "All right!" Then I went out to the Kaiser office. I told the secretary there that I wanted to see the director. And she said, "What for?" And I said, "Because you are going against President Roosevelt's Order 8802. . . . I have just been denied, after having a hundred and twenty hours of welding on my own time and not being paid when you are now paying women to learn to weld while they are working, and they're refusing to hire me." And she said, "Wait a minute and I'll see if you can talk to the director. . . . You'll have to wait." I told her I'd wait all day if necessary. Finally he called me in and I explained to him, and he said, "Oh, no, Mrs. Albrier, we're not discriminating; we have many Negro people working." I said, "Yes, as laborers, but you don't have Negro women or men working as welders and burners in the higher skilled jobs." And he said, "No, we have to go through the union. We have a contract with all the major unions . . . including the Boilermakers Union. . . . I'll send you to a public relations officer in Shipyard 2, and you go there and he will take care of you."

So I went to Shipyard 2 and met the public relations officer and he gave me a slip of paper that said: "Hire Mrs. Albrier." Then he said, "Go to the Boilermakers Union in Richmond." And I said to him, "Now you *call* because I have been there and they said that they were not hiring Negro women. . . ." I went and stood in line behind a great many women . . . all white, and all classes. And they were being trained. They were going into the training school to learn how to weld. And they were paying fifteen dollars to join the union. When I got to the window, the clerk said to me, "We have made no arrangements for you people. . . . You don't have any representation in the union, so you can't work in the shipyard." At the same time, there were two soldiers—two white university men who had just gone into the service—and they said to her: "You mean you're not going to hire this lady? Is that what we're going to fight for? We're supposed to be fighting for democracy." And she said, "It's nothing. . . . Nothing has been made for her representation. . . . They don't take colored in the union." Then I went back to the Shipyard No. 1 and talked again to the director of the yard there. He sent me over to see the public relations man again. And he gives me this note to Mr. Patton, who was the head of this local of the union. . . . I, all over again, went back to the union and Mr. Patton wasn't in. I waited for him and handed him the note. Then he said, "Okay, go to window No. 7." Well, I had seen these other women with fifteen dollars, so I thought that I had to have fifteen dollars. She made out the registration slip—the regular requirements and questions that you answer. When I handed her the fifteen dollars, she said: "You don't have to pay; you're only working on a permit." And I went on into the Kaiser Shipyard No. 1 as a welder.

I was quite a figure in the yards with the welding suit on because I was the first Negro woman in the Kaiser Shipyard in Richmond, one of the biggest ship producers in the United States Navy during the Second World War. . . . But I was interested in all of the other Negro women who were learning to be welders and burners. At that time Berkeley High School was giving a course in burning and welding, and a great many of my friends in the Colored Women's Federated Clubs were going to the school; they finished the required hours and then went to Kaiser's. And they absolutely refused to take them in. They were directed to go to the State Employment Office, and the State Employment Office told them: "Well, you can go over to the Boilermakers Union, but we want to let you know that they're not accepting Negro burners and welders now. And we don't want to see your feelings hurt or see you being discriminated like that." And they advised them not to go. . . . I was legislative chairman of the State Association of Colored Women's Clubs, and I went to the State Employment Office and challenged them on why they did not send these women to the Boilermakers Union and let them turn them down and why they did not make a report of discrimination to the government.

And so we put them on the spot, and we threatened to go to the capital in Sacramento and report this. So they said that they would do that; they would make a requisition of any of the others that came to the government so the government would know. They just were not referring Negro women even though there was this big labor shortage. They were just not referring Negro women to these jobs because the union wouldn't take them. . . .

It was then that I wrote a letter to the President, Franklin Roosevelt, and told him about what was going on out here and the refusal to hire Negro women and men as burners and welders in the shipyards. . . . I received a letter from the War Manpower Commission, Office of Emergency Management, Washington, D.C., Chairman Paul V. McNutt, federal security administrator, dated March 26, 1943: "Your telegram of March 17 addressed to President Roosevelt and relating to difficulties facing Negro workers in the Richmond area has been referred to me for reply. I am discussing this matter with the regional director of the War Manpower Commission and requesting him to take appropriate action. I should appreciate your communicating directly with him in order that he may be kept informed of developments. . . ."

After I got this letter they set up this all-colored auxiliary. . . . The union did not admit the Negro workers, but they set up a separate Jim Crow Negro auxiliary, made you pay the full dues, but gave you no representation, gave you none of the protections or benefits of union membership—including the insurance, the pension plan, union representation and collective bargaining—they just took your money and set it up as a separate all-colored auxiliary.[21]

In 1941 the AFL Metal Trades Department negotiated a master agreement with the Kaiser Company in Portland, Oregon, which obtained a closed-shop contract for the Boilermakers. The effect of the agreement was to give the Boilermakers jurisdiction over 65 percent of the shipyard workers in the United States.[22] The Kaiser Company, one of the largest shipbuilders in America, owned three shipyards in the Portland area and employed 95,000 workers. The majority of Kaiser's employees belonged to Boilermakers Local 72, and the Negro workers were forced to join Boilermakers Auxiliary A-32, which was under the "supervision" of the all-white Local 72.

Late in 1942, as a result of continuing severe manpower shortages, the Kaiser Company began recruiting workers from as far away as New York and transporting them to the Portland yards by special trains. Most of the men recruited in New York City were married and unable to bring their families with them. Among the thousands of workers brought in from other areas were hundreds of Negroes who had been promised skilled jobs at high pay. Once aboard the train to Portland, the Negro workers learned that the only work available to them would be as laborers, and that they would have to join the Boilermakers auxiliary to get those jobs. Sidney Wolf, one of the Negro workers, testified at an FEPC hearing that "I came from New York, with the first load that Kaiser sent here from New York. . . . Out of Chicago a Kaiser representative got on the train, and he started passing out applications, for the men to be reclassified . . .; fortunately, I was sent out as a general helper."[23] When he arrived at the yard in Portland, he found that he would be earning only laborers' pay of 88 cents an hour rather than the helpers' pay of 95 cents he had been promised in New York. He testified that, while most of the Negroes on the train were given laborer classifications, "I had the title as a helper, but I was a laboring man—in fact, I was unloading pipe out of gondolas."[24]

Robert Rhone, another Negro recruited in New York, testified that about 10 percent of the 373 men on the train with him were Negroes and that most of them were given laborer classifications although they had been promised better jobs before boarding the train. Rhone, however, was given the classification of a shipwright welder. He testified before the committee:

> Q. When you arrived in Portland did you find your classification changed, and that you were to start all over again?
>
> A. Not in my case, but in most of the other cases.
>
> Q. To what point were these men reclassified?
>
> A. Regardless of how they were classified on the train, they were made to accept reclassifications later.[25]

Rhone stated that he was told he must join Boilermakers Auxiliary A-32 if he wished to continue his employment. He informed the committee that "[t]o the best of my knowledge, they didn't have any powers in the auxiliary, and I just felt that I didn't like segregation," and he refused to join the union.[26] He received a stopwork notice for nonpayment of union dues and was promptly discharged by the company. Other witnesses at the FEPC hearing testified to being dismissed under similar circumstances. An FEPC examiner summarized the situation:

> The Kaiser Company was quite willing to employ Negroes who offered to work in their shipyards; and the Negroes were well qualified to give the services that were needed.
>
> What was it then, you will ask, which stood between these Negro workers and employment in the shipyard where their work was so urgently, so desperately, needed?
>
> The evidence in this case will provide a clear and short answer to that question. It was a labor union that said no. It was the refusal of the Boilermakers Union to receive Negroes into full membership or to permit them to work in these shipyards unless they joined a Jim-Crow auxiliary organization that stood in the way.[27]

Hundreds of Negro workers who refused to join Auxiliary A-32 received dismissal notices, and many of them filed complaints with the Boilermakers union and the FEPC. The union's response was to continue defending its auxiliary system as a reasonable accommodation for Negro workers employed in jobs under its jurisdiction. When the first complaints of racial discrimination from Negro workers were sent to William Green, president of the American Federation of Labor, and to the Boilermakers international union, J. A. Franklin, a Boilermakers official, replied:

> I am of the opinion, Brother Green, that somebody has been misleading these men, for the reason that our Brotherhood has provided for the admittance of Negroes who are employed in some branch of our trade, through a colored auxiliary lodge. Of course we do not accept

colored members, or even white members, so far as that goes, unless they are employed at some branch of our trade, and if the colored man is competent to perform the work, and demonstrates that he is eligible for membership by competency in employment, there is nothing to prevent him from joining a colored auxiliary.

For your further information I will state that we now have twelve colored auxiliary local unions in existence, so that the charge of discrimination, in my opinion, is without justification.[28]

The manpower shortage at Kaiser was now even more critical. The underutilization of Negro workers—a direct result of the Boilermakers demands—had created a production crisis at the company's three shipyards. The company began to provide training and upgrading for Negro workers who had joined the auxiliary and kept their jobs. The AFL Metal Trades Council of Portland responded to the upgrading of Negro workers by demanding that "all men who have been transferred from one craft to another . . . be returned immediately to their former positions and that they remain in their former positions."[29] Apparently this action seemed excessive even to John Frey, president of the AFL Metal Trades Council, who had repeatedly supported the Boilermakers auxiliary system. Frey wired the employer and the Metal Trades Council of Portland:

Have been informed that Portland Metal Trades Council has informed Oregon shipyard that it must immediately downgrade Negro workmen now employed. This action is contrary to sound judgment and patriotic duty during this time. It is contrary to President Roosevelt's publicly announced policy relative to no racial discrimination. It is contrary to the clause in every shipbuilding contract entered into by the United States Maritime Commission with all shipbuilding which provides that there shall be no racial discrimination. It is contrary to the specific declarations against racial discrimination made by the American Federation of Labor and the Metal Trades Department. It is contrary to public policy. The Portland Metal Trades Council has made an outstanding contribution to shipbuilding and to this great value of trade union cooperation with employers. You cannot afford now to take action which you and your friends cannot afford. I urge you for your own welfare and the integrity of trade unionism during war time to immediately rescind your action. I am convinced that you will not continue in a policy which could only result in disaster.[30]

Franklin of the Boilermakers international union also sent telegrams to Local 72 in Portland, the Metal Trades Council there, and the Kaiser Company asking that Negroes and other workers not be downgraded until a conference of union, company, and government officials could be held.

A meeting was held in Portland, attended by officials of the international union, Local 72, the company, the U.S. Maritime Commission, the War Manpower Commission, the War Production Board, the Shipbuilding Stabilization Committee, and the AFL Metal Trades Council. The discussion among union, company, and government officials resulted in a memorandum that stated in part:

3. To maintain maximum production and good management, there will not be permitted, either by management or by labor, any limitation or restriction against workers because of their race, creed, color or national origin in the process of recruitment, upgrading, training or any other phase or condition of employment. . . .

5. It is understood that the terms of this agreement do not alter, amend or revise any of the terms and conditions of the existing collective bargaining agreement between management and labor.[31]

Although the agreement granted the Negro‑workers limited protection from the proposed downgrading of position, it did not deal with the question of union membership, but tacitly condoned the auxiliary system. The union could continue to require Negroes to join Auxiliary A-32 in order to hold their jobs. Many Negro employees, again informed that they must join the auxiliary unit, refused and were dismissed by the company.

The Fair Employment Practice Committee began receiving complaints from Negro workers discharged for nonpayment of dues to the auxiliary. In 1942 the committee made formal inquiries into the racial practices of the union, and the response of officials of Local 72 in Portland was that "[w]e now have employed in the local shipyards negro workers."[32] Charles MacGowan, president of the Boilermakers union, replied to FEPC inquiries:

There is no foundation for the charge that there has been any discrimination on the part of our local unions against any man on account of race, creed, color, or national origin. And we unequivocally declare that we have fulfilled the letter and spirit of the President's Executive Order No. 8802. In our telephone conversation with you yesterday you repeatedly said that you wanted to get these negroes back to work. We have no specific knowledge of any negroes being held out of work but negroes and whites alike can return to work if and when they pay their dues as provided by the constitution of the International Brotherhood of Boilermakers, Iron Ship Builders and

Helpers of America including the auxiliary constitution controlling the auxiliary of which they are members provided all of them have complied with the requirements of the organization. And if we learn that a single person is not immediately put back to work under the same conditions as any other member of this union, we will rectify the situation at once.[33]

At the hearings in Portland, the attorney for all-white Local 72 attempted to place the responsibility for establishing auxiliaries on the international union. Remarking that the issue was "more than an economic problem," he told the committee:

We have a social problem. Lodge 72 is an organization that exists by virtue of a charter that was given by the International. The ritual . . . is a ritual which should have been referred to the parties responsible for their making. Now we disclaim responsibility for the unfortunate situation in which we find ourselves. Not only do we disclaim it, but I wish further to join in the indictment that has just been uttered . . . against certain international officials, and I regret they are not here to hear what I have to say.[34]

The president of Local 72 testified that "it was the International's problem. It was not our problem. Local 72 cannot change the situation of the Negro. If we could we would. But we cannot. We are bound by the limits of our Constitution."[35]

Evidence presented at the committee's hearings in Portland included full documentation of the exclusion of Negroes who refused to join the auxiliary and of the inferior union status of those who did join. Negro workers at the shipyards were forced either to forfeit to the all-white local the power to determine their conditions of employment or to seek other jobs. For the hundreds of Negroes recruited in New York and transported to the west coast, there was little choice.

The statement made by the company's attorney at the FEPC hearings in Portland acknowledged that "the issue here . . . and I think it is the principal and only issue—is whether or not where a closed shop contract exists, there must be an open union."[36]

A year later the Supreme Court of California was to address itself directly to that question.[37] Because the FEPC had no direct enforcement powers, its Portland hearings and subsequent cease-and-desist directives produced no alteration in the union's discriminatory system. On the west coast, as a consequence of the shipbuilding industry's growth, the Boilermakers had established several auxiliaries, including A-26 in Oakland, A-35 in Los

Angeles, A-32 in the Portland-Vancouver area, and A-41 in Sausalito. By May 18, 1944, the Boilermakers had a national total of thirty-six all-Negro auxiliaries, with a membership of 12,685.[38]

Shortly after its Portland hearings the Fair Employment Practice Committee conducted hearings in Los Angeles, where Boilermakers Local 92 held closed-shop agreements with major shipyards in the area. As in Portland earlier, hundreds of Negro workers had refused to accept the Boilermakers auxiliary in Los Angeles and consequently were dismissed. Walter Edward Williams, a Negro welder, testified at these hearings that after he applied for a job with the California Shipbuilding Corporation, "I didn't discover that they had given me a status in an auxiliary until I observed the word 'auxiliary' on the dues slip."[39] Williams refused to join the auxiliary after he learned that it was unable to elect its own officers, had no grievance committee or business agent, and in fact performed no collective bargaining functions. The auxiliary system, he said, was

> very definitely demoralizing to the greatest majority of Negroes. Because Negroes realize that an auxiliary status, as an auxiliary member of Local 92, is an inferior status, that the auxiliary is an inferior lodge. And most of them are there in the shipyards to work on the production lines, build ships, and they feel that the auxiliary policy of the Boilermakers is a contradiction to the principles which we are fighting for, and which they are working on the production lines to preserve.[40]

Williams organized the Ship Yard Workers Committee for Equal Participation to protest the racial auxiliary units established by the Boilermakers. The committee presented to the FEPC a petition signed by over 1,000 white members of Local 92 which stated that payment of dues to an auxiliary unit "without receiving full membership rights and protection, the same as other workers, constitutes taxation without representation and violates the basic democratic principles of our nation." It concluded: "We, the undersigned, therefore demand that the Jim-Crow Auxiliary Local A-35 be abolished and admitted into Local 92 of the Boilermakers Union with full membership rights and on an equal basis with other workers."[41] Hundreds of Negro members of the auxiliary signed pledge cards refusing to pay additional dues to the Boilermakers until they were admitted into all-white Local 92. All those who refused to pay dues were later dismissed by the employer after the union notified the company of their nonpayment. Andrew

Blakney, a Negro welder employed by the California Shipbuilding Corporation, testified to the committee that he did not join Auxiliary A-35 because "I didn't think it was right. I didn't figure I had any voice, and I had no representative from A-35 out at the shipyard, nobody of my own choosing you know, that I helped choose. I figured it was discrimination against my race."[42] At the time Blakney appeared at the committee's hearings, he had already been dismissed from his job for nonpayment of dues.

When the FEPC issued its summary and findings to the companies and unions involved in the Portland and Los Angeles hearings, it directed the parties to cease and desist from violating the federal executive order and to cease discharging Negroes who refused to join the Boilermakers auxiliaries. Soon after the committee's directives were issued, the Boilermakers union made clear its intent to defy the executive order. In a letter to the Kaiser Company in Portland, Charles MacGowan, on behalf of the Boilermakers union, wrote:

> First of all we desire to direct your attention to Article 2 of the Pacific Coast Master Agreement, particularly Paragraph 1, which reads in part: ". . . and to continue in its employ in said classifications only workmen who are members in good standing of the respective Unions signatory hereto . . . ."
>
> This agreement was entered into in good faith by all of the parties signatory thereto and received the approval of the U.S. Navy Department, U.S. Maritime Commission and the War Production Board. It is still in full force and effect and our International Brotherhood respectfully insists that the provisions of this agreement be adhered to in the future as they have in the past regardless of any opinion to the contrary by the President's Committee on Fair Employment Practice.
>
> Second, it is further our position that the President's Committee on Fair Employment Practice is wholly without Constitutional and legal jurisdiction and power to issue an order having the force of law and for these reasons the said orders are without legal effect.
>
> It is also our position that the President's Executive Order No. 9346 was intended as a directive and was not to be construed as having the force of legislation as it must be so construed to warrant the findings made by the President's Committee on Fair Employment Practice above referred to and to give it the construction placed thereon by the President's Committee on Fair Employment Practice would alienate the goodwill of Organized Labor and its support of the War Effort because of this arrogant attempt to destroy collective bargaining agreements. . . . We must therefore insist that the terms

of the Master Agreement—under which the world's record of ship construction has been established and is being maintained—be rigidly adhered to in the future the same as in the past because we cannot permit any deviation from its terms.[43]

The union's methods of resistance included challenging the committee's legal authority and a continuing refusal to admit Negroes into full membership.[44] However, increasing numbers of Negroes were choosing to lose their jobs rather than join Jim Crow auxiliaries. The Michigan *Chronicle,* in a story datelined Los Angeles, reported:

> Negro shipyard workers here objected to auxiliary status in the AFL unions by refusing this week to join Auxiliary A-35 of the Boilermakers Union Local 92.
> Of the 200 workers present at the meeting held to initiate new members into the auxiliary, only 15 stood up for initiation. The attitude of those who refused jim crow status was expressed by Frederick Jones of the Shipyard Workers Committee for Equal Participation, who asked: "Why would we want to join the auxiliary when there is no opportunity in it for us? Why is it that Local 92 of the Boilermakers takes in all races, white, Chinese, Filipinos, Mexicans—everybody but Negroes? That's not Americanism; it's Nazism."[45]

Because the refusal of the Boilermakers to admit Negroes into full membership contributed significantly to manpower shortages in the shipbuilding industry, the union's racial practices became the target of increasing attacks by the press, government agencies, and spokesmen for the Negro community. At the national convention of the union in 1944, twenty-five Negro leaders of national reputation appealed to the delegates to abandon their auxiliary system and adopt a policy of full integration.[46] Union officials complained that their critics were using the union "as a sounding board to foment strife and turmoil on the issue of social equality, which is in no sense an issue over which a trades union organization can become involved."[47] At the convention, resolutions were adopted which granted limited concessions to the union's all-Negro auxiliaries but which continued their inferior status. The convention agreed to grant auxiliaries representation rights at the union's future national conventions, membership in the Metal Trades Council of the AFL, and equal life insurance coverage. But the resolutions specifically denied auxiliaries the power to elect their own officers, business agents, or grievance committees, forcing them to continue relying on their all-white "supervising" locals for such vital services. Even with the minor concessions allowed the auxiliaries, the 1944 resolutions mainly served to define and further codify the union's discriminatory practices. Auxiliaries remained subject to control by the white locals, and Negro workers remained barred from full union membership.*

Denied relief within the AFL, Negro workers who objected to the racial practices of its affiliates began petitioning the courts for relief. The first court action involving the racial policy of the Boilermakers international union, however, was provoked by one of its own locals. In Providence, Rhode Island, where all-white Local 308 controlled hiring at the Walsh-Kaiser Shipyard, the union relegated Negro workers to Auxiliary A-1.[48] In 1943 Local 308 unanimously voted to abolish the auxiliary and to admit Negro workers under its jurisdiction into full union membership. The international union's officers objected to this divergence from the international's policy and brought suit to enjoin Local 308's inclusion of Negroes. The Michigan *Chronicle* reported:

> In a sweeping opinion here January 7 [1944], Judge Alexander L. Churchill in Superior Court ruled that the auxiliary union arrangement of the International Brotherhood of Boilermakers, Iron Ship-builders and Helpers of America was illegal in Rhode Island.
>
> The auxiliary lodges of the Boilermakers union are set up for Negroes only, and members of the auxiliaries do not have the same rights and protections as regular union members, although paying the same dues.
>
> Judge Churchill's ruling came at the close of a week of argument in his court in which Thurgood Marshall, NAACP special counsel, and Joseph LeCount of this city appeared for certain Negro workers seeking an injunction to restrain Local 308 of the Boilermakers union from discriminating against them.
>
> The action was the result of an election held in December in which Negro members of the union here at the Walsh-Kaiser shipyards were required to vote on a separate ballot marked "C" and deposit the ballots in a special envelope marked "protest" which were then placed in a separate ballot box.

*The FEPC noted: "After public hearing (which the International Brotherhood declined to attend) in November 1943, covering yards in the Portland, Oreg., and Los Angeles areas, the Committee labelled the auxiliary set-up as discrimination in union membership and contrary to the provisions of Executive Order 9346. As to employers, the Committee held that they, by assisting the union through complying with its discharge demands, were likewise guilty of discrimination. Both company and union were ordered to cease and desist from such practices."—*Final Report*, June 28, 1946 (Washington, D.C.: Fair Employment Practice Committee, 1947), p. 21.

All the ballots in the election were impounded by court order and action for a temporary injunction began.

In his opinion, Judge Churchill declared that the Fifth and Fourteenth amendments to the United States Constitution, plus the civil rights law of the state of Rhode Island established a public policy of no discrimination which he was obliged to follow. He also referred to the President's Executive Order 9346 forbidding discrimination in employment and to the policies of the Fair Employment Practice Committee.

"These men [Negroes] are full-fledged members of Local 308," the opinion said.

A remarkable feature of the action was the testimony of officials of Local 308 that they were against discrimination and wanted the Negro workers as members of the regular Local 308. Testimony brought out by Marshall and LeCount established that the International headquarters in Kansas City, Kansas, had ordered the ballots of the Negroes thrown out and had ruled that they could be only auxiliary members.[49]

In the same week that AFL president William Green announced "substantial progress . . . toward the objective of extending Negro workers in the West Coast shipyards full rights and privileges of membership" in the Boilermakers union, a state court issued a temporary injunction against the union and four Los Angeles shipyards ordering them to cease dismissing Negroes who refused to accept the all-Negro auxiliary.[50] Boilermakers Local 6 in Sausalito had demanded that the Marinship Corporation dismiss over 200 Negro workers for nonpayment of dues to Auxiliary A-41, and the Negro workers had filed suit to enjoin their dismissal. In *James* v. *Marinship Corporation*[51] the Supreme Court of California sustained an injunction restraining the Marinship Corporation and Local 6 from dismissing Joseph James and 200 other Negroes who refused to join Auxiliary A-41. The union had been able to demand their dismissal because of its closed-shop contract which stated that any employee working under the union's jurisdiction must be a union member. Negroes were barred from joining all-white Local 6 and so were forced to join the auxiliary or be discharged. In its opinion the court dealt with the question of the union's power to create and maintain subordinate racial auxiliaries in conjunction with a closed-shop contract:

> The fundamental question in this case is whether a closed union coupled with a closed shop is a legitimate objective of organized labor. . . . In our opinion, an arbitrarily closed or partially closed union is incompatible with a closed shop. Where a union has, as in

this case, attained a monopoly of the supply of labor by means of closed shop agreements and other forms of collective labor action, such a union occupies a quasi-public position similar to that of a public service business and it has certain corresponding obligations. It may no longer claim the same freedom from legal restraint enjoyed by golf clubs or fraternal associations. Its asserted right to choose its own members does not merely relate to social relations; it affects the fundamental right to work for a living.[52]

The court therefore ruled that when a union controlled employment, it could not arbitrarily exclude certain groups from full participation in the union. Subsequently the same court, in *Williams* v. *International Brotherhood of Boilermakers,*[53] reaffirmed its *James* opinion and extended the proposition to areas of employment where the union did not have a monopoly on the entire industry but did have a closed-shop agreement with a particular shipyard:

The public interest is directly involved because the unions are seeking to control by arbitrary selection the fundamental right to work. While the need for protection may be greater where the union has secured closed shop contracts covering all the jobs in that locality, this is only an aggravated phase of the general problem. . . . A closed shop agreement with a single employer is in itself a form of monopoly, giving a third party, the union, control over at least the plant of the signatory employer, and although such a labor monopoly is not in itself improper, it carries with it certain responsibilities, and the public clearly has an interest in preventing any abuse of it.[54]

The Boilermakers union then found another way to continue segregating Negro workers under its jurisdiction. According to the FEPC's *Final Report:*

After the California Supreme Court decisions, and following the FEPC post-hearing negotiations, the boilermakers union, in their quadrennial convention, abolished the auxiliary status of their Negro locals, but retained the separate organization of such locals. Conferences with union officials disclosed that under the proposed dissolution of the locals, discrimination against Negro members would not be ended. Under the new arrangement, it would still be possible to assign jobs on the basis of race instead of individual qualifications, thus creating competing interests along racial lines within the same shipyard. The right of universal transfer to other lodges, and hence to other jobs in other sections of the country, would also be governed by the race of the transferring member. That is to say, Negroes would be able to transfer only to Negro lodges and white members only to white lodges. The Committee, therefore, felt that the union's new policy could not serve as a basis for its withdrawal of the order.[55]

The union had altered the form but retained the substance of its nationwide system of anti-Negro practices.

When the Civil Rights Act of 1964 was adopted, shipbuilding activity had greatly declined from its period of peak expansion during World War II and this industry was almost entirely subsidized through vast federal contracts. Soon after Title VII went into effect on July 2, 1965, black workers filed charges with the Equal Employment Opportunity Commission against the nation's largest privately owned shipyard, the Newport News Shipbuilding and Dry Dock Company in Virginia. The commission found "reasonable cause" and its investigation revealed that this major government contractor was responsible for an extensive pattern of racial job discrimination. In 1969, after a widely publicized conciliation agreement failed to eliminate many of the discriminatory practices, black workers filed suit in the federal district court which resulted in a settlement agreement on August 19, 1971.[56]

Before Title VII went into effect black workers in Pascagoula, Mississippi, had filed a series of complaints with the Office of Federal Contract Compliance against the Ingalls Shipbuilding Company, a division of Litton Industries, charging violation of Executive Order 11246 prohibiting job discrimination by government contractors. The Boilermakers union and the AFL-CIO Metal Trades Council held collective bargaining agreements at this large facility, operating almost completely with government contracts. The OFCC and other federal agencies conducted several investigations but failed to act until 1969, when civil rights groups protested the award of a $1.1-billion new contract, because of this company's history of discriminatory practices.[57] After the National Association for the Advancement of Colored People and other organizations requested that the government delay final approval of the new contract until the company took action to eliminate the racial job patterns, an affirmative action agreement with the government was signed by the company and the unions on October 8, 1970.* The most important aspect of this agreement was that for

*Roy Wilkins, executive director of the NAACP, had two discussions with Charles B. Thornton, chairman of the board and chief executive officer of Litton Industries, Inc., on this matter. (Both Wilkins and Thornton served on the National Advisory Commission on Civil

the first time black workers would be permitted to transfer to jobs in the all-white classifications without loss of seniority. The experience of government agencies in the Newport News case, the developing law in Title VII litigation, and pressure on federal agencies by members of Congress to transfer the lucrative contract elsewhere because of discrimination at the Mississippi shipyard were major factors in this breakthrough for black shipyard workers in the Deep South.

However, patterns of racial discrimination in the shipbuilding industry continued into the 1970s. Investigations of the racial practices of the Alabama Dry Dock and Shipbuilding Company, in Mobile, conducted jointly by the Office of Federal Contract Compliance and the U.S. Maritime Administration during the summer and fall of 1970, offer an example. The investigations disclosed that approximately 350 black employees were assigned to less desirable jobs because of their race; minority group persons were underutilized in all white-collar classifications and in most skilled and semiskilled positions; and the Alabama Dry Dock and Shipbuilding Company did not have an adequate affirmative action program to enable black employees to transfer out of these less desirable jobs without loss of pay and seniority.[58]*

Negotiations between federal agencies and the company began in late 1970. In January 1971 the International Union of Marine and Shipbuilding Workers of America, AFL-CIO, and Local 18 in Mobile participated in the negotiations. After a week of conferences the company signed an agreement to rectify each of the job inequities listed by the federal agencies. This agreement, reached by the company and the Federal Government but subject to ratification by the union, was in conformity with decisions of the federal courts which held that, under Title VII, discriminatory provisions in collective bargaining contracts could not be used to deny equal treatment to black workers. The new agreement with federal agencies required the company to promote black workers to more desirable positions without loss of pay or seniority, to provide

---

Disorders by appointment of President Lyndon B. Johnson.) Representatives of the NAACP also met with senators and other public officials interested in the placement of this very large government contract. Interview by author with Roy Wilkins, New York, October 16, 1970.

*Twenty-eight years earlier this same company was found to be violating Executive Order 9346 prohibiting employment discrimination by government contractors. On November 19, 1942, the Fair Employment Practice Committee issued a directive to the Alabama Dry Dock and Shipbuilding Company "instructing it to cease discriminatory hiring practices against Negroes."—*Final Report*, June 28, 1946 (Washington, D.C.: Fair Employment Practice Committee, 1947), p. 27.

them with accelerated training, and to assure them full and equal access to job opportunities and security.

During the following week the company tried to renegotiate its contract with the union in order to conform to the law, but the International Union of Marine and Shipbuilding Workers declared its opposition to the new agreement, the union members voted against ratification, and the negotiations failed. Accordingly, the Maritime Administration notified the company of its intention to withhold further federal contracts, and the company requested a formal hearing as provided by federal regulations.[59] The issue was whether a tradition of discriminatory collective bargaining agreements would prevail over the law requiring equality in employment for black workers and members of other minority groups.

In 1972, after much resistance, seniority lines were renegotiated at this and some other southern shipyards.[60] However, complaints were later pending with the Office of Federal Contract Compliance and the Equal Employment Opportunity Commission charging similar practices of employment discrimination by employers and unions at other shipyards operating with government contracts. In 1973 the EEOC filed an intervention petition in *Stanley Rodney* v. *Avondale Shipyards, Inc.,* in New Orleans. The commission charged that the shipyard ". . . discriminates against blacks in hiring, job assignment and classification, promotion, transfer, wages, and in discharge, discipline and layoff policies."[61] And on May 6, 1975, the commission filed a lawsuit against the Peninsula Shipbuilders Association, the independent labor union representing employees of the huge Newport News Shipbuilding and Dry Dock Company. The commission charged that the union "discriminates against blacks by maintaining a policy of segregating, limiting and classifying its membership by race and failing to have adequate representation of blacks among its members."[62] These cases were examples of the continuing Title VII litigation in the shipbuilding industry during the 1970s.

6

National Defense Industry and the
International Association of Machinists

When the Fair Employment Practice Committee began its investigation of the racial practices of the International Association of Machinists during World War II, the union already had a long history of excluding Negro workers. Its original membership call, dated September 10, 1888, read:

> It is strictly a secret society, in nowise conflicting with one's Religious or Political opinion, holding meetings at least twice per month, admitting none but qualified members which must be (according to Article VII of constitution) a white, free born male citizen of some civilized country. . . .[1]

The National Association of Machinists (later the International Association of Machinists) originally placed the provision requiring racial restriction in the constitution of the Grand Lodge (the international union). In 1895, at the suggestion of AFL leader Samuel Gompers,* the color bar was shifted from the national organization's constitution to the ritual of the local union, where it performed the same function. Soon thereafter the Machinists became affiliated with the American Federation of Labor.[2]

During World War II—a period of acute manpower shortages in the aircraft and other industries where the International Association of Machinists held many labor agreements—the union made few exceptions to its policy of excluding Negroes. Numerous

---

*At the 1894 AFL convention Gompers, who had been president of the organization, was defeated for reelection by John McBride of the United Mine Workers. Gompers was reelected president at the following convention and held the post until his death in December 1924.

FEPC investigations of the racial practices of IAM locals document the consequences of the union's anti-Negro policy.

The Ohio Pattern Works and Foundry Company of Cincinnati had a closed-shop agreement with IAM Lodge 34 and employed no Negro workers. An FEPC report states that "[i]n this case it appears that the union is the chief source of opposition to the use of Negro workers."[3] The IAM local had notified the company that "we wish to advise you . . . after canvassing the employees of your plant who are members of the undersigned union, if you should employ non-white employees, the members of this organization who are now in your employ, shall refuse to work with them and a work stoppage will result."[4] After negotiating with the FEPC, the union agreed to let a small number of Negroes work on a temporary permit basis, but it successfully maintained its policy of excluding Negroes from union membership.

In another FEPC hearing, involving several IAM locals that represented 90 percent of the 13,000 employees of the Western Cartridge Company in East Alton, Illinois, the committee found that not a single Negro was employed at this major defense plant, the largest industrial facility in the area. During the hearings members of the IAM repeatedly interrupted the proceedings and threatened work stoppages if Negroes were employed. The business agent of one local testified: "Well, the best that I have been able to learn from talking to the groups as they have met, that they are very determined that if colored people is brought into the plant, that colored people is going to run the plant. . . . The white people are going to get out of it."[5] Officials of two lodges told the committee that the workers would not tolerate Negro employees at the company and that the white union members would be encouraged to quit if Negroes were employed. A steward of Production Workers Lodge 1654 testified: "I have contacted most of the women in the washroom on all three shifts. With the exception of three women, everyone I have talked to has told me they would walk out if Negro help came in . . . frankly, I would walk out."[6] Rigid opposition from IAM local membership and union officials prevented the employment of Negroes at this important midwestern defense plant. The FEPC noted in its *Final Report:*

> Three hundred Western Cartridge brass mill workers struck for an afternoon and attended the FEPC hearing with demands to be heard against Negroes. Their union leaders threatened to strike if any Negroes were hired. The Western Cartridge management deplored

this display of their workers' intolerance. Nevertheless, FEPC was unable to obtain any change of practice at the Western Cartridge plant.[7]

Another example of how the Machinists union effectively used the threat of a strike to prevent the hiring of Negroes was the action of IAM Lodge 1089 in Cincinnati, Ohio. The local represented workers at the F. H. Lawson Company, which employed only one Negro—as a janitor. A War Manpower Commission report summarizes the position of the union:

> Both [the union president] and [the union treasurer] stated that they are governed by their laws which prohibit Negro membership. Commenting on the attitude of the entire membership, both officials stated that their membership will quit if Negroes are hired. The question of admitting non-white workers has been discussed recently by the union at a regular meeting, resulting in the decision opposing the inclusion of Negro workers.[8]

The majority of the membership of the IAM was employed in aircraft manufacturing and the shipbuilding industry. Because of war production both industries expanded enormously, but the discriminatory practices of the Machinists and other AFL unions excluded Negroes from all but menial jobs. From July 1939 to July 1941 the aircraft industry increased its employment by over 500 percent, and it continued to increase at a rapid rate thereafter.[9] But in 1941, of the 310,000 employees in the aircraft industry fewer than 2,000 were Negroes.[10] In April 1942 there were fewer than 5,300 Negroes employed in forty-nine aircraft plants, and most of them were in menial positions.[11] The IAM by this time had become the dominant union in aircraft manufacturing.

Hundreds of charges of discrimination were filed against aircraft-production plants by Negroes denied employment and excluded from union membership. FEPC hearings on the racial practices of the McDonnell Aircraft Corporation in St. Louis, Missouri, disclosed that the company refused to hire Negroes for production and clerical jobs and that Negroes were not upgraded from their low-paying janitorial jobs.[12] When the company was advertising widely for qualified workers, Negroes applied for jobs as welders, riveters, and sheet-metal workers but were told that "[t]he only thing we have for colored people here is porter, janitor and maid."[13]

John Arthur Taylor, one of the Negro complainants, was a Howard University graduate certified by the U.S. Army and the U.S. Civil Service Commission as qualified to work in a number of technical and administrative positions related to aircraft production. He testified that after reading the company's advertisements for employees he had submitted his application and received no response.[14]

The Vultee Aircraft Company in Nashville, Tennessee, had a collective bargaining agreement with IAM Local Lodge 735. Although the company employed many thousands of workers and over 1,000 trainees, it employed only twenty Negroes, all as janitors and sweepers.[15] In answer to inquiries from the National Association for the Advancement of Colored People in 1941, the company's industrial relations manager replied: "[M]ay we advise that we do not now believe it advisable to include colored people with our regular working force. We may, at a later date, be in a position to add some colored people in minor capacities, such as porters and cleaners."[16] The company consistently refused to employ Negro workers in skilled production jobs, regardless of their qualifications. In an FEPC hearing on charges filed against the company and the union, a committee official reported that "although there are thousands of potential Negro workers available in the Nashville area, the Vultee Company has drawn its workers from the white race exclusively except for a small number of Negro janitors."[17]

One Negro complainant, Mark Miller Latting, had been a qualified mechanic for over twenty years and had attended courses in mechanical engineering at Langston University in Oklahoma and Agricultural and Industrial State College in Nashville. He had worked in Ford and Chrysler plants and had letters of recommendation from both companies when he applied for a job at Vultee. During the hearings he testified that the company interviewer had told him he could not be hired because of insufficient experience. Latting responded to the interviewer:

A. . . . Call out your best engineer and give me a sheet of paper and give me an examination. We will go back in the shop and take it from a chemical or a mathematical standpoint, and if I don't pass I will go, and if I pass, give me a job.

Q. What did he say to that?

A. He said, "Next case."[18]

Other Negro witnesses testified that they had been barred from applying for apprenticeship training because IAM Lodge 735 used the facilities of a local white high school for its training programs.

On the west coast, too, the IAM contributed significantly to the exclusion of Negroes from skilled trades in the aircraft and shipbuilding industries. In three instances, involving locals in San Francisco and Seattle, officials of the international union directly intervened when local lodges, in violation of the union's policy, permitted a small number of Negroes to obtain skilled jobs on a temporary basis, without regular union membership.

Lodge 751 of the IAM represented workers at one of the largest defense plants in the country, the Boeing Aircraft Corporation in Seattle, Washington. When Boeing opened its Seattle manufacturing plant, Lodge 751 was organized. It was soon placed under the direct supervision of the Grand Lodge to make certain that long-established racial restrictions and other IAM policies would continue to be enforced. After local autonomy was restored, the local union remained under the close surveillance of C. L. Bentley, a Grand Lodge representative whose sole duty was to supervise the affairs of Local Lodge 751. Boeing employed over 41,000 workers in 1941, but not a single Negro.[19] A representative of the IAM told reporters, "Organized labor has been called upon to make many sacrifices for defense and has made them gladly, but this [admission of Negroes] is asking too much."[20]

During the war feeling developed among some workers that Negro employment should be permitted at the factory. When the Grand Lodge representative was questioned by the FEPC about the local's refusal to accept Negro members, he replied that they "cannot accept Negroes into full membership because of the dominance of the southern whites in the International organization."[21]

On one occasion an official of the Seattle Urban League accompanied two Negro applicants to a meeting of the lodge. Those present at the meeting voted to admit the Negroes, but their action was later rescinded by the local's executive committee on the ground that the meeting had been dominated by Communists.[22]

The question of the IAM's refusal to allow its local lodges to admit Negroes was repeatedly raised by A. Philip Randolph at AFL conventions. In 1941, calling attention to the NAACP's efforts, Randolph said on the convention floor:

> Paul Frederickson, personnel manager, has written a letter to the National Association for the Advancement of Colored People branch in Seattle, Washington, stating that this company has an agreement with the Machinists union obliging it to employ only union members. Several of the large aircraft corporations holding national defense contracts have changed their policy, and are now employing Negroes, but not Boeing.[23]

Although direct control by the IAM's Grand Lodge over one of its largest local affiliates was publicly condemned by some union members and by the national press, its discriminatory practices continued unchanged until the FEPC referred the matter to President Roosevelt.[24] The agreement then negotiated by the committee, the Grand Lodge, and Lodge 751 provided for the issuance of permits to Negro workers at Boeing so that the local's closed-shop agreement with the company would no longer constitute a total bar to Negro employment. In a later compliance review the FEPC concluded that "the representatives of Local 751 would in the absence of the International directives admit Negroes to membership on an equal basis with whites."[25]

There was a similar situation in IAM Lodge 79, also in Seattle. Following some confusion over the status of Negroes at the IAM's 1940 convention, the officers of Lodge 79 began to interpret the "white-only" clause in the union's ritual as applying to a person's character and not the color of his skin. The local then admitted some thirty Negroes into its membership. The local union's interpretation of the racial prohibition in the ritual was opposed by the Grand Lodge, and Lodge 79 was forced to stop admitting Negroes. The IAM's general vice president wrote to the local union:

> Our Organization as well as other International and National Labor Unions takes the position that the Fair Employment Practice Committee is without authority to compel Labor Unions to accept for members persons not eligible according to the Organization's laws.[26]

After a conference in which the local's business agent told FEPC officials that "the members of Local 79 felt bound by the orders of the International and consequently they would not accept Negroes into membership until they received orders to the contrary from the International Association of Machinists," FEPC examiner Frank Pestana reported:

> The Examiner feels that Hope Lodge [79] representatives are sincere persons, interested in integrating Negroes into war industry, et cetera, and that they have made a sincere effort to by-pass International orders on the matter. They have, however, been rebuked by International representatives and feel that they are not now in a position to fight the issue.
> The Seattle area is affected by an acute labor shortage and employers generally accept Negroes without hesitancy. There is, therefore, very little evidence of any difficulty on the part of qualified Negroes to secure employment as Machinists; Local 79 protects the permit

employees just as it does its regular members. The Examiner was told that the seniority of a permit man is recognized and as between Machinists of equal ability, seniority is the basis for determining who is to be discharged.[27]

The two Seattle locals were among the very few that tried to circumvent the IAM's rigid racial bars. Although Negroes continued to be excluded from union membership, the efforts of these two locals resulted in large numbers of Negroes working on a permit basis. The national leadership of the IAM regarded these temporary work permits as a strategic concession which allowed the union to keep its exclusionary membership policies intact.

In San Francisco, Negroes were not even allowed union permits to work in the shipbuilding industry. IAM Local Lodge 824 maintained a closed-shop contract with the Richmond Shipyards in Richmond, California, and refused to allow the company to employ Negro workers. The FEPC received many complaints charging that Lodge 824 and the Richmond Shipyards were barring Negroes from machinists' positions. Andrew Hudson, a Negro machinist, said in his complaint against the union and the company:

> On November 24, 1944 I went to the hiring hall of the Richmond Shipyards to get work as a machinist. I signed a contract with the Richmond Shipyards in Detroit, but paid my own way to California. When I went to the hiring hall they sent me to the union. When I arrived at the union they said they had a closed shop and that they didn't take any colored. They sent me back to the hiring hall to get some other kind of work. They offered me work as a flanger, but I wanted to work as a machinist, so I never went for clearance.[28]

Fred Chapman, another Negro complainant, stated:

> I was recruited in Detroit, Michigan as a Journeyman Machinist to come to California and work at the Richmond Shipyards in that trade. I was recruited 11/7 and left Detroit on November 8, 1944. When I arrived in Richmond I spent a couple of days filling out forms and when that was completed . . . they sent me to the union. At first the man in the union tried to say that there were no openings, but when I told him I knew that wasn't so, he then explained that the union does not permit Negroes into membership. I went back to the company and they put me to work as a painter. The pay was the same. I worked until today, when I quit, for I do not want to be a painter.[29]

Although the FEPC had repeatedly documented violations of the executive order by the Machinists union and major federal contractors, the government failed to use its powers to eliminate the discriminatory pattern. In large measure this was due to the political alliance between the Roosevelt Administration and organized labor, combined with the acute limitations of the FEPC. As a result there were very few advances made by blacks and other nonwhite workers within the IAM and in the industries under its jurisdiction during World War II.

After Title VII of the Civil Rights Act of 1964 went into effect, the International Association of Machinists and employers with whom it held collective bargaining agreements were joint defendants in lawsuits brought by blacks and other minority workers in both the North and South.* Among the most important of these was the litigation against the Lockheed-Georgia Company and Local Lodge 709 of the IAM initiated in 1968;[30] and in 1973 a suit was filed on behalf of an affected class of 6,000 minority workers against the Lockheed Missile and Space Company and the

---

*The IAM holds collective bargaining rights in many diverse industries. For examples of the variety of issues raised within different contexts in lawsuits against the union, see, among others, *U.S.* v. *East Texas Motor Freight and Teamsters and Machinists,* —— F. Supp. ——, 10 FEP Cases 971, 10 EPD para. 10,345 (N.D. Tex. 1975); *Hardison* v. *Trans World Air Lines, Inc. and Machinists, et al.,* 375 F. Supp. 877, 10 FEP Cases 502 (W.D. Mo. 1974); *Myers* v. *Gilman Paper Co. and Machinists, Locals 446, 453, and 958, et al.,* 392 F. Supp. 413, 10 FEP Cases 220, 9 EPD para. 9920 (S.D. Ga. 1975); *EEOC* v. *United Air Lines, Inc. and Machinists, et al.,* —— F. Supp. —— (Civil Action No. 73–C–972, N.D. Ill. June 26, 1975); *Hughes* v. *Timex Corp. and Machinists, Local 156,* ——F. Supp. ——, 9 FEP Cases 62, 8 EPD para. 9776 (D.D. Ark. 1974); *Cooper* v. *General Dynamics Corp., Convair Aerospace Div. and Machinists, Local 776,* 378 F. Supp. 1258, 8 FEP Cases 567 (N.D. Tex. 1974); *Edison* v. *Rock Hill Printing & Finishing Co. and Textile Workers, Local 710 and Machinists, Local 1779, et al.,* ——F. Supp. ——, 8 FEP Cases 383, 8 EPD para. 9625 (D. S.C. 1974); *EEOC* v. *Eagle Iron Works and Machinists, Local 479,* 367 F. Supp. 817, 6 FEP Cases 1077 (S.D. Iowa 1973), *rehearing denied,* 8 FEP Cases 344, 8 EPD para. 9541 (1974); *Bragg* v. *Robertshaw Controls Co. and Steelworkers, Local 5431 and Machinists Lodge 555,* 355 F. Supp. 345, 6 FEP Cases 251 (E.D. Tenn. 1972); *Moore* v. *Sunbeam Corp. and Machinists, Local 1129,* 459 F.2d 811, 4 FEP Cases 454, 1218, 79 LRRM 2803, 81 LRRM 2158 (7th Cir. 1972); *Newman* v. *Avco Corp. and Machinists Aero Lodge 735,* 451 F.2d 743, 3 FEP Cases 1137 (6th Cir. 1971); *U.S.* v. *Jacksonville Terminal Co.,* 451 F.2d 418, 3 FEP Cases 862 (5th Cir. 1971), *cert. denied,* 406 U.S. 907, 4 FEP Cases 661 (1972); *Brady* v. *Trans World Air Lines, Inc. and Machinists,* 401 F.2d 87, 69 LRRM 2048 (3rd Cir. 1968), *cert. denied,* 393 U.S. 1048, 70 LRRM 2249 (1969); *Gunn* v. *Layne & Bowler, Inc. and Machinists, Local 3,* ——F. Supp. ——, 1 FEP Cases 383, 384, and 385, 69 LRRM 2237, 2238, and 2240 (W.D. Tenn. 1967); *Illinois State Conference of NAACP* v. *Taylor Products, Inc. and Machinists, Lodge 2290,* Civil Action No. 57596 (N.D. Ind., South Bend Division, filed May 1975); *EEOC* v. *Bendix Corp. and Machinists, Local 690,* Civil Action No. 75–32–ORL–CIV–Y (D.C. M.D. Fla., complaint filed Feb. 6, 1975); *EEOC* v. *United Aircraft Corp., Pratt & Whitney Div. and Machinists, Local 743,* Civil Action No. H–74–116 (D.C. D. Conn., complaint filed April 11, 1974); *Luster* v. *Machinists, Local 709,* —— F. Supp. ——, 7 FEP Cases 561, 7 EPD para. 9222 (N.D. Ga. 1973); *Rau* v. *Machinists, Lodge 34,* ——Wis.2d ——, ——N.W.2d ——(Wis. Sup. Ct. No. 5215).

Machinists union in California.[31]

The impact of Title VII litigation upon the IAM has had far-reaching consequences. Although this union continues to resist change, and blacks are still confronted with many problems, as a result of frequent and effective use of the law by minority workers, a ninety-year-old tradition of racial exclusion and discrimination is slowly coming to an end.

7

The Maritime Industry and the
Seafarers' International Union

Accompanying the World War II growth of the Seafarers' International Union was the extension of the racially discriminatory practices of the union on both coasts. The SIU, chartered by the American Federation of Labor in 1938, merged soon thereafter with the older Sailors' Union of the Pacific,* and had AFL jurisdiction over merchant seamen employed on the east, west, and gulf coasts, and later on the Great Lakes.[1] A consequence of its expansion was that Negro workers were even more rigidly restricted to ships' kitchens, despite the fact that Negroes had previously been employed as seamen on the decks and in engine rooms on ships operating out of Atlantic ports. When the government intervened in the maritime industry at the start of World War II, to assure labor-management stability, it froze

---

*The Sailors' Union of the Pacific originated in 1885 as the Coast Seaman's Union, which merged in 1891 with the Steamshipman's Protective Association to form the SUP. Andrew Furuseth, a Norwegian immigrant and the major figure in the early organization of west coast seamen, was one of the most militant white supremacists of his period. Furuseth frequently invoked racist arguments against non-Caucasian workers, as in his warning before a congressional hearing in 1915 that whites would be forced from the sea if black and Asian workers were employed on American ships. He later wrote that "[s]elf-respecting white men will not serve with Negroes."—*Seamen's Journal,* February 1929, p. 35. For many years the SUP formed the core of the SIU and Harry Lundeberg, secretary-treasurer of the Sailors' Union of the Pacific (an autonomous district within the SIU), was also president of the Seafarers' International Union, where he continued the anti-Asian and anti-Negro tradition of Furuseth and other founders of the organization. According to Robert J. Lampman, "[t]he SUP has rarely numbered non-whites in its membership and has never included Negroes, Chinese, or Japanese."—Robert J. Lampman, "Collective Bargaining of West Coast Sailors, 1885–1947" (unpublished doctoral dissertation, University of Wisconsin, 1950), p. 97.

218

"existing practices" specified in union agreements and the discriminatory pattern was further institutionalized. The racial practices of unions in the maritime industry were decisive in determining the status of black workers because of union control of access to jobs through hiring halls.

Although the Seafarers' International Union maintained its discriminatory practices during and after the war, racial discrimination was not accepted among all maritime labor organizations.[2] The National Maritime Union of America, a Congress of Industrial Organizations affiliate with three times the membership of the SIU,[3] did not permit segregated crews or departments aboard ships where it was the collective bargaining agent. Malcolm Ross wrote that "[t]he N.M.U. accepted Negroes in all three departments— deck, engineroom, and stewards'. There were instances where N.M.U. locals broke the nondiscrimination rule, but the union as a whole worked hard at educating the rank and file, and with overall success."[4] The NMU also sponsored complaints to the Fair Employment Practice Committee when one of its members encountered discrimination from a shipping company or from another maritime union. After the committee's satisfactory adjustment of one of the NMU's complaints, the union's port agent wrote: "In behalf of my membership, who are trying to do an all-out job against discrimination, please accept our sincere thanks for the splendid work that your office is doing."[5] The NMU's procedure was to attempt by itself to eliminate a discriminatory practice involving its members, and if it could not effect a satisfactory adjustment, to file a complaint with the FEPC. A committee report summarized one such instance:

> On June 3, 1945, Edward L. Davis was referred to the FEPC office by the National Maritime Union. The NMU had referred Mr. Davis to the St. Lawrence *Victory* as a Second Electrician. He was accepted for work one day until he met the Chief Electrician, who stated he would not work with him. The next day the Negro Second Electrician was laid off the job. The NMU claimed that its efforts to keep the Negro on the job were to no avail and referred the case to FEPC.[6]

The National Maritime Union's efforts to change the racial practices of the maritime industry present a sharp contrast to the policies of the Seafarers' International Union.

Although the SIU on the Atlantic coast segregated Negro seamen and restricted them to jobs in the stewards' department, it nevertheless did accept Negroes into membership; its west coast district, still called the Sailors' Union of the Pacific, did not. One Negro applicant was told by a union official that "they didn't ship colored boys on the West Coast."[7] Negro seamen who were referred by the federal Recruitment and Manning Organization to the Sailors' Union of the Pacific were routinely rejected, their referral slips marked "Not Satisfactory." A memorandum from the Recruitment and Manning Organization contains the union's typical response when Negro seamen were referred: "[A union official] called this office and said that the S.U.P. was not hiring Negroes and were not going to hire them. He also stated that he expected us to use a 'trick' like that and we were attempting to 'cram Negroes down their throats.' "[8]

Although the Seafarers' International Union was not alone in discriminating against Negro seamen,* it was one of the most powerful maritime unions to do so; thus it was instrumental in extending discriminatory practices along the eastern seaboard, on the Great Lakes, and on the gulf coast. Two important factors contributed to the SIU's ability to institutionalize racial discrimination in the maritime industry. One factor—the rapid growth of the merchant marine precipitated by World War II[9]—enabled the union to greatly enlarge its membership. A consequence of the union's increased power was the underemployment of at least 2,000 qualified Negro seamen—and the denial of jobs and training to thousands of other Negroes—during a period of severe manpower shortage in the maritime industry.

The second factor that placed the SIU in a strategic position to enforce patterns of racial segregation was the government's direct control of the maritime fleet. The War Shipping Administration was established early in 1942 to convert the privately owned maritime fleet to wartime use.[10] Shortly afterward it assumed ownership of all ocean-going vessels of U.S. registry. The shipping companies became "general agents" responsible for the operation of their ships. Service agreements executed between the government and the shipping companies contained the following clause: "In any act performed under the agreement, the general agent or subcontractor shall not discriminate against a citizen of the United States on the grounds of race, creed, color or national origin."[11] The agreements further authorized the continuance, or "freezing,"

---

*Other maritime unions with discriminatory policies included the International Organization of Masters, Mates and Pilots, which excluded Negroes by a clause in its constitution. The National Marine Engineers' Beneficial Association and the Marine Firemen, Oilers, Watertenders and Wipers' Union excluded nonwhites by tacit consent.

of the shipping companies' collective bargaining agreements with the maritime unions.

For companies that had collective bargaining agreements with the SIU, the "freezing" clause in the service agreements negated the nondiscrimination provisions. The union was able to maintain that, since segregation and restriction of Negro workers was official union policy before the government seizure, the service agreement constituted an official sanction of union policy and practice. This argument was further bolstered by subsequent agreements signed by the War Shipping Administration and the maritime unions.

The agreements between the government and the unions, called statements of policy, contained this clause: "If the General Agent has contracts with Unions and those contracts require, for example, preference of employment or use of Union hiring halls, the agent would be required to procure men in accordance with the contracts."[12] The statements of policy barred the renegotiation of labor-management contracts for the duration of government ownership. If a union and a shipping company had a closed-shop agreement, the company was required to turn first to the union to fill its manpower requirements. When a union engaged in discriminatory racial practices, the closed-shop agreement was in effect a screening device to prevent Negro workers from obtaining jobs. A standard clause in the Seafarers' union contract provided:

Selection of Personnel: The company agrees to secure its unlicensed personnel . . . through the offices of the union, when available, and with the understanding that the company reserves the right to select personnel for the following positions: On passenger vessels: Chief Steward, chief cook, chief baker, bartender, barber.

Employees of these ratings shall in any event be cleared through the offices of the union.

The Union agrees to furnish capable, competent and satisfactory employees. When replacements requested by the company are not furnished with sufficient promptness to avoid delay in any scheduled sailing, the company is at liberty to hire men wherever possible, with the understanding that men so hired may continue employment with the company, provided they are satisfactory to the union.[13]

The Seafarers' International Union had closed- or preferential-shop contracts with twelve of the major gulf and east coast shipping companies.[14] As these companies expanded during the war, the union's jurisdiction and concurrent enforcement of discriminatory policies expanded also.

To reinforce its commitment to preserve the status quo of employer-employee relationships, the War Shipping Administration formulated "stabilization plans" for the major maritime employment centers in the United States. One such plan covered the New York City area, the maritime industry's most active port at that time. The plan was similar in language and effect to the maritime service agreements:

SECTION 27—

The decision to hire or refer a worker shall be based on qualifications essential for performance of or suitability for the job, and shall be made without discrimination as to race, color . . .

SECTION 29—

Nothing contained in this Program shall be construed to change, modify, or restrict any agreement between any employee, union, or group of employees, or their duly designated representatives, and his or their employer.[15]

As with the service agreement, the stabilization plan contained a nondiscrimination clause but negated its effect with a clause that perpetuated discriminatory employment policies where they had previously existed; while condemning such practices, the government in fact enabled them to be continued and insured that they would be rigidly enforced. As a result of the government's action, discriminatory policies like those of the Seafarers' International Union were codified and practiced as though they had become law. Although the government could have given the nondiscrimination clauses priority over the other clauses in the agreements, it did not do so. Priority remained focused on "stability."

Because of the shortage of workers the War Shipping Administration established a Recruitment and Manning Organization to facilitate recruitment and training of merchant seamen. The organization's primary function was to supplement the maritime unions' recruitment and referral efforts. When unions could not fill positions from their membership rosters, they would place requests with the Recruitment and Manning Organization, which maintained a roster of nonunion seamen, including qualified trainees who had graduated from government-operated merchant marine schools. An FEPC examiner explained how the SIU used this referral system for its own discriminatory purposes:

Usually an operator, when he needs a seaman, calls the union with which he has a contract. Where that union cannot supply the man he needs, the union asks the RMO to send the man. The RMO gets the men from its registry and sends them out to the union on a rotary basis; i.e., the first man who checked in is the first to be sent out. This rotary system is the same as that used by most maritime unions. It was adopted by WSA as the only fair and efficient method. As long as it is followed, assignment is without regard to race, creed, color or national origin.

Even the SIU follows this system, except on a segregated basis. It has a separate hiring hall and separate dispatcher for Negroes. It assigns them only to the stewards' department, and then only if the stewards' department is all-Negro. Our complaints show that the SIU refuses to accept Negroes except as kitchen workers in all-Negro stewards' departments; that it even refuses to allow a qualified and willing white worker to work in an otherwise Negro department; and that its requests for workers specify either "white" or "colored" in order to maintain this segregated scheme.[16]

John Hawk, secretary-treasurer of the SIU, described to a congressional committee how the union placed requests with the Recruitment and Manning Organization:

If we do not have the manpower available, we call the R.M.O., which is set up to supplement the seaman's union. They have a pool of men registered, trainees, etc.

If we want a fireman, we call for a white fireman and if we want a colored fireman we call for a colored fireman. If we want a white steward we call for a white steward or a colored one.[17]

Since the Recruitment and Manning Organization's policy was to refer applicants to the SIU without regard to race or color, the union would reject Negro applicants when it was seeking white workers and reject white applicants when it was seeking to fill a position in an all-Negro stewards' department. The rejected applicants would return to the Recruitment and Manning Organization with their referral cards marked with such notations as: "Negroes only." "We do not mix." "It's a lot easier to ship one utility man than reshipping eleven men in the department." "White crew." "Supply full engine department, if not send white." "Cannot supply one but must supply full department if sending this party." "I ordered white mess. I cannot use this man."[18]

When the SIU placed a "white-only" request with the Recruitment and Manning Organization and was sent a Negro seaman, John Hawk would complain bitterly. On one occasion Hawk called the Recruitment and Manning Organization to say: "We have a statement signed by Admiral Land telling us that RMO was set up to help us: however, you are not cooperating, you are interfering. . . . The problem has been taken up by our membership and they have reaffirmed the policy now in effect in the union."[19] Hawk's interpretation of the executive order was that "[t]he Order is to do away with cases where unions will not let colored men join the union."[20] He stated that neither the President, the government, nor anyone else was going to tell his members whom to live with and that to a seaman a ship was his home.[21] In denying employment to a Negro seaman, Hawk summed up the union's position:

> This is not a Kosher organization or one interested in social reform. As far back as 1942, this Union went on record as being opposed to checkerboard crews—that neither the President nor the FEPC or any other committee would be able to force a white man to live with a Negro. We are not going to become like the N.M.U.[22]

Hawk also remarked that Negroes were by tradition intended for the stewards' department.[23]

The SIU refused to place its Negro members in any position other than those in the stewards' departments. A War Shipping Administration report details the experience of one Negro complainant, J. M. Stevens, a ship's carpenter:

> Mr. Stevens called at this office and alleged that he had been discriminated against twice in employment recently. The following is his story: The first occasion was on June 1, 1944, when he was dispatched by the S.I.U. to the SS *Talisman*. . . . After reporting on this vessel, he was informed by the mate that his services were no longer desirable because the white S.I.U. crew refused to work with him. He was told he would have to get off the ship, and it was suggested that if he dropped the matter the union would dispatch him to another vessel.
>
> The next day he was dispatched by the S.I.U. to the SS *James Harlan*, GAA vessel operated by the Seas Shipping Company. The company accepted him and he went aboard the vessel June second. Two days later the dock delegate informed him the deck crew had a meeting and they said they would not sail with a Negro.
>
> Mr. Stevens contacted the S.I.U. hall and the dispatcher, Mr. Schuler, patrolman, went to the vessel with Mr. Stevens and talked the matter over with the crew. A vote was finally taken and the crew decided to sustain the action taken the previous day. Mr. Stevens said that he asked the deck crew if there were any provisions in the S.I.U. constitution pertaining to segregation, and he was informed that there was nothing in the constitution referring to segregation but that this was a practice of the union.[24]

Another Negro seaman was promised a job in the deck department by an SIU delegate. After paying his $32 initiation fee and reporting to the union's New York City office, he was told: "We don't want any colored in the Deck Department."[25]

Not only were Negro members restricted to jobs in stewards' departments, but they could fill such positions only where those departments were all black. One Negro applicant was referred to the union by the Recruitment and Manning Organization for the position of second cook and baker. The union refused him employment, stating that the stewards' department was all white and that as second cook and baker he would be in a position of authority over white members.[26] To facilitate enforcement of the segregated departments, the union maintained a separate recruiting and dispatching department for Negro workers.[27]

An investigative report of a complaint to the Fair Employment Practice Committee states that one rejected Negro applicant's referral slip was returned with the statement: "This applicant was rejected for the following reason: White crew."[28] The report further states that "[l]ater, the 'colored department' called and said that it was an error because his department could use him. He also informed us that he was having difficulty in manning ships because of the color distinction fostered by the Union."[29] On another occasion, the union requested a second cook and baker from the Recruitment and Manning Organization. A Negro was sent and was told by the union that the position was filled. An hour and a half later the union again requested the same position for the same ship. A white man was sent and was accepted.[30]

The SIU's refusal to comply with the executive order caused many qualified Negro seamen to be unemployed during a period of extreme manpower shortages. FEPC examiner Emanuel Bloch stated:

> Discrimination by the SIU caused the building up of unemployed Negroes in such large numbers that the RMO was finally compelled to deviate from its rotary hiring system and to acquiesce in the SIU's assignment practice although it is violative of Executive Order 9346.[31]

The Recruitment and Manning Organization, in order to employ Negro seamen, began to comply with the union's discriminatory requests. In addition, the War Shipping Administration issued instructions to the RMO that forced it to retreat from the government's declared policy of nondiscrimination. The instructions contained a restatement of the formal policy, but their effect was to sanction deviations from the government's rotary referral system, ostensibly to prevent delay or interference "with the efficient utilization of a vessel":

> Instruction 43 (revised) . . . .
> 3.   Representatives of the Recruitment and Manning Organization shall recruit seamen without regard to race, creed, or color. . . .
> 5.   Seamen registered shall be referred to agents of the War Shipping Administration, operators, and maritime unions in the order in which they are registered *provided that the assignment does not delay the sailing of a vessel on schedule or interfere with the efficient utilization of a vessel in the successful prosecution of the war.*
> 6.   When deviations are made from the rotary system of assignment, to assign men on the grounds of race, creed or color, in order to prevent a delay in sailing, or achieve efficient utilization of a vessel, a report shall be made to the Assistant Deputy Administrator. . . . [Emphasis added.][32]

Testifying at a congressional inquiry, Marshall E. Dimock, assistant deputy administrator for the Recruitment and Manning Organization, explained the reason for the issuance of the instructions:

> Our basic procedure, our basic principle is the rotary hiring system . . . that is the only sound and dependable system that can be used. When this question of the FEPC came up, we took the position at first that we would make no exceptions, we would not give in to pressures or give in to expediency. Then, what happened was that the Negroes on our shipping list—who had come out of our training schools, because since Pearl Harbor about 3,000 of them have been trained—the Negroes began to pile up and they were not being shipped out. Now, we assume one of the purposes of the fair employment practice program is to utilize manpower, to find opportunities for all people who are skilled. These men are skilled, they have gone through the training program just like anybody else, that is, they are trained seamen. We thought under those circumstances, since one of the purposes of the fair employment practice program is to get these men shipped out, that when we were asked specifically to send Negroes we were justified in doing the expedient thing, that is, deviate from our rotary hiring system in supplying those men. Now, what has happened is over a period of time more operators and more unions have come to accept colored seamen without question. The general practice in the industry now is: We want so many ordinary seamen, so many messmen, so many wipers. They do not say whether they want white or black. It is very, very rare to have that happen. It is not even the typical thing in the case of the SIU, although the SIU

does more than any other union. Generally speaking, that practice of taking men by color has almost disappeared from the whole shipping industry. Now, as that situation comes to exist, it will be possible for us to adhere to our rotary hiring system and to get away from this expediency, which we do not like and which we find very difficult to defend, but which, because of the fact that Negro seamen were stacking up and not being used, we have had to do it at times in the past.[33]

The government was now trying to justify a difficult situation it had helped to create. After sanctioning the SIU's practices, the War Shipping Administration had to acquiesce in the union's discriminatory referral system in order to obtain even minimal utilization of the much needed but unemployed Negro seamen. Again, the government's priorities were such that it compromised its own civil rights policies rather than force the union to change its policies.

The FEPC received twenty-six individual complaints against the SIU, as well as many notices of union discrimination from the War Shipping Administration.[34] In reply to the FEPC's first summary of complaints sent to the SIU, secretary-treasurer Hawk challenged the committee: "Moreover, beyond the mere question of procedure, we would be pleased to learn by what authority or penal power we are compelled to respond to any communication of your committee."[35] Hawk added:

We are inclined to resent most bitterly such a course of procedure on the part of any individual, and particularly when it emanates from a government agency which is charged with the fair administration of the law, free from bias, prejudice or ill will. You seem to forget entirely . . . that this organization is composed of many thousands of brave loyal men who have made important sacrifices for the war effort, and who possess the fundamental rights of American citizenship. Although you represent a phase of activity of our sovereign government, your authority is limited by the obscure and ambiguous language of an entirely new and poorly comprehended Executive Order.[36]

Bloch opened the committee hearings by charging "that this union, because of a firm policy of designating certain jobs for Negroes and certain others for white men, has discriminated against Negroes and whites alike. . . ."[37] Before the hearings the union had tried to justify its segregated departments aboard ship by claiming that "mixed crews" would necessitate blacks and whites eating and sleeping together. Bloch replied to this argument:

> Nor are we here requesting that Negro and white seamen live togeth-
> er. That is a matter entirely between the union and the operators. But
> even if such were the result, Negro and white members of other mari-
> time unions sail together and live together at sea. These workers con-
> stitute the majority of the workers in the industry. The WSA training
> program is operated on a non-discriminatory basis. In its training
> schools, Negro and white seamen learn, study, eat, and sleep togeth-
> er, and most of the new workers going into the maritime industry are
> trained in these schools. Again, in its graduate stations, such as the
> Chelsea Station in New York, Negroes and whites are boarded and
> quartered without segregation or discrimination. Yet, a color line is
> arbitrarily drawn at the point of shipping out—and by the SIU—and
> the SIU alone.[38]

Witnesses who had graduated from the government's racially
mixed maritime schools testified to the absence of friction in
them.[39]

Richard Miles, a Negro seaman with eighteen years' experience, explained that Negroes had been barred from the engineroom department when ships began to convert from coal-burning
to oil-burning engines. He stated that between 1935 and 1942 white
men were oilers and water tenders and Negroes were firemen on
coal-burning ships. He was then questioned by the committee on
current practice:

> Q. What kind of vessels are there now?
> A. Oil burners, diesels and motor ships.
> Q. What happened to the Negroes who were firemen on the coal-
> burning vessels?
> A. They were out of a job unless they were in the Stewards'
> Department of the SIU.
> Q. Do you know whether or not any Negro firemen on the coal-
> burning vessels have become firemen on oil-burning vessels?
> A. Not for the SIU.[40]

He described a protest a group of Negro firemen had made to the
SIU in 1940 when they were not allowed to work as firemen on the
new oil-burning ships:

> A. . . . We sent for the Secretary-Treasurer from New Orleans. It
> took four months until he came. We continued writing. . . . We
> didn't get any information and we had a meeting, close to three
> hours. Charles Wade told us plainly; he said, "The whites will not
> ride with you all. Be satisfied as long as you got coal burners." And
> he says, "Otherwise . . . you can go into the steward department.
> You can transfer your book to the steward department."

Q. After there were no more coal burners, did the Negro firemen on those coal burners attempt to obtain firemen's jobs on other ships?

A. They did.

Q. Were they successful?

A. They were not successful.[41]

He also explained why Negroes were firemen on coal-burning ships but not on the easier, cleaner oil-burning and diesel ships:

Q. Can you explain why Negroes were permitted jobs on the coal-burning ships and were denied jobs on the oil-burning ships?

A. Because the whites will not accept that.

Q. Why will they not accept it?

A. Because it was too hard and dirty.

Q. Was it dirty work?

A. It was dirty work.[42]

Harry Fisher, another Negro seaman with five years' experience, spoke of his own referral to the New York office of the SIU:

Q. Will you tell the committee what happened to you after you were referred by the Recruitment and Manning Organization to the SIU?

A. Well, on the morning of the 19th I was in the office and was given an assignment, two white fellows and myself. There were three of us. We were sent to Stone Street, to the union, to go on a ship. All of us were in the steward department, the three of us. On arriving there, this one white fellow who was with me told me, "Let us be friends." I said, "O.K." He said he knew where to go, and I didn't. I didn't belong to the union and he knew. He took me around there and we went up to the sixth floor. On handing the slips to the fellow on the desk, he wrote up the two white fellows first, and he began writing me up, and then he happened to look up. He said, "Harry Fisher?" I said "Yes." He said "You are Harry Fisher?" I said, "Yes." He stopped writing and he handed me my slip back and he said, "That job is taken." I said, "Taken?" He said, "Yes." I said, "What do I tell them when I go back to the office?" He said, "Tell them the job is taken." I started to go out and a tall fellow just went in and he said, "That job is taken?" And the other fellow said, "Forget it."[43]

The Seafarers' International Union refused to participate in the FEPC hearings. The union's attorney read a statement for John Hawk, now denying discrimination and claiming that the committee was acting beyond the scope of its authority.

Before the committee issued its summary of findings and directives to the union, Boris Shishkin, the AFL representative on the committee, sent a memorandum to his fellow members saying that the proper solution of the SIU's case should involve cooperation with the union, not the issuance of directives:

> The hearings conducted by the Committee and the investigation made by its subcommittee on May 18, 1945, of two ships in the New York harbor show that this case is not limited to the simple elements of discrimination present in an ordinary place of employment. The case is not confined solely to the economic questions. The problem of sleeping quarters and eating accommodations goes beyond the simple employment relationship and deserves special attention. . . .
>
> Elimination of discrimination under these conditions should be possible to obtain, provided everything is done to elicit the fullest cooperation from the union leadership in furthering this objective. That, it seems to me, is the most effective approach toward a full and lasting acceptance of non-discrimination on all ships of our Merchant Marine.[44]

Shishkin was urging a course of cooperation with a union which had refused to conciliate on the matter of its racial practices prior to the hearings and later had boycotted them. The committee did not adopt Shishkin's position. Finally, the FEPC directed the union to cease and desist from its discriminatory practices. The *Final Report* of the committee stated:

> FEPC found on evidence at the hearing that SIU maintained segregated hiring halls and that it referred Negroes only to the stewards' department. . . .
>
> FEPC members, before issuing a directive and in deference to SIU assertions that the sailing of mixed deck and engine room crews would be fraught with disaster, visited mixed and segregated crews in New York Harbor. Discussion with the seamen themselves persuaded Committee members that opposition to Negro seamen came largely from shore personnel and not from white seamen. The directive against SIU was the last issued by FEPC. The union never responded to it.[45]

The committee also noted that this was one of its most difficult cases involving racial discrimination.

Refusing to participate in the FEPC hearings, the union instead attacked the committee by joining with its enemies in Congress. Representative Howard Smith, a Virginia Democrat and one of the major spokesmen for southern conservatives in Congress, had formed an *ad hoc* committee entitled the Select

Committee of the House of Representatives to Investigate Acts of Executive Agencies. The Smith committee was established specifically to discredit and denounce the activities of the Fair Employment Practice Committee and other government agencies attempting to enforce a policy of nondiscrimination in employment. Companies and unions which felt themselves "victimized" by the FEPC thus found a sympathetic ear in Congress.[46] John Hawk wrote Chairman Smith requesting a hearing:

> I consider it an urgent obligation to direct the attention of your Committee to a situation which is fast developing to a point where it may hamper the delivery of the cargoes so desperately needed by our fighting forces.
>
> I have reference to the arbitrary, dangerous and unrealistic interpretation being applied to the President's Executive Order establishing the Fair Employment Practice Committee by a pair of starry-eyed fellow-travelers heading the Atlantic Coast District of the Recruitment and Manning Organization of the War Shipping Administration.
>
> These gentlemen . . . are insisting that the President's Order is being violated in connection with the hiring of ships' crews because our Union requires that white seamen shall not be forced to eat and sleep in the same quarters with Negro seamen, and vice versa.
>
> [They] are trying to compel our Union to abandon a sound and tested policy which has resulted in harmonious relationships between Negro and white members over a period of many years. . . .
>
> There is not the slightest vestige of discrimination in the running of our Union. . . .
>
> The Negro members of our Union receive the same wages and voting privileges and enjoy precisely the same working conditions as our white members.
>
> It is this particular section of the President's order which is being twisted and distorted by Messrs. Vincent and Pollatsek [of the Recruitment and Manning Organization] to conform to certain social reformist theories which they are seeking to experiment with at the expense of the American seaman and the war effort, and in defiance of the sober judgment of practical men who have spent the greater part of their lives in the maritime industry.
>
> If the views of these two officials are permitted to prevail—and they have the enthusiastic endorsement of every Communist and sympathizer infesting the waterfront—in other ports throughout the country they inevitably would create a state of chaos in the maritime industry in a critical hour for our country.[47]

Hawk testified at the Smith committee hearings:

> *Mr. Jennings:* As I understand it, your union admits to membership members of the colored race?
>
> *Mr. Hawk:* Yes, sir.
>
> *Mr. Jennings:* What you are protesting against is this procedure or these orders or regulations that require the white members of the union to eat and sleep with men of a different race?
>
> *Mr. Hawk:* That is right. . . . Under that arrangement each race is respectful of the other's rights just as prevails in the armed forces of our country.[48]

The union's objection to "mixed" crews was therefore based on a policy of strict segregation. Hawk reinforced this position:

> *Mr. Hawk:* . . . On some ships where the colored men are employed, it is a full department. We do not mix the crews. In other words, white and colored we do not mix them in one department, for the simple reason that the quarters aboard the ship, the way they are lined up, is generally four in a room, and if you get four mess men aboard the ship these four mess men sleep together.
>
> *Mr. Jennings:* You try to get—
>
> *Mr. Hawk:* All of one color, because we know they have to sleep in the same room. To eliminate any beefs and to carry out the policy of the organization, if a ship has got a colored crew aboard we call on the floor for colored men to man that ship. Now, if we have not got these men, we call the R.M.O. that we want two colored mess men.[49]

The union's complaint focused on Craig Vincent, Atlantic coast representative of the Recruitment and Manning Organization, and on Frank Pollatsek, chief of the organization's New York office. When Hawk was questioned about why he felt they were refusing to fill his discriminatory requests, the following reasons were given:

> *Mr. Hawk:* Fellow travelers. The program of the party right now, one of the main programs is to—
>
> *Mr. Delaney:* In other words, you say fellow travelers and you mean by that these two men are members of the Communist Party?
>
> *Mr. Hawk:* I do not say that.
>
> *Mr. Delaney:* Members of the Communist organization?
>
> *Mr. Hawk:* I say they are sympathizers, fellow travelers are sympathizers. I am not accusing them of being Communists; they might be. They certainly lean towards the policy of the party.
>
> *Mr. Jennings:* You mean the Communist Party?
>
> *Mr. Hawk:* That is right. One of their main programs today is to— well, supposed to be helping the colored man.[50]

Malcolm Ross, chairman of the Fair Employment Practice Committee, wrote some years later:

> Before the war, Negroes comprised 6 per cent of the unlicensed personnel on vessels under American registry. Three-fourths of them had been stewards. There had been, therefore, that one-fourth in the deck department to demonstrate that it was possible for Negroes to be sailors in mixed crews. Back in the 1920's when pay at sea was poor and the job unsought, Negroes could be sailors without anyone rushing to congressional committees with complaints that the sanctity of the American home was being violated.[51]

Through a combination of increased unionization by labor organizations that maintained segregated job classifications and crews, governmental orders preserving discriminatory collective bargaining agreements, and the anti-Negro practices of the Seafarers' International Union and other maritime unions (with the exception of the National Maritime Union and the National Union of Marine Cooks and Stewards), segregation and job discrimination in the merchant marine evolved from an informal custom into a rigid pattern. Despite manpower shortages of merchant seamen, the SIU continued to restrict Negroes to jobs in the stewards' department throughout World War II and afterward.*

In 1968 the Department of Justice, acting on a referral from the Equal Employment Opportunity Commission, investigated the racial practices of the Sailors' Union of the Pacific, the west coast district of the SIU. The San Francisco regional office of the EEOC requested the intervention because it had reason to believe (on the basis of numerous complaints, including those made to the Fair Employment Practice Commission of the state of California) that the union was operating in violation of Title VII of the Civil Rights Act of 1964.[52] After an investigation and extensive negotiation with the union, a conciliation agreement was entered into between the Department of Justice and the SUP. In the agreement, which was

---

*Soon after the New York State Commission Against Discrimination was established in 1945, it received several complaints against the Seafarers' International Union. Because of reluctance to invoke its legal enforcement powers, the commission engaged in interminable conciliation which eventually resulted in a meaningless promise by the defendant union not to discriminate in the future. The *Annual Report* of the National Association for the Advancement of Colored People for 1951 stated that it had intervened "[o]n behalf of Grover Barnes, a Negro member of the Seafarers' International Union, AFL, . . . protesting against its policy of assigning Negro members only to jobs designated as 'Negro.'" The *Report* also noted that the "case involving the union had been before the New York State Commission Against Discrimination for longer than four years."—NAACP *Annual Report*, 43rd year, 1951, p. 35.

to go into effect on July 17, 1968, the union agreed to a procedure for recruitment and admission of black workers and members of other minority groups into the SUP and for employment through the SUP hiring hall. According to officials of the EEOC, the Department of Justice failed to enforce the agreement, and in 1972 Frank A. Quinn, regional director of the Equal Employment Opportunity Commission in San Francisco, wrote:

> Upon the best available information, I am forced to conclude that there has been little, if any, change in the racial practices and racial composition of the Sailors' Union of the Pacific since the FEPC hearings during World War II.[53]

8

The Construction Industry and the
Building Trades Unions

Early in their attempt to regulate the manpower supply during World War II, federal agencies such as the Office of Production Management signed "stabilization agreements" with many craft unions in the construction industry. The government thus became a party to a series of closed-shop contracts with AFL-affiliated unions that denied union membership and jobs to Negro workers. Since government-sponsored projects were the primary source of work in the construction industry during the war, Negro craftsmen in the building trades suffered widespread unemployment and underemployment while there was full employment at unprecedentedly high wages for white workers. Robert C. Weaver wrote:

> In September 1941, the Bureau of Employment Security conducted a survey of Negro workers and the national defense program. It reported that past color bars against Negroes in most skilled and industrial work had relaxed but little, if at all. The employment of Negro artisans in the vast defense construction was limited almost exclusively to carpentry, cement finishing, and, to some extent, bricklaying.[1]

The nationwide pattern of exclusion of Negro workers from defense-related construction projects was a subject of continuing debate at American Federation of Labor conventions. A. Philip Randolph of the Brotherhood of Sleeping Car Porters repeatedly protested the closed-shop agreements negotiated by Building Trades Councils of the AFL and the concurrent refusal of the construction unions to accept Negroes as members. At the AFL's 1941 convention Randolph stated:

I want to cite a few of these cases because the recitation will prove
the advisability of establishing a committee to hear and study discrimination in the labor movement.

Negro painters in Omaha cannot get into the Painters' organization, nor can they secure a charter.

Plasterers and cement finishers in Kansas City, Missouri, cannot
get into the organization nor can they get a charter. . . .

Stabilization pacts between the O.P.M. and certain of the building
trades have resulted in disqualifying qualified colored artisans from
defense employment, and thereby retarding defense efforts.

In St. Louis Negro artisans cannot get work, but white workers
come from outside of St. Louis and are put to work. . . .[2]

During World War II the American Federation of Labor
steadfastly refused to take any action against its building trades
affiliates that either excluded Negro workers or limited Negroes to
segregated locals and engaged in other discriminatory practices.
And as usual, A. Philip Randolph, not the discriminatory unions,
was blamed for the "race problem." For example, a delegate of the
United Association (Plumbers union) replied to Randolph's
charges of discrimination at the 1944 convention:

We don't have any race problem, only the race problem that is
brought up by Delegate Randolph. He goes up and down the length
and breadth of this country preaching social equality. I have no complaints with unions from a national, international or local, who take
Negroes in as members, but I do object to the Pullman Car Porters
or anybody else telling Local 17 of the United Association of Journeymen, Plumbers and Steamfitters that we have to take anybody.
We are the sole judge of who shall become our members.

I think it is high time that people should stop this professional agitation. . . . White people are not raising the race question. It is the
Negroes themselves, and I am in full accord with the committee's
report [rejecting Randolph's proposal of censure].[3]

The pattern of Negro exclusion in the construction industry
existed in all parts of the country. In Savannah, Georgia, one of the
largest employers in the area, the MacEvoy Shipbuilding Corporation, maintained a closed-shop agreement with the Savannah
Building Trades Council of the AFL. The council referred only
white carpenters to the company for employment. Whenever the
supply of local white carpenters was exhausted, the council
imported white carpenters from outside the city rather than
offering employment to the numerous local black craftsmen.[4]

In Birmingham, Alabama, Negro carpenters were excluded from membership in Local 89 of the United Brotherhood of Carpenters and Joiners, AFL. They were forced to form their own all-Negro Local 92 of the Carpenters union and enter into generally unsuccessful competition with all-white Local 89. The business agent for the all-white local testified at a Fair Employment Practice Committee hearing that his local was willing to work with Local 92 only on the condition that the Negro carpenters would work in segregated crews on separate building sites.[5] FEPC investigation disclosed that the Negro union members were refused employment with a large government contractor because "an insufficient number of Negro carpenters were available to make up a complete segregated crew, as required by Local No. 89, the organization of white carpenters in the Negro area."[6] The Negro carpenters, unable to meet the conditions of the white local, were denied employment.

The committee's hearings in Chicago inquiring into the racial practices of the organized plumbing and steamfitting trades clearly demonstrated the effects of such racial exclusion upon Negro craftsmen in northern cities. Edward L. Doty, a Negro plumber in Chicago, was the committee's chief witness at the hearings. He testified that as early as 1912 Negro plumbers and steamfitters had tried to join the all-white Plumbers Local 130 and Steamfitters Local 597 in Chicago. Then, "[a]fter [World War I] was over . . . and many of the white workers had returned home to the jobs that they had previous to going into the Army, the Negro workers in many instances [were] dropped from the job."[7] In the early 1920s Negroes had a great deal of difficulty obtaining training, licensing, and employment from the white-controlled unions and construction firms. Unable to join the white unions, they were forced to organize their own independent unions to train and obtain employment for Negro plumbers and steamfitters. "Still faced with the problem of not having a union card," Doty testified,

> our next problem was becoming members of the local trade unions in Chicago for our crafts. We knocked on the doors of Local 597 of the Steamfitters and Local Union 130 of the Plumbers from the years 1920 to 1926, seeking to become members of the above-named organizations. We were refused at every contact.[8]

Denied union membership or union work permits, Negro craftsmen organized the Cook County Plumbers Union and the Cook County Steamfitters Union, neither of which was affiliated with the AFL or was recognized as a bona fide union by the major

Chicago contracting firms. "From 1926 to 1942 the attitude of Locals 130 and 597 has not changed."[9]

In 1933 and 1934 the Federal Government began to finance the building of many housing projects in Chicago, and the government contractors honored their bargaining agreements by hiring only members of the all-white Plumbers and Steamfitters unions. "We contended," said Doty, "that Negro mechanics should be granted a fair and equitable share of the work in building such projects,"[10] but Negro craftsmen were excluded from employment on the housing projects. Thus Negroes, most severely affected by the Depression, were denied jobs on many construction projects that were created to relieve the effects of the Depression upon workers.

Doty vividly described the long continuity of racial barriers confronting Negro craftsmen in Chicago:

> I went to work in Armour's pipeshop as a pipefitter's helper in 1914 and worked in this capacity from 1914 to 1917. In 1917 I was promoted to a fitter with the tools, receiving a pipefitter's pay. During 1914 and 1915 there were efforts by the white steamfitters' organization to organize the fitters in the pipeshops in the stockyards. We colored men who were employed as pipefitters' helpers tried to become members of this organization. . . . There were approximately 35 to 50 at Armour's, and there were additional Negroes at the other packers—what were known then as the big five—Armour, Wilson, Cudahy, Swift, Morris. To my best knowledge, all these five companies employed Negroes along with the white pipefitters. A fair number of them were desirous of becoming members of this white fitters' organization . . . and on two or three occasions we went to their meetings, and they looked out and saw our faces, and they slammed the door in our faces. We weren't permitted to come into their meetings. . . . Now during this period while we colored men worked in the stockyards, we worked as helpers, we became fitters; working as fitters we worked over a long period of time, and we couldn't see much chance of advancement. We were used to training young white fellows and refugees who were brought from Europe over here—and after these refugees worked here for six months, they became foremen, and we colored men, we worked there year in, year out. We didn't see any prospects for advancement at the stockyards, so we began leaving the yards. We started doing jobs out in the city. . . . We colored men—the police would see us with our tools relating to plumbing work, and on numerous times we were arrested, and we were taken to the police station and detained for a short while, and sometimes we were actually locked up for carrying plumbers' tools

with us—we couldn't work because we didn't have licenses. We couldn't get in the union. We were being harassed by the police.[11]

In 1921 Doty and another black worker, A. W. Dunlop, received formal certification from the Illinois Board of Examiners as journeymen plumbers. They were among the first fully certified Negro plumbers in the state of Illinois. Soon afterward the two men established classes to teach other Negroes preparing for the state licensing test, and approximately fifty received state plumbers' licenses. But, Doty said:

> To our surprise, we found that our problem was just beginning. We had our licenses, but we didn't have a union card. So we went back to the union—the office was at that time down on Randolph Street. They had a little peephole, and they would look through this hole, and evidently they had a string or something on the door. When they would look down the hall and see us, the door would automatically close. So we were stuck on the outside. . . . So, after going down to the local over a long period of time, and getting all kinds of evasive remarks and what appeared to be a runaround, we men got this courage and we said, "Well, after all, these fellows don't seem to want us in their organization, and we've got to live—we've got to eat." So we began to put forth efforts for ourselves. So we set up at that time an organization known as the Chicago Colored Plumbers Protective Association. We were chartered, by the state of Illinois, as an association. This was in 1926. . . . The only employers we could work for were colored employers, and they recognized us because they organized themselves into an association, the New Era Plumbing Contractors Association. . . . But no white contractor would give us work.[12]

After the Negro unions made repeated attempts to gain a share of jobs in the Chicago building industry, they were allowed to join the AFL Pipe Trades District Council of Cook County. Membership in the council conferred the status of "union man" on the members of the all-Negro labor organizations, and in theory left them free to work for unionized construction firms. The concession proved to be a small one, however, because the white locals had closed-shop agreements with the Plumbing Contractors Association, which employed 75 percent of Chicago's plumbers. Thus the Negro craftsmen remained excluded from fully three quarters of the Chicago construction industry.

In 1939 Locals 130 and 597 proposed an agreement, subsequently adopted by the Pipe Trades Council, that placed strict limitations upon the membership of the Negro unions in the council. The Negro unions' membership in the council was conditioned upon their agreement to work exclusively for Negro contracting firms and only on residential buildings to be inhabited by Negro tenants:

> The colored steamfitters and plumbers shall be represented in the Pipe Trades Council of Cook County, Illinois, as a section of Local Union 597 and Local Union 130, United Association, by two (2) delegates, i.e., one (1) plumber and one (1) steamfitter, and such colored steamfitters and plumbers must be employed by colored steamfitting and plumbing contractors, and then only on such buildings as are occupied or are to be occupied by colored owners or tenants, but which building or buildings may be owned by any race of people. They shall work on a probationary working permit or card issued through the Council by Local Union 597 and Local 130. . . .[13]

If the Negro unions had accepted the conditions offered by the white Pipe Trades Council, they would have made their position even worse. Their members had been employed by nonunionized Negro contractors in predominantly Negro residential neighborhoods, with occasional jobs elsewhere. If they signed the agreement, they would be controlled by the white unions and able to work under permits from the white locals exclusively and only on a "probationary" basis. The Negro unions voted not to become parties to the restrictive agreement offered by the Pipe Trades Council.

The all-white Plumbers Local 130 and Steamfitters Local 597 continued to maintain their discriminatory practices in violation of the executive order. At the FEPC hearing Doty testified that "[e]ver since the issuance of the President's executive order . . . there has not been any let-up in the practices of these local unions. The facts are to date: No Negro steamfitters or plumbers are working in the construction of defense buildings in the Chicago area."[14] Exclusion by the white locals had prevented most Negro craftsmen from obtaining employment, Doty said. "We again reiterate that the strain on us and our families is becoming more severe daily . . ., coupled with the mounting cost of living which further aggravates our miserable plight."[15]

Leaders of the two white unions testified at the committee's hearing. William Quirk, business agent for Plumbers Local 130, stated that he knew of no Negroes among the 2,600 members of his union. The president of Steamfitters Local 597 testified that "[i]t is true that we have no Negro members, but it is not true that we do not permit Negroes to become members."[16]

The union officials repeatedly expressed the view that the duty of their unions was to secure full employment for their members before Negroes could be allowed to obtain jobs within their jurisdiction. Quirk stated that priority in employment should be given to the white workers because they had been members of the AFL-affiliated union prior to the promulgation of the executive order:

> Mr. Quirk: I had numerous meetings with the members here representing the Cook County Plumbers' Organization. . . . I told them that when the members of our organization were employed, we would give them work. Unfortunately, since 1931 I have had on my hands from 600 to 1,400 unemployed plumbers. . . .
>
> Chairman Dickerson: Now, will you follow his [President Roosevelt's] program?
>
> Mr. Quirk: If it does not conflict with our organization's record of fifty years. . . .
>
> Chairman Dickerson: Do you feel, Mr. Witness, that Negroes should be denied the right to work as plumbers and steamfitters on defense projects?
>
> Mr. Quirk: I do at the present time because they are not members of our organization and we have our own members unemployed. . . .
>
> Chairman Dickerson: . . . [D]o you think it is fair, Mr. Witness, that in a defense project, Negroes should have to wait until all white people in the union are employed?
>
> Mr. Quirk: I absolutely do, for this reason, that I believe that these men who claim to be plumbers should work their way up into an AF of L organization the same as I did and not overnight drop into $18.60 a day jobs because they claim to be plumbers.[17]

The unions defended their exclusionary practices on this basis while white workers were being accepted into membership and were able to obtain employment in the expanding construction industry.

Since federal agencies failed to enforce the executive order in Chicago and Negro construction workers were experiencing increasing unemployment, the government and the Chicago Housing Authority compromised and instituted a racial hiring formula. The construction firms bidding for contracts on the Cabrini Housing Project in Chicago in 1942 were required to give assurances that a minimum percentage of their payroll would be paid to Negro workers.* The instructions to bidders provided:

> The percentages of Negro labor employed in each skilled trade shall be as nearly as possible in accordance with the ratio of Negro to other labor in each skilled trade as shown by the latest United States labor census for the City of Chicago, and if the contractor pays to the Negro skilled labor at least 3.5 percent of the total amount paid in any period for four weeks under the contract for all skilled labor (irrespective of individual trades) and pays Negro unskilled labor at least 13.2 percent of the total amount paid in any period of four weeks under the contract for the unskilled labor, this shall be considered as prima facie evidence that the contractor has not discriminated against Negro labor. . . . This ratio is to be apportioned to skilled workers in each individual craft first and where workers in a particular craft are not available, the ratio so specified shall be distributed among the other crafts where skilled Negro workers are available so that the total amount of wages paid Negro skilled workers will be at least 3.5 percent in any four weeks' period.[18]

Negroes were therefore to be guaranteed at least 3.5 percent of the skilled jobs available at this project. But the percentages were based on the 1930 census, and by 1942 many more skilled Negro workers had migrated to Chicago and were available for employment. In addition, an official of the Chicago Housing Authority acknowledged that contractors on the project could easily avoid hiring the required percentages of Negroes in each of the skilled trades. By concentrating Negro labor in unskilled classifications, employers were able to fulfill their overall percentage requirements and at the same time allow craft unions such as the Electricians and Plumbers

---

*During the Depression of the 1930s the Federal Government through the Public Works Administration ordered a form of racial job quotas through the "minimum percentage clause" in construction contracts. According to Robert C. Weaver, "[p]ublic housing became the guinea pig for experimenting with developing techniques for assuring the employment of skilled Negro labor on public financed projects during a period of general unemployment. Many problems arose. . . . But experience had shown that a simple non-discrimination clause was not enough. There had to be a definition of discrimination. This was finally provided by establishing a prima facie basis of discrimination, the failure to pay Negro skilled workers (regardless of trades) a minimum percentage of the skilled payroll. The percentage was based upon the latest occupational census with slight variations adjusted to current population movements. This machinery proved effective. It was adopted by the United States Housing Authority when it succeeded the Housing Division of PWA in administering the public housing program. . . . This mechanism for defining and enforcing non-discrimination in employment was a significant development, although not a definitive solution of discrimination on public financed construction."—Robert C. Weaver, *Negro Labor—A National Problem* (New York: Harcourt, Brace & Co., 1946), pp. 11–13. See also Robert C. Weaver, "An Experiment in Negro Labor," *Opportunity*, October 1936, pp. 295–298.

and others to refer white workers exclusively.[19] Thus, even on projects where minority employment problems resulted in intervention by government agencies, Negroes remained excluded from the higher paying, traditionally all-white skilled trades.

One of the major building trades unions in the AFL is the International Brotherhood of Electrical Workers, which excluded Negroes from membership in its industrial as well as in its construction locals during World War II. This practice was a continuation of the union's traditional racial policy. From January to March 1941, the U.S. Employment Service placed 1,066 workers in electrical equipment production jobs, but only five were Negroes.[20]

The FEPC held two formal hearings involving manufacturing companies in which the IBEW was the collective bargaining representative. In both instances, IBEW locals stated their refusal to permit Negroes to work in any capacity other than that of janitor. In Cincinnati, IBEW Local B-1269 had a closed-shop agreement with Victor Electric Products, Inc., and was the sole bargaining representative for all of the company's 526 employees.[21] The company employed only one Negro, as a car unloader outside its plant.

After several complaints were filed against the company and the union, the president of the company responded to FEPC inquiries: "In partial explanation we have a union, Electrical Workers, AFL. On numerous occasions they have been sounded out regarding this matter, and their answer has been consistently and firmly in the negative."[22] The personnel director told officials of the War Manpower Commission that "since an AF of L union is the bargaining agent for all workers in the plant and does not accept non-white members . . . it would be unwise to consider hiring non-white workers at present. In addition, there are no washroom facilities available for non-white women workers."[23] Union officials tacitly encouraged a strike among the membership—in violation of the union's stabilization pact with the government—in the event that the company began to hire Negroes. At the FEPC hearings the president of Local B-1269 predicted a walkout if any Negroes were hired and stated that the officers of the local would not be able to persuade workers to return to their jobs if a strike occurred.[24]

At the committee's second hearing involving the IBEW, also held in Cincinnati, both the officers and the rank and file membership of another IBEW local made it clear that they would not obey the executive order.[25] Local 1061 held a union-shop agreement* with the Crosley Corporation. The company employed over 7,000 workers, only six of whom were Negroes, and all six were employed as janitors or maids. The IBEW local's exclusion of Negroes had the practical effect of denying them employment opportunities except in menial jobs. Responding to FEPC inquiries about the absence of Negroes in production work, the local's president replied: "We don't want the Negroes to stick their foot in the door. We don't want them for competitors in the postwar period. We won't take any."[26] The union's representative took the position that he would be the first to walk out if the company hired any Negro workers, and he added: "I will state again that we represent the voice of the people. The voice of the people is that they will not work with niggers."[27] The racist policies of the union officers were fully supported by a majority of the white rank and file. While the FEPC hearings were in progress, a petition from the union, signed by over 4,000 employees, was presented to the committee: "I for one will not work with colored help. Never have and never will. I am a firm believer that every man or woman has the right to live, whether he is black or white, but the Negro has to be kept in his place. . . . Keep them in their place."[28]

One of the two instances of presidential seizure of facilities because of racial labor disputes during World War II occurred at a large plant of the Western Electric Company. On October 6, 1941, the company hired Negroes for the first time at its manufacturing plant in Point Breeze, Maryland.[29] The two "company unions," the Point Breeze Employees' Association and the Point Breeze Salaried Employees' Association, did not initially object to the employment of Negroes.[30] At that time, in accordance with a municipal code requiring racial segregation of rest rooms, the company installed separate shower, toilet, locker, and cafeteria facilities.[31]

On February 13, 1943, after the racial requirements of the code had been modified, the company desegregated plant facilities.[32] The two unions objected and voted to strike under the War Labor Disputes Act.[33] The National War Labor Board assumed jurisdiction,[34] and the unions' demand for totally segregated facilities was denied by the board in a unanimous decision.[35]

---

*A form of union security which permits the employer to hire whomever he chooses but requires all new employees to become members of the union within a specified period of time, usually thirty days. It also requires the worker to remain a union member or to pay union dues for the duration of the collective bargaining agreement.

On November 16, 1943, the Fair Employment Practice Committee stated:

> The Committee takes the position that in the circumstances of this case, where there are frequent and temporary transfers of workers from department to department, such installations of segregated duplicate facilities cannot but lead to discriminatory employment practices and would be in violation of Executive Order 9346.[36]

On December 13, 1943, the board reaffirmed its decision, and the employees refused to work.[37] Six days later President Roosevelt issued an executive order[38] directing Secretary of War Henry Stimson to assume control of the plant. The order, however, did not direct the Secretary to enforce the FEPC-National War Labor Board ruling but merely "authorized" him to take various steps to obtain the "compliance" of the unions. That same day the War Department took possession of the plant.[39]

After several conferences between War Department officials and union representatives, it was clear that although the unions realized that the strike was unlawful, they refused to urge employees to return to work.[40] To overcome this resistance, Robert Patterson, Acting Secretary of War, asked the War Manpower Commission to deny certificates of availability to striking employees who might try to seek employment elsewhere,[41] and asked the Selective Service System to withdraw the striking employees' draft deferments.[42] By December 27, 1943, production was again normal at the plant, but there were still union threats that the strike would resume when the government departed.[43]

The company began to enlarge toilet and locker areas, which were to be assigned in blocks.[44] John H. Ohly, in his study of governmental seizure of defense facilities, wrote:

> Though there was no formal agreement, the intention to assign lockers to white employees which would adjoin each other and to Negro employees which would also adjoin each other was announced. Though there would be no segregation by rule, in the use of toilet facilities, it was apparent that each employee would use that nearest his locker, which would result in a sort of voluntary segregation.[45]

The War Department, wanting production to continue without further disruption, obtained "grudging approval" for this plan from one FEPC representative.[46]

When the unions renewed an earlier demand for a wage increase before the National War Labor Board, the board inquired into the status of the strike. The unions declared that the strike was temporarily in abeyance as a result of government control.[47] After the company and the War Department informally suggested to the unions that this situation might adversely affect the board's wage-increase decision, the unions agreed to consider the strike at an end.[48] Shortly afterward, on March 23, 1944, government control was terminated.[49]

Here government and company efforts toward integration merely resulted in a more informal system of racial segregation. One commentator later speculated about federal power in general to enforce a policy of nonsegregation: "It might have become fully operative if supported with the same zeal that the Army showed a few months later in introducing Negro operators into the Philadelphia transportation system."[50] (See Chapter 11.) A former official of the National War Labor Board has suggested that the government compromised in the racial controversy because the Western Electric plant held a vital production priority rating as a critically important source of signal wire for the armed forces.[51]

The findings in the FEPC's investigation and hearings on the racial practices of the International Brotherhood of Electrical Workers were indicative of the national pattern of discrimination in the electrical manufacturing industry during World War II. Actively encouraged by officers of the international, locals in virtually every section of the country consistently refused to admit Negroes into membership or apprenticeship training. Throughout the entire war period—when there were critical shortages of electrical workers—the IBEW barred Negroes from its ranks and from employment in its jurisdiction.

In the years between the end of the federal Fair Employment Practice Committee in 1946 and the adoption of the Civil Rights Act of 1964, Negro workers filed many complaints with state and municipal civil rights agencies against the IBEW. Among the most important of those resulting in litigation was a 1953 case, *International Brotherhood of Electrical Workers* v. *Commission on Civil Rights.*[52] When the IBEW became the collective bargaining agent at the Bauer Electric Company in Hartford, Connecticut, it demanded that all Negro production workers be dismissed from their jobs because they could not be admitted into union membership. The Supreme Court of Errors of Connecticut protected the job rights of the Negro employees by sustaining the cease-and-desist order of the State Commission on Civil Rights, whose authority had been challenged by the union.

Significantly, complaints against IBEW locals, including the *Dobbins*[53] case in Cincinnati, were among the first charges to come before the Equal Employment Opportunity Commission in 1965, and the first lawsuit filed by the Department of Justice under Title VII, on February 4, 1966, was jointly against two construction unions in Cleveland—the Sheet Metal Workers International Association and the International Brotherhood of Electrical Workers.[54]

In 1973, the EEOC charged that the IBEW was responsible for discriminatory practices in twelve metropolitan areas, including New York, Washington, Chicago, Dallas, and Los Angeles. Jointly charged with the IBEW was the National Electrical Contractors Association, which consisted of 6,000 affiliated construction companies employing over 200,000 workers.[55]

One of the major areas of litigation under Title VII of the Civil Rights Act of 1964 has been the construction industry. (For an extensive analysis of the application of Title VII to the building trades, see Volume II, Chapter 5.) The large volume of charges filed by black workers against building trades unions and contractors with the Equal Employment Opportunity Commission after 1965, and the many court decisions in this area, indicates the continuing resistance by construction industry employers and labor organizations to the requirements of civil rights laws and federal executive orders.

9

The Trucking Industry and the
International Brotherhood of Teamsters

In the course of many hearings and investigations the Fair Employment Practice Committee found that even after some Negro workers gained membership in restrictive labor unions they continued to experience racial discrimination in several different forms. The desirable, high-paying jobs under the jurisdiction of these unions were invariably reserved for whites.

In the trucking industry during World War II, the International Brotherhood of Teamsters, Chauffeurs, Warehousemen and Helpers of America—then a major union in the AFL—limited Negro workers to intra-city truck-driving jobs or to lower paying work in warehouses and terminals. Defending the practices of a Teamsters local in Birmingham, its president offered testimony at an FEPC hearing that echoed organized labor's disclaimers of discrimination in many other cases: "In the State of Alabama . . . I don't think we can be accused in any way of discrimination. We have here in the City of Birmingham AFL unions with 100 percent Negro membership."[1]

In fact, unionized Negro drivers, in the North as well as in the South, were barred from the better paying, "over-the-road" jobs. Then as now the inter-city or "long-haul" truck drivers organized by the Teamsters union were paid an hourly wage plus a substantial mileage bonus. Annual earnings of over-the-road drivers are much higher than those of drivers limited to trucking within a city, which pays a lower hourly wage and no mileage bonus. This was, and remains in the 1970s, the national pattern.

248

Discrimination within the trucking industry was not confined to the South. During World War II the Teamsters union had nine locals in Detroit.[2] Six admitted Negroes, and those locals had jurisdiction only over intra-city short-haul jobs carrying coal, ashes, and garbage. FEPC chairman Malcolm Ross later wrote that "[i]n Detroit the white truck drivers . . . allowed Negroes to join their union, pay dues, and drive the garbage trucks within the city limits. None of this social equality for the white knights of the long haul."[3]

Teamsters Local 299, one of the largest locals in the city, with more than 6,000 members, had jurisdiction over interstate routes and maintained closed-shop agreements with eleven major long-haul trucking firms. Local 299 excluded Negro workers from membership and actively deterred trucking firms from using Negro drivers on long-haul jobs, even though unorganized Negroes were driving on interstate routes elsewhere in the country, including the South.

The trucking companies in Detroit relied on the U.S. Employment Service for the recruitment and referral of workers. Whenever a Negro was referred to a company that had a labor agreement with Local 299, he was denied employment on the ground that he would have to join the local union, which refused to accept Negro members. Oscar Purvey, a Negro trucker with twelve years' experience driving fruit from Florida to Boston, was referred by the USES to a Detroit company that had an agreement with Local 299.[4] The local refused to grant him membership, and in order to work at his trade he was forced to join Detroit Local 247 instead. The jurisdiction of Local 247, which accepted Negro members, was limited to the hauling of lumber, coal, garbage, and factory rubbish within the city.

Teamsters Local 299—of which James R. Hoffa was then the president—consistently barred Negroes from the most desirable jobs in the industry. The War Manpower Commission, charged during World War II with maintaining an adequate labor supply in essential industries, conducted an investigation in 1944. It reported that "the trucking companies [in Detroit] stated that the uncompromising stand taken by Mr. James Hoffa, president of Local 299, prevented them from complying with the executive order."[5] The report also summarized a conference which officials of the War Manpower Commission had held with Hoffa:

Mr. Hoffa on behalf of the union was of the opinion that there was no discrimination practiced by either the employers or the union. He enumerated the locals which had Negro members, and that therefore the Council did not discriminate, but that Local 299 was not yet ready to accept Negroes as truck drivers. He explained that this was due to the attitude of the members and that he was working to correct this attitude.[6]

It soon became apparent that Hoffa and the local were doing nothing to "correct this attitude." In 1945 an official of the FEPC talked with a representative of one of the trucking firms that had signed a labor agreement with Local 299. His report stated:

I asked her about the person referred to . . . and she remembered him and said that they were desperately in need of help at the time he came out, and they wanted to hire this person, and said they hesitated prior to contacting Local 299. Mr. Calhoun of this local was contacted and he instructed Mr. Trump not to hire non-whites but to tell them that no job opening existed. According to the company representative, Miss Barry, the complainant was a neat, well-mannered person, and they were anxious to hire him. Because of the closed shop agreement they were unable to do so.[7]

The FEPC then held hearings inquiring into Local 299's racial practices, but the union and Hoffa refused to participate. An FEPC memorandum contains Hoffa's response to the notice of the proposed hearings:

James Hoffa . . . phoned yesterday and after asking a couple of questions and receiving answers to same, advised that he did not intend "to be at the god-damn meeting." The questions he asked were: (a) Does the Committee have the power of subpoena, and (b) Does the Committee have the power to invoke criminal penalties.
Both questions were answered in the negative.[8]

At the committee's hearings in Detroit, Negro truck drivers testified that they had been denied membership in Local 299 and therefore had been repeatedly denied employment by firms which offered high-paying jobs on interstate routes. Many testified that they had driven over-the-road routes for trucking firms in other parts of the country. Festus Harrison, a Negro driver, described a typical encounter with Hoffa and Local 299. Harrison, who had twelve years' experience driving moving vans, owned his own truck and equipment and was used by a Detroit trucking company for job assignments. A member of another Teamsters local, he had gone to Local 299's offices to apply for a transfer. He testified that "Mr. Hoffa stated that it was against the policy of the union for Negroes to pull over the road."[9] Harrison persisted in his application, and Hoffa invited him to a meeting of Local 299 so that he could present his request to the membership. He told the FEPC panel what had taken place:

> So then Hoffa gets up and he said, "Now fellows, we have this question of colored drivers over the road." He says, "We have Harrison here. He is here to present his side of the case." . . . I told the fellows, I said, "Fellows, I am just a truck driver like you, trying to make a living. Now we are in a war and we are trying to win. I'd hate to think that I belong to an organization that is less democratic than any other when the President is asking us all to cooperate." In the discussion or talk I pointed out that Crispus Attucks was the first man to die for this country. . . . Then I told them about Pedro that came across with Columbus when he discovered America. And getting back to recent events, just talking to the drivers as I would anyone else, I asked them if any of them had given blood to the Red Cross at a blood bank. One fellow said, "Yes." I told him Doctor Drew, a Negro professor at Howard University, discovered that. In further discussion, I told them, if I was walking down the street and your house was on fire, I said, "You wouldn't refuse me to throw a pail of water on the fire to help put it out." And I said, "If your brother was up on the firing line fighting and a Negro brought a truckload of bullets up there," I said, "I don't believe he would refuse to use them because a Negro brought them."[10]

The membership of Local 299, voting secretly, refused to admit Harrison, and after the incident had been reported in the Detroit press, Hoffa warned him: "You will learn how the union deals with people that do things like this. Now try and get a job."[11] Unable to obtain permanent employment, Harrison was finally forced to let a white friend, a member of Local 299, use his truck and equipment.

Another Negro truck driver described the discriminatory practices of Local 299 at a Senate subcommittee hearing concerning the establishment of a permanent Fair Employment Practice Committee. The Michigan *Chronicle* reported:

> The discriminatory policies and practices of the Teamsters Union and the vicious underhand way in which certain employees go along with them, were brought to light last week when Al Barnes, Navy veteran and Detroiter, testified before the Senate Subcommittee in the interest of a permanent FEPC. . . .

Barnes explained to the committee that he had worked for the Chrysler Corporation in Detroit after his release from the Navy, but had to leave the job because his draft board . . . called him for induction into the army.

Upon his return to the city, after failing to be inducted, Barnes applied to the Employment Service Office. . . . They referred him to the Fleet Carrier Corporation. . . .

Said Barnes, "I immediately went to this company's office. There I was told that they would hire me—but before I could get the job I would have to join the Teamsters Union and that the fee would be $25—if the union would accept me."

"I told the interviewer," Barnes said, "that that would be satisfactory to me, that I would be very glad to join the Union. At this the interviewer smiled and said, 'If they will accept you, you will have a job.' He directed me to Mr. Hoffa, the business agent of the Teamsters Union, Local 299 of the AFL," Barnes said.

Arriving at the Teamsters Union office, Barnes said that he was told that the office was closing and that Mr. Hoffa was not in anyway. "Informed that there was no one else to handle membership, I was told to come back at nine o'clock in the morning," Barnes said.

Barnes testified that he was told at a quarter to nine that Mr. Hoffa was not in, was told the same thing at nine o'clock and on throughout the day. "During this whole day, I stayed until three-thirty p.m., I noticed white men coming in and getting consideration without waiting," Barnes said. "There were no other Negroes that came into this office. It seemed very strange to me that a big union like this, which has contracts with so many companies, couldn't take care of my membership."[12]

Teamsters Local 299, which controlled the desirable long-haul routes out of Detroit, effectively prevented Negroes from obtaining jobs with companies with which it had closed-shop contracts. Negro truckers were forced to seek work hauling industrial waste and garbage at low wages within the city. Many complainants at the FEPC hearing testified that the local refused even to accept transfer applications from Negroes who were members in good standing of other Teamster locals and from others who had many years' experience driving interstate routes in the South.

The racial practices of the Teamsters union in Detroit, as revealed in the FEPC's 1945 investigation, were typical of a national pattern. More than twenty years after the FEPC hearings, complaints filed with the Equal Employment Opportunity Commission against trucking companies and the Teamsters union in several cities showed that the policy of excluding blacks from over-the-road jobs had not changed.* And in a 1971 news release the EEOC stated that it had "charged the entire trucking industry with a 'disgraceful' record of employment discrimination" and asked the Interstate Commerce Commission to exercise its "statutory duty . . . to prohibit employment discrimination by regulated truckers":

> The EEOC statement pointed out that the ICC, with life and death power to license truckers, would be best able to eliminate the shameful pattern of industry discrimination. . . . EEOC argued that "the overwhelming statistical evidence of disparate treatment in employment by the industry establishes a *prima facie* case of discrimination at law." . . . The EEOC position was supported by the Department of Justice, the Department of Transportation, the Office of Federal Contract Compliance and the U.S. Postal Service.[13]

Although in the 1940s the Fair Employment Practice Committee had amassed "overwhelming statistical evidence," it had no power to eliminate the discriminatory job patterns in trucking and other industries that have continued into the 1970s. The Equal Employment Opportunity Commission demonstrated this continuity in its "Initial Statement . . . Before the Interstate Commerce Commission" on "Equal Opportunity in Surface Transportation."[14] The commission indicated a connection between discriminatory employment practices and the pervasive social unrest within black ghettos during the 1960s. Taking note of "an incident in Cincinnati which precipitated racial confrontation," the EEOC said that "[e]mployment discrimination in the trucking industry was the triggering mechanism in this particular instance."[15] The EEOC then quoted a description of the incident from the *Report* of the National Advisory Commission on Civil Disorders (Kerner commission):

> In the 90 degree temperature of Monday, June 12, as throughout the summer, Negro youngsters roamed the streets. . . . Negro youths watched white workers going to work at white-owned stores and businesses. One Negro began to count the number of delivery trucks being driven by Negroes. During the course of the afternoon, of the 52 trucks he counted, only one had a Negro driver. His sampling was

---

*In 1966 the National Association for the Advancement of Colored People filed charges with the EEOC against nine trucking companies in North Carolina, Texas, Ohio, and Tennessee, and local unions affiliated with the Teamsters union. One complaint was from a black veteran of the U.S. Army's long-haul Red Ball Express. "Since last fall," he said, "I've applied eighteen times at five trucking companies for an over-the-road job and in most cases haven't even gotten past the telephone operator."—Lee Berton, "Bias in the Cab," *Wall Street Journal,* March 31, 1966, p.1.

remarkably accurate. According to a study conducted by the Equal Employment Opportunity Commission less than 2 percent of the truck drivers in the Cincinnati area are Negro.[16]

The EEOC drew attention to the social implications of the statistical evidence cited in its "Initial Statement . . .":

> Three years after the [Kerner commission] report, little has changed in the trucking industry, either in Cincinnati or in other parts of the Nation. Pervasive discrimination remains the rule. Cincinnati, with a black population of about 10.3%, has only 300 black employees in its trucking industry. This accounts for 4.4% of a total of 6825 employees in the industry. . . .
>
> Cincinnati is typical of the trucking industry across the Nation. All available information indicates that the trucking industry generally excludes minorities and women or relegates them to the lowest-paying and least prestigious positions in the industry. The desired reaction to the dire prognostication of the Kerner Commission that the United States was fast becoming two separate and unequal societies, one black and one white, was apparently not forthcoming from the trucking industry. Employment discrimination by race, national origin and sex continues unabated. . . .
>
> The teeming ghettos of minorities callously denied equal employment opportunity are being left to fester. Trucking companies in major cities with large minority populations are the worst offenders: Chicago, with a black population of 14.3% and a black participation rate of 15.1% for all industry, employs only 8.8% blacks in trucking.[17]

That the evidence of employment discrimination in the trucking industry is indeed "overwhelming" is borne out in the ample documentation of the EEOC's "Initial Statement . . .":

> Employment statistics for 1970 for the industrial classification of Trucking, Local and Long Distance, show that Negroes constitute only 7.3%, women 8.6% and Spanish-surnamed Americans 2.3% of total employment therein. However, 17.3% of the laborers are Negroes as are 23.8% of the service workers, both low-paying job categories which include jobs like dockmen, greasers, washers, night watchmen, yard workers and janitors.
>
> The best-paid positions for workers in the industry are the over-the-road driving positions. These positions are clearly distinguished from city drivers which are not considered as prestigious and do not pay as well. However, the combined statistics for both over-the-road drivers and city drivers show that only 6.9% are Negroes. It is also an established fact that most of the black drivers are in city driver jobs. . . .

9.5% of all employees in the Nation's workforce are Negro but only 7.3% are Negro in trucking. 4.1% of all white collar jobs are filled by Negroes in all industries but only 2.4% in trucking. Most significantly, while 13.5% of all operatives in industry are Negroes, in the trucking industry, where operatives as drivers earn particularly high wages, only 6.9% are Negroes. Similar comparisons can be drawn for Spanish-surnamed Americans and women. . . .

This is particularly distressing in view of the fact that growth in the trucking industry has been progressing at a rate faster than the overall economic growth of the Nation. Furthermore, the industry is characterized by relatively low level entry skills and high wage rates. Truck drivers constitute over one half of the total jobs. Over-the-road drivers average about $11,000 a year with incomes of $20,000 not uncommon. Demand for truck drivers both now and in the future is substantial. The *Occupational Outlook Handbook* published by the Bureau of Labor Statistics anticipates approximately 8,400 additional job openings for long-haul drivers each year through 1980.[18]

Here the EEOC emphasizes two of the most important aspects of employment discrimination in the trucking industry—the continued growth of an industry which will require increased manpower, and the high wages available to over-the-road drivers who are, with rare exceptions, white.

In further commenting on the wage and status discrepancies between the different job categories open to white and black workers, the EEOC notes:

The appalling total or near total exclusion of Negroes from the trucking industry is reflected again in the following statistics: 2,515 or 68% of the 3,671 trucking establishments reporting to EEOC in 1970 hired less than 1% Negroes in white collar jobs. In Michigan, of 70 firms reporting, 10 had no blacks at all, 37 had no blacks in white collar jobs, 35 had no blacks as craftsmen, and 32 had no blacks as operatives. Ohio, Pennsylvania and, to a lesser extent California, have records which are equally disgraceful. . . .

There are two categories of road drivers, the over-the-road or line drivers and the city or local drivers. The first class averages about $11,500 a year, the latter about $8,000. Unlike the long-haul driver, who spends practically all of his time driving a large tractor trailer, the local driver spends considerable time in loading and unloading the freight which he transports in a smaller vehicle. While many long-haul drivers earn $20,000 or more, few, if any, local drivers earn more than $8,000 a year average.[19]

The commission also takes into account the discriminatory nature of distinctions in educational qualifications for job categories:

> Since trucking does not require a high level of education, differences on that account between minorities and whites cannot explain the exclusion of minorities from trucking. Only 10% of all trucking industry employees are found in jobs requiring more than a high school education. Yet, blacks in trucking have attained 85% of the white educational level (8.3 years as compared to 9.8 years) but earn only 56% of white wages. This suggests that there is no reason for the job segregation of even those few blacks to get past the barriers which block the employment door in trucking.[20]

The commission ascribes the "disgraceful" discrimination against blacks and other minorities in the trucking industry to both the employers and organized labor:

> As stated above, the truck driving jobs are the bulwark of the industry. Practically one out of every two people employed in the industry drives a truck. Drivers are well paid and their interest is jealously protected by the unions. . . .
> Presently, the two most important sources of employees in trucking are either referrals by incumbent employees and pirating employees from other trucking companies or absorbing the employees of a company which has moved its terminal facilities or merged with another carrier. Also, union referral through the shop stewards or hiring hall is also frequently used. All three sources tend to exclude minorities. . . . The traditional word-of-mouth recruiting system by referrals has disastrous implications for . . . minorities. . . . Since Anglo males occupy virtually every high paying job in the trucking industry, they tend to refer other Anglo males for those jobs. Blacks, confined to menial jobs, refer blacks for those jobs. Similarly, one company's hiring the former employees of another has a discriminatory effect since all companies in the industry have traditionally excluded minorities. Use of the union as a source also effectively excludes minorities.[21]

In a footnote, the EEOC "Initial Statement . . ." gives examples of racial bias among officials of local unions within the International Brotherhood of Teamsters:

> E.g., the president of IBT Local 24, Akron, Ohio, was quoted as saying (apparently in reference to Title VII), "To my knowledge, no law has been written yet that says a white has to bed down with Negroes." Expressing an even stronger sentiment, the president of IBT Local 100, Cincinnati, Ohio, posed the question, "Would you like to

climb into a bunk bed that a nigger just got out of?" *Wall Street Journal,* March 3, 1966. The adverse effect of deep-seated feelings such as these is borne out in a case before the EEOC in which a company employed one Negro road driver, but since none of the carrier's 473 white drivers would pair with him, he was forced to work as a local driver. EEOC Case No. At 7–4–471. . . .[22]

Litigation under Title VII against the trucking industry and the Teamsters union began in 1967 in *Bing* v. *Roadway Express.*[23] In this case the plaintiff charged that despite his nine years of experience in driving a variety of vehicles, he was prohibited from transferring from his job as an intra-city driver to a position in the over-the-road classification. It was further charged that the no-transfer provision in the collective bargaining agreement between the employer and the Teamsters union was inherently discriminatory given the total exclusion of blacks among the 300 drivers in the over-the-road classification into which he sought transfer. More than seven years of litigation was required against the employer and the Teamsters union in order to eliminate the discriminatory pattern in the operation of this one trucking company.

In later cases, the statistical evidence of employment discrimination prepared by the Equal Employment Opportunity Commission was recognized by the courts as presenting a "pattern or practice" of unlawful racial discrimination. In 1970, in the case of *Jones* v. *Lee Way Motor Freight,*[24] a federal court noted that "[i]n racial discrimination cases, statistics often demonstrate more than testimony of many witnesses, and they should be given proper effect by the courts."[25] In this case, where there were no black over-the-road or line drivers and all employed blacks were city drivers, the court held that "[i]n light of the large number of line drivers, the statistics establish a prima facie case of discrimination in that during the 1964–1968 period race was a factor in staffing the two drive categories,"[26] and ruled that the practice of hiring separate groups of drivers on a racial basis for over-the-road and intra-city routes was an illegal discriminatory practice.

On January 14, 1971, the Department of Justice filed suit against T.I.M.E.—D.C. Freight, Inc., and the Teamsters union in Lubbock, Texas, charging discrimination against black and Spanish-surnamed persons throughout the trucking company's operation.[27] This company, with headquarters in Lubbock, operates forty-nine terminals in twenty-four states. In May 1972 a consent order required the trucking company to employ more blacks and members of other minority groups in its operations across the country.

During the same period the Justice Department charged Interstate Motor Freight Systems of Michigan—with eighty-one terminals in twenty states and the District of Columbia—and the Teamsters union with discrimination against blacks and Spanish-surnamed workers.[28] As of February 1971 this company had 3,861 employees, of whom ninety-four were members of the two minority groups. According to the government charge, the union's contract with I.M.F.S. perpetuated the effects of discriminatory practices by preventing members of these minority groups from transferring to higher paying and more desirable jobs.

Not surprisingly, among the first suits filed by the EEOC under the 1972 amendments to Title VII was an action against the Preston Trucking Company, of Preston, Maryland.[29] The commission charged that the company violated Title VII, as amended, by using unvalidated tests and screening devices to the detriment of blacks, and using segregated help-wanted ads to the detriment of women.*

In October 1973 the Department of Justice sent letters to the International Brotherhood of Teamsters and 514 trucking companies informing them that government investigation had disclosed a national pattern of hiring and seniority practices that discriminated against blacks and Spanish-surnamed workers in violation of Title VII. J. Stanley Pottinger, head of the Justice Department's Civil Rights Division, told the *Wall Street Journal* that the department had previously tried to eliminate unlawful practices by negotiating with the Teamsters union and Trucking Employers, Inc., but their

---

*Among other cases involving the pattern of discrimination in the trucking industry are *Rodriguez* v. *East Texas Motor Freight,* 505 F.2d 40, 8 FEP Cases 1246 (5th Cir. 1974); *Thornton* v. *East Texas Motor Freight,* 497 F.2d 416, 7 FEP Cases 1245 (6th Cir. 1974); *Black* v. *Central Motor Lines, Inc.,* Civil Action No. 2152 (W.D. N.C. May 31, 1972), consent judgment entered, *affirmed,* 500 F.2d 407, 8 FEP Cases 633 (4th Cir. 1974); *EEOC* v. *Braswell Motor Freight Lines, Inc.,* 8 FEP Cases 754 (N.D. Tex. 1974); *EEOC* v. *McLean Trucking Co.,* ——F. Supp. ——, 7 FEP Cases 302 (W.D. Tenn. 1974); *Cathey, et al.* v. *Johnson Motor Lines, Inc. and Teamsters, et al.,* 398 F. Supp. 1107 (Civil Action No. C-C-72-262, W.D. N.C. Dec. 20, 1974); *Macklin* v. *Spector Freight Systems, Inc., et al.,* 156 U.S. App. D.C. 69, 478 F.2d 979, 5 FEP Cases 994 (D.C. Cir. 1973); *Hairston* v. *McLean Trucking Co.,* 62 F.R.D. 642, 6 FEP Cases 779 (M.D. N.C. 1973); *Sabala* v. *Western Gillette, Inc., et al.,* 362 F. Supp. 1142, 6 FEP Cases 120 (S.D. Tex. 1973); *U.S.* v. *Central Motor Lines, Inc. and Locals 71, 391, and 710, Teamsters,* 325 F. Supp. 478, 3 FEP Cases 354 (W.D. N.C. 1970); *U.S.* v. *Roadway Express, Inc., et al.,* —— F. Supp. —— (Civil Action No. C-68-321, N.D. Ohio), *affirmed,* 457 F.2d 854, 4 FEP Cases 643 (6th Cir. 1972); *Johnson* v. *Georgia Highway Express, Inc.,* 417 F.2d 1122, 2 FEP Cases 231 (5th Cir. 1969); *U.S.* v. *Associated Transport,* Civil Action No. C-99-G-68 (E.D. N.C.), consent decree entered.

responses were "negative" and therefore the department was considering litigation.[30] After further futile negotiations, suit was filed charging that the trucking companies, together with the International Association of Machinists and the International Brotherhood of Teamsters, discriminated against minority workers in several respects, including exclusion from the higher paying jobs in long-haul trucking, as mechanics, and in supervisory positions, and that nonwhites were restricted to employment in intra-city trucking, in terminals, and as warehousemen. On March 20, 1974, seven of the major trucking companies named in the lawsuit entered into a consent decree that required percentage "hiring goals" in filling vacancies and new jobs with black and Spanish-surnamed workers.[31]

In December 1973, in San Francisco, a class action suit asking for $50 million in compensatory back pay was filed on behalf of black and Chicano workers against four locals of the Teamsters, one local of the IAM, and several major trucking companies.[32] The attorney for the minority workers called the trucking industry "one of the most racially exclusionary . . . in the United States."[33]

In 1974 the Court of Appeals for the Fifth Circuit ordered that qualified minority workers limited to city driving be permitted to transfer to more desirable over-the-road jobs as such openings occurred. The court further ruled that the seniority of the nonwhite workers who transferred should date from the time they became qualified for long-haul trucking rather than the time they actually requested transfer.[34] In the same year the Supreme Court refused to set aside a back-pay award to a class of black truck drivers who were subjected to discriminatory racial practices.[35]

Although the law was clear, trucking companies and the Teamsters union continued to violate Title VII and new lawsuits were initiated. Among them was the suit filed by the Equal Employment Opportunity Commission on March 4, 1975, against Borden, Inc., and Local 991 of the Teamsters union in Pensacola, Florida. In this case the EEOC charged that Borden discriminated against black workers in hiring, job assignment, and classification, as well as in promotion and seniority practices; the EEOC also charged that Local 991 discriminated against blacks both in representation and in regard to affirmative action.[36]

These and other cases suggest that despite a later retreat of the courts efforts to eliminate the traditional employment pattern in this industry will continue into the 1980s.

10

Industrial Union Action Against Discrimination: The United Automobile Workers and the United Packinghouse Workers

The history of American labor unions suggests that discriminatory racial practices will most likely become a characteristic of such organizations unless three factors are present: first, a significant concentration of black workers, with their own leaders, in a union's jurisdiction before organizing begins; second, an organizational structure based on industrial unionism; and, finally, a union leadership sensitive to racial issues and involved in social protest. These factors were constructive influences in the development of two advanced industrial unions within the CIO—the United Automobile, Aircraft and Agricultural Implement Workers of America (UAW) and the United Packinghouse Workers of America (UPWA). Both unions' positive responses to executive orders prohibiting discriminatory employment practices during World War II contrasted sharply with the hostile reactions of most labor unions in that period.

In 1944 the UAW and the Fair Employment Practice Committee signed an agreement whereby initial attempts at resolving complaints of racial discrimination against the union would be handled by the union itself. If the union was unable to resolve the conflict, it would cooperate with the FEPC in attempting to reach a satisfactory conclusion. The agreement, which was circulated to local unions, provided that:

> In an effort to promote union cooperation in the adjustment of complaints of discrimination involving the United Automobile, Aircraft

and Agricultural Implement Workers of America, FEPC and UAW-CIO have agreed upon the following case handling procedures for all cases in which the UAW-CIO is the party charged or where a UAW-CIO local or organizing committee is in existence in the plant of the party charged:

1. After the case has been docketed and it appears sufficiently meritorious to warrant a contact with either the employer or the union, send to Mr. Victor G. Reuther, Assistant Director, War Policy Division of the UAW-CIO, a summary of the complaint, the findings to date, and a statement of what action, if any, is or will be required of the UAW-CIO local or organizing committee.

2. Before any such case is referred to the Director of Field Operations as unadjustable at the regional level, send a summary of the case to the War Policy Division, specifying what action is desired from the International UAW-CIO. You may set a reasonable time limit on UAW-CIO action, after which referrals to the Director of Field Operations will be made. . . .

UAW-CIO has agreed that its War Policy Division will:

a. Cooperate with FEPC in the investigation and adjustment of all cases referred or brought to the attention of the UAW-CIO.

b. Issue written instructions to all UAW-CIO personnel designed to implement this cooperative understanding and send copies of those instructions to each FEPC regional and sub-regional office.[1]

The United Auto Workers not only supported the FEPC but also conducted civil rights educational programs among its locals.* A substantial portion of the union's 1944 policy manual was devoted to FEPC activity. For example:

The Constitution of the UAW-CIO states that it is one of the objects of our organization:
"To unite in one organization, regardless of religion, race, creed, color, political affiliation or nationality, all employees under the jurisdiction of the International Union."
The UAW-CIO, therefore, favors the continuation of the work FEPC is doing. . . .
All Local Unions of UAW-CIO are required:

---

*It should be noted that there was an intense factional struggle within the UAW during this period. Socialists, Communists, Trotskyists, and other radicals were deeply involved in the internal political life of the union and educational activity became important within this context. The two major leadership factions were the Addes-Thomas group and the Reuther group, both vying for the support of Negro union members. For a useful but somewhat biased account written by two ardent partisans of the Reuther group, see Irving Howe and B. J. Widick, *The U.A.W. and Walter Reuther* (New York: Random House, 1949).

a. To obey FEPC directives unless and until directed otherwise by the International Office.

b. In each case where FEPC has found discriminatory employment practices in violation of the Executive Orders, local unions should confer with management and seek an immediate correction of such practices in line with FEPC recommendations or directives. . . .

Local Union Presidents and other Local Union Officials should: . . .

d. Prepare and carry out, in cooperation with the FEPC field office in your region, a workable educational program designed to do away with race, color, religious and nationality ill-will among union members and in the union community. . . .[2]

Despite its efforts to cooperate with the FEPC, the UAW was not always successful in implementing this civil rights policy. In January 1943 the union obtained collective bargaining rights in a narrow election victory in the Lockland, Ohio, plant of the Wright Aeronautical Company.[3] Racial segregation was total in this operation—Negroes worked in a separate building manned exclusively by Negro labor. After the union certification election, UAW representatives charged that American Federation of Labor organizers were demagogically provoking racial strife to "embarrass its leadership, render it impotent and [force it to] lose its majority strength in a future election."[4] Hindered by a combination of union factionalism and ineffectual leadership, the UAW was unable to prevent a strike by 15,000 white employees when Negroes were advanced to jobs in the "white building."[5] The white workers eventually returned to work after a series of compromises that provided some gains for Negro workers, but the discriminatory pattern was not eliminated.

In Anderson, Indiana, UAW Local 662 had a collective bargaining agreement with the Delco-Remy Company, a subsidiary of General Motors. The union contract provided for 312 job classifications and restricted Negro employment to five.[6] Burney Woods, president of the Delco-Remy local,

readily admitted the responsibilities of the local in the matter of job restrictions, but seemed uncertain as to the attitude that his Committeemen would take and dubious as to the extent to which the white members of the local would accept and support the championing of the rights of the Negro members. He was doubtful that the company would take any responsibility for a work stoppage which occurred as a result of upgrading Negro workers, and he was not sure what steps could be taken without risking such a stoppage.[7]

An FEPC report records the reactions of white union members to a proposed integrated banquet to express the union's patriotism and support of the war effort:

> An uproar developed within the Delco-Remy union over the question of admitting Negro members to a banquet, dance, and floor show held in celebration of a successful drive to raise funds to purchase two ambulances for the Army. Both the drive and the gala evening were sponsored by the local, and the dance and floor show were held in the newly-purchased union headquarters. The final decision of the local was to bar its Negro members, which it did.[8]

Shortly thereafter the local's executive board passed a resolution that "Negro members be barred from the union hall, clubroom, and all activities, save on regular meeting nights."[9]

In a letter of protest to the FEPC, Robert E. Wilkerson, executive secretary of the Negro Welfare Association in Anderson, wrote:

> Along with these acts of discrimination it is felt by Negro union members of this local that their plight of being relegated to the five most undesirable classifications in the Delco-Remy Division of G.M.C. is due primarily to Local 662 UAW-CIO's passive attitude on the subject. Immigrant southern whites dominate the local, and they are not interested in seeing to Negroes being treated fairly even from the point of view of the union. . . .[10]

Protracted negotiations between the FEPC, the company, and the union failed to change the status of Negro workers.

Despite the official policy of the UAW, strikes by white workers to protest the employment and promotion of Negroes occurred at a number of large auto plants. Among the racially motivated work stoppages in the Detroit area were those at the Timken-Detroit Company and at the River Rouge plant of the Ford Motor Company. Major strikes occurred at plants of the Packard Company, where whites protested the promotion of Negro workers to production jobs; at the Naval Arsenal, then operated by the Hudson Motor Car Company; and also at the Highland Park factory of the Chrysler Corporation.

The UAW leadership defended the job rights of Negro workers at the Packard plant. During this strike, in September 1941, UAW president R. J. Thomas told a meeting of the UAW's National Ford Council:

Negroes pay a dollar a month dues the same as any other union member. Negroes have fought for this organization the same as others. Negroes will fight for it in the future. And still some people ask why Negroes should be upgraded. . . . I have given an ultimatum to the Packard workers that they must go back to work. I am going to make that ultimatum stronger and if it means that large numbers of white workers are going to get fired, that is exactly what is going to happen. This International Union is not going to retreat from that position.[11]

The union's policy was reinforced when Thomas later appeared with a group of UAW officials and crossed the anti-Negro picket lines. But the strike did not end until the Negro workers were temporarily withdrawn from production jobs.*

Later, when Negro women were about to be hired at the Willow Run plant of the Ford Motor Company, Richard T. Leonard, a UAW vice president, called a meeting of white women workers to explain the union's policy toward minorities. Leonard made it clear that the Negro women to be hired would share lunchrooms, toilets, and other facilities with the white women workers on a nondiscriminatory basis. The women voted unanimously to accept the union's policy.[12]

In the midst of these racial conflicts Walter P. Reuther, then a vice president of the United Auto Workers, told the 1942 convention of the Congress of Industrial Organizations:

---

*Action by the UAW leadership at the Chrysler Highland Park plant in 1942 was more successful. In response to the promotion of Negroes into production departments, three work stoppages by white workers took place. The UAW national leadership bluntly told the strikers that if they did not return to work, they would forfeit their jobs. Similar action was taken the same year by the union at the Dodge truck plant when a "wildcat" strike protesting the transfer of Negro workers to war-production employment occurred. At the Hudson naval ordnance plant white workers walked off their jobs on June 18, 1942, after eight Negroes were employed as machine operators. In this instance, the UAW and the Navy Department jointly informed the strikers that if they did not immediately return to work, they would be not only dismissed but denied future employment in all national defense industries. As a consequence, all white workers returned to their jobs. An extensive series of strikes by white workers over the employment of Negroes also occurred at the Packard airplane motor plant beginning in May 1943. After three Negro workers were promoted to the hitherto all-white final motor assembly line, white workers walked off their jobs. On June 3, another walkout took place involving more than 90 percent of the white workers at this major war-production facility. The strike did not end until the Federal Government, management, and the national union leadership jointly invoked strong measures against white workers. The history of these events indicated the necessity for active intervention by the government, and also revealed significant differences on racial matters between the white union membership and the national leadership of the UAW. For an analysis of racially motivated work stoppages and of the status of Negro workers in the auto industry during World War II, see Lloyd H. Bailer, "The Automobile Unions and Negro Labor," *Political Science Quarterly,* December 1944, pp. 548–577.

It is the duty of every delegate here to go back to his respective organization and see that it takes up the fight against racial discrimination, not as a secondary consideration, not as something you think about after you get your closed shop and your wage increases and your seniority agreements; but this fight against racial discrimination must be put at the top of the list with union security and other major demands.[13]

But these declarations of policy often went unheeded by the white membership of the UAW. An eyewitness account by a participant in the events at the Hudson facility indicates the pattern of racial conflicts in Detroit auto plants during World War II:

In early 1944, when this writer became active in union affairs, the majority of Negroes employed at the main plant of the company were janitors. Under the impact of Executive Order 8802, a small number of Negroes had been upgraded from the janitorial force into a production unit of the plant. This group of Negroes, numbering about fifteen, were all located in a single department which machined cast iron parts for a motor assembly. . . .

The local union, while having committed itself policy-wise to the implementation of Executive Order 8802, had done little to force the company to either employ Negroes or to desegregate those already working on production. . . .

. . . [T]he attitude of the chief steward of the district (the district was composed of three machining departments: cast iron, pistons, connecting rods) was to leave the Negroes segregated in the cast iron department. Thus, when an opening developed, the chief steward ignored the Negro workers and upgraded only white workers. There was, at the time, considerable upward mobility as jobs were vacated, but no Negro workers could break out of the cast iron department to get a better-paying classification since all of the better-paying jobs existed outside of the cast iron department.

. . . Problems came to a head when an opening developed on a grinding operation in the piston department. Consulting the seniority lists, this writer found that the highest seniority entitled to upgrading was held by one of the workers in the cast iron department whom we shall call "Smith." Smith was a Negro who had accumulated ten years' seniority as a janitor and brought it over into the cast iron department under the seniority rules prevailing at the plant. This writer realized that Smith was entitled to the upgrading by all trade-union rules but that political expediency required bypassing him. . . .

Smith decided to take the job. After meeting the opposition of the foreman, who warned that there would be trouble, Smith was upgraded according to contractual language. But there was trouble. The attitude of the white workers in the piston department resembled that of a lynch mob. (It was this writer they wanted to lynch as a "nigger-lover," not Smith.) Attempts were made to explain the action on a trade-union basis, particularly to a number of the long-seniority workers who were the "opinion-makers" of the department, but communication was impossible.

Over a period of several months, particularly as Smith worked on the job, the workers of the piston department came to accept the situation. . . .[14]

During this period, Shelton Tappes, a prominent leader of black workers within the UAW and later an international representative of the union, was involved in efforts to obtain the upgrading of Negro workers in several plants. He describes the strikes vividly:

Most of the hate strikes were created by the leaders of white groups who would object to Negroes entering their departments, which heretofore had been all white. They were departments in which semi-skilled work was performed. The only contact most of these departments had had with Negroes was as janitors, cleaners of one kind or other—those who cleaned the machines, or carried out the offal as it is called. These are scraps of grinding operations, scraps from stamping operations and work of that kind. Menial types of work and in some cases assembly operations. Until that time, in plants which had foundries, most Negroes worked in the foundry, and where the machine assembly operations were performed, or the trimming operations were performed, the only way Negroes were employed was in cleaning up and preparing the job for the other workers to perform. During the war, as a result of labor shortages, and in some cases because management had decided to make a move to democratize their setup, they began to move Negroes into more preferred jobs—in some cases through seniority and in others by arbitrary decision. So the resistance came from the white workers, and in many cases they would walk off the job as soon as a Negro was brought in and placed there.

    . . . The walkout at the River Rouge plant of Ford Motor Company was a little different from the others. The Rouge walkout involved the white-collar-type department. . . . It was all pencil-and-paper work, a small amount of typing. The committee in the unit, realizing that a lot of people were being hired directly into these departments and at the same time knowing that a lot of the people who were working in the plant were able to do this kind of work, decided that they would upgrade some people from the plant into this department rather than hire the new people off the street. Hiring went on continuously during the war. At all times they were hiring people. It wasn't seasonal like during the [prewar] automobile production days. This committee upgraded three or four Negro men, young men, into this department. They facilitated all the preliminary work so these men were instructed to come in prepared to work on these jobs the following day. They walked in, and as soon as these men were assigned their jobs and the jobs explained to them—first, the young ladies began to walk out; they walked into the lunchroom one by one and sat down, encouraging others as they went along. It was about an hour before the entire department was in there . . . white women and white men. Mostly white women—about thirty white women, ten white men. People had walked off the job because Negroes had been upgraded.

We got up on a platform and told them that Local 600 was composed of Negroes and whites and that Negroes and whites were responsible for the organization. . . . We gave them a choice—the protesting white workers—of working with Negroes or not working at all. That if they refused to accept the promotion of Negroes they would have to quit their jobs. . . . Literally all of them went back.

. . . In 1944 we had a year in which the race question had been very sharply posed by specific plant conflicts, white workers had expressed their hostility in the Packard, Hudson, and River Rouge situations; but local unions and the international did what had to be done to secure equal rights for Negroes. . . .[15]

After the war, in auto plants outside the Detroit area, the UAW frequently compromised on racial issues, especially in the South. Complaints were filed by Negro UAW members with the President's Committee on Government Contracts charging discriminatory practices by auto industry employers and complaints were also made to the international union charging violations of the UAW's antidiscrimination policy by local unions. Both the Urban League and the National Association for the Advancement of Colored People requested the assistance of the international union to eliminate segregation and discrimination in auto plants in Birmingham, Atlanta, Cleveland, St. Louis, Kansas City, and elsewhere.[16]

In 1952, the UAW revoked the charter of a local in Dallas because it excluded Mexican-American workers. Soon thereafter the local was admitted into the International Association of Machinists with its exclusionary practices intact. Walter Reuther, president of the UAW, in discussing the union's racial policies later stated that "[w]e even expelled a Texas union for excluding Mexicans. That was the only time in our history we had to do that. . . ."[17] In 1960 the UAW placed Local 988, at the International Harvester plant in Memphis, under the trusteeship of the international union because the local insisted on maintaining segregated facilities at its headquarters.[18] However, these were isolated responses by the leadership of the UAW to highly publicized and extreme situations.

A confidential survey based on compliance reports made in 1957 by the President's Committee on Government Contracts of Ford assembly plants in Atlanta, Dallas, Memphis, Kansas City, Missouri, Norfolk-Portsmouth, Virginia, and Long Beach, California, documented discriminatory patterns and noted that there was "a wide regional divergency in the implementation of Ford's stated policy of non-discrimination in employment."[19]

In 1961 the U.S. Commission on Civil Rights in its report on employment stated:

> In Baltimore, each of the companies employed Negroes in production work and not above the semi-skilled level—as assemblers, repairmen, inspectors, and material handlers. In Atlanta, the two automobile assembly plants contacted employed no Negroes in assembly operations. Except for one driver of an inside power truck, all Negro employees observed were engaged in janitorial work—sweeping, mopping, or carrying away trash. Lack of qualified applicants cannot account for the absence of Negroes from automotive assembly jobs in Atlanta.[20]

Black workers and civil rights organizations held public demonstrations in 1964 in Detroit and elsewhere against the discriminatory practices of the General Motors Corporation and took other actions against Ford, Chrysler, and American Motors.[21] During this period there was also a resurgence of black caucus activity inside the union.

The growth of the black labor force in Detroit auto plants in the thirty years since World War II has been dramatic. For example, between 1960 and 1970 Local 3 of the UAW had an increase in black membership of 60 percent; in 1972, blacks constituted over 40 percent of the labor force employed at the River Rouge plant of the Ford Motor Company.[22] By 1973, over two thirds of the 6,900 employees at the Chrysler Corporation's Jefferson-Kercheval plant were black.[23] The large concentration of black workers in the auto industry in Detroit and to a lesser extent in other cities, primarily in the Midwest, has provided the basis for a continuity of black caucus activity within the UAW that is almost as old as the union itself and is an important chapter in black labor history.*

In March 1970 the UAW notified its local unions of a revision in the constitution of the international union affecting utilization of Title VII of the Civil Rights Act. The UAW's constitution, like most union constitutions, specifies that a member cannot file a complaint with a government agency or initiate litigation against the union until all internal remedies have been exhausted. The UAW informed its members of the policy change:

> While the union requires a UAW member to utilize the provisions and procedures set forth in the collective bargaining agreement and the appeals procedures of the UAW constitution, the union cannot in any way prevent the aggrieved member from exercising his "public right" to file a case alleging a practice of discrimination under the provisions of "Title VII of the Civil Rights Act of 1964."[24]

From January 1, 1966, to June 15, 1969, 196 charges against the UAW were filed by its members with the Equal Employment Opportunity Commission or state fair employment practice

*See, for example, interviews with auto workers who led various black caucuses in the UAW from the inception of the union to the late 1960s. Among the interviews conducted by the author in Detroit are the following: Joseph Billups, October 27, 1967; Hodges Mason, November 28, 1967; Shelton Tappes, February 10, 1968; George W. Crockett, March 2, 1968; Robert Battle, March 19, 1968; and Horace Sheffield, July 24, 1968. Transcripts may be examined upon application to the Director, Archives of Labor History and Urban Affairs, Wayne State University, Detroit, Michigan.

Beginning in the late 1950s there was growing discontent among black UAW members on two important issues—continuing exclusion from jobs in the skilled trades and exclusion from major leadership positions within the international union. A resurgence of black caucus activity within the UAW occurred. Several caucuses of black workers emerged during the 1960s, from the moderate Ad Hoc Committee of Concerned UAW Members to the League of Revolutionary Black Workers. An example of direct action by a radical black caucus was the walkout at the Dodge main plant on May 2, 1968, organized by the Dodge Revolutionary Union Movement (DRUM). Subsequently, radical protest groups were formed at other facilities of the Chrysler Corporation, General Motors, and the Ford Motor Company. On several occasions, black workers led by DRUM crippled auto production by a series of wildcat strikes at the Chrysler Corporation's Hamtramck assembly plant. At this installation, where over half of the 7,000 hourly rated workers were black, the caucus attacked not only the Chrysler Corporation but also the UAW itself for its failure to eliminate what the caucus described as "labor-management racism."—*DRUM*, Vol. 1, No. 2 (June 1968), Detroit, Michigan. See also League of Revolutionary Black Workers, *Black Workers Protest UAW Racism—March on Cobo Hall* (leaflet) and *Inner City Voice*, Vol. 2, No. 3 (March 16, 1970) and No. 6 (June 1970); "Our Thing is DRUM," *Leviathan*, June 1970, p. 9. At a major facility of the Ford Motor Company in Mahwah, New Jersey, the United Black Brothers, a group acting independently of the League of Revolutionary Black Workers, organized work stoppages and succeeded in paralyzing all production—winning concessions from management. Similar production disruptions were organized by the Afro-American Employees Committee, which conducted sit-down strikes at the Hotpoint Electric plant in Chicago. Work stoppages also occurred at two plants of the Ford Motor Company in Louisville, Kentucky.

agencies,[25] and the union was named as a defendant in *U.S.* v. *Hayes International Corporation*[26] and in other lawsuits. During the 1970s the UAW and certain of its local unions continued to be involved in litigation under Title VII. Among these cases was the suit filed in 1973 by a local organization of black UAW members against the General Motors Corporation, Detroit Diesel Allison Division, the UAW International Union, and its Local 933 in Indianapolis.[27] The black plaintiffs charged both the company and the union with violating Title VII in regard to sex and race discrimination.

Another example was the suit against the FMS Corporation (John Bean Division), a manufacturer of agricultural equipment in Florida. In this case filed by the EEOC on November 21, 1974, Local 1204 of the UAW was named as codefendant with the employer, who was charged with discriminating "[a]gainst blacks in recruiting, hiring, race-segregated job classifications and departments, discharge, training, promotion, terms and conditions of employment and failure to institute affirmative action programs."[28]

In comparison with most other labor unions, the UAW is distinguished by its formal commitment to civil rights, but during the 1960s and 1970s this was increasingly viewed by its large black membership as an abstraction lacking in concrete application. Whatever argument there may be on this judgment, there is no doubt that the racial issue is a continuing source of contention and conflict within the UAW.

The United Packinghouse Workers of America pledged its support to the FEPC during World War II as did the UAW, and actively opposed white workers' resistance to Negro job advancement in the postwar period and after.* Ralph Helstein, president of

---

*The role of black workers, together with the influence of radical political ideologies, in the formation of the Packinghouse Workers union was unique. Black workers constituted approximately 25 percent of the labor force when, on October 24, 1937, the Packinghouse Workers Organizing Committee of the CIO began its first organizing efforts in Chicago, then the center of the meat packing industry. (On October 18, 1943, the committee was dissolved and the UPWA became a separate union within the CIO.) Large numbers of black workers had originally entered the industry as strikebreakers during the 1920s. See Alma Herbst, *The Negro in the Slaughtering and Meat Packing Industry in Chicago* (Boston: Houghton Mifflin, 1932). The assistant director of the PWOC was Henry ("Hank") Johnson, who was to play a crucial role in the union's early organizing campaigns. Many other black leaders were to emerge later, including Philip Weightman, who became vice president of the international union, and Sam Parks, who served as director of District 1, the union's largest and most important district. He was succeeded by another black worker, Charles A. Hayes, who has held the post for many years. According to Herbert March, a prominent radical organizer for the UPWA in Chicago in its early period, "Wobblies, Communists, Socialists, and other radicals who believed in industrial unionism worked together and became an influential force

the union from 1946 to 1968—when it merged with the Amalgamated Meat Cutters and Butcher Workmen of North America, AFL-CIO—says of the Packinghouse Workers history:

> The Packinghouse Workers Union paid a price for our advanced position on Negro rights. Not only did we lose several locals because of problems with white workers but other labor organizations demagogically used the race issue to attack and raid us. The United Packinghouse Workers reversed the tradition of union racial discrimination in the packinghouse industry. We not only organized Negro workers into the union, but we insisted on full job equality in the shop. We encouraged participation by Negroes as members and leaders within the activities and life of the union itself. There is no question but that our policy created a stronger union. The great test was that after our defeat in the 1948 strike against the industry, the AFL Amalgamated Meat Cutters tried to raid the United Packinghouse Workers in many cities, but failed in every one.[29]*

Describing the role of union leadership in racial conflicts, Helstein added:

> It is the responsibility of union leadership to directly challenge racist sentiments among the white membership, to use the power of the leadership to prevent racist practices. As international president I may not be able to change the racial attitudes of white workers but I can use the prestige and authority of my job to prevent racist actions.[30]

An example of how the UPWA used the arbitration process to obtain jobs for Negroes occurred in 1950 at the Chicago plant of Swift & Company. The union charged that in refusing to employ thirteen Negro women the company had violated Paragraph II of the collective bargaining agreement, which provided that the employer "will give fair and reasonable consideration to any applicant or employee regardless of race, sex, color, creed, nationality or membership in the Union." In submitting the dispute

---

in the growth of the Packinghouse Workers Union, especially in Chicago. But more important was the role of Negro workers. In Chicago, Negro workers became the backbone of the union and eventually provided its most effective leadership."—Interview by author with Herbert March, Los Angeles, July 21, 1968.

*The merger of the UPWA with the Amalgamated Meat Cutters in 1968 was a consequence of basic changes that occurred in packinghouse operations during the 1950s and 1960s. The introduction of a new, sophisticated technology, together with decentralization, eliminated the large concentrations of manpower that had long been a characteristic of this industry. The UPWA membership, based in the slaughterhouses and processing plants, rapidly diminished. The membership of the Meat Cutters union was more diversified and based on the "block-butchers" employed by wholesale suppliers and in retail stores, such as supermarkets, where they were less drastically affected by technological change.

to arbitration, the union demanded that the Negro women be hired with retroactive seniority and back pay. To prevent future violations, the union also insisted that the company be directed to furnish it at regular intervals with the names of all new job applicants and the department and payroll number of those who were hired. The arbitrator ruled that

> the violation of Paragraph II is established beyond question. It seems a fair conclusion from the evidence that during the last two weeks of November, 1950, the Company was not only failing to give female Negro applicants "fair and reasonable consideration," it was failing to give them any consideration whatsoever . . . the Company must be held responsible for the actions of those of its officials who instituted and carried through this policy. The Agreement was violated by those in charge of the employment office of the Chicago plant, and the Company is answerable for the violation. The Arbitrator holds that those Negro applicants whose names were furnished to the Company at the third step of the grievance procedure are entitled to an award directing that they be employed on the first available jobs for which they are qualified with seniority as of November 30, 1950. This holding is necessarily based on a finding that if the aggrieved had not been of the Negro race, they would have been hired on or before that date.[31]

Helstein says:

> We not only forced the company to employ the Negro women but, most significantly, we got back pay and retroactive seniority for them. I believe that our union, in this and other cases, by being adamant on racial issues and insisting on a literal enforcement of the union contract, anticipated legal developments in this field by more than a decade. But, sad to say, we were the only union doing it.[32]

Officials of the United Packinghouse Workers union, both black and white, relate with much pride the many examples of the organization's battles on behalf of black workers and the gains made as a direct result of action by the union. The UPWA succeeded in eliminating segregated plant facilities in several cities in the South and Southwest, although in some instances white workers refused to accept the union's racial policies—as in Moultrie, Georgia, where a Swift local seceded from the UPWA and affiliated to the Amalgamated Meat Cutters, which permitted it to continue its discriminatory practices.[33] In the South as well as the North, the union conducted effective campaigns to obtain the promotion of black workers to jobs with higher status and better pay, and also interceded to obtain initial employment for nonwhites. The UPWA held integrated educational and social functions in the Deep South, often in extremely hostile communities, and the union gave active support to many local and national civil rights struggles.[34]

The United Packinghouse Workers union was directly responsible for important advances in the status of its nonwhite members.[35] From this union's inception it functioned as an interracial organization, with black workers sharing in the leadership of the union. In this fundamental way it was different from most American labor unions, which either actively discriminated against blacks or, at best, regarded their nonwhite membership as a problem to be contained and controlled. In contrast, the leaders of the UPWA—often in opposition to their white members, especially in the South—promoted the interests of black workers at the workplace and in the society as a whole. The uniqueness of this union was that it perceived itself not merely as a collective bargaining agent that provided certain services to its members in return for dues but rather as a labor organization involved in social change.

11

The Philadelphia Transit Strike of 1944

A major problem for black workers in the period of full employment during World War II—and one that would remain central in the postwar years—was the difficulty of moving beyond the traditional black job classifications. This required efforts to change racial employment patterns in many industries. Limited entry into some hitherto all-white classifications came about slowly and was often accompanied by intense racial conflict. Progress was made through a combination of factors, including direct protest by black workers; resort to the judicial process; appeals to the Fair Employment Practice Committee and the War Manpower Commission; and, in a very few instances, through direct intervention by the Federal Government with its extraordinary wartime powers, which included plant seizure and the use of the U.S. Army.

White resistance to Negro job promotion was by no means limited to aircraft production and other war-related industries. Traditional discriminatory patterns were enforced and even intensified in older industries—most dramatically, perhaps, in urban public transportation systems. The FEPC investigated the racial employment practices of transit companies in several cities, including Philadelphia, Washington, D.C., Los Angeles, and San Francisco. White workers employed in the Philadelphia, Washington, and Los Angeles transit systems staged work stoppages— actions that were illegal during the war—over the issue of upgrading Negroes into jobs historically reserved for whites only.

The urban transit cases represent both the triumph and the defeat of the FEPC. Open defiance of the law, in the form of an illegal strike by white workers, caused President Roosevelt to invoke the power of presidential seizure and to order the Army into Philadelphia; similar defiance a short time later failed to persuade President Truman to act in the Washington case, thus seriously undermining the FEPC's effectiveness (and causing the resignation of its most forceful member, Charles H. Houston of the Howard University Law School). In this chapter we will examine the issues, conflicts, and resolution of the Philadelphia transit strike, the most notable instance of governmental action generated by the FEPC. (Chapter 12 deals with other urban transit cases and the varied effects the Philadelphia developments had on them.)

The government's success in Philadelphia in enforcing federal prohibitions against employment discrimination had the immediate effect of securing employment for Negroes as streetcar conductors and operators and bus drivers throughout that city's transit system. The bitter strike of white workers that followed attempts to upgrade Negroes to these positions, and the ensuing government seizure of the transit system, generated, at least in the immediate wartime period, some public condemnation of discriminatory hiring practices and support for government efforts to combat them. The massive display of force, along with sympathetic public opinion, had the added effect in some cases of dissipating potential resistance to subsequent efforts to achieve fair employment for Negroes in the transit systems of other cities. For example, the Los Angeles transit system dispute involving the same issues was settled, after initial resistance, with only a formal FEPC hearing.* The government's success in Philadelphia was important, finally, because it demonstrated for the first time the government's intention to actually enforce its declarations against racial discrimination in employment.

Long before World War II the transit companies of most American cities had informally but effectively designated "platform jobs"—conductor and motorman on streetcars, and bus drivers—as "white men's jobs." Negroes were allowed to work in low-paying maintenance classifications and as car cleaners and porters, but were barred from operating positions and from contact with the

---

*"The Philadelphia seizure by President Roosevelt had favorable consequences. The settlement facilitated an early disposition of long-drawn-out negotiations for the employment of Negroes as operators on the Los Angeles Railway. And the employment of Negroes in Philadelphia proved so satisfactory to the company and so generally accepted by the community that . . . a decade later, the company reported 600 Negroes employed in operations positions. . . ."—John L. Blackman, Jr., *Presidential Seizure in Labor Disputes* (Cambridge, Mass.: Harvard University Press, 1967), p. 192.

public. The racial employment practices of local transit companies were particularly subject to criticism throughout World War II because manpower shortages in many of them seriously hampered the ability of workers in essential industries to get to and from their jobs. Public sentiment was also aroused in some communities because the inferior status of Negro employees could not be shielded from view; it was self-evident to the riding public. Moreover, in Philadelphia a heated interunion rivalry for the right to represent the transit workers kept attention focused on the issue.

As early as 1911 the management of the traction system in Philadelphia had established both a cooperative wage fund for employees and a company-dominated union—the Employees' Co-operative Association,[1] predecessor of the Philadelphia Rapid Transit Employees' Union. For twenty years the employees had been required to invest 10 percent of their wages in the fund.[2] By the mid-1920s employee investment, which had largely been used to purchase company stock, approached control of the company. To forestall that, the management established a holding company which traded holding-company stock to the wage fund in return for traction-company stock. The holding company traded heavily in speculative stock and in 1929 lost $33 million. Further substantial losses in the employees' wage fund were to be a factor in the workers' ultimate rejection of the company union.[3]

On June 1, 1937, the state legislature enacted the Pennsylvania Labor Relations Act (McGinnis Act), the state counterpart of the National Labor Relations Act of 1935. The McGinnis Act protected the right of employees to organize and to bargain collectively through representatives of their own choosing. It defined unfair labor practices by employers as domination, discrimination, discharge, and refusal to bargain. Since the company-controlled Employees' Co-operative Association violated the new law, the employees had the opportunity to elect a lawful bargaining representative.

At the time there were three distinct factions among the workers—one group favored the Philadelphia Rapid Transit Employees' Union, set up to replace the old "company union"; another group, mainly operators, was associated with the Brother-hood of Railroad Trainmen, AFL; and a third favored the CIO's fledgling Transport Workers Union, which was not on the ballot. Soon after the McGinnis Act was passed, the mayor of Philadelphia requested an employee election, allowing a period for campaigning before the actual voting. When the election was finally held, late in 1937, the group that supported the company union won, and the PRT Employees' Union became the collective bargaining agent.

Soon thereafter, intracompany politics helped to divide the employees, as several rival management factions conducted a struggle for control. Each, promising assistance to different union groups, had a following among the employees.

In a joint lawsuit with the Brotherhood of Railroad Trainmen, the Transport Workers Union contested the validity of the union representation election, charging that the company had intervened in behalf of the Philadelphia Rapid Transit Employees' Union. In 1938 a court decision found the election valid and declared the PRT Employees' Union the official representative of the workers. The decision dissipated organized support for the Transport Workers Union, but a very small group, which later had a great influence on unionism in the Philadelphia Transportation Company, remained in close contact with the national headquarters of the TWU and with its president, Michael J. Quill.

By 1941, when a new representation election was scheduled, there was a conflict within the PRT Employees' Union over the issue of "company unionism." The Brotherhood of Railroad Trainmen participated in the election campaign; the Transport Workers Union did not. The narrow victory of the PRT Employees' Union in the second election left labor-management relations within the Philadelphia Transportation Company in a state of uncertainty and turmoil.

At the beginning of World War II, Philadelphia transit workers, for all practical purposes, had a company union. Influenced by the national momentum of union organization, some of the transit workers, like those in other cities, began to join the AFL's Amalgamated Association of Street, Electric Railway and Motor Coach Employees of America. As in many other industries, the collective bargaining agreements that resulted made hitherto informal discriminatory hiring and upgrading practices formal, rigid, and routinely enforceable. After the outbreak of war, an important element in the competition between the AFL's Amalgamated Association and the CIO's Transport Workers Union in organizing urban transit workers was their opposing positions on the employment of Negroes in higher paying and higher status operating jobs. The racial issue was to become the critical factor in various union certification elections, and in Philadelphia it was also the immediate cause of a strike by white workers against the hiring and promotion of Negro workers.

The rapid expansion of war production caused a severe labor shortage in Philadelphia during 1943–1944. The expansion was initially in heavy industry, such as the U.S. Naval Shipyard, the Baldwin Locomotive Works, various steel mills, and electrical manufacturing operations. Companies began large-scale manpower recruitment drives, even importing workers into the city from other areas of the country, particularly the South. The presence of a large number of southern whites, hired in preference to available local Negro labor, exacerbated the bitterness of the racial labor situation in Philadelphia, but the roots of the conflict were already present.[4]

Philadelphia has a long history of anti-Negro sentiment among white workers.* In 1917 a band of white workers beat a Negro to death on the street because he had gotten a job at a local shipyard. Other Negroes were intimidated with threats of similar violence.[5] Many labor unions in Philadelphia remained anti-Negro throughout World War II and afterward. Their discriminatory practices are documented in various studies, hearings, and investigative reports of the Philadelphia Human Relations Committee involving longshore, restaurant and hotel, building trades, and other unions.[6] With the exception of the newer industrial unions, at the beginning of World War II most labor unions in the city either did not admit Negro workers into membership or maintained segregated locals.

In 1943, of the 11,000 employees of the Philadelphia Transportation Company, 537 were Negroes.[7] Until the strike in 1944, not a single Negro had ever been employed in a platform or operating job.

In 1941, soon after President Roosevelt issued Executive Order 8802, creating the Fair Employment Practice Committee, Negroes began to file complaints. In part this was an expression of a new determination among black workers to obtain job advance-

*For a brief history of violence against Negroes in Philadelphia during the nineteenth century, see W. E. B. Du Bois, *The Philadelphia Negro,* Chapter IV. In describing the discriminatory practices of labor unions in Philadelphia at the end of the 1890s, Du Bois writes: "How now has this exclusion been maintained? In some cases by the actual inclusion of the word 'white' among qualifications for entrance into certain trade unions. More often, however, by leaving the matter of color entirely to local bodies, who make no general rule, but invariably fail to admit a colored applicant except under pressing circumstances. This is the most workable system and is adopted by nearly all trade unions. . . . Thus, the carpenters, masons, painters, iron-workers, etc., have succeeded in keeping out nearly all Negro workmen by simply declining to work with non-union men and refusing to let colored men join the union."—W. E. B. Du Bois, *The Philadelphia Negro* (Philadelphia: University of Pennsylvania, 1899), p. 128.

ment, and in part a response to the recent codification of discriminatory practices in the collective bargaining agreement between the union and the company. A group of Negro employees met with the president of the Philadelphia Transportation Company, Ralph Senter, and requested promotion to operating positions.[8] They were told that the company could do nothing without the agreement of the Philadelphia Rapid Transit Employees' Union.[9]

The company further tried to justify its refusal by relying upon a clause in the PTC-PRT Employees' Union agreement which, the company claimed, prevented innovations such as upgrading Negroes to platform positions. The clause stated that "[c]ustoms bearing on employer-employee relationship shall continue in full force and effect until changed by agreement between the parties."[10] This "customs" clause had originally been placed in the first PTC-PRT Employees' Union agreement in 1937 as a device to restate and continue management-employee practices which had existed between the company and the former Employees' Co-operative Association. Until Negro workers filed complaints with the FEPC and protested against their condition, the clause had never been interpreted as a provision freezing the job status of the Negro employees.[11]

The company's new position, specifying the "customs" clause with respect to upgrading Negroes, was an important change. Apparently, with the issuance of Executive Order 8802, both the company and the union anticipated that Negroes would request upgrading and decided to seize upon and interpret this clause of their agreement to prevent Negro job advancement. Racial discrimination was transformed from a general custom into a formal, codified rule.

In January 1942 Negro employees again attacked the discriminatory pattern. An election for a bargaining representative was to be held among the company's nonsupervisory personnel, and the Brotherhood of Railroad Trainmen was again seeking certification. The Pennsylvania Labor Relations Board allowed a group of Negro employees to intervene in its election certification hearings to contest the right of the Brotherhood of Railroad Trainmen to be designated as a bargaining agent.[12] The Negro employees contended that the brotherhood was not legally a "labor organization" under state law since the brotherhood had a "white male" membership clause in its constitution and the Pennsylvania Labor Relations Act defined a "labor organization" as one that did not exclude anyone from membership on the basis of race, creed, or color.[13]

The Pennsylvania Labor Relations Board ruled in favor of the Brotherhood of Railroad Trainmen on the basis that although the brotherhood had a "white male" membership requirement in its constitution, it had explained that the eligibility provision "shall not be construed or applied in any manner or be taken to have any meaning contrary to or in conflict with any state or Federal law."[14] The board also ruled that since September 1, 1937, this eligibility provision had been applied in conformity with state and federal laws.[15] Two months later the PRT Employees' Union defeated the brotherhood and was again certified as the collective bargaining agent for all the company's nonsupervisory employees.[16]

The findings and ruling of the board effectively denied the company's Negro employees any remedy under state law. The board permitted the Brotherhood of Railroad Trainmen, an openly exclusionary union, to participate in certification elections, and also in effect condoned and approved the discriminatory practices of the PRT Employees' Union, which admitted Negroes into membership but prevented their being upgraded to platform jobs.[17]

Having failed in direct negotiations with the company's president and with the Pennsylvania Labor Relations Board, the Negro employees turned to the Philadelphia branch of the National Association for the Advancement of Colored People. On November 20, 1942, the NAACP Action Committee on PTC Employment interceded in their behalf and met with company officials.[18] The company's response to the NAACP was the same as its response to the Negro employees—that the "customs" clause prevented management from upgrading Negro employees. The NAACP then wrote to the PRT Employees' Union requesting a conference. The president of the union, Frank P. Carney, responded: "Your communication was brought before the Union Delegates yesterday, and you are hereby advised that the matter of which you write is not a subject over which the Union has any control. Therefore, no action was taken."[19]

Roosevelt Neal, a Negro employee of the company and a member of the PRT union, later testified before the FEPC about the union's response to the NAACP's letter:

> Well, when the Communications were asked for, I think it was a meeting in February of this year, 1943, the communication was read at that meeting. There was no action taken on the communication at that time, but at the next meeting which was in March, I particularly

asked what answer was sent to the letter that was received from the NAACP and Mr. Carney stated there was no answer sent. So then it came up for brief discussion and I think Mr. Cook made a motion, Harry Cook, that is, a Delegate, made a motion that the letter be ignored, and it was seconded, and finally carried. Then the meeting proceeded for a little further and I think Mr. Smith, a [Negro] Delegate, got up and stated "Gentlemen, that certainly is an insult to us. If you don't want us in the Union you shouldn't try to insult us like that." Then it was reconsidered and I think Mr. Mullin, Joseph Mullin, made a motion that was seconded by Mr. Dure, and the letter I think shortly after that was answered. That is in brief what action was taken.[20]

The Negro employees had finally exhausted all possibilities for relief on the local and state levels and through direct appeals to the company and the union, but meantime, early in 1943, the Federal Government had begun to intercede on their behalf. In January a representative of the War Manpower Commission conferred with Dr. A. A. Mitten, chairman of the company's Industrial Relations Committee.[21] Mitten informed the commission that only a directive from the government to the company could achieve the hiring of Negro workers in hitherto all-white job classifications and the upgrading of Negroes already employed by the company. A week later the company placed a routine request with the U.S. Employment Service for a hundred motormen, specifying "white only."[22] After the company repeatedly refused to withdraw the order, the USES reported the discriminatory specification to the Fair Employment Practice Committee. Between April and October 1943 the committee received twenty-five individual complaints against the company citing racial discrimination in employment and upgrading.[23]

While the company continued to refuse employment to qualified Negro applicants and, in fact, became more adamant in its refusal, its labor shortage increased. It now began a drive to recruit white women as bus drivers and as conductors and motormen on streetcars,[24] at one point distributing 60,000 handbills urging women to apply for such positions. But according to the company, as a result of the great turnover among females employed in these capacities "because of physical inabilities to perform work,"[25] the labor shortage became even worse.

In September the shortage was so acute that the War Manpower Commission issued a "stabilization plan" for the Philadelphia transit industry.[26] Since the Philadelphia Transportation Company operated virtually all public transportation facilities in Philadelphia except taxicabs, the plan was exclusively for the benefit of the PTC. The local transit system was now designated an "essential activity," and under the war-emergency measures of that period employees were severely restricted from seeking jobs elsewhere. All new employees from outside the Philadelphia area were to be hired exclusively through the U.S. Employment Service.[27] The plan also provided that all hiring was to be done without discrimination as to race, creed, color, or national origin, but this mandate was largely nullified by a subsequent provision that "[n]othing in this Plan shall be construed to prejudice existing rights of an employee under any agreement with his employer."[28] The "stabilization plan" thus gave the company and the PRT Employees' Union a further justification to continue barring Negroes from operating positions. By freezing preexisting employment conditions, the plan had the further effect of sanctioning and consolidating the discriminatory employment pattern.

As pressure from the U.S. Employment Service and the Fair Employment Practice Committee increased, the company and the PRT Employees' Union blamed each other for the discriminatory practices. In early October of 1943 the FEPC held separate conferences with the company representative, Dr. A. A. Mitten, and with Frank Carney and Frank Coburn, president and secretary-treasurer of the union. The company indicated a willingness to employ Negro operators provided that they were "acceptable to fellow-workers."[29] Mitten explained that this proviso was necessary because the employment of Negroes would require a change in the "customs" clause, to which the union would have to agree.[30] He anticipated that it would not agree because it had refused "approval" to the employment of Negro platform men the year before. The conference ended with Mitten's assurance that the company would follow any directives issued by the FEPC.

The conference with the PRT Employees' Union officials produced similar hedging and vague assurances. Although the union denied that it had failed to grant "approval" to Negro operators, its officials reaffirmed their discriminatory interpretation of the "customs" clause of their agreement with the company.[31] The union attempted to shift responsibility by stating that the company had made no formal demand for a change in custom to allow the employment of Negroes in jobs they had not customarily held.[32] The union's defense was implicitly an abdication of its responsibility as a collective bargaining agent; the usual justification of organized labor's role is to change employment conditions to benefit its members, and the Negro workers at the Philadelphia Transportation Company were members of the union.

In late October the FEPC began to take steps toward a stipulation of facts, signed by the company and the union, upon which directives could be issued without the necessity of a formal hearing. On November 5, 1943, FEPC chairman Malcolm Ross met separately with officials of the company and the union.[33] The conference with company officials produced an agreed statement of facts signed by the company:

> The War Manpower Commission has designated the Company an essential organization engaged in supplying essential transportation services; and the Company is, therefore, within the jurisdiction conferred upon the President's Committee on Fair Employment Practice. . . . The Company is willing to take whatever steps the Committee may direct to be taken as necessary and appropriate to bring its employment practices in line with the President's Executive Orders.[34]

At a conference with union officials the same day, the union was shown the FEPC's proposed statement of facts, along with its proposed findings and directives:

> The "customs" clause in its contract with the Company has, in effect, frozen certain employment conditions of long-standing and resulted in precluding Negroes from employment or upgrading to jobs or positions which have not been held, customarily, by Negroes in the past. The Union, however, never has advocated any discriminatory steps against Negroes, and the Company has made no formal request that the Union state its position with reference to any change in the Company's customary employment relations as they affect the use of Negroes in jobs which Negroes have not held in the past. The present manpower shortage might well require a reinterpretation of this "customs" clause so as to leave no doubt that it does not preclude the employment or upgrading of Negroes to operating jobs with the Company.[35]

The findings and directives also included the FEPC's interpretation of the "customs" clause:

> (2) The Committee further finds that the ["customs" clause], if intended or interpreted by the union as prohibiting the employment or promotion of qualified Negroes to jobs not formerly held by Negroes with the Company, is in direct conflict with the provisions of Executive Order 9346 and constitutes discrimination by the Union

against Negro employees of the Company and Negro applicants for employment with the Company because of their race or color.[36]

Finally, the findings and directives provided:

> The Committee directs that the Philadelphia Rapid Transit Employees' Union, in the interest of the war effort, shall not interpret any section or provision of its contract with the Philadelphia Transportation Company so as to prohibit, limit, or in any manner interfere with, the employment or upgrading by the Company of qualified Negroes in or to positions as street car and motor coach operators and conductors, motormen, guards, platform attendants, and station cashiers on the Company's elevated and subway lines; or in or to any other job classifications with the Company not presently held by Negroes.[37]

When they examined the committee's proposals union officials did not dispute any of the provisions; nevertheless they declined to sign the document until they had conferred with their delegates.[38] The FEPC allowed the union ten days to consult its members, at which time the proposed findings and directives would be formally issued unless either the company or the union requested a public hearing. Neither did so, and twelve days later the committee issued its proposals,[39] which then became final. During the interim union delegates had met for six hours to discuss the directives but adjourned without taking action.[40]

At this point—while the union was deciding whether or not to sign the directives, as the company had done—public pressure against the union's racial policy began to mount. An editorial in the *Philadelphia Evening Bulletin* asserted:

> The fact is that the company was bound by contract to adhere to its customary employment practices and could change them only by union consent—until an agency of the Federal Government stepped in and issued the present directive. The company announces its willingness to comply. The baby is on the union's doorstep.
>
> The public interest in this matter is to have PTC service adequately, efficiently and safely manned. The color of operator the public has most cause to be disturbed about is green.[41]

After another series of delegates' meetings (in which Negroes did not participate),* the union requested a public hearing before

---

*The policy-making body of the union consisted of 128 "delegates," eight of whom were Negroes representing employees of the maintenance department. The maintenance department did not participate in this series of delegates' meetings, probably because the largest concentration of Negro employees was in that department.

the Fair Employment Practice Committee,[42] despite the committee's time-limit regulations. "It is our understanding," Carney wrote Ross on November 24, "that, because of this request for a hearing, the proposed directive will not go into effect as of November 27, 1943."[43]

This was a significant event. Up to this time the PRT Employees' Union had denied that it opposed equal employment opportunity for Negroes. The union had allowed Negroes to become members and even to become "delegates." It had relied, however, on the "customs" clause in its contract with the company to give an aura of legitimacy to its continuing discriminatory practices. Now that the company had reluctantly acquiesced to pressure from the FEPC and had agreed to obey government directives without a hearing, the union, standing alone in its opposition to the employment of Negroes in operating jobs, publicly demonstrated its resistance by requesting a hearing.

Negro communities in many cities reacted sharply to the union's insistence on continuing its discriminatory practices. The NAACP Action Committee on PTC Employment held a protest march and threatened mass picket lines. These events received nationwide attention, especially in Negro newspapers, which prominently featured dispatches about the issue from the Associated Negro Press.[44]

Sentiment among company employees was divided. Those who supported the PRT Employees' Union's position were outspoken. A week before the scheduled hearing the committee received a petition from the employees in the elevated department purporting to express unanimous employee opposition to the FEPC's directives:

> The Transportation Employees Of the Market St. & Frankford Subway-Elevated Dept.'s Do hereby Disagree with the Order of the President's Committee of Fair Employment Practices in Washington that the Philadelphia Transportation Company Employ Negroes as Bus and Trolley Operators, Conductors, Platform workers and Cashiers.
>
> 1st.
>
> The Philadelphia Transportation Company has over 500 Negroes Employed. We believe that figure is above other Corporations and that the Philadelphia Transportation Company is doing its share and is not Discriminating in any way. . . .
>
> Any Change that the Fair Employment Committee has ordered would surely cause a Major Dissatisfaction to the Public and the

Employees and most likely lead to a Very Serious Situation. Therefore we Deem it Adviseable to leave the present form of Management stand Indefinitely.[45]

The FEPC agreed to the union's request, and hearings began on December 8, 1943, in Philadelphia. The chairman stated that the purpose of the hearing was

> to afford the Philadelphia Rapid Transit Employees' Union an opportunity to show cause why the proposed findings of fact and directives heretofore issued by the President's Committee and served upon the Philadelphia Transportation Company and the Union should not become final and effective.[46]

The only material the union presented was a prepared statement read by Coburn, the union's secretary-treasurer, and the arguments were later repeated in his cross-examination by the committee. The union's first argument was a denial of FEPC jurisdiction on the ground that although the company was "admittedly essential to the war effort," as far as the union knew the company held no contract with any government agency, administrative body, or group, "which seems to be necessary in order for the Fair Employment Practice Committee to make an order."[47]

The company, in signing the directives, had earlier admitted that the committee had the authority to issue its findings and proposals. The union had also implicitly acknowledged the authority of the committee by failing to object when it was shown the proposed directives. (Although argument regarding federal jurisdiction and authority was a minor point advanced by the union, it was later to become a center of controversy before the Smith committee of the House of Representatives, which bitterly opposed the work of the FEPC.)

The union's second point was to protest that it did not engage in anti-Negro practices: "All non-supervisory people employed by the Philadelphia Transportation Company are eligible for membership irrespective of creed, sex, political affiliation, color or racial extraction," and

> [t]his union has a record of industrial peace on the property of the Philadelphia Transportation Company, and this record extends over a period of six years. Peaceable relationships, so far as public order and work stabilization are concerned, have existed. Many of our delegates point out that at the present time while a negro does not replace a white man in a job on the Philadelphia Transportation Company, on the other hand, neither does a white man replace a

negro and many of the negro employees have jobs of some importance.[48]

The union claimed that, rather than practicing discrimination, it was in fact being discriminated against by the FEPC. As an alternative to its being singled out by the committee from among the many unions which did not permit Negro conductors and motormen, the PRT union suggested that there should be a "nation-wide order to all transportation companies or no order at all."[49] In the form of a veiled threat, its statement predicted disrupted service if Negroes should become platform operators:

> The P.R.T. Employees' Union cannot accept responsibility for the chaos and impairment to the transportation of workers to and from the war industries, which we feel will surely follow any attempt to enforce this directive at this time. Efficient mass transportation depends on the co-ordinated efforts of all of the employees.[50]

In further stressing "chaos and impairment" should the directives be enforced, Coburn warned the committee that "[f]orce never enjoys lasting success."[51] The final argument in the union's defense was a plea that the status quo be maintained:

> The members of the P.R.T. Employees' Union definitely do not want this relationship disturbed at this time. For a Government Agency to make an order disturbing this relationship would eventually be most harmful to the war effort because the employees feel they are the employees of the only transportation company and union against which such an order has been made, despite the fact that there are numerous transportation companies in the Country, and in this immediate area, operating under similar conditions and in a fashion similar to the Philadelphia Transportation Company. The employees know that the present employment practices have existed for many, many years and that there have been pleasant relationships among the employees and the public. They feel that it would be a tragic mistake to try to change the known for the unknown at a time as important as this.
> Furthermore, over 1,000 members of the Union and employees of the company are serving in the Armed Forces. The Union feels that the maintenance of a satisfactory employer-employee relationship should not be changed in their absence.[52]

Now, by openly opposing the employment of Negroes for operating jobs, by resorting to the delaying tactic of requesting a hearing after the prescribed time had expired, by challenging FEPC authority, and by threatening "chaos," the union firmly and publicly committed itself to a policy of racial discrimination.

The union's stand at the hearing caused further public protest in Philadelphia. The NAACP Action Committee on PTC Employment appeared at the hearing and testified on its efforts to achieve Negro job upgrading, presenting as evidence the letter from Frank Carney saying the union had no control over the "subject." The NAACP charged that "[i]t is thus clear that the union, in asking for a hearing at the present time, is taking a position diametrically opposite to its own stated position in its letter of March 2, 1943."[53] The Council for Equal Job Opportunity, an association composed of seventeen Philadelphia civic, professional, civil rights, and religious organizations, submitted a statement urging "the P.R.T. Employees' Union to abide by the ruling issued by the FEPC. . . ."[54] The National Urban League submitted a memorandum on the success of integrated local transit in New York City, urging that Philadelphia could enjoy similar success:

> The League wishes to set forth certain facts and conclusions derived from its national observation, dealing particularly with the situation in New York City:
>
> 1. Objection to the use of Negro transit employees in Northern cities arises from certain managements and labor unions and rarely, if at all, from the general public. . . .
> 3. Management is generally loath to move without either the pressure of organized public opinion or intervention of government authority.
> 4. Where leaders of organized labor are themselves sympathetic to the use of Negro workers, they have no trouble in convincing their membership of the desirability and practicability of such a step.
>
> In New York City, Negroes are today employed on all of the publicly owned transportation lines as motormen, conductors, platform guards and inspectors. The League is aware of no instance where friction has arisen either between these Negro workers and the public or between Negroes and their white fellow workers.[55]

The Catholic Intercollegiate Interracial Council of Philadelphia submitted a resolution which stated that "Full Opportunity of Employment is an essential right of the Negro people" and asked the company and the union to "reconsider their stand and to follow the example of other leading cities in the country and open these avenues of employment to qualified Negro men."[56] The CIO Central Labor Council in Philadelphia issued a statement urging immediate acceptance of the FEPC's directives.[57] A week later local church groups sent the company a petition favoring fair employment practices which bore the signature of over 12,500 Philadelphia residents.[58]

The union responded to all these pressures with a fifteen-minute radio broadcast in which its secretary-treasurer defied the directives and again questioned the authority of the FEPC.[59]

The committee issued its final directive on December 27, affirming and giving effect to its earlier findings and directives. The PRT Employees' Union quickly wrote to the committee refusing to comply:

> We have received the directive issued by your Committee against the Philadelphia Transportation Company and the P.R.T. Employees' Union on December 27, 1943.
>
> We respectfully but firmly repeat that under the Constitution and under the Statutes, the directive of the Committee is issued without legal authority. Neither by a broad general appraisal of the law nor by a perusal of the executive order can legal justification of your directive be found. . . .
>
> In addition, we have problems of seniority which must arise as a result of the directive despite any well-intentioned belief on anyone's part that such problems do not exist. We have definite responsibilities to our active employees and especially to those on leave in military service. To break our contract is to break faith. . . .
>
> Finally, it has not yet been demonstrated that the directive is necessary to the war effort in the Philadelphia area or that the directive could be carried out without friction and misunderstanding.
>
> We, therefore, advise you that for the foregoing reasons we cannot comply with the terms of the directive and we are so advising the Philadelphia Transportation Company.[60]

On the same date the union notified the company of its refusal to comply, ordering the company to honor its labor agreement:

> You are hereby advised that the Union cannot comply with the terms of the directive because it is violative of the contract which this Union holds with you. The President's Fair Employment Practice Committee seems to be exceeding legal authority, and the Union takes the position that this directive is beyond the powers of the Committee. The Union wishes to state very definitely that compliance with the directive by the Union cannot be expected at this time. You will, therefore, please take no steps to comply with the directive at this time, it being our contention that such compliance would be violative of our contract and that acquiescence of both employer and employee is needed to carry out the terms of the directive.[61]

The Philadelphia Transportation Company had a direct interest in supporting and maintaining good relations with the PRT Employees' Union, since the union had been formed originally from a company-dominated union and was still to a considerable degree influenced by management. Therefore the company wrote the committee that it, too, refused to comply with the directives:

> [T]he action which these Directives would require to be taken would be in violation of the existing employer-employee contract between the company and the Union. That contract is valid and binding unless and until modified by the mutual consent of the parties or abrogated by Government action legally and constitutionally effective to that end. The contract has not been modified by mutual consent, and inasmuch as the Union has challenged the validity of your Directives, the Company will consider itself bound by its contract and will not take action in violation thereof unless and until the validity of your Committee's Directives, now challenged, shall be finally established.[62]

Without notifying the FEPC,[63] the PRT Employees' Union wrote the Smith committee[64] that "[w]e cannot understand from what source in the terms of the Executive Order itself, the FEPC procures authority to make the directive which it has entered."[65] The Smith committee immediately began *its* hearing, with Frank Coburn testifying that his union was bound by the "customs" clause of its agreement with the company and that a strike would occur if the company obeyed the FEPC directive.[66] In response to a committee member's question whether the union felt itself superior to an order issued by a "nationally formed organization," union president Frank Carney replied, "Yes, sir."[67]

Since the PRT Employees' Union seemed to be able to defy the Fair Employment Practice Committee, the company apparently felt safe in insisting it could not comply with the FEPC's directives because of the union's position. But when the Smith hearings in Washington were announced, growing public sentiment against both the company and the union was expressed. On January 6 the *Philadelphia Inquirer* said, in an editorial titled "Wipe Out P.T.C. Color Line":

> Exclusion of Negroes from jobs as bus and trolley operators and conductors on Philadelphia's transit lines cannot be justified on any valid grounds. The position of the PRT Employees' Union in defying the Government order giving equal status to Negro workers is indefensible.

There is no reason why anyone qualified for conductor's or motor-man's duties should not be assigned to them, regardless of color. Negroes have capably filled posts of greater responsibility and skill. Negroes are given jobs without question on street-car lines in other cities. The P.R.T. union is laying itself open to a grave charge of prejudice in refusing freedom of opportunity to all workers. . . . The company, it may be noted, having first signified its readiness to abide by the committee's decision, has now taken the position that it will not comply until the validity of the FEPC directive has been established by a court test.

A considerable share of the onus of discrimination, however, remains with the P.R.T. Employees' Union. It is not a pleasant thing to be saddled with. The Union officials, if they have not lost all track of common sense, should give up their losing fight forthwith and eradicate the odious color line from the P.T.C. for all time.[68]

The intransigence of the PRT Employees' Union on the racial issue became a major factor in the concurrent interunion rivalry at the transit company. At the beginning of 1944 five groups were competing, overtly or covertly, to become collective bargaining agent for the company's employees in the next election, not yet scheduled but imminent: the PRT Employees' Union; the Transport Workers Union, CIO; the Amalgamated Association of Street, Electric Railway and Motor Coach Employees of America, AFL; the Brotherhood of Railroad Trainmen, AFL; and the International Brotherhood of Teamsters, AFL.

During the campaign the FEPC was relatively inactive in the Philadelphia case, presumably awaiting the outcome of the election before taking further steps.

At this point many employees, bitter at having lost their savings in the Co-operative's wage fund, were encouraged by the dissident management groups to oppose the PRT Employees' Union, hitherto company-protected. The Brotherhood of Railroad Trainmen was receiving support from the company president in an attempt to weaken the position of the Transport Workers Union, which supported the efforts of Negro workers to obtain jobs as operators. Another group, which the personnel director was backing, sympathized with the Amalgamated Association, further splitting support for the Transport Workers Union.

Promotion of Negroes to jobs in the all-white classifications became the central campaign issue. Early in January both the PRT Employees' Union and the Amalgamated Association were circulating petitions declaring that the signatories were white, twenty-

one years of age, and would refuse to work with Negroes.[69] The
FEPC received a petition with approximately 1,700 signatures:

> To whom it may concern: We the undersigned employees of the
> P.T.C. do hereby give fair notice that in the event of employment of
> colored help as operators of street cars and buses with due notice will
> ask for our immediate release from present employment. This notice
> has no affiliation with any political or union organization.[70]

At one of the larger depots a PRT Employees' Union delegate
began soliciting pledges to strike if Negroes were employed as
operators.[71]

As union rivalry increased, only the Transport Workers
Union, CIO, publicly supported the right of Negroes to be
employed as operators. International officers of the TWU,
including Michael Quill, the president, and James J. Fitzsimon,
vice president, came from New York to campaign among the
company's employees, encouraging support for the upgrading and
promotion of Negroes. The CIO's official policy against discrimination had been placed on public record. Philip Murray, president of
the CIO, had just reiterated this position in a telegram to President
Roosevelt supporting the FEPC's orders to end discrimination in
the transit industry. This represented "a decided step forward," he
wrote:

> The Congress of Industrial Organizations was founded upon the
> principle that the benefits of organized effort shall be secured to all
> workers, regardless of race, color, creed or nationality. Therefore, it
> is a source of gratification and encouragement to realize that our
> efforts implement the work of the Fair Employment Practice Com-
> mittee.[72]

At the height of the election campaign, Murray addressed a
meeting of 3,000 PTC workers, telling them the CIO was
"absolutely opposed to anti-Negro discrimination."[73]

On the other hand, the American Federation of Labor, with
three affiliated contending unions—the Amalgamated Association,
the Brotherhood of Railroad Trainmen, and the International
Brotherhood of Teamsters—refused to publicly state its position on
the issue of Negro employment and promotion during the
campaign, although the AFL did nothing to oppose the discriminatory policies of its affiliates.

The PRT Employees' Union was unabashedly conducting a
racist campaign, proclaiming "[w]e'll keep the 'Niggers' off."[74]
Theodore Spaulding, president of the Philadelphia branch of the

NAACP and editor of a local Negro newspaper, the Philadelphia *Afro-American,* met with the Pennsylvania Labor Relations Board to propose that the PRT Employees' Union be barred from participating in the election because of its discriminatory racial practices.[75] The NAACP also met with James Fitzsimon, international vice president of the TWU, to explore the possibility of a court injunction against the PRT Employees' Union,[76] but lack of time and legal complexities forestalled both efforts.*

On February 11, 1944, the Pennsylvania Labor Relations Board finally ordered a March election. A month of violence followed, with organized "goon squads" in action. Toward the end of the campaign, after the Brotherhood of Railroad Trainmen had withdrawn for lack of worker support, the Amalgamated Association and the Transport Workers Union intensified their election efforts. The AFL's Amalgamated Association accused the Transport Workers Union of being "Communist-dominated" and predicted that if the CIO union were elected, its president, Michael Quill, would establish a Pennsylvania branch of the "Communist-controlled" American Labor Party (which was on the ballot in New York State).[77] The Transport Workers Union retorted with a statement that the leadership of the Amalgamated Association was "venal and ineffective."[78] According to Robert C. Weaver, the antagonism resulted in the dissolution of the Philadelphia United Labor Committee, in which the AFL and the CIO had cooperated for eight years.[79] At one point during the campaign, PRT Employees' Union sound trucks blared out: "A vote for CIO is a vote for Niggers on the job."[80]

As the campaign progressed, the Teamsters union also formally withdrew because of insufficient backing among the workers, although it expected to make gains later if the PRT Employees' Union, the Transport Workers Union, or the Amalgamated Association did not receive a decisive margin of victory.†

---

*Theodore Spaulding later stated that it was generally believed that filing a lawsuit would be futile because of the lack of legal precedents in Pennsylvania permitting the disqualification of a discriminatory labor union in a state certification election, and that time would not permit a review by federal appellate courts. (Interview by author with Theodore Spaulding, Philadelphia, October 31, 1967.)

†According to George R. Staab, labor reporter for the *Philadelphia Bulletin* and a close observer of the election and subsequent events, representatives of the Teamsters union gave assistance to those organizing the protest strike against the promotion of blacks, as they believed that if the strike was successful the Teamsters would replace the Transport Workers Union. Staab stated that "[d]uring the election the AFL was waiting in the wings and there is evidence that Ed Crumboch, business agent of the AFL Teamsters Union Local 107, was

When the election was held, on March 14, 1944, most of the company's 500 Negro employees, who worked in the maintenance unit, voted as a bloc for the Transport Workers Union. But even in the transportation unit the TWU won by a large plurality:

> Transportation Unit—TWU, 3,118; PRT Employees' Union, 1,459; Amalgamated, 1,249.
>
> Maintenance Unit—TWU, 1,292; PRT Employees' Union, 356; Amalgamated, 386.
>
> Fifty-five employees voted "No union."[81]

Immediately after the election, the most active opponents of Negro advancement were the leaders and organizers of the two unions that had lost the election; with the aid of the company, they continued to use their organizations as vehicles for creating labor unrest based on antagonism to the promotion of Negro workers.

The FEPC believed the company should begin to upgrade its Negro employees before the old contract expired and the new one was negotiated. Dr. Mitten, at that time the company's personnel director, was reminded on April 6 that the company had agreed to comply with the FEPC directive if it did not violate "the existing employer-employee contract,"[82] and that since there would be no such contract on April 7 (the old contract was due to expire at midnight on the sixth), the committee expected the company to take immediate steps to bring about employment equality. Mitten refused on the ground that with the new contract still being negotiated he feared the Transport Workers Union would think the company was "trying to put one over on them."[83] However, he assured the committee that if the union did not bring up a nondiscrimination clause, "we shall bring it up."[84]

A month after the TWU victory Malcolm Ross formally requested Michael Quill to include a nondiscrimination clause in the new contract the TWU was in the process of negotiating.[85] Quill replied that "[w]e have already started negotiations down there and you can be sure that we will do everything possible to keep the record of the T.W.U. of America in its rightful place as far as the Negro question is concerned."[86]

But contract negotiations were slow and difficult, and no action toward upgrading Negroes was taken by the company, the union, or the FEPC until June 30, 1944, when a contract

---

waiting to pick up the pieces."—Interview by author with George R. Staab, Philadelphia, October 30, 1967.

containing a nondiscrimination clause was produced.[87] The contract was ratified by the membership of the Transport Workers Union at a mass meeting attended by over 2,000 workers in the Philadelphia Town Hall, but the company delayed its signature.[88]

Almost immediately the War Manpower Commission again ordered all industries deemed "essential to the war effort" to hire exclusively through the U.S. Employment Service and further stipulated that discrimination in hiring would not be tolerated. This time company officials agreed to comply, but they made it clear that they were complying with the War Manpower Commission order, not with the FEPC directive. The company posted its notice of compliance on bulletin boards:

> The P.T.C. will obtain new male employees through the U.S. Employment Service. The U.S. Employment Service is required to refer to employers, and this company will accept, those who qualify for open positions without regard to the applicant's race, creed, color or national origin.
>
> In order to provide present employees an opportunity to apply for positions not held heretofore, and to give opportunity in advance of new employees, applications for transfer to fill open positions in various departments will now be accepted.[89]

This was the company's first decisive public indication that it would comply with directives to upgrade Negro workers as operators.

Immediately the leaders and sympathizers of the unions which had withdrawn from or been defeated in the March elections began agitating for a protest strike. Frank Carney, president of the PRT Employees' Union; James McMenamin, organizer for the Brotherhood of Railroad Trainmen; and their followers were still bitter about losing the election. By organizing a strike over the issue of the promotion of Negro workers, they believed they could significantly weaken support for the Transport Workers Union.

Former PRT Employees' Union leaders started holding protest meetings, both on and off company property, urging a strike. Handbills were posted on the company bulletin boards:

> Your buddies are in the Army fighting and dying to protect the life of you and your family, and you are too yellow to protect their jobs until they return. Call a strike and refuse to teach the Negroes, the public is with you, the CIO sold you out.[90]

Other handbills verging on racist hysteria were distributed among company employees:

Your Sons and Buddies that are away Fighting for the Country, are being stabbed in the back on the Home Front by The National Association For the Advancement of Negroes, and the F.E.P.C., which is a 100% Negro Lobby, that was Created by Executive Decree, and financed by the U.S. Treasury, to the tune of 500,000.

During the last War The Prohibitionists Raided the Country While The Boys were away fighting and During this War The Negroes are Raiding the Country while the White Mens backs are turned. The Negroes in this War are Reaping A War Loot Harvest. The Negroes are taking Every Advantage to Gain Control of All the Jobs and Everything Else that belongs to the White People, while they are away fighting. . . . The P.T.C. trolley Men, are the Latest Victims of these Active Negro Lobbies.[91]

The company secretly began training eight Negroes to operate streetcars.[92] Carney and McMenamin addressed a meeting of seventy-five employees in a company carbarn and advised the men to report "sick" if the Negroes were upgraded. A Transport Workers Union leader present urged the men not to strike, but they voted to do so nevertheless. On July 31 fifty men served notice on Mitten that unless they received word by 4:00 a.m. the next day that the issue of Negro upgrading would be submitted to an employee vote, they would call a strike.[93] Mitten did not respond and he also failed to inform the FEPC and the War Manpower Commission of this development.

The strike began at 4:00 a.m., August 1, 1944. When the morning shift of streetcar operators came on duty, a small group of pro-strike leaders and their "flying squads" were waiting at selected locations and urged the men to report "sick."[94] The decision to begin the strike at streetcar barns was strategic. Streetcars were stored in rows on tracks in the carbarns; by immobilizing the cars at the front of each row, a few strikers were able to prevent most of the cars from being operated. Additional flying squads of strikers went to the bus depots to tell the drivers and other employees that the streetcar workers were on strike. Subway and elevated-train operators were willing to work, but company officials shut the power off, saying they feared violence.

The eight Negro trainees were scheduled to make their first runs that same day.[95] Striking employees knew they would be driving but did not know exactly where. When the first car driven by a Negro pulled out of the depot, his passengers, according to an eyewitness account, were two National Guardsmen with bayoneted rifles and two city plainclothesmen with their badges displayed.

About five blocks from the barn the car met a group of white men who taunted the National Guardsmen with shouts of "Nigger-lovers" and "Get that nigger off." A few blocks farther whites gathered on a corner and began smashing the windows of the car with rocks and other objects. The two National Guardsmen had to use their bayonets to prevent white men from jumping onto the car and attacking the driver. Striking workers also tried to push the car off the tracks.*

The company's initial reaction strongly suggested support of the strike and opposition to the Fair Employment Practice Committee and the War Manpower Commission. The company requested (but was denied) permission from the FEPC and the War Manpower Commission to post on its bulletin boards a notice that would, in effect, mean giving in to the strikers' demands:

> Stoppage of P.T.C. service has crippled every war industry in the Philadelphia Area. Service must be restored immediately to prevent critical interference with vital war production.
>
> The first duty of this company is to provide service to the war effort and the public.
>
> Therefore, provisions of the notice dated July 7, 1944, regarding changes in employment practices to comply with the directive of the W.M.C. are suspended.[96]

Company support of the strike was also demonstrated when it not only shut off the power on elevated lines that were still operating but refused to close carbarns being used as meeting places for the strikers.† It had taken no advance action in spite of notice of the strike; and throughout the stoppage it refused to urge employees to go back to work.

Government response to the strike was immediate. Philadelphia ranked "among the most crucial areas of the nation for war production during this period,"[97] and there was a very heavy concentration of vital industries,‡ most of whose workers depended upon the Philadelphia Transportation Company to get to their

---

*This eyewitness account was given to the author by Orrin Evans, who was a reporter for the *Philadelphia Record* at that time. Evans had received information from a private source revealing the time and place where the first car driven by a black motorman would depart and he was there waiting. (Interview by author with Orrin Evans, Philadelphia, October 30, 1967.)

†The only time the company did close its barns was immediately after a meeting of Transport Workers Union members who voted to return to work. The back-to-work attempt failed, and the company reopened the carbarns the next morning.

‡Among these were the Philadelphia Naval Shipyard, the Frankford Arsenal, various private shipyards, military tank factories, steel plants, and many suppliers of vital electrical equipment.

jobs.[98] After the first day of the strike, production losses were estimated at 70 percent on Navy and 50 percent on Army contract work in the city.[99]

The National War Labor Board, whose duty was to prevent interruptions of war production because of labor disputes, had no legal remedy short of government seizure, but Sylvester Garrett, chairman of the regional board in Philadelphia, sent telegrams to the strike leaders ordering them back to work immediately.[100] The Army and Navy also sent telegrams to the strike leaders and to company officials, insisting on the return of the strikers. These initial efforts failed. During the first day of the strike Eli Rock, disputes director of the regional board, along with uniformed officers of the Army and the Navy and officials of the Transport Workers Union, addressed a large meeting of employees at the carbarn at Tenth and Lucerne streets, the largest in the city. As each of them tried to speak, he was howled down by the workers. Describing the assemblage as a "screaming mob" and a "vast uproar," Rock added:

> In perhaps a dozen situations where workers had gone out on strike in violation of the no-strike pledge, and where I had appeared to speak to urge that they return to work pending a consideration of their grievances by the War Labor Board, this was the only time in which I was not permitted to speak. It was doubly difficult because the same treatment was given to the representatives of the Armed Forces.[101]

Rock believed the extreme hostility to government representatives was not spontaneous but planned and organized. As he spoke, he saw McMenamin of the Brotherhood of Railroad Trainmen "passing through the crowd urging strikers on to shout and scream."[102] That evening, amid "sporadic disorders," 3,500 white workers attended a meeting and confirmed their intention of continuing the strike.[103]

The Negro trainees initially believed that the strike resulted from agitation by only a small number of white workers. Lewis Sylvester Thompson, one of the eight and a company employee for nineteen years, said that on that first morning, when he was to drive a streetcar, the 400 men in the barn "were very friendly. They have always been friendly and decent. These are my friends. They're not responsible for this thing. The rank and file don't want anything like this, I know."[104] Rufus G. Lancaster, employed as a porter for eight years, stated that "[i]t's hard to understand: We never had any trouble with anyone, any time before. We think of ourselves as pioneers. And we're going to keep up the spirit. We still want to be trolley operators and I think we will."[105]

On August 2, the second day of the strike, Sylvester Garrett and Eli Rock of the regional board conferred in Washington with William Davis, chairman of the National War Labor Board, and Jonathan Daniels, President Roosevelt's press secretary. Rock gives this account:

> It was concluded after we gave our reports that usual pleas of the Federal Government would be unavailing. All reports indicated that strikers could not be reasoned with on the racial issue, and that no individual labor dispute could compare with this one in its far-reaching impact upon war production, as the transit walkout directly imperiled the operation of many different production installations and industrial enterprises.[106]

The result of the conference was a recommendation to President Roosevelt that the government immediately seize the Philadelphia Transportation Company and all public transportation facilities in Philadelphia.[107] The War Department separately requested the President to designate some agency other than itself to effectuate the takeover.[108]

Because President Roosevelt was abroad, his response to the War Labor Board's seizure request was delayed.* During this interim the strikers were urged by sound truck, newspapers, and radio to return to work. Radio appeals were made by James Fitzsimon of the TWU; Joseph Sharfsin, general counsel for the FEPC; Theodore Spaulding of the local NAACP branch; and by officials of other civic groups.[109] Frank L. McNamee, regional director of the War Manpower Commission, expressed hope that the transit system would be run by company employees, but added that "either the men will do it or the Government will. At no time during this war could a stoppage of work here have caused more damage than at this particular moment."[110]

---

*Will Maslow, director of field operations for the FEPC, explains that on the second day of the strike there was great apprehension within the committee and its staff that the government would fail to act rapidly and decisively. Maslow telephoned Jonathan Daniels at the White House, and Daniels suggested that he report directly to Solicitor General Charles Fahy. Maslow argued to Fahy that the government should act immediately because "Philadelphia was one of the most important military arsenals in the country and the strike was a great blow to the war effort." According to Maslow, the Solicitor General promised that he would recommend swift action by the President. (Interview by author with Will Maslow, New York, February 12, 1968.)

By August 3 about 6,000 employees, virtually the entire work force, were out. Late in the afternoon President Roosevelt's Executive Order 9549[111] was received via overseas radio. It directed Secretary of War Stimson to seize the Philadelphia Transportation Company. Major General Philip Hayes, already in Philadelphia, ordered that the U.S. flag be flown over all carbarns and that notices be posted on all company property stating that the facilities were being operated by the U.S. Government. He announced on the radio: "We shall operate the transit lines on the basis of the conditions that were there before the strike. All the employees will continue in the capacity they held at that time."[112] James McMenamin of the Brotherhood of Railroad Trainmen, now chairman of the strikers' General Emergency Committee, interpreted General Hayes's statement of "conditions that were there before" to mean that the Army would not place Negroes on the platform; on this basis McMenamin ordered the strikers back to work.[113] But after General Hayes explained that although the Negro trainee program had been postponed, it would be reinstated under Army auspices as soon as possible, McMenamin reversed his back-to-work order, telling the men to remain on strike until they had a written guarantee that there would be no Negro operators.[114]

The CIO, the national officers of the Transport Workers Union, and the local Transport Workers leaders continued issuing public statements urging an end to the strike. The national leadership—Quill, Fitzsimon, and secretary-treasurer Douglas MacMahon—went to Philadelphia to try to quell the strike and maintain the union's authority. Quill's first public statement in Philadelphia, on the second day of the strike, was a pledge of support to government efforts; he urged "all PTC employees, as soldiers on the home front, to respond to the call of their Commander-in-Chief."[115]

In addition to using the radio, Fitzsimon toured the carbarns urging the strikers back to work. He said in a press interview:

> I sincerely trust that those employees who are still seriously impeding the successful prosecution of the war will immediately respond to the order and continue at work pending peaceful and lawful negotiations to bring about a settlement of their grievances. They can prove their patriotism and good intentions by going back to buses, subways, and trolley cars without further delay.[116]

At one carbarn Fitzsimon pleaded:

We know that you are good Americans and good union men. Your own future, your wages, your working conditions, and your family's security are at stake. Your country's victory is at stake. You will serve both by getting back on the job at once.[117]

Local 234 of the Transport Workers Union, the certified bargaining agent for the employees, wrote President Roosevelt dissociating itself from the strike:

Mr. President, let us assure you that the interruption of transportation service on the Philadelphia Transportation Company lines was not a strike. It was not a labor dispute. As the rank and file leaders intimately associated with the men and women of PTC, we can assure you that the vast majority of these workers are devoted, loyal, and understanding Americans. They did not want any part of this plot. The national and local leaders of our union condemned this work stoppage. We are unqualifiedly against strikes or other interruption of work in wartime.[118]

On August 4 several hundred Transport Workers Union members reported for work. General Hayes placed a policeman or a soldier on each car, and by 10:00 a.m. service was at 30 percent of normal.[119] By midnight, however, no vehicles were running. After conferring with General Hayes, U.S. Attorney General Francis Biddle ordered the Federal Bureau of Investigation to begin investigating the strike with a view toward prosecution under the Smith-Connally War Labor Disputes Act.[120] After the leaders of the strikers' General Emergency Committee learned of the threatened prosecution they increased their exhortations to keep the strike going: "I am not asking you men to stay out, as the Government has taken over the system and anybody who suggests to stay out is committing a crime against the United States, but your committee has recommended, seconded, and voted unanimously that we stick to our guns."[121] When members of the strikers' committee began to notice that the Army was reluctant to make a strong show of force, the strike leaders interpreted the back-to-work summons as a request rather than an order.[122] Flying squads of strikers continued to threaten workers who tried to return to their jobs.[123]

The "chaos and impairment" that had been threatened by the PRT Employees' Union when the FEPC initially conducted its hearing was now in full swing.[124] During the first day of the strike eleven people had been injured seriously enough to require hospitalization, and over 300 people arrested for "malicious mischief," aggravated assault and battery, and carrying concealed weapons.[125] Hostile whites descended on heavily populated Negro residential sections, where they inflicted the worst violence that occurred during the strike and precipitated over 200 arrests.[126]

John H. Ohly, in his study of presidential seizure of defense facilities, stated:

> By evening [of the first day of the strike] every public transportation vehicle in the city was idle. . . . More serious, still, were indications that the situation might turn from a strike into a race riot. The U.S. Attorney stated early in the day: "If this strike is not settled immediately, Philadelphia will experience one of the worst race riots in the history of the country."[127]

To try to stop the violence and prevent a citywide race war, members of civic groups such as the NAACP, the Catholic Interracial Committee, and the Federation of Churches went into the streets to urge the strikers to cease their harassment. The mayor of Philadelphia activated 10,000 auxiliary policemen and banned the sale of liquor.

The outrageous conduct and statements of the strikers and the danger inherent in the situation provoked Philadelphia's Negro community to protest actions. After a two-day investigation of the hostilities, Roy Wilkins, then assistant secretary of the NAACP, wired Attorney General Biddle:

> I wish to urge strongly that the Department of Justice through the Federal Bureau of Investigation make a special investigation into the activities of James McMenamin, Don Lasher and Frank P. Carney, who are leaders of the so-called committee representing the strikers. Statements attributed to Carney by Philadelphia papers of August 1 and 2 seem to be clearly incitement to riot. Rumor has it that Carney and Lasher were either given or took much time off from work during the past three weeks, devoting their efforts to fomenting racial hatred and stirring up employees to paralyze Philadelphia with the surprise stoppage. Statements attributed to McMenamin in the *New York Herald Tribune* of August 3 came within the category of incitement to riot. Carney and McMenamin have preached open defiance of the federal government as well as the vilest and lowest form of racial hatred. My personal observation among the Negro population of Philadelphia for 36 hours informs me that the statements of these strike leaders have done more to embitter the Negro population and lay the basis for serious clashes than any other aspect of the tie-up. Prompt and effective action by FBI is urged.[128]

The defiance of the law by strike leaders and the disruption of the war effort led to nationwide demands to end the strike. An editorial in the *New York Herald Tribune* placed the blame on race prejudice and a lack of federal remedies:

> There was not a question involved in the strike which had any legitimate standing in a labor dispute. The issue was one of narrow race prejudice, pure and simple. . . . The Smith-Connally Act provides criminal penalties for the leaders of a strike, but only in an industry taken over by the Government. So a gentleman like James McMenamin . . . could exhort his followers against all official or moral mandates, thereby crippling vital war production and promoting race riots, and remain unmolested.[129]

Through the strike the Transport Workers Union strongly supported government measures and repeatedly urged striking employees to return to work; it did not retreat from its antidiscrimination policy. The TWU, as collective bargaining agent for the employees, was much more directly involved in the Philadelphia transit strike than the AFL's Amalgamated Association, but the strike achieved such notoriety that the American Federation of Labor was under considerable public pressure to state its position. The AFL remained silent, although some of the strike organizers were active supporters of the Amalgamated Association. In contrast, the CIO and various affiliated unions publicly condemned the strike. Philip Murray again reiterated the CIO's general policy and urged the strikers to return to work "to help restore their city to normal pursuits and full productive capacity":

> The CIO adopted a wartime policy that is wholly in the best interests of every working man and woman during our country's fight for survival. It is to the everlasting credit of the Transport Workers Union that they upheld the principles of the CIO. The union's adherence to CIO policy will pay the membership dividends in the future as it has in the past.[130]

The South Jersey CIO Industrial Union Council, representing 64,000 members, adopted a resolution urging the Philadelphia Transportation Company employees to return to work immediately.[131] Similar condemnations of the strike were issued by other CIO affiliates in the Philadelphia area.[132] On August 3, 1944, the executive board of the Philadelphia Industrial Union Council, representing 150,000 CIO members, passed a resolution supporting the government's order:

We stand by the order of the President's Fair Employment Practice Committee, demanding that all Americans, regardless of race, creed, or color, be given equal opportunity for employment in all positions of P.T.C. and we demand that all government agencies enforce this order with all means at their command.[133]

Until Saturday, August 5, General Hayes's strategy was based on symbolic seizure, with reliance on persuasion and the support of the Transport Workers Union to end the strike. But government, labor, and citizen appeals had failed to get the strikers back to work.

On Saturday afternoon General Hayes put a new plan into effect. Supported by battle equipment, 5,000 troops armed with bayonets were brought into the city and dispatched to strategic locations. Soldiers were ordered to ride in pairs on each vehicle requiring protection, and the Army had a contingency plan for operating the public transportation system if the strike continued.[134]

The U.S. Attorney General ordered a federal grand jury convened to investigate Smith-Connally Act violations. The Selective Service System ordered local draft boards to cancel the striking employees' draft deferments if they did not return to work. The War Manpower Commission ordered cancellation of certificates of availability for the strikers so that once they were dropped from company rolls they would not be able to take jobs elsewhere. They were to be dropped from company rolls on Monday morning, August 7, 1944, if they did not report for work.

That same day McMenamin, Carney, and two other strike leaders were arrested and charged with violations of the Smith-Connally Act. The historian Louis Ruchames writes that "[t]hese measures brought the consequences of the strike to each striker in a very personal way and proved successful. Workers began to report to work twenty-four hours before the Army deadline."[135] In place of operators who did not report to work that weekend, Army personnel drove the cars, and the operators who did return were accompanied by uniformed and fully equipped soldier guards. The Philadelphia branch of the NAACP offered General Hayes "services and any data in our possession in connection with the Philadelphia Transportation Company situation."[136] And spokesmen for 350 members of the Harlem Transit Guild of New York, composed of Negro employees of the Independent Subway System, sent a telegram to General Hayes offering to supply operators for subways, buses, and streetcars.[137]

After TWU president Michael Quill's initial optimism had been dampened by the failure of the Army seizure to end the strike, he worked actively with General Hayes in developing a plan for the Army to operate the system.* After one meeting during which Hayes, Quill, Fitzsimon, and MacMahon conferred, Quill told the press:

> We pledged our complete support to General Hayes and our Commander-in-Chief, who General Hayes is representing. We have called a meeting of our local officers and shop stewards . . . where we will give a full report of the conference.
> We are confident that normal operation [of the PTC] will be resumed on Monday and that the conspiracy by a small clique of employees will have been defeated by the patriotic P.T.C. men and women who were merely used as pawns in these tragic events.[138]

By Monday, August 7, 90 percent of the company's employees had returned to their posts in response to General Hayes's ultimatum to replace striking workers with specially trained soldiers.[139] Twenty-four strikers were dropped from company rolls, and six were immediately drafted.[140] The strike was over.

The next day Senator Richard Russell of Georgia used the occasion to blame the FEPC for the strike. In a seventy-minute speech on the floor of the Senate, he proclaimed:

> If there had been no Fair Employment Practice Committee, not a single man-hour of war production would have been lost and there would have been no racial disturbances or bitterness. . . .
> It is easy to understand the aggrieved feelings of the employees. They had no recourse to the courts to protect themselves against this creature of executive order when it turned upon them the full power invested in all of the war agencies of the government.[141]

Russell concluded his remarks by calling the FEPC "the most dangerous force in existence in the United States today."[142]

On August 9, the PTC finally signed the contract that the TWU had approved in June. The same day seven of the eight black trainees resumed their training, and a few days later they began to operate cars in the city. The first runs were made without incident. Ohly writes that "the subsequent training went well and by the

---

*In an early plea for the use of government troops, Quill stated that "[i]f the Army wants strong action on the Normandy front, it gets it. There is need for strong action in Philadelphia to protect the workers who are ready and willing to operate the transit system. If troops were ordered into action tomorrow, 95 per cent of the workers now idle would go back."— *Philadelphia Bulletin,* August 5, 1944, p. 1.

14th several of the trainees were operating passenger cars in various sections of the city."[143] Within a few months the company had over 900 Negroes in its employ, including motormen and conductors, and one Negro was on the company's publicity staff.[144] In an election within the Transport Workers Union held shortly after the strike, one Negro was elected vice president of the local and four were elected to the executive committee.[145] These five Negroes were among the forty-man union committee which had negotiated the contract with the company.[146]

The gradual reduction of federal troops had begun on August 10, and on August 17 the government returned the transit lines to the company.[147] The only incident involving federal troops was an attempt by one southern soldier riding guard on a car to segregate the passengers, as was the custom in his home town.[148]

Union rivalry continued for a period after the strike ended. The new TWU contract provided that employees had until August 23 to either join or resign from the union.[149] During that period a small number of workers attempted to organize a mass rejection of the Transport Workers Union. Hundreds of handbills were passed out among the employees:

> FRANKLIN TO ELEANOR,
> YOU KISS THE NIGGERS AND I'LL KISS THE JEWS,
> AND WE'LL STAY IN THE WHITE HOUSE AS LONG AS WE CHOOSE.[150]

In the next union election, held that October, the Transport Workers Union actually increased its membership.[151]

One of the repercussions of the strike was a grand jury indictment of thirty strike leaders, including James McMenamin and Frank Carney. The grand jury was convened and charged by District Court Judge George A. Welsh to determine the identity of the men who organized the strike. "If race hatred was the real reason," he said, "we cannot take it lying down. We must punish the men who called the strike."[152] In its indictment of the strike leaders the grand jury said:

> It seems quite clear that, so far as there was flame or fire in the strike, the chief fuel therefore came from resentment over the upgrading of Negroes to "platform" positions such as none of their race had heretofore held.
>
> The members of this jury wish it to be known that they agree entirely with the viewpoint which holds for this race the right to higher position and wage . . . on the same basis as fellow employees of the white race. We are pleased, therefore, to express our conviction

from the evidence that the great majority of the employees were not interested to strike on this basis. . . .

It is necessary to state there was much antagonism in the strike between representatives of four different labor organs, but chiefly between members of the former Employees' Union and of the new Transport Workers Union. . . .

The jury, after a careful survey of the evidence, finds true bills against 30 such offenders. It is our opinion that all of these individuals are to a more or less degree victims of larger forces under the influence of which they had been affected.[153]

On March 12, 1945, twenty-seven of the thirty defendants pleaded nolo contendere and were fined a hundred dollars each.[154]

The basic cause of the Philadelphia transit strike was the volatile issue of job promotion of Negro workers injected into a complex and intense struggle between competing labor unions. The leaders of the Philadelphia Rapid Transit Employees' Union, the Brotherhood of Railroad Trainmen, and the Amalgamated Association were bitterly opposed to the Congress of Industrial Organizations and its affiliate, the Transport Workers Union, and they used the racial issue in an attempt to defeat the CIO. These labor leaders, with the tacit consent of the American Federation of Labor and the complicity of their international unions and the company management, also provoked the strike in a futile attempt to maintain the racial status quo in employment. Their efforts failed only because of the direct military intervention of the U.S. Government—intervention based upon extraordinary war emergency measures. As such, these measures did not establish a precedent to be invoked in the future.

The NAACP, in "Philadelphia—Postwar Preview?," a full-page editorial in *Crisis,* asked somewhat prophetically:

The great question emerging from the stoppage of work by 6,000 employees of the Philadelphia Transportation Company August 1, assertedly because eight Negroes had been upgraded and were being trained by the company for jobs as motormen, is whether this is a preview of what the Negro may expect in the postwar period.

Are we to have stoppages, street fighting, race-hating speeches, and naked and unchecked race-baiting after the war? Are American citizens who happen not to be white going to be the victims of mobs for the "crime" of wanting to work and maintain themselves as members of society?[155]

The Fair Employment Practice Committee concluded in its *Final Report* that "[o]nce the barriers were down, Negro and white operators worked without incident, the public acceptance of Negro operators was excellent, and the continued hiring of capable Negro operators materially aided in supplying definitely needed manpower."[156]

The history of the Philadelphia transit strike during World War II indicates that the employer, the independent union, and the unions affiliated with the American Federation of Labor were jointly responsible for a bitter strike that paralyzed a major city, with more than a million man-hours of work lost, because of resistance to the promotion of black workers into all-white job classifications. The events in Philadelphia also demonstrated the complexity of the social forces involved in altering a traditional discriminatory labor pattern. Furthermore, they illustrate the potentially decisive role of federal administrative agencies charged with enforcing the law. In the entire history of the FEPC no case showed more clearly the need for the full use of governmental power to achieve compliance with the executive order. Though the Federal Government's intervention in the Philadelphia transit strike was unique to that time and place, it had continuing implications for later civil rights struggles.

12

Los Angeles, Washington, D.C., and
Other Urban Transit Cases

Many complaints of discrimination against Negro employees by urban transit companies had been presented to the Fair Employment Practice Committee before the Philadelphia strike. Black workers in various cities—Pittsburgh, Indianapolis, Gary, Los Angeles, to name a few—charged that they had been barred from employment as conductors, motormen, and in other job classifications. In some instances the FEPC was able to persuade companies to hire Negroes into previously all-white classifications, but in the majority of cases—where the Amalgamated Association of Street, Electric Railway and Motor Coach Employees, AFL, represented the employees—the committee's efforts at negotiation with employers and union officials failed.

The first city in which Negroes joined together as a group to protest against being barred from employment as operators on buses and streetcars was New York. In the late 1930s, with the help of civil rights organizations and other community groups, the Transport Workers Union, CIO, won a major strike in New York City that enabled the union to be recognized as collective bargaining agent for certain groups of transit workers employed by privately owned transit lines. Shortly thereafter, under pressure from the Negro community and with support from the union, some New York transit companies hired Negroes as drivers and conductors for the first time.[1] The New York Omnibus Corporation was the major exception; it employed a small number of Negroes exclusively as car cleaners and, as late as 1941, refused to

upgrade them to operating positions.[2] Adam Clayton Powell, Jr., a
leader in the struggle to open operators' jobs on buses and
streetcars to Negroes, wrote:

> On March 10, five hours after the Transport Workers Union con-
> cluded its 12-day-old strike, we struck. We had supported the white
> men in their union strike. We now carried signs at the crossroads of
> Harlem, "We Stayed Off These Buses for 12 Days That White Men
> Might Have a Decent Standard of Living—Stay Off Them Now for
> Black Men."[3]

Organized pressure from Negroes and white sympathizers
grew. The Harlem Labor Union formed the United Bus Committee
and was joined by representatives from the National Negro
Congress.[4] In the course of mass demonstrations, the number of
protesters picketing at the facilities of the New York Omnibus
Corporation quickly reached 10,000 and the corporation agreed to
hire Negroes as operators.[5] Powell commented:

> For the first time in the history of America a tri-party agreement was
> signed between John D. Ritchie, representing the bus company,
> Michael Quill, representing the Transport Workers Union and I, rep-
> resenting the consumers. The agreement provided that Negroes
> should be integrated into every phase of the company. . . . Letters
> that came from the riding public indicated that the efficiency of the
> Negro driver was just as good as that of the white.[6]

During World War II local transit companies in other cities
expressed willingness to comply with executive orders requiring
fair employment practices, but the results varied. On October 20,
1944, the Springfield Street Railway Company in Springfield,
Massachusetts, agreed to hire Negroes; but as of April 30, 1945, it
did not employ a single Negro.[7] The company attributed the
absence of Negro employees to an absence of Negro applicants.[8]

In Pittsburgh, Pennsylvania, where the employees' union was
the AFL's Amalgamated Association, the Pittsburgh Railways
Company refused to hire Negro operators. A representative of the
company said the employment of Negroes was not considered
practical at that time,[9] and a union spokesman said the union's
only concern was that all workers join the union.[10] After the
company had refused to employ a Negro referred by the U.S.
Employment Service, the War Manpower Commission stopped
referring applicants to the company. By April 1945 the company
had acquiesced and, with the reluctant agreement of the union, had
begun training Negroes to operate buses.[11]

Gary Railways of Gary, Indiana, also refused to employ Negro bus operators during the war years. At a conference with the FEPC on November 18, 1944, company spokesmen explained that their employees, many of whom were recently arrived southerners, had formed a local of the Amalgamated Association,[12] and blamed the union for its refusal to hire Negro operators. Local union officials were actively implementing the Amalgamated Association's policy of opposing employment of Negroes. As of April 30, 1945, the company had hired no Negro operators.[13]

In Indianapolis, Indiana, Local 1070 of the Amalgamated Association had a closed-shop contract with Indianapolis Railways.[14] Negroes were not permitted to join the union, therefore they could not work for the transit company. On November 15, 1944, the FEPC received the complaints of Starling James, president of the Federation of Associated Clubs in Indianapolis, and fifteen qualified Negroes turned away by the company.[15] The transit company's president, Harry Reid, announced that the company was ready and willing to employ Negroes as operators but that Local 1070 of the Amalgamated Association would not permit their employment.[16] The company was reluctant to undertake the expense of training Negroes only to have the union refuse them membership. Indianapolis Railways later agreed to hire Negroes solely on the condition that they be directed to do so after an FEPC public hearing, which the company requested to demonstrate to the public that the union was at fault.[17]

The recognized union at the Kansas City Public Service Company of Kansas City, Missouri, was Division 1287 of the Amalgamated Association.[18] The company employed no Negro transit operators. At a conference early in December 1944 the president of the transit company said that he felt there was public opposition to the employment of Negroes and he was reluctant to act on the issue without the cooperation of the union.[19] The union president announced that he could not commit the union to any particular policy but admitted that for several years "there had been a tacit understanding between the company and the union that certain positions would be reserved for white employees."[20] On December 12, 1944, FEPC representatives met with the local's executive committee and were told that "there might be physical violence against operators who trained Negroes to serve as operators."[21] As a result of acquiescence by the employer and lack of enforcement power by the FEPC, the union was able to convert a discriminatory "tacit understanding" into a formal policy, reinforced with threats of violence. As of April 30, 1945, the company still did not employ Negro operators.[22]

The practice of reserving local transit operators' positions for white men only was also followed by the St. Louis Public Service Company and its union, Local 788 of the Amalgamated Association;[23] by the Portland, Oregon, Traction Company and Division 757 of the Amalgamated Association;[24] and by the Seattle Transit System and Division 587 of the Amalgamated Association.[25]

A similar pattern existed in Los Angeles, where the FEPC had been engaged in futile negotiations for almost two years. The course of events was finally altered by two new factors—the deterioration of the Los Angeles Railway Corporation's service to the public, owing largely to the refusal to utilize available black labor; and the example of the government's seizure of the Philadelphia Rapid Transit Company.

In late 1941 the AFL's Amalgamated Association and the CIO's Transport Workers Union began vying with each other to organize the Los Angeles Railway Corporation's employees.[26] Although no election was held among the workers, there was reason to believe that management unilaterally provided the Amalgamated Association with a closed-shop agreement.[27] Division 1277 of the Amalgamated Association was formed amid hostility between AFL and CIO partisans and suspicions that the AFL union was subservient to management.

The first complaints of Negroes who had been rejected as operators in Los Angeles were received by the War Manpower Commission in October 1942.[28] At a conference with the War Manpower Commission, management predicted serious repercussions among employees and passengers if Negroes were to be hired as operators.[29] The union representative for the bus and streetcar division generally agreed with management's position, but the president of the union and the business agent for the mechanics' division felt that no serious difficulties would occur if Negroes were hired. In this case the transit company initially opposed efforts to employ Negroes, whereas the union was divided on the issue. By February 1943, however, the union had largely come to agree with management. Many members had signed a petition opposing the training of Negroes for operators' jobs, and the union business agent for the operating employees was now in sympathy with them.[30]

At this point management's attitude began to change. Following a conference with the War Manpower Commission, the

Office of Defense Transportation, and the union, on January 15, 1943, the company agreed to comply with Executive Order 8802.[31] On February 9, 1943, the company posted a bulletin to workers stating its intent to comply with the executive order,[32] and on February 17 two Negroes were upgraded to become apprentice mechanics on the night shift.[33] Eighty white workers, striking in protest, suspended all operations for two hours.[34] The superintendent of the mechanics' division then took the two Negroes off the job. P. B. Harris, president of the Los Angeles Railway Corporation, stated that "[w]hen the day shift employees reported, they refused to go to work because of the upgrading of these two employees."[35] On February 23 the company again tried to upgrade three Negroes to a mechanic's classification,[36] but 75 percent of the employees in the shop refused to go to work, and again the Negroes were removed.[37]

The Fair Employment Practice Committee encouraged the company to continue attempts to upgrade Negro workers. An FEPC representative telegraphed Harris urging him to proceed with efforts to promote and advising him to contact Division 1277 of the Amalgamated Association if employees refused to work.[38] Harris wired back that the "[u]nion could give us no assurance that they could prevent walkout in whole or in part. To the contrary, indicated further attempts to upgrade Negro employees would cause partial work stoppages."[39] The union, which a year earlier had anticipated no disturbances, now refused to cooperate and indicated support for the efforts of its white members to prevent the employment of Negroes in "lily-white" job classifications. In July the committee again encouraged the company to comply with the executive order,[40] and Harris again replied that the union's intransigence made compliance impossible: "The union has been, at no time since the sending of this letter, able to assure us that there would be no work stoppage and we have not deemed it advisable to proceed further."[41]

While these negotiations were continuing, the service provided by the Los Angeles Railway Corporation seriously deteriorated. By January 1, 1944, only 493 streetcars were in use out of the 800 that should have been in operation.[42] The situation was similar for buses: 212 were on the streets, while 144 were idle because there was an insufficient number of drivers and maintenance workers.[43]

In late 1943 the company contended that despite its manpower shortages, the union prevented it from hiring qualified Negroes. On November 1, the company, desperate for workers, asked the U.S.

Employment Service to supply men to fill 1,314 vacancies.[44] The positions went largely unfilled. Between January 1 and March 10, 1944, the USES referred sixty qualified Negro car operators; none were hired.[45] A company spokesman told a USES interviewer that "there were certain jobs with this company that were Negroes' jobs and there were certain jobs that were white people's jobs."[46] One Negro woman applicant for a job as conductor testified that she was told by a company representative: " 'Well, Mrs. Slayden, I am from the South' (he tried to put it on a, you know, friendly basis) 'and interested in the Negroes. I have dealt with them all my life and I think the Negro is . . . happier in domestic service.' "[47]

The War Manpower Commission designated the Los Angeles Railway Corporation as "essential" on November 8, 1943,[48] thus giving the company a top-priority rating for manpower referrals. On March 24, 1944, after the company had refused employment to 354 referred Negroes,[49] the commission revoked the company's "essential" classification on the basis of "underutilization of local labor."[50]

Prior to this action the Los Angeles CIO Industrial Union Council had petitioned the War Manpower Commission to revoke the company's referral priority on the grounds that there was an adequate local labor supply and that as a result of the company's refusal to hire Negroes CIO members were losing work time in war plants because of inadequate transportation.[51] The company responded with the charge that the CIO was attempting to undermine the position of the AFL's Amalgamated Association and to supplant that union as collective bargaining agent.[52] In rebuttal the Los Angeles CIO Industrial Union Council replied that it "does not now nor . . . in the future entertain any intention of doing organizational work among LARY employees."[53]

The FEPC held hearings on the racial employment practices of the Los Angeles Railway Corporation on August 8, 1944. Although there was evidence that in practice the union opposed the hiring of Negroes, it was not so charged. The reason for not formally indicting the union was explained in an internal memorandum of the FEPC:

> I recommend that the union not be a party charged. I would have no hesitancy in charging the union if we had any evidence which would support the charges. The difficulty is that the union *officially* has not opposed the hiring of Negroes and what evidence we could get of its insincerity is distinctly of the hearsay variety.[54]

At the hearings the company related the results of its efforts to upgrade Negroes and stated that it was reluctant to try again because it feared more work stoppages.[55] Apparently, after the company's first attempts at upgrading failed, both the company and the union had committed themselves to maintaining the racial status quo. When a company representative was asked what educational programs the company had conducted to impress on the workers the necessity of complying with the executive order, he answered that "we have relied solely upon the union to carry on that educational campaign among the employees themselves; that is, persons below full-time supervision."[56] The same official, asked if the company had checked with the union to see how the program was being carried out, answered: "I think that the union has reported to us that they have carried out throughout their regular meetings, union meetings, and in instructions to their shop stewards, that they have gone forward with the program of the elimination of this irrational prejudice."[57]

When union president Doyle D. McClurg was questioned about the union's attempts to persuade workers to accept Negro platform operators, he responded that during the upgrading of the two Negro workers in 1943, the business agent "got on the benches that day and he begged them to go ahead and work."[58] After the union had allowed representatives of the mayor's office, the Army, and the Navy to speak to its members, McClurg said, "we had gone along and tried to put on this program, which was to no avail because it seems like certain ones had no interest, maybe our idea was right, so then we have left it up to other bodies, to legislative and regulatory bodies, government agencies, to prepare an educational program."[59]

The hearings indicated that the Los Angeles Railway Corporation had placed on the union the responsibility of persuading white workers to accept Negroes, although the union had played an active part in denying them jobs. The union had taken no positive measures of its own, on the ground that it was the government's responsibility. In a final effort at self-exoneration, the company predicted that 90 percent of its workers would strike if Negroes were assigned platform jobs.[60] The union's estimate was 87.5 percent.[61]

On August 9, 1944, the Fair Employment Practice Committee issued a directive to the company to desist from its practice of refusing to hire Negroes as streetcar and motor-coach operators and to cease refusing to upgrade its Negro employees to these and other positions.[62] The same day, the company replied: "We will proceed immediately to take steps to put said directives into effect, and will report to your Regional Director for Region 12 when these steps have been taken and compliance has been effected."[63] Also on the same day, McClurg addressed the membership of the union and stated that the executive committee of Division 1277 intended to comply with the FEPC directive.[64]

The Philadelphia transit strike, involving the same issue, had provoked government seizure only five days before the Los Angeles hearings were held. Both the company and the union were reluctant to risk the same experience. Another factor influencing their decisions was the mounting pressure for compliance both from the government and from civic groups. At a conference of the Fair Employment Practice Committee, the War Manpower Commission, the Army, the Navy, the Maritime Commission, the Selective Service System, the Office of Civil Defense, the War Labor Board, churches, and community organizations including local branches of the National Association for the Advancement of Colored People, all parties offered their full cooperation in obtaining compliance.[65]

By August 23, 1944, the company had one Negro driving a streetcar with two Negro women as conductors; a week later fifteen Negroes were operating streetcars. There was no resentment from the public even when the cars passed through "anti-Negro" areas.[66] More Negroes were later hired, and the discriminatory pattern was abolished. Within a year, an FEPC interoffice memorandum to the director of field operations stated that "[a]s you have been advised previously, the Committee has directed that the cases involved be considered satisfactorily adjusted."[67] Robert C. Weaver later wrote:

> While the effect of the Philadelphia affair on the Los Angeles situation cannot be accurately determined, it seems clear that management and union officials as well as the rank and file of transit workers in Los Angeles were convinced by the determined federal handling of the Philadelphia strike that further resistance against the upgrading of Negroes in Los Angeles was useless.[68]

The resolution of the Philadelphia strike seems to have had a great impact in Los Angeles; it had less influence in San Francisco—and virtually none in Washington, D.C.

Objection by the Amalgamated Association to the hiring of Negroes was adamant in Oakland, San Francisco, and Berkeley. Evidence of discrimination was so abundant there that the FEPC was able to document extensive violations of the executive order by Division 192 of the AFL's Amalgamated Association and the employer, known as the Key System, at its March 19–23, 1945, hearings.[69]

The Key System operated bus and streetcar lines in Oakland and Berkeley and into San Francisco. The company had entered into a union contract with Division 192 of the Amalgamated Association on January 1, 1926.[70] One provision, still in force until January 1, 1941, stipulated the extent of the union's control of employment in the Key System: "The companies agree that all employees covered by this agreement must be members of the Union in good standing, it being understood that the Union has the right to reject applications for cause."[71] In fact the union could deny employment with the company to anyone simply by rejecting a membership application, although it was restricted in theory by the clause requiring it to accept anyone's application for membership except "for cause." Since there were no Negro members of Division 192, and no Negro operators with the Key System, between 1926 and 1941, being a Negro was apparently reason enough to be barred by the union under the "for cause" provision.

But the union was not entirely satisfied with the extent of its control over Key System hiring. When negotiating its 1941–1942 contract with the company, Division 192 proposed elimination of the "for cause" provision, asking instead for "the right to reject any application for membership."[72] Under the terms of this proposal the company would interview potential employees and refer acceptable applicants to the union for clearance; the union could then reject company referrals for any reason whatever. The union would have absolute control over the employment process at the Key System, and the exclusion of Negroes would become a simple matter, requiring no acrobatics in interpreting clauses in the bargaining agreement.

The company refused to sign over to the union such absolute control over its hiring. In its final proposal, which was ultimately accepted by the union, the company imposed a semblance of limitation:

> The Company agrees that all employees covered by this agreement must become members of the Association and remain members in good standing as a condition precedent to continued employment. All new employees shall make application for membership in the Association before becoming regular employees of the Company and acquiring seniority rights. The Association reserves the right to reject

application for membership in accordance with the laws of the Association.[73]

Of course, since the union could establish its own "laws" and then interpret them, the limitation was fictional. If the union might have found it publicly embarrassing to adopt a rule specifically rejecting Negro workers as members, it overcame the difficulty in practice. Not a single Negro was accepted during the period of the contract.

In the next contract, signed June 21, 1943, Division 192 finally got the provision it had tried for two years earlier.[74] In practice, there was now no restriction on its power to reject potential employees of the Key System.

Contract negotiations between the Key System and Division 192 present a pattern of increasing union control over hiring practices. For nearly twenty years there was apparently no necessity for explicit control to exclude Negroes. The tacit arrangement worked well enough until wartime manpower demands placed more pressure on the company to hire Negroes. Then the union began to increase its control over initial hiring as well as job promotion, and to make the control more rigid through renegotiated contracts.

Like the Los Angeles Railway Corporation, the Key System now faced increasingly acute labor shortages. In its 1944 annual report the company described its situation as "critical," because of manpower shortages and poor service.[75] Early that year the company began an extensive advertising campaign to explain its problems to the public and plead for applicants:

> Why Doesn't Somebody Do *Something* About Our Transportation?
>
> We didn't have a ouija board to tell us that the 70 million passengers of 1941 would rise to 119 million in 1943. . . . The fundamental problems are equipment, parts, and manpower. If you know of any man or woman who could enlist as a soldier on the home front by joining the Key System family, whole or part time, whether they need the income or not, please send them to us.[76]

A report of the California Railroad Commission summarized the result of the company's efforts:

> The expenditure for conducting this advertising campaign approximated $52,000 for the year 1943. Even with this program of recruiting, the company was unable to secure and retain enough help to properly man either their shops or equipment.[77]

Despite its labor shortages, the company still did not even refer Negro job applicants to the union for clearance. From 1941 to

1945 it referred 27,000 white applicants to the union.[78] But in 1945 the company referred eight Negroes to the union, and in each instance the union denied them membership;[79] according to the closed-shop agreement, this meant they could not be employed.

The president of Division 192, Alfred Brown, took the position that there was no need to employ Negroes. An FEPC report describes Brown's attitude at a union-government conference:

> Mr. Brown expressed complete disagreement with the statements by [War Manpower Commission] and Army representatives, that failure to utilize Negroes was interfering with proper utilization of manpower. He stated that there was no good reason why Negroes should be used as operators, they were not needed.[80]

At the FEPC hearings Brown explained that his union had authorized a subcommittee composed of the president, the vice president, and the financial secretary to make preliminary approval for membership of potential employees referred by the company.[81] Subcommittee approval was tantamount to union approval, but subcommittee disapproval denied the applicant employment with the company until the union membership met and voted on his application. In the operation of this system whites were routinely approved; Negroes were systematically denied subcommittee clearance.[82] The eight Negroes referred by the company in 1945 were denied clearance and were then rejected by a vote of the rank and file membership.[83] Brown told an FEPC representative why his subcommittee never approved Negroes:

> *A.* . . . I know my membership. I know that they won't accept a Negro, and consequently I would not be performing my function if I approved the Negro before having him voted upon by the general membership.
>
> *Q.* In other words, Mr. Brown, if the man is colored you would not pass him merely because he's colored?
>
> *A.* That's right. I know my membership.[84]

The union, which had obtained full control over employment procedures with the company through the series of closed-shop contracts, had developed an expedient method of systematically rejecting Negroes. When the applicant's petition came before the full union for a vote, Brown would state that he thought it was his "duty" to inform the membership that the person they were voting upon was a Negro.[85]

Division 192 of the Amalgamated Association included the following passage in its membership oath:

> I will be respectful in work and action to every woman and be considerate to the widow and orphan, the weak and defenseless, and never discriminate against a fellow-worker on account of creed, color or nationality.[86]

It might be assumed that members of the union, given their systematic exclusion of Negroes, were violating their oath. Brown was questioned about how he could reconcile his union's oath with its discriminatory practice:

> *Q.* Is it a violation of that obligation for any member or officer of Division 192, to vote against any Negro referred by the Key System because of race?
>
> *A.* It is not.
>
> *Q.* Will you explain that answer?
>
> *A.* It is very simple: It states in there "against a fellow-worker." A fellow-worker is not a fellow-worker until such time as they become a fellow-worker. In our particular organization a rat, or skunk, or anybody who might be working in some other capacity, is not a fellow-worker in the sense as defined in the obligation.[87]

Brown further explained:

> I mean anybody who works in any other capacity, such as a laborer, a machinist, or anything else, in the meaning of the obligation is not a fellow-worker until such time as he becomes a fellow-worker in the industry in which we are working.[88]

Brown added that this definition also applied to job applicants.[89]

The union had perfected a tautology—members pledged not to discriminate against "fellow-workers"; the union defined "fellow-workers" as only those already engaged in their occupation and holding union membership. As a final insult to credulity, when asked "[w]ould a man's race be one of the factors you would consider" in refusing to admit applicants, Brown replied that "[i]t would not."[90]

The union responded with indignation to the FEPC hearings. In its official paper, *Wheels,* it denounced the committee:

> The Cause of Racial Tolerance Suffered Serious Harm In Oakland During The Days Of March 19th To March 23rd. This damage to inter-racial friendliness and understanding resulted from the deception and dictator-like manner in which officials of the President's Committee on Fair Employment Practice conducted the proceedings

involving the Key System and Div. 192, Amalgamated Association of Street, Electric Railway and Motor Coach Employees of America.

So biased and unfair were the actions of representatives of FEPC, so shameless were their violations of legal ethics and even the commonest standards of good manners, that the Committee has Earned the Distrust And The Fear of all persons in California who are working for an improvement in relations between peoples of the white and black and yellow races. No subterfuge was too mean, no trick was too shoddy to be left out of the performance of FEPC officials during the hearings.[91]

In the same article the union insisted that it was sympathetic with "racial tolerance":

Racial tolerance and friendliness are praiseworthy human aims, but they can only be obtained by intelligence and cooperation among the people concerned. It was for this reason that Division 192 volunteered to appear before the FEPC. The committee's charges that the Key System and Division 192 discriminate against Negroes are unfounded and have been denied by both the Company and the Union.[92]

The hearings had no discernible effect on the company or the union. Both continued to deny employment to Negroes. Several months after the hearings an FEPC memorandum reported:

There has been a good deal of undercurrent resentment within the Negro community because the Key System has not hired qualified Negro applicants as platform personnel, despite an expressed need for workers.

On October 3rd, Mr. Ray Thompson—who was present at the Key System Hearings—and who, as chairman of the Shipyard Committee Against Discrimination, was very cooperative with our office, disclosed some tentative plans for action in the East Bay.

Mr. Thompson stated it was "now or never" that Negroes had a chance to get jobs with the Key System, particularly since "merchants from small East Bay towns are asking for more service to their communities." He added that the Shipyard Committee Against Discrimination planned to change its name and, with support from other groups, picket both the Union and the Company, with signs bearing charges of "collusion" and other statements, including "in a friendly way" a question as to why FEPC hadn't acted. . . .

Whether or not the projected plans mentioned above materialize, in my opinion the feeling of the Negro community is aroused on this point and Mr. Thompson's reaction is merely symptomatic of a more generally felt let-down attitude.[93]

Developments in the transit industry of the San Francisco-Oakland Bay area followed a familiar pattern. Increased pressure to hire Negro operators provoked increased union resistance and management's acquiescence to it. During the entire period of World War II no Negroes were employed as operators or mechanics with the Key System.

The Capital Transit Company, operating the major mass-transportation system in Washington, D.C., also refused to hire Negro operators during the war years. Government efforts to persuade the company to hire Negroes as car operators and conductors began as early as 1942, but although Capital Transit suffered severe manpower shortages, FEPC chairman Malcolm Ross was later to describe the Capital Transit case as a "spectacular FEPC failure."[94]

Until 1942 the company had placed discriminatory job orders with the U.S. Employment Service, specifying "white only."[95] On July 15, 1942, the FEPC received a complaint from the USES that the company had not employed qualified Negroes as bus operators, streetcar conductors, motormen, and checkers.[96] Negotiations between the committee and Capital Transit began in October 1942, and on December 1 the committee directed the company to comply with Executive Order 8802.[97] The company then agreed to cease placing discriminatory job orders with the USES, but later evidence showed that the company did not honor the agreement and applications from Negro workers were filed away without consideration.[98]

The company had an agreement with Division 689 of the Amalgamated Association that required membership in good standing in the union as a condition of continued employment with the company.[99] The union agreed to receive into membership all eligible employees "according to the laws of the Association."[100] Under the terms of the agreement, after ninety days of employment each employee was required to become and remain a union member and was subject to a compulsory dues checkoff by the company.[101] Although Negroes were admitted into the union, they were limited to menial jobs only and were prevented both by the company and by the union from being upgraded to the position of operator or conductor. In 1942, when the government first became interested in the discriminatory practices at the company, the local union wrote its international president, W. D. Mahon, asking for advice on its "race problem." He replied:

I know of no complaints in our organization anywhere over this matter. There was some little complaint in San Francisco some time ago, but that has disappeared and there is nothing of it at the present time. In many places colored men are employed in this line of transportation and in many of our organizations there have been colored men for years holding membership.

You ask regarding the records concerning accidents and so on. There is no record by any company that I know of kept concerning the difference of accidents between colored and white, and there is no difference so far as I can find out in that line of work. Their records show the same as anyone else's so far as their work is concerned. I again would call your attention to the fact that it is a serious matter. I realize how some of your membership, being Southerners, feel on this matter, but you must take into consideration the fact that we are now engaged in a war in which the colored man is called upon to do the same line of duty that the white man is called upon to do, and any discrimination that would attract public attention at this time would be very detrimental and especially coming out of Washington. So I would suggest that your members realize the situation and try to meet it in line with the policy of the organization.[102]

This letter conveniently ignored the fact that many affiliated divisions were directly responsible for discriminatory practices throughout the country and were actively resisting compliance with the federal executive order. It is revealing, however, in that it discusses records "concerning the difference of accidents between colored and white." Apparently the local's membership believed that Negroes were inherently less qualified than whites to be platform operators and sought to buttress this notion with reference to accidents, but not even the sympathetic international president could supply supporting statistics.

Subsequent to the FEPC's directive to the company, acting committee chairman Earl Dickerson was informed that the committee was to be recognized.[103] At the request of the White House, the Capital Transit Company hearings were postponed, and no action was taken until May 27, 1943, when President Roosevelt issued Executive Order 9346, which expanded the jurisdiction and authority of the Fair Employment Practice Committee.[104]

In February 1943 the Capital Transit Company made its only attempt to hire a Negro platform operator. B. A. Simmons, former chauffeur to then Assistant Secretary of State Dean Acheson, was trained as a motorman by the company for three days.[105] According to Simmons, when he arrived at the carbarn to begin work, the conductor he was assigned to work with said: "I refuse to work with a black man. I have told all of you that I won't work with a black man and I still won't work with a black man."[106] Simmons was then placed on ten other cars but the response was similar—"I would not work with a nigger."[107] After a half-hour work stoppage by the white operators, Simmons was removed; and, as FEPC chairman Malcolm Ross wrote, "the traffic jam was cleared for the triumphant procession of Nordic-operated trolleys behind it."[108]

The next attempt to obtain compliance with the executive order was made by the government. Edmund L. Jones, an FEPC attorney, reported the outcome of a conference between the company and the executive board of Division 689: "The members of the union Board urged that some individuals of national prominence be requested to explain to the men the reason for the . . . insistence by the government that the program proposed by the FEPC be adopted."[109] In response, Otto Reyer of the Office of Defense Transportation and Paul V. McNutt, chairman of the War Manpower Commission, addressed 2,000 union members.[110] "That meeting was a very stormy one," despite the union president's request for a show of courtesy among the rank and file.[111] Malcolm Ross commented that "[a] discussion of race differences always puts forward hecklers intoxicated with their own private hates. The McNutt meeting was ever so well intentioned. It wound up with insults to the featured speakers and a confirmation in the minds of Capital Transit workers from Virginia and North Carolina that they were in the saddle."[112] In this futile attempt at education of white workers through a dialogue with government officials, the workers were left with the feeling that the government had polled their opinion and that their decision against the employment of Negroes would be binding. The attitude was reinforced by the fact that for a full year no visible steps were taken to employ Negroes.

Because of increasing manpower shortages, the company's service deteriorated. In an effort to forestall conflict over employment of Negroes the company tried to increase the workload of its existing manpower by converting its two-man cars into one-man cars,[113] and it asked the Office of Defense Transportation for 150 new one-man cars.[114] It also asked the War Labor Board for permission to give bonuses to the operators to deter them from seeking employment elsewhere.[115] In efforts to increase its labor force, the company lowered qualifications and sought to recruit women and even soldiers on furlough.[116] It began running overcrowded buses,[117] and it appealed to the Public Utilities Commission for an extension of designated "rush hour" periods.[118] The personnel director testified before the Public Utilities Commission that "I don't think there is going to be much hope of getting help for at least six months,"[119] and the appeal was granted. A company report to the War Manpower Commission dated November 18, 1943, details the crisis:

> We are not making any progress. We are barely able to replace those leaving. Experience during the past month indicates that the trend is downward and that it will be increasingly difficult to even obtain replacements, much less to build up additions. The total number of employees on November 18, 1943, was the same as on May 1, 1943. At the same time, there is still a shortage of about 600 for replacements alone.
>
> The difficulty of obtaining qualified personnel for street car-bus operation is increasing; not only is the number of applicants smaller but the caliber of the applicants is much poorer. We seem to be approaching the bottom of the barrel. For a while in September and October, we were able to recruit a number of women to operate street cars and buses. The turnover among the women is very great, however, and the net results are very discouraging.[120]

After its abortive attempt in February, Capital Transit refused to consider hiring Negroes. The company even used an FEPC recommendation to justify its position. On July 17, 1943, the committee had recommended to the company a number of men "who have background training and experience in the business of integrating Negroes in industries."[121] From the list the company selected Paul S. Lunt, an industrial relations consultant, to begin an "educational program." His first task was to "investigate" the attitudes of the workers. A letter from the committee to Capital Transit described the duties of the consultant: ". . . 'to investigate' . . . means that you intend through the medium of consultants to take steps looking toward an early employment of Negroes on buses and streetcars."[122] The committee made it clear that the consultant's work was to constitute merely the first step in a continuing program. The company replied that "the first step is to secure information as to the attitude of our employees in the matter and to ascertain the reasons therefor, so that later steps can be taken in the light of that information,"[123] and the committee agreed.

Beginning in September 1943, Lunt interviewed between 200 and 250 men at their homes; he issued his report to the company on January 10, 1944.[124] His method had been to announce himself as a company interviewer interested in polling the workers' opinions. The conclusion of his "unguided survey" was that 70 percent of the platform men would strike if Negroes were hired.[125] Thereafter the company used this report—which was supposed to be a "first step" toward hiring Negroes—as a defense and justification of its practices.

Malcolm Ross, later realizing that the opinion poll had been a mistake, wrote:

> The company seemed to be sitting very pretty, for FEPC itself had agreed to the making of the survey. This was out of a policy for patience. The company had said it wanted to place Negroes. It had tried once and failed. The survey would be a first step in a new and careful approach. But when the sociologist turned in reams of statistics to show that a majority would strike, the company said: There! See! It can't be done.[126]

The impact on the Negro community of the company's and the union's resistance to hiring Negro platform operators was reflected in the black press. The nationally distributed Pittsburgh *Courier* carried two photographs of male and female Negro conductors on the Detroit Street Railway system. The caption read: "Detroit Refutes—Has Capital Transit an Answer for This?"[127] The same newspaper ran an angry editorial calling for united protest action against the discriminatory practices of the Capital Transit Company and pointed out that

> [i]t so happened that the four-point edict, revealing "irrefutable" handicaps of the Negro, as faked by Capital Transit, collapsed like a deck of cards when subjected to the withering fire power of the FEPC. . . . We need only to recall that Tulsa is a Southern city where Negroes have served as platform men with success for 15 years. Tulsa happens, also, to be the site where one of America's bloodiest race riots occurred a generation ago. . . .
>
> Thus, stripped of every pretense, isolated and proved guilty by FEPC in defying President Roosevelt, and met with an unprecedented unanimity of vigorous action by the colored population—what leg will Capital Transit have to stand on?
>
> The answer is an emphatic finality. None![128]

Other black newspapers protested too. The Washington, D.C., *Afro-American* editorially criticized the FEPC as well as the company for the protracted negotiations and attacked the committee's failure to act decisively.[129]

On January 15-16, 1945, three years after it received its first complaint against Capital Transit, the Fair Employment Practice

Committee held a hearing to investigate the racial practices of the company. Division 689 refused to participate at all. The company, relying heavily on Paul Lunt's prediction of a 70-percent walkout, defended its position on the ground that Washington, as the nation's capital and center of government activity, could not be allowed to suffer a crippling strike even for the cause of racial equality.

In public testimony Frank N. Johnson, a Negro applicant who had been refused employment with the company, recounted how the company treated Negro applicants and described the racial attitudes of Alexander Shapiro, the company's personnel director:

> I walked into the employment office and stated that I wanted an application for a bus or street car operator. The first fellow who approached me didn't say anything. He went in another room and got a fellow and brought him out there and he told me that it wasn't the policy of the company to accept applications from colored people, that he would be glad to entertain the idea of accepting an application from me for some other sort of work. I did not want to file an application for any other type of work at that time, and I asked to see his superior.
>
> Another gentleman came out and told me the same thing: in other words, that he could not accept my application.
>
> After I insisted on seeing the chief of personnel, they finally took me over to Mr. Shapiro's office. Mr. Shapiro said he was quite surprised to know that I thought that I could get a job as a street car operator or bus operator, because it was certainly contrary to custom, as I knew. He asked me where I was from. I told him I was from Virginia and I had lived around in Washington for a while. Then he said, "You know that that sort of thing is absurd and out of the question." He said, "If we hired Negroes here as street car or bus operators," he says, "every . . . employee that we have would strike," and he asked me didn't I think so. I told Mr. Shapiro that I didn't think that all of them would strike, but if they did strike, that it would, indeed, be a very fine thing, because it would show the rest of the world what kind of democracy we were actually fighting for. We discussed the situation about bus drivers, or potential bus drivers being imported here, brought in from the South, fellows who had no knowledge of the city at all, and I said to Mr. Shapiro that there were many fellows around town here who were graduates of Miner Teachers College, Dunbar, and even Howard University, who would possibly consider bus driving for the Capital Transit Company because of the attractive salary involved, that those fellows, no doubt because of their being local and because of their educational qualifications and

that sort of thing, should be superior to those fellows who were brought here from the farms of the South. He admitted all this, but said it was just impossible to entertain the idea of employing Negroes as bus drivers and, therefore, he would have to refuse to take my application, because of customs existing here at that time.[130]

A representative of the employer acknowledged that the company had done very little to impress upon the workers the urgent need to relieve manpower shortages by hiring Negro operators:

> In all of our contacts, in all of my own personal contacts with the union and their representatives, while I haven't entered into acrimonious debate and discussion with them, I have tried little by little to instill in their minds the fact that here was a situation, a trend, and a program which we ought to think of as something that we would go along with eventually. In that I haven't been very successful, I will admit.[131]

The union was quite accurate in its appraisal of the situation. Neither the company nor the union was "eventually" forced to comply with the executive order. The FEPC never issued a directive. When the employees of the company struck over a wage dispute on November 21, 1945, the government seized control of the company.[132] The FEPC decided that this was the opportune time to issue directives and have them enforced, as they had been in Philadelphia, and on November 23 it voted to issue firm directives to the company.[133] But on November 24, without consulting the committee, President Harry S. Truman countermanded the decision.[134]

Charles H. Houston—the distinguished civil rights attorney and vice dean of the Howard University Law School—asked President Truman to put his instructions to the committee in writing. His request was ignored.[135] Houston also asked the President to give the committee an opportunity to confer with him, but this too was ignored.[136]*

---

*Houston's unique contribution to the development of civil rights law, as well as his influence in developing a generation of black legal advocates, deserves further study. See Genna Rae McNeil, "Charles Hamilton Houston," *Black Law Journal,* Vol. 3 (1974), pp. 123–131; Walter J. Leonard, "The Development of the Black Bar," *Annals of the American Academy of Political and Social Sciences,* May 1973, pp. 134–143; Kenneth S. Tollett, "Black Lawyers, Their Education and the Black Community," *Howard Law Journal,* Vol. 17, No. 2 (1972), pp. 326–357. See also Herbert Hill and Jack Greenberg, *Citizen's Guide to Desegregation: A Study of Social and Legal Change in American Life* (Boston: The Beacon Press, 1955), pp. 56–61.

On December 3, 1945, in an angry letter of resignation from the FEPC, Houston described to the President how government inaction negated the official policy of nondiscrimination:

My Dear Mr. President:

I hereby resign as a member of the President's Committee on Fair Employment Practice, effective immediately.

On November 23, 1945, in the Capital Transit Company Case, No. 70 on the Committee docket, the Committee voted to issue its decision which directs Capital Transit to cease and desist from practices and policies which have resulted in the denial of employment to Negroes, because of race, as conductors, motormen, bus operators and traffic checkers. This merely effectuates the nondiscriminatory employment policy declared for industries essential to the prosecution of the war by Executive Order No. 9346.

Without notice to the Committee or a chance for the Committee to present its views, on November 24 you ordered the Committee not to issue the decision. November 25 on behalf of the Committee I wrote you asking that you give the Committee opportunity to confer with you. The return registry receipt shows the letter delivered to The White House November 26. To date we have not received even an acknowledgment of the letter.

. . . Since the effect of your intervention in the Capital Transit case is not to eliminate the discrimination but to condone it, to that extent you not only repudiate the Committee, but more important, you nullify the Executive Orders themselves. . . .

The issue of the Capital Transit case far transcends the question whether a few Negro workers shall be placed on the platforms of street cars and buses and as traffic checkers on the Capital Transit system. It raises the fundamental question of the basic government attitude toward minorities. The failure of the Government to enforce democratic practices and to protect minorities in its own capital makes its expressed concern for national minorities abroad somewhat specious, and its interference in the domestic affairs of other countries very premature.[137]

President Truman accepted Houston's resignation on December 7:

Dear Mr. Houston:

Your letter of December third has been received.

When it was found necessary under the wartime powers conferred upon the President by the Congress, to seize the Capital Transit property, the conditions under which the property was to be operated were the same as those of any other property so seized. The law requires that when the Government seizes a property under such circumstances, it shall be operated under the terms and conditions of employment which were in effect at the time possession of such plant, mine, or facility was so taken.

In view of this apparent contradiction between the law and the order which the Fair Employment Practice Committee proposed to issue, it was thought best to suggest that the order be temporarily postponed. The property was not seized for the purpose of enforcing the aims of the Fair Employment Practice Committee, laudable as these aims are, but to guarantee transportation for the citizens of Washington and vicinity.

As anxious as I am for Congress to pass legislation for a permanent Fair Employment Practice Committee, I cannot contravene an Act of Congress in order to carry out the present Committee's aims. Under the circumstances it was felt the issuance of the proposed order would prove injurious to the accomplishments desired by all of us who are honestly interested in promoting the welfare of minority groups.

I regret that you were unwilling to approach the problem from this viewpoint. As suggested in your letter, your resignation is accepted, to be effective immediately.[138]

President Truman in effect gave governmental assurance to the company and the union that they would be free to continue their discriminatory practices. Malcolm Ross wrote:

I have no bad dreams about the Capital Transit case. The game was over by that time. The war was won. Temporary Washington was packing its grips. Controls were being relaxed from one end of Pennsylvania Avenue to the other. . . . Peace shifts gears from patriotism to politics.

FEPC quietly expired during that period. It kept its offices open for six months more. Actually it became moribund when Charles Houston's gallant refusal to compromise tried to force action on a similar high plane from people who were busy with other matters and who had never completely understood the importance of being straightforward in support of minority rights.[139]*

In its *Final Report* the committee observed that "[c]ases involving street-railway systems ran the gamut of FEPC experience from compliance after informal negotiations to outright refusal to obey the Executive order."[140] The major offender, in addition to the employers, was the Amalgamated Association of Street, Electric

*On May 8, 1945, the war ended in Europe; and the Japanese surrender on August 14, 1945, concluded World War II. President Truman's refusal to act in the Capital Transit case as Roosevelt had in Philadelphia was an expression of the change in domestic political priorities. The FEPC was under increasing attack in Congress, and retreat by the Truman Administration on civil rights issues was underway. (See Chapter 14.)

Railway and Motor Coach Employees of America, AFL. Many of its local divisions refused to admit Negroes into membership; virtually all of them refused to allow Negroes to be hired for or upgraded to operators' or mechanics' jobs. Where companies acquiesced in the discriminatory practices of labor organizations, union resistance usually remained in the background. But where employers tried to relieve labor shortages by hiring Negroes for operating jobs, the union became an increasingly active force in open opposition to Negro advancement. In several cities it succeeded in preventing enforcement of federal executive orders requiring the elimination of discriminatory employment practices.

In the 1970s, as the black population was increasingly concentrated in the cities, urban transit systems were employing significant numbers of black workers. A 1970 survey found that black workers comprised 40.3 percent of the transit industry labor force in nine large cities.[141] The study concludes:

> The transit industry is thus likely to continue to become an industry serving blacks and operated by blacks in major metropolitan areas. In terms of employment, this has already occurred in Detroit where a majority of the transit labor force is Negro. In New York a majority of the workers are Negro or Puerto Rican, with more than 40 percent black. In Houston and Washington, the Negro employment ratio exceeds 40 percent; in Chicago and Los Angeles, it is in excess of 30 percent; and in Philadelphia, about 25 percent. It is likely that for the industry as a whole, approximately 30 percent of the employees were black in 1970.[142]

Although there has been a substantial increase in black employment in this area, black transit workers face new problems. Beginning in the late 1960s, and increasingly in the 1970s, black workers in many municipal transit systems found it necessary to protest against the absence of black leadership in the Amalgamated Transit Union, AFL-CIO—successor to the AFL's Amalgamated Association—whose general executive board consisted entirely of white officers despite the large nonwhite membership. Black caucuses have been formed within local unions in Washington, Richmond, Norfolk, and Chicago, among others. In 1968, in Chicago, the black caucus within the Amalgamated Transit Union organized two work stoppages, which paralyzed the bus system, in protest against the exclusion of blacks from union offices.* Black

---

*Wayman Benson, chairman of the caucus, stated that "[t]his is nothing different from the old plantation system. Here you have a union with about 65–70 percent blacks and the

caucuses have also emerged within the Transport Workers Union, AFL-CIO, in several cities including New York and San Francisco.

In 1968 a predominantly black caucus known as the Muni Drivers Association developed within the Transport Workers Union in San Francisco. After the association unsuccessfully challenged the leadership of Transport Workers Local 250-A, the union expelled five leaders of the independent caucus, and during January 1971, nineteen bus drivers who supported the caucus were dismissed from their jobs. Leaders of the Muni Drivers Association claimed that the discharges were reprisals by the Transport Workers Union.[143]

In 1969 a black transit workers' caucus challenged the leadership of the Transport Workers Union in New York City, and in 1971 filed pledge cards with the New York State Public Employment Relations Board in an effort to displace Local 100 of the TWU (where black and Puerto Rican workers constituted over 50 percent of the membership) as collective bargaining agent for New York City transit workers. In 1972 this group, the Rank and File Committee for a Democratic Union—led by Joseph Carnegie, a retired black subway conductor—obtained a court order requiring a new representation election.[144] The Rank and File Committee also filed suit in federal district court charging "conspiratorial racial discrimination in employment" against the Metropolitan Transit Authority and Local 100 of the Transport Workers Union.[145] The complaint asked for an injunction against the Metropolitan Transit Authority and the union on the ground that they "systematically discriminate in their hiring, assignment and promotion practices" against members of minority groups.[146]

These developments in Chicago, San Francisco, New York, and other cities indicate that in the 1970s minority workers, although widely employed in city transit systems, are confronted with two related problems, exclusion from skilled jobs in machine shops and denial of access to leadership, in both major transit unions. It may be anticipated that with the increasing concentration of nonwhite workers in urban transit operations, there will be

---

leadership virtually all white. How long do you think we can stand for this?"—Quoted in *The Movement,* September 1968, p. 6. After a second walkout began, on August 28, 1968, the Chicago Transit Authority obtained an injunction that resulted in the suspension of 149 drivers and also prevented the Concerned Rapid Transit Workers, the caucus of black subway employees, from joining the bus drivers' strike. But although defeated in the courts, the black caucus eventually succeeded in having blacks appointed as vice president, assistant recording secretary, and assistant financial secretary-treasurer, and in addition obtained four positions on the executive board of the local union.

intensified efforts to racially integrate the remaining "lily-white" occupational enclaves in the skilled classifications, and to achieve shared leadership within the transit unions.

13

The Railroad Industry and the
Railway Labor Unions

When the Fair Employment Practice Committee began its extensive investigation of job discrimination in the railroad industry, it found a historical pattern of anti-Negro practices in both operating and nonoperating crafts. The "Big Four" railroad brotherhoods, organized in the two decades during and after the Civil War,* had become the dominant labor unions in the railroad industry. All four of them enforced "white-only" restrictions.[1] The Brotherhood of Locomotive Engineers constitution provided that "[n]o person shall become a member of the Brotherhood of Locomotive Engineers unless he is a white man 21 years of age,"[2] and the constitution of the Brotherhood of Locomotive Firemen and Enginemen required that applicants for membership be "born white."[3] The nonoperating railroad unions had similar restrictions, although some admitted Negroes on a segregated basis.†

---

*The Big Four operating unions were the Brotherhood of Locomotive Engineers, founded in 1863; the Brotherhood (later: the Order) of Railroad Conductors, 1868; the Brotherhood of Locomotive Firemen (later: and Enginemen), 1873; and the Brotherhood of Railroad Trainmen, 1883.

†Railway labor is divided into operating and nonoperating classifications. The operating crafts consist of two major groups: enginemen and trainmen. The enginemen classification includes engineers and firemen. Trainmen are divided into two classes: brakemen who work on the road and those who work in railroad yards. Workers in the nonoperating crafts are represented by the International Association of Machinists, the Switchmen's Union of North America, the Order of Railroad Telegraphers, the Brotherhood of Railway Carmen, the Brotherhood of Maintenance of Way Employees, and the Brotherhood of Railway and Steamship Clerks. At the time of the FEPC investigations these AFL affiliates either excluded Negroes by clauses in their constitutions or limited Negroes to segregated units.

334

From the Civil War period through the early 1900s large numbers of Negroes were employed by the railroads, primarily in the South,[4] as locomotive firemen, brakemen, baggagemen, freight handlers, and in railroad repair shops. But they were not employed as engineers, switchmen, or conductors, the highest paying and highest status jobs in the railroad industry. In some instances companies were eager to hire black workers because they could be paid less than whites.

Early in their history all-white railroad unions began to demand that lower paid, unorganized Negro workers be removed from jobs in the industry. In 1887 white switchmen walked off the job in the Southern Pacific Railroad yard at Houston to protest working alongside Negroes[5] and the white switchmen of the Houston and Texas Central Railroad staged a sympathy walkout at the same yard. Having recently owned slaves, the Houston and Texas Central Railroad was accustomed to using black labor; it was now hiring white and Negro switchmen and paying them equal wages. In 1890 the white foremen of the switchmen's crew sent an appeal to the railroad management:

> Much discord and dissatisfaction has arisen amongst us, owing to the employment of negro switchmen in the Houston yard. We feel that this is an injustice to us, both morally and socially. . . . We consider it a consideration due us, as faithful employees of the company, that this negro labor be removed, thereby removing from amongst us our only cause for dissatisfaction. . . . If you cannot remove this objection, and have employment to offer us in any other department, we will gladly accept it; if not, please accept our resignations. We cannot, and will not be objects of derision any longer.[6]

When the company rejected their appeal, the switchmen quit. A joint committee of the Brotherhood of Railroad Trainmen, the Brotherhood of Railroad Conductors, the Switchmen's Mutual Aid Association, and the Brotherhood of Locomotive Firemen formally protested to the company:

> *Article 1*—The mere fact of negroes being employed in train, yard and locomotive departments of this company is causing many of our most worthy members to leave the service. . . . We term it an injustice to subject us to an association which is directly antagonistic to our organization and taste. Therefore, we earnestly request that all negroes employed in train, yard and locomotive departments of the Houston and Texas Central Railroad system be removed and white men employed in their stead.[7]

Again the company refused to accept their collective demands, and the Brotherhood of Locomotive Firemen's magazine commented:

> It will be observed that the officers of the road claim that the employment of negroes at Houston, in the yards of the road, were employed on the occasion of an emergency, and notwithstanding the admission, that crews of negroes must have white men to oversee them (as in old plantation times), a tacit admission of their inferiority—they are placed on an equality with white men in the matter of wages, and in all other matters, so far as the railroad is concerned.[8]

In a news story on the white railroad employees' efforts to force Negroes out of their jobs, the *Houston Daily Post* reported:

> The Houston and Texas Central Railroad Company prior to emancipation owned slaves. Its employees had also owned slaves. These negroes had worked in various capacities, as firemen, brakemen, etc. After emancipation they were put on the payroll of the company. From the day of its creation as a corporation, therefore, the Houston and Texas Central Railroad Company has employed negroes. It was no innovation in this respect. Negro labor was and is the ordinary labor of the country. With the influx of railroad men from other states, and the intensification of the competition for employment, these negroes have been gradually crowded out of the service of the company. . . .[9]

In this union-management contest, the power to enforce a final decision still rested with the railroad companies; at that time the railroad brotherhoods were not strong enough to remove all Negro employees from the yards. The companies continued to employ Negro firemen and trainmen because they had done so in the past and because Negroes were generally paid lower wages.

In 1909 the Brotherhood of Locomotive Firemen and Enginemen organized a strike against the Georgia Railroad in an attempt to evict black workers from their jobs. During the course of this strike, which lasted for almost six weeks, Negro firemen and other black railroad workers were the frequent victims of mob violence. The company had replaced ten members of the union, who had been paid $1.75 a day, with Negro workers paid $1.25 a day. It had also granted Negroes equal seniority rights, with the result that many Negroes were assigned better runs because of their greater seniority.[10] By custom, only whites were employed as engineers; since engineers were recruited from the firemen's ranks, the Brotherhood of Locomotive Firemen and Enginemen feared that Negroes would soon be making inroads into the classification of engineer, bringing the wage level down. The union struck and was able to halt the railroad's service.[11]

The alternative of admitting Negroes to union membership and demanding equal wages for all employees in the same job category, depending on seniority, was rejected by the union. The brotherhood contended that Negro firemen could not be trusted to perform their duties adequately; the Georgia Railroad management argued that it employed Negroes because they could be paid less and that "[w]e give the white man more because we do not wish to bring his scale down to the level of a Negro."[12] During the strike the union agreed to arbitration of the dispute, and a railway arbitration board decided that equal wages should be paid to white and Negro firemen, hostlers, and hostlers' helpers. The decision appeared to be in the black railroadmen's favor, but it was actually a victory for the Brotherhood of Locomotive Firemen and Enginemen. The railroad companies employed Negroes in various categories because they were paid less for their labor; naturally, the companies made no effort to establish equal wages. It could be assumed that if forced to pay equal wages the railroads would hire whites exclusively, or so the union reasoned. The brotherhood's magazine anticipated that "[i]f this course [of equal pay] is followed by the company, and the incentive for employing Negroes is thus removed, the strike will not have been in vain."[13]

By 1910 the railroad brotherhoods had become powerful enough to obtain recognition and collective bargaining contracts with many railroad companies. Wage differentials still existed between white and Negro firemen and trainmen, and rather than bargain for equal pay for all potential union members, the unions centered their efforts on completely eliminating Negroes from those job classifications. Labor strikes and the collective bargaining process became the means to that end.

In 1911 the Brotherhood of Locomotive Firemen and Enginemen protested to the Cincinnati, New Orleans and Texas Pacific Railroad (the Queen and Crescent line) because the company granted Negroes within each job classification equal seniority rights with white workers. Since the Negro firemen could not be promoted, they were able to accumulate greater seniority than whites in that classification and thus work on the more desirable runs.[14] The brotherhood struck, and its journal gave the reason:

The strike is due to the action of that company in subordinating white firemen to negro firemen, placing the latter on preferred runs and gradually displacing their white firemen with negroes. As the negroes are not eligible to promotion to engineers these preferred runs have been thus permanently blocked and white firemen required to remain upon heavy freight runs, locals, etc.[15]

During the strike white workers committed acts of violence against Negroes, and some Negro firemen were murdered. W. E. B. Du Bois commented in *Crisis:*

The significance of the strike and resultant murders of colored firemen on the Cincinnati Southern Railroad should not be overlooked. . . . It should be borne in mind that the colored firemen are not "scabs" or strikebreakers, but regularly employed workmen. There is no complaint of their inefficiency or their unwillingness to join with their white fellow employees in organizing for betterment. It is simply this: they are called upon to accept a permanent and fixed status at the bottom—in jobs that white men do not (at present) desire—and the railroad is required to ratify the "understanding" and enforce it. It looks like an extension and exemplification of the recently announced policy as to political offices—in effect, that no colored man may hold a position when white people object, or, if you please to so state it more boldly, any place that a white man wants.

One peculiar feature of the strike situation is that, although all traffic is interfered with, and the dispatches say that on some sections of the road no freight is moving, so far there has been no cry raised as to interference with interstate commerce, nor any of the United States troops rushed to the scene. However, the railroad is standing by its employees, which is encouraging.[16]

It did not stand by them for long. When the strike ended, the agreement between the Brotherhood of Locomotive Firemen and Enginemen and the Cincinnati, New Orleans and Texas Pacific Railroad provided that Negro firemen would not be employed at all north of Oakdale and Chattanooga, Tennessee; that the percentage of all Negro firemen employed by the railroad would not increase beyond the number recorded as of January 1, 1911; and that they could have no more than half the passenger runs or half the preferred freight runs.[17] This contract served as a model for subsequent collective bargaining agreements in the industry, which were to be the primary method used for the next forty years to force black railroad workers from their jobs.

The pattern of racial discrimination had been set. Over the following decades the railroad brotherhoods would use their growing collective bargaining strength to reach agreements setting specific numerical limitations and other restrictions on Negro employment,* and since the Negro railroadman was excluded from the brotherhoods, he would have no voice in the collective bargaining process.†

Soon after the strike against the Cincinnati, New Orleans and Texas Pacific Railroad was settled, the Brotherhood of Locomotive Firemen and Enginemen threatened a strike against the Southern Railroad of Georgia for similar reasons. But the strike was avoided as the company agreed to the major demands of the union. The settlement fixed a point north of which Negro firemen would not be employed and established a pay differential between white and Negro firemen of 30 percent.[18] The brotherhood and three other southern railroads signed an agreement that provided:

> (1) On each division the proportion of colored firemen shall not exceed the percentage given below, provided that white firemen are available for employment. These percentages, though varying on each division, represent for all of the divisions taken together only 33 $1/_3$ percent colored. The proposed percentage on each division shall be reached by the employment of white in preference to colored firemen, when vacancies occur or new men are employed. . . .
>
> (2) When vacancies occur in passenger, preferred freight, or local freight service, or whenever new runs are made in any of these services, assignments shall be made in such a way that the percentage

---

*"The agreements on the Queen and Crescent and the Southern of Georgia roads marked the beginning of a definite attempt by the white brotherhoods to stop the extension of Negro employment in engine service. Ultimately Negroes were to be eliminated from the fireman's craft, but in the meantime the brotherhood planned to direct its efforts to the more practical program of confining Negro employment to certain districts and of limiting the proportion of Negroes to the percentage in the service on a given date."—Sterling D. Spero and Abraham L. Harris, *The Black Worker* (New York: Columbia University Press, 1931), pp. 292–293.

†Black railroad workers, over a period of many years, attempted to build independent unions of their own. The interesting but inadequately studied history of black railway labor organizations begins at the turn of the century. Among these are the Colored Locomotive Firemen's Association, founded in 1902, and the Railway Men's Benevolent Industrial Association, founded in 1915. By 1920 the latter claimed 15,000 members in 187 locals. Other black railway labor organizations, such as the Association of Colored Railway Trainmen and Locomotive Firemen, the Colored Trainmen of America, the Interstate Order of Colored Locomotive Firemen, and the Southern Association of Colored Railway Trainmen and Firemen, were also formed during this period. Black workers, excluded from membership in the AFL's Railway Mail Association, formed the National Alliance of Postal Employees in 1913, and in 1915 a broader union of black railway workers was founded—the Railway Men's Benevolent Association. Although this effort to bring the main groups of black railway workers into one organization failed, the National Alliance of Postal and Federal Employees continues, as does the Brotherhood of Sleeping Car Porters; the United Transport Service Employees; and the Brotherhood of Dining Car Employees, a division of the Hotel and Restaurant Employees and Bartenders International Union.

of colored firemen in each of these services shall be brought down to
the percentage provided for each district . . . .

(3) The percentage of colored firemen above provided for each
division shall be applied alike to road service and to yard service.

(4) No colored firemen or hostlers to be employed on the St. Louis-
Louisville Division, nor any increase to be made over the percentage
of colored employees on the Appalachia Division as of June 1, 1911.[19]

The Brotherhood of Railroad Trainmen also adopted the
practice of setting percentages for the maximum number of
Negroes to be employed, and negotiated an agreement with the
Southern Railroad Association that froze the percentage of Negro
trainmen and yardmen:

No larger percentage of Negro trainmen or yardmen will be
employed on any division or in any yard than was employed on January 1, 1910. If on any roads this percentage is now larger than on
January 1, 1910, this agreement does not contemplate the discharge
of any Negroes to be replaced by whites; but as vacancies are filled or
new men employed, whites are to be taken on until the percentage of
January first is again reached.

Negroes are not to be employed as baggagemen, flagmen or yard
foremen, but in any case in which they are now employed, they are
not to be discharged to make places for whites, but when the positions they occupy become vacant, whites shall be employed in their
places.[20]

In addition, "[w]here no differences in the rates of pay between
white and colored employees exists, the restriction as to percentage
of Negroes to be employed does not apply."[21] The implication of
this last provision was that if Negroes were not available as cheaper
labor than whites, the companies would have no reason to hire
them.

During World War I, because of growing pressure from the
railroad unions and also because of expanding employment
opportunities in other industries, Negroes began leaving railroad
jobs in large numbers. To stem the exodus, which was threatening
to intensify an acute labor shortage in an essential industry, the
government's director general of the railroads issued an order
effective June 1, 1918, establishing that "colored men employed as
firemen, trainmen, and switchmen shall be paid the same rates as
are paid white men in the same capacities."[22] The purpose of this
order was to induce Negro railroadmen to remain in the industry,
but its effect was to reduce the incentive of employers to hire
Negroes. As a result of the general decline in employment in the

postwar period (by 1920–1921 railroad employment had fallen from 2 million to 1.6 million[23]) the brotherhoods intensified their efforts to eliminate black workers from railroad employment. To contrast 1914 and 1929, the percentage of Negro firemen on the Southern Railway dropped from 80 to 33; on the Atlantic Coast Line, from 90 to 50; and on the Seaboard Air Line Railway, from 90 to 25.[24]

In 1910 the total number of locomotive firemen in the United States had been 76,381, and Negro firemen were 6.8 percent of that number.[25] By 1940 the total had fallen to 47,410, of which Negro firemen were only 5 percent.[26] In the South, between 1910 and 1940 the percentage of Negro firemen fell steadily from 41.6 to 29.5 percent.[27] There were 165,530 railroad trainmen in the United States in 1910, 41.1 percent of whom were Negroes.[28] By 1940 the total number was reduced to 113,736 and the percentage of Negroes to 2.5.[29] In the South the percentage of Negro trainmen fell from 29.8 percent in 1910 to 15.1 percent in 1940.[30]

By the 1920s, as a result of the racial practices of the railroad unions, enforced by labor-management restrictive agreements and at times by violence, Negro railroad workers were entirely barred from the conductors', switchmen's, and engineers' classifications and were eventually displaced from other jobs in the firemen's and trainmen's classifications.

When the Railway Labor Act became law in 1926, the power of the railroad labor unions was legally sanctioned and strengthened, but the vital interests of Negro railroad workers were ignored. Government sanction of discriminatory collective bargaining agreements contributed heavily to this displacement of Negro employees. The Railway Labor Act of 1926 was adopted primarily:

(1) To avoid any interruption to commerce . . .

(2) to forbid any limitation upon freedom of association among employees or any denial, as a condition of employment or otherwise, of the right of employees to join a labor organization. . . .[31]

To encourage collective bargaining in the railroad industry, the Act urged the companies and unions "to make and maintain agreements concerning rates of pay, rules, and working conditions, and to settle all disputes, whether arising out of the application of such agreements or otherwise. . . ."[32] The Act guaranteed the right of employees to organize into unions, and it established a National Mediation Board, composed of three presidential appointees, to certify such unions as collective bargaining agents for a particular "craft or class."[33] The Act also established the National Railroad Adjustment Board, to be composed of eighteen representatives of railroad companies and eighteen representatives of railroad unions, which was to settle disputes "growing out of grievances or out of the interpretation or application of agreements concerning rates of pay, rules, or working conditions. . . ."[34]

The new law, enacted to stabilize labor-management relations and especially to eliminate railroad strikes, operated to the disadvantage of Negro railroad employees. Since Negroes were excluded from membership in the Big Four brotherhoods and other railroad unions, and since these national unions were designated by the National Mediation Board as sole collective bargaining agents in their jurisdictions, black railroad workers were effectively excluded from the collective bargaining process. In 1944, Herbert R. Northrup wrote:

> The National Mediation Board often designates as exclusive bargaining agent for Negroes a union which excludes Negroes, or affords them only inferior status. It assists parties to reach agreements which result in the displacement of colored workers. It has refused to take the racial policies of unions into consideration in determining appropriate bargaining units, thus consigning smaller groups of Negroes to the domination of discriminatory unions. And finally, evidence has been presented which seriously questions the impartiality of the Mediation Board, especially in disputes involving Negro workers and the Big Four Brotherhoods.
>
> The record of the National Railroad Adjustment Board is even more open to criticism. Composed of partisans, appointed, for the most part, by organizations which do not afford Negroes equal status, it has denied aggrieved Negro workers even a hearing, let alone justice. Its ruling that a craft of workers "own" a particular type of work whether or not such workers ever performed that work in the past, threatens to eliminate Negro trainmen from the industry. Since judicial review of the Adjustment Board's decisions is available only to the winning, and never to the losing party, the Board is virtually a labor court which can enforce its decisions however inequitable.[35]

For the unions to retain their status as exclusive certified collective bargaining agents, and thereby exclude Negroes from railroad employment, they needed to maintain a white majority in each craft on every railroad over which they wanted to preserve jurisdiction. They accomplished this through contractual power and physical violence. In the same year the Railway Labor Act was passed, the president of the Brotherhood of Locomotive Firemen and Enginemen told the union's annual convention that he hoped to be able to report at the next meeting that "not a single Negro remained on the left side of an engine cab."[36]

After being certified and thereby encouraged by the government, the unions renewed their efforts to force the occupational eviction of Negro railroad workers. In 1928 the Brotherhood of Locomotive Firemen and Enginemen, the Brotherhood of Locomotive Engineers, the Order of Railroad Conductors, and the Brotherhood of Railroad Trainmen signed an agreement with the St. Louis-San Francisco Railway Company:

> The four train service organizations have insisted and demanded for several years that St. Louis-San Francisco Railway Company have an understanding with them that in the future the Company would not employ any more Negroes in train, engine and yard service, but not including train porters. This demand and request upon the part of the organizations has been based upon the allegation that colored firemen under arrangements prevent and make almost impossible opportunity for the training of white firemen to become engineers and limit their opportunities so to do; that colored employees cannot render them intelligent service; that constant friction and irritation arises out of the whole situation and various other reasons. . . .
>
> In accordance with the above it is agreed that effective March 14, 1928, in the future hiring of employees in train, engine and yard service but not including train porters, only white men shall be employed.[37]

This typical agreement remained in force until 1941.

There had been intermittent violence on railroads in the lower Mississippi Valley since 1916. In 1931 a reign of terror against Negro railroadmen began that lasted for three years. The Depression was forcing cutbacks in railroad employment, and with their greater seniority Negro firemen and trainmen were retaining their jobs while whites with less seniority were being discharged. Between September 7, 1931, and July 10, 1934, ten Negroes were killed and eleven were fired at or wounded; two of those killed had been shot at previously.[38] Horace R. Cayton and George S. Mitchell, in their study "Murders of Negro Firemen," described how the automatic stoker converted the fireman's job into an easier, cleaner, more desirable position, how shifts in traffic routes created new openings for the Negro firemen and trainmen with high seniority, and how these changes caused whites to seek the rapid elimination of all Negro railroadmen:

Firemen's work a generation or two ago was dirtier and harder than it is at present. In those days it was a Negro's job; the whites wouldn't have it. Engineers, who have always been white, picked their own Negro firemen, and kept them for years. . . . [B]y the rules of seniority, Negroes with seniority might "roll" men, white or colored, in the places next below their own when contraction set in, and Negroes are said to have used this right. . . .

The scene was thus set for organized white aggression. Many tactics were used. White firemen and engineers at various times in the past tried to persuade Negroes to sign over to representatives of the local groups of their two crafts a formal right to bargain for the Negroes. On at least one occasion railroad officials called in Negroes who had been induced to sign petitions to that effect, told them that the petition would be disregarded as having been obtained unfairly, and warned them to sign nothing presented to them by white road service men. The whites, unable to trick the Negroes into signing away their seniority, turned to intimidation and then to murder. In the case of Aaron Williams, it was said by persons who had known him well that he had been one of those men whom the company had told fifteen years before to sign no petitions brought him by whites. On the afternoon of the day he was murdered two white men had come to his home, and offered him a new document to sign. On his wife's advice he had refused. That night he was killed in the Vicksburg yard, with slugs from a shot gun. Murder need not have been the object in every case; a threat to shoot this man or that might have been expected to drive him off the job from fear; the general terror must have been calculated to produce a wholesale trek of Negro firemen. In actual fact, Negroes stayed on their runs.[39]

Cayton and Mitchell also report to what extent those responsible for the violence were brought to justice:

Attempts at exposing the members of the gang have been suspiciously feeble, and the actual prosecutions have been few. Negroes believe that at some points the police, the white firemen, and the railroad's own detectives have worked, or rather agreed not to work cooperatively. The railroad did offer a reward of $5,000 for information leading to the arrest and conviction of anyone implicated in the murders of certain of the men, and it has renewed this offer in the case of Woody Barrett. Agents of the Department of Justice have at one time or another been called in on the cases. By the fall of 1934 four men had been arrested. Fingerprints found on exploded shells at the point where Will Harvey was killed led to the arrest of Charles B. Coon, a white fireman, who was charged with the crime. Coon had on him at the time of his arrest a seniority list of the firemen, with the names of those thus far killed checked. He was acquitted. B. G.

Gunner, a white fireman, was tried for the killing of Clarence Book-er, and acquitted. Reatie Lee, a white railwayman, was acquitted by a jury in six minutes, when tried for the wounding of Ernest Clark. He sued for false arrest, and was restored to his railroad job. The only convictions have been those of Matt Lewis, a white fireman, and M. F. Varnado, white (not a fireman), who were found guilty of assault and battery in the wounding of Ernest Clark. Varnado is said to have confessed to receiving a fee of $100.00 for the job. Lewis had driven Varnado to the spot where the shooting occurred. Varnado was given five years in the Mississippi State penitentiary, and Matt Lewis was given a year in the Court House jail, with six months off for good behavior.[40]

In "Murder for the Job," a report in the *Nation,* the killing of Negro firemen in Mississippi was vividly recounted:

Frank Kincaid, Negro fireman on the Mississippi division of the Illinois Central Railroad, climbed into the cab of "The Creole" as crews were being changed late one night in Canton, twenty-five miles north of Jackson, the capital of Mississippi. Against the lighted window he made a perfect target for a gunman in the darkness outside. A shotgun belched a load of buckshot into the Negro's head and he fell back into the coal tender to die. A white man took his place, and "The Creole" pulled out for New Orleans.

To Mississippi newspapers and the correspondents of such outside journals as the Memphis *Commercial-Appeal* and the Birmingham *Age-Herald,* it was just another Negro murder, barely worth a paragraph. A week later, however, they had a strangely similar paragraph to print:

Ed Cole, a Negro fireman on the same division, stepped at night from his cab to throw a switch at Water Valley junction. From behind the curtains of an unlighted automobile that drew up beside the track a shotgun roared, and Ed fell over the switch to die. A white man took his place in the cab.

Mississippi, in its own primitive way, had begun to deal with the unemployment problem. Dust had been blown from the shotgun, the whip, and the noose, and Ku Klux Klan practices were being resumed in the certainty that dead men not only tell no tales but create vacancies. . . .[41]

A Negro fireman later testified before the Fair Employment Practice Committee about the direct connection between the violence and the railroad unions:

Q. . . . [W]hen the Negro firemen were being shot out of the cabs, [did] you have any idea as to who was doing the shooting?

A. Well, yes ma'am, I have an idea who done the shooting, but I couldn't prove it. But it was proved that the Brotherhood of Locomotive Firemen and Enginemen hired the public to shoot Negro firemen out of the cabs, and the brakemen that was over there, and they paid them $500 to everyone they killed and $150 for every one that was scared off the job.[42]

During this period technological advances were changing the nature of certain jobs in the railroad industry, making the work more agreeable and further contributing to racial occupational eviction. The automatic stoker, for example—which relieved the railroad fireman from the task of shoveling coal into the engines and made the job of fireman a "white man's" job—became standard equipment. In September 1937 the Interstate Commerce Commission ruled that by July 1943 all engines in fast passenger and freight service (designated "preferred runs" in railroad-union agreements) must have mechanical stokers.[43] Northrup wrote that "[s]oon thereafter, the firemen entered into a secret agreement with the Gulf, Mobile & Ohio Railroad whereby in return for preference given members of its organization on stokerized engines, it waived its right to request and to obtain a higher wage scale."[44]

But it was the introduction of the diesel engine that stimulated the most intense and systematic campaign to displace black workers. Before the advent of the diesel, the fireman's job was still among the dirtiest, hottest, and lowest paid in the railroad industry. Working on the new engines not only brought higher wages but conferred higher status. As diesels began to replace coal burners, the railroad brotherhoods systematically accelerated their efforts to force black workers out of their traditional fireman's jobs by negotiating collective bargaining agreements stipulating that wherever a diesel engine replaced a coal-burning engine a white man must replace a Negro, regardless of seniority.

In 1938 the Brotherhood of Locomotive Firemen and Enginemen signed an agreement with the Seaboard Air Line Railway that provided:

> When Diesel-electric locomotives are substituted for steam locomotives on regular assigned run or runs, then held by a fireman not in line of promotion, this will create a vacancy which will be filled by firemen in line of promotion who will be allowed preference over such run or runs in accordance with their seniority. A fireman thereby displaced will exercise his seniority rights.[45]

Since engineers and conductors were drawn from the firemen and the trainmen, respectively, and since Negroes were not promoted to engineers' and conductors' jobs, Negro trainmen and firemen were uniformly those "not in line of promotion." "Promotable" meant white; "nonpromotable" meant Negro. Thus the Seaboard agreement prevented Negro firemen, without exception, from working on diesel engines.

In 1938 the Brotherhood of Locomotive Firemen and Enginemen made an agreement with the Illinois Central Railroad Company and its subsidiary, the Yazoo and Mississippi Valley Railroad Company, which provided restrictive quotas for white and Negro firemen:

> . . . (h) Engines in preferred service shall be manned by one-half white firemen, regardless of their seniority. This has reference to both passenger and freight service. Colored firemen have rights in passenger and preferred service when senior to white firemen, but only to the extent of one-half of the service.[46]

In 1940 this agreement was revised and approved by the National Mediation Board:

> Engines in preferred service shall be manned by fifty-five percent white firemen, regardless of their seniority. Colored firemen have rights in preferred service when senior to white firemen, but only to the extent of forty-five percent. . . .
>
> In applying the above rule, the white fireman will be given the odd job, for example, with a total of 10 preferred service jobs, the white firemen would be entitled to fifty-five percent or 5.5 jobs, and the colored firemen forty-five percent or 4.5 jobs. In this case, the jobs would be divided 6 to the white firemen and 4 to the colored firemen.[47]

In 1941 the Brotherhood of Locomotive Firemen and Enginemen signed an agreement with nine southern railroads providing:

> *Whereas*, Diesel-electric engines are being placed in operation on lines of Carriers named below, and
>
> *Whereas*, it seems desirable that when fireman (helper) is required on such Diesel-electric locomotives as are specified in the Chicago Agreement of February 28, 1937, as requiring the services of a fireman (helper), such fireman (helper) shall be a promotable man. . . .
>
> (5) Where Diesel-electric locomotives are hereafter substituted for steam locomotives, or where Diesel electric locomotives are now in operation on run or runs, assignment or assignments, occupied by other than promotable men, that shall be deemed to create a vacancy, and shall, where it may be done in accordance with the provisions of

this memorandum, be filled under the rules by the promotable man entitled thereto, such promotable man to be placed on same in accordance with the rules of the schedule of wages and working conditions as to filling vacancies. Any fireman displaced shall place himself under the rules of the schedule of wages and working conditions and as specified herein.[48]

This agreement too, like all railroad labor contracts, was approved by the National Mediation Board. As a participant in the certification process, the government was not only giving approval to but assisting in the enforcement of labor-management agreements that effectively barred Negro firemen from diesel-electric engines by instituting racially restricted quota systems to limit the numbers of employable Negroes and by circumventing established lines of seniority.

Technological innovation was followed by an expansion of the labor force in the railroad industry. The decline in railroad jobs that had begun after World War I and intensified during the Depression was reversed with the increase in national defense production during the late 1930s. To keep pace with nationwide industrial expansion, the railroads throughout the country would require a larger labor force. Faced simultaneously with the railroad unions' persistent efforts to evict Negro workers from desirable job classifications and the need for more workers in the industry, the government vacillated between its aims of effecting a smooth transition to defense production and of mobilizing all available manpower. Since Negro workers had in the past constituted a significant part of the railroad labor force, there was some initial government resistance to union demands that would have prevented Negroes from moving into job vacancies.

A major development in the brotherhoods' use of the collective bargaining process to force Negroes out of railroad jobs was the Southeastern Carriers Conference Agreement (Washington Agreement) and its subsidiary agreements. Late in 1940 the Brotherhood of Locomotive Firemen and Enginemen submitted to twenty-one major railroads a proposal whose goal was the consolidation of promotional and seniority systems that would give preference to whites for all new job vacancies. The brotherhood's draft provided:

1. Only promotable men will be employed for service as locomotive firemen or for service as helpers on other than steam power.

2. When new runs or jobs are established in any service, only promotable firemen or helpers will be assigned to them.

3. When permanent vacancies occur on established runs or jobs in any service, only promotable firemen or helpers will be assigned to them.

4. It is understood that promotable firemen or helpers on other than steam power are those who are in line for promotion under present rules and practices to the position of locomotive engineer.[49]

The Fair Employment Practice Committee, which later held hearings on the racial employment practices of the railroad industry, stated in its summary, findings, and directives that "[h]ad the carriers agreed to the Brotherhood's first three proposals, it is clear that Negro firemen would have been rapidly eliminated. Being non-promotable, no more could have been employed and those already on the rosters could not have survived the proscription against their assignment to new runs and permanent vacancies."[50]

When the carriers rejected the four proposals, application for mediation was made on January 15, 1941, to the National Mediation Board. The final agreement certified by the board provided in part that:

1. On each railroad party hereto the proportion of non-promotable firemen, and helpers on other than steam power, shall not exceed fifty percent in each class of service established as such on each individual carrier. This agreement does not sanction the employment of non-promotable men on any seniority district on which non-promotable men are not now employed. . . .

7. It is expressly understood that in making this agreement representatives of the employees do not waive and are in no way prejudiced in the right to request agreements on the individual carriers here represented which will restrict the employment of helpers on other than steam power to promotable men; and it is agreed that this question is to be renegotiated to a conclusion with the individual carriers.[51]

The FEPC detailed in its summary, findings, and directives the consequences for Negro workers of the agreement that was finally signed:

Under the agreement . . . it is apparent that the situation is only slightly less serious than that intended to be created by the Brotherhoods. In the first place, according to the Agreement, white firemen are virtually guaranteed at least 50% of the jobs in each class of service, regardless of seniority, whereas there is no floor whatever under the number of Negro firemen. Secondly, the Agreement ended the employment of Negro firemen wherever their numbers exceeded 50%

of the total, and despite the existing firemen shortage. The carriers and the union have preferred to struggle along with insufficient and inexperienced men rather than utilize the services of experienced Negro firemen ready and willing to work. Thirdly, the Agreement sanctions prior contracts in force on some roads under which employment of Negro firemen is more severely restricted or has been eliminated entirely. . . . Fourthly, the percentage rule and the provision relating to vacancies and new runs have so greatly impaired the seniority rights of Negro firemen and inflated those of junior white firemen that the better jobs have become or are rapidly becoming the monopoly of the white firemen. Consequently, Negroes have been and are being relegated to the lowest paid, least desirable jobs, to part time work and to extra and even emergency status.[52]

The formula established by the Washington Agreement eliminated Negro workers less "rapidly" than had been originally proposed, but it was a major development in the systematic displacement of Negro firemen.

In February 1941 the Brotherhood of Locomotive Firemen and Enginemen negotiated with several railroads supplementary agreements which further hastened the elimination of Negro employees. An agreement between the brotherhood and the Southern Railway Company and eight other southern railroads provided:

(5) Where Diesel-electric locomotives are hereafter substituted for steam locomotives, or where Diesel-electric locomotives are now in operation . . . occupied by other than promotable men, that shall be deemed to create a vacancy, and shall . . . be filled under the rules by the promotable men. . . .[53]

The brotherhood subsequently negotiated a similar agreement with the Central of Georgia Railroad Company:

On and after October 1, 1941 all new runs or vacancies on any seniority district will be bulletined for each class of service as follows:

First run or vacancy for promotable men.

Second run or vacancy seniority to govern.

That is, runs or vacancies to be filled alternatively, first by promotable men and second seniority to govern, until the proper percentage is reached.

When a promotable fireman vacates a run gained by percentages, the run vacated will continue to be filled by a promotable man until the proper percentage is reached, and non-promotable men will not be permitted to exercise seniority to positions acquired by a promotable man until the proper percentage is reached. . . .[54]

Such labor agreements caused Negro railroadmen to file complaints with the FEPC. A Negro fireman's complaint against the Louisville & Nashville Railroad Company stated:

> I began working as a fireman July 23, 1913, and am presently employed on the Birmingham and Mineral Division.
> Sometime about June 8, 1942 or June 9, 1942 run No. 148 . . . became vacant as a result of the death of J. S. Maxey, a colored fireman, and I filed my bid for the same. My bid was not recognized and the run was given to a junior white fireman who had been in service about three months. As a result of the denial of my bid in favor of a junior white fireman I was compelled to remain on my night job.
> I am not allowed to exercise my seniority against a white fireman no matter how short the period or term of his service. On the other hand a white fireman can roll me or any colored fireman at any time.[55]

Eight complaints by Negro brakemen were filed against the Louisville & Nashville Railroad. One complainant, who had been a brakeman for the railroad for twenty-nine years, said:

> As a brakeman we are restricted and cannot become flagmen although the white brakemen have this privilege. The white brakemen can be advanced or promoted to flagmen and conductors but such advancement is not open to the colored brakemen.
> The seniority of the brakemen (colored) is restricted to the job of brakeman and can only be exercised against colored, while the white brakeman can work all over the train. Then too when a colored brakeman is on the Extra Board and a flagman vacancy occurs, if the colored brakeman is first up (next out) he is passed around and the white brakeman taken. . . . [T]he white brakeman, as a result, in many instances has 2 or 3 trips before the colored brakeman has any or at best one.[56]

When the FEPC notified the company of these complaints, the railroad responded:

> These agreements do (a) restrict the proportion of Negro locomotive firemen and helpers to 50 percent or less in each class of service, (b) eliminate the hiring of Negro locomotive firemen and helpers until such proportion or percentage is established, and (c) provide for filling of new runs or vacancies created as specified in the agreements by "promotable men," who under present rules and practices are not and may not be Negroes.

It is true that until the 50 percent ratio has been reached in the several classes of service on the above named divisions of labor, Negro locomotive firemen are not permitted to exercise full seniority rights as are exercised by white firemen.

Because of the . . . 50 percent rule . . . Negro locomotive firemen have been displaced by white locomotive firemen, their juniors in service. . . .[57]

The railroad also stated that because of agreements with the International Association of Machinists, the company hired no Negro workers in its repair shops; because of agreements with the Brotherhood of Railway and Steamship Clerks, no Negroes were employed as freight and storeroom employees; and because of agreements with the Brotherhood of Railroad Trainmen, no Negroes were upgraded from waiter to steward in dining-car service.[58] The railroad concluded its letter with a defense of these agreements:

The railroad did not create and is not responsible for the political and social aspects of the people whom it serves. . . . The prevailing usages, customs, and traditions of the South will not yet countenance the employment by this railroad of negroes in positions of authority over white persons. . . .[59]

In a complaint charging racial wage differentials at the Louisiana and Arkansas Railway Company, the Association of Colored Railway Trainmen and Locomotive Firemen wrote the FEPC:

The discrimination herein charged lies in the exploitation of Negro labor by the Railway Company by refusing to pay to the Negro firemen and brakemen standard wages equal to that paid to white firemen and brakemen performing the same work, and the intimidation of the Negro firemen and brakemen with suggestions of displacement by whites if the company is forced to pay them standard wages.[60]

Negro firemen were paid $1.71 to $2.30 per day less than white firemen and Negro brakemen $2.02 to $2.71 per day less than white brakemen on the railroad. The association also informed the committee that "[w]hite firemen and brakemen are paid time and a half for all overtime; Negroes are not, but are paid straight time only."[61]

Seventeen complaints were filed with the FEPC against the Brotherhood of Railway Carmen of America and the Baltimore and Ohio Railroad. The union had excluded Negroes from regular membership but had established separate Negro auxiliaries under the control of the white locals. One such auxiliary, Booker T. Washington Lodge No. 331 of the Brotherhood of Railway Carmen of America, wrote the committee:

> Our local, No. 331 of the Brotherhood of Railway Carmen of America, was organized during the summer of 1942 by Mr. George O'Brien, General Vice-President. Mr. O'Brien promised us then our promotions would be dealt with from then on on the basis of seniority rights. This promise has not been fulfilled. . . . [T]he local chairman of the white local (No. 1010) Mr. F. Woody stated that our grievances were none of his business and he would not act on them. Meanwhile white members of [Local] 1010 were being promoted although they had only 6 years seniority, while our members with as much as 23 years seniority were passed over. We appealed . . . all we got as a result of these letters was buck passing and deliberate disregard or refusal to even answer the letters.
>
> In view of these facts, it appears to me . . . that the Brotherhood of Railway Carmen of America and the B. & O. Railroad Company have cooperated in violating the President's Executive Order 8802.
>
> I am attaching a copy of Clause C Section 7 of Subordinate Lodge Constitution of the Brotherhood of Railway Carmen which indicates the discriminatory policy of the union in organizing Negro members into *separate* locals, privileged to pay dues, but denied representation—except through the grievances committee of the nearest white local. In our case this meant simply complete denial of representation.[62]

The subordinate lodge's constitution provided that "[o]n railroads where the employment of colored persons has become a permanent institution, they shall be admitted to membership in separate lodges . . . under the jurisdiction of, and represented by the delegate of the nearest white local."[63]*

---

*In January 1953 all-white Lodge 364 of the Railway Carmen in Washington, D.C., voted to admit three Negro carmen who had refused to join all-Negro Lodge 716. This resulted from the union being "under attack by non-union Negro carmen at the Union Station, and by the CIO United Railroad Workers, which is challenging the AFL union's jurisdiction over the carmen at the Washington terminal."—*Washington Post,* January 29, 1953, p. 7. For a description of the racial practices of labor unions at the beginning of the 1950s, see Lloyd H. Bailer, "Organized Labor and Racial Minorities," *Annals of the American Academy of Political and Social Science,* March 1951, pp. 101–107. Competition between AFL and CIO unions in industries where the bloc vote of black workers in certification elections was often decisive caused some AFL affiliates to relax their traditional discriminatory practices. With the merger between the AFL and the CIO in 1955, such rivalry was eliminated. For a description of continuing discriminatory practices after the unification of the two labor groups, see Herbert Hill, "Racism Within Organized Labor: A Report of Five Years of the AFL-CIO, 1955–1960," *Journal of Negro Education,* Spring 1961, pp. 109–118.

A Negro fireman whose seniority dated from 1917 filed a complaint against the Brotherhood of Locomotive Firemen and Enginemen and the Gulf, Mobile and Ohio Railroad Company:

> 3. That white firemen constituted the majority of the craft of firemen. . . . By virtue of their majority numbers, the white firemen, acting under the authority of the Railway Labor Act of 1934, selected the Brotherhood of Locomotive Firemen and Enginemen as the bargaining agent for all of the firemen on the road. The Brotherhood . . . restricts its membership to white firemen and enginemen. . . .
>
> 5. That when he requested from the management of the company the reason for his displacement by a junior fireman he was advised that the displacement was in accordance with an agreement negotiated by the management with the Brotherhood . . . which provided that white firemen should be given preference on all stoker fired locomotives.[64]

Complaints were also filed against the Brotherhood of Railway and Steamship Clerks and the Brotherhood of Railroad Trainmen in connection with their agreements with the Pennsylvania Railroad Company. The constitution of the Brotherhood of Railway and Steamship Clerks provided: "Eligibility: All white persons, male or female, of good moral character, who have had actual experience . . . shall be eligible to membership."[65] The brotherhood later amended its regulations to provide that "[a]ll colored persons, of good moral character . . . who at the time of making application are in the employ of such company shall be eligible to membership."[66] In practice this meant limiting Negro workers to segregated units and to jobs in segregated classifications. complaint against the brotherhood by a Negro auxiliary protesting its inferior membership status noted that "[t]his unjust and undemocratic practice of which we complain is more particularly hurtful as we are frequently required to train and instruct inexperienced white workers, without seniority, in the performance of duties in positions which are denied to us because of our race and color."[67]

In a summary of complaints sent to the Pennsylvania Railroad Company, the FEPC charged:

> 5. That the Brotherhood of Railroad Shop Crafts of America is the representative or bargaining agent for persons employed by the company as machinists or machinist helpers, machine operators and painters.

6. It is alleged that the opposition of the Brotherhood to the employment of Negroes as machinists, machine operators, helpers and painters has been assigned as one of the grounds or reasons upon which the company bases the refusal to employ Negroes in the said categories of employment.

7. That the Brotherhood of Railroad Trainmen is the bargaining agent or representative for the trainmen, brakemen, and supervisors of dining car service employed by the company. The Brotherhood of Railroad Trainmen will not admit Negroes to membership in its organization.[68]

Replying to a request from the committee for information regarding the racial composition of the railroad's employees, the general counsel of the Pennsylvania Railroad Company wrote: "I am not sending you the seniority lists covering trainmen and switchmen at Chicago, Illinois, inasmuch as these rosters are quite voluminous and there are no Negroes employed on the Chicago Terminal as trainmen or switchmen."[69]

Complaints were also filed against the New York Central Railroad and the Brotherhood of Railway Carmen of America. This brotherhood's constitution read:

Qualification for membership . . .
Any white person between the ages of 16 and 65 . . .
On railroads where the employment of colored persons has become a permanent institution, they shall be admitted to separate lodges.[70]

A Negro auxiliary protested the provision in the brotherhood's agreement with the New York Central which stated succinctly that "[w]hite helpers capable of understanding the English language will be given preference in employment."[71] In answer to the committee's summary of complaints, the New York Central wrote:

If we correctly read the signs of the times, the present feeling or state of mind of a large majority of the employees of the New York Central and of the public served by its railroads makes it inadvisable to employ negroes in certain railroad occupations or to upgrade them in certain other occupations. The New York Central employs negroes where, under the then existing circumstances and conditions, they can best do the work; it employs white men where they can best do the work.

In determining who can best do the work, it must take into account not only . . . education, training, skills, and capacity . . . but as well the nature and relationship that will exist among the several men who will work on the job and their contacts with the public. . . .

> To employ negroes in certain occupations on the New York Central Railroad would, it is believed, disrupt the present harmonious relations between the railroad company and its employees.[72]

The company admitted that it did not hire Negroes as trainmen, brakemen, or dining-car stewards but denied "that it is because of race": "New York Central avers that its failure to employ negro dining car stewards is the result of long-standing custom."[73]

A complaint filed with the FEPC by a black union, the International Association of Railway Employees, against the Southern Railway Company and the Brotherhood of Railroad Trainmen was accompanied by a letter:

> [T]he members of our race have been . . . denied jobs of switchmen for which our forefathers sacrificed their life and limb in order that this nation might have one of the greatest railroad systems of the world. . . .
>
> . . . After serving about 25 years in the railroad industry and 22 years of it with the Southern Railroad, I am able to prove that the Negroes are being denied more than any other human being in employment. . . . [W]hy then are we barred from the jobs that we have been holding over 100 years? . . .
>
> Now, you see just what we are up against—barred from representation by the Railway Labor Act and denied from employment by our officers. For what cause? None other than: "We are black."[74]

In its answer to the FEPC's summary of complaints, the Southern Railway pointed out that it was a signatory to the Washington Agreement and was bound by the percentage restrictions of Negro employees established under the agreement. The company went on to defend its discriminatory agreements with all the railroad brotherhoods:

> The question of whether an applicant for employment as locomotive fireman is "competent" is one left to the operating offices in charge of hiring. "Competent" . . . does not consist alone of manual dexterity or ability to do a single job . . . there must be ability to work harmoniously with others engaged in the joint undertaking. . . . The employment of white firemen on the crews tends to greater harmony. . . . This Company has no negro in its employ as conductor. The reason is (1) the white employees would not permit (2) the public served would not permit and (3) this Company does not regard them as competent under all the surrounding circumstances and conditions.
>
> This respondent's binding agreements with the labor organizations representing its employees . . . are made in the light of the social

environment as it exists in the South and deals realistically and fairly with the racial problems referred to above. This respondent is not at liberty to disregard or violate these agreements.[75]

The Seaboard Air Line Railway was also served complaints by the FEPC for having signed the Washington Agreement and for refusing to hire Negro railroadmen. The company responded:

Locomotive engineers are recruited entirely from the ranks of firemen. . . . It has been found necessary in recent years to employ only white firemen.

The Seaboard has not in recent years employed negroes as trainmen for the reason that, since conductors are recruited entirely from trainmen, an adequate supply of conductors requires that only white trainmen be employed.

Because of contractual obligations the Seaboard does not permit negro trainmen to work as flagmen or baggagemen, or to be promoted to the position of conductor.

Intrinsic in the management's selection of firemen is the basic fact that . . . negroes are not employed as locomotive engineers on the Seaboard. Engineers are invariably chosen from Seaboard's firemen. . . .

That negroes are not qualified as locomotive engineers is a condition resulting from complex and delicate considerations of compelling force in the areas traversed by the Seaboard, for which the railroad is not responsible but which it cannot disregard. It would be impractical to place a negro engineer in a place of authority over a white fireman.[76]

When the Illinois Central System was notified of the committee's summary of complaints, the company answered that "[t]he Illinois Central System employs negroes exclusively as red caps, waiters, train porters and elevator operators."[77]

Complaints against the Norfolk & Western Railway Company charged that, because of the company's agreements with the Brotherhood of Railroad Trainmen, Negroes were not hired for the positions of road brakeman and car retarder. Four complaints were filed against the Louisiana and Arkansas Railway Company for maintaining pay differentials for firemen based on color. Three complaints of the many against the Pennsylvania Railroad Company came from Negro women who were refused jobs as cleaning women because, as the railroad explained, it "didn't have toilet facilities for colored women."[78]

A complaint by the Joint Council of Dining Car Employees, a black union, against the Missouri, Kansas and Texas Railroad

Company stated that the company refused to upgrade Negro waiters with seniority to the position of dining-car steward. Fifteen complaints against the Atlantic Coast Line Railroad Company came from Negro firemen who charged that, as a result of the Washington Agreement's restrictive quotas, they had been taken off their regular jobs and given work on the "extra board," which meant irregular assignments. Three other Negro firemen complained to the committee that they had applied for work on the Yazoo and Mississippi Valley Railroad Company and been told that it "had signed an agreement not to hire any more colored firemen." Complaints were filed against the Boston and Albany Railroad and the Illinois Central Railroad alleging refusal to upgrade Negro waiters to the position of steward in dining-car service.

There were also charges against the Union Pacific Railroad, the Sheet Metal Workers' International Association, and the International Association of Machinists that the company and the unions had agreed not to promote Negroes to the position of machinist in the railroad's repair shops. And there were complaints of discrimination against the Jacksonville Terminal Company and the Atlanta Joint Terminal, both of which had signed the Washington Agreement.[79]

When, in Washington, on September 15, 1943, the FEPC finally held its public hearings on the railroad industry—after a delay of eight months*—it had complaints of race discrimination against twenty-two railroads and fourteen labor unions.† The railroad companies were collectively represented by legal counsel, but the unions refused to send any representatives. The only

---

*The hearings were originally scheduled for January 1943 but were postponed indefinitely by Director Paul McNutt of the War Manpower Commission. When the FEPC was reorganized under Executive Order 9346, the hearings were rescheduled for September 1943.

†Among the railroads included were the New York Central, the Baltimore and Ohio, the Pennsylvania, the Union Pacific, the Georgia, the Central of Georgia, the Seaboard, the Southern, the Jacksonville Terminal, the Atlanta Joint Terminals, the St. Louis-San Francisco, the Atlantic Coast Line, the Chesapeake and Ohio, the Louisville & Nashville, and the Illinois Central. Among the unions included were the Brotherhood of Locomotive Firemen and Enginemen, the Brotherhood of Locomotive Engineers, the Brotherhood of Railroad Trainmen, the Brotherhood of Railway Carmen of America, the International Association of Machinists, the International Brotherhood of Boilermakers, Iron Ship Builders and Helpers of America, the Sheetmetal Workers' International Association, and the International Brotherhood of Blacksmiths, Drop Forgers and Helpers. Six additional companies and one union agreed to comply, and the directives concerning them were not made public by the FEPC.

testimony introduced by the railroads was that of their attorney, Sidney S. Alderman:

> The railroads cannot undertake to push the solutions of these problems beyond that reached by the civilization as a whole.
>
> The larger portion of the railroads cited by this Committee operate in the South, in a society and civilization vexed with some of the most delicate and difficult racial problems the world has ever known.
>
> In dealing with these problems, the South has adopted by law the solution of segregation of the races. The railroads are not responsible for that solution and cannot undertake to pass upon or question its wisdom.
>
> The prevailing manners and customs of the various sections of the country would not countenance the employment by the railroads of Negroes in all types of positions.
>
> Neither the employees nor the patrons of the railroads could be expected to change overnight their long-standing views regarding racial problems, and any attempt to force them to do so by governmental decree would not fail to do harm rather than good.[80]

The spokesman for the railroads also pointedly reminded the committee that the employers had entered into labor agreements "under the Railway Labor Act and earlier controlling United States labor laws, and often with government assistance and approval," and that the railroads were "not at liberty to disregard or violate these agreements."[81]

The FEPC's chief counsel, Bartley C. Crum, described the hearings to the press as "[t]he most important ever held so far as minority groups are concerned either in this country or abroad."[82] At the hearings he said:

> Contractual agreements between the unions and the employers, witnessed by an agency of the United States Government . . . have not only barred all doors of advancement to Negro workers already on the pay roll, but have crowded hundreds of others out of railroad employment into a new and uncertain search for a livelihood.[83]

During the four days of hearings FEPC counsel detailed the charges against the railroads and unions, and witnesses described the discrimination practiced against them. One Negro fireman for the Atlantic Coast Line Railway testified that he had been refused the opportunity to exercise his seniority in seeking a job aboard a diesel engine:

> *Q.* Did you take it up with the Brotherhood [of Locomotive Firemen and Enginemen]?
>
> *A.* Yes, sir.

Q. What did he [the local chairman] do?

A. He said that it was a white man's job; not only that, but he was going to take the niggers off Diesel jobs that showed up.[84]

In his testimony against the Norfolk and Southern Railway, Joseph C. Waddy, general counsel of the Association of Colored Trainmen and Locomotive Firemen, described the circumstances under which that railroad signed the Washington Agreement and its supplements:

> Mr. Kennedy [general superintendent of the Norfolk and Southern Railway] indicated to me that . . . his company had first taken the position and had communicated to the Brotherhood [of Locomotive Firemen and Enginemen] that they were hiring no Negroes anyway, and that under their present hiring policies it would only be a matter of time before all Negroes would be off the road anyway, and they didn't want to enter into the policy which would accelerate the process of getting Negroes off the road, but nevertheless, because of the pressure, they signed the Southeastern Carriers Conference Agreement on the road.[85]

The supplemental agreement to which Waddy referred stated that "[i]t is understood and agreed that the phrase 'non-promotable' carried in paragraph 1 of the above quoted agreement refers only to colored firemen."[86]

The effect of the lack of Negro representation in the collective bargaining process was described in the evidence against the St. Louis-San Francisco Railway Company. Will Whitfield, a Negro fireman working for the railroad, was questioned:

Q. Now, at the time that you were first employed on the railroad [1905], what was the approximate percentage of Negro locomotive firemen employed on the railroad?

A. About 95 percent.

Q. What is it now?

A. Less than 1 percent.

Q. Did the Brotherhood of Locomotive Firemen and Enginemen ever give you any notice that in 1928 they were going to negotiate an agreement which would bind the railroad not to hire any more Negro locomotive firemen?

A. No.

Q. Suppose there is a contest between you and a white locomotive fireman; will they [the brotherhood] handle that?

A. No, sir.[87]

Throughout the hearings, none of the evidence introduced by counsel for the FEPC was refuted by the railroads' spokesman, and the cited unions continued their refusal to participate at all. The committee's summary, findings, and directives[88] found a "refusal to employ Negroes as locomotive firemen, trainmen, switchmen, yardmen, dining car stewards, mechanics, machinists, and helpers."[89] The committee ordered the carriers and the unions to cease and desist from their discriminatory practices and to set aside their discriminatory labor agreements, particularly the Washington Agreement. They were also informed that the matter would be referred to the President if the railroads and unions continued to violate the executive order.

Fourteen southern railroads responded to the committee's directives with a letter stating that they had no influence over the railroad unions and that

> [i]t is wholly impracticable, and indeed impossible for these railroads to put into effect your Committee's Directives addressed against them. Any attempt on their part to comply with those Directives, for instance, to promote negroes to locomotive engineers or train conductors, would inevitably disrupt their present peaceful and cooperative relations with their employees, would antagonize the traveling and shipping public served by them, would substitute conditions of chaos for the present condition of harmony, would result in stoppages of transportation, and would most gravely and irreparably impair the whole war effort of the country. These railroads cannot assume the responsibility for precipitating such disastrous results.
>
> These railroads are ready at any time to confer with their employees of various crafts and classes to ascertain whether, under the orderly and controlling procedures of the Railway Labor Act, any more generally satisfactory solution of the racial problems of employment can be worked out by mutual agreement. However, frankness compels these railroads very respectfully to state to your Committee that it is utterly unrealistic to suppose that these railroads and their employees can agree to comply with the breadth of your Directives or that problems of such delicacy, controlled and governed by a special Act of Congress, can be solved out-of-hand by the fist of your Committee's Directives. . . .[90]

The railroads not only refused to obey the FEPC's directives but also challenged the constitutionality of the committee's power to issue them:

> And, finally, with great respect the undersigned railroads submit that your Committee was and is wholly without constitutional power to

make and issue the Directives which it made and issued, and for this reason the said Directives are without legal effect.[91]

Since the committee lacked any enforcement power beyond referral to the President, its chief weapon was publicity. Malcolm Ross, its chairman, responded to the railroad companies' letter with the following statement:

> The fireman problem, and the problems of upgrading, job assignments and seniority rights of Negroes in the operating divisions and the shops were the subject of four days of FEPC hearings in September. The railroad unions chose to ignore the hearings. The carriers made a perfunctory appearance. Their letter now makes a bid for public disapproval of FEPC by viewing with alarm alleged pretensions of Negroes to be engineers and conductors. The plain fact is that this issue—necessarily covered because complaints were received and no rebuttal offered—is dormant and could remain so if the railroads offer justice to Negro railroadmen in the classifications where reason and public policy both urge it. Certainly it is not the part of candor to seize upon the most delicate issue in order to avoid the many basic problems squarely placed before the railroads.
>
> The Southeastern Carriers' Conference Agreement, which the Committee found in violation of Executive Order 9346, was concerned with the hiring and use of Negroes as firemen and not with their promotion from firemen to engineers. The railroads now advance obligations under the Railway Labor Act as barriers to changing the discriminatory Southeastern Carriers' Conference Agreement. There is no conflict of jurisdiction here. The Agreement was reached with the Brotherhoods in 1941, and by mutual agreement it can be altered or discarded. In asking both parties to make this move, the FEPC is not suggesting anything which cannot be done in conformity with the Railway Labor Act and the procedures adopted by the National Mediation Board. There are extremely serious Negro problems on American railroads. The FEPC did not invent them. It tried, honestly and with the war need for railroad workers in mind, to find out what is wrong and to direct remedial action.[92]

The committee sent the case to President Roosevelt, but instead of taking action to enforce the executive order, the President announced on January 3, 1944, that he had appointed a special committee to conciliate the issue with the companies, the unions, and the FEPC. The committee consisted of Chief Justice Walter P. Stacy of the Supreme Court of North Carolina; Judge William H. Holly of the U.S. district court in Chicago; and Frank J. Lausche, the mayor of Cleveland. After several meetings with the parties involved, the FEPC reported that it "was not successful in bringing about compliance with the [FEPC's] directives, and no report of its progress was made other than an interim statement in May, 1944. Thus, the situation respecting the 14 railroads and 7 unions remains today what it was when the [FEPC] referred the case to the President."[93]* Beyond publicizing the acknowledged discriminatory practices of the railroad companies and labor unions, the FEPC hearings and directives accomplished nothing. The committee had no enforcement power, the President did not act, and both the carriers and the unions successfully defied the committee. Later, its *Final Report* described the hearings as "among the Committee's outstanding failures."[94]

In the same year Negro railroad employees were seeking redress through litigation in two cases that would be decided by the Supreme Court, *Steele* v. *Louisville & Nashville R.R. Co.*[95] and *Tunstall* v. *Brotherhood of Locomotive Firemen and Enginemen.*[96] Bester William Steele had been a fireman in Alabama on the Decatur-Montgomery division of the Louisville & Nashville Railroad Company since 1910, and when the railroad signed the Washington Agreement with the Brotherhood of Locomotive Firemen and Enginemen, Steele was taken off his "preferred run" and given a job on a less desirable "local freight," thus being denied his seniority rights.[97] In his testimony at the FEPC hearing, and later in court, he stated that Negroes comprised 98 percent of the firemen in his district when he was first hired in 1910, and that they were systematically displaced by whites as a result of the Southeastern Carriers' Conference Agreement. Steele sued the railroad and the brotherhood to enjoin the enforcement of the Washington Agreement and the supplemental agreements, maintaining that the Railway Labor Act imposed a duty upon the certified collective bargaining agent of a craft or class to represent all members of the craft fairly and impartially.

Tom Tunstall, a Negro fireman with the Norfolk & Southern Railway Company, had also been displaced from his job by a white fireman with less seniority, as a result of the Washington Agreement. Tunstall sued the Brotherhood of Locomotive Firemen and Enginemen to enjoin enforcement of the agreement, claiming that the union "has always been disloyal to the Negro minority

*When the committee certified the cases to President Roosevelt, certain railroads named in the original directives were not included because they indicated a willingness to negotiate with the committee. Of the seven unions named, four did not reply and three responded by stating that they would refuse to comply with the directives.

firemen, refused to give them notice, hearing or a chance to vote on policy matters adversely affecting their interests, refused to report to them on action taken, has constantly sought to drive them out of employment in order to obtain a monopoly and the most favored jobs for its own members; and has refused to give them fair, honest and impartial representation under the Railway Labor Act."[98] The United States entered both the *Steele* and *Tunstall* cases as *amicus curiae,* arguing on behalf of the Negro firemen that the Railway Labor Act did impose a duty upon the Brotherhood of Locomotive Firemen and Enginemen to represent the Negro nonmember firemen fairly and impartially:

> The right of the organization chosen by the majority to be the exclusive representative of a bargaining unit exists only by reason of the Railway Labor Act. Implicit in the grant of such right is a correlative duty of the representative to act in behalf of all the employees in the unit without discrimination. Congress would not have incapacitated a minority or an individual from representing itself or his own interests without imposing upon the craft representative a duty to serve on behalf of the craft. . . and not merely for the benefit of certain portions of it favored as a result of discrimination against others.
>
> The terms of the statute and its history support this interpretation. The word "representative" normally connotes action on behalf of those to be represented. The Act fulfills its purpose of peacefully settling disputes on a voluntary basis only when the employees have confidence that their representative in the negotiations is acting in their interest. And the Congress which incorporated the principle of majority rule in the Railway Labor Act and the National Labor Relations Act believed that, although the minority was deprived of separate representation, it was not harmed inasmuch as it was to receive all the advantages which the majority obtained for itself. Clearly Congress did not intend the grant of exclusive authority to a representative to result in discrimination against individuals or minorities.
>
> Upon the allegations in the complaints in these cases, the Brotherhood has entered into and is enforcing agreements which discriminate against the Negro firemen because of their race. This discrimination in the Brotherhood's conduct as representative is aggravated by its refusal to admit the colored firemen to membership, so that they do not have the protection which would flow from participation in the formulation of union policy. In these circumstances, the Brotherhood is obviously not acting in good faith as the representative of the entire craft. This does not mean that a labor union as a private organization has no power to fix its own membership requirements. But when it seeks *o exercise the exclusive statutory right, it must carry out the obligation to represent fairly which is inherent in that right.[99]

On December 18, 1944, the Supreme Court announced its decisions in the *Steele* and *Tunstall* cases. The Court ruled that the Railway Labor Act did impose a duty upon the brotherhood to represent fairly the Negro firemen over whom it had jurisdiction:

> The Brotherhood has acted and asserts the right to act as exclusive bargaining representative of the firemen's craft. It is alleged that in that capacity it is under an obligation and duty imposed by the Act to represent the Negro firemen impartially and in good faith; but instead,... it has been hostile and disloyal to the Negro firemen, has deliberately discriminated against them, and has sought to deprive them of their seniority rights and to drive them out of employment in their craft, all in order to create a monopoly of employment for Brotherhood members. . . . So long as a labor union assumes to act as the statutory representative of a craft, it cannot rightly refuse to perform the duty, which is inseparable from the power of representation conferred upon it, to represent the entire membership of the craft.Wherever necessary. . . the union is required to consider requests of non-union members of the craft . . . with respect to collective bargaining with the employer. . . .[100]

The Court's opinion was narrowly restricted in application to the brotherhood's duty toward Negroes already employed by the railroads. It did not rule that the Railway Labor Act was unconstitutional in its application, that the brotherhood was required by the Fifth Amendment to accept Negro members, or that the brotherhood's "impartiality" was to extend to potential Negro railroad employees. Justice Frank Murphy wrote in his concurring opinion in the *Steele* case:

> The utter disregard for the dignity and the well-being of colored citizens shown by this record is so pronounced as to demand the invocation of constitutional condemnation. To decide the case and to analyze the statute solely upon the basis of legal niceties, while remaining mute and placid as to the obvious and oppressive deprivation of constitutional guarantees, is to make the judicial function something less than it should be.[101]

The FEPC's *Final Report,* in discussing the shortcomings of the Court's opinion in the *Steele* and *Tunstall* cases, concluded that the decisions would have little practical effect on the discriminatory practices of the carriers and the unions:

> Although the Court's opinions left no doubt as to the illegality of the discriminatory agreements, the agreements are so numerous and apply to so many railroads that to invalidate them by litigation would require a multiplicity of suits and the expenditure of much time and money. Moreover, the Steele and Tunstall cases touch only on the

rights of Negroes after they have been hired. They do not affect discrimination which bars Negroes from employment in the first place.
Hence it is fair to conclude that, as a practical matter, only an
administrative agency with the necessary authority can deal successfully with the problems presented by such discriminatory agreements.[102]

The committee's plea for an administrative agency "with the
necessary authority" was made in its *Final Report* on June 28,
1946, the last day of its existence.

The limitations of the *Steele* and *Tunstall* decisions were
demonstrated by a 1945 FEPC investigation of the racial practices
of the Texas and New Orleans Railroad Company and the
Brotherhood of Railroad Trainmen.[103] The railroad had employed
Negro yardmen for seventy years, and in 1937 it signed an
agreement with the Brotherhood of Railroad Trainmen that it
would cease to do so, although Negroes previously hired as
yardmen were to be protected. The railroad's seniority list,
introduced into evidence, showed that in 1932 the company
employed forty-five Negro yardmen; in 1935, thirty-five Negro
yardmen; in 1944, twenty-seven Negro yardmen; and in 1945,
twenty-three Negro yardmen.[104] Counsel for the railroad denied
any discrimination: "We have not been motivated by any prejudice
against niggers or by any desire to discriminate against them."[105]

This hearing was unlike the previous FEPC hearings involving
railroads in that the Brotherhood of Railroad Trainmen participated. The brotherhood's attorney admitted that the union refused
membership to Negroes: "The organization is something past 60
years in age. It was organized in the State of New York in 1883,
and has consistently since its organization, and down to this time,
prescribed that the membership be limited to white males between
the ages of 18 and 65 years."[106] He also said that "[t]here have been
no Negro switchmen employed since the first day of May, 1937,"
and he defended the racial policies of the union by arguing that
"[t]he custom and practice of segregation of races in this
community [the South] is a very old one."[107] Despite the fact that
the brotherhood had directly prevented the hiring of any Negro
yardmen for the past eight years, the union's counsel added, "I
think those of us living here have every respect for the Negro and
there is no disposition on the part of anyone to take from him any
of his economic rights or any of his political rights or any of his
social rights."[108]

Charles H. Houston, in describing the consequences of these developments, said in an address to the 1949 convention of the National Association for the Advancement of Colored People:

> Inch by inch and yard by yard, down through the years the brotherhoods have been choking off the employment rights of Negro train and engine service employees. In 1890 the Trainmen, the Conductors, the Firemen and Switchmen's Mutual Aid Association demanded that all Negroes in the train, yard, and locomotive service of the Houston and Texas Central Railway System be removed and white men employed in their places. In 1898 the Trainmen tried to get all the Negro brakemen removed from the Missouri Pacific System. In 1899 the four Brotherhoods had all the colored porters on the Gulf, Colorado and Santa Fe Railway passenger trains removed and replaced by white brakemen. . . . In 1909 the Firemen's Brotherhoods staged a bitter and violent strike against Negro firemen on the Georgia Railroad, demanding white supremacy and the replacement of Negro firemen by whites. In 1910 the Trainmen and the Conductors negotiated what is called the Washington Agreement with most of the Southeast railroads providing that no more Negroes were to be employed as garageman, flagman, or yard foreman; they followed up in 1911 by negotiating a similar agreement with some of the railroads in the Mississippi Valley.[109]

Houston described a similar "history of aggression of the big four Brotherhoods against Negro firemen and brakemen" in many northern states as well. Direct action was taken by the railway brotherhoods to force Negroes out of jobs on the Michigan Central as early as 1863 and on the New York, New Haven and Hartford Railway, the Baltimore and Ohio, and other lines during World War I.[110]

This pattern, which had begun as early as 1863, when the railway labor unions forced Negroes out of jobs on the Michigan Central, continued into the period of World War II, as documented by the investigation and hearings of the Fair Employment Practice Committee. When collective bargaining was instituted in the industry, all facets of the bargaining process operated to the disadvantage of the Negro. The railroad unions excluded Negroes from membership and jobs; yet those same unions received government sanction as collective bargaining agents, and labor agreements which restricted Negro employment were approved by the Federal Government.*

*Discriminatory labor contracts negotiated by railroads and labor unions during the 1940s were often continued into the 1960s. Soon after Title VII went into effect, black workers

At the beginning of the 1970s the long struggle of black railroad workers against discriminatory employment practices in the railway industry entered a new phase. As a result of the decision of the U.S. Court of Appeals for the Eighth Circuit in *Norman* v. *Missouri Pacific Railroad*,[111] black workers were freed from the frustrating barriers of the Railway Labor Act and were able to seek their employment rights under Title VII of the Civil Rights Act of 1964. The appeals court stated:

> We, therefore, do not think the plaintiffs are confined to their administrative remedies, which appear without further examination to be inadequate, under the Railway Labor Act. The enactment of Title VII provides a more extensive and broader ground for relief, specifically oriented towards the elimination of discriminatory employment practices based upon race, color, religion, sex or national origin. Title VII is cast in broad, all-inclusive terms setting up statutory rights against discrimination based *inter alia* upon race.[112]

---

filed complaints with the EEOC seeking relief from restrictive labor-management agreements. In several cases the commission found reasonable cause and its investigations revealed a continuation of the racial patterns documented by the FEPC during World War II. In 1966, for example, the EEOC found reasonable cause in a complaint against an employer and Local 616 of the International Brotherhood of Firemen, Oilers, Helpers, Roadhouse and Railway Shop Laborers in Fort Worth, Texas, because they enforced a 1945 agreement at the Texarkana yard of the St. Louis-Southwestern Railway Lines which prevented black workers from advancing beyond the position of laborer. The railroad employed 132 persons at this yard, nine of whom were blacks employed as laborers. In 1965, Benjamin F. Grant, a black laborer, applied for the vacant position of hostler helper. He received no further information on his application until he learned that the job had been awarded to a white fireman. The company had originally claimed that Grant was rejected because he was too old for the position. However, the successful white applicant was two years older than Grant.

The railroad contended that Grant had been ineligible for the position because the company was bound by a labor agreement with Local 616 dated September 19, 1945, which limited promotions to the position of hostler only to firemen. In practice this meant that only white workers were eligible for promotion. The investigation disclosed that the company employed no black firemen and that, in fact, it had never employed black firemen. The investigative report states that "[t]he effect of the rule established by the memorandum is to effectively deny Negroes access to the job of Hostler Helper." In its finding of reasonable cause, the commission concluded that Local 616 as well as the company were jointly responsible for perpetuating a discriminatory agreement: "The white employee was given the job despite the fact that he had less seniority than the Charging Party, despite the fact that he was older than the Charging Party, and despite the fact that the Charging Party's job duties as a laborer were often similar to those of a fireman, thereby satisfying the experience requirement. The 'Memorandum of Agreement' of 1945 is therefore clearly an instrument of discrimination and has been used to effectively exclude Negroes from the position of Hostler Helper. The parties to that agreement, the company and the union, are therefore found to be in violation of Title VII of the Civil Rights Act of 1964."—EEOC Case No. 6–5–5177, filed November 1, 1966. See also EEOC Case No. 6–6–5651, filed October 17, 1966, involving the Chesapeake and Ohio Railway Company and Local 637 of the International Brotherhood of Firemen and Oilers.

In the years before this decision black workers confined to the job of train porter had protested both in and out of the courts that their work and that of the white brakemen was identical except for pay and promotional opportunities, and that the separate classifications established under the Railway Labor Act were in fact simply segregated work units.* Litigation between the train porters and the railroads and the unions representing the brakemen began in 1946 with *Howard* v. *Thompson.*[113] The Brotherhood of Railroad Trainmen sought to pressure the railroads into abolishing the jobs of the train porters and replacing them with white brakemen. The Supreme Court's decision in *Howard,* which saved the porters from the predatory raid, held that the Railway Labor Act prohibited the brakemen's agents from destroying Negro workers' jobs in favor of white workers. However, the Supreme Court reinforced the denial of any remedy to the black workers in *Howard,* holding that "*disputed* questions of reclassification of the craft of 'train porters' are committed by the Railway Labor Act to the National Mediation Board."[114] Thus the Supreme Court held that even the federal courts lacked jurisdiction to order a merger of the all-white and all-black classifications.

In a later decision marking a second phase of *Howard,*[115] the eighth circuit court held that the train porters could retain their accumulated seniority but denied them relief in seeking to be classified as brakemen. The court ruled that only the National Mediation Board had the power to make such craft or class determinations and that the dispute should be settled by the Railroad Adjustment Board rather than in the courts. The effect of this ruling was to relegate black workers to the dubious protection of the Railway Labor Act, which had created as its administrative agencies the National Mediation Board and the Railroad Adjustment Board—agencies composed of representatives from the same railroads and unions that in the past and currently were engaged in systematic aggression against black workers.

In the second *Norman* decision by the Court of Appeals for the Eighth Circuit, the court observed that "[i]t appears clear, however, that even though train porters are foreclosed from judicial relief by way of merger or reclassification of craft, the plaintiffs

---

*While performing the work of porter on passenger trains, the Negro train porter was frequently required to perform all the functions of a brakeman but denied the classification and wages of that craft, historically restricted to whites. Blacks classified as train porters were required to take the same training and examinations as the white brakemen.

have certain protections under the Railway Labor Act and under Title VII of the Civil Rights Act of 1964."[116] In *Norman* the black train porters had filed suit under Title VII, claiming that the establishment of separate classifications was in fact segregation and was thus in violation of Title VII. The district court had dismissed the suit on the basis of the earlier *Howard* decisions, holding that the relief sought could be granted only by the National Mediation Board.[117] In 1969 the eighth circuit reversed and remanded the case to the district court for consideration under Title VII, stating that "[t]he Railroad is not exempt from the provisions of Title VII."[118]

With this decision, the controversy between black and white workers over separate classifications began anew.* In 1970 William H. Brown, III, then the chairman of the Equal Employment Opportunity Commission, bluntly told the American Railroad Association that the industry "has demonstrated insufficient progress in providing equal employment opportunities for minorities and women. . . . [T]he industry employs a lower percentage of blacks and Spanish-surnamed Americans than the nation-wide average for all industries and . . . no improvement was registered from 1966 to 1969." In "an industry characterized by powerful unions, the railroads historically restricted the opportunity of minorities to move upward through segregated unions, dual job

---

*A suit filed in the U.S. district court in Lake Charles, Louisiana, involving the Brotherhood of Locomotive Engineers and the Missouri Pacific Railroad illustrates the complexities of contemporary litigation involving black employment on the railroads. In 1972 the brotherhood's local union, which had historically excluded blacks from membership and limited them to jobs as firemen and porters, entered into a new collective bargaining agreement. Conscious of the requirements of Title VII, the company and the union eliminated traditional discriminatory provisions from the new agreement and negotiated amendments that for the first time allowed blacks to enter the all-white seniority line and thus be employed as brakemen and engineers with full seniority retention. Soon thereafter a group of white union members filed suit against the union and the railroad to have the nondiscriminatory bargaining agreement declared invalid. The NAACP, representing the black workers, intervened in defense of the new union contract and on February 6, 1974, the court dismissed the white workers' suit. District Judge Edwin F. Hunter, Jr., noted that "[p]rior to 1964 all of the Railroad Engineers in the DeQuincy Division were white and all of its Firemen in both portions of the Division which I've just described were Negro. . . . [Y]ou had to be Black to be a fireman and no fireman could ever become an engineer in the DeQuincy Division. . . . If [intervening defendants] and these other people had been white, they could and would have been engineers much earlier. . . ." The judge observed that the new agreement merged and consolidated the hitherto racially segregated seniority rosters and that "I just cannot, in view of the jurisprudence, find anything illegal about it. I would think that if they hadn't made some sort of provision in regard to seniority to undo the effects of past discrimination that the contract would have been invalid."—*J. C. Miller, et al. v. Missouri Pacific Co.*, Civil Action No. 18,675 (W.D. La.). The material quoted above does not appear in the published order of the court. It is found in "Portion of Proceedings before the Honorable Edwin F. Hunter, Jr., United States District Judge, at Lake Charles, Louisiana, on the 6th day of February 1974."

progressions, and exclusion from certain work classifications. . . . [T]he effects of . . . discriminatory practices persist through . . . testing, arbitrary education requirements, and seniority systems."[119]

In 1971 the U.S. Court of Appeals for the Fifth Circuit ruled that a railroad seniority structure that had been developed through fifty years of collective bargaining agreements was not immune to remedial measures intended to provide relief to black workers. In *U.S. v. Jacksonville Terminal Co.*[120] the court held that work rules and other provisions in union contracts in the railroad industry were no less susceptible to court-ordered remedies and relief from racial discrimination than those in other industries. According to the appellate court, union agreements do not "carry the authoritative imprimatur and moral force of sacred scripture, or even of mundane legislation." Furthermore, in the legal context of Title VII the railroad industry and its labor unions could not be deemed "a state within a state."[121]

Since discriminatory practices continue, the courts are granting under Title VII the relief that has been denied under the Railway Labor Act. The irony, of course, is that railroad employment is rapidly diminishing. In 1974, at the time of the court's decision in *Norman*,[122] passenger train operations were curtailed throughout the country, and attrition among the plaintiffs due to retrenchment had reduced from sixteen to three those train porters who qualified for promotion.

On February 26, 1975, while other cases were pending in the federal courts, the Equal Employment Opportunity Commission filed a suit in New Mexico against the Atchison, Topeka & Santa Fe Railway and fifteen local and international unions charging that the company and labor organizations discriminated against "Spanish-surnamed Americans in testing, arrest record inquiry, non-job related physical requirements, recruiting, hiring, promotion, layoff and recall, wages, transfer and segregated job classifications."[123] Later in 1975, in *Claiborne* v. *Illinois Central R.R.*[124] a district court awarded punitive damages to the black plaintiffs. Although punitive damages are rarely ordered by the courts in Title VII litigation,[125] in this case the court stated that "[s]ince punitive damages would further the aims of Title VII by deterring violations and by encouraging plaintiffs to seek relief by increasing their recovery, the implication of punitive damages will further the broad remedial effect that Congress intended under Title VII."[126]

On January 9, 1976, after extensive litigation, a federal court ordered the payment of $120,000 as compensatory back pay to forty-three black railroad workers who had sued the Birmingham Southern Railroad and Local 1887 of the United Transportation Union, AFL-CIO. As a result of the decision in *Jack A. Gamble et al.* v. *Birmingham Southern Railroad*,[127] black workers, many of whom had twenty to thirty years' work experience with the railroad but had been denied advancement into the all-white seniority lines, could for the first time be promoted beyond entry-level switchmen's jobs and into the conductor's classification. Although working in a declining industry, blacks, Chicanos, and members of other minority groups were continuing through litigation the struggle against the old employment patterns of the railroads and the railway labor unions.

14

Epilogue: The End of the
Fair Employment Practice Committee

The Fair Employment Practice Committee, established in June 1941 by Executive Order 8802 and revised in 1943 by Executive Order 9346, was conceived as a temporary measure during a period of national rearmament and war. President Roosevelt established the FEPC to defuse a nationwide black protest movement against discrimination and to accelerate mobilization of manpower for defense production. During World War II some members of Congress sought to extend the committee's operations into the postwar period on a permanent basis, with greater enforcement powers. As early as July 20, 1942, the first attempt to establish the FEPC as a statutory agency was made. The bill, introduced by Representative Vito Marcantonio of New York, received so little support that it was never reported out of committee. In January 1944 the National Council for a Permanent FEPC was formed. The council, which consisted of a coalition of minority, religious, civic, and fraternal organizations and some labor unions, conducted educational programs and sponsored fair employment practice legislation.

In 1946 a filibuster in the Senate prevented consideration of a fair employment proposal introduced by Senator Dennis Chavez of New Mexico. In 1950 Congressman Adam Clayton Powell, Jr., of New York introduced an FEPC bill which was defeated, and in 1954 the Dawson-Scanlon bill in the House of Representatives proposing a federal agency to eliminate job discrimination with the same power and authority as the National Labor Relations Board was rejected. Over a period of twenty years, many attempts to secure enactment of fair employment practice legislation failed.

The World War II FEPC budget came from funds approved by Congress for the operation of wartime executive agencies.* In 1944, Senator Richard B. Russell of Georgia was chairman of the subcommittee of the Senate Committee on Appropriations before which the Senate version of a new appropriations bill was pending. Russell, a powerful member of the committee and a resolute opponent of fair employment practice legislation, introduced an amendment to the appropriations bill which provided that no funds could be allotted to any agency established by an executive order and in existence for more than one year "if the Congress has not appropriated any money specifically for such an agency . . . or specifically authorized the expenditure of funds by it."[1]

In June 1944 the Russell amendment, which was to have a dire effect on the FEPC's operations, was adopted. Commenting on the significance of the amendment, Louis Ruchames wrote:

> Although couched in the most general terms and applicable to all executive agencies, the amendment was undoubtedly directed at the FEPC. Indeed, Senator Russell remarked soon after its introduction that he hoped it would wipe out the agency.[2]

Although Russell did not then succeed in eliminating the FEPC, he had crippled its operations and paved the way for its demise, even as proponents of a permanent, statutory FEPC were trying to get a bill enacted.

In August and September of 1944, soon after the Philadelphia transit strike ended, a subcommittee of the Senate Committee on Education and Labor held hearings on one of the pending bills to establish a permanent commission.[3] The proposed bill defined discrimination in employment by employers and labor unions as an "unfair employment practice" and called for a permanent fair employment practice administrative agency that would be empowered to obtain court injunctions against offending employers and unions.†

---

*For data on FEPC appropriations, see Independent Offices Appropriation Act, 1945, Title II, Sec. 213 (Russell amendment), The Act of June 27, 1944, ch. 286, 58 Stat. 361 at 387 (1944), 31 U.S.C. Sec. 696 (1954); National War Agency Appropriation Act, 1945, The Act of June 28, 1944, ch. 301, 58 Stat. 533 (1944); National War Agencies Appropriation Act, 1946, The Act of July 17, 1945, ch. 319, 59 Stat. 473 (1945).

†The bill provided: "Section 3(b). It shall be an unfair employment practice for any labor union within the scope of this act—(1) to refuse membership to any person because of such person's race, creed, color, national origin or ancestry; (2) to expel from membership any

Management groups and business interests uniformly opposed such legislation, while organized labor was divided. The Senate subcommittee invited both national labor organizations to state their views at its hearings. The testimony of the American Federation of Labor and the Congress of Industrial Organizations (which were then separate organizations) illustrates their different formal policies on racial discrimination in employment at that time.

Philip Murray, president of the CIO, was represented by James B. Carey, secretary-treasurer of the CIO and chairman of its Committee to Abolish Discrimination, who appeared before the Senate subcommittee to affirm the CIO's support of the proposed bill. Carey testified:

> I come before your subcommittee to urge a favorable and early report on S. 2048, a bill to make the Fair Employment Practice Committee a permanent Government agency. . . .
>
> The Negro people and other minority groups have made their contribution to victory in the war. Their record in the armed forces and on the home front is second to none. Are we to allow them to slip back now into the category of second-class citizens that our racists would like to see them occupy?
>
> The Fair Employment Commission proposed in this bill is a strong answer to this antidemocratic proposition. There is nothing in the bill that runs counter to any American freedom. On the contrary, everything that it provides will serve to strengthen that freedom by strengthening the unity of the people who partake of it.[4]

William Green, president of the American Federation of Labor, did not send a representative. Instead, the AFL responded to the Senate subcommittee with a letter from W. C. Hushing, its National Legislative Committee chairman: "Your telegram to President Green of September 4, requesting him to make a statement in regard to S. 2048, was referred to me and I am pleased to incorporate hereinafter the report of the executive council of the American Federation of Labor to the 1943 convention, which sets forth our attitude."[5]

---

person because of such person's race . . .; (3) to discriminate against any member, employer, or employee because of such person's race . . . ." It covered labor unions with five or more members and employers with five or more employees and proposed the use of injunctions to obtain compliance. The bill was defeated in committee. (S. 2048, *A Bill to Prohibit Discrimination in Employment Because of Race, Creed, Color, National Origin or Ancestry,* 78th Cong., 2d Sess. (1944).)

The AFL's statement acknowledged in general terms the need to eliminate discrimination:

> Insistent need for elimination of race discrimination in employment and wage standards is . . . dictated, not only by the democratic principle to which the labor movement is pledged, but also by the need to assure economic justice to all workers through stability of wages and employment after the war.[6]

However, after these generalities the statement expressed opposition to government action to prevent the discriminatory racial practices of labor unions:

> The executive council does not believe, however, that imposition of any policy, no matter how salutary, through compulsory Government control of freely constituted associations of workers, accords with the basic right of freedom of association among the American people. While it endorses without reservation the policy of nondiscrimination in employment, the executive council takes strong exception to the compulsory imposition upon unions of this or any other policy interfering with the self-government of labor organizations.[7]

The American Federation of Labor opposed all efforts during this period to enact an enforceable fair employment law. Boris Shishkin, AFL representative on the FEPC, succinctly expressed the labor organization's policy in November 1944, at a Howard University conference, The Postwar Industrial Outlook for Negroes, when he stated that "labor would oppose any regulation of unions, even to prevent discrimination."[8] He added that legislation prohibiting racial and religious discrimination by unions "would open the door to much broader regulations of unions and labor spokesmen could not support it."[9]

In 1945 the same Senate subcommittee again had before it two bills proposing a permanent FEPC. One bill was substantially the same as that of the year before, calling for a strong commission which could actively prosecute violators through court-enforced injunctions. The other bill proposed an FEPC which would be limited to the functions of study, proposal, and recommendation to the President.

George L-P Weaver, director of the CIO's Committee to Abolish Discrimination, reaffirmed the CIO's support of a "[f]ederal FEPC with enforcement powers. . . . We realize that the maintenance of special groups of workers at depressed levels is a constant threat to workers at higher levels."[10] In contrast, the AFL opposed government intervention against employment discrimination, especially where it involved labor unions. Together with opposition from employers, southern members of Congress, and other conservative political figures, the AFL contributed to the defeat of a permanent federal fair employment commission.

After the surrender of Japan in August 1945 the Fair Employment Practice Committee continued in existence for almost another year, but at a greatly reduced level of operations. In its *Final Report* the FEPC explained the conditions under which its functions slowly came to a halt:

> The National War Agencies Appropriation Act, 1946, approved by Congress on July 17, 1945, included a $250,000 appropriation for the Committee on Fair Employment Practice. The act provided that this sum be used "for completely terminating the functions and duties of the Committee . . ." and provided further, "That if and until the Committee . . . is continued by an Act of Congress the amount named . . . may be used for its continued operation until an additional appropriation shall have been provided". . . .
>
> The Committee's decreased appropriation necessitated two early cuts in staff, one in August and another in December 1945. . . . In addition, as of that date, all field offices except those in Detroit, Chicago, and St. Louis had been closed. Further cuts followed in March and on May 3, it became necessary to put all employees on leave without pay status. Except for volunteer work, active operation ceased on that date [May 3, 1946]. The Committee, however, has remained in being through June 28.[11]

The committee described its findings about the situation of Negro and other minority workers:

> The minority groups most frequently subjected to discrimination during the war, as recorded by charges filed with FEPC, were Negroes, Jews, Mexican-Americans, and a scattering of religious creeds, as well as Nisei, aliens and citizens of recent origin. . . .
>
> Negroes, comprising the largest group, filed 80 percent of FEPC complaints. In general, discrimination against workers among the 3,000,000 Mexican-Americans in this country parallels that against Negro workers, so that facts stated about the problems of one may stand for both. . . .
>
> However, the seniority of colored workers is less than that of white workers in those industries which have continued into the postwar period because Negro workers entered war production very late. . . . They were unable, because of racial barriers, to transfer to other employment. And their low seniority, in those industries in which they are still employed, subjects them to the risk of further displacement by returning veterans. . . .[12]

The committee also gave warning of the very serious problems ahead for minority group workers in the postwar economy:

> The wartime gains of Negro, Mexican-American and Jewish workers are being lost through an unchecked revival of discriminatory practices.
>
> To many returning minority group veterans, civilian life presents a dismal picture. The things [they] looked forward to most—a job and a decent place in which to live—are hardest to find. . . .
>
> Fewer Negro than white GI's said they were satisfied to return to their old employment. Many hoped for something different and better. . . .
>
> . . . [A] majority of veterans—and nearly three-fourths of Negro veterans—do not try to get their old jobs back. Instead, they seek work in line with new skills they have acquired in the services. . . .
>
> It is now clear that Negro workers have lost large parts of their wartime employment gains and are finding that peacetime industry offers only the traditional openings of the years before 1940. City after city is reported as a loose labor market. The job competition which has been feared and which a few have sought to avoid, is here.[13]

On June 28, 1946, the committee, its appropriations exhausted and its official duties over, submitted its "Letter of Transmittal and Resignation" to President Truman. In it the FEPC cautioned that "[c]onformity to the national policy of nondiscrimination will come only when fair employment practice legislation has been adopted by the Congress" and that "[t]he mere existence of a Federal policy . . . will not in itself result in fair employment practices. . . ."[14] The committee therefore recommended that the President "continue to urge upon the Congress the passage of legislation which will guarantee equal job opportunity to all workers without discrimination because of race, color, religious belief, or national origin" and that the Federal Government "take steps not only to promulgate its policy more widely, but to enforce it as well."[15]

President Truman promptly issued a "Letter of Acceptance" of the resignations of the committee members: "The degree of effectiveness which the Fair Employment Practice Committee was able to attain has shown once and for all that it is possible to equalize job opportunity by governmental action, and, thus, eventually to eliminate the influence of prejudice in the field of employment." The President went on to convey to the members of the committee "my appreciation of the devotion they have brought to this war-time task,"[16] but he made no comment on their recommendations for congressional legislation and for enforcement provisions to end discriminatory employment practices in the postwar period.* With presidential acceptance of its members' resignations, the Fair Employment Practice Committee came to an end.

On December 3, 1951, President Truman issued Executive Order 10308, creating the President's Committee on Government Contract Compliance. This committee, which had no powers and was limited exclusively to advisory functions, issued a report twelve years after the formation of the Fair Employment Practice Committee. The 1953 report charged that the nondiscrimination clause included in every contract made by an agency or department of the Federal Government was now

> almost forgotten, dead and buried under thousands of words of standard legal and technical language in Government procurement contracts. . . . [O]n several occasions contracting agencies to which cases were referred stated they felt a sufficient inquiry had been made by sending a representative to the plant to ask what apparently amounted to the simple question—"Are you discriminating against Negroes?" When the obvious answer "No" was recorded, the inquiry was considered closed by the agency.[17]

The demise of the Fair Employment Practice Committee in 1946 was followed by almost two decades of federal executive and legislative inaction on the issue of employment discrimination. Beginning with its 1954 decision in *Brown* v. *Board of Education,*[18] the Supreme Court initiated a new era in constitutional law that led to important civil rights litigation, but neither the executive branch nor Congress acted against racial discrimination in employment.

During the Eisenhower Administration civil rights matters were given a low priority. In 1953 Executive Order 10479 was issued, followed by Executive Order 10557 in 1954. Although these

---

*A study of the civil rights record of the Truman Administration concludes that President Truman "raised the art of civil rights advocacy to new heights while shying away from anything that resembled a substantive program. . . . [His] sponsorship and endorsement of a civil rights program from 1948 on was not synonymous with active support for its passage. He, his supporters, and his opponents in Congress were participants in a civil rights drama in which ritualized action characterized the role performances of the players from the White House down." The author states that integration of the military establishment "was undoubtedly President Truman's greatest civil rights achievement—and it illustrates the intelligent use of executive power to change, within admittedly narrow limits, a racist social structure."—William C. Berman, *The Politics of Civil Rights in the Truman Administration* (Columbus, Ohio: Ohio State University Press, 1970), pp. 238–239.

orders expanded the obligations of federal contractors, the President's Committee on Government Contracts, under the chairmanship of Vice President Richard M. Nixon, limited itself to public relations pronouncements that changed nothing for black workers and other minorities.

The Kennedy Administration acted on some civil rights issues, notably that of enfranchising southern blacks, but it failed to take action against job discrimination. In 1961 President Kennedy issued Executive Order 10925, which required equal employment opportunity within federal agencies and in the enterprises of government contractors, and also established the President's Committee on Equal Employment Opportunity. This was supplemented in 1963 by Executive Order 11114, covering federally assisted construction. Although the President's committee had greater enforcement powers than earlier agencies, the Administration relied upon voluntary approaches such as the "Plans for Progress" program. Sanctions were not imposed and the executive orders were not enforced.

In 1965 President Lyndon B. Johnson issued Executive Order 11246, which further extended the obligations of federal contractors and resulted in the establishment of the Office of Federal Contract Compliance within the Department of Labor. However, "voluntary compliance" was again substituted for enforcement. The history of federal efforts to eliminate employment discrimination through executive orders has been largely a history of administrative nullification, and the potential of these orders was never realized.*

*Many studies document the failure of federal contract compliance. The Equal Employment Opportunity Commission, in a study of discrimination in white-collar jobs in New York City, disclosed that government contractors participating in the "Plans for Progress" program had a worse record of minority employment than those without government contracts (*Hearings Before the United States Equal Employment Opportunity Commission on Discrimination in White Collar Employment,* January 15–18, 1968, pp. 171– 174). A detailed survey of government contractors in five southwestern states made by the Institute of Industrial Relations, University of California, Los Angeles, revealed that among companies reporting to the EEOC "the pattern of minority employment is better for each minority group among employers who do not contract work for the government than it is among prime contractors who have agreed to nondiscrimination clauses in their contracts with the federal government." The study included California and Texas, states with high concentrations of government contracts held by large corporate enterprises (*Spanish-American Employment in the Southwest,* Staff of the Institute of Industrial Relations, University of California, Los Angeles, A Study Prepared for the Colorado Civil Rights Commission and the Equal Employment Opportunity Commission, September 1968). For detailed analyses of contract compliance by federal agencies, see the five reports issued by the U.S. Commission on Civil Rights, *The Federal Civil Rights Enforcement Effort,* October 1970, May 1971, November 1971, January 1973, and July 1975. See also Jerolyn R. Lyle,

Congress failed to act until the racial upheavals of the early 1960s led to the passage of the Civil Rights Act of 1964. The Act included Title VII, which established that black workers, women, and members of other minority groups had the right to earn a living free of discrimination and that illegal practices by employers and labor unions must be eliminated. Because administrative agencies failed to obtain compliance with the law it became necessary to seek enforcement through the judicial system. As a result of extensive litigation, a new perception of the nature of employment discrimination was to emerge in the federal courts together with new legal remedies that were to have far-reaching consequences. The development of the law of equal employment opportunity during the 1960s and 1970s brought renewed hope for economic justice, without which all other civil rights advances are diminished.

"Differences in the Occupational Standing of Black Workers Among Industries and Cities" (Washington, D.C.: Equal Employment Opportunity Commission, 1970); Barbara R. Bergmann and Jerolyn R. Lyle, "The Occupational Standing of Negroes by Areas and Industries," *Journal of Human Resources,* Fall 1971; Robert B. McKersie, "Minority Employment Patterns in an Urban Labor Market: The Chicago Experience" (Washington, D.C.: Equal Employment Opportunity Commission, 1972); Herbert Hill, "Whose Law— Whose Order? The Failure of Federal Contract Compliance," in Charles V. Hamilton, ed., *The Black Experience in American Politics* (New York: G. P. Putnam's Sons, 1973), pp. 325–331.

The bibliography and appendices may
be found in the companion volume.

Reference Notes

Introduction

1. 42 U.S.C. Section 2000(e) *et seq.*, as amended Public Law No. 92–261 (March 24, 1972).
2. Leonard Price Stavisky, "Negro Craftsmanship in Early America," *American Historical Review*, January 1949, pp. 315, 325; Stavisky, "The Origins of Negro Craftsmanship in Colonial America," *Journal of Negro History*, October 1947, pp. 417–429.
3. See Marcus W. Jernegan, "Slavery and the Beginnings of Industrialism in the American Colonies," *American Historical Review*, January 1920, p. 228, for evidence of Negro carpenters, coopers, and other mechanics as indicated in the inventories and wills of the period.
4. Stavisky, "Negro Craftsmanship in Early America," *supra* note 2, pp. 322–325.
5. Jernegan, *supra* note 3, pp. 232–234.
6. *Ibid.*
7. Eugene D. Genovese, *Roll, Jordan, Roll* (New York: Pantheon Books, 1974), p. 338.
8. *Compendium of the Census of 1850,* p. 94; cited in Charles H. Wesley, *Negro Labor in the United States, 1850–1925* (New York: Russell & Russell, 1967; originally published in 1927), p. 25.
9. Lorenzo J. Greene and Carter G. Woodson, *The Negro Wage Earner* (Washington, D.C.: Association for the Study of Negro Life and History, 1930), p. 10.
10. *Id.*, pp. 11–12.
11. Booker T. Washington, *The Story of the Negro*, Vol. II, p. 63; cited in Sterling D. Spero and Abram L. Harris, *The Black Worker* (New York: Columbia University Press, 1931), p. 5.
12. Spero and Harris, *supra* note 11, p. 6.
13. Ulrich B. Phillips, *American Negro Slavery,* Chap. XX; cited in Spero and Harris, *supra* note 11, pp. 5–6.
14. Richard C. Wade, *Slavery in the Cities* (New York: Oxford University Press, 1964), p. 38.
15. Frederick Douglass, *Narrative of the Life of Frederick Douglass, An American Slave* (Cambridge, Mass.: Harvard University Press, 1960), pp. 138–139.

16. *A Digest of All the Ordinances of the City of Savannah . . . which were in Force on the 1st January 1858*, pp. 417–418; cited in Wade, *supra* note 14, p. 41.

17. Dawson and DeSaussure, *Census of Charleston 1848*, pp. 31–35; cited in Leonard Price Stavisky, "Industrial Realism in Ante-Bellum Charleston," *Journal of Negro History*, July 1951, p. 311.

18. Wade, *supra* note 14, p. 33.

19. Greene and Woodson, *supra* note 9, p. 13.

20. Wade, *supra* note 14, p. 33.

21. Francis and Theresa Pulszky, *White, Red, Black Sketches of American Society in the United States During the Visit of Their Guests*, Vol. II, p. 98; cited in Wade, *supra* note 14, p. 36.

22. Greene and Woodson, *supra* note 9, p. 17.

23. *Id.*, p. 13.

24. *De Bow's Review*, February 1852, p. 183. *De Bow's Review* was published from 1846 to 1880, first in Charleston and later in New Orleans.

25. Wade, *supra* note 14, p. 33.

26. *Id.*, p. 36.

27. *Charleston Mercury*, November 19, 1853; cited in Wesley, *supra* note 8, p. 7.

28. Greene and Woodson, *supra* note 9, p. 13.

29. Charles Nordhoff, *America for Free Workingmen*, p. 7; cited in Wesley, *supra* note 8, p. 15.

30. Ethel Armes, *The Story of Coal and Iron in Alabama*, pp. 77–78; cited in Wesley, *supra* note 8, p. 104.

31. Herbert R. Northrup, *Organized Labor and the Negro* (New York: Harper & Brothers, 1944), p. 102.

32. Wade, *supra* note 14, p. 43.

33. Robert S. Starobin, *Industrial Slavery in the Old South* (New York: Oxford University Press, 1970), p. 231.

34. Wesley, *supra* note 8, p. 142.

35. See Starobin, *supra* note 33, Chap. 4.

36. Cited in John Stephens Durham, "The Labor Unions and the Negro," *Atlantic Monthly*, February 1898, pp. 222–231.

37. Spero and Harris, *supra* note 11, pp. 7–8.

38. For an interesting discussion of this development, see Starobin, *supra* note 33, Chap. 4.

39. *Frederick Douglass' Paper*, March 4, 1853.

40. Wesley, *supra* note 8, p. 148.

41. *Id.*, p. 145.

42. Paul B. Worthman and James R. Green, "Black Workers in the New South, 1865–1915," in Nathan I. Huggins et al., eds., *Issues in the Afro-American Experience* (New York: Harcourt Brace Jovanovich, 1971), pp. 52–53.

43. Spero and Harris, *supra* note 11, p. 15.

44. *Locomotive Firemen's Magazine*, December 1890, p. 1094.

45. "The Georgia Railroad Strike," *Outlook*, June 5, 1909, p. 310; cited in Spero and Harris, *supra* note 11, p. 289.

46. *Id.*, p. 291.

47. Gunnar Myrdal, *An American Dilemma*, Vol. 1 (New York: Harper & Brothers, 1944), p. 206.

48. *Sixteenth Annual Report of the Commission on Labor, Strikes and Lockouts* (Washington, D.C.: Bureau of Labor, 1901), pp. 413–465; cited in Wesley, *supra* note 8, p. 237.
49. Spero and Harris, *supra* note 11, p. 14.
50. C. Vann Woodward, *The Strange Career of Jim Crow,* 2nd ed. (New York: Oxford University Press, 1966), p. 98.
51. C. Vann Woodward, *Origins of the New South, 1877–1913* (Baton Rouge, La.: Louisiana State University Press, 1951), p. 360.
52. Frenise A. Logan, "The Economic Status of the Town Negro in Post-Reconstruction North Carolina," *North Carolina Historical Review,* October 1958, p. 454.
53. Robert C. Weaver, *Negro Labor, A National Problem* (New York: Harcourt, Brace & Co., 1946), p. 6.
54. Philadelphia *Press,* quoted in *The Christian Recorder,* July 12, 1894.
55. Federation of Organized Trades and Labor Unions, Fourteenth Annual Convention, *Proceedings,* 1894, p. 55.
56. American Federation of Labor, Tenth Annual Convention, *Proceedings,* 1890, p. 31.
57. Roger W. Shugg, "The New Orleans General Strike of 1892," *Louisiana Historical Quarterly,* April 1938, pp. 543–547.
58. Letter to Frank D. Hamlin, April 30, 1890; letter to Charles W. Murphy, May 16, 1890; letter to Fred J. Carr, December 8, 1891; Samuel Gompers' Letter-Books, AFL Archives, Washington, D.C.
59. *Report to the Sixteenth American Federation of Labor Convention,* 1896, p. 19.
60. Samuel Gompers, *American Federationist,* September 1905, p. 636.
61. Cigar Makers Union, *International Proceedings,* 1865, p. 60.
62. The meaning of the elimination in 1871 of Article IX, the exclusion clause in the constitution of the Cigar Makers Union, is explained in *The Working Man's Advocate,* November 25, 1871, p. 1.
63. Frank E. Wolfe, *Admission to American Trade Unions* (Baltimore: Johns Hopkins University Press, 1912), p. 114.
64. *Constitution of the Brotherhood of Locomotive Firemen and Enginemen,* 1906, Section 162, pp. 77–78.
65. *Constitution of the Brotherhood of Railway Carmen of America,* adopted 1890, revised August 1921, Section 6, Clause (a), p. 41.
66. "Handbook of American Trade Unions," Bulletin 506 (Washington, D.C.: U.S. Department of Commerce, Bureau of Labor Statistics, 1929), p. 80.
67. *Constitution and General Rules of the Order of Sleeping Car Conductors,* effective April 1, 1925, Article XVI, p. 26.
68. *Supra* note 66, p. 104.
69. *Id.,* p. 208.
70. *Electrical World,* April 1903, p. 102.
71. Woodward, *supra* note 51, p. 360.
72. Durham, *supra* note 36, pp. 222–231.
73. *Ibid.*
74. Ira De A. Reid, *Negro Membership in American Labor Unions* (New York: National Urban League, 1930).
75. *First Report,* July 1943–December 1944 (Washington, D.C.: Fair Employment Practice Committee, 1945), pp. 81–82.

76. Petition of Negro steelworkers employed at the Atlantic Steel Company, Atlanta, Georgia, to Boyd Wilson, international representative, United Steelworkers of America, CIO, February 5, 1958. (Copy in NAACP files. NAACP file material cited hereinafter is in the National Association for the Advancement of Colored People Papers, Manuscript Division, Library of Congress.)

77. Complaint of James Mills to the President's Committee on Government Contracts, June 30, 1958. Complaint of Mid Duncan to PCGC, June 30, 1958. Complaint of Nathaniel Brown to PCGC, June 30, 1958. Complaint of Julius C. Wynn to PCGC, June 30, 1958. (Copies in NAACP files.)

78. *Atlantic Steel Co. and United Steelworkers of America Local No. 2401,* NLRB Case No. R–2964, Motion to Rescind Certification, filed October 29, 1962; Affidavit of Nathaniel Brown to the NLRB, filed October 29, 1962; Affidavit of J. C. Wynn to the NLRB, filed October 29, 1962; *Atlantic Steel Co., et al.,* Memorandum Supporting Motion, filed October 29, 1962. The NLRB regional director refused to issue complaints for the reason that "[t]he evidence fails to show that Respondent has, within six months prior to the filing of the charge herein, failed to entertain or process any grievance presented to it or that it has interpreted any claim adversely to the complainant. I am, therefore, refusing to issue complaint in this matter." Of course, the substance of the blacks' complaints was that because of the restrictions upon transfer into all-white departments and the dual system of classification and wages for identical jobs performed, violations were occurring on a day-to-day basis. The regional director refused to interpret the violations as continuing in nature, and thus dismissed the charges on a technicality.

79. Carl Brent Swisher, *The Growth of Constitutional Power in the United States* (Chicago: University of Chicago Press, 1946), p. 238.

80. Alfred W. Blumrosen, "Legal Process and Labor Law," in William M. Evan, ed., *Law and Sociology* (Glencoe, Ill.: Free Press of Glencoe, 1962), p. 211.

81. C. Wright Mills, *The New Men of Power* (New York: Harcourt, Brace, & Co., 1948), pp. 229, 230, 232.

82. *Alexander* v. *Gardner-Denver Co.,* 346 F. Supp. 1012, 4 FEP Cases 1205 (D. Colo. 1971); *affirmed,* 466 F.2d 1209, 4 FEP Cases 1210 (10th Cir. 1972); *reversed,* 415 U.S. 987, 7 FEP Cases 81 (1974).

83. The opinion of the Supreme Court in the *Civil Rights Cases* written by Justice Joseph P. Bradley contains the phrase "badges and incidents" of slavery. *Civil Rights Cases,* 109 U.S. 3 (1883).

84. *Current Population Reports,* Series P–60, No. 86, Consumer Income, "Characteristics of the Low-Income Population: 1971"; and Series P–60, No. 88, "Characteristics of the Low-Income Population: 1972" (Washington, D.C.: U.S. Bureau of the Census, 1972 and 1973, respectively).

85. *Unemployment in Poverty Areas, 1973* (Washington, D.C.: U.S. Bureau of Labor Statistics, August 28, 1974), p. 2.

86. *Current Population Reports,* Series P–60, No. 98, "Characteristics of the Low-Income Population: 1973" (Washington, D.C.: U.S. Bureau of the Census, 1975), p. 1.

87. *Current Population Reports,* Special Studies, P–23, No. 48, "The Social and Economic Status of the Black Population in the United States, 1973" (Washington, D.C.: U.S. Bureau of the Census, 1974), Table 30, p. 46.

88. "The Employment Situation: February 1975," U.S. Department of Labor, press release, Washington, D.C., p. 2. See also James Reston, "41% of Black Teen-agers Jobless!" *The New York Times,* February 23, 1975, Section 4, p. 13.
89. *Current Population Reports,* Special Studies, P–23, No. 54, "The Social and Economic Status of the Black Population in the United States, 1974" (Washington, D.C.: U.S. Bureau of the Census, 1975), Table 9, p. 25.
90. *Ibid.*
91. *Ibid.*
92. *Ibid.*
93. *Ibid.*
94. *Current Population Reports,* Series P–23, No. 42, "The Social and Economic Status of the Black Population in the United States, 1971" (Washington, D.C.: U.S. Bureau of the Census, 1972), Table 17, p. 30.
95. *Equal Employment Opportunity Report Number 1,* Part 1 (Washington, D.C.: Equal Employment Opportunity Commission, 1966), p. 3.
96. Cited in Michael Meyerson, "ILGWU, Fighting for Lower Wages," *Ramparts,* October 1969, p. 51. Dr. Keyserling confirmed the existence of the study in an interview with David Gumpert, *Wall Street Journal,* December 30, 1970, p. 22; see also *Report of the General Executive Board to the 32nd Convention,* International Ladies' Garment Workers' Union, May 12, 1965, p. 116.
97. *Report of the National Advisory Commission on Civil Disorders* (Washington, D.C.: U.S. Government Printing Office, March 1, 1968), p. 124.

Chapter 1

1. Vern Countryman, *Discrimination and the Law* (Chicago: University of Chicago Press, 1965), p. 1.
2. 437 F.2d 1286 (5th Cir. 1971); *petition for rehearing en banc granted, argued* October 19, 1971; *reversed and remanded per curiam,* 461 F.2d 1171 (5th Cir. 1972).
3. 437 F.2d p. 1292.
4. See *Arkansas Oak Flooring Co.,* v. *U.M.W.* 351 U.S. 62, 37 LRRM 2828 (1956).
5. 334 U.S. 1 (1948).
6. 323 U.S. 192, 15 LRRM 708 (1944).
7. *Id.,* p. 202, 15 LRRM p. 712.
8. Neil M. Herring, "Judicial Remedies for Racial Discrimination by Labor Unions," Preliminary Draft of a Divisional Essay (New Haven, Conn.: Yale University Law School, Labor Law Division, March 1963), p. 54. See also Neil M. Herring, "The 'Fair Representation' Doctrine: An Effective Weapon Against Union Racial Discrimination?" *Maryland Law Review,* Spring 1964, pp. 113, 146–162; and Sanford Jay Rosen, "The Law and Racial Discrimination in Employment," in Arthur M. Ross and Herbert Hill, eds., *Employment, Race and Poverty* (New York: Harcourt, Brace & World, 1967).
9. Countryman, *supra* note 1, p. 22.

10. Timothy L. Jenkins, "Study of Federal Efforts to End Job Bias: A History, a Status Report, and a Prognosis," *Howard Law Journal,* Summer 1968, pp. 259, 262.
11. Samuel C. Jackson, "Using the Law to Attack Discrimination in Employment," *Washburn Law Journal,* Winter 1969, pp. 191–192.
12. See Testimony of Herbert Hill, national labor director, NAACP, before the New York State Advisory Committee, U.S. Commission on Civil Rights, *Hearings on Racial Discrimination in the Construction Industry in New York State,* Albany, N.Y. (October 21, 1970), NAACP document; Herbert Hill, "Twenty Years of State Fair Employment Practice Commissions: A Critical Analysis with Recommendations," *Buffalo Law Review,* Fall 1964, pp. 22–69.
13. *Lefkowitz, etc.* v. *Farrell, et al.* (New York State Commission for Human Rights, Case No. C 9287–63), *affirmed sub nom. New York State Commission for Human Rights* v. *Farrell,* 43 Misc.2d 958, 252 N.Y.S.2d 649, 1 FEP Cases 100, 59 LRRM 3050 (N.Y. Sup. Ct. 1964), *affirmed,* 24 A.D.2d 128, 264 N.Y.S.2d 489, 1 FEP Cases 112, 60 LRRM 2509 (N.Y. App. Div. First Dept. 1965).
14. *Equal Employment Opportunity Commission, et al.* v. *Local 638 and Local 28 of the Sheet Metal Workers International Association, et al.,* 401 F. Supp. 467, 12 FEP Cases ——, 10 EPD para. 10,347 (S.D. N.Y. July 18, 1975).
15. *Hunter* v. *Sullivan Dress Shop,* C–1439–46, New York State Commission Against Discrimination (1947).
16. *Holmes* v. *Falikman,* C–7580–61, New York State Commission for Human Rights (1963).
17. These included EEOC Charge Nos. TNY 9–0648, 2–1463, 9–0059, and 1–1754. In at least one of the cases in which the EEOC found reasonable cause—Charge No. YNK 3–063—the international union itself was a respondent.
18. EEOC Charge No. TNY 1–1413, filed March 25, 1971.
19. These included Chicago (EEOC Charge No. TCH 8–0277); Kansas City, Missouri (EEOC Charge No. TKC 1–1101); Memphis (TME 1–1091); San Francisco (TSF 3–0853); Baltimore (TBA 3–0084); Philadelphia (TPA 2–0165); Cleveland (TCL 1–0805); Atlanta (TAT 0–1245); Charlotte (TCT 2–0468, 2–0043, 1–0002, 1–0004, 1–0006, 1–0008, 1–0010); and Birmingham (TBI 0–0954, 1–0357, 1–0195, 1–0873, 9–0098, 2–0875).
20. 43 U.S.C. Section 2000e *et seq.*
21. Public Law 92–261.
22. See *Heart of Atlanta Motel, Inc.* v. *U.S.,* 379 U.S. 241 (1964).
23. 347 U.S. 483 (1954).
24. 251 F. Supp. 184, 1 FEP Cases 120, 61 LRRM 2458 (N.D. Tenn. 1966). See also *Jenkins* v. *United Gas Corp.,* 400 F.2d 28, 33, 1 FEP Cases 364, 367, 69 LRRM 2152, 2155 (5th Cir. 1968); *Oatis* v. *Crown-Zellerbach Corp.,* 398 F.2d 496, 499, 1 FEP Cases 328, 330, 68 LRRM 2781, 2784 (5th Cir. 1968); *Bowe* v. *Colgate-Palmolive Co.,* 416 F.2d 711, 715, 2 FEP Cases 121, 123 (7th Cir. 1969); *Johnson* v. *Georgia Highway Express, Inc.,* 417 F.2d 1122, 2 FEP Cases 231 (5th Cir. 1969); *Carr* v. *Conoco Plastics,* 423 F.2d 57, 2 FEP Cases 388 (5th Cir. 1970), *cert. denied,* 400 U.S. 951, 2 FEP Cases 1120 (1970); *Albemarle Paper Co.,* v. *Moody* 422 U.S. 405, 414, n. 8, 10 FEP Cases 1181, 1186, n. 8 (1975).

25. *First Annual Report* (Washington, D.C.: Equal Employment Opportunity Commission, March 1, 1967), p. 56.
26. 380 U.S. 1 (1965).
27. 400 U.S. 1004, 3 FEP Cases 70 (1971).
28. 421 F.2d 888, 2 FEP Cases 377 (5th Cir. 1970).
29. *Supra* note 23.
30. 433 F.2d 421, 2 FEP Cases 1017 (8th Cir. 1970).
31. *McDonnell Douglas Corp.* v. *Green*, 411 U.S. 792, 5 FEP Cases 965 (1973).
32. 400 F.2d 28, 1 FEP Cases 364, 69 LRRM 2152 (5th Cir. 1968).
33. *Id.*, p. 32, 1 FEP Cases p. 366, 69 LRRM p. 2154.
34. Brief for the United States and the EEOC as *Amicus Curiae, Jenkins* v. *United Gas, supra* note 32, p. 13.
35. *Supra* note 32, p. 33, 1 FEP Cases p. 367, 69 LRRM p. 2155.
36. *Id.*, p. 31, 1 FEP Cases p. 365, 69 LRRM p. 2154 (footnotes omitted).
37. *Id.*, p. 35, 1 FEP Cases p. 368, 69 LRRM pp. 2156–2157.
38. 313 F.2d 284 (5th Cir. 1963).
39. *Supra* note 32, p. 34, 1 FEP Cases p. 368, 69 LRRM p. 2156.
40. 431 F.2d 455, 2 FEP Cases 788, 912 (5th Cir. 1970).
41. *Id.*, n. 1.
42. *Id.*, pp. 460–461, 2 FEP Cases p. 792.
43. *Id.*, pp. 462–463, 2 FEP Cases pp. 793–794.
44. *Supra* note 28.
45. *Id.*, p. 891, 2 FEP Cases p. 378.
46. *Id.*, p. 894, 2 FEP Cases pp. 380, 381.
47. *Ibid.*
48. 1 FEP Cases 383, 384, 385, 69 LRRM 2237, 2238, 2240 (W. D. Tenn. 1967).
49. 316 F. Supp. 401, 2 FEP Cases 821 (C.D. Calif. 1970), *affirmed as modified,* 472 F.2d 631, 5 FEP Cases 267, 5 EPD para. 8089 (9th Cir. 1972).
50. *Id.*, p. 403, 2 FEP Cases p. 822.
51. *Ibid.*
52. 279 F. Supp. 505, 1 FEP Cases 260, 67 LRRM 2098 (E.D. Va. 1968).
53. See, for example, *United States* v. *Local 189, Papermakers & Paperworkers, and Crown Zellerbach Corp.,* 416 F.2d 980, 1 FEP Cases 875, 71 LRRM 3070 (5th Cir. 1969), *cert. denied,* 397 U.S. 919, 2 FEP Cases 426 (1970); *Robinson* v. *Lorillard Corp.,* 444 F.2d 791, 798, 3 FEP Cases 653, 657–658 (4th Cir. 1971), *cert. dismissed,* 404 U.S. 1006 (1971); *United States* v. *Bethlehem Steel Corp.,* 446 F.2d 652, 657–659, 3 FEP Cases 589, 592–593 (2nd Cir. 1971); *United States* v. *Georgia Power Co.,* 474 F.2d 906, 5 FEP Cases 587 (5th Cir. 1973); *Johnson* v. *Goodyear Tire & Rubber Co.,* 491 F.2d 1364, 7 FEP Cases 627 (5th Cir. 1974); *Pettway* v. *American Cast Iron Pipe Co.,* 494 F.2d 211, 7 FEP Cases 1115 (5th Cir. 1974).
54. See, for example, *Dobbins* v. *Electrical Workers (IBEW), Local 212,* 292 F. Supp. 413, 1 FEP Cases 387, 2 FEP Cases 180 (S.D. Ohio 1968); *United States* v. *Sheet Metal Workers, Local 36,* 416 F.2d 123, 2 FEP Cases 127 (8th Cir. 1969); *EEOC* v. *Plumbers, Local 189 (Mechanical Contractors Association of Central Ohio, Inc.),* 311 F. Supp. 468, 2 FEP Cases 170 (S.D. Ohio 1970), *vacated on other grounds,* 438 F.2d 408, 3 FEP Cases 193 (6th Cir. 1971), *cert. denied,* 404 U.S. 832, 3 FEP Cases 1030 (1971).
55. 416 F.2d 980, 1 FEP Cases 875, 71 LRRM 3070 (5th Cir. 1969), *affirming* 282 F. Supp. 39, 1 FEP Cases 820, 71 LRRM 2738 (E.D. La. 1968).

56. 431 F.2d 245, 2 FEP Cases 895 (10th Cir. 1970), *reversing* 300 F. Supp. 653, 2 FEP Cases 102 (D. Okla. 1969); *cert. denied*, 401 U.S. 954, 3 FEP Cases 193 (1971).
57. *Id.*, pp. 247–248, 2 FEP Cases p. 897.
58. See also *Gunn* v. *Layne & Bowler, Inc., supra* note 48; and *Johnson* v. *Georgia Highway*, 417 F.2d 1122, 2 FEP Cases 231 (5th Cir. 1969), *reversing* 47 F.R.D. 327, 1 FEP Cases 637, 70 LRRM 2664 (N.D. Ga. 1968).
59. 291 F. Supp. 786, 1 FEP Cases 440, 69 LRRM 2601, 300 F. Supp. 709, 1 FEP Cases 759, 71 LRRM 2406, 304 F. Supp. 1116, 2 FEP Cases 177 (D. Mich. 1969–70); *reversed*, 429 F.2d 324, 2 FEP Cases 687, 869 (6th Cir. 1970); *affirmed per curiam*, 402 U.S. 689, 3 FEP Cases 508, 3 EPD para. 8216 (1971).
60. *Supra* note 28.
61. 428 F.2d 303, 2 FEP Cases 725 (5th Cir. 1970).
62. 416 F.2d 711, 2 FEP Cases 121 (7th Cir. 1969).
63. See *Carey* v. *Westinghouse Electric Corp.*, 375 U.S. 261, 55 LRRM 2042 (1964).
64. The Supreme Court's affirmance by a court divided equally creates no precedent. See *Durant* v. *Essex Co.*, 7 Wall. 107, 110, 19 L.Ed. 154, 157 (1869); *Ohio, ex rel. Eaton* v. *Price*, 364 U.S. 263, 264, 80 S. Ct. 1463, 1474 (1960). Nor, of course, does it indicate the grounds on which any of the justices agree or disagree.
65. 346 F. Supp. 1012, 4 FEP Cases 1205 (D. Colo. 1971); *affirmed*, 466 F.2d 1209, 4 FEP Cases 1210 (10th Cir. 1972); *reversed*, 415 U.S. 36, 94 S. Ct. 1011, 7 FEP Cases 81 (1974).
66. 401 U.S. 424, 3 FEP Cases 175 (1971).
67. *New York Times*, March 21, 1971.
68. *Supra* note 66, p. 433, 3 FEP Cases p. 178.

Chapter 2

1. *Prigg* v. *Pennsylvania*, 16 Pet. (U.S.) 539 (1842); and *Ableman* v. *Booth*, 21 How. (U.S.) 506 (1859), respectively.
2. *Scott* v. *Sandford*, 19 How. (U.S.) 393 (1857).
3. *Ibid.*
4. The *Civil Rights Cases*, 109 U.S. 3 (1883). See also *Hodges* v. *United States*, 203 U.S. 1 (1906).
5. 392 U.S. 409 (1968).
6. *Id.*, p. 445.
7. 14 Stat. 27 (1866).
8. *Ibid.*
9. *Ibid.*
10. Senate Executive Doc. No. 2, 39th Cong., 1st Sess., Vol. II, p. 32.
11. *Id.*, p. 22.
12. *Id.*, p. 21.
13. James M. McPherson, *The Struggle for Equality* (Princeton, N.J.: Princeton University Press, 1964), p. 41.

14. George R. Bentley, *A History of the Freedmen's Bureau* (Philadelphia: University of Pennsylvania Press, 1955), p. 132.
15. *Id.,* p. 151.
16. John Hope Franklin, *Reconstruction After the Civil War* (Chicago: University of Chicago Press, 1961), pp. 48–49.
17. *Congressional Globe,* 39th Cong., 1st Sess. (1866), p. 1160.
18. *Id.,* p. 1159.
19. *Id.,* p. 1833.
20. Milton R. Konvitz, *The Constitution and Civil Rights* (New York: Columbia University Press, 1947), pp. 4–5.
21. 18 Stat. L. 140 (1870).
22. 18 Stat. L. 335 (1875).
23. 10 *Congressional Record* 952 (February 3, 1875).
24. Konvitz, *supra* note 20, pp. 6–7.
25. *Supra* note 4.
26. *Ibid.*
27. *Ibid.*
28. *Ibid.*
29. *Ibid.*
30. *Ibid.*
31. *Ibid.*
32. 203 U.S. 1 (1906).
33. *Supra* note 5.
34. *Id.,* p. 413.
35. *Id.,* p. 421.
36. *Id.,* p. 422.
37. *Id.,* pp. 426–427.
38. *Id.,* pp. 427–428.
39. *Id.,* p. 436.
40. *Id.,* p. 444.
41. *Id.,* p. 415.
42. *Id.,* pp. 416–417.
43. *Johnson* v. *Railway Express Agency Inc.,* 421 U.S. 454, 10 FEP Cases 817 (May 19, 1975).
44. See Note, "Racial Discrimination in Employment Under the Civil Rights Act of 1866," *University of Chicago Law Review,* Spring 1969, p. 615.
45. 292 F. Supp. 413, 1 FEP Cases 387, 69 LRRM 2313 (S.D. Ohio 1968).
46. *Ibid.*
47. 437 F.2d 1011, 3 FEP Cases 99 (5th Cir. 1971).
48. *Ibid.*
49. 438 F.2d 757, 3 FEP Cases 146 (3rd Cir. 1971).
50. ——F. Supp.——, 2 FEP Cases 995, 997 (E.D. Pa. 1970).
51. 438 F.2d 757, 760, 3 FEP Cases 146, 148.
52. 431 F.2d 1097, 2 FEP Cases 942 (5th Cir. 1970); *cert. denied,* 401 U.S. 948, 3 FEP Cases 193, 3 EPD para. 8127 (1971).
53. 427 F.2d 476, 2 FEP Cases 574 (7th Cir. 1970); *reversing and remanding* 301 F. Supp. 663, 1 FEP Cases 858, 71 LRRM 2886 (N.D. Ill. 1969); *cert. denied sub nom.,* 400 U.S. 911, 2 FEP Cases 1059 (1970).
54. *Ibid.*
55. *Waters* (II), 502 F.2d 1309, 8 FEP Cases 577 (7th Cir. 1974).

56. *Supra* note 43.
57. 304 F. Supp. 603, 2 FEP Cases 198 (E.D. La. 1969).
58. *Ibid.*
59. *Ibid.*
60. *Supra* note 57, pp. 609–610, 2 FEP Cases p. 203.
61. *Id.*, p. 611, 2 FEP Cases p. 204.
62. *Supra* note 53.
63. *Supra* note 5.
64. 427 F.2d 476, 482, 2 FEP Cases 574, 578 (7th Cir. 1970).
65. *Id.*, p. 483, 2 FEP Cases p. 579.
66. *Id.*, p. 485, 2 FEP Cases p. 580.
67. *Id.*, p. 488, 2 FEP Cases p. 583.
68. *Supra* note 52.
69. *Quarles* v. *Philip Morris, Inc.*, 279 F. Supp. 505, 1 FEP Cases 260, 67 LRRM 2098 (E.D. Va. 1968).
70. *Local 189, United Papermakers and Paperworkers, AFL-CIO, and Crown Zellerbach* v. *United States*, 416 F.2d 980, 1 FEP Cases 875, 71 LRRM 3070 (5th Cir. 1969); *affirming* 282 F. Supp. 39, 1 FEP Cases 820, 71 LRRM 2738 (E.D. La. 1968); *cert. denied*, 397 U.S. 919, 2 FEP Cases 426 (1970).
71. Department of Justice Memorandum submitted by Senator Joseph Clark on April 8, 1964, in *The Civil Rights Act of 1964* (Washington, D.C.: BNA Books, 1964), p. 326.
72. Interpretive Memorandum of Senators Joseph Clark and Clifford Case, *supra* note 71, p. 329.
73. *Supra* note 69.
74. *Ibid.*
75. *Ibid.*
76. *Supra* note 70.
77. 429 F.2d 498, 2 FEP Cases 820 (5th Cir. 1970).
78. William B. Gould, "The Emerging Law Against Racial Discrimination in Employment," *Northwestern University Law Review*, July-August 1969, p. 362. See also Alfred W. Blumrosen, "Seniority and Equal Employment Opportunity: A Glimmer of Hope," *Rutgers Law Review*, Winter 1969, pp. 268–317; William B. Gould, "Seniority and the Black Worker—Reflections on *Quarles* and Its Implications," *Texas Law Review*, June 1969, p. 1039; Peter B. Doeringer, "Promotion Systems and Equal Employment Opportunity," *Proceedings of the Nineteenth Annual Winter Meeting* (Madison, Wis.: Industrial Relations Research Association, 1967), pp. 228–289.
79. *Sixth Annual Report* (Washington, D.C.: Equal Employment Opportunity Commission, March 30, 1972), p. 27.
80. *Brown* v. *Gaston County Dyeing Machine Co.*, 457 F.2d 1377, 4 FEP Cases 514 (4th Cir. 1972), *cert. denied*, 409 U.S. 982, 5 FEP Cases 149 (1972).
81. *Johnson* v. *Goodyear Tire & Rubber Co.*, 491 F.2d 1364, 7 FEP Cases 627 (5th Cir. 1974).
82. *Carpenters Union, Local 600 (Mechanical Handling Systems, Inc.)* v. *NLRB*, 365 U.S. 651, 47 LRRM 2900 (1965).
83. *Supra* note 43.
84. *EEOC* v. *Detroit Edison Co.*, 515 F.2d 301, 10 FEP Cases 239, 1063 (6th Cir. 1975).
85. *Supra* note 45.

86. *Supra* note 53.
87. *Waters, et al.* v. *Wisconsin Steel Works of International Harvester Co.*, 8 FEP Cases 234 (N.D. Ill. 1973), *affirmed in part, reversed in part, and remanded in part*, 502 F.2d 1309, 8 FEP Cases 577, 8 EPD para. 9658 (7th Cir. 1974).
88. 452 F.2d 315, 4 FEP Cases 121 (8th Cir. 1972); *cert. denied*, 406 U.S. 950, 4 FEP Cases 771, 4 EPD para. 7818; *judgment entered*, ——F. Supp. ——, 9 FEP Cases 1191, 4 EPD para. 7853 (D. Minn. 1972).
89. *Ibid.*
90. *Ibid.*
91. *Ibid.*
92. *Chance* v. *Board of Examiners*, 496 F.2d 820, 7 FEP Cases 1207 (2nd Cir. 1974).
93. *Supra* note 53.
94. *Supra* note 49.
95. *Supra* note 43.

Chapter 3

1. 49 Stat. 449 (1935); 61 Stat. 136 (1947), as amended; 29 U.S.C. Sections 151–68 (1958), as amended; 29 U.S.C. Sections 153–64 (Supp. II, 1959–1960).
2. 44 Stat. 577 (1926), 45 U.S.C. Sections 151–88, as amended.
3. See *Glover* v. *St. Louis & San Francisco Railroad*, 393 U.S. 324, 70 LRRM 2097 (1968).
4. *Independent Metal Workers, Locals 1 and 2*, 147 NLRB 1573, 56 LRRM 1289 (1964).
5. NLRA Sections 9(c)(1) and 11, as amended; 29 U.S.C. Sections 159(c)(1) and 161 (1970).
6. NLRA Section 10(c), as amended; 29 U.S.C. Section 160(c) (1970).
7. NLRA Section 10(e), as amended; 29 U.S.C. Section 160(e) (1970).
8. See, *e.g.*, National Industrial Recovery Act, Chap. 90, 48 Stat. 195 (1933); Wagner-Peyser Act, Chap. 49, 48 Stat. 113, as amended, 29 U.S.C. Section 49 *et seq.* (Supp, III 1973); Fair Labor Standards Act, Chap. 676, 52 Stat. 1060, as amended, 29 U.S.C. Section 201 *et seq.* (Supp. III 1973).
9. Interviews by author with Henry Lee Moon, Frank Horne, and Ted Poston, New York, June 10–19, 1968.
10. *Opportunity*, March 1934, p. 73.
11. Allen F. Kifer, *The Negro Under the New Deal* (Ann Arbor, Mich.: University Microfilms), No. 61–3124, p. 226.
12. *Crisis*, September 1934, pp. 262 *et seq.*
13. John P. Davis, in *Crisis*, October 1934, p. 298.
14. *Crisis*, September 1934, p. 279.
15. Robert C. Weaver, "A Wage Differential Based on Race," *Crisis*, August 1934, p. 236.
16. T. Arnold Hill, "Old Settings in New Scenes," *Opportunity*, February 1934, p. 58.
17. Kifer, *supra* note 11, p. 226.

18. John P. Davis, "The Maid-Well Garment Case," *Crisis,* December 1934, p. 356.
19. See *Schechter Poultry Corp.* v. *United States,* 294 U.S. 495 (1935).
20. W. E. B. Du Bois, "The AF of L," *Crisis,* December 1933, p. 292.
21. *Ibid.*
22. Urban League Memorandum, "Negro Working Population and National Recovery," January 4, 1937.
23. Roy Wilkins to Horace R. Cayton, October 30, 1934; cited in Horace R. Cayton and George S. Mitchell, *Black Workers and the New Unions* (Chapel Hill, N.C.: University of North Carolina Press, 1939), pp. 413–414.
24. Jesse O. Thomas, "Negro Workers and Organized Labor," *Opportunity,* September 1934, p. 278.
25. Baltimore *Afro-American,* April 14, 1934, p. 4, col. 2.
26. Raymond Wolters, *Negroes and the Great Depression: The Problem of Economic Recovery* (Westport, Conn.: Greenwood Publishing Corp., 1970), pp. 176–177.
27. AFL, *Report of Proceedings, 1934 Convention,* pp. 330–332.
28. Walter White to William Green, NAACP press release, September 26, 1935.
29. Statement by John Brophy, November 15, 1935, NAACP files.
30. John Brophy, *A Miner's Life* (Madison, Wis.: University of Wisconsin Press, 1964), p. 246.
31. Walter White to John L. Lewis, November 27, 1935, NAACP files.
32. Wolters, *supra* note 26, p. 185.
33. Roy Wilkins, memorandum to NAACP office staff, March 23, 1934.
34. Harry E. Davis to Walter White, March 20, 1934.
35. T. Arnold Hill to Walter White, April 3, 1934.
36. T. Arnold Hill, "Labor Marches On," *Opportunity,* April 1934, pp. 120–121.
37. Wolters, *supra* note 26, p. 184.
38. *Id.,* p. 185.
39. *Id.,* pp. 185–186.
40. *Id.,* p. 187.
41. FEPC *Hearings.* In the Matter of a *Hearing to Hear Evidence of Complaints of Racial Discrimination in Employment on Certain Railroads in the United States.* No case number. Transcript of proceedings held in Washington, D.C., on September 15–18, 1943. Exhibits, correspondence, reports, docketed cases, summaries, findings, directives, summaries of complaints, operational statistics for cases docketed and closed, agreements between individual railroad companies and unions, resolutions against railroad discrimination, complaints and agreements on railroad employment, seniority lists, and questionnaires on discriminatory employment practices in the railroad industry. Record Group 228, National Archives Building, Washington, D.C. See Charles Zaid, *Preliminary Inventory No. 147,* Records of the Committee on Fair Employment Practice (Washington, D.C.: The National Archives, 1962).
42. *Final Report,* June 28, 1946 (Washington, D.C.: Fair Employment Practice Committee, 1947), p. 12.
43. Supreme Court of the United States, October Term, 1944, Nos. 37 and 45, Brief for the United States as *Amicus Curiae,* pp. 11–12.
44. 323 U.S. 192, 15 LRRM 708 (1944).
45. 323 U.S. 210, 15 LRRM 715 (1944).

46. 323 U.S. 192, 202–203, 15 LRRM 708 (1944).
47. Harry H. Wellington, *Labor and the Legal Process* (New Haven, Conn.: Yale University Press, 1968), p. 145.
48. *Ibid.*
49. Since the 1870s, the Fourteenth Amendment had been used to invalidate judicial action as constituting state action violative of procedural due process, and it was used to invalidate injunctions as state action violative of substantive due process in several labor cases where the injunction infringed upon freedom of speech of pickets—for example, in *AFL* v. *Swing,* 312 U.S. 321, 7 LRRM 307 (1941). The equal protection clause had been applied to state action by the executive branch of state government—in *Yick Wo* v. *Hopkins,* 118 U.S. 356—and to state action by the legislative branch—for example, in *Missouri ex rel. Gaines* v. *Canada,* 305 U.S. 337. A company town ban on solicitation, enforced by criminal trespass sanctions and used to bar Jehovah's Witnesses, had been held to constitute state action in violation of the due process clause of the Fourteenth Amendment in *Marsh* v. *Alabama,* 326 U.S. 501 (1946). State action to enforce a racially discriminatory private contract was first prohibited in *Shelley* v. *Kraemer,* 344 U.S. 1 (1948).
50. Wellington, *supra* note 47, pp. 148–149.
51. 323 U.S. 192, 208–209, 15 LRRM 708, 715 (1944).
52. *Ibid.*
53. *Ibid.*
54. *Id.,* p. 204, 15 LRRM 713.
55. "The Law and Racial Discrimination in Employment," in Arthur M. Ross and Herbert Hill, eds., *Employment, Race, and Poverty* (New York: Harcourt, Brace & World, 1967), pp. 488–489.
56. *Ibid.*
57. 338 U.S. 232, 25 LRRM 2033 (1949).
58. 343 U.S. 768, 30 LRRM 2258 (1952). See also *Betts* v. *Easley,* 169 P.2d 831, 18 LRRM 2145 (Kans. Sup. Ct. 1946).
59. *Id.,* p. 774, 30 LRRM p. 2261.
60. *Id.,* pp. 773–774, 30 LRRM p. 2260.
61. 200 F.2d 302, 31 LRRM 2152 (3rd Cir. 1952).
62. 346 U.S. 840 (1953).
63. 223 F.2d 739, 36 LRRM 2290 (5th Cir. 1955).
64. In *Wallace Corporation* v. *NLRB,* 323 U.S. 248, 15 LRRM 697 (1944), the Supreme Court noted the similarities in the purpose of the National Labor Relations Act and the Railway Labor Act in that both provide for the certification of a collective bargaining agent and both foster and guarantee the bargaining process. The Court held that the duty of fair representation applied to both acts. This position was reaffirmed in *Ford Motor Company* v. *Huffman,* 345 U.S. 330, 31 LRRM 2548 (1953), a nonracial case.
65. 350 U.S. 892, 37 LRRM 2068 (1955).
66. 355 U.S. 41, 41 LRRM 2089 (1957).
67. 262 F.2d 359, 43 LRRM 2159 (6th Cir. 1958).
68. *Id.,* p. 363, 43 LRRM p. 2162.
69. 359 U.S. 935, 43 LRRM 2668 (1959). See Alfred W. Blumrosen's analysis of this case in *Ohio State Law Journal,* Winter 1961, pp. 21–38.
70. NLRA Section 9, as amended, 29 U.S.C. Section 159 (1970).

71. NLRA Section 10, as amended, 29 U.S.C. Section 160 (1970).
72. NLRA Section 8, as amended, 29 U.S.C. Section 158 (1970).
73. *General Cable Corp.*, 139 NLRB 1123, 51 LRRM 1444 (1962); *Medo Photo Supply Corp.* v. *NLRB*, 321 U.S. 678, 684, 14 LRRM 581, 584 (1944). See also *J. I. Case Co.* v. *NLRB*, 321 U.S. 332, 14 LRRM 501 (1944).
74. NLRA Sections 8 and 10, as amended, 29 U.S.C. Sections 158 and 160 (1970).
75. 62 NLRB 1075, 16 LRRM 242 (1945).
76. *Id.*, p. 1083, 16 LRRM 244.
77. See also *Veneer Products, Inc.*, 81 NLRB 492, 23 LRRM 1373 (1949); and *Atlanta Oak Flooring Company*, 62 NLRB 973, 16 LRRM 235 (1945).
78. *Tenth Annual Report* (Washington, D.C.: National Labor Relations Board, 1945).
79. *Ibid.*
80. 344 U.S. 1 (1948).
81. 344 U.S. 24 (1948).
82. 218 F.2d 913, 35 LRRM 2578 (9th Cir. 1955); *cert. denied, sub nom.*, *Union of Marine Cooks and Stewards* v. *NLRB*, 349 U.S. 909, 930, 36 LRRM 2099 (1955).
83. *Id.*, n. 3, p. 917, 35 LRRM 2581.
84. *Id.*, p. 916.
85. *Id.*, p. 914.
86. Labor Management Relations Act (Taft-Hartley Act), Chap. 120, 61 Stat. 136 (1947), as amended, 29 U.S.C. Section 141 *et seq.* (1970). Section 101 of the Taft-Hartley Act, 29 U.S.C. 158(a)(3), as amended, and (b)(2) (1970), prohibits the closed shop.
87. 93 *Congressional Record* 4193 (1947).
88. Taft-Hartley Act, Section 101, 29 U.S.C. Section 158(b)(1)(A) and (b)(2) (1970).
89. *Mountain Pacific, Seattle & Tacoma Chapters (Associated General Contractors)*, 119 NLRB 883, 41 LRRM 1460 (1958); *enforcement denied*, 270 F.2d 425, 44 LRRM 2802 (9th Cir. 1959).
90. *Local 357, Teamsters* v. *NLRB*, 365 U.S. 667, 47 LRRM 2906 (1961).
91. Michael I. Sovern, "The National Labor Relations Act and Racial Discrimination," *Columbia Law Review*, April 1962, pp. 563, 574.
92. 140 NLRB 54, 51 LRRM 1546 (1962).
93. *Id.*, p. 55, 51 LRRM 1546. The "clear court decisions" cited were *Brown* v. *Board of Education*, 349 U.S. 294 (1955); *Boynton* v. *Virginia*, 364 U.S. 454 (1960); *Bailey* v. *Patterson*, 369 U.S. 31 (1962); and *Burton* v. *Wilmington Parking Authority*, 365 U.S. 715 (1961). *Id.*, p. 55, n. 3.
94. *Id.*, p. 55.
95. *Ibid.*
96. Interview by author with Mrs. Barbara A. Morris, New York, April 26, 1972.
97. 140 NLRB 181, 51 LRRM 1584 (1962); *enforcement denied*, 326 F.2d 172, 54 LRRM 2715 (2nd Cir. 1963).
98. *Atlantic Steel Co. and United Steelworkers of America Local No. 2401*, NLRB Case No. R–2964, Motion to Rescind Certification, filed October 29, 1962; Affidavit of J. C. Wynn to the NLRB, filed October 29, 1962; Affidavit of Nathaniel Brown to the NLRB, filed October 29, 1962; *Atlantic*

Steel Co., et al., Memorandum Supporting Motion, filed October 29, 1962. See also Memorandum to Roy Wilkins, executive secretary, NAACP, from Herbert Hill, labor secretary, NAACP, re: The Atlantic Steel Co., Atlanta, Georgia, May 27, 1958. NAACP files.

99. National Labor Relations Board, press release, April 9, 1963.
100. *Independent Metal Workers, Locals 1 and 2*, 147 NLRB 1573, 56 LRRM 1289 (1964).
101. Robert L. Carter, "The National Labor Relations Board and Racial Discrimination," *Law in Transition Quarterly*, Spring 1965, pp. 89–90.
102. Report of trial examiner in 147 NLRB 1573, 56 LRRM 1289, 1291 (1964).
103. Brief of American Civil Liberties Union as *Amicus Curiae* before the NLRB, Case Nos. 23–CB–429 and 23–RC–1758, filed July 15, 1963.
104. *Ibid.*
105. *Ibid.*
106. *Ibid.*
107. 147 NLRB 1573, 1577, 56 LRRM 1289, 1294 (1964).
108. For example, see *Atlanta Oak Flooring Co.*, 62 NLRB 973, 16 LRRM 235 (1945); and *Larus & Brother Co.*, 62 NLRB 1075, 16 LRRM 242 (1945).
109. *Id.*, pp. 1577–1578, 56 LRRM 1294.
110. Wellington, *supra* note 47, pp. 152–153.
111. 147 NLRB 1573, 1577, 56 LRRM 1289, 1294.
112. 148 NLRB 897, 57 LRRM 1083 (1964).
113. 148 NLRB 897, 57 LRRM 1083, 1085 (1964).
114. 368 F.2d 12, 63 LRRM 2395 (5th Cir. 1966).
115. *Id.*, p. 16, 63 LRRM p. 2397.
116. NLRA Sections 8 (practices) and 10 (enforcement), as amended, 29 U.S.C. 158 and 160 (1970).
117. *Id.*, p. 17, 63 LRRM p. 2398.
118. *Id.*, p. 21.
119. *Id.*, p. 21, 63 LRRM p. 2401.
120. *Id.*, p. 23, 63 LRRM p. 2402.
121. *Ibid.*
122. *Ibid.*
123. *Farmers' Cooperative Compress*, 169 NLRB 290, 67 LRRM 1266 (1968), *sub nom. Packinghouse, Food & Allied Workers (UPWA) v. NLRB*, 416 F.2d 1126, 70 LRRM 2489 (D.C. Cir. 1969); *cert. denied*, 396 U.S. 903, 72 LRRM 2095 (1969); *decision on remand*, 194 NLRB No. 3, 78 LRRM 1465, 1972 CCH NLRB para. 23, 643 (November 12, 1971).
124. In doing so, the board ignored the clear thesis of *Central of Georgia Ry. Co. v. Jones*, 229 F.2d 648, 37 LRRM 2435 (5th Cir. 1956).
125. 416 F.2d 1126, 1134, 70 LRRM 2489, 2493 (1969).
126. *Id.*, p. 1135, 70 LRRM p. 2494.
127. *Id.*, pp. 1135–1136, 70 LRRM 2495–2496.
128. William B. Gould, "The Emerging Law Against Racial Discrimination in Employment," *Northwestern Law Review*, July-August 1969, pp. 359–385.
129. NLRA Section 10(c), as amended, 29 U.S.C. Section 160(c) (1970).
130. See 416 F.2d 1136.
131. 368 F.2d 12, 63 LRRM 2395 (5th Cir. 1966).
132. *Id.*, p. 24.
133. *Ibid.*

134. *Ibid.*
135. Letter from NLRB general counsel Arnold Ordman to Senator Jacob Javits, November 18, 1966. Sent with covering letter from Senator Javits to Herbert Hill, labor director, NAACP, November 27, 1966. NAACP files.
136. 185 NLRB 642, 75 LRRM 1139 (1970).
137. 185 NLRB 642, 75 LRRM 1139, 1143.
138. *Ibid.*
139. *Ibid.*
140. 416 F.2d 711, 2 FEP Cases 121 (7th Cir. 1969).
141. 272 F. Supp. 332, 1 FEP Cases 201, 65 LRRM 2714 (S.D. Ind. 1967), *affirmed in part and reversed in part,* 416 F.2d 711, 2 FEP Cases 121, 223 (7th Cir. 1969).
142. *Id.,* p. 715, 2 FEP Cases p. 123.
143. *Ibid.*
144. 414 F.2d 73, 1 FEP Cases 863, 71 LRRM 2940 (8th Cir. 1969).
145. *Id.,* pp. 74–75, 1 FEP Cases p. 864, 71 LRRM p. 2941.
146. See *Brotherhood of R.R. Trainmen* v. *Howard,* 343 U.S. 768, 30 LRRM 2258 (1942); *Howard* v. *Thompson,* 72 F. Supp. 695, 20 LRRM 2706 (E.D. Mo. 1947); *Neal* v. *System Board of Adjustment (Missouri Pac. R.R.),* 348 F.2d 722, 59 LRRM 2840 (8th Cir. 1965); *Howard* v. *St. Louis-S.F. Ry.,* 361 F.2d 905, 62 LRRM 2531 (8th Cir. 1966); *Nunn* v. *Missouri Pac. R.R.,* 248 F. Supp. 304, 1 FEP Cases 115, 60 LRRM 2573 (E.D. Mo. 1966).
147. *Brotherhood of Railroad Trainmen* v. *Howard,* 343 U.S. 768, 30 LRRM 2258 (1942).
148. In *Howard* v. *Thompson,* 72 F. Supp. 695, 20 LRRM 2706 (E.D. Mo. 1947).
149. 361 F.2d 905, 62 LRRM 2531 (8th Cir. 1966).
150. 248 F. Supp. 304, 1 FEP Cases 115, 60 LRRM 2573 (E.D. Mo. 1966).
151. 348 F.2d 722, 59 LRRM 2840 (8th Cir. 1965).
152. 414 F.2d 73, 78, 1 FEP Cases 863, 866, 71 LRRM 2940, 2943 (8th Cir. 1969).
153. *Id.,* p. 82, 1 FEP Cases p. 870, 71 LRRM p. 2947.
154. *Supra* note 149, Appellants' Brief, pp. 11–12.
155. *Id.,* p. 13.
156. 497 F.2d 594, 8 FEP Cases 594 (8th Cir. 1974), *cert. denied,* 420 U.S. 908, 9 FEP Cases 240 (1975).
157. 42 U.S.C. Section 2000e-5 (Supp. III 1973).
158. 42 U.S.C. Section 2000e-5(e) (Supp. III 1973).
159. 42 U.S.C. Section 2000e-5(b) (Supp. III 1973).
160. Economic Employment Opportunity Act, Public Law No. 92–261, 86 Stat. 103 (1972), as amended, 42 U.S.C. Section 2000e *et seq.* (Supp. III 1973).
161. NLRA Section 10(e), as amended, 29 U.S.C. Section 160(e) (1970).
162. NLRA Section 11, as amended, 29 U.S.C. Section 161 (1970).
163. NLRA Section 10(c), as amended, 29 U.S.C. Section 160(c) (1970).
164. NLRA Section 3(d), as amended, 29 U.S.C. Section 153(d) (1970).
165. Labor-Management Reporting and Disclosure Act (Landrum-Griffin Act), Public Law No. 86–257 (1959), 29 U.S.C. Sections 153, 158–160, 164, 186–187, 401 *et seq.* (1970). Section 158(b)(7) makes certain picketing aimed at forcing the employer to recognize or bargain with the union an unfair labor practice.

166. The RLA, unlike the NLRA, contains no specific provisions for injunctive relief.
167. Taft-Hartley Act, Section 101, adding Section 9(f) and (g) to the NLRA.
168. *Id.*, adding Section 9(h) to the NLRA.
169. *Id.*, adding Section 9(f), (g), and (h) to the NLRA.
170. *Id.*, adding Section 9(g) to the NLRA. If an employer or a complying union filed a petition, the NLRB allowed the noncomplying union to be put on the ballot, but it could not be certified even if it won.
171. *Supra* note 169.
172. *Supra* note 129.
173. 29 U.S.C. Section 431 (1970).
174. 29 U.S.C. Section 439 (1970) provides fines and imprisonment; Section 440 provides injunctive relief.
175. Leo Weiss, "Federal Remedies for Racial Discrimination by Labor Unions," *Georgetown Law Journal,* Spring 1962, pp. 457, 476–477.
176. See *Hughes Tool Co.,* 147 NLRB 1573, 1577, 56 LRRM 1289 (1964). See also *Pioneer Bus Co.,* 140 NLRB 54, 51 LRRM 1546 (1962).
177. 169 P.2d 831, 18 LRRM 2145 (Kans. Sup. Ct. 1946).
178. *Id.*, pp. 838–839, 18 LRRM p. 2150.
179. Ross and Hill, *supra* note 55, pp. 493–494.
180. 29 U.S.C. Section 157 (1970).
181. 29 U.S.C. Section 159(a) (1970).
182. 148 NLRB 1402, 57 LRRM 1170 (1964), *aff'd in part and remanded,* 349 F.2d 1, 59 LRRM 2784 (9th Cir. 1965), *on remand,* 166 NLRB 551, 65 LRRM 1502 (1967), *rev'd,* 419 F.2d 216, 72 LRRM 2866 (9th Cir. 1965), *on remand.*
183. 192 NLRB 173, 77 LRRM 1669 (1971), *rev'd,* 485 F.2d 917, 83 LRRM 2738 (D.C. Cir. 1973), *rev'd sub nom. Emporium Capwell Co.* v. *Western Addition Community Organization,* 420 U.S. 50, 9 FEP Cases 195, 88 LRRM 2660 (1975). The decision of the court of appeals provoked numerous critical responses. See, for example, *Harvard Law Review,* Vol. 87 (1974), p. 656.
184. *Supra* note 182..
185. *Ibid.*
186. *Supra* note 183.
187. Brief for the United States Equal Employment Opportunity Commission as *Amicus Curiae, Western Addition Community Org.* v. *NLRB (Emporium Capwell Co.), supra* note 183, pp. 5–6.
188. *Id.*, pp. 8, 10, 11.
189. *Id.*, pp. 18, 25, 26.
190. *Western Addition Community Org.* v. *NLRB (Emporium Capwell Co.),* 485 F.2d 917, 83 LRRM 2738 (D.C. Cir. 1973).
191. *Supra* note 183.
192. *Ibid.*
193. *Ibid.*
194. *Supra* note 189.
195. *Supra* note 183.
196. *Id.*, p. 53, 9 FEP Cases p. 196, 88 LRRM p. 2662 (footnote omitted).
197. *Id.*, pp. 72–73, 9 FEP Cases p. 204, 88 LRRM p. 2669.
198. *Id.*, pp. 73–75, 9 FEP Cases p. 204, 88 LRRM pp. 2669–2670.

199. *Id.,* p. 75, 9 FEP Cases p. 205, 88 LRRM p. 2670.
200. 303 U.S. 552, 9 FEP Cases 464, 82 LRRM 592 (1938).
201. *Id.,* p. 561, 9 FEP Cases p. 467, 82 LRRM p. 595.
202. *NLRB* v. *Mansion House Management Corp.,* 473 F.2d 471, 9 FEP Cases 358, 82 LRRM 2608 (8th Cir. 1973).
203. *Id.,* p. 477, 9 FEP Cases p. 363, 82 LRRM p. 2613.
204. *Id.,* p. 472, 9 FEP Cases p. 359, 82 LRRM p. 2609.
205. As that guarantee is incorporated in the due process clause of the Fifth Amendment. *Id.* The involvement of the NLRB as a government instrumentality was noted by the court in applying the state action concept in *Mansion House:* "When a governmental agency recognizes such a union to be the bargaining representative, it significantly becomes a willing participant in the union's discriminatory practices. Although the union itself is not a governmental instrumentality, the National Labor Relations Board is. . . . The Board seeks enforcement of its order requiring collective bargaining in a federal court. Obviously, judicial enforcement of private discrimination cannot be sanctioned."
206. 473 F.2d p. 473, 9 FEP Cases p. 360, 82 LRRM p. 2610.
207. "NLRB Sets Procedures in Discrimination Claims Cases Involving Union," National Labor Relations Board, press release, June 11, 1974.
208. *Ibid.*
209. *Ibid.*
210. *Bekins Moving & Storage Co. of Florida, Inc. and Freight Drivers, Warehousemen and Helpers, Local Union No. 390, an Affiliate of the International Brotherhood of Teamsters, Chauffeurs, Warehousemen and Helpers of America,* 211 NLRB No. 7, 86 LRRM 1323, Case No. 12–RC–4352, June 11, 1974.
211. *Ibid.*
212. *Ibid.*
213. *Grant's Furniture Plaza,* 213 NLRB No. 80, 87 LRRM 1175, 1177 (1974).
214. *Bell and Howell Co.,* 213 NLRB No. 79, 87 LRRM 1172 (1974).
215. *Williams Enterprises, Inc.,* 212 NLRB No. 132, 87 LRRM 1045 (1974).
216. See *Taylor* v. *Armco Steel Corp.,* 429 F.2d 498, 2 FEP Cases 820 (5th Cir. 1970).
217. *Jenkins* v. *United Gas,* 400 F.2d 28, 1 FEP Cases 364, 69 LRRM 2152 (5th Cir. 1968).
218. *Supra* note 44.
219. 415 U.S. 36, 51, 7 FEP Cases 81, 87 (1974).
220. *Supra* note 217.
221. *Supra* note 219.
222. 150 NLRB 312, 57 LRRM 1535 (1964).
223. *Supra* note 100.
224. NLRA Sections 8(b)(1)(A), (2), and (3), as amended, 29 U.S.C. Sections 158(b)(1)(A), (2), and (3).
225. 345 U.S. 330, 31 LRRM 2548 (1952).
226. *Supra* note 222.
227. *Ibid.*
228. *Supra* note 123.
229. 416 F.2d 1126, 1133, n. 11, 9 FEP Cases 317, 321, n. 11, 70 LRRM 2489, 2493, n. 11.

230. The Hruska amendment, Amendment No. 877 to S.2515, 92d Cong., 2d Sess. (1972), printed in *Legislative History of the Equal Employment Opportunity Act of 1972*, 92d Cong., 2d Sess. (Washington, D.C.: Senate Committee on Labor and Public Welfare, 1972), p. 1382. For the vote, see pp. 1556–1557.

231. *Supra* note 219, p. 51, 7 FEP Cases p. 87.

Chapter 4

1. *First Report,* July 1943–December 1944 (Washington, D.C.: Fair Employment Practice Committee, 1945), p. 13.

2. Irving Bernstein, *The Lean Years* (A History of the American Worker 1920–1933) (Boston: Houghton Mifflin Company, 1960), p. 257.

3. Raymond Wolters, *Negroes and the Great Depression* (Westport, Conn.: Greenwood Publishing Corporation, 1970), pp. 90–91.

4. Robert C. Weaver, *Negro Labor—A National Problem* (New York: Harcourt, Brace & Co., 1946), pp. 18–19.

5. *Ibid.*

6. Gunnar Myrdal, *An American Dilemma,* Vol. I (New York: Harper & Brothers, 1944), p. 412.

7. Letter from W. Gerard Tuttle, manager, industrial relations, Vultee Aircraft Corporation, to Robert S. Robinson, executive secretary, National Negro Congress, August 2, 1940. Photostat in NAACP files.

8. *PM,* May 7, 1941. Quoted in Herbert Garfinkel, *When Negroes March: The March on Washington Movement in the Organizational Politics for FEPC* (Glencoe, Ill.: The Free Press, 1959), p. 17.

9. American Federation of Labor, *Report of Proceedings, 1940 Convention,* Statement of A. Philip Randolph, pp. 511 *et seq.*

10. American Federation of Labor, *Report of Proceedings, 1941 Convention,* Resolution No. 18, pp. 476–477.

11. American Federation of Labor, *Report of Proceedings, 1942 Convention,* Resolution No. 14, "Race Discrimination in Trade Unions," introduced by A. Philip Randolph and Milton P. Webster, p. 580.

12. Myrdal, *supra* note 6, p. 402.

13. 3 C. F. R. 957 (1941).

14. 3 C. F. R. 1280 (1943).

15. *Supra* note 1, p. 7.

16. *Id.,* p. 6.

17. Charles Zaid, *Preliminary Inventory No. 147,* Records of the Committee on Fair Employment Practice (Washington, D.C.: The National Archives, 1962), p. 4.

18. *Supra* note 1, p. 39.

19. *Id.,* p. 41.

20. *Ibid.*

21. *Id.,* p. 39.

22. *Ibid.*

23. *Id.,* p. 41.

24. *Id.*, pp. 41–42.
25. Weaver, *supra* note 4, pp. 35–36, 134.
26. *Final Report,* June 28, 1946 (Washington, D.C.: Fair Employment Practice Committee, 1947), p. 1.
27. *Supra* note 1, p. 89.

Chapter 5

All FEPC material cited here is in Record Group 228, National Archives Building, Washington, D.C. See Charles Zaid, *Preliminary Inventory No. 147,* Records of the Committee on Fair Employment Practice (Washington, D.C.: The National Archives, 1962).

1. According to testimony presented at FEPC *Hearings* in Birmingham, Ala., June 18–20, 1942, during World War I there were 380,000 shipyard workers, 10 percent of whom were Negroes, 20 percent of them skilled. By March 1, 1943, 8.4 percent of the shipyard workers were Negroes, 3.1 percent skilled. See note 12 *infra.*
2. Cited in Robert C. Weaver, *Negro Labor—A National Problem* (New York: Harcourt, Brace & Co., 1946), pp. 19–20.
3. *Ibid.*
4. Malcolm Ross, *All Manner of Men* (New York: Reynal and Hitchcock, 1948), p. 143.
5. *Ibid.*
6. International Brotherhood of Boilermakers, *Report of Proceedings, 1937 Convention* (Kansas City, Mo.: September 1937). See also *Report of the International President and Executive Council to the Sixteenth Consolidated Convention of the International Brotherhood of Boilermakers, Iron Ship Builders, and Helpers of America* (Kansas City, Mo.: September 1937). Copies in the National Archives.
7. Ross, *supra* note 4, p. 145.
8. Bylaws of the International Brotherhood Governing Auxiliary Lodges, adopted by the 1937 Boilermakers convention, effective January 1, 1938, Article VI.
9. *Id.,* Article II, Section 15.
10. FEPC Birmingham *Hearings.* No case number. Transcript of proceedings held in Birmingham, Ala., on June 18–20, 1942, with summaries, findings, and directives relating to the National Training Program in Alabama, Tennessee, and Georgia; Vultee Aircraft, Inc.; Gulf Shipbuilding Corporation; Alabama Drydock and Shipbuilding Corporation; and National Defense Training. FEPC Statement of the Case Against Gulf Shipbuilding Corporation, p. 214.
11. FEPC Complaint Against Delta Shipbuilding Corporation at *Hearings, supra* note 10, p. 496.
12. *Ibid.*
13. Testimony of James B. McCollum at *Hearings, supra* note 10.
14. FEPC Statement, *supra* note 10, p. 217.

15. American Federation of Labor, *Report of Proceedings, 1940 Convention*, pp. 508–511.
16. American Federation of Labor, *Report of Proceedings, 1941 Convention*, pp. 478–479.
17. *Id.*, p. 536.
18. American Federation of Labor, *Report of Proceedings, 1943 Convention*, pp. 432–434.
19. American Federation of Labor, *Report of Proceedings, 1944 Convention*, p. 495.
20. Michigan *Chronicle*, December 9, 1944, p. 1.
21. Interview by author with Mrs. Frances Albrier, Berkeley, Calif., November 3, 1968. Transcript in Archives of Labor History and Urban Affairs, Wayne State University, Detroit, Mich.
22. FEPC *Hearings*. Oregon Shipbuilding Corporation, Vancouver and Swan Island Shipyards, and International Brotherhood of Boiler Makers, Iron Ship Builders, Welders and Helpers of America (Boilermakers union). No case number. Transcript of proceedings held in Portland, Oreg., on November 15–16, 1943, with accompanying correspondence, exhibits, court order, union bylaws, summary with findings and directives, newspaper clippings, and a petition, dated January 22, 1944, of the Kaiser Company, Inc., and the Oregon Shipbuilding Corporation for a rehearing. Testimony of Marvin Harrison, FEPC examiner, p. 11.
23. Testimony of Sidney Wolf at *Hearings, supra* note 22, pp. 110 *et seq.*
24. *Ibid.*
25. Testimony of Robert Rhone at *Hearings, supra* note 22, pp. 117 *et seq.*
26. *Ibid.*
27. Statement of Marvin Harrison at *Hearings, supra* note 22, p. 12.
28. Letter from J. A. Franklin to William Green, September 23, 1941, introduced at *Hearings, supra* note 22, p. 273.
29. Testimony of Edgar Kaiser at *Hearings, supra* note 22, p. 285.
30. Telegram from John Frey to Edgar Kaiser, October 22, 1942, introduced at *Hearings, supra* note 22, pp. 291–292.
31. Memorandum of November 10–11, 1942, conference, introduced at *Hearings, supra* note 22, pp. 302–305.
32. Letter from Tom Ray, secretary of Local 72, to the FEPC, March 22, 1942, introduced at *Hearings, supra* note 22, p. 271.
33. Telegram from Charles MacGowan to Monsignor Francis Haas, FEPC chairman, August 27, 1943, introduced at *Hearings, supra* note 22, p. 266.
34. Statement of Leland Turner at *Hearings, supra* note 22, p. 31.
35. Testimony of Charles Robinson at *Hearings, supra* note 22, p. 51.
36. Statement of Gordon Johnson at *Hearings, supra* note 22, p. 62.
37. *James* v. *Marinship Corp.*, 25 Cal.2d 721, 155 P.2d 329, 15 LRRM 798 (1945); *Williams* v. *International Brotherhood of Boilermakers*, 27 Cal.2d 586, 165 P.2d 903, 17 LRRM 771 (1946); see also *Thompson* v. *Moore Drydock Company*, 27 Cal.2d 595, 165 P.2d 901, 17 LRRM 776 (1946).
38. Confidential FEPC Memorandum, May 18, 1944.
39. FEPC *Hearings*. Western Pipe and Steel Company, Consolidated Steel Corporation (Shipbuilding Division), California Shipbuilding Corporation, Kaiser Company, Inc., Oregon Shipbuilding Corporation, and Auxiliary Lodge No. A–35 and Subordinate Lodge 92 of the International

Brotherhood of Boiler Makers, Iron Ship Builders and Helpers of America, AFL. No case number. Transcript of proceedings held in Los Angeles, Calif., on November 19–20, 1943, with accompanying correspondence on a rehearing and a petition of the California Shipbuilding Corporation for a rehearing, dated January 22, 1944. Testimony of Walter Edward Williams, pp. 38 *et seq.*

40. *Ibid.*
41. *Ibid.*
42. Testimony of Andrew Blakney at *Hearings, supra* note 39, pp. 100 *et seq.*
43. Letter from Charles MacGowan to Kaiser Company, December 14, 1943. Copy in *Hearings, supra* note 39.
44. Charles MacGowan, president of the International Brotherhood, wrote Representative Howard Smith complaining of the FEPC's demands upon the union. At the Smith committee hearings the Boilermakers union was invited to testify about the FEPC's "illegal" hearings and directives to the union.
45. Michigan *Chronicle,* December 25, 1943, p. 1.
46. *Id.,* February 12, 1944.
47. Quoted in FEPC Memorandum from Frank D. Reeves to George M. Johnson, FEPC deputy chairman, February 24, 1944.
48. FEPC Office Memorandum, September 14, 1943, re: Kaiser Shipyard, Providence, R.I.
49. Michigan *Chronicle,* January 15, 1944.
50. The Michigan *Chronicle,* June 17, 1944, carried adjoining news reports on p. 8: "William Green Cites Progress of Boilermakers"; "Injunction Stops Boilermakers in West Coast Issue."
51. *Supra* note 37.
52. *Id.,* 25 Cal.2d 721, 731, 15 LRRM 798, 802, 803.
53. 27 Cal.2d 586, 165 P.2d 903, 17 LRRM 771 (1946).
54. *Id.,* 27 Cal.2d 586, 591–592, 17 LRRM 771, 773, 774.
55. *Final Report,* June 28, 1946 (Washington, D.C.: Fair Employment Practice Committee, 1947), p. 21.
56. *Hiawatha Darden, et al.* v. *Newport News Shipbuilding and Dry Dock Company, et al.,* CA No. 95–69–NN (D.C. E. Va., Newport News Division, complaint filed August 9, 1969).
57. William Chapman, "Shipyard Gets Pact Despite Bias Case," *Washington Post,* May 23, 1969.
58. Interview by author with John Heneghan, director of civil rights, Maritime Administration, Washington, D.C., December 29, 1971.
59. *Ibid.*
60. Interview by author with John Heneghan, director of civil rights, Maritime Administration, Washington, D.C., April 11, 1972.
61. Equal Employment Opportunity Commission, news release, August 29, 1973.
62. Report of Philadelphia Regional Litigation Center, EEOC, *News* (Washington, D.C.: Equal Employment Opportunity Commission, October 6, 1975), p. 21.

Chapter 6

All FEPC material cited here is in Record Group 228, National Archives Building, Washington, D.C. See Charles Zaid, *Preliminary Inventory No. 147*, Records of the Committee on Fair Employment Practice (Washington, D.C.: The National Archives, 1962).

1. "Order of United Machinists and Mechanical Engineers of America," photographic reproduction in Mark Perlman, *The Machinists* (Cambridge, Mass.: Harvard University Press, 1961), frontispiece.

2. AFL Incoming Correspondence: James O'Connell, president of the National Association of Machinists, to John McBride, president of the AFL, March 25, 1895; James O'Connell to Samuel Gompers, February 26, 1896; James O'Connell to Frank Morrison, March 20, 1903. Material cited from archival correspondence is taken from Bernard Mandel, "Samuel Gompers and the Negro Workers, 1886–1914," *Journal of Negro History*, January 1955, pp. 34–60; Philip S. Foner, *History of the Labor Movement in the United States*, Vol. II (New York: International Publishers, 1955), pp. 348–349. See also Frank E. Wolfe, "Admission to American Trade Unions," Johns Hopkins University Studies in Historical and Political Science, Series XXX (Baltimore: Johns Hopkins Press, 1912), p. 120; Herbert Hill, "The Racial Practices of Organized Labor—The Age of Gompers and After," in Arthur M. Ross and Herbert Hill, eds., *Employment, Race, and Poverty* (New York: Harcourt, Brace & World, 1967), pp. 365–402.

3. FEPC Staff Memorandum from Clarence Mitchell to William McKnight, August 11, 1944.

4. Letter from IAM Lodge 34 to the president of the Ohio Pattern Works and Foundry Company, September 29, 1944.

5. FEPC *Hearings*. In the Matter of Western Cartridge Company, Case No. 71. Transcript of proceedings held in East Alton, Ill., on January 31, 1945, and February 23 and 24, 1945, with accompanying correspondence, statements of company's position and charges, and agreement between Western Cartridge Company and the American Federation of Labor and affiliated organizations, p. 148.

6. *Id.*, pp. 390 *et seq.*

7. *Final Report*, June 28, 1946 (Washington, D.C.: Fair Employment Practice Committee, 1947), p. 19.

8. Memorandum from John Bader, area director, War Manpower Commission, to Edward Lawson, state director, War Manpower Commission, introduced at *Hearings, supra* note 5, p. 11.

9. Robert C. Weaver, *Negro Labor—A National Problem* (New York: Harcourt, Brace & Co., 1946), p. 37.

10. *Ibid.*

11. *Ibid.*

12. FEPC *Hearings*. In the Matter of McDonnell Aircraft Corporation, Case No. 65. Transcript of proceedings held in St. Louis, Mo., on August 2, 1944, with accompanying correspondence.

13. Testimony of Complainant Dorothy Burton at *Hearings, supra* note 12, p. 37.

14. *Supra* note 12.

15. FEPC Birmingham *Hearings*. No case number. Transcript of proceedings held in Birmingham, Ala., on June 18–20, 1942, with summaries, findings, and directives relating to the National Training Program in Alabama, Tennessee, and Georgia; Vultee Aircraft, Inc.; Gulf Shipbuilding Corporation; Alabama Drydock and Shipbuilding Corporation; and National Defense Training, pp. 107 *et seq.*

16. Letter from G. S. Hastings, manager of industrial relations at Vultee Aircraft, Inc., February 6, 1941, submitted at *Hearings, supra* note 15, p. 107.

17. Statement of E. G. Trimble, FEPC attorney, at *Hearings, supra* note 15, pp. 107 *et seq.*

18. Testimony of Mark Miller Latting at *Hearings, supra* note 15, pp. 131 *et seq.*

19. FEPC *Hearings.* Complaints of Discrimination in Employment in Defense Industries Because of Race, Creed, Color, or National Origin. No case number. Transcript of proceedings held in Los Angeles, Calif., on October 20–21, 1941.

20. Quoted in Louis Ruchames, *Race, Jobs & Politics—The Story of FEPC* (New York: Columbia University Press, 1953), p. 12.

21. FEPC Request for Further Action, from Harry Kingman, regional director, to Will Maslow, director of field operations, May 27, 1944.

22. Weaver, *supra* note 9, p. 116.

23. American Federation of Labor, *Report of Proceedings, 1941 Convention,* p. 477. A heated debate developed in this convention after the delegates of the Brotherhood of Sleeping Car Porters introduced their antidiscrimination resolution and A. Philip Randolph arose to sustain the charges of anti-Negro practices by AFL unions and to attack the acquiescence of the federation in these matters. Philip Taft, in his book *The AF of L From the Death of Gompers to the Merger* (New York: Harper and Bros., 1959), seriously distorts Randolph's position by selectively quoting excerpts that make it appear as if Randolph were praising the AFL for not discriminating against Negroes. Compare Taft's elliptical quotation, p. 446, with the *Report of Proceedings,* pp. 490–491.

24. Weaver, *supra* note 9, p. 117.

25. *Supra* note 21.

26. Letter from IAM General Vice President Eric Peterson to Local 79, *supra* note 21.

27. *Supra* note 21.

28. Complaint of Andrew Hudson, December 4, 1944.

29. Complaint of Fred Chapman, December 1, 1944.

30. *Ralph Banks, et al.* v. *Lockheed-Georgia Company (A Division of Lockheed Aircraft Corporation) and Local No. 709, International Association of Machinists and Aerospace Workers, AFL-CIO,* 46 F.R.D. 442, 1 FEP Cases 323 (D.C. N. Ga. 1968); 53 F.R.D. 283, 4 FEP Cases 117 (D.C. N. Ga. 1971).

31. *Lockheed Minority Solidarity Coalition* v. *Lockheed Missile and Space Company (A Division of Lockheed Aircraft Corporation) and the International Association of Machinists and Aerospace Workers and its District Lodge 508 and affiliated Locals 2225, 2226, 2227, and 2228 ("Machinists"),* CA No. C–73–2006 (D.C. N. Calif., CBR filed November 9, 1973).

Chapter 7

All FEPC material cited here is in Record Group 228, National Archives Building, Washington, D.C. See Charles Zaid, *Preliminary Inventory No. 147*, Records of the Committee on Fair Employment Practice (Washington, D.C.: The National Archives, 1962).

1. The Sailors' Union of the Pacific was thereafter the SIU's west coast district. The SIU recruited members on the east and gulf coasts and the Great Lakes.

2. Complaints of discrimination filed with the FEPC against the Longshoremen and Warehousemen's Union, CIO, and the Marine Cooks and Stewards' Association of the Pacific Coast were dismissed for lack of merit. However, complaints against the SIU; the Sailors' Union of the Pacific; the Marine Engineers' Beneficial Association; the Masters, Mates and Pilots' Union; and the Marine Firemen, Oilers, Watertenders and Wipers' Association were considered to have merit. The FEPC proceeded with formal hearings only against the Seafarers' International Union.

3. During World War II the SIU had approximately 25,000 members, 2,000 of whom were Negroes. The NMU had 85,000 members, 8,000 of them Negroes.

4. Malcolm Ross, *All Manner of Men* (New York: Reynal and Hitchcock, 1948), p. 106.

5. Letter from Oliver Boutte, NMU port agent at Long Beach, Calif., contained in FEPC Final Disposition Report, re: The Barber Line Steamship Company, May 23, 1945.

6. FEPC Final Disposition Report, re: Inner Ocean Steamship Company and the Marine Engineers' Beneficial Association, July 5, 1945. The association was opposed to the employment of Negroes in skilled jobs but in this instance, faced with the opposition of the FEPC and the NMU, it acquiesced in the employment of a Negro electrician.

7. Memorandum from Craig Vincent, regional director, to Marshall Dimock, director of the Recruitment and Manning Organization, War Shipping Administration, re: Complaint of Alfred Govetin, March 8, 1944.

8. Memorandum from Craig Vincent, regional director, to Marshall Dimock, director of the Recruitment and Manning Organization, War Shipping Administration, February 22, 1944.

9. The merchant marine expanded from a small, privately owned cargo-shipping industry before the war to a force of 169,000 men by 1944. The government's referral agency, the Recruitment and Manning Organization's maritime offices in New York, remained open and active twenty-four hours a day, seven days a week. An October 1944 press release from the organization demonstrates that, as with other war industries, a manpower shortage was developing in the maritime industry: "The need for additional experienced seamen at this stage of the war is so great that the Atlantic Coast offices of R.M.O. of the W.S.A. have found it necessary to operate on a basis of less than three days' manpower supply instead of the normal two weeks' reserve. . . . Increased need for shipping for the Pacific operations are foreseen. To meet all such demands, the merchant marine fleet is still being expanded. . . . An additional 8,000 experienced seamen and officers now working in port jobs on the East Coast must return to sea duty during

the remaining three months of this year so that the Merchant Marine can continue doing its job at capacity."

10. The War Shipping Administration was established February 7, 1942, by Executive Order 9054.

11. FEPC *Hearings.* Seafarers' International Union of North America. Case No. 67. Transcript of proceedings held in New York, on October 10, 1944, with accompanying correspondence and exhibits, pp. 6 *et seq.*

12. Statements of policy were signed May 4, 1942, and copies are reprinted in FEPC *Hearings, supra* note 11, p. 7. John Hawk, SIU secretary-treasurer, later told the Smith committee that the statement of policy was "a guarantee from the Government that the contracts that the unions have with the operators will be lived up to, frozen and lived up to for the duration of the war. Now, the unions in turn gave up voluntarily their right to strike."— *Hearings,* U.S. House of Representatives, Special Committee to Investigate Executive Agencies, February 25, 1944, p. 2321.

13. *Hearings,* U.S. House of Representatives, Special Committee to Investigate Executive Agencies, February 25, 1944, pp. 2331–2332.

14. *Supra* note 11. Summary of Evidence against the SIU. Among the larger companies that had agreements with the SIU were the Waterman Steamship Corporation of Mobile, Alabama; the Alcoa Steamship Company, Inc.; the Seatrain Management Corporation; A. H. Bull & Company; Arnold Bernstein Shipping Company, Inc.; and the McAllister Lighterage Line, Inc.; all of New York. On July 14, 1944, the Waterman Steamship Corporation wrote to the FEPC: "Several years ago we had an agreement with the Seafarers International Union that we would employ one-half white and one-half colored Stewards' Departments on our vessels. Apparently by having such an agreement we were violating the Fair Employment practice [*sic*], so in view of this we want to discontinue this practice. . . ."

15. War Manpower Commission Employment Stabilization Program for the New York City Area, *supra* note 11, p. 90.

16. Opening Statement of Emanuel Bloch, FEPC examiner, *supra* note 11, pp. 7–8.

17. Statement of John Hawk before the U.S. House of Representatives, Special Committee to Investigate Executive Agencies, February 25, 1944, p. 2324.

18. From the FEPC Complaint to SIU, March 4, 1944.

19. Memorandum from Craig Vincent, regional representative, to Marshall Dimock, director of the War Shipping Administration, February 11, 1943.

20. *Ibid.*

21. *Ibid.*

22. Quoted in letter from Frederick Farr, port representative for Maritime Labor Relations, WSA, to Hubert Wyckoff, assistant deputy administrator, Maritime Labor Relations, WSA, re: Complaint of J. M. Stevens, June 23, 1944.

23. *Ibid.*

24. War Shipping Administration Memorandum from Hubert Wyckoff, assistant deputy administrator for Maritime Labor Relations, to Malcolm Ross, chairman, FEPC, June 22, 1944.

25. Complaint of Osborne S. Roberts, FEPC File No. 2–UR–857.

26. Complaint of L. Johnson, FEPC File No. 2–UR–401.

27. Memorandum from Craig Vincent, regional representative, to Marshall Dimock, director, Recruitment and Manning Organization, December 9, 1942.
28. Complaint of Edmund Jones, FEPC File No. 2–UR–402.
29. *Ibid.*
30. FEPC File No. 2–UR–678, February 17, 1944.
31. Opening Statement of Emanuel Bloch, FEPC examiner, *supra* note 11, pp. 11–12.
32. War Shipping Administration, Instruction 43 (revised), to the Recruitment and Manning Organization, May 15, 1944.
33. Smith committee hearings. Statement of Marshall E. Dimock, Recruitment and Manning Organization, War Shipping Administration, before the Select Committee of the House of Representatives to Investigate Executive Agencies, March 1, 1944, Washington, D.C., pp. 2385–2386.
34. The FEPC had operating agreements with the War Shipping Administration (and other government agencies) whereby the agency would attempt to settle the matter satisfactorily in the first instance and would notify the FEPC of its failure if settlement could not be effected.
35. Letter from John Hawk, secretary-treasurer of the SIU, to the FEPC, March 23, 1944.
36. *Ibid.*
37. *Supra* note 11, p. 4.
38. *Id.*, p. 13.
39. Edward Helfeld, a white merchant seaman who had graduated from the government training school at Sheepshead Bay, N.Y., stated that although whites and blacks ate, slept, and studied together, their relationship was "harmonious," and there were "no tensions." *Supra* note 11, pp. 134 *et seq.* Robert Adams, a Negro graduate of the school at New London, Conn., testified to similar circumstances. *Supra* note 11, pp. 162 *et seq.*
40. Statement of Richard G. Miles, *supra* note 11, p. 158.
41. *Id.*, pp. 159–160.
42. *Id.*, pp. 161–162.
43. Statement of Harry Fisher, *supra* note 11, pp. 171–172.
44. Memorandum from Boris Shishkin to the FEPC, May 22, 1945.
45. *Final Report,* June 28, 1946 (Washington, D.C.: Fair Employment Practice Committee, 1947), p. 22.
46. The Smith committee heard testimony from railroad companies and unions, the Philadelphia Transportation Company, and the Seafarers' International Union, among others. Members of the committee were later influential in obtaining the demise of the FEPC.
47. Letter from John Hawk to Representative Howard Smith, January 28, 1944, contained in Hawk's testimony before the Smith committee, *supra* note 33, pp. 2313 *et seq.*
48. Statements by John Hawk, *supra* note 33, pp. 2315–2316.
49. *Id.*, pp. 2325–2326.
50. *Id.*, p. 2345.
51. Ross, *supra* note 4, p. 106.
52. Interview by author with Frank A. Quinn, Regional Director, EEOC, San Francisco, October 14, 1971.
53. Letter to author from Frank A. Quinn, June 5, 1972.

Chapter 8

All FEPC material cited here is in Record Group 228, National Archives Building, Washington, D.C. See Charles Zaid, *Preliminary Inventory No. 147,* Records of the Committee on Fair Employment Practice (Washington, D.C.: The National Archives, 1962).

1. Robert C. Weaver, *Negro Labor—A National Problem* (New York: Harcourt, Brace & Co., 1946), p. 19.
2. American Federation of Labor, *Report of Proceedings, 1941 Convention,* pp. 476–477.
3. American Federation of Labor, *Report of Proceedings, 1944 Convention,* pp. 496–497.
4. FEPC Birmingham *Hearings.* No case number. Transcript of proceedings held in Birmingham, Ala., on June 18–20, 1942, with summaries, findings, and directives relating to the National Training Program in Alabama, Tennessee, and Georgia; Vultee Aircraft, Inc.; Gulf Shipbuilding Corporation; Alabama Drydock and Shipbuilding Corporation; and National Defense Training, p. 664.
5. Testimony of L. M. Cooper, business agent for Carpenters Local 89, *supra* note 5, p. 389.
6. Quote from FEPC Complaint, *supra* note 5, p. 364.
7. FEPC *Hearings.* Cook County Plumbers' Union. No case number. Transcript of proceedings held in Chicago on April 4, 1942. (Complaints of Negro Plumbers Against the Chicago Journeymen Plumbers Union Local 130 and of Negro Steamfitters Against the Steamfitters Protective Association Local 597.) Testimony of Edward L. Doty, pp. 9 *et seq.*
8. *Ibid.*
9. *Ibid.*
10. *Ibid.*
11. Interview by author with Edward L. Doty, Chicago, November 2, 1967. Transcript in Archives of Labor History and Urban Affairs, Wayne State University, Detroit, Mich.
12. *Ibid.*
13. *Supra* note 7, p. 25.
14. *Id.,* pp. 9 *et seq.*
15. *Ibid.*
16. Testimony of Wilson Frankland, president of the Steamfitters Protective Association, *supra* note 7, p. 139.
17. Testimony of William Quirk, business agent of Plumbers Local 130, *supra* note 7, pp. 132–154.
18. Testimony of Elizabeth Wood, executive secretary of the Chicago Housing Authority, *supra* note 7, pp. 105 *et seq.*
19. *Ibid.*
20. Weaver, *supra* note 1, pp. 19–20.
21. FEPC *Hearings.* Victor Electric Products, Inc. Case No. 75. Transcript of proceedings held in Cincinnati, Ohio, on March 17, 1945, with brief and exhibits, p. 17.
22. *Id.,* p. 15.
23. *Id.,* p. 9.
24. *Id.,* p. 65.

25. FEPC *Hearings.* Crosley Corporation. Case No. 72. Transcript of proceedings held in Cincinnati, Ohio, on March 15, 1945, with accompanying correspondence and brief.
26. *Id.,* p. 61.
27. *Id.,* p. 82.
28. *Id.,* pp. 141–142.
29. John H. Ohly, "History of Plant Seizures During World War II" (3 volumes of unpublished manuscript, Office of the Chief of Military History, Department of the Army, 1946), Vol. III, Appendix Z–1–a.
30. *Ibid.*
31. *Ibid.*
32. *Ibid.*
33. *Ibid.*
34. John L. Blackman, Jr., *Presidential Seizure in Labor Disputes* (Cambridge, Mass.: Harvard University Press, 1967), p. 133.
35. *Ibid.*
36. Ohly, *supra* note 29.
37. *Ibid.*
38. Executive Order 9408, 8 F.R. 16958 (1943).
39. Ohly, *supra* note 29.
40. *Ibid.*
41. Copy of letter from Robert Patterson to Paul V. McNutt, chairman, national War Manpower Commission, December 23, 1943, *supra* note 30, Appendix BB–17.
42. Copy of letter from Robert Patterson to Major General Louis B. Hershey, director of Selective Service, December 23, 1943, *supra* note 29, Appendix BB–18.
43. Ohly, *supra* note 29.
44. *Ibid.*
45. *Ibid.*
46. Blackman, *supra* note 34, p. 134.
47. Ohly, *supra* note 29.
48. *Ibid.*
49. *Ibid.*
50. Blackman, *supra* note 34, p. 134.
51. Interview by author with Eli Rock, disputes director of Third Regional Office of the War Labor Board during World War II, Philadelphia, February 27, 1968. Author's files.
52. 140 Conn. 537, 102 A.2d 366, 1 FEP Cases 5, 33 LRRM 2307 (1953).
53. *Dobbins v. Local 212, Electrical Workers,* 292 F. Supp. 413, 1 FEP Cases 387, 69 LRRM 2313 (S.D. Ohio 1968), *amended in part,* 2 FEP Cases 180 (1969).
54. *United States v. Local 36, Sheet Metal Workers, and Local 1, Electrical Workers,* 416 F.2d 123, 2 FEP Cases 127 (8th Cir. 1969).
55. Tim O'Brien, "Two New Groups Charged With Job Bias by the EEOC," *Washington Post,* September 21, 1973, p. 3.

Chapter 9

All FEPC material cited here is in Record Group 228, National Archives Building, Washington, D.C. See Charles Zaid, *Preliminary Inventory No. 147,* Records of the Committee on Fair Employment Practice (Washington, D.C.: The National Archives, 1962).

1. FEPC Birmingham *Hearings.* No case number. Transcript of proceedings held in Birmingham, Ala., on June 18–20, 1942, with summaries, findings, and directives relating to the National Training Program in Alabama, Tennessee, and Georgia; Vultee Aircraft, Inc.; Gulf Shipbuilding Corporation; Alabama Drydock and Shipbuilding Corporation; and National Defense Training. Testimony of John Bushby, p. 82.

2. FEPC *Hearings.* International Brotherhood of Teamsters, Chauffeurs, Warehousemen, and Helpers of America, Local 299, et al. (the White Star Trucking Company, the Mannion Express Company, Shippers Dispatch, Inc., the McFarren Cartage Company, the Opland Trucking Company, the Detroit Delivery Company, the Dealers Transport Company, Associate Truck Lines, Inc., Fourteenth Avenue Cartage Company, U.S. Truck Company, Inc., and the Douglas Trucking Lines, Inc.). Case No. 84. Transcript of proceedings held in Detroit, on June 2, 1945, with accompanying correspondence, p. 7.

3. Malcolm Ross, *All Manner of Men* (New York: Reynal and Hitchcock, 1948), p. 103.

4. Testimony of Oscar Purvey, *supra* note 2, pp. 104 *et seq.*

5. War Manpower Commission Report to Regional Director Robert C. Goodwin, August 9, 1944, *supra* note 2, p. 20.

6. *Id.,* p. 22.

7. Testimony of Lethia Clore, FEPC examiner, *supra* note 2, p. 120.

8. Memorandum from Simon Stickgold and Frank Reeves, FEPC attorneys, to Maceo Hubbard, FEPC Legal Division, May 23, 1945, re: Developments in the Teamsters Union *Hearings.*

9. Testimony of Festus Harrison, *supra* note 2, pp. 222 *et seq.*

10. *Ibid.*

11. *Ibid.*

12. Michigan *Chronicle,* September 16, 1944, p. 1.

13. Equal Employment Opportunity Commission, news release, December 3, 1971.

14. Brief Before the Interstate Commerce Commission, "Equal Opportunity in Surface Transportation," Initial Statement of the Equal Employment Opportunity Commission (*Ex Parte* No. 278), filed December 1, 1971.

15. *Id.,* p. 5; quoted from *Report* of the National Advisory Commission on Civil Disorders (Washington, D.C.: U.S. Government Printing Office, March 1968).

16. *Ibid.*

17. *Supra* note 14, pp. 6, 7, 15.

18. *Id.,* pp. 8, 10, 11.

19. *Id.,* pp. 18, 19.

20. *Id.,* p. 12.

21. *Id.,* pp. 18, 29–31.

22. *Id.,* p. 31.

23. *Bing* v. *Roadway Express, Inc.,* 485 F.2d 441, 6 FEP Cases 677 (5th Cir. 1973).
24. *Jones* v. *Lee Way Motor Freight,* 431 F.2d 245, 2 FEP Cases 895 (10th Cir. 1970), *cert. denied,* 401 U.S. 954, 3 FEP Cases 193 (1971).
25. *Id.,* p. 24, n. 45.
26. *Ibid.*
27. *United States* v. *T.I.M.E.-D.C., Inc., et al.,* consent decree entered, ——F. Supp. ——, 4 EPD para. 7831 (N.D. Tex. May 12, 1972), *remanded for other reasons,* 417 F.2d 299, 11 FEP Cases 66 (5th Cir. 1975).
28. *U.S.* v. *Interstate Motor Freight Systems of Michigan,* CA No. G–137–72 (W.D. Mich., complaint filed May 11, 1972), partial consent decree entered June 29, 1972 (issue of seniority pending).
29. *E.E.O.C.* v. *Preston Trucking Company of Maryland,* CA No. 72–632–M (D. Md., complaint filed June 20, 1972), consent decree entered June 25, 1973.
30. *Wall Street Journal,* October 31, 1973, p. 3.
31. *U.S.* v. *Trucking Employers, Inc., et al.,* ——F. Supp. ——, consent decree entered March 20, 1974 (CA No. 74–453).
32. *Leon Jones, et al.* v. *Pacific Intermountain Express, et al.,* ——F. Supp. ——, 10 FEP Cases 913, 914 (N.D. Calif. 1975).
33. *San Francisco Chronicle,* December 21, 1973.
34. *Rodriguez* v. *East Texas Motor Freight,* 505 F.2d 40, 8 FEP Cases 1246 (5th Cir. 1974). See also *Herrera* v. *Yellow Freight System, Inc.,* 505 F.2d 66, 8 FEP Cases 1266, 8 EPD para. 9812 (5th Cir. 1974); and *Resendis* v. *Lee Way Motor Freight, Inc.,* 505 F.2d 69, 8 FEP Cases 1268, 8 EPD para. 9813 (5th Cir. 1974).
35. *Franks* v. *Bowman Transportation Co.,* 495 F.2d 398, 8 FEP Cases 66, 7 EPD para. 9401, *rehearing denied,* 8 EPD para. 9580 (5th Cir. 1974), *cert. denied sub nom.,* 419 U.S. 1050, 8 FEP Cases 1280 (1974).
36. Report of Atlanta Regional Litigation Center, EEOC, *News* (Washington, D.C.: Equal Employment Opportunity Commission, July 11, 1975), p. 14.

Chapter 10

All FEPC material cited here is in Record Group 228, National Archives Building, Washington, D.C. See Charles Zaid, *Preliminary Inventory No. 147,* Records of the Committee on Fair Employment Practice (Washington, D.C.: The National Archives, 1962).

1. UAW-CIO Agreement, FEPC Field Instruction No. 38, August 26, 1944.
2. UAW-CIO Policy Manual, July 1, 1944.
3. FEPC Summary of Strike at Wright Aeronautical Company, based on a report by William McKnight.
4. *Ibid.*
5. *Ibid.*
6. FEPC Internal Memorandum from Joy Schultz to Elmer Henderson, re: Progress Report on the Delco-Remy Cases, January 25, 1945, p. 5.
7. *Id.,* p. 4.
8. *Id.,* p. 5.

9. *Id.,* p. 8.
10. *Ibid.*
11. Frank Winn, "Labor Tackles the Race Question," *Antioch Review,* Fall 1943, pp. 341–360.
12. *Id.,* pp. 354–355.
13. *Id.,* p. 342.
14. William H. Friedland, "Attitude Change Toward Negroes by White Shop-Level Leaders of the United Automobile Workers Union" (unpublished master's thesis submitted to the Graduate Council of Wayne State University in partial fulfillment of the requirements for the Master of Arts degree in the Department of Sociology and Anthropology, 1952), pp. 29–32. Copy in Archives of Labor History and Urban Affairs, Wayne State University, Detroit, Mich.
15. Interview by author with Shelton Tappes, international representative, UAW, Detroit, October 27, 1967. Transcript in Archives of Labor History and Urban Affairs, Wayne State University, Detroit, Mich.
16. Letter from Jacob Seidenberg, executive director, President's Committee on Government Contracts, to Herbert Hill, labor secretary, NAACP, July 2, 1957, re: Investigation of Hayes Aircraft Corp., Birmingham; letter from Irving Bluestone, administrative assistant to Leonard Woodcock, vice president, UAW, to Herbert Hill, labor secretary, NAACP, August 14, 1957, re: Hayes Aircraft Corp., Birmingham; letter from Jacob Seidenberg, executive director, President's Committee on Government Contracts, to Frank Hunter, October 19, 1959, re: Complaint filed against Hayes Aircraft Corp.; letter from Jerry R. Holleman, executive vice chairman, President's Committee on Equal Employment Opportunity, to Clyde L. Robertson, May 3, 1962, re: Complaint against Chevrolet Atlanta plant of General Motors Corp., File No. C–4–1–513; letter from James H. Brown, international representative, National Ford Dept. UAW, to Calvin C. Alsobrook, November 1, 1962, acknowledging receipt of 13 "Employment Survey Forms" signed by Negro applicants for employment at the Ford Atlanta assembly plant. "Racial Hiring Policies Cleveland Tank Plant, General Motors Corporation and the Cleveland Diesel Engine Division (G.M.)," a report by the Urban League of Cleveland submitted to the President's Committee on Government Contracts, June 1954. Letter from Charles J. Patterson, Urban League of Cleveland, to Jacob Seidenberg, executive director, President's Committee on Government Contracts, September 20, 1954. Report of General Motors Survey by Charles J. Patterson, industrial field secretary, Urban League of Cleveland, January 1955. Memorandum to Leonard Woodcock, director, General Motors Dept. UAW, from Herbert Hill, labor secretary, NAACP, June 3, 1957, re: Status of Negro Workers, General Motors Corporation, St. Louis, Mo.; letter from William H. Oliver, co-director Fair Practices Dept. UAW, to Herbert Hill, labor secretary, NAACP, December 31, 1957, and letter from Leonard Woodcock, vice president, UAW, and director, General Motors Dept., to Herbert Hill, labor secretary, NAACP, January 13, 1958, re: General Motors Corporation, St. Louis, Mo.; See also NAACP Annual Report, 1957, pp. 51–52; letter from Percy H. Williams, assistant executive director, President's Committee on Equal Employment Opportunity, to Robert Lee Stovall, Jr., October 3, 1962, re: Complaint against General Motors Corp.,

Kansas City, Kansas, File No. C–4–2–1190; letter from Hobart Taylor, Jr., executive vice chairman, President's Committee on Equal Employment Opportunity, to Leonard H. Carter, regional field secretary, NAACP, January 7, 1963, re: Charges of discrimination against General Motors Corp., Kansas City, Kansas. Copies in author's files.

17. *President's Report,* UAW, 1955, p. 84–D.
18. Clark Porteous, "International Takes Over Local 988," Memphis *Press-Scimitar,* February 10, 1960. "Statement to all members of Local 988, UAW" from the board of administration, Pat Greathouse, chairman, vice president, UAW, Robert Johnston, international executive board member, UAW, Douglas Fraser, international executive board member, UAW, May 2, 1960; "Statement to all members of Local 988, UAW, from the Board of Administration," June 3, 1960; letter from John L. Holcombe, commissioner, Bureau of Labor-Management Reports, U.S. Department of Labor, to Walter P. Reuther, president, international union, UAW-CIO, May 23, 1960, together with substance of action by the bureau dismissing complaint filed against trusteeship imposed upon Local 988; letter from William J. Beckham, administrative assistant to the president, UAW, to Herbert Hill, labor secretary, NAACP, July 25, 1960; interviews by author with George Holloway, member Shop Committee, Local 988, UAW, in Memphis on May 26, 1961, in Atlantic City on March 21, 1964, and in Baltimore on November 3, 1967; interview by author with Carl Shier, international representative, UAW, member of National Harvester Council-UAW in Chicago on November 27, 1966. Copies in author's files.
19. Memorandum to members of the Sub-Committee on Review from Jacob Seidenberg, executive director, re: The Attached Compliance Review Reports, "For Administrative Purposes Only," n.d.; Summary of Compliance Review Report, Ford Motor Company, Atlanta, GSA–1, 1956–1957, S-C.R. April 22, 1957; Summary of Compliance Review Report, Ford Motor Company, Long Beach, California, GSA–4, S-C.R. April 22, 1957; Summary of Compliance Review Report, Ford Motor Company, Kansas City, Mo., GSA–6, 1956–1957, S-C.R. April 22, 1957; Summary of Compliance Review Report, Ford Motor Company, Dallas, GSA–7, 1956–1957, S-C.R. April 22, 1957; Summary of Compliance Review Report, Ford Motor Company, Memphis, GSA–10, 1956–1957, S-C.R. April 22, 1957; Summary of Compliance Review Report, Ford Motor Company, Chicago, GSA–15, 1956–1957, S-C.R. April 22, 1957; Summary of Compliance Review Survey, Ford Motor Company, GSA–18, 1956–1957, S-C.R. April 22, 1957.
20. *Employment,* Report No. 3 (Washington, D.C.: U.S. Commission on Civil Rights, 1961), p. 65.
21. "NAACP Plans a G.M. Job Drive," *New York Times,* April 9, 1964; Fred Porterfield, "GM Pickets Tell Why They March," Detroit *Free Press,* May 5, 1964; "NAACP May Picket Ford, Chrysler, Too," Detroit *News,* May 5, 1964; "NAACP Asks Auto Industry to Form Panel for Negro Jobs," *New York Times,* June 11, 1964; Gene Roberts, "Auto Firms Asked to Act on Bias," Detroit *Free Press,* June 14, 1964.
22. Interview by author with UAW officials, Detroit, October, 17–19, 1973.
23. *Ibid.*
24. UAW Administrative Letter, Vol. 22, March 19, 1970, Letter No. 6.

25. Minutes of UAW National Advisory Council on Anti-Discrimination, June 27–28, 1969.
26. 295 F. Supp. 803, 1 FEP Cases 665, 70 LRRM 2926 (N.D. Ala. 1968).
27. *Movement for Opportunity and Equality* v. *General Motors Corp., Detroit Diesel Allison Division, United Automobile, Aerospace, and Agricultural Implement Workers of America, International Union, Local 933,* CA No. IP 73–C–412 (D.C. S. Ind., Indianapolis Division, August 23, 1973).
28. Report of Atlanta Regional Litigation Center, EEOC, *News* (Washington, D.C.: Equal Employment Opportunity Commission, July 11, 1975), p. 8.
29. Interview by author with Ralph Helstein, Chicago, April 27, 1967.
30. *Ibid.*
31. Arbitration of Grievance No. 1367, Local 28, UPWA Against Swift & Co., Chicago, Winter 1950.
32. *Supra* note 29.
33. *Ibid.*
34. Interview by author with Charles A. Hayes, director, District 1, UPWA, Chicago, March 30, 1967; interview by author with Richard C. Saunders, president, Local 100, UPWA, Chicago, April 1, 1967; interview by author with Ralph Helstein, president, international union, UPWA, Chicago, April 27 and 29, 1967; interview by author with Jess Prosten, director of organization and contract enforcement, UPWA, Chicago, April 29, 1967; interview by author with Russell R. Lasley, vice president, UPWA, Chicago, April 29, 1967; interview by author with Herbert March, former organizer, UPWA, Los Angeles, July 21, 1968. See also the following publications: *Minorities in the UPWA,* A History of Negroes and Mexican Americans in the Packing Industry, Anti-Discrimination Department, UPWA, June 1951, mimeo; "Action Against Jim Crow, UPWA's Fight for Equal Rights," n.d.; "Discrimination Fight to Reach All Local Unions," *Packinghouse Worker,* July 1952; "Report of UPWA's Anti-Discrimination Conference," *Packinghouse Worker,* December 1953; Leslie F. Orear and Stephen H. Diamond, *Out of the Jungle* (The Packinghouse Workers Fight for Justice and Equality) (Chicago: The Hyde Park Press, 1968).
35. For a study of the racial practices of the United Packinghouse Workers union, see John Hope, II, *Equality of Opportunity—A Union Approach to Fair Employment* (Washington, D.C.: Public Affairs Press, 1956). See also Erdman B. Palmore, "The Introduction of Negroes into White Departments," *Human Organization,* Spring 1955; Brendon Sexton, "The Intervention of the Union in the Plant," *Journal of Social Issues,* Vol. ix, No. 1 (1953), pp. 7–11.

Chapter 11

All FEPC material cited here is in Record Group 228, National Archives Building, Washington, D.C. See Charles Zaid, *Preliminary Inventory No. 147.* Records of the Committee on Fair Employment Practice (Washington, D.C.: The National Archives, 1962).

1. Robert C. Weaver, *Negro Labor—A National Problem* (New York: Harcourt, Brace & Co., 1946), pp. 155–156. See also Stanley Frazier, "Collective Bargaining in Philadelphia Local Transit" (unpublished bachelor's thesis, Princeton University, April 19, 1954).

2. *Ibid.*

3. *Ibid.*

4. See W. E. B. Du Bois, *The Philadelphia Negro: A Social Study* (Philadelphia: University of Pennsylvania, 1899; reissued in a paperback edition, New York: Schocken Books, 1967), Chaps. IV and IX.

5. Interviews by author with George R. Staab, labor reporter for the *Philadelphia Bulletin,* Philadelphia, October 30, 1967; and with Orrin Evans, Philadelphia, October 30, 1967. Before joining the staff of the *Bulletin,* Mr. Evans had a long career as a reporter for other newspapers, including the Negro press, in the Philadelphia area.

6. Public hearing, "Stenographic Transcript of Testimony Before the Philadelphia Commission on Human Relations in re: Investigation into Alleged Discriminatory Employment Practices by Hotels and Restaurants in Center City Philadelphia," commencing November 30, 1959, Philadelphia, Commission on Human Relations; "Summary of Testimony—Hotel and Restaurant Hearings," The Division of Public Law and Employment, Philadelphia: Commission on Human Relations, November 4, 1960; "Findings of Facts, Conclusions and Action of the Commission on Human Relations in re: Investigative Public Hearings into Alleged Discriminatory Practices by the Hotel and Restaurant Industry in Philadelphia," Philadelphia: Commission on Human Relations, April 7, 1961; "Interim Report, Hotel and Restaurant Survey," Memorandum, Philadelphia: Commission on Human Relations, February 17, 1965; "Status of Hotel and Restaurant Survey," Memorandum, Philadelphia: Commission on Human Relations, July 12, 1965; "The Philadelphia Entertainment Industry: A Study of Non-White Employment Patterns," Philadelphia: Commission on Human Relations, 1962; Memorandum, "Investigation of Waterfront Employment Patterns and Practices," from Terry C. Chisholm to All Commissioners, Philadelphia: Commission on Human Relations, June 19, 1963; "The Philadelphia Waterfront—General Information," Memorandum, Philadelphia: Commission on Human Relations, June 25, 1963; "Recent Developments in Waterfront Investigations," Memorandum, Philadelphia: Commission on Human Relations, July 2, 1963; "Memorandum of Agreement Between the Philadelphia Marine Trade Association and the International Longshoremen's Association, Local 1291, and the Commission on Human Relations," Philadelphia: Commission on Human Relations, October 1, 1964; "Conciliation Order, City of Philadelphia Commission on Human Relations, and Local 1242, International Longshoremen's Association, the Philadelphia Marine Trade Association," Philadelphia: Commission on Human Relations, September 20, 1966; Special Report, "Progress in Waterfront Cases," March 1, 1967; Memorandum, "Résumé of Philadelphia Waterfront Employment Practices," from Richard J. Levin, Division of Public Law and Employment, to the Commission, Philadelphia: Commission on Human Relations, n.d.; "Resolution Authorizing Public Hearings Regarding Discrimination by Employers, Labor Unions and Others in Public Works Projects in the City of Philadelphia," Philadelphia: Commis-

sion on Human Relations, April 2, 1963; "Conclusions and Recommenda-
tions Pertaining to Employment Discrimination on Certain City Work
Contracts and in the Construction Trades," Philadelphia: Commission on
Human Relations, May 20, 1963.

7. FEPC Statement of Facts, October 23, 1943. Legal Division Hearings, Case
   No. 55.
8. FEPC Chronological Summary of Philadelphia Transportation Company
   Case, filed at Smith committee hearings, January 11, 1944. The summary
   reports that between August 1941 and November 1942 repeated efforts were
   made by Negro PTC employees to obtain upgrading. The company placed
   responsibility on the PRT Employees' Union and continued to advertise for
   streetcar and bus operators.
9. FEPC, *Weekly News Digest,* Vol. 1, No. 14 (March 3, 1944).
10. *Supra* note 8.
11. FEPC *Hearings.* Philadelphia Transit Employees' Union. Case No. 55.
    Transcript of proceedings held in Philadelphia on December 8, 1943, with
    prepared papers, summary of evidence with opinion and orders, grand jury
    report and indictment, summary with findings and directives, and exhibits.
    Testimony of Raleigh Johnson, pp. 39 *et seq.* Mr. Johnson was a Negro
    electrical welder for the company who had been a member of the Co-
    operative Association and later the PRT Employees' Union. He stated that
    it was the common understanding among the union members that the
    "customs" clause was simply a device to incorporate the rules and
    regulations which had been in effect between the company and the former
    association. When asked if the clause was ever previously understood to be
    relevant to racial employment practices, he replied: "It was never my
    understanding. We were always led to believe just the opposite, we were one
    big family."
12. FEPC Internal Memorandum from Will Maslow to Malcolm Ross,
    chairman, re: Philadelphia Transportation Company, December 8, 1943.
13. *Ibid.*
14. *Ibid.*
15. *Ibid.*
16. Agreement between the PTC and the PRT Employees' Union, March 2,
    1943.
17. *Supra* note 12. Maslow stated: "It would seem that a union which admits
    Negroes to membership but otherwise discriminates against them, for
    example, by opposing their upgrading to platform men, would not be
    violating the Pennsylvania Labor Relations Act, except under an extreme
    reading of that statute."
18. *Supra* note 8.
19. Letter from Frank Carney, president of PRT Employees' Union, to Carolyn
    Moore, executive secretary of NAACP Action Committee on PTC
    Employment, March 2, 1943, *supra* note 11.
20. Testimony of Roosevelt Neal, *supra* note 11, p. 51.
21. *Supra* note 8.
22. *Ibid.*
23. *Ibid.*
24. U.S. Employment Service report, September 1943.
25. *Ibid.*

26. FEPC Internal Memorandum from Will Maslow to Malcolm Ross, re: War Manpower Commission Stabilization Plan for Philadelphia, December 2, 1943.
27. *Ibid.*
28. *Ibid.*
29. *Supra* note 8.
30. *Ibid.*
31. *Ibid.*
32. *Ibid.*
33. *Ibid.*
34. FEPC Summary of the Evidence, with Findings and Directives in the Matter of P.T.C. and P.R.T. Employees' Union, *supra* note 11.
35. *Ibid.*
36. *Ibid.*
37. *Ibid.*
38. *Supra* note 8.
39. *Ibid.*
40. Weaver, *supra* note 1, p. 159.
41. *Philadelphia Evening Bulletin,* November 22, 1943, p. 18.
42. Weaver, *supra* note 1, p. 159.
43. Letter from Frank Carney to Malcolm Ross, November 24, 1943.
44. See, for example, Michigan *Chronicle,* November 13, 1943, p. 1, and December 4, 1943, p. 3.
45. Dated December 1, 1943.
46. Statement of Malcolm Ross, *supra* note 11, pp. 4–5.
47. Statement of PRT Employees' Union Concerning the Directive Order of the FEPC, *supra* note 11.
48. *Ibid.*
49. *Ibid.*
50. *Ibid.*
51. *Ibid.*
52. *Ibid.*
53. NAACP statement, *supra* note 11.
54. *Supra* note 11.
55. *Ibid.*
56. *Ibid.*
57. Weaver, *supra* note 1, p. 160.
58. *Ibid.*
59. December 14, 1943, 10:30 p.m., on station WCAU. Coburn prefaced his defiance of the FEPC with these remarks: "We are a democratic union, operating on democratic principles, and we do not believe in or practice discrimination. We have no resentment for Negroes, or any other group, seeking advancement." Transcript in FEPC files, *supra* note 11.
60. Letter from Frank Carney, president of PRT Employees' Union, to Malcolm Ross, January 3, 1944.
61. The text of the letter from the union to the company is in a letter to Malcolm Ross from Ralph Senter, president of the PTC, January 4, 1944.
62. *Ibid.*
63. *Supra* note 8. "January 6, 1944—Washington newspapers state Smith Committee will investigate FEPC Directives to P.T.C. This was the FEPC's

first notice that a hearing was scheduled in the matter." The hearing was held five days later.

64. The Select Committee of the House of Representatives to Investigate Executive Agencies Exceeding Their Jurisdiction, Howard W. Smith (D-Va.), chairman.

65. The text of the union's letter to the Smith committee is in the FEPC Internal Memorandum from George Johnson to George Crockett, January 15, 1944. The memorandum states: "The Smith Committee construed this letter to be a complaint and held a public hearing."

66. Hearings Before the Special Committee to Investigate Executive Agencies, January 11, 1944, p. 1992.

67. *Id.,* p. 1986.

68. *Philadelphia Inquirer,* January 6, 1944, p. 18.

69. FEPC Internal Memorandum from Milo Manly, examiner, to G. James Fleming, regional director, January 7, 1944.

70. Original in FEPC files.

71. *Supra* note 69. "So far, all indications are that the men at this location will not strike." Another memorandum stated: "It is our opinion that the rank and file white workers are much less aroused and bitter at the present time than they were in the initial stages of this case; they do not seem willing to go along with their paid officers who have reportedly threatened to strike rather than observe FEPC's directive. In fact, several of the men have been outspoken against their officers 'defying the President'; others point out . . . that they have worked alongside Negroes . . . for years."

72. Michigan *Chronicle,* January 1, 1944, p. 3.

73. *Ibid.*

74. Douglas MacMahon, "The Real Philadelphia Story," *New Masses,* August 29, 1944. Also, according to George Staab, PRT Employees' Union leaders told employees: "A victory for the CIO Transport Workers Union means Negro drivers." *Supra* note 5.

75. FEPC Internal Memorandum from G. James Fleming to George Crockett, January 6, 1944.

76. *Ibid.*

77. Weaver, *supra* note 1, p. 161.

78. *Ibid.*

79. *Ibid.*

80. Nathan Glazer and Frederick Hoffman, "Behind the Philadelphia Strike," *Politics,* November 1944, p. 307.

81. Results of PTC election, March 14, 1944, as reported by FEPC Summary of the Evidence, with Findings and Directives in the Matter of P.T.C. and P.R.T. Employees' Union, *supra* note 11.

82. FEPC Internal Memorandum from G. James Fleming to Will Maslow, re: Conversation with Mitten, April 6, 1944.

83. *Ibid.*

84. *Ibid.*

85. FEPC Letter from Ross to Quill, April 12, 1944.

86. Letter from Quill to Ross, April 20, 1944.

87. FEPC Internal Memorandum from G. James Fleming to Will Maslow, July 4, 1944.

88. MacMahon, *supra* note 74.

89. PTC Notice to All Employees, July 7, 1944.
90. Quoted in Louis Ruchames, *Race, Jobs & Politics—The Story of FEPC* (New York: Columbia University Press, 1953), p. 109.
91. *PM,* July 12, 1944, p. 1
92. FEPC Internal Memorandum from G. James Fleming to Malcolm Ross, August 5, 1944. One of the workers had nineteen years of seniority with the company and was to lose eleven cents an hour by starting anew as a streetcar operator.
93. Ruchames, *supra* note 90, p. 110.
94. Weaver, *supra* note 1, p. 163.
95. FEPC Internal Memorandum from G. James Fleming to Malcolm Ross, July 31, 1944.
96. Quoted in Ruchames, *supra* note 90, p. 113.
97. Interview by author with Eli Rock, attorney, Philadelphia, February 27, 1968. At the time of the strike Rock was disputes director for the regional office of the War Labor Board.
98. Because of strict wartime rationing of oil and gasoline, the use of automobiles was severely curtailed.
99. *Philadelphia Bulletin,* August 2, 1944, p. 1.
100. *Supra* note 97.
101. *Ibid.*
102. *Ibid.*
103. *Supra* note 8.
104. Quoted in Ruchames, *supra* note 90, pp. 114–115.
105. *Ibid.*
106. *Supra* note 97.
107. *Ibid.*
108. John H. Ohly, "History of Plant Seizures During World War II," 3 vols. (unpublished manuscript, Office of the Chief of Military History, Department of the Army, 1946), pp. 305–306. Ohly writes: "This request was ignored, as it should have been."
109. *Philadelphia Bulletin,* August 3, 1944, p. 1.
110. *Ibid.*
111. 9 Fed. Reg. 9878 (1944).
112. *Supra* note 109.
113. *Ibid.*
114. *Ibid.*
115. *Ibid.*
116. *Philadelphia Bulletin,* August 4, 1944, p. 1.
117. *Ibid.*
118. MacMahon, *supra* note 74.
119. Ohly, *supra* note 108, p. 303.
120. *Supra* note 116. The act imposed criminal penalties on anyone engaging in a strike at a government-operated facility.
121. Statement of Frank Thompson, a member of the General Emergency Committee. *Supra* note 120.
122. Weaver, *supra* note 1, p. 167.
123. Ruchames, *supra* note 90, p. 116.
124. Statement of PRT Employees' Union Concerning the Directive Order of the FEPC, *supra* note 11.

125. *Supra* note 99.
126. *Ibid.*
127. Ohly, *supra* note 108, p. 300.
128. Minutes of the Meeting of the Board of Directors, NAACP, September 11, 1944. Theodore Spaulding, president of the Philadelphia branch of the NAACP, provides an account of the involvement of the association in efforts to upgrade Negro workers and of the subsequent strike in "Philadelphia Hate Strike," *Crisis*, September 1944, pp. 281–283, 301.
129. *New York Herald Tribune*, August 4, 1944, p. 28.
130. *Philadelphia Record*, August 4, 1944, p. 1.
131. *Ibid.*
132. *Ibid.*
133. *Philadelphia Bulletin*, August 3, 1944, p. 1.
134. The stages and rationale of military activity are outlined in Ohly, *supra* note 108, pp. 305–306.
135. Ruchames, *supra* note 90, p. 117.
136. *Philadelphia Record*, August 6, 1944, p. 1.
137. *Philadelphia Bulletin*, August 7, 1944, p. 1.
138. *Ibid.*
139. Ohly, *supra* note 108, p. 309.
140. *Id.*, pp. 310–311.
141. *Philadelphia Bulletin*, August 9, 1944, p. 1.
142. *Ibid.*
143. Ohly, *supra* note 108, p. 312.
144. FEPC Internal Memorandum from G. James Fleming to Malcolm Ross, December 28, 1944. Fleming wrote that the company "felt that public acceptance of Negro operators was excellent as there were no negative incidents reported . . . the company is perfectly satisfied with the performance of the Negro operators."
145. *Ibid.*
146. *Ibid.*
147. Ohly, *supra* note 108, p. 113.
148. Michigan *Chronicle*, August 12, 1944, p. 1.
149. Weaver, *supra* note 1, p. 169.
150. Quoted in Weaver, *supra* note 1.
151. Ruchames, *supra* note 90, p. 117.
152. Michigan *Chronicle*, October 14, 1944, p. 1.
153. *Philadelphia Record*, October 5, 1944, p. 1.
154. *Philadelphia Record*, March 13, 1945, p. 1. Under the Smith-Connally Act they could have received a $5,000 fine and one year in jail.
155. *Crisis*, September 1944, p. 280.
156. *Final Report*, June 28, 1946 (Washington, D.C.: Fair Employment Practice Committee, 1947), pp. 14–15.

Chapter 12

All FEPC material cited here is in Record Group 228, National Archives Building, Washington, D.C. See Charles Zaid, *Preliminary*

Inventory No. 147, Records of the Committee on Fair Employment Practice (Washington, D.C.: The National Archives, 1962).

1. Adam Clayton Powell, Jr., *Marching Blacks* (New York: Dial Press, 1945), p. 102.
2. *Ibid.*
3. *Ibid.*
4. *Ibid.*
5. *Ibid.*
6. *Id.*, pp. 102–103.
7. FEPC Internal Memorandum from Hayes Beall, senior fair practice examiner, to Will Maslow, director of field operations, re: Status of Recent FEPC Transit Cases, April 30, 1945.
8. *Ibid.*
9. *Ibid.*
10. *Ibid.*
11. *Ibid.*
12. *Id.*, p. 3.
13. *Ibid.*
14. FEPC Internal Memorandum, April 25, 1945.
15. *Ibid.*
16. *Supra* note 7, p. 3.
17. *Supra* note 14.
18. *Supra* note 7, p. 3.
19. *Ibid.*
20. *Ibid.*
21. *Ibid.*
22. *Ibid.*
23. *Id.*, p. 4. At a conference with the FEPC, the union's president "was noncommittal with respect to the union's attitude towards the employment of Negroes as operators."
24. *Id.*, p. 5. In 1944 the company sent Division 757 a communication stating: "It is the purpose and intention of this Company to abide by the Fair Employment Practice prescribed by the President's Committee. Applicants for employment will be accepted for employment on cars, buses, and maintenance forces of the company solely on the basis of their qualifications and without regard to their race, creed, color or national origin." On April 30, 1945, the FEPC stated: "To date, the submission of the above statement had not been followed by the actual employment of workers against whom there has been discrimination."
25. *Ibid.*
26. Robert C. Weaver, *Negro Labor—A National Problem* (New York: Harcourt, Brace & Co., 1946), p. 171.
27. *Id.*, pp. 171–172, citing as his source "observers who were on the scene." Weaver reports that "[a]lthough the exact nature of any such maneuver cannot be established, this much is known: there was no bargaining election in which workers had a chance to select their own union."
28. FEPC Timetable of Events (of major local transit cases), n.d.
29. Weaver, *supra* note 26, p. 173.
30. *Ibid.* The union had no objection to Negroes becoming members of the union, for according to the union president's testimony at the FEPC

hearing, the union had approximately 250 Negro members. The union's objection, however, was to Negroes occupying the better jobs over which the union had jurisdiction—those of operators and conductors.

31. FEPC *Hearings. Los Angeles Railway Corporation* v. *Complaints of Alfonso Edwards, James H. Herod, Jr., Charles M. Robinson, Sidney L. Robinson, James E. Savoy, Nona S. Slayden, and others.* Case No. 66. Transcript of proceedings held in Los Angeles on August 8, 1944, with accompanying correspondence, exhibits, agreement, findings with directives, excerpts from contracts, statements of complaints, and regional cases. Letter from P. B. Harris to Thomas F. Neblett, regional chairman, War Labor Board, February 26, 1943, pp. 197–204.
32. *Id.,* pp. 190–193.
33. Letter from Harris to Neblett, *supra* note 31.
34. Weaver, *supra* note 26, p. 173.
35. Letter from Harris to Neblett, *supra* note 31.
36. *Ibid.*
37. *Ibid.*
38. Telegram from Lawrence Cramer to P. B. Harris, February 23, 1943, *supra* note 31, p. 207.
39. Telegram from P. B. Harris to Lawrence Cramer, February 24, 1943, *supra* note 31, p. 207.
40. Telegram from Monsignor Francis J. Haas, chairman, FEPC, to P. B. Harris, July 9, 1943, *supra* note 31, p. 212.
41. Letter from P. B. Harris to Monsignor Francis J. Haas, July 13, 1943, *supra* note 31, p. 212.
42. Weaver, *supra* note 26, p. 175.
43. *Ibid.*
44. FEPC Complaint Against the Los Angeles Railway Corporation, July 1, 1944, *supra* note 31, pp. 31–35.
45. *Ibid.*
46. Testimony of Mrs. Cortez Strange, regarding conversation of December 1, 1943, *supra* note 31, pp. 46–47.
47. Testimony of Mrs. Nona S. Slayden, *supra* note 31, pp. 98–99.
48. Testimony of Thomas Campbell, regional director, War Manpower Commission, *supra* note 31, pp. 114–122.
49. *Ibid.*
50. *Ibid.*
51. Weaver, *supra* note 26, p. 176.
52. *Ibid.*
53. Quoted in Weaver, *supra* note 26, p. 177.
54. FEPC Internal Memorandum from Maceo Hubbard to George M. Johnson, deputy chairman, July 20, 1944.
55. *Supra* note 31, p. 187.
56. Testimony of Mr. Neary, *supra* note 31, p. 227.
57. *Ibid.*
58. Testimony of Doyle D. McClurg, president of Division 1277, *supra* note 31, p. 266.
59. *Id.,* pp. 268–269.
60. Malcolm Ross, *All Manner of Men* (New York: Reynal and Hitchcock, 1948), p. 155.

61. *Ibid.*
62. FEPC Summary of Findings and Directives to Los Angeles Railway Corporation, August 9, 1944.
63. Letter from P. B. Harris to FEPC, August 9, 1944.
64. FEPC Internal Memorandum from Carol Coan and C. L. Golightly to John A. Davis, September 5, 1944.
65. *Ibid.* The conference was held August 18, 1944.
66. *Ibid.*
67. FEPC Internal Memorandum from George M. Johnson, deputy chairman, Legal Division, to Will Maslow, director of field operations, March 22, 1945.
68. Weaver, *supra* note 26, pp. 180–181.
69. FEPC *Hearings.* Key System and Division 192, Amalgamated Association of Street, Electric Railway and Motor Coach Employees of America. Case No. 81. Transcript of proceedings held on March 19–23, 1945, at Oakland, Calif., and on April 16, 1945, at San Francisco, with accompanying correspondence; newspaper clippings; a survey of the attitudes of platform operators, submitted on behalf of the Key System in March 1945; and a *Report on Results of Operation of the Key System,* by the Railroad Commission of the State of California, dated August 28, 1944.
70. Testimony of Alfred E. Brown, president and business agent for Division 192, *supra* note 69, p. 44.
71. *Id.,* pp. 99–100.
72. Data on negotiations for 1941–1942 contract between Division 192 and Key System, *supra* note 69.
73. *Ibid.*
74. Testimony of Alfred E. Brown, *supra* note 69, pp. 99–100.
75. The Key System Annual Report, issued December 31, 1944.
76. February 1, 1944, publication by Key System.
77. August 31, 1944, California Railroad Commission Report on the Service, Equipment, Manpower, and Track of Key System.
78. Testimony of Alfred E. Brown, *supra* note 69, pp. 55–56.
79. *Id.,* p. 59.
80. FEPC Summary of Meeting of Government Agency Representatives with Executive Committee of Division 192, December 23, 1944.
81. Testimony of Alfred E. Brown, *supra* note 69, pp. 55–56.
82. *Id.,* p. 59.
83. *Id.,* pp. 67, 75.
84. Testimony of Frank Pestana, FEPC examiner, regarding December 1944 conversation with Alfred E. Brown, *supra* note 69, pp. 150–151.
85. *Id.,* p. 152.
86. Testimony of Alfred E. Brown, *supra* note 69, p. 80.
87. *Ibid.*
88. Testimony of Alfred E. Brown, *supra* note 69, p. 81.
89. *Id.,* p. 84.
90. *Id.,* p. 88.
91. *Wheels,* August 5, 1945. *Wheels* was the official organ of Division 192, Amalgamated Association of Street, Electric Railway and Motor Coach Employees of America, p. 1.
92. *Ibid.*

93. FEPC Confidential Memorandum to Malcolm Ross, FEPC chairman, from Bernard Ross, acting regional director, re: Activity Regarding Key System, October 5, 1945.
94. Ross, *supra* note 60, p. 156.
95. FEPC *Hearings*. Capital Transit Company. Case No. 70. Transcript of proceedings held in Washington, D.C., on January 15–16, 1945, with accompanying correspondence, newspaper clippings, and statistical charts. Statement of Mrs. Evelyn Cooper, FEPC examiner, p. 10.
96. Stipulation of Facts between FEPC and Capital Transit Company, signed December 27, 1943.
97. War Manpower Commission, news release, December 1, 1942.
98. Statement of Mrs. Evelyn Cooper, *supra* note 95, pp. 12–13.
99. *Supra* note 96.
100. *Ibid.*
101. *Ibid.*
102. Letter to Division 689 from W. D. Mahon, international president of the Amalgamated Association of Street, Electric Railway and Motor Coach Employees of America, August 7, 1942, *supra* note 95, pp. 231–232.
103. Louis Ruchames, *Race, Jobs & Politics—The Story of FEPC* (New York: Columbia University Press, 1953), pp. 55–56.
104. *Id.,* p. 56.
105. Testimony of B. A. Simmons, *supra* note 95, pp. 271–274.
106. *Ibid.*
107. *Ibid.*
108. Ross, *supra* note 60, p. 157.
109. Statement of Edmund L. Jones, *supra* note 95, pp. 19–20.
110. *Ibid.*
111. *Ibid.*
112. Ross, *supra* note 60, p. 157.
113. Statement of Mrs. Evelyn Cooper, *supra* note 95, p. 14.
114. *Ibid.*
115. *Ibid.*
116. *Supra* note 95, pp. 21–22.
117. Testimony of Edward A. Roberts, director of passenger operations, Office of Defense Transportation, *supra* note 95, p. 60.
118. Public Utilities Order No. 2311, June 25, 1942, *supra* note 95, pp. 36–37.
119. Mrs. Evelyn Cooper, summarizing testimony of Alexander Shapiro, director of personnel at the Capital Transit Company, before the Public Utilities Commission, *supra* note 95, p. 223.
120. *Supra* note 95, p. 5.
121. Letter from FEPC to Capital Transit Company, July 17, 1943, *supra* note 95, p. 223.
122. Letter to Capital Transit Company from FEPC, August 14, 1943, *supra* note 95, p. 224.
123. Letter from Capital Transit Company to FEPC, August 25, 1943, *supra* note 95, p. 225.
124. Testimony of Paul S. Lunt, *supra* note 95, pp. 105 *et seq.*
125. *Ibid.*
126. Ross, *supra* note 60, p. 159.
127. Pittsburgh *Courier,* September 4, 1943, p. 1.

128. *Ibid.*
129. Washington *Afro-American,* September 4, 1943, p. 1.
130. Testimony of Frank N. Johnson, *supra* note 95, pp. 292–293.
131. Testimony of E. D. Merril, *supra* note 95, p. 399.
132. Ruchames, *supra* note 103, p. 132.
133. *Ibid.*
134. *Ibid.*
135. Ross, *supra* note 60, p. 162.
136. Ruchames, *supra* note 103, p. 132.
137. Letter from Charles H. Houston to President Harry S. Truman, December 3, 1945.
138. Letter from President Harry S. Truman to Charles H. Houston, December 7, 1945.
139. Ross, *supra* note 60, p. 162.
140. *Final Report,* June 28, 1946 (Washington, D.C.: Fair Employment Practice Committee, 1947), p. 14.
141. Philip W. Jeffress, *The Negro in the Urban Transit Industry,* Report No. 18 in the series *The Racial Policies of American Industry* (Industrial Research Unit, Wharton School of Finance and Commerce, 1970; distributed by University of Pennsylvania Press, Philadelphia), Table 21, p. 63.
142. *Id.,* p. 64. See also p. 101.
143. Interview by author with George Brady, leader of Muni Drivers Association, San Francisco, September 4, 1971. The record of expulsion is in *Reporter's Transcript of Proceedings, June 9–10, 1970, in the Matter of Charges Brought Against George Brady, David Nelson, Robert Coats, Jonnie Gilbert, and Ted Walker, Before the Trial Committee of the Transport Workers of America, AFL-CIO, Local 250–A,* San Francisco, Calif.
144. For news reports on the development of this black workers' caucus, see "Transit Workers Form Rights Unit," *New York Times,* June 9, 1968; "Transit Rebels Call on the Rank and File," *New York Post,* December 16, 1969; "TA [Transit Authority], TWU Sued by Workers," *New York Post,* May 21, 1971; "Transit Workers Act to Replace Bargaining Unit," *New York Times,* October 1, 1971; "Bus and Subway Service Called Normal as Wildcat Strike Ends," *New York Times,* January 9, 1972; and "TWU Rebels Seek Election," *New York Post,* January 21, 1972.
145. *Winn, et al.* v. *N.Y.C. Transit Authority, et al.,* CA No. 71-CIV-2261 (S.D. N.Y.).
146. Interview by author with Joseph Carnegie, leader of the Rank and File Committee for a Democratic Union, New York, February 22, 1971.

Chapter 13

All FEPC material cited here is in Record Group 228, National Archives Building, Washington, D.C. See Charles Zaid, *Preliminary Inventory No. 147,* Records of the Committee on Fair Employment Practice (Washington, D.C.: The National Archives, 1962).

1. The railroad brotherhoods were independent organizations not affiliated with the AFL. For an analysis of racially restrictive membership provisions in union constitutions during the 1930s and 1940s, see Herbert Northrup, *Organized Labor and the Negro* (New York: Harper & Brothers, 1944), pp. 2–5. See also Frank E. Wolfe, "Admission to American Trade Unions," Johns Hopkins University Studies in Historical and Political Science, Series XXX (Baltimore: Johns Hopkins University Press, 1912).

2. FEPC *Hearings*. Railroads. No case number. Transcript of proceedings held in Washington, D.C., on September 15–18, 1943, to hear evidence on complaints of racial discrimination in employment on certain railroads of the United States. Exhibits, correspondence, reports, docketed cases, summaries, findings, directives, summaries of complaints, operational statistics for cases docketed and closed, agreements between individual railroad companies and unions, resolutions against railroad discrimination, complaints and agreements on railroad employment seniority lists, and questionnaires on discriminatory employment practices in the railroad industry. Copies of union constitutions were introduced as evidence at these *Hearings*. President's Committee on Fair Employment Practice, *A Hearing to Hear Evidence on Complaints of Racial Discrimination on Certain Railroads of the United States* (Washington, D.C.: Alderson Publishing Co., 1943), p. 413.

3. *Ibid.*

4. Sterling D. Spero and Abraham L. Harris, in *The Black Worker* (New York: Columbia University Press, 1931), p. 284, wrote: "The employment of Negroes in these crafts has been confined almost entirely to the South. It was usual before the world war [World War I] for southern railroads to employ Negro firemen on from 50 to 60 per cent of their runs, while some roads employed 85 to 90 per cent colored firemen, or practically the entire firing force exclusive of apprentice engineers. In 1920, according to calculations based upon the census, Negroes constituted 27.4 per cent of the firemen, 27.1 per cent of the brakemen, and 12.3 per cent of the switchmen in the southern states. . . ."

5. *Locomotive Firemen's Magazine,* December 1890, p. 1094.

6. *Id.,* pp. 1094–1095.

7. *Id.,* p. 1095.

8. *Ibid.*

9. *Houston Daily Post,* October 9, 1890.

10. "The Georgia Railroad Strike," *Outlook,* June 5, 1909, p. 310; cited in Spero and Harris, *supra* note 4, p. 289.

11. *Ibid.*

12. *Locomotive Firemen's Magazine,* August 1909, p. 257; cited in Spero and Harris, *supra* note 4, p. 290.

13. *Ibid.*

14. Spero and Harris, *supra* note 4, p. 291.

15. *Locomotive Firemen's Magazine,* April 1911, p. 519; cited in Spero and Harris, *supra* note 4, p. 291.

16. "The Firemen's Strike," editorial by W. E. B. Du Bois, *Crisis,* May 1911.

17. Spero and Harris, *supra* note 4, p. 292.

18. *Ibid.*

19. Article 29, Section D, "Percentage of Colored Firemen," Agreement Between the Southern Railway Company, the Northern Alabama Railway Company, and the Knoxville and Augusta Railroad Company, and the Brotherhood of Locomotive Firemen and Enginemen, n.d.

20. Agreement Between the Brotherhood of Railroad Trainmen and the Southern Railway Association, January 10, 1910. Quoted in Spero and Harris, *supra* note 4, p. 293.

21. *Ibid.*

22. General Order No. 27, Report of the Director General of Railroads, 1918, p. 15. Quoted in Spero and Harris, *supra* note 4, p. 294.

23. Herbert R. Northrup, *Organized Labor and the Negro* (New York: Harper & Brothers, 1944), pp. 50–51.

24. "The Elimination of Negro Firemen on American Railways—A Study of the Evidence Adduced at the Hearing Before the President's Committee on Fair Employment Practices," *Lawyers Guild Review*, March-April, 1944, p. 33.

25. U.S. Census of Occupations 1910–1940; reported in Northrup, *supra* note 23, p. 53.

26. *Ibid.*

27. *Ibid.*

28. *Ibid.*

29. *Ibid.*

30. *Ibid.*

31. Section 151 (a), General Purposes of the Railway Labor Act, 45 U.S.C.A., Sections 151 *et seq.* The act was amended in 1951 to include Section 151, Eleventh, which permits a union shop.

32. 45 U.S.C.A., Section 152, First.

33. 45 U.S.C.A., Section 152, Fourth and Ninth.

34. 45 U.S.C.A., Section 153, First (i).

35. Northrup, *supra* note 23, pp. 100–101.

36. Speech at the Detroit convention of the Brotherhood of Locomotive Firemen and Enginemen, 1926. Quoted in Spero and Harris, *supra* note 4, p. 307.

37. Memorandum of Understanding of Responsibility for and Duties Under an Agreement Made Between the Four Train Service Organizations and the St. Louis-San Francisco Railway Company, March 14, 1928.

38. Horace R. Cayton and George S. Mitchell, *Black Workers and the New Unions* (Chapel Hill, N.C.: University of North Carolina Press, 1939), p. 440, Appendix B.

39. *Id.*, pp. 441–442.

40. *Id.*, p. 444.

41. Milton Butler, "Murder for the Job," *Nation*, July 12, 1933, p. 44.

42. Testimony of Will Whitfield, *supra* note 2, p. 485.

43. Northrup, *supra* note 23, p. 67.

44. *Ibid.*

45. Supplemental Agreement Effective December 1, 1938, Between the Brotherhood of Locomotive Firemen and Enginemen and the Seaboard Air Line Railway.

46. Provision of the September 1, 1938, Agreement is contained in the Mediation Agreement between the union and the companies, Docket Case

No. A–755, National Mediation Board, applied for December 30, 1939, signed June 24, 1940, effective July 1, 1940.

47. *Ibid.*
48. Memorandum Agreement, February 26, 1941, Between the Brotherhood of Locomotive Firemen and Enginemen and the Southern Railway Company; the Cincinnati, New Orleans and Texas Pacific Railway Company; the Alabama Great Southern Railroad Company; New Orleans and Northeastern Railroad Company; New Orleans Terminal Company; Georgia Southern and Florida Railway Company; St. Johns River Terminal Company; Harriman and Northeastern Railroad Company; and the Cincinnati, Burnside and Cumberland River Railway Company.
49. Brotherhood of Locomotive Firemen and Enginemen Proposals to Twenty-One Railroads, submitted to the National Mediation Board as Docket Case No. A–905.
50. FEPC Summary, Findings, and Directives Concerning Signatories to the Washington Agreement, issued November 18, 1943, and made public December 1, 1943.
51. The Washington Agreement was signed February 18, 1941, effective February 22, 1941, between the Brotherhood of Locomotive Firemen and Enginemen and twenty-one railroads, including the Atlantic Coast Line, the Atlanta Joint Terminals, the Central of Georgia, the Georgia Railroad, the Jacksonville Terminal Co., the Louisville & Nashville Railroad Company, the Norfolk Southern Railroad Company, the St. Louis-San Francisco Railway Company, the Seaboard Air Line Railroad Company, and the Southern Railway Company.
52. *Supra* note 50, pp. 4–5.
53. Memorandum Agreement Between the Brotherhood of Locomotive Firemen and Enginemen and nine southern railroads, February 26, 1941.
54. Supplement to the Agreement Between the Central of Georgia Railway Company and the Brotherhood of Locomotive Firemen and Enginemen, November 3, 1941.
55. Complaint of Edward Nunn, July 25, 1942, *supra* note 2.
56. Complaint of Harry Curry, July 1942, *supra* note 2.
57. Letter from Edward Jouett, vice president and general counsel of the Louisville & Nashville Railroad, to Bartley Crum, FEPC special counsel, September 13, 1943, *supra* note 2.
58. *Ibid.*
59. *Ibid.*
60. Affidavit supporting the complaint of the Association of Colored Trainmen and Locomotive Firemen, May 30, 1942, *supra* note 2.
61. *Ibid.*
62. Letter from the chairman of Booker T. Washington Lodge No. 331 of the Brotherhood of Railway Carmen of America, November 12, 1942, *supra* note 2.
63. *Ibid.* The Subordinate Lodge Constitution was attached to the chairman's letter.
64. Complaint of Ed Teague, May 30, 1942, *supra* note 2.
65. Article 35, Section 1(a) of the constitution of the union was contained in a complaint by a Negro auxiliary, Lodge No. 6208, August 13, 1943, *supra* note 2.

66. *Ibid.* Article 10, Section 1(a) of the Regulations of the union was contained in Lodge No. 6208's complaint.
67. *Ibid.*
68. FEPC Summary of Complaints against the Pennsylvania Railroad Company.
69. Letter from John Dickinson, general counsel for the Pennsylvania Railroad, to Bartley Crum, FEPC special counsel, September 10, 1943.
70. Constitution of the Brotherhood of Railway Carmen of America, appended to a complaint against the brotherhood by their Auxiliary Lodge No. 309, November 3, 1942, *supra* note 2.
71. *Ibid.*
72. New York Central's Answer to the FEPC Summary of Complaints, September 15, 1943.
73. *Ibid.*
74. Letter from George Palmer, general chairman of the International Association of Railway Employees, June 17, 1943, *supra* note 2.
75. Answer of the Southern Railway Company to Summary of Complaints, September 13, 1943, *supra* note 2.
76. Answer of the Seaboard Air Line Railway Company to the FEPC's Summary of Complaints, *supra* note 2.
77. Answer of the Illinois Central System, September 11, 1943, *supra* note 2.
78. Complaint of Mildred Johnson, January 1943, *supra* note 2.
79. *Supra* note 50.
80. Statement of Sidney Alderman, *supra* note 2, pp. 32–37.
81. *Ibid.*
82. *New York Times,* September 17, 1943.
83. Opening Statement of Bartley C. Crum, *supra* note 2, p. 17.
84. Statement of V. T. Snowden, *supra* note 2, p. 218.
85. Statement of Joseph C. Waddy, *supra* note 2, p. 363.
86. Copy of the Supplemental Agreement Between the Norfolk and Southern and the Brotherhood of Locomotive Firemen and Enginemen, *supra* note 2, p. 371.
87. Statement of Will Whitfield, *supra* note 2, pp. 479–481.
88. The summary, findings, and directives were issued November 18, 1943, and the committee allowed a seven-day grace period during which the directives would not be made public. For the six companies and one union which agreed to comply, the directives were never made public.
89. *Final Report,* June 28, 1946 (Washington, D.C.: Fair Employment Practice Committee, 1947), p. 12.
90. Copies of the letter from the fourteen southern railroads dated December 13, 1943, *supra* note 2.
91. *Ibid.*
92. Fair Employment Practice Committee press release, December 13, 1943.
93. *Supra* note 89, p. 13.
94. *Id.,* p. 12.
95. 323 U.S. 192, 15 LRRM 708 (1944).
96. *Id.,* p. 210, 15 LRRM p. 715 (1944).
97. Supreme Court of the United States, October Term, 1943, No. 826, On Writ of Certiorari to the Supreme Court of Alabama and Brief in Support Thereof.

98. Supreme Court of the United States, October Term, 1944, No. 37, Brief for Petitioner, p. 4.
99. Supreme Court of the United States, Nos. 37 and 45, October Term, 1944, Brief for the United States as *Amicus Curiae*, pp. 11–12.
100. *Supra* note 95, p. 204, 15 LRRM p. 713.
101. *Id.*, p. 208, 15 LRRM p. 715.
102. *Supra* note 89, pp. 13–14.
103. FEPC *Hearing.* Texas and New Orleans Railroad Company and the Brotherhood of Railroad Trainmen. Case Nos. 82 and 91. Transcript of proceedings held in Houston, on May 4, 1945, with accompanying correspondence and exhibits.
104. *Id.*, pp. 33–35.
105. *Id.*, p. 61.
106. Statement of Charles Murphy, *supra* note 103, p. 65.
107. *Id.*, p. 62.
108. *Id.*, p. 63.
109. Charles H. Houston, "Foul Employment on the Rails" (based on a report to the Fortieth Annual Convention of the NAACP, Los Angeles, July 1949), *Crisis,* October 1949, p. 269.
110. *Id.*, p. 271.
111. *Norman* v. *Missouri-Pacific Railroad,* 414 F.2d 73, 1 FEP Cases 863, 71 LRRM 2940 (8th Cir. 1969), *on remand,* 8 FEP Cases 155 (D.C. E. Ark. 1973), *affirmed,* 497 F.2d 594, 8 FEP Cases 156 (8th Cir. 1974), *cert. denied,* 420 U.S. 908, 9 FEP Cases 240 (1975).
112. *Id.*, p. 83, 1 FEP Cases p. 87, 71 LRRM p. 2947.
113. 72 F. Supp. 695, 20 LRRM 2706 (E.D. Mo. 1947); *Howard* v. *St. Louis-San Francisco Railway Company,* 191 F.2d 442, 28 LRRM 2590 (8th Cir. 1951); *Brotherhood of Railway Trainmen* v. *Howard,* 343 U.S. 768, 30 LRRM 2258 (1952).
114. 343 U.S. 768, 775, 30 LRRM 2258, 2261 (1952).
115. *Howard* v. *St. Louis-San Francisco Railway Company,* 361 F.2d 905, 62 LRRM 2531 (8th Cir. 1966), *cert. denied,* 385 U.S. 986, 63 LRRM 2559 (1966).
116. 414 F.2d 73, 78, 1 FEP Cases 863, 866, 71 LRRM 2940, 2943.
117. ——F. Supp. ——, 1 FEP Cases 331, 68 LRRM 2796 (D. Mo. 1968).
118. *Supra* note 116, p. 79, 1 FEP Cases p. 867, 71 LRRM p. 2944.
119. Equal Employment Opportunity Commission, news release, December 9, 1970.
120. *U.S.* v. *Jacksonville Terminal Co.,* 316 F. Supp. 567, 2 FEP Cases 610, 611 (D.C. Fla. 1970); *aff'd in part, rev'd in part, and rem'd,* 451 F.2d. 418, 3 FEP Cases 862 (5th Cir. 1971); *cert. denied sub nom; Railroad Trainmen* v. *U.S.,* 406 U.S. 906, 4 FEP Cases 661, 4 EPD para. 774 (1972); *order issued on remand,* 356 F. Supp. 177, 6 FEP Cases 850, 6 EPD para. 8724; *enforcement directed,* ——F. Supp. ——, 6 FEP Cases 856, 6 EPD para. 8829 (D.C. Fla. 1973).
121. *Ibid.*
122. *Supra* note 111.
123. Report of Denver Regional Litigation Center, EEOC, *News* (Washington, D.C.: Equal Employment Opportunity Commission, July 11, 1975), p. 39.
124. 401 F. Supp. 1022, 11 FEP Cases 811 (D.C. E. La. 1975).

125. See *Van Hoomissen* v. *Xerox Corp.*, 368 F. Supp. 829, 6 FEP Cases 1231 (D.C. N. Calif. 1973); and *EEOC* v. *Detroit Edison Co.*, 515 F.2d 301, 10 FEP Cases 239, 1063 (6th Cir. 1975).
126. *Supra* note 124.
127. *Jack A. Gamble et al.* v. *Birmingham Southern Railroad*, CA No. 68–597 (N.D. Ala. Jan. 9, 1976).

Chapter 14

1. Quoted in Louis Ruchames, *Race, Jobs & Politics—The Story of FEPC* (New York: Columbia University Press, 1953), p. 87.
2. *Ibid.*
3. Hearings Before a Subcommittee of the Committee on Education and Labor, United States Senate, 78th Congress, 2nd Session, S. 2048—A Bill to Prohibit Discrimination in Employment Because of Race, Creed, Color, National Origin or Ancestry. August 30, 31, and September 6, 7, and 8, 1944.
4. *Id.*, pp. 116–122.
5. *Id.*, pp. 194–195.
6. *Ibid.*
7. *Ibid.*
8. Michigan *Chronicle*, November 11, 1944, p. 1.
9. *Ibid.*
10. Hearings Before a Subcommittee of the Committee on Education and Labor, United States Senate, 79th Congress, 1st Session, S. 101—A Bill to Prohibit Discrimination in Employment Because of Race, Creed, Color, National Origin or Ancestry; and S. 459—A Bill to Establish a Fair Employment Practice Commission and to Aid in Eliminating Discrimination in Employment Because of Race, Creed, or Color. March 12, 13, and 14, 1945.
11. *Final Report*, June 28, 1946 (Washington, D.C.: Fair Employment Practice Committee, 1947), pp. ix-x.
12. *Id.*, pp. x-xi.
13. *Id.*, pp. viii, 86, 87, 88, 96.
14. *Id.*, p. vi.
15. *Ibid.*
16. *Id.*, p. vii.
17. *Equal Economic Opportunity, A Report by the President's Committee on Government Contract Compliance* (The Truman Committee Report) (Washington, D.C.: U.S. Government Printing Office, 1953), p. 3.
18. 347 U.S. 483 (1954).

Table of Cases

A

Ableman v. Booth 390

Adams v. Richardson (HEW) 164n

Alabama; see Marsh v.

Albemarle Paper Co. v. Moody 53n, 388

Alexander v. Gardner-Denver Co. 27, 61, 144n, 165, 166-167, 386

Alpha Portland Cement v. Reese 89n

Alyeska v. Wilderness Society 88n

American Cast Iron Pipe Co.; see Pettway v.

American Federation of Labor v. Swing 395

American Mailing Corp. 162n

American Marine Corporation; see Clark v.

American Tobacco Company 97n

Arkansas Oak Flooring v. United Mine Workers 125n, 387

Armco Steel Corp.; see Taylor v.

Asbestos Workers, Local 53 v. Vogler 122n

Asbestos Workers Local 53 and Paul Vogler, Jr. 142

Associated Transport; U.S. v. 258n

Atlanta Oak Flooring Company 132, 396, 397

Atlantic Steel Co. and United Steelworkers of America Local No. 2401 386, 396

Avco Corp.; see Newman v.

Avondale Shipyards, Inc.; see Rodney, Stanley v.

B

Bailey v. Patterson 396

Banks, Ralph, et al. v. Lockheed-Georgia Company (A Division of Lockheed Aircraft Corporation) and Local No. 709, International Association of Machinists and Aerospace Workers, AFL-CIO 406

Baton Rouge Marine Contracting Co.; see Boudreaux v.

Baugh Construction Co.; see Washington v.

Bekins Moving & Storage Co. of Florida, Inc. and Freight Drivers, Warehousemen and Helpers, Local Union No. 390, an Affiliate of the International Brotherhood of Teamsters, Chauffeurs, Warehousemen and Helpers of America 168n, 400

Bell and Howell Co. 161, 400

Bendix Corp. and Machinists, Local 690; EEOC v. 216n

Bethlehem Alameda Shipyard, Inc. 97n, 107n

Bethlehem Steel Corp.; U.S. v. 163n, 389

Betts v. Easley 130, 149, 150, 395

Beverly v. Lone Star Lead Construction Corp. 52n, 80n, 84n

Bing v. Roadway Express, Inc 257, 413

435

Name Index

443

Topical Index

[Appendices and bibliography appear in Volume II.]

A

B